**JIST's _Best Jobs_ Series**

# 300 Best Jobs Without a Four-Year Degree

## Developed by Michael Farr and LaVerne L. Ludden, Ed.D.

### _With database work by Laurence Shatkin, Ph.D._

### Also in JIST's _Best Jobs_ Series
▲ _Award-winning Best Jobs for the 21st Century_
▲ _200 Best Jobs for College Graduates_

**jIST**
Works

## 300 Best Jobs Without a Four-Year Degree

© 2003 by JIST Publishing, Inc.

Published by JIST Works, an imprint of JIST Publishing, Inc.
8902 Otis Avenue
Indianapolis, IN 46216-1033

Phone: 1-800-648-JIST      Fax: 1-800-JIST-FAX      E-mail: info@jist.com

Visit our Web site at www.jist.com for information on JIST, free job search information, book excerpts, and ordering information on our many products.

---

**Some Other Books by the Authors**

*Michael Farr and LaVerne L. Ludden*

Best Jobs for the 21st Century

200 Best Jobs for College Graduates

Enhanced Occupational Outlook Handbook

Guide for Occupational Exploration

*Michael Farr*

The Quick Resume & Cover Letter Book

America's Top Resumes for America's Top Jobs

Getting the Job You Really Want

The Very Quick Job Search

---

Quantity discounts are available for JIST books. Please call our sales department at 1-800-648-JIST for a free catalog and more information.

Editors: Stephanie Koutek, Susan Pines
Cover and Interior Designer: Aleata Howard
Page Layout Coordinator: Carolyn J. Newland
Proofreader: Jeanne Clark

Printed in Canada
06 05 04 03 02     9 8 7 6 5 4 3 2 1

Library of Congress Cataloging-in-Publication Data is on file with the Library of Congress.

ISBN 1-56370-861-2

# This Is a Big Book, But It Is Very Easy to Use

This book is designed to help you explore career options in a variety of interesting ways. The nice thing about it is that you don't have to read it all. Instead, we designed it to allow you to browse and find information that most interests you.

The Table of Contents will give you a good idea of what's inside and how to use the book, so we suggest you start there. The first part is made up of interesting lists that will help you explore jobs based on pay, interests, education level, personality type, and many other criteria. The second part provides descriptions for the 300 jobs that met our criteria for this book (high pay, fast growth, or large number of openings). Just find a job that interests you in one of the lists in Part I and look up its description in Part II. Simple.

## How We Selected the 300 Best Jobs Without a Four-Year Degree

Deciding on the "best" job is a choice that only you can make, but objective criteria can help you identify jobs that are, for example, better paying than other jobs with similar duties. We sorted through the data for *all* major jobs and selected only those jobs that meet the following criteria:

1. **They do not require a four-year college degree.** The U.S. Department of Labor assigns a minimum level of training or education for entry into each job they track. This book excludes all jobs that require a four-year college degree or above. We included jobs requiring up to but not more than a two-year associate's degree—including those requiring short-term to long-term on-the-job training, work experience in a related field, and/or formal or informal training lasting from several weeks to several years. There were 605 jobs that met this criteria.

2. **They have the highest combined scores for earnings, growth, and number of openings.** For the 605 jobs that met our first criteria, we collected data from a variety of government sources and created three lists that organized the jobs from highest to lowest on three measures:

   ▲ Annual earnings

   ▲ Projected growth rate through 2010

   ▲ Number of job openings per year

*(continued)*

We then assigned a number to the relative positions of the 605 jobs on each list. We combined each job's position numbers from the three lists and sorted the jobs by total score. The 300 jobs with the highest combined score for earnings, growth rate, and number of openings per year are included in this book. They comprise the lists in Part I, and descriptions for each are located in Part II.

We are not suggesting that all of these jobs are good ones for you to consider—some will not be. But the 300 jobs that met our criteria cover such a wide range that you are likely to find one or more that interest you. The jobs that met our criteria are more likely than average to have higher pay, faster projected growth, and a larger number of openings than other jobs at similar levels of education and training.

## Some Things You Can Do with This Book

▲ Identify more interesting or better-paying jobs that don't require additional training or education.

▲ Develop long-term career plans that may require additional training, education, or experience.

▲ Explore and select a training or educational program that relates to a career objective.

▲ Find reliable earnings information to negotiate pay.

▲ Prepare for interviews.

These are a few of the many ways you can use this book. We hope you find it as interesting to browse as we did to put together. We have tried to make it easy to use and as interesting as occupational information can be.

When you are done with this book, pass it along or tell someone else about it. We wish you well in your career and in your life.

Credits and Acknowledgments: While the authors created this book, it is based on the work of many others. The occupational information is based on data obtained from the U.S. Department of Labor and the U.S. Census Bureau. These sources provide the most authoritative occupational information available. The job titles and their related descriptions are from the O*NET database, which was developed by researchers and developers under the direction of the U.S. Department of Labor. They, in turn, were assisted by thousands of employers who provided details on the nature of work in the many thousands of job samplings used in the database's development. We used the most recent version of the O*NET database, release 4.0, which was first available in April 2002. We appreciate and thank the staff of the U.S. Department of Labor for their efforts and expertise in providing such a rich source of data.

# Table of Contents

## Summary of Major Sections

**Introduction.** Very short review to help you better understand and use the book. *Starts on page 1.*

**Part I. The Best Jobs Lists: Jobs That Don't Require a Four-Year Degree.** Very useful for exploring career options! Lists are arranged into easy-to-use groups. The first group of lists presents the 300 jobs that do not require a four-year degree and that have the highest rankings based on earnings, projected growth, and number of openings. More specialized lists follow, presenting the best jobs by age, gender, level of education or training, personality type, and interest. The column starting at right presents all the list titles within groups. *Starts on page 9.*

**Part II. Descriptions of the 300 Best Jobs That Don't Require a Four-Year Degree.** Provides complete descriptions of the jobs that met our criteria for a combination of high pay, fast growth, and large number of openings. *Starts on page 127.*

**Appendix.** Provides descriptions of the skills referenced in the job descriptions in Part II. *Starts on page 447.*

## Part I. The Best Jobs Lists: Jobs That Don't Require a Four-Year Degree ................... 9

The many interesting lists in this book are organized into the major groupings below. Simply find the lists that interest you, turn to the page number indicated, and browse the lists to find jobs that interest you. Then look up job descriptions in Part II. Easy!

### Best Jobs Overall: Jobs with the Highest Pay, Fastest Growth, and Most Openings ................ 10

### Best Jobs with High Percentages of Workers Age 16–24, Workers Age 55 and Over, Part-Time Workers, Self-Employed Workers, Women, and Men ................................... 35

## Best Jobs Based on Personality Types ................... 92

## Best Jobs Based on Interests ................................ 105

## Part II. Descriptions of the 300 Best Jobs That Don't Require a Four-Year Degree ........... 127

Descriptions for all of the jobs that met our criteria for this book are included in this part of the book. They are presented in alphabetical order here, along with the page numbers where you will find them, and they also appear in alphabetical order in this part. We suggest that you use the lists in Part I to identify job titles that interest you and then locate their descriptions in Part II.

# Introduction

We want to keep our introduction short to encourage you to actually read or at least scan it. For this reason, we don't provide many details on the technical issues we had to solve in order to create this book. Instead, we give you short explanations that will help you understand the information presented in the book and use it well as a career exploration or planning tool.

## Why We Created This Book

Several years ago we wrote a book titled *Best Jobs for the 21st Century*. It was very well received and has since been revised. It covered all major jobs at all levels of education and training and included only those with earnings, projected growth rate, and number of job openings over certain criteria that we set. And it is a very good book for those who want to consider jobs at all levels of education and training. Although the book covered 500 jobs, it left out many jobs that don't require a four-year college degree that we think should be considered.

So we decided that the world needed a good book for the many people who want to get ahead or change jobs—but who do not have a four-year college degree and are not planning to obtain one in the next few years.

This is that book.

## Where the Information Came From

The information we used in creating this book came from three major sources:

▲ The U.S. Department of Labor—We used a variety of data sources to construct the information in this book. Most came from various databases of information provided by the U.S. Department of Labor. We started with the jobs included in the Department of Labor's O*NET (Occupational Information Network) database. The O*NET includes data on about 1,000 occupations and is now the primary source of detailed information on occupations. The Labor Department updates the O*NET on a regular basis, and we used the most recent one available—O*NET version 4.

▲ The U.S. Census Bureau—Because we wanted to include earnings, growth, number of openings, and other data not in the O*NET, we cross-referenced information on earnings developed by the U.S. Bureau of Labor Statistics (BLS) and the U.S. Census Bureau. This information on earnings is the most reliable data we could obtain. For data on projected growth and number of openings, the BLS uses a slightly different system of job titles than the O*NET uses. We were able to link the BLS data to many of the O*NET job titles in this book and tie growth and earnings information to the job titles in this book.

▲ US—That's "us," the authors. We did many things to help make all the data useful and present it to you in a way that is more understandable than any boring database format.

# How the Best Jobs in This Book Were Selected

The "This Is a Big Book…" statement at the beginning of this book includes a brief description of how we selected the jobs we included in this book. Here are a few more details:

1. We began by creating our own database of information from the O*NET and the Census Bureau and other sources to include the information we wanted. This database covered about 1,000 job titles at all levels of education and training.

2. We cut our initial list to include only those jobs requiring up to but not more than a two-year associate's degree. A total of 605 jobs met this criteria; they require short- to long-term on-the-job training, apprenticeship, work experience, career or vocational school training, or a two-year associate's degree.

3. Next, we created three lists that ranked all 605 of these jobs based on three major criteria: annual earnings, projected growth through 2010, and number of job openings projected per year. Each of these lists was then sorted from highest to lowest, and the jobs were assigned a number score from 605 (highest pay, for example) to 1 (lowest pay, for example).

4. We then added the number scores for each job from all three lists and created a new list that presented all 605 jobs in order from highest to lowest total score for all three measures.

5. To emphasize jobs that tend to pay more, are likely to grow more rapidly, and have more job openings, we selected the 300 job titles with the highest total scores from our final list. These jobs are the focus of this book.

For example, Registered Nurses has the highest combined score for earnings, growth, and number of job openings, so Registered Nurses is listed first in our "The 300 Best Jobs That Don't Require a Four-Year Degree" list even though it is not the best-paying job (which is Traffic Controllers), the fastest-growing job (which is Desktop Publishers), or the job with the most openings (which is Cashiers).

# Understand the Limits of the Data in This Book

In this book we use the most reliable and up-to-date earnings, projected growth, number of openings, and other information available. Some came from the U.S. Department of Labor source known as Occupation and Employment Statistics, and others came from the Current Population Survey from the Census Bureau. As you look at the data, keep in mind that they are estimates. They give you a general idea about the number of workers employed, annual earnings, rate of job growth, and annual job openings.

Understand that a problem with data is that it is only true on the average. Just as there is no precisely average person, there is no such thing as a statistically average example of a particular job. We say this because data, while helpful, can also be misleading.

Take, for example, the yearly earnings information in this book. This is highly reliable data obtained from a very large U.S. working population sample by the Bureau of Labor Statistics. It tells us the average annual pay received by people in various job titles (actually, it is the median annual pay, which means that half earned more and half less).

This sounds great, except that half of all people in that occupation earned less than that amount. For example, people entering the occupation or with a few years of work experience often earn much less than the average amount. People who live in rural areas or who work for smaller employers typically earn less than those who do similar work in cities (where the cost of living is higher) or for bigger employers. People in certain areas of the country earn less than those in others. Other factors also influence how much you are likely to earn in a given job in your area. For example, Lawn Service Managers have median earnings of $33,720, but those in cold climate areas would work only part of the year.

So, in reviewing the information in this book, please understand the limitations of data. You need to use common sense in career decision-making as in most other things in life. Even so, we hope that you find the information helpful and interesting.

# Part I. The Best Jobs Lists: Jobs That Don't Require a Four-Year Degree

Sixty lists are included in Part I of this book—look in the Table of Contents for a complete list of them. Although there are a lot of lists, they are not difficult to understand because they have clear titles and are organized into groupings of related lists.

Depending on your situation, some of the jobs lists in Part I will interest you more than others. For example, if you are young, you may be interested in finding out about the best-paying jobs that employ high percentages of young people. Other lists show jobs at various levels of training, experience, or education that you might consider in your career planning.

Whatever your situation, we suggest you use the lists that make sense for you to help explore career options. Following are the names of each group of lists along with short comments on each group. You will find additional information in a brief introduction provided at the beginning of each group of lists in Part I. Comments are also provided at the beginning of many of the lists.

Here is an overview of each major group of lists in Part I.

# Best Jobs Overall: Jobs with the Highest Pay, Fastest Growth, and Most Openings

Four lists are in this group, and they are the ones that most people want to see first. The first list presents all 300 jobs that are included in this book in order of their total scores for earnings, growth, and number of job openings. These jobs are used in the more specialized lists that follow. Three more lists in this group present the 100 best-paying jobs, the 100 fastest-growing jobs, and the 100 jobs with the most openings.

# Best Jobs with High Percentages of Workers Age 16–24, Workers Age 55 and Over, Part-Time Workers, Self-Employed Workers, Women, and Men

This group includes a total of 30 lists that are arranged into subgroups of five lists for each population covered. For example, the first subgroup presents five lists for workers age 16 to 24. The first list in this subgroup presents jobs with a high percentage of workers age 16 to 24. In this case, we set the criteria of 20 percent or higher of workers age 16 to 24, and 52 jobs met this criteria. This list is then followed by more specialized lists:

▲ Best Jobs Overall for Workers Age 16–24—This list includes the 25 jobs with the highest total combined scores for earnings, growth, and number of openings.

▲ Best-Paying Jobs for Workers Age 16–24—A list of the 25 jobs with the highest pay.

▲ Fastest-Growing Jobs for Workers Age 16–24—A list of 25 jobs that are projected to grow the fastest through 2010.

▲ Jobs with the Most Openings for Workers Age 16–24—A list of 25 jobs that are projected to have the most openings per year.

In a similar way, five lists are provided for each of the other subgroups of special populations in this grouping.

# Best Jobs Based on Levels of Education, Training, and Experience

Each of the six lists in this group presents jobs that require different levels of education or training. The jobs are all from our list of 300 best jobs used throughout this book. One list is provided for each level of education and training up to and including a two-year associate's degree.

The levels are those used by the U.S. Department of Labor, and they represent the minimum level of education or training typically required for entry to that job. The number of jobs in each list varies based on how many of the jobs in our top 300 require each of the levels. The lists cover jobs for the following levels: associate's degree, postsecondary vocational training, work experience in a related job, long-term on-the-job training, moderate-term on-the-job training, and short-term on-the-job training. The introduction to this group of lists in Part I describes these levels and provides other information.

# Best Jobs Based on Personality Types

This group provides one list of jobs for each of six personality types, based on a system that is used in a variety of popular career exploration inventories. The lists present the jobs in order of their total combined scores for earnings, growth, and number of openings. We explain the six personality types in the introduction to these lists.

# Best Jobs Based on Interests

There are 14 lists in this group, and they contain all of the jobs from our 300 best jobs list that fall within each of 14 major areas of interest. The number of jobs varies by list, and the lists are organized from highest to lowest total combined score for earnings, growth, and number of openings.

# Part II. Descriptions of the 300 Best Jobs That Don't Require a Four-Year Degree

This part of the book provides a brief but information-packed description for each of the 300 best jobs that met our criteria for this book. The descriptions are presented in alphabetical order. This structure makes it easy to look up a job that you've identified in a list from Part I and you want to learn more about.

We used the most current information from a variety of government sources to create the descriptions. Although we've tried to make the descriptions easy to understand, the sample job description that follows—and the explanation of each of its parts—may help you better understand and use the descriptions.

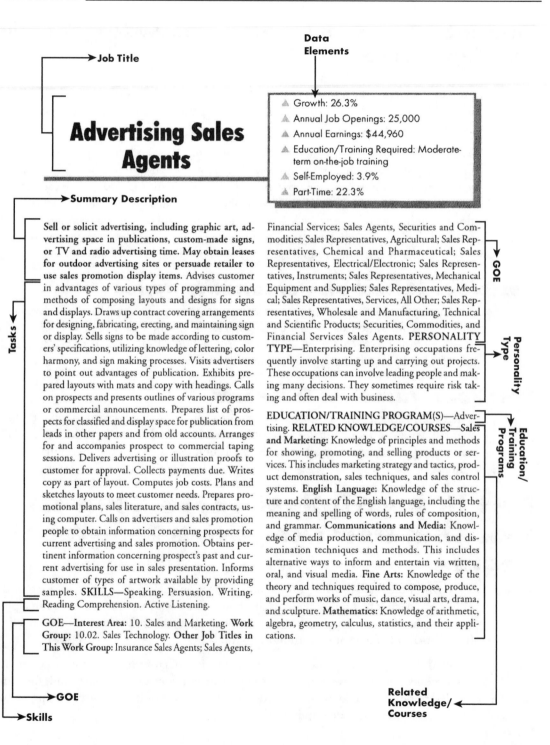

**Job Title**

**Data Elements**

# Advertising Sales Agents

▲ Growth: 26.3%
▲ Annual Job Openings: 25,000
▲ Annual Earnings: $44,960
▲ Education/Training Required: Moderate-term on-the-job training
▲ Self-Employed: 3.9%
▲ Part-Time: 22.3%

**Summary Description**

**Tasks**

Sell or solicit advertising, including graphic art, advertising space in publications, custom-made signs, or TV and radio advertising time. May obtain leases for outdoor advertising sites or persuade retailer to use sales promotion display items. Advises customer in advantages of various types of programming and methods of composing layouts and designs for signs and displays. Draws up contract covering arrangements for designing, fabricating, erecting, and maintaining sign or display. Sells signs to be made according to customers' specifications, utilizing knowledge of lettering, color harmony, and sign making processes. Visits advertisers to point out advantages of publication. Exhibits prepared layouts with mats and copy with headings. Calls on prospects and presents outlines of various programs or commercial announcements. Prepares list of prospects for classified and display space for publication from leads in other papers and from old accounts. Arranges for and accompanies prospect to commercial taping sessions. Delivers advertising or illustration proofs to customer for approval. Collects payments due. Writes copy as part of layout. Computes job costs. Plans and sketches layouts to meet customer needs. Prepares promotional plans, sales literature, and sales contracts, using computer. Calls on advertisers and sales promotion people to obtain information concerning prospects for current advertising and sales promotion. Obtains pertinent information concerning prospect's past and current advertising for use in sales presentation. Informs customer of types of artwork available by providing samples. **SKILLS**—Speaking. Persuasion. Writing. Reading Comprehension. Active Listening.

**GOE**—Interest Area: 10. Sales and Marketing. **Work Group:** 10.02. Sales Technology. **Other Job Titles in This Work Group:** Insurance Sales Agents; Sales Agents, Financial Services; Sales Agents, Securities and Commodities; Sales Representatives, Agricultural; Sales Representatives, Chemical and Pharmaceutical; Sales Representatives, Electrical/Electronic; Sales Representatives, Instruments; Sales Representatives, Mechanical Equipment and Supplies; Sales Representatives, Medical; Sales Representatives, Services, All Other; Sales Representatives, Wholesale and Manufacturing, Technical and Scientific Products; Securities, Commodities, and Financial Services Sales Agents. **PERSONALITY TYPE**—Enterprising. Enterprising occupations frequently involve starting up and carrying out projects. These occupations can involve leading people and making many decisions. They sometimes require risk taking and often deal with business.

**EDUCATION/TRAINING PROGRAM(S)**—Advertising. **RELATED KNOWLEDGE/COURSES**—**Sales and Marketing:** Knowledge of principles and methods for showing, promoting, and selling products or services. This includes marketing strategy and tactics, product demonstration, sales techniques, and sales control systems. **English Language:** Knowledge of the structure and content of the English language, including the meaning and spelling of words, rules of composition, and grammar. **Communications and Media:** Knowledge of media production, communication, and dissemination techniques and methods. This includes alternative ways to inform and entertain via written, oral, and visual media. **Fine Arts:** Knowledge of the theory and techniques required to compose, produce, and perform works of music, dance, visual arts, drama, and sculpture. **Mathematics:** Knowledge of arithmetic, algebra, geometry, calculus, statistics, and their applications.

**GOE**

**Personality Type**

**Education/ Training Programs**

**Related Knowledge/ Courses**

**GOE**

**Skills**

Here are details on each of the major parts of the job descriptions you will find in Part II:

▲ Job Title—This is the job title for the job as defined by the U.S. Department of Labor and used in its O*NET database.

▲ Data Elements—This information comes from various government databases for this occupation, as explained elsewhere in this Introduction.

▲ Summary Description and Tasks—The bold sentences provide a summary description of the occupation. This is followed by a listing of tasks that are generally performed by people who work in the job.

▲ Skills—The government provides data on many skills; we decided to list only those that were most important for each job rather than list pages of unhelpful details. For each job, we identified any skill with a rating that was higher than the average rating for that skill for all jobs. If there were more than five, we included only those five with the highest ratings, and we present them from highest to lowest score. We include up to seven skills if scores were tied for fifth place. And, finally, at least one skill is listed for each job, even if the rating for that skill is lower than the average for all jobs. You can find definitions for the skills in the Appendix.

▲ GOE—This information cross-references the *Guide for Occupational Information* (or the *GOE*), a system that organizes jobs based on interests and is used in a variety of career information systems. We use the new third edition of the *Guide for Occupational Exploration,* as published by JIST. The description includes the major Interest Area the job fits into, its more specific Work Group, and a list of related job titles that are in this same GOE Work Group. This will help you identify other jobs that relate to similar interests or require similar skills. You can find more information on the *GOE* and its Interest Areas in the introduction to the lists of jobs based on interests in Part I.

▲ Personality Type—This part gives the name of the personality type that most closely matches each job as well as a brief definition of this personality type. You can find more information on the personality types in the introduction to the lists of jobs based on personality types in Part I.

▲ Education/Training Programs—This entry provides the name of the educational or training program or programs listed for the job in a related government data source called the *Classification of Instruction Programs (CIP)*. This information can help you identify sources of formal or informal training for a job that interests you.

▲ Related Knowledge/Courses—This entry can help you understand the most important knowledge areas that are required for a job and the types of courses or programs you will likely need to take to prepare for it. We used information in the Department of Labor's O*NET database for this entry. We went through a process similar to the one we used for Skills (earlier in this list) to determine which entries were most important for each job.

# Sources of Additional Information

Hundreds of sources of career information are available; here are a few we consider most helpful for getting additional information on the jobs listed in this book.

## Print References

▲ *O*NET Dictionary of Occupational Titles*—Revised on a regular basis, this book provides good descriptions for all jobs listed in the U.S. Department of Labor's O*NET database (about 1,000 jobs, at all levels of education and training), plus lists of related job titles in other major career information sources, educational programs, and other information. Published by JIST.

▲ *Guide for Occupational Exploration,* Third Edition—This new edition of the *GOE* is cross-referenced in the descriptions provided in Part II. The *GOE* book provides helpful information to consider on each of the interest areas and work groups as well as descriptions of all O*NET jobs within each group, and it has many other features useful for exploring career options. Published by JIST.

▲ *Enhanced Occupational Outlook Handbook*—Updated regularly, this handbook provides thorough descriptions for 260 major jobs, descriptions for the O*NET jobs that are related to each, thousands of additional descriptions of more specialized jobs, and other information. Published by JIST.

## Internet Resources

▲ The U.S. Department of Labor Web site—The U.S. Department of Labor Web site (http://www.bls.gov) provides a lot of career information, including links to other pages that provide information on the jobs covered in this book. The site is a bit formal and, well, confusing, but it will take you to the major sources of government career information if you explore its options.

▲ O*NET site—Go to http://www.onetcenter.org for a variety of information on the O*NET database, including additional detailed information on the O*NET job titles presented in Part II of this book.

▲ CareerOINK.com—This site (at http://www.careeroink.com) is operated by JIST and includes lots of free information on all major jobs, easy-to-use crosswalks between major career information systems, links from military to civilian jobs, sample resumes, and many other features.

## Thanks

Thanks for reading this introduction. You are surely a more thorough person than someone who jumped into the book without reading it—and you will likely get more out of the book.

We wish you a satisfying career and, more importantly, a satisfying life.

# Part I

# The Best Jobs Lists: Jobs That Don't Require a Four-Year Degree

This part contains a lot of interesting lists, and it's a good place for you to start using the book. Here are some suggestions for using the lists to explore career options:

▲ The Table of Contents at the beginning of this book presents a complete listing of the list titles in this section. The lists are arranged in easy-to-use groups. You can browse the lists or use the Table of Contents to find those that interest you most.

▲ We organized the lists into sensible groups and gave them clear titles, so most require little explanation. We provide comments for each group of lists to inform you of the selection criteria we used or other details we think you may want to know.

▲ This part contains a large variety of lists to meet many different interests and needs. Some lists will help you identify jobs based on your interests or personality type; others provide information on jobs by education or training needed, jobs with high percentages of men or women, and many other criteria. The Table of Contents also provides page numbers for these lists.

▲ As you review the lists, one or more of the occupations may appeal to you enough that you want to seek additional information. As this happens, mark that occupation (or, if someone else will be using this book, write it on a separate sheet of paper) so that you can look up the description of that job in Part II.

*(continued)*

*(continued)*

▲ Keep in mind that all jobs in these lists met our basic criteria for being included in this book. All lists, therefore, emphasize occupations with high pay, high growth, or large numbers of openings. These measures are easily quantified and are often presented in lists of best jobs in the newspapers and other media. While earnings, growth, and openings are important, there are other factors to consider in your career planning. For example, location, liking the people you work with, having an opportunity to serve others, and enjoying your work are a few of many factors that may define the ideal job for you. These measures are difficult or impossible to quantify and so are not used in this book, so you will need to consider the importance of these issues yourself.

▲ All data in this book comes from government sources, including the U.S. Department of Labor and the Census Bureau. The earnings figures are based on the average annual pay received by full-time workers. Some occupations have high percentages of part-time workers, and those workers would receive, of course, proportionately less pay on a weekly or annual basis. The earnings also represent the national averages, and actual pay rates can vary greatly by location, amount of previous work experience, and other factors.

We hope you find these lists both interesting and helpful. They can help you explore your career options in a variety of interesting ways. We suggest you find the ones that are most helpful to you and focus your attention on them. Enjoy!

# Best Jobs Overall: Jobs with the Highest Pay, Fastest Growth, and Most Openings

We consider the four lists that follow to be our premier lists. They are the lists that are most often mentioned in the media and the ones that most readers want to see. The first list presents the jobs with the highest combined scores for pay, growth, and number of openings that do not require a four-year college degree. This is a very popular list because it represents jobs with the very highest quantifiable measures from our labor market. Three additional lists present jobs with the highest scores in each of three measures: annual earnings, projected percentage growth, and largest number of openings. As you review these lists, keep in mind that the lists include jobs with the highest measures from a database of jobs that included all major jobs that don't require a four-year degree in our economy. Jobs that did not make it onto the list of 300 best jobs are not included in the descriptions in Part II.

# The 300 Best Jobs That Don't Require a Four-Year Degree

This is the list that most people want to know about. It includes the 300* jobs that don't require a four-year college degree that have the highest overall combined ratings for earnings, projected growth, and number of openings.

A wide variety of jobs are on the list. Among the top 20 are jobs in sales, education, law enforcement, entertainment, construction, administration, and transportation. The top 20 also include several management and supervisory jobs, proving that these kinds of jobs do exist for people without a college degree.

Details on the ranking process: The Introduction provides a more detailed review of how we selected the jobs on this list, but here is a quick review. We started with about a thousand jobs and eliminated those that required more than a two-year associate's degree. This left a list of about 600 jobs. We then sorted these jobs into three lists in order of highest pay, fastest growth, and largest number of openings. The occupations on each list were given scores corresponding to their ranking on the list. This scoring process was continued for each occupation on each of the three lists. The three scores for each job were combined, resulting in a total score for each occupation. Then a new list was created based on the total score of each occupation. The 300 jobs with the highest total scores are presented in the list that follows.

Registered Nurses was the occupation with the best total score, and it is on the top of the list. The other occupations follow in descending order based on their total scores. Many jobs had tied scores and were simply listed one after another, so there are often only very small or even no differences between the scores of jobs that are near each other on a list. All other jobs lists in this book use these jobs as their source list. You can find descriptions for each of these jobs beginning on page 127.

* Two jobs had the same score as the 300th job in the list. So, to be perfectly fair, this book title might have been a less memorable "302 Best Jobs Without a Four-Year Degree." To avoid this unnatural situation, we simply dropped those last two job titles from the 300 Best Jobs That Don't Require a Four-Year Degree list and the three lists of 100 jobs that follow. We did, however, include those two jobs in the more specialized lists you will find later in this section, and we included their descriptions in Part II. The two jobs tied for last place in the list are Station Installers and Repairers, Telephone ($42,520 / -3.1% / 9,000) and Telecommunications Facility Examiners ($42,520 / -3.1% / 9,000).

# The 300 Best Jobs That Don't Require a Four-Year Degree

| Job | Annual Earnings | Percent Growth | Annual Openings |
|-----|-----------------|----------------|-----------------|
| 1. Registered Nurses | $46,410 | 25.6% | 140,000 |
| 2. Advertising Sales Agents | $44,960 | 26.3% | 25,000 |
| 3. Musicians, Instrumental | $44,520 | 20.1% | 33,000 |
| 4. Singers | $44,520 | 20.1% | 33,000 |
| 5. First-Line Supervisors and Manager/Supervisors—Construction Trades Workers | $47,740 | 16.5% | 43,000 |
| 6. First-Line Supervisors and Manager/Supervisors—Extractive Workers | $47,740 | 16.5% | 43,000 |
| 7. Electricians | $42,210 | 17.3% | 66,000 |
| 8. First-Line Supervisors/Managers of Mechanics, Installers, and Repairers | $46,560 | 16.0% | 38,000 |
| 9. Actors | $41,570 | 26.7% | 20,000 |
| 10. Paralegals and Legal Assistants | $38,790 | 33.2% | 23,000 |
| 11. Tractor-Trailer Truck Drivers | $32,810 | 19.8% | 240,000 |
| 12. Truck Drivers, Heavy | $32,810 | 19.8% | 240,000 |
| 13. Storage and Distribution Managers | $58,200 | 20.2% | 13,000 |
| 14. Transportation Managers | $58,200 | 20.2% | 13,000 |
| 15. Highway Patrol Pilots | $40,590 | 23.2% | 21,000 |
| 16. Police Patrol Officers | $40,590 | 23.2% | 21,000 |
| 17. Sheriffs and Deputy Sheriffs | $40,590 | 23.2% | 21,000 |
| 18. Legal Secretaries | $35,370 | 20.3% | 36,000 |
| 19. First-Line Supervisors/Managers of Transportation and Material-Moving Machine and Vehicle Operators | $43,120 | 19.9% | 17,000 |
| 20. Claims Examiners, Property and Casualty Insurance | $44,000 | 15.1% | 25,000 |
| 21. Insurance Adjusters, Examiners, and Investigators | $44,000 | 15.1% | 25,000 |
| 22. Correctional Officers and Jailers | $32,680 | 32.4% | 30,000 |
| 23. Adjustment Clerks | $26,530 | 32.4% | 359,000 |
| 24. Customer Service Representatives, Utilities | $26,530 | 32.4% | 359,000 |
| 25. Dental Hygienists | $51,980 | 37.1% | 5,000 |
| 26. Licensed Practical and Licensed Vocational Nurses | $30,470 | 20.3% | 58,000 |
| 27. Heating and Air Conditioning Mechanics | $34,180 | 22.3% | 21,000 |

# The 300 Best Jobs That Don't Require a Four-Year Degree

| Job | Annual Earnings | Percent Growth | Annual Openings |
|---|---|---|---|
| 28. Refrigeration Mechanics | $34,180 | 22.3% | 21,000 |
| 29. Automotive Master Mechanics | $30,780 | 18.0% | 104,000 |
| 30. Automotive Specialty Technicians | $30,780 | 18.0% | 104,000 |
| 31. Radiologic Technologists and Technicians | $37,290 | 23.1% | 13,000 |
| 32. Food Service Managers | $34,350 | 15.0% | 55,000 |
| 33. Roofers | $31,670 | 19.4% | 38,000 |
| 34. First-Line Supervisors, Administrative Support | $39,410 | 9.4% | 146,000 |
| 35. First-Line Supervisors, Customer Service | $39,410 | 9.4% | 146,000 |
| 36. Telecommunications Line Installers and Repairers | $38,050 | 27.6% | 9,000 |
| 37. Architectural Drafters | $37,100 | 20.8% | 12,000 |
| 38. Civil Drafters | $37,100 | 20.8% | 12,000 |
| 39. Production, Planning, and Expediting Clerks | $32,520 | 17.9% | 36,000 |
| 40. Sheet Metal Workers | $35,050 | 23.0% | 13,000 |
| 41. Painters, Construction and Maintenance | $29,610 | 19.1% | 67,000 |
| 42. Pipe Fitters | $40,170 | 10.2% | 49,000 |
| 43. Pipelaying Fitters | $40,170 | 10.2% | 49,000 |
| 44. Plumbers | $40,170 | 10.2% | 49,000 |
| 45. Bill and Account Collectors | $26,670 | 25.3% | 71,000 |
| 46. Physical Therapist Assistants | $34,370 | 44.8% | 9,000 |
| 47. First-Line Supervisors/Managers of Helpers, Laborers, and Material Movers, Hand | $36,910 | 18.9% | 14,000 |
| 48. Flight Attendants | $45,220 | 18.4% | 8,000 |
| 49. Brazers | $29,080 | 19.3% | 51,000 |
| 50. Solderers | $29,080 | 19.3% | 51,000 |
| 51. Welder-Fitters | $29,080 | 19.3% | 51,000 |
| 52. Welders and Cutters | $29,080 | 19.3% | 51,000 |
| 53. Welders, Production | $29,080 | 19.3% | 51,000 |
| 54. Self-Enrichment Education Teachers | $31,070 | 18.5% | 34,000 |
| 55. Structural Iron and Steel Workers | $39,140 | 18.4% | 12,000 |
| 56. Athletes and Sports Competitors | $62,960 | 22.5% | 3,000 |
| 57. Executive Secretaries and Administrative Assistants | $32,520 | 11.5% | 185,000 |

*(continued)*

*(continued)*

## The 300 Best Jobs That Don't Require a Four-Year Degree

| Job | Annual Earnings | Percent Growth | Annual Openings |
|---|---|---|---|
| 58. Sales Representatives, Wholesale and Manufacturing, Except Technical and Scientific Products | $46,770 | 5.7% | 86,000 |
| 59. Construction Laborers | $26,940 | 17.0% | 236,000 |
| 60. Fitness Trainers and Aerobics Instructors | $28,750 | 40.3% | 19,000 |
| 61. Aircraft Mechanics and Service Technicians | $40,550 | 16.7% | 11,000 |
| 62. First-Line Supervisors/Managers of Non-Retail Sales Workers | $56,850 | 5.8% | 41,000 |
| 63. Coaches and Scouts | $33,470 | 17.6% | 19,000 |
| 64. Sales Representatives, Agricultural | $58,630 | 7.5% | 24,000 |
| 65. Sales Representatives, Chemical and Pharmaceutical | $58,630 | 7.5% | 24,000 |
| 66. Sales Representatives, Electrical/Electronic | $58,630 | 7.5% | 24,000 |
| 67. Sales Representatives, Instruments | $58,630 | 7.5% | 24,000 |
| 68. Sales Representatives, Mechanical Equipment and Supplies | $58,630 | 7.5% | 24,000 |
| 69. Sales Representatives, Medical | $58,630 | 7.5% | 24,000 |
| 70. Electrical Drafters | $40,420 | 23.3% | 5,000 |
| 71. Electronic Drafters | $40,420 | 23.3% | 5,000 |
| 72. Boat Builders and Shipwrights | $35,100 | 8.2% | 161,000 |
| 73. Brattice Builders | $35,100 | 8.2% | 161,000 |
| 74. Carpenter Assemblers and Repairers | $35,100 | 8.2% | 161,000 |
| 75. Construction Carpenters | $35,100 | 8.2% | 161,000 |
| 76. Rough Carpenters | $35,100 | 8.2% | 161,000 |
| 77. Ship Carpenters and Joiners | $35,100 | 8.2% | 161,000 |
| 78. Brickmasons and Blockmasons | $41,140 | 12.5% | 18,000 |
| 79. Calibration and Instrumentation Technicians | $41,210 | 10.8% | 22,000 |
| 80. Electrical Engineering Technicians | $41,210 | 10.8% | 22,000 |
| 81. Electronics Engineering Technicians | $41,210 | 10.8% | 22,000 |
| 82. First-Line Supervisors/Managers of Police and Detectives | $57,900 | 13.1% | 9,000 |
| 83. Human Resources Assistants, Except Payroll and Timekeeping | $29,400 | 19.3% | 25,000 |
| 84. Respiratory Therapists | $38,220 | 34.8% | 4,000 |

# The 300 Best Jobs That Don't Require a Four-Year Degree

| Job | Annual Earnings | Percent Growth | Annual Openings |
|---|---|---|---|
| 85. Social and Human Service Assistants | $23,840 | 54.2% | 45,000 |
| 86. Chemical Technicians | $37,080 | 15.0% | 13,000 |
| 87. Truck Drivers, Light or Delivery Services | $24,620 | 19.2% | 153,000 |
| 88. Appraisers, Real Estate | $41,700 | 18.0% | 6,000 |
| 89. First-Line Supervisors and Manager/ Supervisors—Landscaping Workers | $33,720 | 20.1% | 10,000 |
| 90. Lawn Service Managers | $33,720 | 20.1% | 10,000 |
| 91. Automatic Teller Machine Servicers | $32,860 | 14.2% | 24,000 |
| 92. Data Processing Equipment Repairers | $32,860 | 14.2% | 24,000 |
| 93. Office Machine and Cash Register Servicers | $32,860 | 14.2% | 24,000 |
| 94. Real Estate Sales Agents | $37,950 | 9.5% | 28,000 |
| 95. Security Guards | $19,470 | 35.4% | 242,000 |
| 96. Irradiated-Fuel Handlers | $31,630 | 32.8% | 9,000 |
| 97. Receptionists and Information Clerks | $20,780 | 23.7% | 269,000 |
| 98. Child Support, Missing Persons, and Unemployment Insurance Fraud Investigators | $49,830 | 16.4% | 4,000 |
| 99. Criminal Investigators and Special Agents | $49,830 | 16.4% | 4,000 |
| 100. Immigration and Customs Inspectors | $49,830 | 16.4% | 4,000 |
| 101. Police Detectives | $49,830 | 16.4% | 4,000 |
| 102. Police Identification and Records Officers | $49,830 | 16.4% | 4,000 |
| 103. Landscaping and Groundskeeping Workers | $20,030 | 29.0% | 193,000 |
| 104. Interviewers, Except Eligibility and Loan | $22,360 | 33.4% | 53,000 |
| 105. Biological Technicians | $32,970 | 26.4% | 7,000 |
| 106. Bus and Truck Mechanics and Diesel Engine Specialists | $33,210 | 14.2% | 20,000 |
| 107. Commercial Pilots | $51,370 | 26.9% | 1,000 |
| 108. Mechanical Drafters | $40,330 | 15.4% | 8,000 |
| 109. Dental Assistants | $26,740 | 37.2% | 16,000 |
| 110. Desktop Publishers | $32,700 | 66.7% | 5,000 |
| 111. Demonstrators and Product Promoters | $24,460 | 24.9% | 34,000 |
| 112. Nursing Aides, Orderlies, and Attendants | $19,100 | 23.5% | 268,000 |
| 113. First-Line Supervisors/Managers of Retail Sales Workers | $32,170 | 8.1% | 206,000 |
| 114. Private Detectives and Investigators | $30,650 | 23.5% | 9,000 |

*(continued)*

*(continued)*

## The 300 Best Jobs That Don't Require a Four-Year Degree

| Job | Annual Earnings | Percent Growth | Annual Openings |
|---|---|---|---|
| 115. Fitters, Structural Metal—Precision | $28,490 | 19.5% | 20,000 |
| 116. Metal Fabricators, Structural Metal Products | $28,490 | 19.5% | 20,000 |
| 117. Home Health Aides | $18,110 | 47.3% | 120,000 |
| 118. Telemarketers | $21,460 | 22.2% | 145,000 |
| 119. Teacher Assistants | $18,770 | 23.9% | 256,000 |
| 120. Chemical Equipment Controllers and Operators | $36,310 | 14.9% | 9,000 |
| 121. Chemical Equipment Tenders | $36,310 | 14.9% | 9,000 |
| 122. Occupational Therapist Assistants | $34,860 | 39.7% | 3,000 |
| 123. Medical and Clinical Laboratory Technicians | $28,970 | 19.0% | 19,000 |
| 124. Cardiovascular Technologists and Technicians | $34,960 | 34.9% | 3,000 |
| 125. Combined Food Preparation and Serving Workers, Including Fast Food | $14,240 | 30.5% | 737,000 |
| 126. First-Line Supervisors/Managers of Production and Operating Workers | $43,020 | 1.0% | 71,000 |
| 127. Environmental Science and Protection Technicians, Including Health | $35,830 | 24.5% | 3,000 |
| 128. Real Estate Brokers | $60,080 | 9.6% | 8,000 |
| 129. Numerical Control Machine Tool Operators and Tenders, Metal and Plastic | $28,780 | 19.7% | 15,000 |
| 130. Office Clerks, General | $22,290 | 15.9% | 676,000 |
| 131. Surgical Technologists | $29,660 | 34.7% | 8,000 |
| 132. Emergency Medical Technicians and Paramedics | $24,740 | 31.3% | 19,000 |
| 133. Nuclear Medicine Technologists | $44,850 | 22.4% | 1,000 |
| 134. Medical Secretaries | $24,460 | 19.0% | 40,000 |
| 135. Bus Drivers, Transit and Intercity | $27,250 | 17.4% | 24,000 |
| 136. Personal and Home Care Aides | $15,960 | 62.5% | 84,000 |
| 137. Cooks, Restaurant | $18,880 | 21.7% | 158,000 |
| 138. Dispatchers, Except Police, Fire, and Ambulance | $30,410 | 22.2% | 8,000 |
| 139. Medical Assistants | $23,840 | 57.0% | 18,700 |
| 140. Hotel, Motel, and Resort Desk Clerks | $17,100 | 33.4% | 73,000 |
| 141. Nuclear Equipment Operation Technicians | $61,970 | 20.7% | fewer than 500 |
| 142. Nuclear Monitoring Technicians | $61,970 | 20.7% | fewer than 500 |
| 143. Ceiling Tile Installers | $35,580 | 9.4% | 19,000 |
| 144. Drywall Installers | $35,580 | 9.4% | 19,000 |

# The 300 Best Jobs That Don't Require a Four-Year Degree

| Job | Annual Earnings | Percent Growth | Annual Openings |
|---|---|---|---|
| 145. Refuse and Recyclable Material Collectors | $26,020 | 16.6% | 34,000 |
| 146. Elevator Installers and Repairers | $46,240 | 17.2% | 2,000 |
| 147. Mobile Heavy Equipment Mechanics, Except Engines | $34,790 | 14.0% | 11,000 |
| 148. Camera Operators, Television, Video, and Motion Picture | $33,860 | 25.8% | 3,000 |
| 149. Reinforcing Iron and Rebar Workers | $37,800 | 17.5% | 4,000 |
| 150. Medical Records and Health Information Technicians | $24,430 | 49.0% | 14,000 |
| 151. Library Technicians | $24,230 | 19.5% | 29,000 |
| 152. Painters, Transportation Equipment | $32,910 | 17.5% | 8,000 |
| 153. Combination Machine Tool Operators and Tenders, Metal and Plastic | $29,350 | 14.7% | 21,000 |
| 154. Combination Machine Tool Setters and Set-Up Operators, Metal and Plastic | $29,350 | 14.7% | 21,000 |
| 155. Coroners | $44,140 | 8.9% | 9,000 |
| 156. Environmental Compliance Inspectors | $44,140 | 8.9% | 9,000 |
| 157. Equal Opportunity Representatives and Officers | $44,140 | 8.9% | 9,000 |
| 158. Government Property Inspectors and Investigators | $44,140 | 8.9% | 9,000 |
| 159. Licensing Examiners and Inspectors | $44,140 | 8.9% | 9,000 |
| 160. Pressure Vessel Inspectors | $44,140 | 8.9% | 9,000 |
| 161. Packers and Packagers, Hand | $17,030 | 19.3% | 242,000 |
| 162. Reservation and Transportation Ticket Agents | $26,140 | 14.5% | 39,000 |
| 163. Travel Clerks | $26,140 | 14.5% | 39,000 |
| 164. Automotive Body and Related Repairers | $33,710 | 10.2% | 18,000 |
| 165. Interpreters and Translators | $33,550 | 23.8% | 3,000 |
| 166. Grader, Bulldozer, and Scraper Operators | $36,170 | 6.9% | 25,000 |
| 167. Operating Engineers | $36,170 | 6.9% | 25,000 |
| 168. Tile and Marble Setters | $36,580 | 15.6% | 5,000 |
| 169. Counter and Rental Clerks | $18,670 | 19.4% | 150,000 |
| 170. Amusement and Recreation Attendants | $15,480 | 32.4% | 62,000 |
| 171. Pharmacy Technicians | $21,600 | 36.4% | 22,000 |
| 172. Industrial Truck and Tractor Operators | $26,090 | 11.3% | 91,000 |

*(continued)*

*(continued)*

## The 300 Best Jobs That Don't Require a Four-Year Degree

| Job | Annual Earnings | Percent Growth | Annual Openings |
|---|---|---|---|
| 173. Machinists | $31,610 | 9.1% | 28,000 |
| 174. Water and Liquid Waste Treatment Plant and System Operators | $32,450 | 18.1% | 6,000 |
| 175. First-Line Supervisors/Managers of Food Preparation and Serving Workers | $24,600 | 12.7% | 136,000 |
| 176. Taxi Drivers and Chauffeurs | $18,920 | 24.4% | 37,000 |
| 177. Waiters and Waitresses | $14,750 | 18.3% | 596,000 |
| 178. Helpers—Installation, Maintenance, and Repair Workers | $22,620 | 18.5% | 35,000 |
| 179. Electro-Mechanical Technicians | $38,630 | 14.5% | 4,000 |
| 180. Semiconductor Processors | $27,170 | 32.4% | 7,000 |
| 181. Freight, Stock, and Material Movers, Hand | $20,460 | 13.9% | 519,000 |
| 182. Grips and Set-Up Workers, Motion Picture Sets, Studios, and Stages | $20,460 | 13.9% | 519,000 |
| 183. Stevedores, Except Equipment Operators | $20,460 | 13.9% | 519,000 |
| 184. Photographers, Scientific | $27,420 | 17.0% | 13,000 |
| 185. Professional Photographers | $27,420 | 17.0% | 13,000 |
| 186. Paperhangers | $32,490 | 20.2% | 3,000 |
| 187. Electrical and Electronics Repairers, Commercial and Industrial Equipment | $37,190 | 9.2% | 10,000 |
| 188. Cleaners of Vehicles and Equipment | $17,380 | 18.8% | 86,000 |
| 189. Electrical Power-Line Installers and Repairers | $44,490 | 9.3% | 5,000 |
| 190. Aviation Inspectors | $44,200 | 11.3% | 3,000 |
| 191. Freight Inspectors | $44,200 | 11.3% | 3,000 |
| 192. Marine Cargo Inspectors | $44,200 | 11.3% | 3,000 |
| 193. Motor Vehicle Inspectors | $44,200 | 11.3% | 3,000 |
| 194. Public Transportation Inspectors | $44,200 | 11.3% | 3,000 |
| 195. Railroad Inspectors | $44,200 | 11.3% | 3,000 |
| 196. Food Preparation Workers | $16,180 | 16.9% | 231,000 |
| 197. Housekeeping Supervisors | $27,830 | 14.2% | 18,000 |
| 198. Janitorial Supervisors | $27,830 | 14.2% | 18,000 |
| 199. Medical Equipment Repairers | $37,470 | 14.9% | 3,000 |
| 200. Forest Fire Fighters | $35,260 | 8.9% | 12,000 |
| 201. Municipal Fire Fighters | $35,260 | 8.9% | 12,000 |

# The 300 Best Jobs That Don't Require a Four-Year Degree

| Job | Annual Earnings | Percent Growth | Annual Openings |
|---|---|---|---|
| 202. Weighers, Measurers, Checkers, and Samplers, Recordkeeping | $26,250 | 17.9% | 13,000 |
| 203. Plasterers and Stucco Masons | $35,170 | 11.9% | 7,000 |
| 204. Soldering and Brazing Machine Operators and Tenders | $29,730 | 15.1% | 9,000 |
| 205. Soldering and Brazing Machine Setters and Set-Up Operators | $29,730 | 15.1% | 9,000 |
| 206. Welding Machine Operators and Tenders | $29,730 | 15.1% | 9,000 |
| 207. Welding Machine Setters and Set-Up Operators | $29,730 | 15.1% | 9,000 |
| 208. Gaming Dealers | $15,550 | 32.4% | 28,000 |
| 209. First-Line Supervisors/Managers of Personal Service Workers | $30,350 | 15.1% | 8,000 |
| 210. Janitors and Cleaners, Except Maids and Housekeeping Cleaners | $19,080 | 13.5% | 507,000 |
| 211. Retail Salespersons | $20,260 | 12.4% | 1,124,000 |
| 212. Dragline Operators | $33,480 | 14.8% | 5,000 |
| 213. Excavating and Loading Machine Operators | $33,480 | 14.8% | 5,000 |
| 214. Numerical Tool and Process Control Programmers | $37,690 | 16.6% | 2,000 |
| 215. Chefs and Head Cooks | $28,550 | 9.0% | 35,000 |
| 216. Glaziers | $32,360 | 14.8% | 6,000 |
| 217. Library Assistants, Clerical | $19,380 | 19.7% | 26,000 |
| 218. Cartoonists | $35,770 | 13.4% | 4,000 |
| 219. Fire Inspectors | $42,800 | 15.1% | 1,000 |
| 220. Painters and Illustrators | $35,770 | 13.4% | 4,000 |
| 221. Sculptors | $35,770 | 13.4% | 4,000 |
| 222. Sketch Artists | $35,770 | 13.4% | 4,000 |
| 223. Cashiers | $15,730 | 14.2% | 1,125,000 |
| 224. Construction and Building Inspectors | $39,730 | 15.0% | 2,000 |
| 225. Fire Inspectors and Investigators | $42,800 | 15.1% | 1,000 |
| 226. Packaging and Filling Machine Operators and Tenders | $21,700 | 14.4% | 56,000 |
| 227. Maintenance and Repair Workers, General | $29,420 | 4.7% | 103,000 |
| 228. Forest Fire Fighting and Prevention Supervisors | $52,990 | 7.2% | 5,000 |
| 229. Municipal Fire Fighting and Prevention Supervisors | $52,990 | 7.2% | 5,000 |

*(continued)*

*(continued)*

## The 300 Best Jobs That Don't Require a Four-Year Degree

| Job | Annual Earnings | Percent Growth | Annual Openings |
|---|---|---|---|
| 230. Stonemasons | $32,380 | 20.8% | 2,000 |
| 231. Paving, Surfacing, and Tamping Equipment Operators | $30,090 | 15.5% | 6,000 |
| 232. Extruding and Drawing Machine Setters, Operators, and Tenders, Metal and Plastic | $25,030 | 13.5% | 23,000 |
| 233. Bakers, Bread and Pastry | $21,050 | 16.8% | 25,000 |
| 234. Bakers, Manufacturing | $21,050 | 16.8% | 25,000 |
| 235. Food Servers, Nonrestaurant | $16,170 | 16.4% | 85,000 |
| 236. Aircraft Rigging Assemblers | $38,150 | 14.2% | 2,000 |
| 237. Aircraft Structure Assemblers, Precision | $38,150 | 14.2% | 2,000 |
| 238. Aircraft Systems Assemblers, Precision | $38,150 | 14.2% | 2,000 |
| 239. Billing, Cost, and Rate Clerks | $25,480 | 8.5% | 69,000 |
| 240. Billing, Posting, and Calculating Machine Operators | $25,480 | 8.5% | 69,000 |
| 241. Counter Attendants, Cafeteria, Food Concession, and Coffee Shop | $15,030 | 14.4% | 216,000 |
| 242. Statement Clerks | $25,480 | 8.5% | 69,000 |
| 243. Hairdressers, Hairstylists, and Cosmetologists | $20,710 | 13.0% | 78,000 |
| 244. Lodging Managers | $34,800 | 9.3% | 8,000 |
| 245. Transit and Railroad Police | $41,560 | 16.5% | fewer than 500 |
| 246. Shipping, Receiving, and Traffic Clerks | $23,340 | 9.3% | 133,000 |
| 247. Court Clerks | $27,780 | 12.0% | 14,000 |
| 248. Municipal Clerks | $27,780 | 12.0% | 14,000 |
| 249. Tapers | $38,680 | 8.3% | 6,000 |
| 250. Production Helpers | $19,350 | 11.9% | 143,000 |
| 251. Production Laborers | $19,350 | 11.9% | 143,000 |
| 252. Carpet Installers | $33,030 | 10.5% | 7,000 |
| 253. Helpers—Brickmasons, Blockmasons, Stonemasons, and Tile and Marble Setters | $25,780 | 14.1% | 14,000 |
| 254. Pile-Driver Operators | $41,570 | 14.0% | 1,000 |
| 255. Nonfarm Animal Caretakers | $17,600 | 21.6% | 20,000 |
| 256. Tree Trimmers and Pruners | $25,590 | 16.3% | 11,000 |
| 257. Bus Drivers, School | $21,430 | 11.6% | 63,000 |
| 258. Bookkeeping, Accounting, and Auditing Clerks | $26,950 | 2.0% | 298,000 |

# The 300 Best Jobs That Don't Require a Four-Year Degree

| Job | Annual Earnings | Percent Growth | Annual Openings |
|---|---|---|---|
| 259. Helpers—Electricians | $22,740 | 13.3% | 27,000 |
| 260. Postal Service Mail Carriers | $36,830 | 2.4% | 13,000 |
| 261. Design Printing Machine Setters and Set-Up Operators | $30,090 | 5.5% | 24,000 |
| 262. Embossing Machine Set-Up Operators | $30,090 | 5.5% | 24,000 |
| 263. Engraver Set-Up Operators | $30,090 | 5.5% | 24,000 |
| 264. Letterpress Setters and Set-Up Operators | $30,090 | 5.5% | 24,000 |
| 265. Marking and Identification Printing Machine Setters and Set-Up Operators | $30,090 | 5.5% | 24,000 |
| 266. Offset Lithographic Press Setters and Set-Up Operators | $30,090 | 5.5% | 24,000 |
| 267. Precision Printing Workers | $30,090 | 5.5% | 24,000 |
| 268. Printing Press Machine Operators and Tenders | $30,090 | 5.5% | 24,000 |
| 269. Screen Printing Machine Setters and Set-Up Operators | $30,090 | 5.5% | 24,000 |
| 270. Veterinary Technologists and Technicians | $22,730 | 39.3% | 6,000 |
| 271. Costume Attendants | $24,790 | 19.1% | 8,000 |
| 272. Travel Guides | $30,990 | 9.5% | 10,000 |
| 273. Heat Treating, Annealing, and Tempering Machine Operators and Tenders, Metal and Plastic | $28,020 | 13.4% | 9,000 |
| 274. Heaters, Metal and Plastic | $28,020 | 13.4% | 9,000 |
| 275. Heating Equipment Setters and Set-Up Operators, Metal and Plastic | $28,020 | 13.4% | 9,000 |
| 276. Residential Advisors | $21,600 | 24.0% | 9,000 |
| 277. Pest Control Workers | $24,020 | 22.1% | 7,000 |
| 278. Marking Clerks | $20,650 | 8.5% | 467,000 |
| 279. Order Fillers, Wholesale and Retail Sales | $20,650 | 8.5% | 467,000 |
| 280. Stock Clerks and Order Fillers | $20,650 | 8.5% | 467,000 |
| 281. Stock Clerks, Sales Floor | $20,650 | 8.5% | 467,000 |
| 282. Stock Clerks—Stockroom, Warehouse, or Storage Yard | $20,650 | 8.5% | 467,000 |
| 283. Audio-Visual Collections Specialists | $35,590 | 13.6% | 2,000 |
| 284. Casting Machine Set-Up Operators | $23,630 | 9.8% | 38,000 |

*(continued)*

*(continued)*

# The 300 Best Jobs That Don't Require a Four-Year Degree

| Job | Annual Earnings | Percent Growth | Annual Openings |
|---|---|---|---|
| 285. Coating, Painting, and Spraying Machine Operators and Tenders | $25,140 | 11.9% | 18,000 |
| 286. Coating, Painting, and Spraying Machine Setters and Set-Up Operators | $25,140 | 11.9% | 18,000 |
| 287. Metal Molding, Coremaking, and Casting Machine Operators and Tenders | $23,630 | 9.8% | 38,000 |
| 288. Metal Molding, Coremaking, and Casting Machine Setters and Set-Up Operators | $23,630 | 9.8% | 38,000 |
| 289. Plastic Molding and Casting Machine Operators and Tenders | $23,630 | 9.8% | 38,000 |
| 290. Plastic Molding and Casting Machine Setters and Set-Up Operators | $23,630 | 9.8% | 38,000 |
| 291. Physical Therapist Aides | $20,930 | 46.3% | 7,000 |
| 292. Avionics Technicians | $41,600 | 9.8% | 2,000 |
| 293. Child Care Workers | $16,350 | 10.6% | 370,000 |
| 294. Bartenders | $16,150 | 13.4% | 84,000 |
| 295. Septic Tank Servicers and Sewer Pipe Cleaners | $28,930 | 16.5% | 4,000 |
| 296. Pipelayers | $30,220 | 11.9% | 6,000 |
| 297. Air Traffic Controllers | $79,460 | 7.2% | 2,000 |
| 298. Crane and Tower Operators | $35,340 | 8.6% | 5,000 |
| 299. Central Office and PBX Installers and Repairers | $42,520 | −3.1% | 9,000 |
| 300. Communication Equipment Mechanics, Installers, and Repairers | $42,520 | −3.1% | 9,000 |

# The 100 Best-Paying Jobs That Don't Require a Four-Year Degree

From the 300 jobs that met our criteria for this book, this list shows the 100 with the highest earnings. This is a very popular list for obvious reasons. It includes jobs at all levels of training, although many of the better-paying jobs do require technical training and/or work experience.

For example, the highest-paying job on the list is Air Traffic Controllers, a job that requires considerable training and on-the-job experience. Among the top 25, seven are in sales and others require management, supervision, or technical skills.

We mention in the Introduction that earnings can vary considerably by region of the country, by amount of experience, and because of many other factors, so do keep this in mind as you review this and any other list. Entry-level workers, for example, would typically be paid considerably less than the amounts listed here.

## The 100 Best-Paying Jobs That Don't Require a Four-Year Degree

| Job | Annual Earnings |
|---|---|
| 1. Air Traffic Controllers | $79,460 |
| 2. Athletes and Sports Competitors | $62,960 |
| 3. Nuclear Equipment Operation Technicians | $61,970 |
| 4. Nuclear Monitoring Technicians | $61,970 |
| 5. Real Estate Brokers | $60,080 |
| 6. Sales Representatives, Agricultural | $58,630 |
| 7. Sales Representatives, Chemical and Pharmaceutical | $58,630 |
| 8. Sales Representatives, Electrical/Electronic | $58,630 |
| 9. Sales Representatives, Instruments | $58,630 |
| 10. Sales Representatives, Mechanical Equipment and Supplies | $58,630 |
| 11. Sales Representatives, Medical | $58,630 |
| 12. Storage and Distribution Managers | $58,200 |
| 13. Transportation Managers | $58,200 |
| 14. First-Line Supervisors/Managers of Police and Detectives | $57,900 |
| 15. First-Line Supervisors/Managers of Non-Retail Sales Workers | $56,850 |
| 16. Forest Fire Fighting and Prevention Supervisors | $52,990 |
| 17. Municipal Fire Fighting and Prevention Supervisors | $52,990 |

*(continued)*

(continued)

## The 100 Best-Paying Jobs That Don't Require a Four-Year Degree

| Job | Annual Earnings |
|---|---|
| 18. Dental Hygienists | $51,980 |
| 19. Commercial Pilots | $51,370 |
| 20. Child Support, Missing Persons, and Unemployment Insurance Fraud Investigators | $49,830 |
| 21. Criminal Investigators and Special Agents | $49,830 |
| 22. Immigration and Customs Inspectors | $49,830 |
| 23. Police Detectives | $49,830 |
| 24. Police Identification and Records Officers | $49,830 |
| 25. First-Line Supervisors and Manager/Supervisors—Construction Trades Workers | $47,740 |
| 26. First-Line Supervisors and Manager/Supervisors—Extractive Workers | $47,740 |
| 27. Sales Representatives, Wholesale and Manufacturing, Except Technical and Scientific Products | $46,770 |
| 28. First-Line Supervisors/Managers of Mechanics, Installers, and Repairers | $46,560 |
| 29. Registered Nurses | $46,410 |
| 30. Elevator Installers and Repairers | $46,240 |
| 31. Flight Attendants | $45,220 |
| 32. Advertising Sales Agents | $44,960 |
| 33. Nuclear Medicine Technologists | $44,850 |
| 34. Musicians, Instrumental | $44,520 |
| 35. Singers | $44,520 |
| 36. Electrical Power-Line Installers and Repairers | $44,490 |
| 37. Aviation Inspectors | $44,200 |
| 38. Freight Inspectors | $44,200 |
| 39. Marine Cargo Inspectors | $44,200 |
| 40. Motor Vehicle Inspectors | $44,200 |
| 41. Public Transportation Inspectors | $44,200 |
| 42. Railroad Inspectors | $44,200 |
| 43. Coroners | $44,140 |
| 44. Environmental Compliance Inspectors | $44,140 |
| 45. Equal Opportunity Representatives and Officers | $44,140 |
| 46. Government Property Inspectors and Investigators | $44,140 |
| 47. Licensing Examiners and Inspectors | $44,140 |

# The 100 Best-Paying Jobs That Don't Require a Four-Year Degree

| Job | Annual Earnings |
|---|---|
| 48. Pressure Vessel Inspectors | $44,140 |
| 49. Claims Examiners, Property and Casualty Insurance | $44,000 |
| 50. Insurance Adjusters, Examiners, and Investigators | $44,000 |
| 51. First-Line Supervisors/Managers of Transportation and Material-Moving Machine and Vehicle Operators | $43,120 |
| 52. First-Line Supervisors/Managers of Production and Operating Workers | $43,020 |
| 53. Fire Inspectors | $42,800 |
| 54. Fire Inspectors and Investigators | $42,800 |
| 55. Central Office and PBX Installers and Repairers | $42,520 |
| 56. Communication Equipment Mechanics, Installers, and Repairers | $42,520 |
| 57. Electricians | $42,210 |
| 58. Appraisers, Real Estate | $41,700 |
| 59. Avionics Technicians | $41,600 |
| 60. Actors | $41,570 |
| 61. Pile-Driver Operators | $41,570 |
| 62. Transit and Railroad Police | $41,560 |
| 63. Calibration and Instrumentation Technicians | $41,210 |
| 64. Electrical Engineering Technicians | $41,210 |
| 65. Electronics Engineering Technicians | $41,210 |
| 66. Brickmasons and Blockmasons | $41,140 |
| 67. Highway Patrol Pilots | $40,590 |
| 68. Police Patrol Officers | $40,590 |
| 69. Sheriffs and Deputy Sheriffs | $40,590 |
| 70. Aircraft Mechanics and Service Technicians | $40,550 |
| 71. Electrical Drafters | $40,420 |
| 72. Electronic Drafters | $40,420 |
| 73. Mechanical Drafters | $40,330 |
| 74. Pipe Fitters | $40,170 |
| 75. Pipelaying Fitters | $40,170 |
| 76. Plumbers | $40,170 |
| 77. Construction and Building Inspectors | $39,730 |
| 78. First-Line Supervisors, Administrative Support | $39,410 |
| 79. First-Line Supervisors, Customer Service | $39,410 |

*(continued)*

(continued)

## The 100 Best-Paying Jobs That Don't Require a Four-Year Degree

| Job | Annual Earnings |
| --- | --- |
| 80. Structural Iron and Steel Workers | $39,140 |
| 81. Paralegals and Legal Assistants | $38,790 |
| 82. Tapers | $38,680 |
| 83. Electro-Mechanical Technicians | $38,630 |
| 84. Respiratory Therapists | $38,220 |
| 85. Aircraft Rigging Assemblers | $38,150 |
| 86. Aircraft Structure Assemblers, Precision | $38,150 |
| 87. Aircraft Systems Assemblers, Precision | $38,150 |
| 88. Telecommunications Line Installers and Repairers | $38,050 |
| 89. Real Estate Sales Agents | $37,950 |
| 90. Reinforcing Iron and Rebar Workers | $37,800 |
| 91. Numerical Tool and Process Control Programmers | $37,690 |
| 92. Medical Equipment Repairers | $37,470 |
| 93. Radiologic Technologists and Technicians | $37,290 |
| 94. Electrical and Electronics Repairers, Commercial and Industrial Equipment | $37,190 |
| 95. Architectural Drafters | $37,100 |
| 96. Civil Drafters | $37,100 |
| 97. Chemical Technicians | $37,080 |
| 98. First-Line Supervisors/Managers of Helpers, Laborers, and Material Movers, Hand | $36,910 |
| 99. Postal Service Mail Carriers | $36,830 |
| 100. Tile and Marble Setters | $36,580 |

# The 100 Fastest-Growing Jobs That Don't Require a Four-Year Degree

From the 300 jobs that met our criteria for this book, this list presents the 100 jobs that are projected to have the highest percentage increase in the numbers of people employed through 2010.

Fourteen of the top 25 jobs are in the healthcare field, an industry that is growing quickly and that will provide many opportunities. But you will see a variety of rapidly growing jobs in many different fields as you go through this list. Some of these jobs have average or lower earnings, but some have good earnings—and training requirements vary tremendously, from short-term on-the-job training to technical training that may require up to two years.

## The 100 Fastest-Growing Jobs That Don't Require a Four-Year Degree

| Job | Percent Growth |
|---|---|
| 1. Desktop Publishers | 66.7% |
| 2. Personal and Home Care Aides | 62.5% |
| 3. Medical Assistants | 57.0% |
| 4. Social and Human Service Assistants | 54.2% |
| 5. Medical Records and Health Information Technicians | 49.0% |
| 6. Home Health Aides | 47.3% |
| 7. Physical Therapist Aides | 46.3% |
| 8. Physical Therapist Assistants | 44.8% |
| 9. Fitness Trainers and Aerobics Instructors | 40.3% |
| 10. Occupational Therapist Assistants | 39.7% |
| 11. Veterinary Technologists and Technicians | 39.3% |
| 12. Dental Assistants | 37.2% |
| 13. Dental Hygienists | 37.1% |
| 14. Pharmacy Technicians | 36.4% |
| 15. Security Guards | 35.4% |
| 16. Cardiovascular Technologists and Technicians | 34.9% |
| 17. Respiratory Therapists | 34.8% |
| 18. Surgical Technologists | 34.7% |
| 19. Hotel, Motel, and Resort Desk Clerks | 33.4% |
| 20. Interviewers, Except Eligibility and Loan | 33.4% |
| 21. Paralegals and Legal Assistants | 33.2% |

(continued)

(continued)

## The 100 Fastest-Growing Jobs That Don't Require a Four-Year Degree

| Job | Percent Growth |
|---|---|
| 22. Irradiated-Fuel Handlers | 32.8% |
| 23. Adjustment Clerks | 32.4% |
| 24. Amusement and Recreation Attendants | 32.4% |
| 25. Correctional Officers and Jailers | 32.4% |
| 26. Customer Service Representatives, Utilities | 32.4% |
| 27. Gaming Dealers | 32.4% |
| 28. Semiconductor Processors | 32.4% |
| 29. Emergency Medical Technicians and Paramedics | 31.3% |
| 30. Combined Food Preparation and Serving Workers, Including Fast Food | 30.5% |
| 31. Landscaping and Groundskeeping Workers | 29.0% |
| 32. Telecommunications Line Installers and Repairers | 27.6% |
| 33. Commercial Pilots | 26.9% |
| 34. Actors | 26.7% |
| 35. Biological Technicians | 26.4% |
| 36. Advertising Sales Agents | 26.3% |
| 37. Camera Operators, Television, Video, and Motion Picture | 25.8% |
| 38. Registered Nurses | 25.6% |
| 39. Bill and Account Collectors | 25.3% |
| 40. Demonstrators and Product Promoters | 24.9% |
| 41. Environmental Science and Protection Technicians, Including Health | 24.5% |
| 42. Taxi Drivers and Chauffeurs | 24.4% |
| 43. Residential Advisors | 24.0% |
| 44. Teacher Assistants | 23.9% |
| 45. Interpreters and Translators | 23.8% |
| 46. Receptionists and Information Clerks | 23.7% |
| 47. Nursing Aides, Orderlies, and Attendants | 23.5% |
| 48. Private Detectives and Investigators | 23.5% |
| 49. Electrical Drafters | 23.3% |
| 50. Electronic Drafters | 23.3% |
| 51. Highway Patrol Pilots | 23.2% |
| 52. Police Patrol Officers | 23.2% |
| 53. Sheriffs and Deputy Sheriffs | 23.2% |
| 54. Radiologic Technologists and Technicians | 23.1% |

## The 100 Fastest-Growing Jobs That Don't Require a Four-Year Degree

| Job | Percent Growth |
|---|---|
| 55. Sheet Metal Workers | 23.0% |
| 56. Athletes and Sports Competitors | 22.5% |
| 57. Nuclear Medicine Technologists | 22.4% |
| 58. Heating and Air Conditioning Mechanics | 22.3% |
| 59. Refrigeration Mechanics | 22.3% |
| 60. Dispatchers, Except Police, Fire, and Ambulance | 22.2% |
| 61. Telemarketers | 22.2% |
| 62. Pest Control Workers | 22.1% |
| 63. Cooks, Restaurant | 21.7% |
| 64. Nonfarm Animal Caretakers | 21.6% |
| 65. Architectural Drafters | 20.8% |
| 66. Civil Drafters | 20.8% |
| 67. Stonemasons | 20.8% |
| 68. Nuclear Equipment Operation Technicians | 20.7% |
| 69. Nuclear Monitoring Technicians | 20.7% |
| 70. Legal Secretaries | 20.3% |
| 71. Licensed Practical and Licensed Vocational Nurses | 20.3% |
| 72. Paperhangers | 20.2% |
| 73. Storage and Distribution Managers | 20.2% |
| 74. Transportation Managers | 20.2% |
| 75. First-Line Supervisors and Manager/Supervisors—Landscaping Workers | 20.1% |
| 76. Lawn Service Managers | 20.1% |
| 77. Musicians, Instrumental | 20.1% |
| 78. Singers | 20.1% |
| 79. First-Line Supervisors/Managers of Transportation and Material-Moving Machine and Vehicle Operators | 19.9% |
| 80. Tractor-Trailer Truck Drivers | 19.8% |
| 81. Truck Drivers, Heavy | 19.8% |
| 82. Library Assistants, Clerical | 19.7% |
| 83. Numerical Control Machine Tool Operators and Tenders, Metal and Plastic | 19.7% |
| 84. Fitters, Structural Metal—Precision | 19.5% |
| 85. Library Technicians | 19.5% |
| 86. Metal Fabricators, Structural Metal Products | 19.5% |

*(continued)*

*(continued)*

## The 100 Fastest-Growing Jobs That Don't Require a Four-Year Degree

| Job | Percent Growth |
| --- | --- |
| 87. Counter and Rental Clerks | 19.4% |
| 88. Roofers | 19.4% |
| 89. Brazers | 19.3% |
| 90. Human Resources Assistants, Except Payroll and Timekeeping | 19.3% |
| 91. Packers and Packagers, Hand | 19.3% |
| 92. Solderers | 19.3% |
| 93. Welder-Fitters | 19.3% |
| 94. Welders and Cutters | 19.3% |
| 95. Welders, Production | 19.3% |
| 96. Truck Drivers, Light or Delivery Services | 19.2% |
| 97. Costume Attendants | 19.1% |
| 98. Painters, Construction and Maintenance | 19.1% |
| 99. Medical and Clinical Laboratory Technicians | 19.0% |
| 100. Medical Secretaries | 19.0% |

# The 100 Jobs with the Most Openings That Don't Require a Four-Year Degree

From the 300 jobs that met our criteria for this book, this list presents the 100 jobs that are projected to have the largest number of job openings per year.

Jobs with many openings present several advantages that may be attractive to you. Because there are many openings, these jobs can be easier to obtain, particularly for those just entering the job market. These jobs may also offer more opportunities for part-time or short-term employment or the ability to move from one employer to another with relative ease. Though some of these jobs have average or below-average pay, some also pay quite well and can provide good long-term career opportunities or the ability to move up to more responsible roles.

## The 100 Jobs with the Most Openings That Don't Require a Four-Year Degree

| Job | Annual Openings |
|---|---|
| 1. Cashiers | 1,125,000 |
| 2. Retail Salespersons | 1,124,000 |
| 3. Combined Food Preparation and Serving Workers, Including Fast Food | 737,000 |
| 4. Office Clerks, General | 676,000 |
| 5. Waiters and Waitresses | 596,000 |
| 6. Freight, Stock, and Material Movers, Hand | 519,000 |
| 7. Grips and Set-Up Workers, Motion Picture Sets, Studios, and Stages | 519,000 |
| 8. Stevedores, Except Equipment Operators | 519,000 |
| 9. Janitors and Cleaners, Except Maids and Housekeeping Cleaners | 507,000 |
| 10. Marking Clerks | 467,000 |
| 11. Order Fillers, Wholesale and Retail Sales | 467,000 |
| 12. Stock Clerks and Order Fillers | 467,000 |
| 13. Stock Clerks, Sales Floor | 467,000 |
| 14. Stock Clerks—Stockroom, Warehouse, or Storage Yard | 467,000 |
| 15. Child Care Workers | 370,000 |
| 16. Adjustment Clerks | 359,000 |
| 17. Customer Service Representatives, Utilities | 359,000 |
| 18. Bookkeeping, Accounting, and Auditing Clerks | 298,000 |
| 19. Receptionists and Information Clerks | 269,000 |
| 20. Nursing Aides, Orderlies, and Attendants | 268,000 |
| 21. Teacher Assistants | 256,000 |

*(continued)*

*(continued)*

# The 100 Jobs with the Most Openings That Don't Require a Four-Year Degree

| Job | Annual Openings |
|---|---|
| 22. Packers and Packagers, Hand | 242,000 |
| 23. Security Guards | 242,000 |
| 24. Tractor-Trailer Truck Drivers | 240,000 |
| 25. Truck Drivers, Heavy | 240,000 |
| 26. Construction Laborers | 236,000 |
| 27. Food Preparation Workers | 231,000 |
| 28. Counter Attendants, Cafeteria, Food Concession, and Coffee Shop | 216,000 |
| 29. First-Line Supervisors/Managers of Retail Sales Workers | 206,000 |
| 30. Landscaping and Groundskeeping Workers | 193,000 |
| 31. Executive Secretaries and Administrative Assistants | 185,000 |
| 32. Boat Builders and Shipwrights | 161,000 |
| 33. Brattice Builders | 161,000 |
| 34. Carpenter Assemblers and Repairers | 161,000 |
| 35. Construction Carpenters | 161,000 |
| 36. Rough Carpenters | 161,000 |
| 37. Ship Carpenters and Joiners | 161,000 |
| 38. Cooks, Restaurant | 158,000 |
| 39. Truck Drivers, Light or Delivery Services | 153,000 |
| 40. Counter and Rental Clerks | 150,000 |
| 41. First-Line Supervisors, Administrative Support | 146,000 |
| 42. First-Line Supervisors, Customer Service | 146,000 |
| 43. Telemarketers | 145,000 |
| 44. Production Helpers | 143,000 |
| 45. Production Laborers | 143,000 |
| 46. Registered Nurses | 140,000 |
| 47. First-Line Supervisors/Managers of Food Preparation and Serving Workers | 136,000 |
| 48. Shipping, Receiving, and Traffic Clerks | 133,000 |
| 49. Home Health Aides | 120,000 |
| 50. Automotive Master Mechanics | 104,000 |
| 51. Automotive Specialty Technicians | 104,000 |
| 52. Maintenance and Repair Workers, General | 103,000 |
| 53. Industrial Truck and Tractor Operators | 91,000 |

## The 100 Jobs with the Most Openings That Don't Require a Four-Year Degree

| Job | Annual Openings |
|---|---|
| 54. Cleaners of Vehicles and Equipment | 86,000 |
| 55. Sales Representatives, Wholesale and Manufacturing, Except Technical and Scientific Products | 86,000 |
| 56. Food Servers, Nonrestaurant | 85,000 |
| 57. Bartenders | 84,000 |
| 58. Personal and Home Care Aides | 84,000 |
| 59. Hairdressers, Hairstylists, and Cosmetologists | 78,000 |
| 60. Hotel, Motel, and Resort Desk Clerks | 73,000 |
| 61. Bill and Account Collectors | 71,000 |
| 62. First-Line Supervisors/Managers of Production and Operating Workers | 71,000 |
| 63. Billing, Cost, and Rate Clerks | 69,000 |
| 64. Billing, Posting, and Calculating Machine Operators | 69,000 |
| 65. Statement Clerks | 69,000 |
| 66. Painters, Construction and Maintenance | 67,000 |
| 67. Electricians | 66,000 |
| 68. Bus Drivers, School | 63,000 |
| 69. Amusement and Recreation Attendants | 62,000 |
| 70. Licensed Practical and Licensed Vocational Nurses | 58,000 |
| 71. Packaging and Filling Machine Operators and Tenders | 56,000 |
| 72. Food Service Managers | 55,000 |
| 73. Interviewers, Except Eligibility and Loan | 53,000 |
| 74. Brazers | 51,000 |
| 75. Solderers | 51,000 |
| 76. Welder-Fitters | 51,000 |
| 77. Welders and Cutters | 51,000 |
| 78. Welders, Production | 51,000 |
| 79. Pipe Fitters | 49,000 |
| 80. Pipelaying Fitters | 49,000 |
| 81. Plumbers | 49,000 |
| 82. Social and Human Service Assistants | 45,000 |
| 83. First-Line Supervisors and Manager/Supervisors—Construction Trades Workers | 43,000 |
| 84. First-Line Supervisors and Manager/Supervisors—Extractive Workers | 43,000 |

*(continued)*

*(continued)*

## The 100 Jobs with the Most Openings That Don't Require a Four-Year Degree

| Job | Annual Openings |
|---|---|
| 85. First-Line Supervisors/Managers of Non-Retail Sales Workers | 41,000 |
| 86. Medical Secretaries | 40,000 |
| 87. Reservation and Transportation Ticket Agents | 39,000 |
| 88. Travel Clerks | 39,000 |
| 89. Casting Machine Set-Up Operators | 38,000 |
| 90. First-Line Supervisors/Managers of Mechanics, Installers, and Repairers | 38,000 |
| 91. Metal Molding, Coremaking, and Casting Machine Operators and Tenders | 38,000 |
| 92. Metal Molding, Coremaking, and Casting Machine Setters and Set-Up Operators | 38,000 |
| 93. Plastic Molding and Casting Machine Operators and Tenders | 38,000 |
| 94. Plastic Molding and Casting Machine Setters and Set-Up Operators | 38,000 |
| 95. Roofers | 38,000 |
| 96. Taxi Drivers and Chauffeurs | 37,000 |
| 97. Legal Secretaries | 36,000 |
| 98. Production, Planning, and Expediting Clerks | 36,000 |
| 99. Chefs and Head Cooks | 35,000 |
| 100. Helpers—Installation, Maintenance, and Repair Workers | 35,000 |

# Best Jobs with High Percentages of Workers Age 16–24, Workers Age 55 and Over, Part-Time Workers, Self-Employed Workers, Women, and Men

The data we used to create this book included information that allowed us to compile more specialized sets of lists that include high percentages of younger workers, older workers, part-time workers, self-employed workers, women, and men. As with the other lists, these lists start with the jobs included in the list of 300 jobs with the highest overall scores that don't require a four-year college degree.

We have created five lists for each group. For example, the best jobs lists for younger workers include

▲ Jobs with the Highest Percentage of Workers Age 16–24

▲ Best Jobs Overall for Workers Age 16–24

▲ Best-Paying Jobs for Workers Age 16–24

▲ Fastest-Growing Jobs for Workers Age 16–24

▲ Jobs with the Most Openings for Workers Age 16–24

As in the previous groupings, the Best Jobs Overall list is based on the jobs' combined scores for pay, growth, and number of openings.

We hope you find these lists interesting and useful. Do note that we are not suggesting that you should use the lists to limit your choices. For example, many jobs with a high percentage of women would provide excellent opportunities for, and should be considered by, men who find them interesting.

## Best Jobs with a High Percentage of Workers Age 16–24

Workers age 16–24 make up 16 percent of the workforce, but jobs in the lists that follow include at least 20 percent of these workers. A total of 52 occupations met this criteria.

While young workers are employed in virtually all major occupations, the ones with the highest percentage of workers age 16–24 tend to be in entry-level, part-time, seasonal, or service jobs. This makes sense in that many young workers have not yet settled into careers or are working while going to school. The jobs they get tend to be relatively easy to obtain but have relatively low wages.

More than half (54 percent) of the jobs on these lists pay less than $10 an hour, while less than 8 percent pay more than $15 an hour and none pay more than $17 an hour. These low-paying jobs are often referred to as entry-level jobs because they offer inexperienced workers an opportunity to enter the labor market. Many young people work in them to earn some money, gain basic job skills, and use their experience to move up to better-paying jobs.

## Jobs with the Highest Percentage of Workers Age 16–24

| Job | Percent Workers 16–24 |
|---|---|
| 1. Cashiers | 51.8% |
| 2. Counter Attendants, Cafeteria, Food Concession, and Coffee Shop | 51.1% |
| 3. Waiters and Waitresses | 47.2% |
| 4. Freight, Stock, and Material Movers, Hand | 46.4% |
| 5. Amusement and Recreation Attendants | 46.1% |
| 6. Gaming Dealers | 46.1% |
| 7. Counter and Rental Clerks | 44.8% |
| 8. Helpers—Brickmasons, Blockmasons, Stonemasons, and Tile and Marble Setters | 43.9% |
| 9. Helpers—Electricians | 43.9% |
| 10. Combined Food Preparation and Serving Workers, Including Fast Food | 40.1% |
| 11. Food Preparation Workers | 40.1% |
| 12. Food Servers, Nonrestaurant | 39.4% |
| 13. Cleaners of Vehicles and Equipment | 38.9% |
| 14. Library Assistants, Clerical | 38.4% |
| 15. Bakers, Bread and Pastry | 38.2% |
| 16. Cooks, Restaurant | 38.2% |
| 17. Demonstrators and Product Promoters | 33.1% |
| 18. Retail Salespersons | 33.1% |
| 19. Telemarketers | 33.1% |
| 20. Nonfarm Animal Caretakers | 30.7% |
| 21. Grips and Set-Up Workers, Motion Picture Sets, Studios, and Stages | 30.1% |
| 22. Helpers—Installation, Maintenance, and Repair Workers | 30.1% |
| 23. Production Helpers | 30.1% |
| 24. Production Laborers | 30.1% |
| 25. Stevedores, Except Equipment Operators | 30.1% |
| 26. Landscaping and Groundskeeping Workers | 29.6% |

# Jobs with the Highest Percentage of Workers Age 16–24

| Job | Percent Workers 16–24 |
|---|---|
| 27. Tree Trimmers and Pruners | 29.4% |
| 28. Receptionists and Information Clerks | 29.0% |
| 29. Hotel, Motel, and Resort Desk Clerks | 27.9% |
| 30. Costume Attendants | 26.8% |
| 31. Reservation and Transportation Ticket Agents | 26.8% |
| 32. Travel Clerks | 26.8% |
| 33. Travel Guides | 26.8% |
| 34. Interviewers, Except Eligibility and Loan | 24.3% |
| 35. Dental Assistants | 23.8% |
| 36. Physical Therapist Aides | 22.4% |
| 37. Physical Therapist Assistants | 22.4% |
| 38. Roofers | 22.4% |
| 39. Metal Molding, Coremaking, and Casting Machine Operators and Tenders | 22.0% |
| 40. Metal Molding, Coremaking, and Casting Machine Setters and Set-Up Operators | 22.0% |
| 41. Office Clerks, General | 22.0% |
| 42. Plastic Molding and Casting Machine Operators and Tenders | 22.0% |
| 43. Plastic Molding and Casting Machine Setters and Set-Up Operators | 22.0% |
| 44. Packers and Packagers, Hand | 21.8% |
| 45. Marking Clerks | 21.5% |
| 46. Packaging and Filling Machine Operators and Tenders | 21.5% |
| 47. Teacher Assistants | 21.3% |
| 48. Carpet Installers | 20.9% |
| 49. Production, Planning, and Expediting Clerks | 20.7% |
| 50. Shipping, Receiving, and Traffic Clerks | 20.1% |
| 51. Bartenders | 20.0% |
| 52. Bill and Account Collectors | 20.0% |

# Best Jobs Overall for Workers Age 16–24

| Job | Percent Workers 16–24 | Annual Earnings | Percent Growth | Annual Openings |
|---|---|---|---|---|
| 1. Roofers | 22.4% | $31,670 | 19.4% | 38,000 |
| 2. Production, Planning, and Expediting Clerks | 20.7% | $32,520 | 17.9% | 36,000 |
| 3. Bill and Account Collectors | 20.0% | $26,670 | 25.3% | 71,000 |
| 4. Physical Therapist Assistants | 22.4% | $34,370 | 44.8% | 9,000 |
| 5. Receptionists and Information Clerks | 29.0% | $20,780 | 23.7% | 269,000 |
| 6. Landscaping and Groundskeeping Workers | 29.6% | $20,030 | 29.0% | 193,000 |
| 7. Interviewers, Except Eligibility and Loan | 24.3% | $22,360 | 33.4% | 53,000 |
| 8. Dental Assistants | 23.8% | $26,740 | 37.2% | 16,000 |
| 9. Demonstrators and Product Promoters | 33.1% | $24,460 | 24.9% | 34,000 |
| 10. Telemarketers | 33.1% | $21,460 | 22.2% | 145,000 |
| 11. Teacher Assistants | 21.3% | $18,770 | 23.9% | 256,000 |
| 12. Combined Food Preparation and Serving Workers, Including Fast Food | 40.1% | $14,240 | 30.5% | 737,000 |
| 13. Office Clerks, General | 22.0% | $22,290 | 15.9% | 676,000 |
| 14. Cooks, Restaurant | 38.2% | $18,880 | 21.7% | 158,000 |
| 15. Hotel, Motel, and Resort Desk Clerks | 27.9% | $17,100 | 33.4% | 73,000 |
| 16. Packers and Packagers, Hand | 21.8% | $17,030 | 19.3% | 242,000 |
| 17. Reservation and Transportation Ticket Agents | 26.8% | $26,140 | 14.5% | 39,000 |
| 18. Travel Clerks | 26.8% | $26,140 | 14.5% | 39,000 |
| 19. Counter and Rental Clerks | 44.8% | $18,670 | 19.4% | 150,000 |
| 20. Amusement and Recreation Attendants | 46.1% | $15,480 | 32.4% | 62,000 |
| 21. Waiters and Waitresses | 47.2% | $14,750 | 18.3% | 596,000 |
| 22. Helpers—Installation, Maintenance, and Repair Workers | 30.1% | $22,620 | 18.5% | 35,000 |
| 23. Freight, Stock, and Material Movers, Hand | 46.4% | $20,460 | 13.9% | 519,000 |
| 24. Grips and Set-Up Workers, Motion Picture Sets, Studios, and Stages | 30.1% | $20,460 | 13.9% | 519,000 |
| 25. Stevedores, Except Equipment Operators | 30.1% | $20,460 | 13.9% | 519,000 |

# Best-Paying Jobs for Workers Age 16–24

| Job | Percent Workers 16–24 | Annual Earnings |
|---|---|---|
| 1. Physical Therapist Assistants | 22.4% | $34,370 |
| 2. Carpet Installers | 20.9% | $33,030 |
| 3. Production, Planning, and Expediting Clerks | 20.7% | $32,520 |
| 4. Roofers | 22.4% | $31,670 |
| 5. Travel Guides | 26.8% | $30,990 |
| 6. Dental Assistants | 23.8% | $26,740 |
| 7. Bill and Account Collectors | 20.0% | $26,670 |
| 8. Reservation and Transportation Ticket Agents | 26.8% | $26,140 |
| 9. Travel Clerks | 26.8% | $26,140 |
| 10. Helpers—Brickmasons, Blockmasons, Stonemasons, and Tile and Marble Setters | 43.9% | $25,780 |
| 11. Tree Trimmers and Pruners | 29.4% | $25,590 |
| 12. Costume Attendants | 26.8% | $24,790 |
| 13. Demonstrators and Product Promoters | 33.1% | $24,460 |
| 14. Metal Molding, Coremaking, and Casting Machine Operators and Tenders | 22.0% | $23,630 |
| 15. Metal Molding, Coremaking, and Casting Machine Setters and Set-Up Operators | 22.0% | $23,630 |
| 16. Plastic Molding and Casting Machine Operators and Tenders | 22.0% | $23,630 |
| 17. Plastic Molding and Casting Machine Setters and Set-Up Operators | 22.0% | $23,630 |
| 18. Shipping, Receiving, and Traffic Clerks | 20.1% | $23,340 |
| 19. Helpers—Electricians | 43.9% | $22,740 |
| 20. Helpers—Installation, Maintenance, and Repair Workers | 30.1% | $22,620 |
| 21. Interviewers, Except Eligibility and Loan | 24.3% | $22,360 |
| 22. Office Clerks, General | 22.0% | $22,290 |
| 23. Packaging and Filling Machine Operators and Tenders | 21.5% | $21,700 |
| 24. Telemarketers | 33.1% | $21,460 |
| 25. Bakers, Bread and Pastry | 38.2% | $21,050 |

# Fastest-Growing Jobs for Workers Age 16–24

| Job | Percent Workers 16–24 | Percent Growth |
|---|---|---|
| 1. Physical Therapist Aides | 22.4% | 46.3% |
| 2. Physical Therapist Assistants | 22.4% | 44.8% |
| 3. Dental Assistants | 23.8% | 37.2% |
| 4. Hotel, Motel, and Resort Desk Clerks | 27.9% | 33.4% |
| 5. Interviewers, Except Eligibility and Loan | 24.3% | 33.4% |
| 6. Amusement and Recreation Attendants | 46.1% | 32.4% |
| 7. Gaming Dealers | 46.1% | 32.4% |
| 8. Combined Food Preparation and Serving Workers, Including Fast Food | 40.1% | 30.5% |
| 9. Landscaping and Groundskeeping Workers | 29.6% | 29.0% |
| 10. Bill and Account Collectors | 20.0% | 25.3% |
| 11. Demonstrators and Product Promoters | 33.1% | 24.9% |
| 12. Teacher Assistants | 21.3% | 23.9% |
| 13. Receptionists and Information Clerks | 29.0% | 23.7% |
| 14. Telemarketers | 33.1% | 22.2% |
| 15. Cooks, Restaurant | 38.2% | 21.7% |
| 16. Nonfarm Animal Caretakers | 30.7% | 21.6% |
| 17. Library Assistants, Clerical | 38.4% | 19.7% |
| 18. Counter and Rental Clerks | 44.8% | 19.4% |
| 19. Roofers | 22.4% | 19.4% |
| 20. Packers and Packagers, Hand | 21.8% | 19.3% |
| 21. Costume Attendants | 26.8% | 19.1% |
| 22. Cleaners of Vehicles and Equipment | 38.9% | 18.8% |
| 23. Helpers—Installation, Maintenance, and Repair Workers | 30.1% | 18.5% |
| 24. Waiters and Waitresses | 47.2% | 18.3% |
| 25. Production, Planning, and Expediting Clerks | 20.7% | 17.9% |

# Jobs with the Most Openings for Workers Age 16–24

| Job | Percent Workers 16–24 | Annual Openings |
|---|---|---|
| 1. Cashiers | 51.8% | 1,125,000 |
| 2. Retail Salespersons | 33.1% | 1,124,000 |
| 3. Combined Food Preparation and Serving Workers, Including Fast Food | 40.1% | 737,000 |
| 4. Office Clerks, General | 22.0% | 676,000 |
| 5. Waiters and Waitresses | 47.2% | 596,000 |
| 6. Freight, Stock, and Material Movers, Hand | 46.4% | 519,000 |
| 7. Grips and Set-Up Workers, Motion Picture Sets, Studios, and Stages | 30.1% | 519,000 |
| 8. Stevedores, Except Equipment Operators | 30.1% | 519,000 |
| 9. Marking Clerks | 21.5% | 467,000 |
| 10. Receptionists and Information Clerks | 29.0% | 269,000 |
| 11. Teacher Assistants | 21.3% | 256,000 |
| 12. Packers and Packagers, Hand | 21.8% | 242,000 |
| 13. Food Preparation Workers | 40.1% | 231,000 |
| 14. Counter Attendants, Cafeteria, Food Concession, and Coffee Shop | 51.1% | 216,000 |
| 15. Landscaping and Groundskeeping Workers | 29.6% | 193,000 |
| 16. Cooks, Restaurant | 38.2% | 158,000 |
| 17. Counter and Rental Clerks | 44.8% | 150,000 |
| 18. Telemarketers | 33.1% | 145,000 |
| 19. Production Helpers | 30.1% | 143,000 |
| 20. Production Laborers | 30.1% | 143,000 |
| 21. Shipping, Receiving, and Traffic Clerks | 20.1% | 133,000 |
| 22. Cleaners of Vehicles and Equipment | 38.9% | 86,000 |
| 23. Food Servers, Nonrestaurant | 39.4% | 85,000 |
| 24. Bartenders | 20.0% | 84,000 |
| 25. Hotel, Motel, and Resort Desk Clerks | 27.9% | 73,000 |

# Best Jobs with a High Percentage of Workers Age 55 and Over

Workers age 55 and over make up about 12.5 percent of the labor market. We included occupations in this list if the percent of workers 55 and over was 15 percent or higher. A total of 36 jobs met these criteria and are included in this group of lists.

One use for these lists is to help you identify careers that might be interesting as you decide to change careers or approach retirement. Some occupations are on the lists because they are attractive to older workers wanting part-time work to supplement their retirement income. For example, we think that the job of Lawn Service Managers is on the list because the job pays pretty well, can be done less than full time and on a flexible schedule, and lends itself to self-employment. After occupations on the lists (such as Musicians, Instrumental) take many years of training and experience. After a person is established in that career, the person often works in that occupation until retirement.

## Jobs with the Highest Percentage of Workers Age 55 and Over

| Job | Percent Workers 55 and Over |
|---|---|
| 1. First-Line Supervisors and Manager/Supervisors—Landscaping Workers | 36.1% |
| 2. Lawn Service Managers | 35.2% |
| 3. Appraisers, Real Estate | 26.8% |
| 4. Real Estate Brokers | 26.8% |
| 5. Real Estate Sales Agents | 26.8% |
| 6. Bus Drivers, School | 23.3% |
| 7. Bus Drivers, Transit and Intercity | 23.3% |
| 8. Personal and Home Care Aides | 21.7% |
| 9. Private Detectives and Investigators | 21.7% |
| 10. Security Guards | 21.7% |
| 11. Social and Human Service Assistants | 21.7% |
| 12. Taxi Drivers and Chauffeurs | 21.6% |
| 13. Housekeeping Supervisors | 20.4% |
| 14. Janitorial Supervisors | 20.4% |
| 15. Musicians, Instrumental | 19.4% |
| 16. Singers | 19.4% |
| 17. Weighers, Measurers, Checkers, and Samplers, Recordkeeping | 18.4% |

# Jobs with the Highest Percentage of Workers Age 55 and Over

| Job | Percent Workers 55 and Over |
|---|---|
| 18. Bookkeeping, Accounting, and Auditing Clerks | 18.3% |
| 19. Pest Control Workers | 17.7% |
| 20. Janitors and Cleaners, Except Maids and Housekeeping Cleaners | 17.6% |
| 21. Library Assistants, Clerical | 17.0% |
| 22. Automatic Teller Machine Servicers | 16.4% |
| 23. Child Support, Missing Persons, and Unemployment Insurance Fraud Investigators | 16.4% |
| 24. Transit and Railroad Police | 16.4% |
| 25. Aviation Inspectors | 15.2% |
| 26. Construction and Building Inspectors | 15.2% |
| 27. Coroners | 15.2% |
| 28. Crane and Tower Operators | 15.2% |
| 29. Environmental Compliance Inspectors | 15.2% |
| 30. Equal Opportunity Representatives and Officers | 15.2% |
| 31. Government Property Inspectors and Investigators | 15.2% |
| 32. Immigration and Customs Inspectors | 15.2% |
| 33. Licensing Examiners and Inspectors | 15.2% |
| 34. Marine Cargo Inspectors | 15.2% |
| 35. Pressure Vessel Inspectors | 15.2% |
| 36. Public Transportation Inspectors | 15.2% |

# Best Jobs Overall for Workers Age 55 and Over

| Job | Percent Workers 55 and Over | Annual Earnings | Percent Growth | Annual Openings |
|---|---|---|---|---|
| 1. Musicians, Instrumental | 19.4% | $44,520 | 20.1% | 33,000 |
| 2. Singers | 19.4% | $44,520 | 20.1% | 33,000 |
| 3. Social and Human Service Assistants | 21.7% | $23,840 | 54.2% | 45,000 |
| 4. Appraisers, Real Estate | 26.8% | $41,700 | 18.0% | 6,000 |
| 5. First-Line Supervisors and Manager/ Supervisors—Landscaping Workers | 36.1% | $33,720 | 20.1% | 10,000 |
| 6. Lawn Service Managers | 35.2% | $33,720 | 20.1% | 10,000 |
| 7. Real Estate Sales Agents | 26.8% | $37,950 | 9.5% | 28,000 |
| 8. Security Guards | 21.7% | $19,470 | 35.4% | 242,000 |
| 9. Automatic Teller Machine Servicers | 16.4% | $32,860 | 14.2% | 24,000 |
| 10. Immigration and Customs Inspectors | 15.2% | $49,830 | 16.4% | 4,000 |
| 11. Child Support, Missing Persons, and Unemployment Insurance Fraud Investigators | 16.4% | $49,830 | 16.4% | 4,000 |
| 12. Private Detectives and Investigators | 21.7% | $30,650 | 23.5% | 9,000 |
| 13. Real Estate Brokers | 26.8% | $60,080 | 9.6% | 8,000 |
| 14. Bus Drivers, Transit and Intercity | 23.3% | $27,250 | 17.4% | 24,000 |
| 15. Personal and Home Care Aides | 21.7% | $15,960 | 62.5% | 84,000 |
| 16. Coroners | 15.2% | $44,140 | 8.9% | 9,000 |
| 17. Environmental Compliance Inspectors | 15.2% | $44,140 | 8.9% | 9,000 |
| 18. Equal Opportunity Representatives and Officers | 15.2% | $44,140 | 8.9% | 9,000 |
| 19. Government Property Inspectors and Investigators | 15.2% | $44,140 | 8.9% | 9,000 |
| 20. Licensing Examiners and Inspectors | 15.2% | $44,140 | 8.9% | 9,000 |
| 21. Pressure Vessel Inspectors | 15.2% | $44,140 | 8.9% | 9,000 |
| 22. Taxi Drivers and Chauffeurs | 21.6% | $18,920 | 24.4% | 37,000 |
| 23. Aviation Inspectors | 15.2% | $44,200 | 11.3% | 3,000 |
| 24. Marine Cargo Inspectors | 15.2% | $44,200 | 11.3% | 3,000 |
| 25. Public Transportation Inspectors | 15.2% | $44,200 | 11.3% | 3,000 |

# Best-Paying Jobs for Workers Age 55 and Over

| Job | Percent Workers 55 and Over | Annual Earnings |
|---|---|---|
| 1. Real Estate Brokers | 26.8% | $60,080 |
| 2. Child Support, Missing Persons, and Unemployment Insurance Fraud Investigators | 16.4% | $49,830 |
| 3. Immigration and Customs Inspectors | 15.2% | $49,830 |
| 4. Musicians, Instrumental | 19.4% | $44,520 |
| 5. Singers | 19.4% | $44,520 |
| 6. Aviation Inspectors | 15.2% | $44,200 |
| 7. Marine Cargo Inspectors | 15.2% | $44,200 |
| 8. Public Transportation Inspectors | 15.2% | $44,200 |
| 9. Coroners | 15.2% | $44,140 |
| 10. Environmental Compliance Inspectors | 15.2% | $44,140 |
| 11. Equal Opportunity Representatives and Officers | 15.2% | $44,140 |
| 12. Government Property Inspectors and Investigators | 15.2% | $44,140 |
| 13. Licensing Examiners and Inspectors | 15.2% | $44,140 |
| 14. Pressure Vessel Inspectors | 15.2% | $44,140 |
| 15. Appraisers, Real Estate | 26.8% | $41,700 |
| 16. Transit and Railroad Police | 16.4% | $41,560 |
| 17. Construction and Building Inspectors | 15.2% | $39,730 |
| 18. Real Estate Sales Agents | 26.8% | $37,950 |
| 19. Crane and Tower Operators | 15.2% | $35,340 |
| 20. First-Line Supervisors and Manager/Supervisors— Landscaping Workers | 36.1% | $33,720 |
| 21. Lawn Service Managers | 35.2% | $33,720 |
| 22. Automatic Teller Machine Servicers | 16.4% | $32,860 |
| 23. Private Detectives and Investigators | 21.7% | $30,650 |
| 24. Housekeeping Supervisors | 20.4% | $27,830 |
| 25. Janitorial Supervisors | 20.4% | $27,830 |

## Fastest-Growing Jobs for Workers Age 55 and Over

| Job | Percent Workers 55 and Over | Percent Growth |
|---|---|---|
| 1. Personal and Home Care Aides | 21.7% | 62.5% |
| 2. Social and Human Service Assistants | 21.7% | 54.2% |
| 3. Security Guards | 21.7% | 35.4% |
| 4. Taxi Drivers and Chauffeurs | 21.6% | 24.4% |
| 5. Private Detectives and Investigators | 21.7% | 23.5% |
| 6. Pest Control Workers | 17.7% | 22.1% |
| 7. First-Line Supervisors and Manager/Supervisors— Landscaping Workers | 36.1% | 20.1% |
| 8. Lawn Service Managers | 35.2% | 20.1% |
| 9. Musicians, Instrumental | 19.4% | 20.1% |
| 10. Singers | 19.4% | 20.1% |
| 11. Library Assistants, Clerical | 17.0% | 19.7% |
| 12. Appraisers, Real Estate | 26.8% | 18.0% |
| 13. Weighers, Measurers, Checkers, and Samplers, Recordkeeping | 18.4% | 17.9% |
| 14. Bus Drivers, Transit and Intercity | 23.3% | 17.4% |
| 15. Transit and Railroad Police | 16.4% | 16.5% |
| 16. Child Support, Missing Persons, and Unemployment Insurance Fraud Investigators | 16.4% | 16.4% |
| 17. Immigration and Customs Inspectors | 15.2% | 16.4% |
| 18. Construction and Building Inspectors | 15.2% | 15.0% |
| 19. Automatic Teller Machine Servicers | 16.4% | 14.2% |
| 20. Housekeeping Supervisors | 20.4% | 14.2% |
| 21. Janitorial Supervisors | 20.4% | 14.2% |
| 22. Janitors and Cleaners, Except Maids and Housekeeping Cleaners | 17.6% | 13.5% |
| 23. Bus Drivers, School | 23.3% | 11.6% |
| 24. Aviation Inspectors | 15.2% | 11.3% |
| 25. Marine Cargo Inspectors | 15.2% | 11.3% |

# Jobs with the Most Openings for Workers Age 55 and Over

| Job | Percent Workers 55 and Over | Annual Openings |
|---|---|---|
| 1. Janitors and Cleaners, Except Maids and Housekeeping Cleaners | 17.6% | 507,000 |
| 2. Bookkeeping, Accounting, and Auditing Clerks | 18.3% | 298,000 |
| 3. Security Guards | 21.7% | 242,000 |
| 4. Personal and Home Care Aides | 21.7% | 84,000 |
| 5. Bus Drivers, School | 23.3% | 63,000 |
| 6. Social and Human Service Assistants | 21.7% | 45,000 |
| 7. Taxi Drivers and Chauffeurs | 21.6% | 37,000 |
| 8. Musicians, Instrumental | 19.4% | 33,000 |
| 9. Singers | 19.4% | 33,000 |
| 10. Real Estate Sales Agents | 26.8% | 28,000 |
| 11. Library Assistants, Clerical | 17.0% | 26,000 |
| 12. Automatic Teller Machine Servicers | 16.4% | 24,000 |
| 13. Bus Drivers, Transit and Intercity | 23.3% | 24,000 |
| 14. Housekeeping Supervisors | 20.4% | 18,000 |
| 15. Janitorial Supervisors | 20.4% | 18,000 |
| 16. Weighers, Measurers, Checkers, and Samplers, Recordkeeping | 18.4% | 13,000 |
| 17. First-Line Supervisors and Manager/Supervisors—Landscaping Workers | 36.1% | 10,000 |
| 18. Lawn Service Managers | 35.2% | 10,000 |
| 19. Coroners | 15.2% | 9,000 |
| 20. Environmental Compliance Inspectors | 15.2% | 9,000 |
| 21. Equal Opportunity Representatives and Officers | 15.2% | 9,000 |
| 22. Government Property Inspectors and Investigators | 15.2% | 9,000 |
| 23. Licensing Examiners and Inspectors | 15.2% | 9,000 |
| 24. Pressure Vessel Inspectors | 15.2% | 9,000 |
| 25. Private Detectives and Investigators | 21.7% | 9,000 |

# Best Jobs with a High Percentage of Part-Time Workers

Starting with the 300 jobs that met our criteria for this book, we ran lists that included only those with 30 percent or more of part-time workers. A total of 43 jobs met this criteria and are included in this group of lists.

If you want to work part time, these lists will be helpful in identifying where most others are finding opportunities for this kind of work. Many people prefer to work less than full time. For example, people who are attending school or who have young children may prefer part-time work due to its flexibility. People also work part time for money-related reasons, such as supplementing income from a full-time job or working two or more part-time jobs because one desirable full-time job is not available.

Many of these jobs can be learned quickly, offer flexible work schedules, are easy to obtain, and offer other desirable advantages. Although many people think of part-time jobs as requiring low skills and providing low pay, this is not always the case. Some of these jobs pay quite well, require substantial training or experience, or are growing quickly.

## Jobs with the Highest Percentage of Part-Time Workers

| Job | Percent Part-Time Workers |
|---|---|
| 1. Counter Attendants, Cafeteria, Food Concession, and Coffee Shop | 62.9% |
| 2. Library Assistants, Clerical | 61.7% |
| 3. Food Servers, Nonrestaurant | 58.2% |
| 4. Combined Food Preparation and Serving Workers, Including Fast Food | 57.4% |
| 5. Food Preparation Workers | 57.4% |
| 6. Cashiers | 57.2% |
| 7. Waiters and Waitresses | 57.0% |
| 8. Musicians, Instrumental | 53.5% |
| 9. Singers | 53.5% |
| 10. Counter and Rental Clerks | 50.8% |
| 11. Amusement and Recreation Attendants | 48.8% |
| 12. Gaming Dealers | 48.8% |
| 13. Teacher Assistants | 46.8% |
| 14. Flight Attendants | 45.7% |
| 15. Child Care Workers | 43.4% |
| 16. Bus Drivers, School | 43.3% |
| 17. Bus Drivers, Transit and Intercity | 43.3% |

# Jobs with the Highest Percentage of Part-Time Workers

| Job | Percent Part-Time Workers |
|---|---|
| 18. Bartenders | 43.1% |
| 19. Fitness Trainers and Aerobics Instructors | 42.5% |
| 20. Self-Enrichment Education Teachers | 42.5% |
| 21. Personal and Home Care Aides | 42.4% |
| 22. Social and Human Service Assistants | 42.4% |
| 23. Demonstrators and Product Promoters | 40.2% |
| 24. Retail Salespersons | 40.2% |
| 25. Telemarketers | 40.2% |
| 26. Costume Attendants | 40.1% |
| 27. Dental Assistants | 39.7% |
| 28. Bakers, Bread and Pastry | 38.5% |
| 29. Cooks, Restaurant | 38.5% |
| 30. Freight, Stock, and Material Movers, Hand | 38.4% |
| 31. Nonfarm Animal Caretakers | 38.1% |
| 32. Hairdressers, Hairstylists, and Cosmetologists | 36.5% |
| 33. Receptionists and Information Clerks | 35.1% |
| 34. Physical Therapist Aides | 34.5% |
| 35. Physical Therapist Assistants | 34.5% |
| 36. Bookkeeping, Accounting, and Auditing Clerks | 32.8% |
| 37. Interviewers, Except Eligibility and Loan | 32.5% |
| 38. Janitors and Cleaners, Except Maids and Housekeeping Cleaners | 32.3% |
| 39. Reservation and Transportation Ticket Agents | 31.7% |
| 40. Travel Clerks | 31.7% |
| 41. Travel Guides | 31.7% |
| 42. Office Clerks, General | 30.7% |
| 43. Pest Control Workers | 30.4% |

# Best Jobs Overall for Part-Time Workers

| Job | Percent Part-Time Workers | Annual Earnings | Percent Growth | Annual Openings |
|---|---|---|---|---|
| 1. Musicians, Instrumental | 53.5% | $44,520 | 20.1% | 33,000 |
| 2. Singers | 53.5% | $44,520 | 20.1% | 33,000 |
| 3. Physical Therapist Assistants | 34.5% | $34,370 | 44.8% | 9,000 |
| 4. Flight Attendants | 45.7% | $45,220 | 18.4% | 8,000 |
| 5. Self-Enrichment Education Teachers | 42.5% | $31,070 | 18.5% | 34,000 |
| 6. Fitness Trainers and Aerobics Instructors | 42.5% | $28,750 | 40.3% | 19,000 |
| 7. Social and Human Service Assistants | 42.4% | $23,840 | 54.2% | 45,000 |
| 8. Receptionists and Information Clerks | 35.1% | $20,780 | 23.7% | 269,000 |
| 9. Interviewers, Except Eligibility and Loan | 32.5% | $22,360 | 33.4% | 53,000 |
| 10. Dental Assistants | 39.7% | $26,740 | 37.2% | 16,000 |
| 11. Demonstrators and Product Promoters | 40.2% | $24,460 | 24.9% | 34,000 |
| 12. Telemarketers | 40.2% | $21,460 | 22.2% | 145,000 |
| 13. Teacher Assistants | 46.8% | $18,770 | 23.9% | 256,000 |
| 14. Combined Food Preparation and Serving Workers, Including Fast Food | 57.4% | $14,240 | 30.5% | 737,000 |
| 15. Office Clerks, General | 30.7% | $22,290 | 15.9% | 676,000 |
| 16. Bus Drivers, Transit and Intercity | 43.3% | $27,250 | 17.4% | 24,000 |
| 17. Personal and Home Care Aides | 42.4% | $15,960 | 62.5% | 84,000 |
| 18. Cooks, Restaurant | 38.5% | $18,880 | 21.7% | 158,000 |
| 19. Reservation and Transportation Ticket Agents | 31.7% | $26,140 | 14.5% | 39,000 |
| 20. Travel Clerks | 31.7% | $26,140 | 14.5% | 39,000 |
| 21. Counter and Rental Clerks | 50.8% | $18,670 | 19.4% | 150,000 |
| 22. Amusement and Recreation Attendants | 48.8% | $15,480 | 32.4% | 62,000 |
| 23. Waiters and Waitresses | 57.0% | $14,750 | 18.3% | 596,000 |
| 24. Freight, Stock, and Material Movers, Hand | 38.4% | $20,460 | 13.9% | 519,000 |
| 25. Food Preparation Workers | 57.4% | $16,180 | 16.9% | 231,000 |

# Best-Paying Jobs for Part-Time Workers

| Job | Percent Part-Time Workers | Annual Earnings |
| --- | --- | --- |
| 1. Flight Attendants | 45.7% | $45,220 |
| 2. Musicians, Instrumental | 53.5% | $44,520 |
| 3. Singers | 53.5% | $44,520 |
| 4. Physical Therapist Assistants | 34.5% | $34,370 |
| 5. Self-Enrichment Education Teachers | 42.5% | $31,070 |
| 6. Travel Guides | 31.7% | $30,990 |
| 7. Fitness Trainers and Aerobics Instructors | 42.5% | $28,750 |
| 8. Bus Drivers, Transit and Intercity | 43.3% | $27,250 |
| 9. Bookkeeping, Accounting, and Auditing Clerks | 32.8% | $26,950 |
| 10. Dental Assistants | 39.7% | $26,740 |
| 11. Reservation and Transportation Ticket Agents | 31.7% | $26,140 |
| 12. Travel Clerks | 31.7% | $26,140 |
| 13. Costume Attendants | 40.1% | $24,790 |
| 14. Demonstrators and Product Promoters | 40.2% | $24,460 |
| 15. Pest Control Workers | 30.4% | $24,020 |
| 16. Social and Human Service Assistants | 42.4% | $23,840 |
| 17. Interviewers, Except Eligibility and Loan | 32.5% | $22,360 |
| 18. Office Clerks, General | 30.7% | $22,290 |
| 19. Telemarketers | 40.2% | $21,460 |
| 20. Bus Drivers, School | 43.3% | $21,430 |
| 21. Bakers, Bread and Pastry | 38.5% | $21,050 |
| 22. Physical Therapist Aides | 34.5% | $20,930 |
| 23. Receptionists and Information Clerks | 35.1% | $20,780 |
| 24. Hairdressers, Hairstylists, and Cosmetologists | 36.5% | $20,710 |
| 25. Freight, Stock, and Material Movers, Hand | 38.4% | $20,460 |

# Fastest-Growing Jobs for Part-Time Workers

| Job | Percent Part-Time Workers | Percent Growth |
|---|---|---|
| 1. Personal and Home Care Aides | 42.4% | 62.5% |
| 2. Social and Human Service Assistants | 42.4% | 54.2% |
| 3. Physical Therapist Aides | 34.5% | 46.3% |
| 4. Physical Therapist Assistants | 34.5% | 44.8% |
| 5. Fitness Trainers and Aerobics Instructors | 42.5% | 40.3% |
| 6. Dental Assistants | 39.7% | 37.2% |
| 7. Interviewers, Except Eligibility and Loan | 32.5% | 33.4% |
| 8. Amusement and Recreation Attendants | 48.8% | 32.4% |
| 9. Gaming Dealers | 48.8% | 32.4% |
| 10. Combined Food Preparation and Serving Workers, Including Fast Food | 57.4% | 30.5% |
| 11. Demonstrators and Product Promoters | 40.2% | 24.9% |
| 12. Teacher Assistants | 46.8% | 23.9% |
| 13. Receptionists and Information Clerks | 35.1% | 23.7% |
| 14. Telemarketers | 40.2% | 22.2% |
| 15. Pest Control Workers | 30.4% | 22.1% |
| 16. Cooks, Restaurant | 38.5% | 21.7% |
| 17. Nonfarm Animal Caretakers | 38.1% | 21.6% |
| 18. Musicians, Instrumental | 53.5% | 20.1% |
| 19. Singers | 53.5% | 20.1% |
| 20. Library Assistants, Clerical | 61.7% | 19.7% |
| 21. Counter and Rental Clerks | 50.8% | 19.4% |
| 22. Costume Attendants | 40.1% | 19.1% |
| 23. Self-Enrichment Education Teachers | 42.5% | 18.5% |
| 24. Flight Attendants | 45.7% | 18.4% |
| 25. Waiters and Waitresses | 57.0% | 18.3% |

# Jobs with the Most Openings for Part-Time Workers

| Job | Percent Part-Time Workers | Annual Openings |
|---|---|---|
| 1. Cashiers | 57.2% | 1,125,000 |
| 2. Retail Salespersons | 40.2% | 1,124,000 |
| 3. Combined Food Preparation and Serving Workers, Including Fast Food | 57.4% | 737,000 |
| 4. Office Clerks, General | 30.7% | 676,000 |
| 5. Waiters and Waitresses | 57.0% | 596,000 |
| 6. Freight, Stock, and Material Movers, Hand | 38.4% | 519,000 |
| 7. Janitors and Cleaners, Except Maids and Housekeeping Cleaners | 32.3% | 507,000 |
| 8. Child Care Workers | 43.4% | 370,000 |
| 9. Bookkeeping, Accounting, and Auditing Clerks | 32.8% | 298,000 |
| 10. Receptionists and Information Clerks | 35.1% | 269,000 |
| 11. Teacher Assistants | 46.8% | 256,000 |
| 12. Food Preparation Workers | 57.4% | 231,000 |
| 13. Counter Attendants, Cafeteria, Food Concession, and Coffee Shop | 62.9% | 216,000 |
| 14. Cooks, Restaurant | 38.5% | 158,000 |
| 15. Counter and Rental Clerks | 50.8% | 150,000 |
| 16. Telemarketers | 40.2% | 145,000 |
| 17. Food Servers, Nonrestaurant | 58.2% | 85,000 |
| 18. Bartenders | 43.1% | 84,000 |
| 19. Personal and Home Care Aides | 42.4% | 84,000 |
| 20. Hairdressers, Hairstylists, and Cosmetologists | 36.5% | 78,000 |
| 21. Bus Drivers, School | 43.3% | 63,000 |
| 22. Amusement and Recreation Attendants | 48.8% | 62,000 |
| 23. Interviewers, Except Eligibility and Loan | 32.5% | 53,000 |
| 24. Social and Human Service Assistants | 42.4% | 45,000 |
| 25. Reservation and Transportation Ticket Agents | 31.7% | 39,000 |

# Best Jobs with a High Percentage of Self-Employed Workers

About 10 percent of all working people are self-employed or own their own business. This substantial part of our workforce gets little mention in most career books.

The jobs in the lists in this section all have 20 percent or more self-employed workers. Fifty jobs met this requirement. Many jobs in these lists, such as the various types of photographers or artists, are held by people who operate one- or two-person businesses and who may also do this work part time. Those in other occupations, such as Carpet Installers, often work on a per-job basis under the supervision of others.

As you will see from these lists, self-employed people hold a wide range of jobs at all levels of pay and skill. Many are in the construction trades, but many other fields are also represented. Also, while the lists do not include data on age and gender, older workers and women make up a rapidly growing part of the self-employed population. For example, some highly experienced older workers set up consulting and other small businesses following a layoff or as an alternative to full retirement. Large numbers of women are forming small businesses or creating self-employment opportunities as an alternative to traditional employment.

## Jobs with the Highest Percentage of Self-Employed Workers

| Job | Percent Self-Employed Workers |
|-----|-------------------------------|
| 1. Real Estate Sales Agents | 69.4% |
| 2. Real Estate Brokers | 63.1% |
| 3. Paperhangers | 60.2% |
| 4. Cartoonists | 56.7% |
| 5. Painters and Illustrators | 56.7% |
| 6. Sculptors | 56.7% |
| 7. Sketch Artists | 56.7% |
| 8. Photographers, Scientific | 51.9% |
| 9. Professional Photographers | 51.9% |
| 10. Lodging Managers | 51.5% |
| 11. Tile and Marble Setters | 49.4% |
| 12. Carpet Installers | 48.5% |
| 13. Hairdressers, Hairstylists, and Cosmetologists | 48.5% |
| 14. Painters, Construction and Maintenance | 46.5% |
| 15. Musicians, Instrumental | 45.4% |

## Jobs with the Highest Percentage of Self-Employed Workers

| Job | Percent Self-Employed Workers |
|---|---|
| 16. Singers | 45.4% |
| 17. Child Care Workers | 39.4% |
| 18. Private Detectives and Investigators | 39.3% |
| 19. First-Line Supervisors/Managers of Retail Sales Workers | 38.7% |
| 20. First-Line Supervisors and Manager/Supervisors—Landscaping Workers | 37.8% |
| 21. Lawn Service Managers | 37.8% |
| 22. First-Line Supervisors and Manager/Supervisors—Construction Trades Workers | 37.4% |
| 23. First-Line Supervisors and Manager/Supervisors—Extractive Workers | 37.4% |
| 24. Actors | 36.8% |
| 25. Food Service Managers | 33.8% |
| 26. First-Line Supervisors/Managers of Personal Service Workers | 31.1% |
| 27. Coaches and Scouts | 30.0% |
| 28. Boat Builders and Shipwrights | 28.6% |
| 29. Brattice Builders | 28.6% |
| 30. Carpenter Assemblers and Repairers | 28.6% |
| 31. Construction Carpenters | 28.6% |
| 32. Nonfarm Animal Caretakers | 28.6% |
| 33. Rough Carpenters | 28.6% |
| 34. Ship Carpenters and Joiners | 28.6% |
| 35. Brickmasons and Blockmasons | 28.3% |
| 36. Roofers | 27.5% |
| 37. Athletes and Sports Competitors | 27.2% |
| 38. Medical Equipment Repairers | 27.2% |
| 39. First-Line Supervisors/Managers of Non-Retail Sales Workers | 27.0% |
| 40. Taxi Drivers and Chauffeurs | 27.0% |
| 41. Stonemasons | 26.1% |
| 42. Camera Operators, Television, Video, and Motion Picture | 24.4% |
| 43. Storage and Distribution Managers | 21.9% |
| 44. Transportation Managers | 21.9% |
| 45. Interpreters and Translators | 21.5% |
| 46. Tapers | 20.7% |
| 47. Ceiling Tile Installers | 20.4% |
| 48. Drywall Installers | 20.4% |
| 49. Heating and Air Conditioning Mechanics | 20.0% |
| 50. Refrigeration Mechanics | 20.0% |

# Best Jobs Overall for Self-Employed Workers

| Job | Percent Self-Employed Workers | Annual Earnings | Percent Growth | Annual Openings |
|---|---|---|---|---|
| 1. Musicians, Instrumental | 45.4% | $44,520 | 20.1% | 33,000 |
| 2. Singers | 45.4% | $44,520 | 20.1% | 33,000 |
| 3. First-Line Supervisors and Manager/ Supervisors—Construction Trades Workers | 37.4% | $47,740 | 16.5% | 43,000 |
| 4. First-Line Supervisors and Manager/ Supervisors—Extractive Workers | 37.4% | $47,740 | 16.5% | 43,000 |
| 5. Actors | 36.8% | $41,570 | 26.7% | 20,000 |
| 6. Storage and Distribution Managers | 21.9% | $58,200 | 20.2% | 13,000 |
| 7. Transportation Managers | 21.9% | $58,200 | 20.2% | 13,000 |
| 8. Heating and Air Conditioning Mechanics | 20.0% | $34,180 | 22.3% | 21,000 |
| 9. Refrigeration Mechanics | 20.0% | $34,180 | 22.3% | 21,000 |
| 10. Food Service Managers | 33.8% | $34,350 | 15.0% | 55,000 |
| 11. Roofers | 27.5% | $31,670 | 19.4% | 38,000 |
| 12. Painters, Construction and Maintenance | 46.5% | $29,610 | 19.1% | 67,000 |
| 13. Athletes and Sports Competitors | 27.2% | $62,960 | 22.5% | 3,000 |
| 14. First-Line Supervisors/Managers of Non-Retail Sales Workers | 27.0% | $56,850 | 5.8% | 41,000 |
| 15. Coaches and Scouts | 30.0% | $33,470 | 17.6% | 19,000 |
| 16. Boat Builders and Shipwrights | 28.6% | $35,100 | 8.2% | 161,000 |
| 17. Brattice Builders | 28.6% | $35,100 | 8.2% | 161,000 |
| 18. Carpenter Assemblers and Repairers | 28.6% | $35,100 | 8.2% | 161,000 |
| 19. Construction Carpenters | 28.6% | $35,100 | 8.2% | 161,000 |
| 20. Rough Carpenters | 28.6% | $35,100 | 8.2% | 161,000 |
| 21. Ship Carpenters and Joiners | 28.6% | $35,100 | 8.2% | 161,000 |
| 22. Brickmasons and Blockmasons | 28.3% | $41,140 | 12.5% | 18,000 |
| 23. First-Line Supervisors and Manager/ Supervisors—Landscaping Workers | 37.8% | $33,720 | 20.1% | 10,000 |
| 24. Lawn Service Managers | 37.8% | $33,720 | 20.1% | 10,000 |
| 25. Real Estate Sales Agents | 69.4% | $37,950 | 9.5% | 28,000 |

# Best-Paying Jobs for Self-Employed Workers

| Job | Percent Self-Employed Workers | Annual Earnings |
|---|---|---|
| 1. Athletes and Sports Competitors | 27.2% | $62,960 |
| 2. Real Estate Brokers | 63.1% | $60,080 |
| 3. Storage and Distribution Managers | 21.9% | $58,200 |
| 4. Transportation Managers | 21.9% | $58,200 |
| 5. First-Line Supervisors/Managers of Non-Retail Sales Workers | 27.0% | $56,850 |
| 6. First-Line Supervisors and Manager/Supervisors—Construction Trades Workers | 37.4% | $47,740 |
| 7. First-Line Supervisors and Manager/Supervisors—Extractive Workers | 37.4% | $47,740 |
| 8. Musicians, Instrumental | 45.4% | $44,520 |
| 9. Singers | 45.4% | $44,520 |
| 10. Actors | 36.8% | $41,570 |
| 11. Brickmasons and Blockmasons | 28.3% | $41,140 |
| 12. Tapers | 20.7% | $38,680 |
| 13. Real Estate Sales Agents | 69.4% | $37,950 |
| 14. Medical Equipment Repairers | 27.2% | $37,470 |
| 15. Tile and Marble Setters | 49.4% | $36,580 |
| 16. Cartoonists | 56.7% | $35,770 |
| 17. Painters and Illustrators | 56.7% | $35,770 |
| 18. Sculptors | 56.7% | $35,770 |
| 19. Sketch Artists | 56.7% | $35,770 |
| 20. Ceiling Tile Installers | 20.4% | $35,580 |
| 21. Drywall Installers | 20.4% | $35,580 |
| 22. Boat Builders and Shipwrights | 28.6% | $35,100 |
| 23. Brattice Builders | 28.6% | $35,100 |
| 24. Carpenter Assemblers and Repairers | 28.6% | $35,100 |
| 25. Construction Carpenters | 28.6% | $35,100 |

## Fastest-Growing Jobs for Self-Employed Workers

| Job | Percent Self-Employed Workers | Percent Growth |
|---|---|---|
| 1. Actors | 36.8% | 26.7% |
| 2. Camera Operators, Television, Video, and Motion Picture | 24.4% | 25.8% |
| 3. Taxi Drivers and Chauffeurs | 27.0% | 24.4% |
| 4. Interpreters and Translators | 21.5% | 23.8% |
| 5. Private Detectives and Investigators | 39.3% | 23.5% |
| 6. Athletes and Sports Competitors | 27.2% | 22.5% |
| 7. Heating and Air Conditioning Mechanics | 20.0% | 22.3% |
| 8. Refrigeration Mechanics | 20.0% | 22.3% |
| 9. Nonfarm Animal Caretakers | 28.6% | 21.6% |
| 10. Stonemasons | 26.1% | 20.8% |
| 11. Storage and Distribution Managers | 21.9% | 20.2% |
| 12. Transportation Managers | 21.9% | 20.2% |
| 13. Paperhangers | 60.2% | 20.2% |
| 14. Musicians, Instrumental | 45.4% | 20.1% |
| 15. Singers | 45.4% | 20.1% |
| 16. First-Line Supervisors and Manager/ Supervisors—Landscaping Workers | 37.8% | 20.1% |
| 17. Lawn Service Managers | 37.8% | 20.1% |
| 18. Roofers | 27.5% | 19.4% |
| 19. Painters, Construction and Maintenance | 46.5% | 19.1% |
| 20. Coaches and Scouts | 30.0% | 17.6% |
| 21. Photographers, Scientific | 51.9% | 17.0% |
| 22. Professional Photographers | 51.9% | 17.0% |
| 23. First-Line Supervisors and Manager/ Supervisors—Construction Trades Workers | 37.4% | 16.5% |
| 24. First-Line Supervisors and Manager/ Supervisors—Extractive Workers | 37.4% | 16.5% |
| 25. Tile and Marble Setters | 49.4% | 15.6% |

## Jobs with the Most Openings for Self-Employed Workers

| Job | Percent Self-Employed Workers | Annual Openings |
|---|---|---|
| 1. Child Care Workers | 39.4% | 370,000 |
| 2. First-Line Supervisors/Managers of Retail Sales Workers | 38.7% | 206,000 |
| 3. Boat Builders and Shipwrights | 28.6% | 161,000 |
| 4. Brattice Builders | 28.6% | 161,000 |
| 5. Carpenter Assemblers and Repairers | 28.6% | 161,000 |
| 6. Construction Carpenters | 28.6% | 161,000 |
| 7. Rough Carpenters | 28.6% | 161,000 |
| 8. Ship Carpenters and Joiners | 28.6% | 161,000 |
| 9. Hairdressers, Hairstylists, and Cosmetologists | 48.5% | 78,000 |
| 10. Painters, Construction and Maintenance | 46.5% | 67,000 |
| 11. Food Service Managers | 33.8% | 55,000 |
| 12. First-Line Supervisors and Manager/Supervisors—Construction Trades Workers | 37.4% | 43,000 |
| 13. First-Line Supervisors and Manager/Supervisors—Extractive Workers | 37.4% | 43,000 |
| 14. First-Line Supervisors/Managers of Non-Retail Sales Workers | 27.0% | 41,000 |
| 15. Roofers | 27.5% | 38,000 |
| 16. Taxi Drivers and Chauffeurs | 27.0% | 37,000 |
| 17. Musicians, Instrumental | 45.4% | 33,000 |
| 18. Singers | 45.4% | 33,000 |
| 19. Real Estate Sales Agents | 69.4% | 28,000 |
| 20. Heating and Air Conditioning Mechanics | 20.0% | 21,000 |
| 21. Refrigeration Mechanics | 20.0% | 21,000 |
| 22. Actors | 36.8% | 20,000 |
| 23. Nonfarm Animal Caretakers | 28.6% | 20,000 |
| 24. Coaches and Scouts | 30.0% | 19,000 |
| 25. Ceiling Tile Installers | 20.4% | 19,000 |

# Best Jobs with a High Percentage of Women

We knew we would create some controversy when we first included the best jobs lists with high percentages of men and women. But these lists are not meant to restrict women or men from considering job options—our reason for including these lists is exactly the opposite. We hope the lists help people see possibilities that they might not otherwise have considered. For example, we suggest that women browse the lists of jobs that employ high percentages of men. Many of these occupations pay quite well, and women who want to do them and who have or obtain the necessary education and training should consider them.

We created the lists by sorting the jobs that met the criteria for this book and including only those employing 70 percent or more of men or women. Of the 300 best jobs, 55 jobs met this criteria for women and 160 jobs did so for men.

The lists that follow present the occupations employing high percentages of women. In comparing these lists to those with a high percentage of men, you may notice some distinct differences beyond the obvious. For example, the jobs with high percentages of women are growing at an average rate of 34 percent—much faster than those with a high percentage of men, which are growing at an average rate of 23 percent. The number of annual job openings shows a similar pattern. Occupations with a high percentage of men average 53,960 openings per year, while more than twice that number of openings, 124,108, exist in occupations with a high percentage of women.

This discrepancy might explain why men have had more problems than women in adapting to an economy dominated by service and information-based jobs. Many women may simply be better prepared for these jobs, possessing more appropriate skills for the jobs that are now growing rapidly and have the most job openings. Economists have long noticed that men over 50 who are laid off find it very difficult to locate new jobs. Looking over our lists based on gender, you can see why this might be so. Older males employed in manufacturing, trade, and other traditionally male jobs often develop few of the skills needed in most occupations that are now rapidly growing. If they lose these jobs because of downsizing or any other reason, they may find that fewer similar jobs are available. The results are longer lengths of unemployment, new employment in lower-paying jobs, forced withdrawal from the labor market, and other fates not suffered by many women who have skills that are more in demand.

Perhaps you can come to other conclusions, but there is a variety of evidence that women equipped with skills in demand are doing quite well in the labor market. And it is increasingly true that people of either gender without these skills are less likely to find the best jobs.

## Jobs with the Highest Percentage of Women

| Job | Percent Women |
|---|---|
| 1. Legal Secretaries | 98.8% |
| 2. Medical Secretaries | 98.8% |
| 3. Dental Assistants | 96.6% |
| 4. Child Care Workers | 95.2% |
| 5. Licensed Practical and Licensed Vocational Nurses | 94.9% |
| 6. Receptionists and Information Clerks | 94.2% |
| 7. Registered Nurses | 93.8% |
| 8. Teacher Assistants | 92.8% |
| 9. Bookkeeping, Accounting, and Auditing Clerks | 92.0% |
| 10. Hairdressers, Hairstylists, and Cosmetologists | 90.8% |
| 11. Home Health Aides | 88.9% |
| 12. Nursing Aides, Orderlies, and Attendants | 88.9% |
| 13. Reservation and Transportation Ticket Agents | 88.4% |
| 14. Travel Clerks | 88.4% |
| 15. Travel Guides | 88.4% |
| 16. Hotel, Motel, and Resort Desk Clerks | 87.3% |
| 17. Communication Equipment Mechanics, Installers, and Repairers | 86.6% |
| 18. Telecommunications Facility Examiners | 86.6% |
| 19. Personal and Home Care Aides | 85.1% |
| 20. Social and Human Service Assistants | 85.1% |
| 21. Billing, Cost, and Rate Clerks | 82.4% |
| 22. Flight Attendants | 81.6% |
| 23. Cardiovascular Technologists and Technicians | 81.5% |
| 24. Dental Hygienists | 81.5% |
| 25. Emergency Medical Technicians and Paramedics | 81.5% |
| 26. Medical Assistants | 81.5% |
| 27. Medical Records and Health Information Technicians | 81.5% |
| 28. Pharmacy Technicians | 81.5% |
| 29. Surgical Technologists | 81.5% |
| 30. Interviewers, Except Eligibility and Loan | 81.0% |
| 31. Occupational Therapist Assistants | 81.0% |
| 32. Office Clerks, General | 80.0% |
| 33. Cashiers | 79.8% |
| 34. Paralegals and Legal Assistants | 79.8% |
| 35. Physical Therapist Aides | 78.5% |

*(continued)*

(continued)

## Jobs with the Highest Percentage of Women

| Job | Percent Women |
|---|---|
| 36. Physical Therapist Assistants | 78.5% |
| 37. Waiters and Waitresses | 78.5% |
| 38. Human Resources Assistants, Except Payroll and Timekeeping | 78.1% |
| 39. Library Assistants, Clerical | 77.6% |
| 40. Statement Clerks | 77.1% |
| 41. Medical and Clinical Laboratory Technicians | 76.8% |
| 42. Billing, Posting, and Calculating Machine Operators | 75.5% |
| 43. Customer Service Representatives, Utilities | 75.5% |
| 44. Stock Clerks and Order Fillers | 75.5% |
| 45. Claims Examiners, Property and Casualty Insurance | 74.8% |
| 46. Court Clerks | 74.8% |
| 47. Insurance Adjusters, Examiners, and Investigators | 74.8% |
| 48. Municipal Clerks | 74.8% |
| 49. Adjustment Clerks | 74.6% |
| 50. Combined Food Preparation and Serving Workers, Including Fast Food | 74.4% |
| 51. Food Preparation Workers | 74.4% |
| 52. Respiratory Therapists | 74.2% |
| 53. Nuclear Medicine Technologists | 74.0% |
| 54. Radiologic Technologists and Technicians | 74.0% |
| 55. Counter Attendants, Cafeteria, Food Concession, and Coffee Shop | 73.4% |

# Best Jobs Overall Employing 70 Percent or More Women

| Job | Percent Women | Annual Earnings | Percent Growth | Annual Openings |
|---|---|---|---|---|
| 1. Registered Nurses | 93.8% | $46,410 | 25.6% | 140,000 |
| 2. Paralegals and Legal Assistants | 79.8% | $38,790 | 33.2% | 23,000 |
| 3. Legal Secretaries | 98.8% | $35,370 | 20.3% | 36,000 |
| 4. Claims Examiners, Property and Casualty Insurance | 74.8% | $44,000 | 15.1% | 25,000 |
| 5. Insurance Adjusters, Examiners, and Investigators | 74.8% | $44,000 | 15.1% | 25,000 |
| 6. Customer Service Representatives, Utilities | 75.5% | $26,530 | 32.4% | 359,000 |
| 7. Adjustment Clerks | 74.6% | $26,530 | 32.4% | 359,000 |
| 8. Dental Hygienists | 81.5% | $51,980 | 37.1% | 5,000 |
| 9. Licensed Practical and Licensed Vocational Nurses | 94.9% | $30,470 | 20.3% | 58,000 |
| 10. Radiologic Technologists and Technicians | 74.0% | $37,290 | 23.1% | 13,000 |
| 11. Physical Therapist Assistants | 78.5% | $34,370 | 44.8% | 9,000 |
| 12. Flight Attendants | 81.6% | $45,220 | 18.4% | 8,000 |
| 13. Human Resources Assistants, Except Payroll and Timekeeping | 78.1% | $29,400 | 19.3% | 25,000 |
| 14. Respiratory Therapists | 74.2% | $38,220 | 34.8% | 4,000 |
| 15. Social and Human Service Assistants | 85.1% | $23,840 | 54.2% | 45,000 |
| 16. Receptionists and Information Clerks | 94.2% | $20,780 | 23.7% | 269,000 |
| 17. Interviewers, Except Eligibility and Loan | 81.0% | $22,360 | 33.4% | 53,000 |
| 18. Dental Assistants | 96.6% | $26,740 | 37.2% | 16,000 |
| 19. Nursing Aides, Orderlies, and Attendants | 88.9% | $19,100 | 23.5% | 268,000 |
| 20. Home Health Aides | 88.9% | $18,110 | 47.3% | 120,000 |
| 21. Teacher Assistants | 92.8% | $18,770 | 23.9% | 256,000 |
| 22. Occupational Therapist Assistants | 81.0% | $34,860 | 39.7% | 3,000 |
| 23. Medical and Clinical Laboratory Technicians | 76.8% | $28,970 | 19.0% | 19,000 |
| 24. Cardiovascular Technologists and Technicians | 81.5% | $34,960 | 34.9% | 3,000 |
| 25. Combined Food Preparation and Serving Workers, Including Fast Food | 74.4% | $14,240 | 30.5% | 737,000 |

# Best-Paying Jobs Employing 70 Percent or More Women

| Job | Percent Women | Annual Earnings |
|---|---|---|
| 1. Dental Hygienists | 81.5% | $51,980 |
| 2. Registered Nurses | 93.8% | $46,410 |
| 3. Flight Attendants | 81.6% | $45,220 |
| 4. Nuclear Medicine Technologists | 74.0% | $44,850 |
| 5. Claims Examiners, Property and Casualty Insurance | 74.8% | $44,000 |
| 6. Insurance Adjusters, Examiners, and Investigators | 74.8% | $44,000 |
| 7. Communication Equipment Mechanics, Installers, and Repairers | 86.6% | $42,520 |
| 8. Telecommunications Facility Examiners | 86.6% | $42,520 |
| 9. Paralegals and Legal Assistants | 79.8% | $38,790 |
| 10. Respiratory Therapists | 74.2% | $38,220 |
| 11. Radiologic Technologists and Technicians | 74.0% | $37,290 |
| 12. Legal Secretaries | 98.8% | $35,370 |
| 13. Cardiovascular Technologists and Technicians | 81.5% | $34,960 |
| 14. Occupational Therapist Assistants | 81.0% | $34,860 |
| 15. Physical Therapist Assistants | 78.5% | $34,370 |
| 16. Travel Guides | 88.4% | $30,990 |
| 17. Licensed Practical and Licensed Vocational Nurses | 94.9% | $30,470 |
| 18. Surgical Technologists | 81.5% | $29,660 |
| 19. Human Resources Assistants, Except Payroll and Timekeeping | 78.1% | $29,400 |
| 20. Medical and Clinical Laboratory Technicians | 76.8% | $28,970 |
| 21. Court Clerks | 74.8% | $27,780 |
| 22. Municipal Clerks | 74.8% | $27,780 |
| 23. Bookkeeping, Accounting, and Auditing Clerks | 92.0% | $26,950 |
| 24. Dental Assistants | 96.6% | $26,740 |
| 25. Adjustment Clerks | 74.6% | $26,530 |

# Fastest-Growing Jobs Employing 70 Percent or More Women

| Job | Percent Women | Percent Growth |
|---|---|---|
| 1. Personal and Home Care Aides | 85.1% | 62.5% |
| 2. Medical Assistants | 81.5% | 57.0% |
| 3. Social and Human Service Assistants | 85.1% | 54.2% |
| 4. Medical Records and Health Information Technicians | 81.5% | 49.0% |
| 5. Home Health Aides | 88.9% | 47.3% |
| 6. Physical Therapist Aides | 78.5% | 46.3% |
| 7. Physical Therapist Assistants | 78.5% | 44.8% |
| 8. Occupational Therapist Assistants | 81.0% | 39.7% |
| 9. Dental Assistants | 96.6% | 37.2% |
| 10. Dental Hygienists | 81.5% | 37.1% |
| 11. Pharmacy Technicians | 81.5% | 36.4% |
| 12. Cardiovascular Technologists and Technicians | 81.5% | 34.9% |
| 13. Respiratory Therapists | 74.2% | 34.8% |
| 14. Surgical Technologists | 81.5% | 34.7% |
| 15. Hotel, Motel, and Resort Desk Clerks | 87.3% | 33.4% |
| 16. Interviewers, Except Eligibility and Loan | 81.0% | 33.4% |
| 17. Paralegals and Legal Assistants | 79.8% | 33.2% |
| 18. Customer Service Representatives, Utilities | 75.5% | 32.4% |
| 19. Adjustment Clerks | 74.6% | 32.4% |
| 20. Emergency Medical Technicians and Paramedics | 81.5% | 31.3% |
| 21. Combined Food Preparation and Serving Workers, Including Fast Food | 74.4% | 30.5% |
| 22. Registered Nurses | 93.8% | 25.6% |
| 23. Teacher Assistants | 92.8% | 23.9% |
| 24. Receptionists and Information Clerks | 94.2% | 23.7% |
| 25. Nursing Aides, Orderlies, and Attendants | 88.9% | 23.5% |

# Jobs with the Most Openings Employing 70 Percent or More Women

| Job | Percent Women | Annual Openings |
|---|---|---|
| 1. Cashiers | 79.8% | 1,125,000 |
| 2. Combined Food Preparation and Serving Workers, Including Fast Food | 74.4% | 737,000 |
| 3. Office Clerks, General | 80.0% | 676,000 |
| 4. Waiters and Waitresses | 78.5% | 596,000 |
| 5. Stock Clerks and Order Fillers | 75.5% | 467,000 |
| 6. Child Care Workers | 95.2% | 370,000 |
| 7. Customer Service Representatives, Utilities | 75.5% | 359,000 |
| 8. Adjustment Clerks | 74.6% | 359,000 |
| 9. Bookkeeping, Accounting, and Auditing Clerks | 92.0% | 298,000 |
| 10. Receptionists and Information Clerks | 94.2% | 269,000 |
| 11. Nursing Aides, Orderlies, and Attendants | 88.9% | 268,000 |
| 12. Teacher Assistants | 92.8% | 256,000 |
| 13. Food Preparation Workers | 74.4% | 231,000 |
| 14. Counter Attendants, Cafeteria, Food Concession, and Coffee Shop | 73.4% | 216,000 |
| 15. Registered Nurses | 93.8% | 140,000 |
| 16. Home Health Aides | 88.9% | 120,000 |
| 17. Personal and Home Care Aides | 85.1% | 84,000 |
| 18. Hairdressers, Hairstylists, and Cosmetologists | 90.8% | 78,000 |
| 19. Hotel, Motel, and Resort Desk Clerks | 87.3% | 73,000 |
| 20. Billing, Cost, and Rate Clerks | 82.4% | 69,000 |
| 21. Statement Clerks | 77.1% | 69,000 |
| 22. Billing, Posting, and Calculating Machine Operators | 75.5% | 69,000 |
| 23. Licensed Practical and Licensed Vocational Nurses | 94.9% | 58,000 |
| 24. Interviewers, Except Eligibility and Loan | 81.0% | 53,000 |
| 25. Social and Human Service Assistants | 85.1% | 45,000 |

# Best Jobs with a High Percentage of Men

We suggest you read the introductory material in the "Best Jobs with a High Percentage of Women" section to better understand the purpose of publishing the following lists. As we state in that section, we are not suggesting that the best jobs lists for men include the only jobs that men should consider.

For example, Flight Attendants and Registered Nurses, two jobs that employ high percentages of women, are in short supply, and the few available are highly recruited and often find jobs quickly. Just as women should consider careers typically held by men, many men should consider career opportunities usually associated with women. This is particularly true now, since occupations with high percentages of women workers are growing more rapidly than occupations in our similar lists for men.

In the Best Jobs Overall list for men, note that 13 of the best jobs are in the construction, transportation, and repair fields, whereas 13 of the best jobs overall for women are in the health field. This difference confirms the concerns of many educators, counselors, and social advocates about sexual stereotyping of occupations. In many cases, both men and women would be well advised to consider occupations typically held by the opposite gender.

Another thing we noticed is that many jobs with high percentages of men have significantly higher earnings than jobs with high percentages of women. The average pay for all jobs in the list for women was only 77 percent of the average for men. This indicates that women interested in improving their earnings may want to seriously consider jobs traditionally dominated by men.

## Jobs with the Highest Percentage of Men

| Job | Percent Men |
|---|---|
| 1. Roofers | 99.8% |
| 2. Excavating and Loading Machine Operators | 99.7% |
| 3. Bus and Truck Mechanics and Diesel Engine Specialists | 99.6% |
| 4. Pipe Fitters | 99.3% |
| 5. Plumbers | 99.3% |
| 6. Septic Tank Servicers and Sewer Pipe Cleaners | 99.3% |
| 7. Heating and Air Conditioning Mechanics | 99.2% |
| 8. Refrigeration Mechanics | 99.2% |
| 9. Boat Builders and Shipwrights | 99.0% |
| 10. Brattice Builders | 99.0% |

_(continued)_

*(continued)*

## Jobs with the Highest Percentage of Men

| Job | Percent Men |
|---|---|
| 11. Carpenter Assemblers and Repairers | 99.0% |
| 12. Ceiling Tile Installers | 99.0% |
| 13. Construction Carpenters | 99.0% |
| 14. Rough Carpenters | 99.0% |
| 15. Ship Carpenters and Joiners | 99.0% |
| 16. Automotive Master Mechanics | 98.9% |
| 17. Automotive Specialty Technicians | 98.9% |
| 18. Automotive Body and Related Repairers | 98.8% |
| 19. Brickmasons and Blockmasons | 98.7% |
| 20. Stonemasons | 98.7% |
| 21. Reinforcing Iron and Rebar Workers | 98.6% |
| 22. Structural Iron and Steel Workers | 98.6% |
| 23. Operating Engineers | 98.3% |
| 24. Electrical Power-Line Installers and Repairers | 98.2% |
| 25. Electricians | 98.2% |
| 26. Mobile Heavy Equipment Mechanics, Except Engines | 98.2% |
| 27. Carpet Installers | 98.0% |
| 28. Fire Inspectors | 98.0% |
| 29. Fire Inspectors and Investigators | 98.0% |
| 30. Forest Fire Fighters | 98.0% |
| 31. Municipal Fire Fighters | 98.0% |
| 32. Drywall Installers | 97.9% |
| 33. Tapers | 97.9% |
| 34. Glaziers | 97.7% |
| 35. Paving, Surfacing, and Tamping Equipment Operators | 97.7% |
| 36. Plasterers and Stucco Masons | 97.7% |
| 37. Tile and Marble Setters | 97.7% |
| 38. Crane and Tower Operators | 97.5% |
| 39. Grader, Bulldozer, and Scraper Operators | 97.3% |
| 40. Painters, Construction and Maintenance | 97.3% |
| 41. Paperhangers | 97.3% |
| 42. Refuse and Recyclable Material Collectors | 97.1% |
| 43. Construction Laborers | 97.0% |
| 44. Electrical and Electronics Repairers, Commercial and Industrial Equipment | 96.9% |

## Jobs with the Highest Percentage of Men

| Job | Percent Men |
|---|---|
| 45. Pipelayers | 96.9% |
| 46. Pipelaying Fitters | 96.9% |
| 47. Commercial Pilots | 96.8% |
| 48. Helpers—Brickmasons, Blockmasons, Stonemasons, and Tile and Marble Setters | 96.6% |
| 49. Helpers—Electricians | 96.6% |
| 50. Machinists | 95.5% |
| 51. Tractor-Trailer Truck Drivers | 95.5% |
| 52. Truck Drivers, Heavy | 95.5% |
| 53. Truck Drivers, Light or Delivery Services | 95.5% |
| 54. Welder-Fitters | 95.5% |
| 55. Welders and Cutters | 95.5% |
| 56. Welders, Production | 95.5% |
| 57. Welding Machine Operators and Tenders | 95.5% |
| 58. Welding Machine Setters and Set-Up Operators | 95.5% |
| 59. Aircraft Mechanics and Service Technicians | 95.2% |
| 60. Water and Liquid Waste Treatment Plant and System Operators | 94.8% |
| 61. Office Machine and Cash Register Servicers | 94.3% |
| 62. Elevator Installers and Repairers | 94.2% |
| 63. Landscaping and Groundskeeping Workers | 94.1% |
| 64. Aircraft Rigging Assemblers | 93.5% |
| 65. Aircraft Structure Assemblers, Precision | 93.5% |
| 66. Aircraft Systems Assemblers, Precision | 93.5% |
| 67. Fitters, Structural Metal—Precision | 93.5% |
| 68. Industrial Truck and Tractor Operators | 93.1% |
| 69. Sheet Metal Workers | 92.8% |
| 70. Maintenance and Repair Workers, General | 92.5% |
| 71. Medical Equipment Repairers | 92.5% |
| 72. Avionics Technicians | 92.4% |
| 73. First-Line Supervisors and Manager/Supervisors—Construction Trades Workers | 91.0% |
| 74. First-Line Supervisors and Manager/Supervisors—Extractive Workers | 91.0% |
| 75. First-Line Supervisors/Managers of Helpers, Laborers, and Material Movers, Hand | 91.0% |

*(continued)*

*(continued)*

## Jobs with the Highest Percentage of Men

| Job | Percent Men |
|-----|-------------|
| 76. First-Line Supervisors/Managers of Mechanics, Installers, and Repairers | 91.0% |
| 77. First-Line Supervisors/Managers of Production and Operating Workers | 91.0% |
| 78. First-Line Supervisors/Managers of Transportation and Material-Moving Machine and Vehicle Operators | 91.0% |
| 79. Irradiated-Fuel Handlers | 90.4% |
| 80. Pile-Driver Operators | 90.4% |
| 81. Taxi Drivers and Chauffeurs | 89.8% |
| 82. Chemical Equipment Controllers and Operators | 89.7% |
| 83. Chemical Equipment Tenders | 89.7% |
| 84. Dragline Operators | 89.5% |
| 85. Tree Trimmers and Pruners | 89.2% |
| 86. Cleaners of Vehicles and Equipment | 88.3% |
| 87. First-Line Supervisors/Managers of Police and Detectives | 88.0% |
| 88. Forest Fire Fighting and Prevention Supervisors | 88.0% |
| 89. Municipal Fire Fighting and Prevention Supervisors | 88.0% |
| 90. Grips and Set-Up Workers, Motion Picture Sets, Studios, and Stages | 87.0% |
| 91. Helpers—Installation, Maintenance, and Repair Workers | 87.0% |
| 92. Production Helpers | 87.0% |
| 93. Production Laborers | 87.0% |
| 94. Stevedores, Except Equipment Operators | 87.0% |
| 95. Criminal Investigators and Special Agents | 86.5% |
| 96. Highway Patrol Pilots | 86.5% |
| 97. Police Detectives | 86.5% |
| 98. Police Identification and Records Officers | 86.5% |
| 99. Police Patrol Officers | 86.5% |
| 100. Telecommunications Line Installers and Repairers | 85.1% |
| 101. Calibration and Instrumentation Technicians | 85.0% |
| 102. Electrical Engineering Technicians | 85.0% |
| 103. Electronics Engineering Technicians | 85.0% |
| 104. Combination Machine Tool Operators and Tenders, Metal and Plastic | 84.6% |
| 105. Combination Machine Tool Setters and Set-Up Operators, Metal and Plastic | 84.6% |
| 106. Metal Fabricators, Structural Metal Products | 84.6% |
| 107. Numerical Control Machine Tool Operators and Tenders, Metal and Plastic | 84.6% |
| 108. Sheriffs and Deputy Sheriffs | 84.3% |

## Jobs with the Highest Percentage of Men

| Job | Percent Men |
|---|---|
| 109. Private Detectives and Investigators | 84.2% |
| 110. Security Guards | 84.2% |
| 111. Design Printing Machine Setters and Set-Up Operators | 83.9% |
| 112. Letterpress Setters and Set-Up Operators | 83.9% |
| 113. Marking and Identification Printing Machine Setters and Set-Up Operators | 83.9% |
| 114. Offset Lithographic Press Setters and Set-Up Operators | 83.9% |
| 115. Printing Press Machine Operators and Tenders | 83.9% |
| 116. Screen Printing Machine Setters and Set-Up Operators | 83.9% |
| 117. Central Office and PBX Installers and Repairers | 83.8% |
| 118. Station Installers and Repairers, Telephone | 83.8% |
| 119. Automatic Teller Machine Servicers | 83.3% |
| 120. Child Support, Missing Persons, and Unemployment Insurance Fraud Investigators | 83.3% |
| 121. Transit and Railroad Police | 83.3% |
| 122. Coating, Painting, and Spraying Machine Operators and Tenders | 83.2% |
| 123. Coating, Painting, and Spraying Machine Setters and Set-Up Operators | 83.2% |
| 124. Painters, Transportation Equipment | 83.2% |
| 125. Data Processing Equipment Repairers | 81.6% |
| 126. Correctional Officers and Jailers | 81.1% |
| 127. Freight, Stock, and Material Movers, Hand | 79.9% |
| 128. Architectural Drafters | 79.6% |
| 129. Civil Drafters | 79.6% |
| 130. Electrical Drafters | 79.6% |
| 131. Electronic Drafters | 79.6% |
| 132. Mechanical Drafters | 79.6% |
| 133. Casting Machine Set-Up Operators | 77.6% |
| 134. Embossing Machine Set-Up Operators | 77.6% |
| 135. Engraver Set-Up Operators | 77.6% |
| 136. Heat Treating, Annealing, and Tempering Machine Operators and Tenders, Metal and Plastic | 77.4% |
| 137. Heaters, Metal and Plastic | 77.4% |
| 138. Heating Equipment Setters and Set-Up Operators, Metal and Plastic | 77.4% |
| 139. Extruding and Drawing Machine Setters, Operators, and Tenders, Metal and Plastic | 76.9% |
| 140. Lawn Service Managers | 76.1% |

(continued)

*(continued)*

## Jobs with the Highest Percentage of Men

| Job | Percent Men |
|---|---|
| 141. First-Line Supervisors and Manager/Supervisors—Landscaping Workers | 75.3% |
| 142. Precision Printing Workers | 75.1% |
| 143. Camera Operators, Television, Video, and Motion Picture | 72.4% |
| 144. Photographers, Scientific | 72.4% |
| 145. Professional Photographers | 72.4% |
| 146. Aviation Inspectors | 71.8% |
| 147. Construction and Building Inspectors | 71.8% |
| 148. Coroners | 71.8% |
| 149. Environmental Compliance Inspectors | 71.8% |
| 150. Equal Opportunity Representatives and Officers | 71.8% |
| 151. Government Property Inspectors and Investigators | 71.8% |
| 152. Immigration and Customs Inspectors | 71.8% |
| 153. Licensing Examiners and Inspectors | 71.8% |
| 154. Marine Cargo Inspectors | 71.8% |
| 155. Pressure Vessel Inspectors | 71.8% |
| 156. Public Transportation Inspectors | 71.8% |
| 157. Storage and Distribution Managers | 71.8% |
| 158. Transportation Managers | 71.8% |
| 159. Shipping, Receiving, and Traffic Clerks | 71.6% |
| 160. Semiconductor Processors | 71.5% |

## Best Jobs Overall Employing 70 Percent or More Men

| Job | Percent Men | Annual Earnings | Percent Growth | Annual Openings |
|---|---|---|---|---|
| 1. First-Line Supervisors and Manager/ Supervisors—Construction Trades Workers | 91.0% | $47,740 | 16.5% | 43,000 |
| 2. First-Line Supervisors and Manager/ Supervisors—Extractive Workers | 91.0% | $47,740 | 16.5% | 43,000 |
| 3. Electricians | 98.2% | $42,210 | 17.3% | 66,000 |
| 4. First-Line Supervisors/Managers of Mechanics, Installers, and Repairers | 91.0% | $46,560 | 16.0% | 38,000 |
| 5. Tractor-Trailer Truck Drivers | 95.5% | $32,810 | 19.8% | 240,000 |
| 6. Truck Drivers, Heavy | 95.5% | $32,810 | 19.8% | 240,000 |
| 7. Storage and Distribution Managers | 71.8% | $58,200 | 20.2% | 13,000 |
| 8. Transportation Managers | 71.8% | $58,200 | 20.2% | 13,000 |
| 9. Highway Patrol Pilots | 86.5% | $40,590 | 23.2% | 21,000 |
| 10. Police Patrol Officers | 86.5% | $40,590 | 23.2% | 21,000 |
| 11. Sheriffs and Deputy Sheriffs | 84.3% | $40,590 | 23.2% | 21,000 |
| 12. First-Line Supervisors/Managers of Transportation and Material-Moving Machine and Vehicle Operators | 91.0% | $43,120 | 19.9% | 17,000 |
| 13. Correctional Officers and Jailers | 81.1% | $32,680 | 32.4% | 30,000 |
| 14. Heating and Air Conditioning Mechanics | 99.2% | $34,180 | 22.3% | 21,000 |
| 15. Refrigeration Mechanics | 99.2% | $34,180 | 22.3% | 21,000 |
| 16. Automotive Master Mechanics | 98.9% | $30,780 | 18.0% | 104,000 |
| 17. Automotive Specialty Technicians | 98.9% | $30,780 | 18.0% | 104,000 |
| 18. Roofers | 99.8% | $31,670 | 19.4% | 38,000 |
| 19. Telecommunications Line Installers and Repairers | 85.1% | $38,050 | 27.6% | 9,000 |
| 20. Architectural Drafters | 79.6% | $37,100 | 20.8% | 12,000 |
| 21. Civil Drafters | 79.6% | $37,100 | 20.8% | 12,000 |
| 22. Sheet Metal Workers | 92.8% | $35,050 | 23.0% | 13,000 |
| 23. Painters, Construction and Maintenance | 97.3% | $29,610 | 19.1% | 67,000 |
| 24. Pipe Fitters | 99.3% | $40,170 | 10.2% | 49,000 |
| 25. Plumbers | 99.3% | $40,170 | 10.2% | 49,000 |

# Best-Paying Jobs Employing 70 Percent or More Men

| Job | Percent Men | Annual Earnings |
|---|---|---|
| 1. Storage and Distribution Managers | 71.8% | $58,200 |
| 2. Transportation Managers | 71.8% | $58,200 |
| 3. First-Line Supervisors/Managers of Police and Detectives | 88.0% | $57,900 |
| 4. Forest Fire Fighting and Prevention Supervisors | 88.0% | $52,990 |
| 5. Municipal Fire Fighting and Prevention Supervisors | 88.0% | $52,990 |
| 6. Commercial Pilots | 96.8% | $51,370 |
| 7. Criminal Investigators and Special Agents | 86.5% | $49,830 |
| 8. Police Detectives | 86.5% | $49,830 |
| 9. Police Identification and Records Officers | 86.5% | $49,830 |
| 10. Child Support, Missing Persons, and Unemployment Insurance Fraud Investigators | 83.3% | $49,830 |
| 11. Immigration and Customs Inspectors | 71.8% | $49,830 |
| 12. First-Line Supervisors and Manager/Supervisors— Construction Trades Workers | 91.0% | $47,740 |
| 13. First-Line Supervisors and Manager/Supervisors— Extractive Workers | 91.0% | $47,740 |
| 14. First-Line Supervisors/Managers of Mechanics, Installers, and Repairers | 91.0% | $46,560 |
| 15. Elevator Installers and Repairers | 94.2% | $46,240 |
| 16. Electrical Power-Line Installers and Repairers | 98.2% | $44,490 |
| 17. Aviation Inspectors | 71.8% | $44,200 |
| 18. Marine Cargo Inspectors | 71.8% | $44,200 |
| 19. Public Transportation Inspectors | 71.8% | $44,200 |
| 20. Coroners | 71.8% | $44,140 |
| 21. Environmental Compliance Inspectors | 71.8% | $44,140 |
| 22. Equal Opportunity Representatives and Officers | 71.8% | $44,140 |
| 23. Government Property Inspectors and Investigators | 71.8% | $44,140 |
| 24. Licensing Examiners and Inspectors | 71.8% | $44,140 |
| 25. Pressure Vessel Inspectors | 71.8% | $44,140 |

# Fastest-Growing Jobs Employing 70 Percent or More Men

| Job | Percent Men | Percent Growth |
|---|---|---|
| 1. Security Guards | 84.2% | 35.4% |
| 2. Irradiated-Fuel Handlers | 90.4% | 32.8% |
| 3. Correctional Officers and Jailers | 81.1% | 32.4% |
| 4. Semiconductor Processors | 71.5% | 32.4% |
| 5. Landscaping and Groundskeeping Workers | 94.1% | 29.0% |
| 6. Telecommunications Line Installers and Repairers | 85.1% | 27.6% |
| 7. Commercial Pilots | 96.8% | 26.9% |
| 8. Camera Operators, Television, Video, and Motion Picture | 72.4% | 25.8% |
| 9. Taxi Drivers and Chauffeurs | 89.8% | 24.4% |
| 10. Private Detectives and Investigators | 84.2% | 23.5% |
| 11. Electrical Drafters | 79.6% | 23.3% |
| 12. Electronic Drafters | 79.6% | 23.3% |
| 13. Highway Patrol Pilots | 86.5% | 23.2% |
| 14. Police Patrol Officers | 86.5% | 23.2% |
| 15. Sheriffs and Deputy Sheriffs | 84.3% | 23.2% |
| 16. Sheet Metal Workers | 92.8% | 23.0% |
| 17. Heating and Air Conditioning Mechanics | 99.2% | 22.3% |
| 18. Refrigeration Mechanics | 99.2% | 22.3% |
| 19. Stonemasons | 98.7% | 20.8% |
| 20. Architectural Drafters | 79.6% | 20.8% |
| 21. Civil Drafters | 79.6% | 20.8% |
| 22. Paperhangers | 97.3% | 20.2% |
| 23. Storage and Distribution Managers | 71.8% | 20.2% |
| 24. Transportation Managers | 71.8% | 20.2% |
| 25. First-Line Supervisors and Manager/Supervisors—Landscaping Workers | 75.3% | 20.1% |

## Jobs with the Most Openings Employing 70 Percent or More Men

| Job | Percent Men | Annual Openings |
|---|---|---|
| 1. Grips and Set-Up Workers, Motion Picture Sets, Studios, and Stages | 87.0% | 519,000 |
| 2. Stevedores, Except Equipment Operators | 87.0% | 519,000 |
| 3. Freight, Stock, and Material Movers, Hand | 79.9% | 519,000 |
| 4. Security Guards | 84.2% | 242,000 |
| 5. Tractor-Trailer Truck Drivers | 95.5% | 240,000 |
| 6. Truck Drivers, Heavy | 95.5% | 240,000 |
| 7. Construction Laborers | 97.0% | 236,000 |
| 8. Landscaping and Groundskeeping Workers | 94.1% | 193,000 |
| 9. Boat Builders and Shipwrights | 99.0% | 161,000 |
| 10. Brattice Builders | 99.0% | 161,000 |
| 11. Carpenter Assemblers and Repairers | 99.0% | 161,000 |
| 12. Construction Carpenters | 99.0% | 161,000 |
| 13. Rough Carpenters | 99.0% | 161,000 |
| 14. Ship Carpenters and Joiners | 99.0% | 161,000 |
| 15. Truck Drivers, Light or Delivery Services | 95.5% | 153,000 |
| 16. Production Helpers | 87.0% | 143,000 |
| 17. Production Laborers | 87.0% | 143,000 |
| 18. Shipping, Receiving, and Traffic Clerks | 71.6% | 133,000 |
| 19. Automotive Master Mechanics | 98.9% | 104,000 |
| 20. Automotive Specialty Technicians | 98.9% | 104,000 |
| 21. Maintenance and Repair Workers, General | 92.5% | 103,000 |
| 22. Industrial Truck and Tractor Operators | 93.1% | 91,000 |
| 23. Cleaners of Vehicles and Equipment | 88.3% | 86,000 |
| 24. First-Line Supervisors/Managers of Production and Operating Workers | 91.0% | 71,000 |
| 25. Painters, Construction and Maintenance | 97.3% | 67,000 |

# Best Jobs Based on Levels of Education, Training, and Experience

The lists in this section separate the 300 jobs that met our criteria for this book into lists based on the education or training typically required for entry. Unlike many of the other lists, we did not include separate lists for highest pay, growth, or number of openings. Instead, we provided one list that includes all the occupations in our database that fit into each of the education levels and ranked the occupations by their total score (combining earnings, growth, and job openings).

You can use these lists in a variety of ways. For example, they can help you identify a job with higher potential but with a similar level of education to the job you now hold.

You can also use these lists to figure out additional job possibilities that would open up if you were to get additional training, education, or work experience. For example, maybe you are a high school graduate working in the health care field. There are many jobs in this field at all levels of education. You can identify the job you're interested in and the related training you need so you can move ahead in the health care field.

The lists of jobs by education should also help you when you're planning your education. For example, you might be thinking about a job in the construction field, but you aren't sure what kind of work you want to do. The lists show that a job as a Drywall Installer requires moderate-term on-the-job training and pays $35,580, while various carpenter jobs require long-term on-the-job training but pay an average of $35,100. If you want higher earnings without lengthy training, this information might make a difference in your choice.

As you review these lists, keep in mind that they do not include jobs that typically require a four-year college degree or more. Many of the jobs in the lists that follow are related to and can help you prepare for jobs requiring a four-year degree. If you are considering jobs requiring education beyond an associate's degree, we suggest you refer to the books and resources listed in the front of this book.

## The Education Levels

Here are brief descriptions used by the U.S. Department of Labor for the training and education levels used in the lists that follow:

▲ **Associate's degree**—This degree typically requires two years of full-time academic work beyond high school.

▲ **Postsecondary vocational training**—This requirement involves training that lasts at least a few months but usually less than one year. In a few instances, there may be as many as four years of training.

▲ **Work experience in a related occupation**—This type of job requires a worker to have experience—usually several years of experience—in a related occupation (such as police detectives, who are selected based on their experience as police patrol officers).

▲ **Long-term on-the-job training**—This type of job requires more than 12 months of on-the-job training or combined work experience and formal classroom instruction. This includes occupations that use formal apprenticeships for training workers that may take up to four years. It also includes intensive occupation-specific, employer-sponsored training like police academies. Furthermore, it includes occupations that require natural talent that must be developed over many years.

▲ **Moderate-term on-the-job training**—Occupations that require this type of training can be performed adequately after a 1- to 12-month period of combined on-the-job and informal training. Typically, untrained workers observe experienced workers perform tasks and are gradually moved into progressively more difficult assignments.

▲ **Short-term on-the-job training**—It is possible to work in these occupations and achieve an average level of performance within a few days or weeks through on-the-job training.

# Another Warning About the Data

We warned you in the Introduction to use caution in interpreting the data we use, and we want to do it again here. The occupational data we use is the most accurate available anywhere, but it has its limitations. For example, the education or training requirements for entry into a job are those typically required as a minimum—but some people working in those jobs may have considerably more or different credentials. For example, most Registered Nurses now have a four-year bachelor's degree, although the two-year associate's degree is the minimum level of training this job requires.

In a similar way, people with jobs that require long-term on-the-job training typically earn more than people with jobs that require short-term on-the-job training. However, some people with short-term on-the-job training do earn more than the average for the highest-paying occupations listed in this book. On the other hand, some people with long-term on-the-job training earn much less than the average shown in this book—this is particularly true early in a person's career.

So as you browse the lists that follow, please use them as a way to be encouraged rather than discouraged. Education and training are very important for success in the labor market of the future, but so are ability, drive, initiative, and, yes, luck.

Having said this, we encourage you to get as much education and training as you can. It used to be that you got your schooling and never went back, but this is not a good attitude to have now. You will probably need to continue learning new things throughout your working life. You can do so by going to school, and this is a good thing for many people to do. But there are also many other ways to learn, such as workshops, certification programs, employer training, professional conferences, Internet training, reading related books and magazines, and many others. Upgrading your computer and other technical skills is particularly important in our rapidly changing workplace, and you avoid doing so at your peril.

As one of our grandfathers used to say, "The harder you work, the luckier you get." It is just as true now as it was then.

# Best Jobs Requiring an Associate's Degree

An associate's degree usually requires two years of full-time academic work. Twenty-two jobs met this requirement. The average annual earnings are $38,960. The average rate of growth is just under 27 percent, and the average number of openings annually is about 15,500.

## Best Jobs Requiring an Associate's Degree

| Job | Annual Earnings | Percent Growth | Annual Openings |
|---|---|---|---|
| 1. Registered Nurses | $46,410 | 25.6% | 140,000 |
| 2. Paralegals and Legal Assistants | $38,790 | 33.2% | 23,000 |
| 3. Dental Hygienists | $51,980 | 37.1% | 5,000 |
| 4. Radiologic Technologists and Technicians | $37,290 | 23.1% | 13,000 |
| 5. Physical Therapist Assistants | $34,370 | 44.8% | 9,000 |
| 6. Calibration and Instrumentation Technicians | $41,210 | 10.8% | 22,000 |
| 7. Electrical Engineering Technicians | $41,210 | 10.8% | 22,000 |
| 8. Electronics Engineering Technicians | $41,210 | 10.8% | 22,000 |
| 9. Respiratory Therapists | $38,220 | 34.8% | 4,000 |
| 10. Chemical Technicians | $37,080 | 15.0% | 13,000 |
| 11. Biological Technicians | $32,970 | 26.4% | 7,000 |
| 12. Occupational Therapist Assistants | $34,860 | 39.7% | 3,000 |
| 13. Medical and Clinical Laboratory Technicians | $28,970 | 19.0% | 19,000 |
| 14. Cardiovascular Technologists and Technicians | $34,960 | 34.9% | 3,000 |
| 15. Environmental Science and Protection Technicians, Including Health | $35,830 | 24.5% | 3,000 |
| 16. Nuclear Medicine Technologists | $44,850 | 22.4% | 1,000 |
| 17. Nuclear Equipment Operation Technicians | $61,970 | 20.7% | fewer than 500 |
| 18. Nuclear Monitoring Technicians | $61,970 | 20.7% | fewer than 500 |
| 19. Medical Records and Health Information Technicians | $24,430 | 49.0% | 14,000 |
| 20. Electro-Mechanical Technicians | $38,630 | 14.5% | 4,000 |
| 21. Semiconductor Processors | $27,170 | 32.4% | 7,000 |
| 22. Veterinary Technologists and Technicians | $22,730 | 39.3% | 6,000 |
| Average | $38,960 | 26.8% | 15,455 |

# Best Jobs Requiring Postsecondary Vocational Training

Postsecondary vocational training typically consists of a few months to a year of full-time academic work. There were 37 jobs that met this requirement. The average annual earnings are $34,062. The average rate of growth is 18 percent, and the average number of openings annually is about 27,800.

## Best Jobs Requiring Postsecondary Vocational Training

| Job | Annual Earnings | Percent Growth | Annual Openings |
|---|---|---|---|
| 1. Legal Secretaries | $35,370 | 20.3% | 36,000 |
| 2. Licensed Practical and Licensed Vocational Nurses | $30,470 | 20.3% | 58,000 |
| 3. Automotive Master Mechanics | $30,780 | 18.0% | 104,000 |
| 4. Automotive Specialty Technicians | $30,780 | 18.0% | 104,000 |
| 5. Architectural Drafters | $37,100 | 20.8% | 12,000 |
| 6. Civil Drafters | $37,100 | 20.8% | 12,000 |
| 7. Brazers | $29,080 | 19.3% | 51,000 |
| 8. Solderers | $29,080 | 19.3% | 51,000 |
| 9. Welder-Fitters | $29,080 | 19.3% | 51,000 |
| 10. Welders and Cutters | $29,080 | 19.3% | 51,000 |
| 11. Welders, Production | $29,080 | 19.3% | 51,000 |
| 12. Fitness Trainers and Aerobics Instructors | $28,750 | 40.3% | 19,000 |
| 13. Aircraft Mechanics and Service Technicians | $40,550 | 16.7% | 11,000 |
| 14. Electrical Drafters | $40,420 | 23.3% | 5,000 |
| 15. Electronic Drafters | $40,420 | 23.3% | 5,000 |
| 16. Appraisers, Real Estate | $41,700 | 18.0% | 6,000 |
| 17. Automatic Teller Machine Servicers | $32,860 | 14.2% | 24,000 |
| 18. Data Processing Equipment Repairers | $32,860 | 14.2% | 24,000 |
| 19. Office Machine and Cash Register Servicers | $32,860 | 14.2% | 24,000 |
| 20. Real Estate Sales Agents | $37,950 | 9.5% | 28,000 |
| 21. Bus and Truck Mechanics and Diesel Engine Specialists | $33,210 | 14.2% | 20,000 |
| 22. Commercial Pilots | $51,370 | 26.9% | 1,000 |
| 23. Mechanical Drafters | $40,330 | 15.4% | 8,000 |

## Best Jobs Requiring Postsecondary Vocational Training

| Job | Annual Earnings | Percent Growth | Annual Openings |
|-----|-----------------|----------------|-----------------|
| 24. Desktop Publishers | $32,700 | 66.7% | 5,000 |
| 25. Surgical Technologists | $29,660 | 34.7% | 8,000 |
| 26. Emergency Medical Technicians and Paramedics | $24,740 | 31.3% | 19,000 |
| 27. Medical Secretaries | $24,460 | 19.0% | 40,000 |
| 28. Mobile Heavy Equipment Mechanics, Except Engines | $34,790 | 14.0% | 11,000 |
| 29. Electrical and Electronics Repairers, Commercial and Industrial Equipment | $37,190 | 9.2% | 10,000 |
| 30. Gaming Dealers | $15,550 | 32.4% | 28,000 |
| 31. Chefs and Head Cooks | $28,550 | 9.0% | 35,000 |
| 32. Hairdressers, Hairstylists, and Cosmetologists | $20,710 | 13.0% | 78,000 |
| 33. Avionics Technicians | $41,600 | 9.8% | 2,000 |
| 34. Central Office and PBX Installers and Repairers | $42,520 | −3.1% | 9,000 |
| 35. Communication Equipment Mechanics, Installers, and Repairers | $42,520 | −3.1% | 9,000 |
| 36. Station Installers and Repairers, Telephone | $42,520 | −3.1% | 9,000 |
| 37. Telecommunications Facility Examiners | $42,520 | −3.1% | 9,000 |
| *Average* | *$34,062* | *18.0%* | *27,784* |

# Best Jobs Requiring Work Experience in a Related Job

Jobs in this list require a worker to have experience in a related occupation. An example is Police Detectives, who are selected based on their experience as Police Patrol Officers. Forty jobs met this requirement. The average annual earnings are $43,047. The average rate of growth is almost 14 percent, and the average number of openings annually is about 29,200.

## Best Jobs Requiring Work Experience in a Related Job

| Job | Annual Earnings | Percent Growth | Annual Openings |
|---|---|---|---|
| 1. First-Line Supervisors and Manager/Supervisors—Construction Trades Workers | $47,740 | 16.5% | 43,000 |
| 2. First-Line Supervisors and Manager/Supervisors—Extractive Workers | $47,740 | 16.5% | 43,000 |
| 3. First-Line Supervisors/Managers of Mechanics, Installers, and Repairers | $46,560 | 16.0% | 38,000 |
| 4. Storage and Distribution Managers | $58,200 | 20.2% | 13,000 |
| 5. Transportation Managers | $58,200 | 20.2% | 13,000 |
| 6. First-Line Supervisors/Managers of Transportation and Material-Moving Machine and Vehicle Operators | $43,120 | 19.9% | 17,000 |
| 7. Food Service Managers | $34,350 | 15.0% | 55,000 |
| 8. First-Line Supervisors, Administrative Support | $39,410 | 9.4% | 146,000 |
| 9. First-Line Supervisors, Customer Service | $39,410 | 9.4% | 146,000 |
| 10. First-Line Supervisors/Managers of Helpers, Laborers, and Material Movers, Hand | $36,910 | 18.9% | 14,000 |
| 11. Self-Enrichment Education Teachers | $31,070 | 18.5% | 34,000 |
| 12. First-Line Supervisors/Managers of Non-Retail Sales Workers | $56,850 | 5.8% | 41,000 |
| 13. First-Line Supervisors/Managers of Police and Detectives | $57,900 | 13.1% | 9,000 |
| 14. First-Line Supervisors and Manager/Supervisors—Landscaping Workers | $33,720 | 20.1% | 10,000 |
| 15. Lawn Service Managers | $33,720 | 20.1% | 10,000 |
| 16. Child Support, Missing Persons, and Unemployment Insurance Fraud Investigators | $49,830 | 16.4% | 4,000 |
| 17. Criminal Investigators and Special Agents | $49,830 | 16.4% | 4,000 |

# Best Jobs Requiring Work Experience in a Related Job

| Job | Annual Earnings | Percent Growth | Annual Openings |
|---|---|---|---|
| 18. Immigration and Customs Inspectors | $49,830 | 16.4% | 4,000 |
| 19. Police Detectives | $49,830 | 16.4% | 4,000 |
| 20. Police Identification and Records Officers | $49,830 | 16.4% | 4,000 |
| 21. First-Line Supervisors/Managers of Retail Sales Workers | $32,170 | 8.1% | 206,000 |
| 22. Private Detectives and Investigators | $30,650 | 23.5% | 9,000 |
| 23. First-Line Supervisors/Managers of Production and Operating Workers | $43,020 | 1.0% | 71,000 |
| 24. Real Estate Brokers | $60,080 | 9.6% | 8,000 |
| 25. First-Line Supervisors/Managers of Food Preparation and Serving Workers | $24,600 | 12.7% | 136,000 |
| 26. Aviation Inspectors | $44,200 | 11.3% | 3,000 |
| 27. Freight Inspectors | $44,200 | 11.3% | 3,000 |
| 28. Marine Cargo Inspectors | $44,200 | 11.3% | 3,000 |
| 29. Motor Vehicle Inspectors | $44,200 | 11.3% | 3,000 |
| 30. Public Transportation Inspectors | $44,200 | 11.3% | 3,000 |
| 31. Railroad Inspectors | $44,200 | 11.3% | 3,000 |
| 32. Housekeeping Supervisors | $27,830 | 14.2% | 18,000 |
| 33. Janitorial Supervisors | $27,830 | 14.2% | 18,000 |
| 34. First-Line Supervisors/Managers of Personal Service Workers | $30,350 | 15.1% | 8,000 |
| 35. Fire Inspectors | $42,800 | 15.1% | 1,000 |
| 36. Construction and Building Inspectors | $39,730 | 15.0% | 2,000 |
| 37. Fire Inspectors and Investigators | $42,800 | 15.1% | 1,000 |
| 38. Forest Fire Fighting and Prevention Supervisors | $52,990 | 7.2% | 5,000 |
| 39. Municipal Fire Fighting and Prevention Supervisors | $52,990 | 7.2% | 5,000 |
| 40. Lodging Managers | $34,800 | 9.3% | 8,000 |
| Average | $43,047 | 13.9% | 29,150 |

# Best Jobs Requiring Long-Term On-the-Job Training

These jobs require a worker to have more than 12 months of on-the-job training or combined work experience and formal classroom instruction. The jobs also include occupations that use formal apprenticeships that may take up to four years and intensive occupation-specific, employer-sponsored training. There were 62 jobs that met this requirement. The average annual earnings are $38,129. The average rate of growth is just under 15 percent, and the average number of openings annually is about 32,800.

## Best Jobs Requiring Long-Term On-the-Job Training

| Job | Annual Earnings | Percent Growth | Annual Openings |
|-----|----------------:|---------------:|----------------:|
| 1. Musicians, Instrumental | $44,520 | 20.1% | 33,000 |
| 2. Singers | $44,520 | 20.1% | 33,000 |
| 3. Electricians | $42,210 | 17.3% | 66,000 |
| 4. Actors | $41,570 | 26.7% | 20,000 |
| 5. Highway Patrol Pilots | $40,590 | 23.2% | 21,000 |
| 6. Police Patrol Officers | $40,590 | 23.2% | 21,000 |
| 7. Sheriffs and Deputy Sheriffs | $40,590 | 23.2% | 21,000 |
| 8. Claims Examiners, Property and Casualty Insurance | $44,000 | 15.1% | 25,000 |
| 9. Insurance Adjusters, Examiners, and Investigators | $44,000 | 15.1% | 25,000 |
| 10. Heating and Air Conditioning Mechanics | $34,180 | 22.3% | 21,000 |
| 11. Refrigeration Mechanics | $34,180 | 22.3% | 21,000 |
| 12. Telecommunications Line Installers and Repairers | $38,050 | 27.6% | 9,000 |
| 13. Pipe Fitters | $40,170 | 10.2% | 49,000 |
| 14. Pipelaying Fitters | $40,170 | 10.2% | 49,000 |
| 15. Plumbers | $40,170 | 10.2% | 49,000 |
| 16. Flight Attendants | $45,220 | 18.4% | 8,000 |
| 17. Structural Iron and Steel Workers | $39,140 | 18.4% | 12,000 |
| 18. Athletes and Sports Competitors | $62,960 | 22.5% | 3,000 |
| 19. Coaches and Scouts | $33,470 | 17.6% | 19,000 |
| 20. Boat Builders and Shipwrights | $35,100 | 8.2% | 161,000 |
| 21. Brattice Builders | $35,100 | 8.2% | 161,000 |
| 22. Carpenter Assemblers and Repairers | $35,100 | 8.2% | 161,000 |
| 23. Construction Carpenters | $35,100 | 8.2% | 161,000 |
| 24. Rough Carpenters | $35,100 | 8.2% | 161,000 |
| 25. Ship Carpenters and Joiners | $35,100 | 8.2% | 161,000 |
| 26. Brickmasons and Blockmasons | $41,140 | 12.5% | 18,000 |
| 27. Numerical Control Machine Tool Operators and Tenders, Metal and Plastic | $28,780 | 19.7% | 15,000 |

# Best Jobs Requiring Long-Term On-the-Job Training

| Job | Annual Earnings | Percent Growth | Annual Openings |
|---|---|---|---|
| 28. Cooks, Restaurant | $18,880 | 21.7% | 158,000 |
| 29. Elevator Installers and Repairers | $46,240 | 17.2% | 2,000 |
| 30. Reinforcing Iron and Rebar Workers | $37,800 | 17.5% | 4,000 |
| 31. Coroners | $44,140 | 8.9% | 9,000 |
| 32. Environmental Compliance Inspectors | $44,140 | 8.9% | 9,000 |
| 33. Equal Opportunity Representatives and Officers | $44,140 | 8.9% | 9,000 |
| 34. Government Property Inspectors and Investigators | $44,140 | 8.9% | 9,000 |
| 35. Licensing Examiners and Inspectors | $44,140 | 8.9% | 9,000 |
| 36. Pressure Vessel Inspectors | $44,140 | 8.9% | 9,000 |
| 37. Automotive Body and Related Repairers | $33,710 | 10.2% | 18,000 |
| 38. Interpreters and Translators | $33,550 | 23.8% | 3,000 |
| 39. Tile and Marble Setters | $36,580 | 15.6% | 5,000 |
| 40. Water and Liquid Waste Treatment Plant and System Operators | $32,450 | 18.1% | 6,000 |
| 41. Machinists | $31,610 | 9.1% | 28,000 |
| 42. Photographers, Scientific | $27,420 | 17.0% | 13,000 |
| 43. Professional Photographers | $27,420 | 17.0% | 13,000 |
| 44. Electrical Power-Line Installers and Repairers | $44,490 | 9.3% | 5,000 |
| 45. Forest Fire Fighters | $35,260 | 8.9% | 12,000 |
| 46. Municipal Fire Fighters | $35,260 | 8.9% | 12,000 |
| 47. Plasterers and Stucco Masons | $35,170 | 11.9% | 7,000 |
| 48. Numerical Tool and Process Control Programmers | $37,690 | 16.6% | 2,000 |
| 49. Glaziers | $32,360 | 14.8% | 6,000 |
| 50. Cartoonists | $35,770 | 13.4% | 4,000 |
| 51. Painters and Illustrators | $35,770 | 13.4% | 4,000 |
| 52. Sculptors | $35,770 | 13.4% | 4,000 |
| 53. Sketch Artists | $35,770 | 13.4% | 4,000 |
| 54. Maintenance and Repair Workers, General | $29,420 | 4.7% | 103,000 |
| 55. Stonemasons | $32,380 | 20.8% | 2,000 |
| 56. Bakers, Bread and Pastry | $21,050 | 16.8% | 25,000 |
| 57. Bakers, Manufacturing | $21,050 | 16.8% | 25,000 |
| 58. Aircraft Rigging Assemblers | $38,150 | 14.2% | 2,000 |
| 59. Aircraft Structure Assemblers, Precision | $38,150 | 14.2% | 2,000 |
| 60. Aircraft Systems Assemblers, Precision | $38,150 | 14.2% | 2,000 |
| 61. Transit and Railroad Police | $41,560 | 16.5% | fewer than 500 |
| 62. Air Traffic Controllers | $79,460 | 7.2% | 2,000 |
| *Average* | *$38,129* | *14.8%* | *32,758* |

# Best Jobs Requiring Moderate-Term On-the-Job Training

Occupations that require this type of training can be performed adequately after one month to one year of combined on-the-job training and informal training. There were 78 jobs that met this requirement. The average annual earnings are $32,566. The average rate of growth is 15.6 percent, and the average number of openings annually is slightly more than 42,300.

## Best Jobs Requiring Moderate-Term On-the-Job Training

| Job | Annual Earnings | Percent Growth | Annual Openings |
|---|---|---|---|
| 1. Advertising Sales Agents | $44,960 | 26.3% | 25,000 |
| 2. Tractor-Trailer Truck Drivers | $32,810 | 19.8% | 240,000 |
| 3. Truck Drivers, Heavy | $32,810 | 19.8% | 240,000 |
| 4. Correctional Officers and Jailers | $32,680 | 32.4% | 30,000 |
| 5. Adjustment Clerks | $26,530 | 32.4% | 359,000 |
| 6. Customer Service Representatives, Utilities | $26,530 | 32.4% | 359,000 |
| 7. Roofers | $31,670 | 19.4% | 38,000 |
| 8. Sheet Metal Workers | $35,050 | 23.0% | 13,000 |
| 9. Painters, Construction and Maintenance | $29,610 | 19.1% | 67,000 |
| 10. Executive Secretaries and Administrative Assistants | $32,520 | 11.5% | 185,000 |
| 11. Sales Representatives, Wholesale and Manufacturing, Except Technical and Scientific Products | $46,770 | 5.7% | 86,000 |
| 12. Construction Laborers | $26,940 | 17.0% | 236,000 |
| 13. Sales Representatives, Agricultural | $58,630 | 7.5% | 24,000 |
| 14. Sales Representatives, Chemical and Pharmaceutical | $58,630 | 7.5% | 24,000 |
| 15. Sales Representatives, Electrical/Electronic | $58,630 | 7.5% | 24,000 |
| 16. Sales Representatives, Instruments | $58,630 | 7.5% | 24,000 |
| 17. Sales Representatives, Mechanical Equipment and Supplies | $58,630 | 7.5% | 24,000 |
| 18. Sales Representatives, Medical | $58,630 | 7.5% | 24,000 |
| 19. Social and Human Service Assistants | $23,840 | 54.2% | 45,000 |
| 20. Irradiated-Fuel Handlers | $31,630 | 32.8% | 9,000 |
| 21. Dental Assistants | $26,740 | 37.2% | 16,000 |
| 22. Demonstrators and Product Promoters | $24,460 | 24.9% | 34,000 |
| 23. Fitters, Structural Metal—Precision | $28,490 | 19.5% | 20,000 |
| 24. Metal Fabricators, Structural Metal Products | $28,490 | 19.5% | 20,000 |
| 25. Chemical Equipment Controllers and Operators | $36,310 | 14.9% | 9,000 |
| 26. Chemical Equipment Tenders | $36,310 | 14.9% | 9,000 |

# Best Jobs Requiring Moderate-Term On-the-Job Training

| Job | Annual Earnings | Percent Growth | Annual Openings |
|---|---|---|---|
| 27. Bus Drivers, Transit and Intercity | $27,250 | 17.4% | 24,000 |
| 28. Dispatchers, Except Police, Fire, and Ambulance | $30,410 | 22.2% | 8,000 |
| 29. Medical Assistants | $23,840 | 57.0% | 18,700 |
| 30. Ceiling Tile Installers | $35,580 | 9.4% | 19,000 |
| 31. Drywall Installers | $35,580 | 9.4% | 19,000 |
| 32. Camera Operators, Television, Video, and Motion Picture | $33,860 | 25.8% | 3,000 |
| 33. Painters, Transportation Equipment | $32,910 | 17.5% | 8,000 |
| 34. Combination Machine Tool Operators and Tenders, Metal and Plastic | $29,350 | 14.7% | 21,000 |
| 35. Combination Machine Tool Setters and Set-Up Operators, Metal and Plastic | $29,350 | 14.7% | 21,000 |
| 36. Grader, Bulldozer, and Scraper Operators | $36,170 | 6.9% | 25,000 |
| 37. Operating Engineers | $36,170 | 6.9% | 25,000 |
| 38. Pharmacy Technicians | $21,600 | 36.4% | 22,000 |
| 39. Paperhangers | $32,490 | 20.2% | 3,000 |
| 40. Medical Equipment Repairers | $37,470 | 14.9% | 3,000 |
| 41. Soldering and Brazing Machine Operators and Tenders | $29,730 | 15.1% | 9,000 |
| 42. Soldering and Brazing Machine Setters and Set-Up Operators | $29,730 | 15.1% | 9,000 |
| 43. Welding Machine Operators and Tenders | $29,730 | 15.1% | 9,000 |
| 44. Welding Machine Setters and Set-Up Operators | $29,730 | 15.1% | 9,000 |
| 45. Dragline Operators | $33,480 | 14.8% | 5,000 |
| 46. Excavating and Loading Machine Operators | $33,480 | 14.8% | 5,000 |
| 47. Paving, Surfacing, and Tamping Equipment Operators | $30,090 | 15.5% | 6,000 |
| 48. Extruding and Drawing Machine Setters, Operators, and Tenders, Metal and Plastic | $25,030 | 13.5% | 23,000 |
| 49. Tapers | $38,680 | 8.3% | 6,000 |
| 50. Carpet Installers | $33,030 | 10.5% | 7,000 |
| 51. Pile-Driver Operators | $41,570 | 14.0% | 1,000 |
| 52. Bookkeeping, Accounting, and Auditing Clerks | $26,950 | 2.0% | 298,000 |
| 53. Design Printing Machine Setters and Set-Up Operators | $30,090 | 5.5% | 24,000 |
| 54. Embossing Machine Set-Up Operators | $30,090 | 5.5% | 24,000 |
| 55. Engraver Set-Up Operators | $30,090 | 5.5% | 24,000 |

*(continued)*

*(continued)*

# Best Jobs Requiring Moderate-Term On-the-Job Training

| Job | Annual Earnings | Percent Growth | Annual Openings |
|---|---|---|---|
| 56. Letterpress Setters and Set-Up Operators | $30,090 | 5.5% | 24,000 |
| 57. Marking and Identification Printing Machine Setters and Set-Up Operators | $30,090 | 5.5% | 24,000 |
| 58. Offset Lithographic Press Setters and Set-Up Operators | $30,090 | 5.5% | 24,000 |
| 59. Precision Printing Workers | $30,090 | 5.5% | 24,000 |
| 60. Printing Press Machine Operators and Tenders | $30,090 | 5.5% | 24,000 |
| 61. Screen Printing Machine Setters and Set-Up Operators | $30,090 | 5.5% | 24,000 |
| 62. Travel Guides | $30,990 | 9.5% | 10,000 |
| 63. Heat Treating, Annealing, and Tempering Machine Operators and Tenders, Metal and Plastic | $28,020 | 13.4% | 9,000 |
| 64. Heaters, Metal and Plastic | $28,020 | 13.4% | 9,000 |
| 65. Heating Equipment Setters and Set-Up Operators, Metal and Plastic | $28,020 | 13.4% | 9,000 |
| 66. Residential Advisors | $21,600 | 24.0% | 9,000 |
| 67. Pest Control Workers | $24,020 | 22.1% | 7,000 |
| 68. Audio-Visual Collections Specialists | $35,590 | 13.6% | 2,000 |
| 69. Coating, Painting, and Spraying Machine Operators and Tenders | $25,140 | 11.9% | 18,000 |
| 70. Coating, Painting, and Spraying Machine Setters and Set-Up Operators | $25,140 | 11.9% | 18,000 |
| 71. Casting Machine Set-Up Operators | $23,630 | 9.8% | 38,000 |
| 72. Metal Molding, Coremaking, and Casting Machine Operators and Tenders | $23,630 | 9.8% | 38,000 |
| 73. Metal Molding, Coremaking, and Casting Machine Setters and Set-Up Operators | $23,630 | 9.8% | 38,000 |
| 74. Plastic Molding and Casting Machine Operators and Tenders | $23,630 | 9.8% | 38,000 |
| 75. Plastic Molding and Casting Machine Setters and Set-Up Operators | $23,630 | 9.8% | 38,000 |
| 76. Septic Tank Servicers and Sewer Pipe Cleaners | $28,930 | 16.5% | 4,000 |
| 77. Pipelayers | $30,220 | 11.9% | 6,000 |
| 78. Crane and Tower Operators | $35,340 | 8.6% | 5,000 |
| *Average* | *$32,566* | *15.6%* | *42,342* |

# Best Jobs Requiring Short-Term On-the-Job Training

It is possible to work in these occupations and achieve an average level of performance within a few days or weeks through on-the-job training. Sixty-three jobs met this requirement. The average annual earnings for these jobs are $21,476, the average rate of growth is 18.5 percent, and the average number of openings annually is 212,492. While there are exceptions, many of these jobs do not have higher-than-average earnings or are not projected to grow more rapidly than the average for all jobs. Even so, these jobs can have advantages that make them of interest to many people.

## Best Jobs Requiring Short-Term On-the-Job Training

| Job | Annual Earnings | Percent Growth | Annual Openings |
|---|---|---|---|
| 1. Production, Planning, and Expediting Clerks | $32,520 | 17.9% | 36,000 |
| 2. Bill and Account Collectors | $26,670 | 25.3% | 71,000 |
| 3. Human Resources Assistants, Except Payroll and Timekeeping | $29,400 | 19.3% | 25,000 |
| 4. Truck Drivers, Light or Delivery Services | $24,620 | 19.2% | 153,000 |
| 5. Security Guards | $19,470 | 35.4% | 242,000 |
| 6. Receptionists and Information Clerks | $20,780 | 23.7% | 269,000 |
| 7. Landscaping and Groundskeeping Workers | $20,030 | 29.0% | 193,000 |
| 8. Interviewers, Except Eligibility and Loan | $22,360 | 33.4% | 53,000 |
| 9. Nursing Aides, Orderlies, and Attendants | $19,100 | 23.5% | 268,000 |
| 10. Home Health Aides | $18,110 | 47.3% | 120,000 |
| 11. Telemarketers | $21,460 | 22.2% | 145,000 |
| 12. Teacher Assistants | $18,770 | 23.9% | 256,000 |
| 13. Combined Food Preparation and Serving Workers, Including Fast Food | $14,240 | 30.5% | 737,000 |
| 14. Office Clerks, General | $22,290 | 15.9% | 676,000 |
| 15. Personal and Home Care Aides | $15,960 | 62.5% | 84,000 |
| 16. Hotel, Motel, and Resort Desk Clerks | $17,100 | 33.4% | 73,000 |
| 17. Refuse and Recyclable Material Collectors | $26,020 | 16.6% | 34,000 |
| 18. Library Technicians | $24,230 | 19.5% | 29,000 |
| 19. Packers and Packagers, Hand | $17,030 | 19.3% | 242,000 |
| 20. Reservation and Transportation Ticket Agents | $26,140 | 14.5% | 39,000 |
| 21. Travel Clerks | $26,140 | 14.5% | 39,000 |
| 22. Counter and Rental Clerks | $18,670 | 19.4% | 150,000 |

(continued)

(continued)

## Best Jobs Requiring Short-Term On-the-Job Training

| Job | Annual Earnings | Percent Growth | Annual Openings |
|---|---|---|---|
| 23. Amusement and Recreation Attendants | $15,480 | 32.4% | 62,000 |
| 24. Industrial Truck and Tractor Operators | $26,090 | 11.3% | 91,000 |
| 25. Taxi Drivers and Chauffeurs | $18,920 | 24.4% | 37,000 |
| 26. Waiters and Waitresses | $14,750 | 18.3% | 596,000 |
| 27. Helpers—Installation, Maintenance, and Repair Workers | $22,620 | 18.5% | 35,000 |
| 28. Freight, Stock, and Material Movers, Hand | $20,460 | 13.9% | 519,000 |
| 29. Grips and Set-Up Workers, Motion Picture Sets, Studios, and Stages | $20,460 | 13.9% | 519,000 |
| 30. Stevedores, Except Equipment Operators | $20,460 | 13.9% | 519,000 |
| 31. Cleaners of Vehicles and Equipment | $17,380 | 18.8% | 86,000 |
| 32. Food Preparation Workers | $16,180 | 16.9% | 231,000 |
| 33. Weighers, Measurers, Checkers, and Samplers, Recordkeeping | $26,250 | 17.9% | 13,000 |
| 34. Janitors and Cleaners, Except Maids and Housekeeping Cleaners | $19,080 | 13.5% | 507,000 |
| 35. Retail Salespersons | $20,260 | 12.4% | 1,124,000 |
| 36. Library Assistants, Clerical | $19,380 | 19.7% | 26,000 |
| 37. Cashiers | $15,730 | 14.2% | 1,125,000 |
| 38. Packaging and Filling Machine Operators and Tenders | $21,700 | 14.4% | 56,000 |
| 39. Food Servers, Nonrestaurant | $16,170 | 16.4% | 85,000 |
| 40. Billing, Cost, and Rate Clerks | $25,480 | 8.5% | 69,000 |
| 41. Billing, Posting, and Calculating Machine Operators | $25,480 | 8.5% | 69,000 |
| 42. Counter Attendants, Cafeteria, Food Concession, and Coffee Shop | $15,030 | 14.4% | 216,000 |
| 43. Statement Clerks | $25,480 | 8.5% | 69,000 |
| 44. Shipping, Receiving, and Traffic Clerks | $23,340 | 9.3% | 133,000 |
| 45. Court Clerks | $27,780 | 12.0% | 14,000 |
| 46. Municipal Clerks | $27,780 | 12.0% | 14,000 |
| 47. Production Helpers | $19,350 | 11.9% | 143,000 |
| 48. Production Laborers | $19,350 | 11.9% | 143,000 |
| 49. Helpers—Brickmasons, Blockmasons, Stonemasons, and Tile and Marble Setters | $25,780 | 14.1% | 14,000 |

# Best Jobs Requiring Short-Term On-the-Job Training

| Job | Annual Earnings | Percent Growth | Annual Openings |
|---|---|---|---|
| 50. Nonfarm Animal Caretakers | $17,600 | 21.6% | 20,000 |
| 51. Tree Trimmers and Pruners | $25,590 | 16.3% | 11,000 |
| 52. Bus Drivers, School | $21,430 | 11.6% | 63,000 |
| 53. Helpers—Electricians | $22,740 | 13.3% | 27,000 |
| 54. Postal Service Mail Carriers | $36,830 | 2.4% | 13,000 |
| 55. Costume Attendants | $24,790 | 19.1% | 8,000 |
| 56. Marking Clerks | $20,650 | 8.5% | 467,000 |
| 57. Order Fillers, Wholesale and Retail Sales | $20,650 | 8.5% | 467,000 |
| 58. Stock Clerks and Order Fillers | $20,650 | 8.5% | 467,000 |
| 59. Stock Clerks, Sales Floor | $20,650 | 8.5% | 467,000 |
| 60. Stock Clerks—Stockroom, Warehouse, or Storage Yard | $20,650 | 8.5% | 467,000 |
| 61. Physical Therapist Aides | $20,930 | 46.3% | 7,000 |
| 62. Child Care Workers | $16,350 | 10.6% | 370,000 |
| 63. Bartenders | $16,150 | 13.4% | 84,000 |
| *Average* | *$21,476* | *18.5%* | *212,492* |

# Best Jobs Based on Personality Types

Several popular career assessment inventories organize jobs into groupings based on personality types. The most-used system is one that presents six personality types: Realistic, Investigative, Artistic, Social, Enterprising, and Conventional. This system is used in the *Self Directed Search (SDS),* developed by John Holland, and many other inventories.

If you have used one of these career exploration systems, the following lists may help. Even if you have not, you may find the concept of personality types—and the jobs that are related to them—helpful to you.

We've ranked the jobs within each grouping based on their total combined scores for earnings, growth, and annual openings. Like the job lists for education levels, there is only one list for each personality type.

Here are brief descriptions for each of the six personality types presented in these lists:

- ▲ **Artistic.** These occupations frequently involve working with forms, designs, and patterns. They often require self-expression, and the work can be done without following a clear set of rules.

- ▲ **Conventional.** These occupations frequently involve following set procedures and routines. These occupations can include working with data and details more than with ideas. Usually there is a clear line of authority to follow.

- ▲ **Enterprising.** These occupations frequently involve starting up and carrying out projects. These occupations can involve leading people and making many decisions. They sometimes require risk taking and often deal with business.

- ▲ **Investigative.** These occupations frequently involve working with ideas and require an extensive amount of thinking. These occupations can involve searching for facts and figuring out problems mentally.

- ▲ **Realistic.** These occupations frequently involve work activities that include practical, hands-on problems and solutions. They often deal with plants, animals, and real-world materials like wood, tools, and machinery. Many of the occupations require working outside and do not involve a lot of paperwork or working closely with others.

- ▲ **Social.** These occupations frequently involve working with, communicating with, and teaching people. These occupations often involve helping or providing service to others.

## Best Jobs for Artistic Personality Types

| Job | Annual Earnings | Percent Growth | Annual Openings |
|---|---|---|---|
| 1. Musicians, Instrumental | $44,520 | 20.1% | 33,000 |
| 2. Singers | $44,520 | 20.1% | 33,000 |
| 3. Actors | $41,570 | 26.7% | 20,000 |
| 4. Camera Operators, Television, Video, and Motion Picture | $33,860 | 25.8% | 3,000 |
| 5. Interpreters and Translators | $33,550 | 23.8% | 3,000 |
| 6. Photographers, Scientific | $27,420 | 17.0% | 13,000 |
| 7. Professional Photographers | $27,420 | 17.0% | 13,000 |
| 8. Cartoonists | $35,770 | 13.4% | 4,000 |
| 9. Painters and Illustrators | $35,770 | 13.4% | 4,000 |
| 10. Sculptors | $35,770 | 13.4% | 4,000 |
| 11. Sketch Artists | $35,770 | 13.4% | 4,000 |
| 12. Costume Attendants | $24,790 | 19.1% | 8,000 |

# Best Jobs for Conventional Personality Types

| Job | Annual Earnings | Percent Growth | Annual Openings |
|---|---|---|---|
| 1. Legal Secretaries | $35,370 | 20.3% | 36,000 |
| 2. Claims Examiners, Property and Casualty Insurance | $44,000 | 15.1% | 25,000 |
| 3. Adjustment Clerks | $26,530 | 32.4% | 359,000 |
| 4. Customer Service Representatives, Utilities | $26,530 | 32.4% | 359,000 |
| 5. Production, Planning, and Expediting Clerks | $32,520 | 17.9% | 36,000 |
| 6. Bill and Account Collectors | $26,670 | 25.3% | 71,000 |
| 7. Executive Secretaries and Administrative Assistants | $32,520 | 11.5% | 185,000 |
| 8. Electrical Drafters | $40,420 | 23.3% | 5,000 |
| 9. Human Resources Assistants, Except Payroll and Timekeeping | $29,400 | 19.3% | 25,000 |
| 10. Receptionists and Information Clerks | $20,780 | 23.7% | 269,000 |
| 11. Immigration and Customs Inspectors | $49,830 | 16.4% | 4,000 |
| 12. Police Identification and Records Officers | $49,830 | 16.4% | 4,000 |
| 13. Interviewers, Except Eligibility and Loan | $22,360 | 33.4% | 53,000 |
| 14. Office Clerks, General | $22,290 | 15.9% | 676,000 |
| 15. Medical Secretaries | $24,460 | 19.0% | 40,000 |
| 16. Dispatchers, Except Police, Fire, and Ambulance | $30,410 | 22.2% | 8,000 |
| 17. Hotel, Motel, and Resort Desk Clerks | $17,100 | 33.4% | 73,000 |
| 18. Medical Records and Health Information Technicians | $24,430 | 49.0% | 14,000 |
| 19. Library Technicians | $24,230 | 19.5% | 29,000 |
| 20. Licensing Examiners and Inspectors | $44,140 | 8.9% | 9,000 |
| 21. Reservation and Transportation Ticket Agents | $26,140 | 14.5% | 39,000 |
| 22. Travel Clerks | $26,140 | 14.5% | 39,000 |
| 23. Counter and Rental Clerks | $18,670 | 19.4% | 150,000 |
| 24. Pharmacy Technicians | $21,600 | 36.4% | 22,000 |
| 25. Freight Inspectors | $44,200 | 11.3% | 3,000 |
| 26. Marine Cargo Inspectors | $44,200 | 11.3% | 3,000 |
| 27. Weighers, Measurers, Checkers, and Samplers, Recordkeeping | $26,250 | 17.9% | 13,000 |
| 28. Library Assistants, Clerical | $19,380 | 19.7% | 26,000 |
| 29. Fire Inspectors | $42,800 | 15.1% | 1,000 |
| 30. Cashiers | $15,730 | 14.2% | 1,125,000 |
| 31. Construction and Building Inspectors | $39,730 | 15.0% | 2,000 |
| 32. Billing, Cost, and Rate Clerks | $25,480 | 8.5% | 69,000 |

## Best Jobs for Conventional Personality Types

| Job | Annual Earnings | Percent Growth | Annual Openings |
|---|---|---|---|
| 33. Billing, Posting, and Calculating Machine Operators | $25,480 | 8.5% | 69,000 |
| 34. Statement Clerks | $25,480 | 8.5% | 69,000 |
| 35. Shipping, Receiving, and Traffic Clerks | $23,340 | 9.3% | 133,000 |
| 36. Court Clerks | $27,780 | 12.0% | 14,000 |
| 37. Municipal Clerks | $27,780 | 12.0% | 14,000 |
| 38. Bookkeeping, Accounting, and Auditing Clerks | $26,950 | 2.0% | 298,000 |
| 39. Postal Service Mail Carriers | $36,830 | 2.4% | 13,000 |
| 40. Marking Clerks | $20,650 | 8.5% | 467,000 |
| 41. Order Fillers, Wholesale and Retail Sales | $20,650 | 8.5% | 467,000 |
| 42. Stock Clerks—Stockroom, Warehouse, or Storage Yard | $20,650 | 8.5% | 467,000 |
| 43. Audio-Visual Collections Specialists | $35,590 | 13.6% | 2,000 |
| 44. Air Traffic Controllers | $79,460 | 7.2% | 2,000 |

# Best Jobs for Enterprising Personality Types

| Job | Annual Earnings | Percent Growth | Annual Openings |
|---|---|---|---|
| 1. Advertising Sales Agents | $44,960 | 26.3% | 25,000 |
| 2. First-Line Supervisors and Manager/Supervisors— Construction Trades Workers | $47,740 | 16.5% | 43,000 |
| 3. First-Line Supervisors and Manager/Supervisors— Extractive Workers | $47,740 | 16.5% | 43,000 |
| 4. First-Line Supervisors/Managers of Mechanics, Installers, and Repairers | $46,560 | 16.0% | 38,000 |
| 5. Paralegals and Legal Assistants | $38,790 | 33.2% | 23,000 |
| 6. Storage and Distribution Managers | $58,200 | 20.2% | 13,000 |
| 7. Transportation Managers | $58,200 | 20.2% | 13,000 |
| 8. First-Line Supervisors/Managers of Transportation and Material-Moving Machine and Vehicle Operators | $43,120 | 19.9% | 17,000 |
| 9. Insurance Adjusters, Examiners, and Investigators | $44,000 | 15.1% | 25,000 |
| 10. Food Service Managers | $34,350 | 15.0% | 55,000 |
| 11. First-Line Supervisors, Administrative Support | $39,410 | 9.4% | 146,000 |
| 12. First-Line Supervisors, Customer Service | $39,410 | 9.4% | 146,000 |
| 13. First-Line Supervisors/Managers of Helpers, Laborers, and Material Movers, Hand | $36,910 | 18.9% | 14,000 |
| 14. Flight Attendants | $45,220 | 18.4% | 8,000 |
| 15. Athletes and Sports Competitors | $62,960 | 22.5% | 3,000 |
| 16. Sales Representatives, Wholesale and Manufacturing, Except Technical and Scientific Products | $46,770 | 5.7% | 86,000 |
| 17. First-Line Supervisors/Managers of Non-Retail Sales Workers | $56,850 | 5.8% | 41,000 |
| 18. Coaches and Scouts | $33,470 | 17.6% | 19,000 |
| 19. Sales Representatives, Agricultural | $58,630 | 7.5% | 24,000 |
| 20. Sales Representatives, Chemical and Pharmaceutical | $58,630 | 7.5% | 24,000 |
| 21. Sales Representatives, Electrical/Electronic | $58,630 | 7.5% | 24,000 |
| 22. Sales Representatives, Instruments | $58,630 | 7.5% | 24,000 |
| 23. Sales Representatives, Mechanical Equipment and Supplies | $58,630 | 7.5% | 24,000 |
| 24. Sales Representatives, Medical | $58,630 | 7.5% | 24,000 |
| 25. First-Line Supervisors/Managers of Police and Detectives | $57,900 | 13.1% | 9,000 |
| 26. Appraisers, Real Estate | $41,700 | 18.0% | 6,000 |
| 27. Lawn Service Managers | $33,720 | 20.1% | 10,000 |

# Best Jobs for Enterprising Personality Types

| Job | Annual Earnings | Percent Growth | Annual Openings |
|---|---|---|---|
| 28. Real Estate Sales Agents | $37,950 | 9.5% | 28,000 |
| 29. Child Support, Missing Persons, and Unemployment Insurance Fraud Investigators | $49,830 | 16.4% | 4,000 |
| 30. Criminal Investigators and Special Agents | $49,830 | 16.4% | 4,000 |
| 31. Police Detectives | $49,830 | 16.4% | 4,000 |
| 32. Demonstrators and Product Promoters | $24,460 | 24.9% | 34,000 |
| 33. First-Line Supervisors/Managers of Retail Sales Workers | $32,170 | 8.1% | 206,000 |
| 34. Private Detectives and Investigators | $30,650 | 23.5% | 9,000 |
| 35. Telemarketers | $21,460 | 22.2% | 145,000 |
| 36. First-Line Supervisors/Managers of Production and Operating Workers | $43,020 | 1.0% | 71,000 |
| 37. Government Property Inspectors and Investigators | $44,140 | 8.9% | 9,000 |
| 38. First-Line Supervisors/Managers of Food Preparation and Serving Workers | $24,600 | 12.7% | 136,000 |
| 39. Public Transportation Inspectors | $44,200 | 11.3% | 3,000 |
| 40. Housekeeping Supervisors | $27,830 | 14.2% | 18,000 |
| 41. Janitorial Supervisors | $27,830 | 14.2% | 18,000 |
| 42. Gaming Dealers | $15,550 | 32.4% | 28,000 |
| 43. First-Line Supervisors/Managers of Personal Service Workers | $30,350 | 15.1% | 8,000 |
| 44. Retail Salespersons | $20,260 | 12.4% | 1,124,000 |
| 45. Chefs and Head Cooks | $28,550 | 9.0% | 35,000 |
| 46. Hairdressers, Hairstylists, and Cosmetologists | $20,710 | 13.0% | 78,000 |
| 47. Lodging Managers | $34,800 | 9.3% | 8,000 |
| 48. Transit and Railroad Police | $41,560 | 16.5% | fewer than 500 |
| 49. Travel Guides | $30,990 | 9.5% | 10,000 |
| 50. Bartenders | $16,150 | 13.4% | 84,000 |

## Best Jobs for Investigative Personality Types

| Job | Annual Earnings | Percent Growth | Annual Openings |
|---|---|---|---|
| 1. Respiratory Therapists | $38,220 | 34.8% | 4,000 |
| 2. Cardiovascular Technologists and Technicians | $34,960 | 34.9% | 3,000 |
| 3. Environmental Science and Protection Technicians, Including Health | $35,830 | 24.5% | 3,000 |
| 4. Nuclear Medicine Technologists | $44,850 | 22.4% | 1,000 |
| 5. Coroners | $44,140 | 8.9% | 9,000 |
| 6. Environmental Compliance Inspectors | $44,140 | 8.9% | 9,000 |

## Best Jobs for Realistic Personality Types

| Job | Annual Earnings | Percent Growth | Annual Openings |
|---|---|---|---|
| 1. Electricians | $42,210 | 17.3% | 66,000 |
| 2. Tractor-Trailer Truck Drivers | $32,810 | 19.8% | 240,000 |
| 3. Truck Drivers, Heavy | $32,810 | 19.8% | 240,000 |
| 4. Highway Patrol Pilots | $40,590 | 23.2% | 21,000 |
| 5. Correctional Officers and Jailers | $32,680 | 32.4% | 30,000 |
| 6. Heating and Air Conditioning Mechanics | $34,180 | 22.3% | 21,000 |
| 7. Refrigeration Mechanics | $34,180 | 22.3% | 21,000 |
| 8. Automotive Master Mechanics | $30,780 | 18.0% | 104,000 |
| 9. Automotive Specialty Technicians | $30,780 | 18.0% | 104,000 |
| 10. Roofers | $31,670 | 19.4% | 38,000 |
| 11. Telecommunications Line Installers and Repairers | $38,050 | 27.6% | 9,000 |
| 12. Architectural Drafters | $37,100 | 20.8% | 12,000 |
| 13. Civil Drafters | $37,100 | 20.8% | 12,000 |
| 14. Sheet Metal Workers | $35,050 | 23.0% | 13,000 |
| 15. Painters, Construction and Maintenance | $29,610 | 19.1% | 67,000 |
| 16. Pipe Fitters | $40,170 | 10.2% | 49,000 |
| 17. Pipelaying Fitters | $40,170 | 10.2% | 49,000 |
| 18. Plumbers | $40,170 | 10.2% | 49,000 |
| 19. Brazers | $29,080 | 19.3% | 51,000 |
| 20. Solderers | $29,080 | 19.3% | 51,000 |
| 21. Welder-Fitters | $29,080 | 19.3% | 51,000 |
| 22. Welders and Cutters | $29,080 | 19.3% | 51,000 |
| 23. Welders, Production | $29,080 | 19.3% | 51,000 |
| 24. Structural Iron and Steel Workers | $39,140 | 18.4% | 12,000 |
| 25. Construction Laborers | $26,940 | 17.0% | 236,000 |
| 26. Electronic Drafters | $40,420 | 23.3% | 5,000 |
| 27. Boat Builders and Shipwrights | $35,100 | 8.2% | 161,000 |
| 28. Brattice Builders | $35,100 | 8.2% | 161,000 |
| 29. Carpenter Assemblers and Repairers | $35,100 | 8.2% | 161,000 |
| 30. Construction Carpenters | $35,100 | 8.2% | 161,000 |
| 31. Rough Carpenters | $35,100 | 8.2% | 161,000 |
| 32. Ship Carpenters and Joiners | $35,100 | 8.2% | 161,000 |
| 33. Brickmasons and Blockmasons | $41,140 | 12.5% | 18,000 |
| 34. Calibration and Instrumentation Technicians | $41,210 | 10.8% | 22,000 |
| 35. Electrical Engineering Technicians | $41,210 | 10.8% | 22,000 |

*(continued)*

(continued)

# Best Jobs for Realistic Personality Types

| Job | Annual Earnings | Percent Growth | Annual Openings |
|---|---|---|---|
| 36. Electronics Engineering Technicians | $41,210 | 10.8% | 22,000 |
| 37. Chemical Technicians | $37,080 | 15.0% | 13,000 |
| 38. Truck Drivers, Light or Delivery Services | $24,620 | 19.2% | 153,000 |
| 39. First-Line Supervisors and Manager/Supervisors— Landscaping Workers | $33,720 | 20.1% | 10,000 |
| 40. Automatic Teller Machine Servicers | $32,860 | 14.2% | 24,000 |
| 41. Data Processing Equipment Repairers | $32,860 | 14.2% | 24,000 |
| 42. Office Machine and Cash Register Servicers | $32,860 | 14.2% | 24,000 |
| 43. Irradiated-Fuel Handlers | $31,630 | 32.8% | 9,000 |
| 44. Landscaping and Groundskeeping Workers | $20,030 | 29.0% | 193,000 |
| 45. Biological Technicians | $32,970 | 26.4% | 7,000 |
| 46. Bus and Truck Mechanics and Diesel Engine Specialists | $33,210 | 14.2% | 20,000 |
| 47. Commercial Pilots | $51,370 | 26.9% | 1,000 |
| 48. Mechanical Drafters | $40,330 | 15.4% | 8,000 |
| 49. Desktop Publishers | $32,700 | 66.7% | 5,000 |
| 50. Fitters, Structural Metal—Precision | $28,490 | 19.5% | 20,000 |
| 51. Metal Fabricators, Structural Metal Products | $28,490 | 19.5% | 20,000 |
| 52. Chemical Equipment Controllers and Operators | $36,310 | 14.9% | 9,000 |
| 53. Chemical Equipment Tenders | $36,310 | 14.9% | 9,000 |
| 54. Medical and Clinical Laboratory Technicians | $28,970 | 19.0% | 19,000 |
| 55. Combined Food Preparation and Serving Workers, Including Fast Food | $14,240 | 30.5% | 737,000 |
| 56. Numerical Control Machine Tool Operators and Tenders, Metal and Plastic | $28,780 | 19.7% | 15,000 |
| 57. Surgical Technologists | $29,660 | 34.7% | 8,000 |
| 58. Bus Drivers, Transit and Intercity | $27,250 | 17.4% | 24,000 |
| 59. Cooks, Restaurant | $18,880 | 21.7% | 158,000 |
| 60. Nuclear Equipment Operation Technicians | $61,970 | 20.7% | fewer than 500 |
| 61. Nuclear Monitoring Technicians | $61,970 | 20.7% | fewer than 500 |
| 62. Ceiling Tile Installers | $35,580 | 9.4% | 19,000 |
| 63. Drywall Installers | $35,580 | 9.4% | 19,000 |
| 64. Refuse and Recyclable Material Collectors | $26,020 | 16.6% | 34,000 |
| 65. Elevator Installers and Repairers | $46,240 | 17.2% | 2,000 |
| 66. Mobile Heavy Equipment Mechanics, Except Engines | $34,790 | 14.0% | 11,000 |
| 67. Reinforcing Iron and Rebar Workers | $37,800 | 17.5% | 4,000 |
| 68. Painters, Transportation Equipment | $32,910 | 17.5% | 8,000 |

## Best Jobs for Realistic Personality Types

| Job | Annual Earnings | Percent Growth | Annual Openings |
|---|---|---|---|
| 69. Combination Machine Tool Operators and Tenders, Metal and Plastic | $29,350 | 14.7% | 21,000 |
| 70. Combination Machine Tool Setters and Set-Up Operators, Metal and Plastic | $29,350 | 14.7% | 21,000 |
| 71. Pressure Vessel Inspectors | $44,140 | 8.9% | 9,000 |
| 72. Packers and Packagers, Hand | $17,030 | 19.3% | 242,000 |
| 73. Automotive Body and Related Repairers | $33,710 | 10.2% | 18,000 |
| 74. Grader, Bulldozer, and Scraper Operators | $36,170 | 6.9% | 25,000 |
| 75. Operating Engineers | $36,170 | 6.9% | 25,000 |
| 76. Tile and Marble Setters | $36,580 | 15.6% | 5,000 |
| 77. Amusement and Recreation Attendants | $15,480 | 32.4% | 62,000 |
| 78. Industrial Truck and Tractor Operators | $26,090 | 11.3% | 91,000 |
| 79. Water and Liquid Waste Treatment Plant and System Operators | $32,450 | 18.1% | 6,000 |
| 80. Machinists | $31,610 | 9.1% | 28,000 |
| 81. Taxi Drivers and Chauffeurs | $18,920 | 24.4% | 37,000 |
| 82. Helpers—Installation, Maintenance, and Repair Workers | $22,620 | 18.5% | 35,000 |
| 83. Electro-Mechanical Technicians | $38,630 | 14.5% | 4,000 |
| 84. Semiconductor Processors | $27,170 | 32.4% | 7,000 |
| 85. Freight, Stock, and Material Movers, Hand | $20,460 | 13.9% | 519,000 |
| 86. Grips and Set-Up Workers, Motion Picture Sets, Studios, and Stages | $20,460 | 13.9% | 519,000 |
| 87. Stevedores, Except Equipment Operators | $20,460 | 13.9% | 519,000 |
| 88. Paperhangers | $32,490 | 20.2% | 3,000 |
| 89. Electrical and Electronics Repairers, Commercial and Industrial Equipment | $37,190 | 9.2% | 10,000 |
| 90. Cleaners of Vehicles and Equipment | $17,380 | 18.8% | 86,000 |
| 91. Electrical Power-Line Installers and Repairers | $44,490 | 9.3% | 5,000 |
| 92. Aviation Inspectors | $44,200 | 11.3% | 3,000 |
| 93. Motor Vehicle Inspectors | $44,200 | 11.3% | 3,000 |
| 94. Railroad Inspectors | $44,200 | 11.3% | 3,000 |
| 95. Food Preparation Workers | $16,180 | 16.9% | 231,000 |
| 96. Medical Equipment Repairers | $37,470 | 14.9% | 3,000 |
| 97. Forest Fire Fighters | $35,260 | 8.9% | 12,000 |
| 98. Municipal Fire Fighters | $35,260 | 8.9% | 12,000 |
| 99. Plasterers and Stucco Masons | $35,170 | 11.9% | 7,000 |

*(continued)*

(continued)

# Best Jobs for Realistic Personality Types

| Job | Annual Earnings | Percent Growth | Annual Openings |
|---|---|---|---|
| 100. Soldering and Brazing Machine Operators and Tenders | $29,730 | 15.1% | 9,000 |
| 101. Soldering and Brazing Machine Setters and Set-Up Operators | $29,730 | 15.1% | 9,000 |
| 102. Welding Machine Operators and Tenders | $29,730 | 15.1% | 9,000 |
| 103. Welding Machine Setters and Set-Up Operators | $29,730 | 15.1% | 9,000 |
| 104. Janitors and Cleaners, Except Maids and Housekeeping Cleaners | $19,080 | 13.5% | 507,000 |
| 105. Dragline Operators | $33,480 | 14.8% | 5,000 |
| 106. Excavating and Loading Machine Operators | $33,480 | 14.8% | 5,000 |
| 107. Numerical Tool and Process Control Programmers | $37,690 | 16.6% | 2,000 |
| 108. Glaziers | $32,360 | 14.8% | 6,000 |
| 109. Packaging and Filling Machine Operators and Tenders | $21,700 | 14.4% | 56,000 |
| 110. Maintenance and Repair Workers, General | $29,420 | 4.7% | 103,000 |
| 111. Forest Fire Fighting and Prevention Supervisors | $52,990 | 7.2% | 5,000 |
| 112. Municipal Fire Fighting and Prevention Supervisors | $52,990 | 7.2% | 5,000 |
| 113. Stonemasons | $32,380 | 20.8% | 2,000 |
| 114. Paving, Surfacing, and Tamping Equipment Operators | $30,090 | 15.5% | 6,000 |
| 115. Extruding and Drawing Machine Setters, Operators, and Tenders, Metal and Plastic | $25,030 | 13.5% | 23,000 |
| 116. Bakers, Bread and Pastry | $21,050 | 16.8% | 25,000 |
| 117. Bakers, Manufacturing | $21,050 | 16.8% | 25,000 |
| 118. Aircraft Rigging Assemblers | $38,150 | 14.2% | 2,000 |
| 119. Aircraft Structure Assemblers, Precision | $38,150 | 14.2% | 2,000 |
| 120. Aircraft Systems Assemblers, Precision | $38,150 | 14.2% | 2,000 |
| 121. Tapers | $38,680 | 8.3% | 6,000 |
| 122. Production Helpers | $19,350 | 11.9% | 143,000 |
| 123. Production Laborers | $19,350 | 11.9% | 143,000 |
| 124. Carpet Installers | $33,030 | 10.5% | 7,000 |
| 125. Helpers—Brickmasons, Blockmasons, Stonemasons, and Tile and Marble Setters | $25,780 | 14.1% | 14,000 |
| 126. Pile-Driver Operators | $41,570 | 14.0% | 1,000 |
| 127. Nonfarm Animal Caretakers | $17,600 | 21.6% | 20,000 |
| 128. Tree Trimmers and Pruners | $25,590 | 16.3% | 11,000 |
| 129. Bus Drivers, School | $21,430 | 11.6% | 63,000 |
| 130. Helpers—Electricians | $22,740 | 13.3% | 27,000 |
| 131. Design Printing Machine Setters and Set-Up Operators | $30,090 | 5.5% | 24,000 |

# Best Jobs for Realistic Personality Types

| Job | Annual Earnings | Percent Growth | Annual Openings |
|---|---|---|---|
| 132. Embossing Machine Set-Up Operators | $30,090 | 5.5% | 24,000 |
| 133. Engraver Set-Up Operators | $30,090 | 5.5% | 24,000 |
| 134. Letterpress Setters and Set-Up Operators | $30,090 | 5.5% | 24,000 |
| 135. Marking and Identification Printing Machine Setters and Set-Up Operators | $30,090 | 5.5% | 24,000 |
| 136. Offset Lithographic Press Setters and Set-Up Operators | $30,090 | 5.5% | 24,000 |
| 137. Precision Printing Workers | $30,090 | 5.5% | 24,000 |
| 138. Printing Press Machine Operators and Tenders | $30,090 | 5.5% | 24,000 |
| 139. Screen Printing Machine Setters and Set-Up Operators | $30,090 | 5.5% | 24,000 |
| 140. Heat Treating, Annealing, and Tempering Machine Operators and Tenders, Metal and Plastic | $28,020 | 13.4% | 9,000 |
| 141. Heaters, Metal and Plastic | $28,020 | 13.4% | 9,000 |
| 142. Heating Equipment Setters and Set-Up Operators, Metal and Plastic | $28,020 | 13.4% | 9,000 |
| 143. Pest Control Workers | $24,020 | 22.1% | 7,000 |
| 144. Stock Clerks, Sales Floor | $20,650 | 8.5% | 467,000 |
| 145. Coating, Painting, and Spraying Machine Operators and Tenders | $25,140 | 11.9% | 18,000 |
| 146. Coating, Painting, and Spraying Machine Setters and Set-Up Operators | $25,140 | 11.9% | 18,000 |
| 147. Casting Machine Set-Up Operators | $23,630 | 9.8% | 38,000 |
| 148. Metal Molding, Coremaking, and Casting Machine Operators and Tenders | $23,630 | 9.8% | 38,000 |
| 149. Metal Molding, Coremaking, and Casting Machine Setters and Set-Up Operators | $23,630 | 9.8% | 38,000 |
| 150. Plastic Molding and Casting Machine Operators and Tenders | $23,630 | 9.8% | 38,000 |
| 151. Plastic Molding and Casting Machine Setters and Set-Up Operators | $23,630 | 9.8% | 38,000 |
| 152. Avionics Technicians | $41,600 | 9.8% | 2,000 |
| 153. Septic Tank Servicers and Sewer Pipe Cleaners | $28,930 | 16.5% | 4,000 |
| 154. Pipelayers | $30,220 | 11.9% | 6,000 |
| 155. Crane and Tower Operators | $35,340 | 8.6% | 5,000 |
| 156. Central Office and PBX Installers and Repairers | $42,520 | −3.1% | 9,000 |
| 157. Communication Equipment Mechanics, Installers, and Repairers | $42,520 | −3.1% | 9,000 |
| 158. Station Installers and Repairers, Telephone | $42,520 | −3.1% | 9,000 |
| 159. Telecommunications Facility Examiners | $42,520 | −3.1% | 9,000 |

# Best Jobs for Social Personality Types

| Job | Annual Earnings | Percent Growth | Annual Openings |
|---|---|---|---|
| 1. Registered Nurses | $46,410 | 25.6% | 140,000 |
| 2. Police Patrol Officers | $40,590 | 23.2% | 21,000 |
| 3. Sheriffs and Deputy Sheriffs | $40,590 | 23.2% | 21,000 |
| 4. Dental Hygienists | $51,980 | 37.1% | 5,000 |
| 5. Licensed Practical and Licensed Vocational Nurses | $30,470 | 20.3% | 58,000 |
| 6. Physical Therapist Assistants | $34,370 | 44.8% | 9,000 |
| 7. Self-Enrichment Education Teachers | $31,070 | 18.5% | 34,000 |
| 8. Fitness Trainers and Aerobics Instructors | $28,750 | 40.3% | 19,000 |
| 9. Social and Human Service Assistants | $23,840 | 54.2% | 45,000 |
| 10. Security Guards | $19,470 | 35.4% | 242,000 |
| 11. Dental Assistants | $26,740 | 37.2% | 16,000 |
| 12. Nursing Aides, Orderlies, and Attendants | $19,100 | 23.5% | 268,000 |
| 13. Home Health Aides | $18,110 | 47.3% | 120,000 |
| 14. Teacher Assistants | $18,770 | 23.9% | 256,000 |
| 15. Occupational Therapist Assistants | $34,860 | 39.7% | 3,000 |
| 16. Emergency Medical Technicians and Paramedics | $24,740 | 31.3% | 19,000 |
| 17. Personal and Home Care Aides | $15,960 | 62.5% | 84,000 |
| 18. Medical Assistants | $23,840 | 57.0% | 18,700 |
| 19. Equal Opportunity Representatives and Officers | $44,140 | 8.9% | 9,000 |
| 20. Waiters and Waitresses | $14,750 | 18.3% | 596,000 |
| 21. Food Servers, Nonrestaurant | $16,170 | 16.4% | 85,000 |
| 22. Counter Attendants, Cafeteria, Food Concession, and Coffee Shop | $15,030 | 14.4% | 216,000 |
| 23. Residential Advisors | $21,600 | 24.0% | 9,000 |
| 24. Physical Therapist Aides | $20,930 | 46.3% | 7,000 |
| 25. Child Care Workers | $16,350 | 10.6% | 370,000 |

# Best Jobs Based on Interests

The lists that follow organize the 300 jobs that met the criteria for this book into 14 interest areas that are used in a variety of career exploration systems. The lists provide a very useful way to quickly identify jobs based on your interests.

The lists can help you identify jobs that are related to ones you have had in the past or that require similar skills to those you want to use in the future. Within each interest grouping, occupations are arranged in order of their total scores based on earnings, growth, and number of openings.

The system of interest areas is called the *Guide for Occupational Exploration,* or *GOE,* and it was developed by the U.S. Department of Labor as an intuitive way to assist in career exploration. The lists that follow use the revised *GOE* groupings as presented in the *Guide for Occupational Exploration,* Third Edition, published by JIST.

Brief descriptions follow for each of the 14 interest areas used in the lists. Simply find the area or areas that interest you most and then use the lists in this section to identify jobs that are likely to interest you. Then, as with most of our lists, simply look up the job descriptions in Part II for the jobs that interest you most. Note that the descriptions for each of the interest areas may use sample jobs that are not among those described in this book.

▲ **Arts, Entertainment, and Media**—*An interest in creatively expressing feelings or ideas, in communicating news or information, or in performing.* You can satisfy this interest in several creative, verbal, or performing activities. For example, if you enjoy literature, perhaps writing or editing would appeal to you. Do you prefer to work in the performing arts? If so, you could direct or perform in drama, music, or dance. If you especially enjoy the visual arts, you could become a critic in painting, sculpture, or ceramics. You may want to use your hands to create or decorate products. You may prefer to model clothes or develop sets for entertainment. Or you may want to participate in sports professionally as an athlete or coach.

▲ **Science, Math, and Engineering**—*An interest in discovering, collecting, and analyzing information about the natural world; in applying scientific research findings to problems in medicine, the life sciences, and the natural sciences; in imagining and manipulating quantitative data; and in applying technology to manufacturing, transportation, mining, and other economic activities.* You can satisfy this interest by working with the knowledge and processes of the sciences. You may enjoy researching and developing new knowledge in mathematics, or perhaps solving problems in the physical or life sciences would appeal to you. You may wish to study engineering and help create new machines, processes, and structures. If you want to work with scientific equipment and procedures, you could seek a job in a research or testing laboratory.

▲ **Plants and Animals**—*An interest in working with plants and animals, usually outdoors.* You can satisfy this interest by working in farming, forestry, fishing, and related fields. You may like doing physical work outdoors, such as on a farm. You may enjoy animals; perhaps training or taking care of animals would appeal to you. If you have management ability, you could own, operate, or manage a farm or related business.

▲ **Law, Law Enforcement, and Public Safety**—*An interest in upholding people's rights or in protecting people and property by using authority, inspecting, or monitoring.* You can satisfy this interest by working in law, law enforcement, fire fighting, and related fields. For example, if you enjoy mental challenge and intrigue, you could investigate crimes or fires for a living. If you enjoy working with verbal skills, you may want to defend citizens in court or research deeds, wills, and other legal documents. You may prefer to fight fires and respond to other emergencies. Or, if you want more routine work, perhaps a job in guarding or patrolling would appeal to you; if you have management ability, you could seek a leadership position in law enforcement and the protective services. Work in the military gives you the chance to use technical and/or leadership skills while serving your country.

▲ **Mechanics, Installers, and Repairers**—*An interest in applying mechanical and electrical/electronic principles to practical situations by use of machines or hand tools.* You can satisfy this interest working with a variety of tools, technologies, materials, and settings. If you enjoy making machines run efficiently or fixing them when they break down, you could seek a job installing or repairing such devices as copiers, aircraft engines, automobiles, or watches. You may instead prefer to deal directly with certain materials and find work cutting and shaping metal or wood. Or if electricity and electronics interest you, you could install cables, troubleshoot telephone networks, or repair videocassette recorders. If you prefer routine or physical work in settings other than factories, perhaps work repairing tires or batteries would appeal to you.

▲ **Construction, Mining, and Drilling**—*An interest in assembling components of buildings and other structures or in using mechanical devices to drill or excavate.* If construction interests you, you can find fulfillment in the many building projects that are being undertaken at all times. If you like to organize and plan, you can find careers in management. On the other hand, you can play a more direct role in putting up and finishing buildings by doing jobs such as plumbing, carpentry, masonry, painting, or roofing. You may like working at a mine or oilfield, operating the powerful drilling or digging equipment. There are also several jobs that let you put your hands to the task.

▲ **Transportation**—*An interest in operations that move people or materials.* You can satisfy this interest by managing a transportation service, by helping vehicles keep on their assigned schedules and routes, or by driving or piloting a vehicle. If you enjoy taking responsibility, perhaps managing a rail line would appeal to you. If you work well with details and can take pressure on the job, you might consider being an air traffic controller. Or would you rather get out on the highway, on the water, or up in the air? If so, then you could drive a truck from state to state, sail down the Mississippi on a barge, or fly a crop duster over a cornfield. If you prefer to stay closer to home, you could drive a delivery van, taxi, or school bus. You can use your physical strength to load freight and arrange it so it gets to its destination in one piece.

▲ **Industrial Production**—*An interest in repetitive, concrete, organized activities most often done in a factory setting.* You can satisfy this interest by working in one of many industries that mass-produce goods or for a utility that distributes electric power, gas, telephone service, and related services. You may enjoy manual work, using your hands or hand tools. Perhaps you prefer to operate machines. You may like to inspect, sort, count, or weigh products. Using your training and experience to set up machines or supervise other workers may appeal to you.

▲ **Business Detail**—*An interest in organized, clearly defined activities requiring accuracy and attention to details, primarily in an office setting.* You can satisfy this interest in a variety of jobs in which you attend to the details of a business operation. You may enjoy using your math skills; if so, perhaps a job in billing, computing, or financial record-keeping would satisfy you. If you prefer to deal with people, you may want a job in which you meet the public, talk on the telephone, or supervise other workers. You may like to do word processing on a computer, turn out copies on a duplicating machine, or work out sums on a calculator. Perhaps a job in filing or recording would satisfy you. Or you may wish to use your training and experience to manage an office.

▲ **Sales and Marketing**—*An interest in bringing others to a particular point of view by personal persuasion, using sales and promotional techniques.* You can satisfy this interest in a variety of sales and marketing jobs. If you like using technical knowledge of science or agriculture, you may enjoy selling technical products or services. Or perhaps you are more interested in selling business-related services such as insurance coverage, advertising space, or investment opportunities. Real estate offers several kinds of sales jobs. Perhaps you'd rather work with something you can pick up and show to people. You may work in stores, sales offices, or customers' homes.

▲ **Recreation, Travel, and Other Personal Services**—*An interest in catering to the personal wishes and needs of others so that they may enjoy cleanliness, good food and drink, comfortable lodging away from home, and enjoyable recreation.* You can satisfy this interest by providing services for the convenience, feeding, and pampering of others in hotels, restaurants, airplanes, and so on. If you enjoy improving the appearance of others, perhaps working in the hair and beauty care field would satisfy you. You may wish to provide personal services such as taking care of small children, tailoring garments, or ushering. Or you may use your knowledge of the field to manage workers who are providing these services.

▲ **Education and Social Service**—*An interest in teaching people or improving their social or spiritual well-being.* You can satisfy this interest by teaching students, who may be preschoolers, retirees, or any age between. Or if you are interested in helping people sort out their complicated lives, you may find fulfillment as a counselor, social worker, or religious worker. Working in a museum or library may give you opportunities to expand people's understanding of the world. If you also have an interest in business, you may find satisfaction in managerial work in this field.

▲ **General Management and Support**—*An interest in making an organization run smoothly.* You can satisfy this interest by working in a position of leadership or by specializing in a function that contributes to the overall effort. The organization may be a profit-making business, a non-profit, or a government agency. If you especially enjoy working with people, you may find fulfillment from working in human resources. An interest in numbers may cause you to consider accounting, finance, budgeting, or purchasing. Or perhaps you would enjoy managing the organization's physical resources (such as land, buildings, equipment, and utilities).

▲ **Medical and Health Services**—*An interest in helping people be healthy.* You can satisfy this interest by working in a health-care as a doctor, therapist, or nurse. You might specialize in one of the many different parts of the body or types of care, or you might be a generalist who deals with the whole patient. If you like technology, you might find satisfaction working with X rays, one of the electronic means of diagnosis, or clinical laboratory testing. You might work with healthy people, helping them stay in condition through exercise and eating right. If you like to organize, analyze, and plan, a managerial role might be right for you.

# Best Jobs for People Interested in Arts, Entertainment, and Media

| Job | Annual Earnings | Percent Growth | Annual Openings |
|---|---|---|---|
| 1. Musicians, Instrumental | $44,520 | 20.1% | 33,000 |
| 2. Singers | $44,520 | 20.1% | 20,000 |
| 3. Actors | $41,570 | 26.7% | 3,000 |
| 4. Athletes and Sports Competitors | $62,960 | 22.5% | 33,000 |
| 5. Fitness Trainers and Aerobics Instructors | $28,750 | 40.3% | 4,000 |
| 6. Coaches and Scouts | $33,470 | 17.6% | 4,000 |
| 7. Desktop Publishers | $32,700 | 66.7% | 4,000 |
| 8. Camera Operators, Television, Video, and Motion Picture | $33,860 | 25.8% | 3,000 |
| 9. Interpreters and Translators | $33,550 | 23.8% | 13,000 |
| 10. Professional Photographers | $27,420 | 17.0% | 4,000 |
| 11. Cartoonists | $35,770 | 13.4% | 19,000 |
| 12. Painters and Illustrators | $35,770 | 13.4% | 19,000 |
| 13. Sculptors | $35,770 | 13.4% | 5,000 |
| 14. Sketch Artists | $35,770 | 13.4% | 3,000 |
| 15. Costume Attendants | $24,790 | 19.1% | 8,000 |

## Best Jobs for People Interested in Science, Math, and Engineering

| Job | Annual Earnings | Percent Growth | Annual Openings |
|-----|-----------------|----------------|-----------------|
| 1. Architectural Drafters | $37,100 | 20.8% | 12,000 |
| 2. Civil Drafters | $37,100 | 20.8% | 12,000 |
| 3. Electrical Drafters | $40,420 | 23.3% | 5,000 |
| 4. Electronic Drafters | $40,420 | 23.3% | 5,000 |
| 5. Calibration and Instrumentation Technicians | $41,210 | 10.8% | 22,000 |
| 6. Electrical Engineering Technicians | $41,210 | 10.8% | 22,000 |
| 7. Electronics Engineering Technicians | $41,210 | 10.8% | 22,000 |
| 8. Chemical Technicians | $37,080 | 15.0% | 13,000 |
| 9. Biological Technicians | $32,970 | 26.4% | 7,000 |
| 10. Mechanical Drafters | $40,330 | 15.4% | 8,000 |
| 11. Environmental Science and Protection Technicians, Including Health | $35,830 | 24.5% | 3,000 |
| 12. Nuclear Equipment Operation Technicians | $61,970 | 20.7% | fewer than 500 |
| 13. Pressure Vessel Inspectors | $44,140 | 8.9% | 9,000 |
| 14. Electro-Mechanical Technicians | $38,630 | 14.5% | 4,000 |
| 15. Photographers, Scientific | $27,420 | 17.0% | 13,000 |
| 16. Numerical Tool and Process Control Programmers | $37,690 | 16.6% | 2,000 |
| 17. Construction and Building Inspectors | $39,730 | 15.0% | 2,000 |

## Best Jobs for People Interested in Plants and Animals

| Job | Annual Earnings | Percent Growth | Annual Openings |
|---|---|---|---|
| 1. First-Line Supervisors and Manager/ Supervisors—Landscaping Workers | $33,720 | 20.1% | 10,000 |
| 2. Lawn Service Managers | $33,720 | 20.1% | 10,000 |
| 3. Landscaping and Groundskeeping Workers | $20,030 | 29.0% | 193,000 |
| 4. Nonfarm Animal Caretakers | $17,600 | 21.6% | 20,000 |
| 5. Tree Trimmers and Pruners | $25,590 | 16.3% | 11,000 |
| 6. Veterinary Technologists and Technicians | $22,730 | 39.3% | 6,000 |
| 7. Pest Control Workers | $24,020 | 22.1% | 7,000 |

# Best Jobs for People Interested in Law, Law Enforcement, and Public Safety

| Job | Annual Earnings | Percent Growth | Annual Openings |
|---|---|---|---|
| 1. Paralegals and Legal Assistants | $38,790 | 33.2% | 23,000 |
| 2. Highway Patrol Pilots | $40,590 | 23.2% | 21,000 |
| 3. Police Patrol Officers | $40,590 | 23.2% | 21,000 |
| 4. Sheriffs and Deputy Sheriffs | $40,590 | 23.2% | 21,000 |
| 5. Correctional Officers and Jailers | $32,680 | 32.4% | 30,000 |
| 6. First-Line Supervisors/Managers of Police and Detectives | $57,900 | 13.1% | 9,000 |
| 7. Security Guards | $19,470 | 35.4% | 242,000 |
| 8. Criminal Investigators and Special Agents | $49,830 | 16.4% | 4,000 |
| 9. Immigration and Customs Inspectors | $49,830 | 16.4% | 4,000 |
| 10. Police Detectives | $49,830 | 16.4% | 4,000 |
| 11. Police Identification and Records Officers | $49,830 | 16.4% | 4,000 |
| 12. Child Support, Missing Persons, and Unemployment Insurance Fraud Investigators | $49,830 | 16.4% | 4,000 |
| 13. Private Detectives and Investigators | $30,650 | 23.5% | 9,000 |
| 14. Emergency Medical Technicians and Paramedics | $24,740 | 31.3% | 19,000 |
| 15. Nuclear Monitoring Technicians | $61,970 | 20.7% | fewer than 500 |
| 16. Environmental Compliance Inspectors | $44,140 | 8.9% | 9,000 |
| 17. Equal Opportunity Representatives and Officers | $44,140 | 8.9% | 9,000 |
| 18. Government Property Inspectors and Investigators | $44,140 | 8.9% | 9,000 |
| 19. Licensing Examiners and Inspectors | $44,140 | 8.9% | 9,000 |
| 20. Aviation Inspectors | $44,200 | 11.3% | 3,000 |
| 21. Marine Cargo Inspectors | $44,200 | 11.3% | 3,000 |
| 22. Public Transportation Inspectors | $44,200 | 11.3% | 3,000 |
| 23. Forest Fire Fighters | $35,260 | 8.9% | 12,000 |
| 24. Municipal Fire Fighters | $35,260 | 8.9% | 12,000 |
| 25. Fire Inspectors | $42,800 | 15.1% | 1,000 |
| 26. Fire Inspectors and Investigators | $42,800 | 15.1% | 1,000 |
| 27. Forest Fire Fighting and Prevention Supervisors | $52,990 | 7.2% | 5,000 |
| 28. Municipal Fire Fighting and Prevention Supervisors | $52,990 | 7.2% | 5,000 |
| 29. Transit and Railroad Police | $41,560 | 16.5% | fewer than 500 |

# Best Jobs for People Interested in Being Mechanics, Installers, and Repairers

| Job | Annual Earnings | Percent Growth | Annual Openings |
|---|---|---|---|
| 1. First-Line Supervisors/Managers of Mechanics, Installers, and Repairers | $46,560 | 16.0% | 38,000 |
| 2. Heating and Air Conditioning Mechanics | $34,180 | 22.3% | 21,000 |
| 3. Refrigeration Mechanics | $34,180 | 22.3% | 21,000 |
| 4. Automotive Master Mechanics | $30,780 | 18.0% | 104,000 |
| 5. Automotive Specialty Technicians | $30,780 | 18.0% | 104,000 |
| 6. Telecommunications Line Installers and Repairers | $38,050 | 27.6% | 9,000 |
| 7. Aircraft Mechanics and Service Technicians | $40,550 | 16.7% | 11,000 |
| 8. Data Processing Equipment Repairers | $32,860 | 14.2% | 24,000 |
| 9. Office Machine and Cash Register Servicers | $32,860 | 14.2% | 24,000 |
| 10. Bus and Truck Mechanics and Diesel Engine Specialists | $33,210 | 14.2% | 20,000 |
| 11. Elevator Installers and Repairers | $46,240 | 17.2% | 2,000 |
| 12. Mobile Heavy Equipment Mechanics, Except Engines | $34,790 | 14.0% | 11,000 |
| 13. Painters, Transportation Equipment | $32,910 | 17.5% | 8,000 |
| 14. Automotive Body and Related Repairers | $33,710 | 10.2% | 18,000 |
| 15. Helpers—Installation, Maintenance, and Repair Workers | $22,620 | 18.5% | 35,000 |
| 16. Electrical and Electronics Repairers, Commercial and Industrial Equipment | $37,190 | 9.2% | 10,000 |
| 17. Electrical Power-Line Installers and Repairers | $44,490 | 9.3% | 5,000 |
| 18. Railroad Inspectors | $44,200 | 11.3% | 3,000 |
| 19. Medical Equipment Repairers | $37,470 | 14.9% | 3,000 |
| 20. Maintenance and Repair Workers, General | $29,420 | 4.7% | 103,000 |
| 21. Helpers—Electricians | $22,740 | 13.3% | 27,000 |
| 22. Avionics Technicians | $41,600 | 9.8% | 2,000 |
| 23. Central Office and PBX Installers and Repairers | $42,520 | −3.1% | 9,000 |
| 24. Communication Equipment Mechanics, Installers, and Repairers | $42,520 | −3.1% | 9,000 |
| 25. Station Installers and Repairers, Telephone | $42,520 | −3.1% | 9,000 |
| 26. Telecommunications Facility Examiners | $42,520 | −3.1% | 9,000 |

# Best Jobs for People Interested in Construction, Mining, and Drilling

| Job | Annual Earnings | Percent Growth | Annual Openings |
|---|---|---|---|
| 1. First-Line Supervisors and Manager/Supervisors—Construction Trades Workers | $47,740 | 16.5% | 43,000 |
| 2. First-Line Supervisors and Manager/Supervisors—Extractive Workers | $47,740 | 16.5% | 43,000 |
| 3. Electricians | $42,210 | 17.3% | 66,000 |
| 4. Roofers | $31,670 | 19.4% | 38,000 |
| 5. Sheet Metal Workers | $35,050 | 23.0% | 13,000 |
| 6. Painters, Construction and Maintenance | $29,610 | 19.1% | 67,000 |
| 7. Pipe Fitters | $40,170 | 10.2% | 49,000 |
| 8. Pipelaying Fitters | $40,170 | 10.2% | 49,000 |
| 9. Plumbers | $40,170 | 10.2% | 49,000 |
| 10. Structural Iron and Steel Workers | $39,140 | 18.4% | 12,000 |
| 11. Construction Laborers | $26,940 | 17.0% | 236,000 |
| 12. Boat Builders and Shipwrights | $35,100 | 8.2% | 161,000 |
| 13. Brattice Builders | $35,100 | 8.2% | 161,000 |
| 14. Carpenter Assemblers and Repairers | $35,100 | 8.2% | 161,000 |
| 15. Construction Carpenters | $35,100 | 8.2% | 161,000 |
| 16. Rough Carpenters | $35,100 | 8.2% | 161,000 |
| 17. Ship Carpenters and Joiners | $35,100 | 8.2% | 161,000 |
| 18. Brickmasons and Blockmasons | $41,140 | 12.5% | 18,000 |
| 19. Ceiling Tile Installers | $35,580 | 9.4% | 19,000 |
| 20. Drywall Installers | $35,580 | 9.4% | 19,000 |
| 21. Reinforcing Iron and Rebar Workers | $37,800 | 17.5% | 4,000 |
| 22. Grader, Bulldozer, and Scraper Operators | $36,170 | 6.9% | 25,000 |
| 23. Operating Engineers | $36,170 | 6.9% | 25,000 |
| 24. Tile and Marble Setters | $36,580 | 15.6% | 5,000 |
| 25. Grips and Set-Up Workers, Motion Picture Sets, Studios, and Stages | $20,460 | 13.9% | 519,000 |
| 26. Paperhangers | $32,490 | 20.2% | 3,000 |
| 27. Plasterers and Stucco Masons | $35,170 | 11.9% | 7,000 |
| 28. Excavating and Loading Machine Operators | $33,480 | 14.8% | 5,000 |
| 29. Glaziers | $32,360 | 14.8% | 6,000 |
| 30. Stonemasons | $32,380 | 20.8% | 2,000 |
| 31. Paving, Surfacing, and Tamping Equipment Operators | $30,090 | 15.5% | 6,000 |

## Best Jobs for People Interested in Construction, Mining, and Drilling

| Job | Annual Earnings | Percent Growth | Annual Openings |
|---|---|---|---|
| 32. Tapers | $38,680 | 8.3% | 6,000 |
| 33. Carpet Installers | $33,030 | 10.5% | 7,000 |
| 34. Helpers—Brickmasons, Blockmasons, Stonemasons, and Tile and Marble Setters | $25,780 | 14.1% | 14,000 |
| 35. Pile-Driver Operators | $41,570 | 14.0% | 1,000 |
| 36. Septic Tank Servicers and Sewer Pipe Cleaners | $28,930 | 16.5% | 4,000 |
| 37. Pipelayers | $30,220 | 11.9% | 6,000 |

## Best Jobs for People Interested in Transportation

| Job | Annual Earnings | Percent Growth | Annual Openings |
|---|---|---|---|
| 1. Tractor-Trailer Truck Drivers | $32,810 | 19.8% | 240,000 |
| 2. Truck Drivers, Heavy | $32,810 | 19.8% | 240,000 |
| 3. Transportation Managers | $58,200 | 20.2% | 13,000 |
| 4. First-Line Supervisors/Managers of Transportation and Material-Moving Machine and Vehicle Operators | $43,120 | 19.9% | 17,000 |
| 5. Truck Drivers, Light or Delivery Services | $24,620 | 19.2% | 153,000 |
| 6. Commercial Pilots | $51,370 | 26.9% | 1,000 |
| 7. Bus Drivers, Transit and Intercity | $27,250 | 17.4% | 24,000 |
| 8. Taxi Drivers and Chauffeurs | $18,920 | 24.4% | 37,000 |
| 9. Stevedores, Except Equipment Operators | $20,460 | 13.9% | 519,000 |
| 10. Freight Inspectors | $44,200 | 11.3% | 3,000 |
| 11. Bus Drivers, School | $21,430 | 11.6% | 63,000 |
| 12. Air Traffic Controllers | $79,460 | 7.2% | 2,000 |

# Best Jobs for People Interested in Industrial Production

| Job | Annual Earnings | Percent Growth | Annual Openings |
|---|---|---|---|
| 1. First-Line Supervisors/Managers of Helpers, Laborers, and Material Movers, Hand | $36,910 | 18.9% | 14,000 |
| 2. Brazers | $29,080 | 19.3% | 51,000 |
| 3. Solderers | $29,080 | 19.3% | 51,000 |
| 4. Welder-Fitters | $29,080 | 19.3% | 51,000 |
| 5. Welders and Cutters | $29,080 | 19.3% | 51,000 |
| 6. Welders, Production | $29,080 | 19.3% | 51,000 |
| 7. Irradiated-Fuel Handlers | $31,630 | 32.8% | 9,000 |
| 8. Fitters, Structural Metal—Precision | $28,490 | 19.5% | 20,000 |
| 9. Metal Fabricators, Structural Metal Products | $28,490 | 19.5% | 20,000 |
| 10. Chemical Equipment Controllers and Operators | $36,310 | 14.9% | 9,000 |
| 11. Chemical Equipment Tenders | $36,310 | 14.9% | 9,000 |
| 12. First-Line Supervisors/Managers of Production and Operating Workers | $43,020 | 1.0% | 71,000 |
| 13. Numerical Control Machine Tool Operators and Tenders, Metal and Plastic | $28,780 | 19.7% | 15,000 |
| 14. Refuse and Recyclable Material Collectors | $26,020 | 16.6% | 34,000 |
| 15. Combination Machine Tool Operators and Tenders, Metal and Plastic | $29,350 | 14.7% | 21,000 |
| 16. Combination Machine Tool Setters and Set-Up Operators, Metal and Plastic | $29,350 | 14.7% | 21,000 |
| 17. Packers and Packagers, Hand | $17,030 | 19.3% | 242,000 |
| 18. Industrial Truck and Tractor Operators | $26,090 | 11.3% | 91,000 |
| 19. Water and Liquid Waste Treatment Plant and System Operators | $32,450 | 18.1% | 6,000 |
| 20. Machinists | $31,610 | 9.1% | 28,000 |
| 21. Semiconductor Processors | $27,170 | 32.4% | 7,000 |
| 22. Freight, Stock, and Material Movers, Hand | $20,460 | 13.9% | 519,000 |
| 23. Motor Vehicle Inspectors | $44,200 | 11.3% | 3,000 |
| 24. Soldering and Brazing Machine Operators and Tenders | $29,730 | 15.1% | 9,000 |
| 25. Soldering and Brazing Machine Setters and Set-Up Operators | $29,730 | 15.1% | 9,000 |
| 26. Welding Machine Operators and Tenders | $29,730 | 15.1% | 9,000 |
| 27. Welding Machine Setters and Set-Up Operators | $29,730 | 15.1% | 9,000 |

(continued)

*(continued)*

# Best Jobs for People Interested in Industrial Production

| Job | Annual Earnings | Percent Growth | Annual Openings |
|---|---|---|---|
| 28. Dragline Operators | $33,480 | 14.8% | 5,000 |
| 29. Packaging and Filling Machine Operators and Tenders | $21,700 | 14.4% | 56,000 |
| 30. Extruding and Drawing Machine Setters, Operators, and Tenders, Metal and Plastic | $25,030 | 13.5% | 23,000 |
| 31. Bakers, Manufacturing | $21,050 | 16.8% | 25,000 |
| 32. Aircraft Rigging Assemblers | $38,150 | 14.2% | 2,000 |
| 33. Aircraft Structure Assemblers, Precision | $38,150 | 14.2% | 2,000 |
| 34. Aircraft Systems Assemblers, Precision | $38,150 | 14.2% | 2,000 |
| 35. Production Helpers | $19,350 | 11.9% | 143,000 |
| 36. Production Laborers | $19,350 | 11.9% | 143,000 |
| 37. Design Printing Machine Setters and Set-Up Operators | $30,090 | 5.5% | 24,000 |
| 38. Embossing Machine Set-Up Operators | $30,090 | 5.5% | 24,000 |
| 39. Engraver Set-Up Operators | $30,090 | 5.5% | 24,000 |
| 40. Letterpress Setters and Set-Up Operators | $30,090 | 5.5% | 24,000 |
| 41. Marking and Identification Printing Machine Setters and Set-Up Operators | $30,090 | 5.5% | 24,000 |
| 42. Offset Lithographic Press Setters and Set-Up Operators | $30,090 | 5.5% | 24,000 |
| 43. Precision Printing Workers | $30,090 | 5.5% | 24,000 |
| 44. Printing Press Machine Operators and Tenders | $30,090 | 5.5% | 24,000 |
| 45. Screen Printing Machine Setters and Set-Up Operators | $30,090 | 5.5% | 24,000 |
| 46. Heat Treating, Annealing, and Tempering Machine Operators and Tenders, Metal and Plastic | $28,020 | 13.4% | 9,000 |
| 47. Heaters, Metal and Plastic | $28,020 | 13.4% | 9,000 |
| 48. Heating Equipment Setters and Set-Up Operators, Metal and Plastic | $28,020 | 13.4% | 9,000 |
| 49. Coating, Painting, and Spraying Machine Operators and Tenders | $25,140 | 11.9% | 18,000 |
| 50. Coating, Painting, and Spraying Machine Setters and Set-Up Operators | $25,140 | 11.9% | 18,000 |
| 51. Casting Machine Set-Up Operators | $23,630 | 9.8% | 38,000 |

## Best Jobs for People Interested in Industrial Production

| Job | Annual Earnings | Percent Growth | Annual Openings |
|---|---|---|---|
| 52. Metal Molding, Coremaking, and Casting Machine Operators and Tenders | $23,630 | 9.8% | 38,000 |
| 53. Metal Molding, Coremaking, and Casting Machine Setters and Set-Up Operators | $23,630 | 9.8% | 38,000 |
| 54. Plastic Molding and Casting Machine Operators and Tenders | $23,630 | 9.8% | 38,000 |
| 55. Plastic Molding and Casting Machine Setters and Set-Up Operators | $23,630 | 9.8% | 38,000 |
| 56. Crane and Tower Operators | $35,340 | 8.6% | 5,000 |

# Best Jobs for People Interested in Business Detail

| Job | Annual Earnings | Percent Growth | Annual Openings |
|---|---|---|---|
| 1. Legal Secretaries | $35,370 | 20.3% | 36,000 |
| 2. Adjustment Clerks | $26,530 | 32.4% | 359,000 |
| 3. Customer Service Representatives, Utilities | $26,530 | 32.4% | 359,000 |
| 4. First-Line Supervisors, Administrative Support | $39,410 | 9.4% | 146,000 |
| 5. First-Line Supervisors, Customer Service | $39,410 | 9.4% | 146,000 |
| 6. Production, Planning, and Expediting Clerks | $32,520 | 17.9% | 36,000 |
| 7. Bill and Account Collectors | $26,670 | 25.3% | 71,000 |
| 8. Executive Secretaries and Administrative Assistants | $32,520 | 11.5% | 185,000 |
| 9. Human Resources Assistants, Except Payroll and Timekeeping | $29,400 | 19.3% | 25,000 |
| 10. Automatic Teller Machine Servicers | $32,860 | 14.2% | 24,000 |
| 11. Receptionists and Information Clerks | $20,780 | 23.7% | 269,000 |
| 12. Interviewers, Except Eligibility and Loan | $22,360 | 33.4% | 53,000 |
| 13. Office Clerks, General | $22,290 | 15.9% | 676,000 |
| 14. Medical Secretaries | $24,460 | 19.0% | 40,000 |
| 15. Dispatchers, Except Police, Fire, and Ambulance | $30,410 | 22.2% | 8,000 |
| 16. Medical Records and Health Information Technicians | $24,430 | 49.0% | 14,000 |
| 17. Travel Clerks | $26,140 | 14.5% | 39,000 |
| 18. Counter and Rental Clerks | $18,670 | 19.4% | 150,000 |
| 19. Weighers, Measurers, Checkers, and Samplers, Recordkeeping | $26,250 | 17.9% | 13,000 |
| 20. Cashiers | $15,730 | 14.2% | 1,125,000 |
| 21. Billing, Cost, and Rate Clerks | $25,480 | 8.5% | 69,000 |
| 22. Billing, Posting, and Calculating Machine Operators | $25,480 | 8.5% | 69,000 |
| 23. Statement Clerks | $25,480 | 8.5% | 69,000 |
| 24. Shipping, Receiving, and Traffic Clerks | $23,340 | 9.3% | 133,000 |
| 25. Court Clerks | $27,780 | 12.0% | 14,000 |
| 26. Municipal Clerks | $27,780 | 12.0% | 14,000 |
| 27. Bookkeeping, Accounting, and Auditing Clerks | $26,950 | 2.0% | 298,000 |
| 28. Postal Service Mail Carriers | $36,830 | 2.4% | 13,000 |
| 29. Marking Clerks | $20,650 | 8.5% | 467,000 |
| 30. Order Fillers, Wholesale and Retail Sales | $20,650 | 8.5% | 467,000 |
| 31. Stock Clerks and Order Fillers | $20,650 | 8.5% | 467,000 |
| 32. Stock Clerks—Stockroom, Warehouse, or Storage Yard | $20,650 | 8.5% | 467,000 |

# Best Jobs for People Interested in Sales and Marketing

| Job | Annual Earnings | Percent Growth | Annual Openings |
|---|---|---|---|
| 1. Advertising Sales Agents | $44,960 | 26.3% | 25,000 |
| 2. Sales Representatives, Wholesale and Manufacturing, Except Technical and Scientific Products | $46,770 | 5.7% | 86,000 |
| 3. First-Line Supervisors/Managers of Non-Retail Sales Workers | $56,850 | 5.8% | 41,000 |
| 4. Sales Representatives, Agricultural | $58,630 | 7.5% | 24,000 |
| 5. Sales Representatives, Chemical and Pharmaceutical | $58,630 | 7.5% | 24,000 |
| 6. Sales Representatives, Electrical/Electronic | $58,630 | 7.5% | 24,000 |
| 7. Sales Representatives, Instruments | $58,630 | 7.5% | 24,000 |
| 8. Sales Representatives, Mechanical Equipment and Supplies | $58,630 | 7.5% | 24,000 |
| 9. Sales Representatives, Medical | $58,630 | 7.5% | 24,000 |
| 10. Real Estate Sales Agents | $37,950 | 9.5% | 28,000 |
| 11. Demonstrators and Product Promoters | $24,460 | 24.9% | 34,000 |
| 12. First-Line Supervisors/Managers of Retail Sales Workers | $32,170 | 8.1% | 206,000 |
| 13. Telemarketers | $21,460 | 22.2% | 145,000 |
| 14. Real Estate Brokers | $60,080 | 9.6% | 8,000 |
| 15. Retail Salespersons | $20,260 | 12.4% | 1,124,000 |
| 16. Stock Clerks, Sales Floor | $20,650 | 8.5% | 467,000 |

# Best Jobs for People Interested in Recreation, Travel, and Other Personal Services

| Job | Annual Earnings | Percent Growth | Annual Openings |
|---|---|---|---|
| 1. Food Service Managers | $34,350 | 15.0% | 55,000 |
| 2. Flight Attendants | $45,220 | 18.4% | 8,000 |
| 3. Combined Food Preparation and Serving Workers, Including Fast Food | $14,240 | 30.5% | 737,000 |
| 4. Personal and Home Care Aides | $15,960 | 62.5% | 84,000 |
| 5. Cooks, Restaurant | $18,880 | 21.7% | 158,000 |
| 6. Hotel, Motel, and Resort Desk Clerks | $17,100 | 33.4% | 73,000 |
| 7. Reservation and Transportation Ticket Agents | $26,140 | 14.5% | 39,000 |
| 8. Amusement and Recreation Attendants | $15,480 | 32.4% | 62,000 |
| 9. First-Line Supervisors/Managers of Food Preparation and Serving Workers | $24,600 | 12.7% | 136,000 |
| 10. Waiters and Waitresses | $14,750 | 18.3% | 596,000 |
| 11. Cleaners of Vehicles and Equipment | $17,380 | 18.8% | 86,000 |
| 12. Food Preparation Workers | $16,180 | 16.9% | 231,000 |
| 13. Housekeeping Supervisors | $27,830 | 14.2% | 18,000 |
| 14. Janitorial Supervisors | $27,830 | 14.2% | 18,000 |
| 15. Gaming Dealers | $15,550 | 32.4% | 28,000 |
| 16. First-Line Supervisors/Managers of Personal Service Workers | $30,350 | 15.1% | 8,000 |
| 17. Janitors and Cleaners, Except Maids and Housekeeping Cleaners | $19,080 | 13.5% | 507,000 |
| 18. Chefs and Head Cooks | $28,550 | 9.0% | 35,000 |
| 19. Bakers, Bread and Pastry | $21,050 | 16.8% | 25,000 |
| 20. Food Servers, Nonrestaurant | $16,170 | 16.4% | 85,000 |
| 21. Counter Attendants, Cafeteria, Food Concession, and Coffee Shop | $15,030 | 14.4% | 216,000 |
| 22. Hairdressers, Hairstylists, and Cosmetologists | $20,710 | 13.0% | 78,000 |
| 23. Lodging Managers | $34,800 | 9.3% | 8,000 |
| 24. Travel Guides | $30,990 | 9.5% | 10,000 |
| 25. Bartenders | $16,150 | 13.4% | 84,000 |

# Best Jobs for People Interested in Education and Social Service

| Job | Annual Earnings | Percent Growth | Annual Openings |
|-----|-----------------|----------------|-----------------|
| 1. Self-Enrichment Education Teachers | $31,070 | 18.5% | 34,000 |
| 2. Social and Human Service Assistants | $23,840 | 54.2% | 45,000 |
| 3. Teacher Assistants | $18,770 | 23.9% | 256,000 |
| 4. Library Technicians | $24,230 | 19.5% | 29,000 |
| 5. Library Assistants, Clerical | $19,380 | 19.7% | 26,000 |
| 6. Residential Advisors | $21,600 | 24.0% | 9,000 |
| 7. Audio-Visual Collections Specialists | $35,590 | 13.6% | 2,000 |
| 8. Child Care Workers | $16,350 | 10.6% | 370,000 |

## Best Jobs for People Interested in General Management and Support

| Job | Annual Earnings | Percent Growth | Annual Openings |
|---|---|---|---|
| 1. Storage and Distribution Managers | $58,200 | 20.2% | 13,000 |
| 2. Claims Examiners, Property and Casualty Insurance | $44,000 | 15.1% | 25,000 |
| 3. Insurance Adjusters, Examiners, and Investigators | $44,000 | 15.1% | 25,000 |
| 4. Appraisers, Real Estate | $41,700 | 18.0% | 6,000 |

# Best Jobs for People Interested in Medical and Health Services

| Job | Annual Earnings | Percent Growth | Annual Openings |
|---|---|---|---|
| 1. Registered Nurses | $46,410 | 25.6% | 140,000 |
| 2. Dental Hygienists | $51,980 | 37.1% | 5,000 |
| 3. Licensed Practical and Licensed Vocational Nurses | $30,470 | 20.3% | 58,000 |
| 4. Radiologic Technologists and Technicians | $37,290 | 23.1% | 13,000 |
| 5. Physical Therapist Assistants | $34,370 | 44.8% | 9,000 |
| 6. Respiratory Therapists | $38,220 | 34.8% | 4,000 |
| 7. Dental Assistants | $26,740 | 37.2% | 16,000 |
| 8. Nursing Aides, Orderlies, and Attendants | $19,100 | 23.5% | 268,000 |
| 9. Home Health Aides | $18,110 | 47.3% | 120,000 |
| 10. Occupational Therapist Assistants | $34,860 | 39.7% | 3,000 |
| 11. Medical and Clinical Laboratory Technicians | $28,970 | 19.0% | 19,000 |
| 12. Cardiovascular Technologists and Technicians | $34,960 | 34.9% | 3,000 |
| 13. Surgical Technologists | $29,660 | 34.7% | 8,000 |
| 14. Nuclear Medicine Technologists | $44,850 | 22.4% | 1,000 |
| 15. Medical Assistants | $23,840 | 57.0% | 18,700 |
| 16. Coroners | $44,140 | 8.9% | 9,000 |
| 17. Pharmacy Technicians | $21,600 | 36.4% | 22,000 |
| 18. Physical Therapist Aides | $20,930 | 46.3% | 7,000 |

# Part II

# Descriptions of the 300 Best Jobs That Don't Require a Four-Year Degree

This part provides descriptions for all the jobs included in one or more of the lists in Part I. The book's introduction gives more details on how to use and interpret the job descriptions, but here are the highlights, along with some additional information:

▲ The job descriptions that follow met our criteria for inclusion in this book, as we describe in the Introduction. The jobs in this book do not require a four-year college degree and are among the 300 highest total scores for earnings, projected growth, and number of job openings. Many good jobs do not meet one or more of these criteria, but we think the jobs that do are the best ones to consider in your career planning.

▲ The job descriptions are arranged in alphabetical order by job title. This approach allows you to quickly find a description if you know its title from one of the lists in Part I. Part I features many interesting lists that will help you identify job titles to explore in more detail. If you have not browsed the lists in Part I, consider spending some time there. The lists are interesting and will help you identify job titles you can look up in the descriptions that follow.

▲ Refer to the Introduction, beginning on page 1, for details on interpreting the job descriptions' content.

(continued)

*(continued)*

▲ The *GOE* job description section includes a subsection titled Other Job Titles in This Work Group to help you identify similar jobs. In some cases, the list of jobs here can be very long, and when this happens, we limit the number of job titles listed to a reasonable number followed by "others" as the last entry. If you want to see the complete list of job titles, consult the "Sources of Additional Information" section in the Introduction for details on how to obtain them.

▲ When reviewing the descriptions, keep in mind that the jobs meet our criteria for being among the top 300 jobs based on their total scores for earnings, growth, and number of openings—but one or more of these measures may not be among the highest. For example, an occupation that has high pay may be included, even though growth rate and number of job openings are below average.

"Well," you might ask, "doesn't this mean that at least some 'bad' jobs are described in this part?" Our answer is yes and no. Some jobs with high scores for all measures, such as Registered Nurses—the job with the highest total for pay, growth, and number of openings —would be a very bad job for people who dislike or are not good at that sort of work. On the other hand, many people love working as Child Care Workers even though that job has lower earnings, a lower projected growth rate, and fewer openings. Descriptions for both jobs are included in this book.

Most likely, somewhere an ex-registered nurse works as a child care worker and loves it. Some who do so may even have figured out how to make more money (say, by running a small child care center), have a more flexible schedule, have more fun, or have other advantages not available in their previous career.

The point is that each job is right for some people at the right time in their lives. We are all likely to change careers and jobs several times, and it's not always money that motivates us. So browse the job descriptions that follow and know that somewhere there is a good place for you. We hope you find it.

# Actors

- ▲ Growth: 26.7%
- ▲ Annual Job Openings: 20,000
- ▲ Annual Earnings: $41,570
- ▲ Education/Training Required: Long-term on-the-job training
- ▲ Self-Employed: 36.8%
- ▲ Part-Time: 25.3%

**Play parts in stage, television, radio, video, or motion picture productions for entertainment, information, or instruction. Interpret serious or comic role by speech, gesture, and body movement to entertain or inform audience. May dance and sing.** Portrays and interprets role, using speech, gestures, and body movements, to entertain radio, film, television, or live audience. Performs humorous and serious interpretations of emotions, actions, and situations, using only body movements, facial expressions, and gestures. Reads from script or book to narrate action, inform, or entertain audience, utilizing few or no stage props. Prepares for and performs action stunts for motion picture, television, or stage production. Constructs puppets and ventriloquist dummies and sews accessory clothing, using hand tools and machines. Writes original or adapted material for drama, comedy, puppet show, narration, or other performance. Signals start and introduces performers to stimulate excitement and to coordinate smooth transition of acts during circus performance. Manipulates string, wire, rod, or fingers to animate puppet or dummy in synchronization to talking, singing, or recorded program. Sings or dances during dramatic or comedy performance. Dresses in comical clown costume and makeup and performs comedy routines to entertain audience. Reads and rehearses role from script to learn lines, stunts, and cues as directed. Tells jokes, performs comic dances and songs, impersonates mannerisms and voice of others, contorts face, and uses other devices to amuse audience. Performs original and stock tricks of illusion to entertain and mystify audience, occasionally including audience members as participants. **SKILLS**—Speaking. Monitoring. Reading Comprehension. Coordination. Active Learning. Social Perceptiveness.

**GOE—Interest Area:** 01. Arts, Entertainment, and Media. **Work Group:** 01.05. Performing Arts. **Other Job Titles in This Work Group:** Choreographers; Composers; Dancers; Directors—Stage, Motion Pictures, Television, and Radio; Music Arrangers and Orchestrators; Music Directors; Music Directors and Composers; Musicians and Singers; Musicians, Instrumental; Public Address System and Other Announcers; Radio and Television Announcers; Singers; Talent Directors. **PERSONALITY TYPE**—Artistic. Artistic occupations frequently involve working with forms, designs, and patterns. They often require self-expression, and the work can be done without following a clear set of rules.

**EDUCATION/TRAINING PROGRAM(S)**—Acting and Directing; Drama/Theater Arts, General; Drama/Theater Literature, History and Criticism; Dramatic/Theater Arts and Stagecraft, Other. **RELATED KNOWLEDGE/COURSES—Fine Arts:** Knowledge of the theory and techniques required to compose, produce, and perform works of music, dance, visual arts, drama, and sculpture. **English Language:** Knowledge of the structure and content of the English language, including the meaning and spelling of words, rules of composition, and grammar. **Communications and Media:** Knowledge of media production, communication, and dissemination techniques and methods. This includes alternative ways to inform and entertain via written, oral, and visual media. **Psychology:** Knowledge of human behavior and performance; individual differences in ability, personality, and interests; learning and motivation; psychological research methods; and the assessment and treatment of behavioral and affective disorders. **Building and Construction:** Knowledge of materials, methods, and tools involved in the construction or repair of houses, buildings, or other structures such as highways and roads.

# Adjustment Clerks

▲ Growth: 32.4%

▲ Annual Job Openings: 359,000

▲ Annual Earnings: $26,530

▲ Education/Training Required: Moderate-term on-the-job training

▲ Self-Employed: 0.2%

▲ Part-Time: 12.6%

Investigate and resolve customers' inquiries concerning merchandise, service, billing, or credit rating. Examine pertinent information to determine accuracy of customers' complaints and responsibility for errors. Notify customers and appropriate personnel of findings, adjustments, and recommendations, such as exchange of merchandise, refund of money, credit to customers' accounts, or adjustment to customers' bills. Reviews claims adjustments with dealer, examines parts claimed to be defective, and approves or disapproves of dealer's claim. Notifies customer and designated personnel of findings and recommendations, such as exchanging merchandise, refunding money, or adjustment of bill. Examines weather conditions and number of days in billing period and reviews meter accounts for errors which might explain high utility charges. Writes work order. Prepares reports showing volume, types, and disposition of claims handled. Compares merchandise with original requisition and information on invoice and prepares invoice for returned goods. Orders tests to detect product malfunction and determines if defect resulted from faulty construction. Trains dealers or service personnel in construction of products, service operations, and customer service. **SKILLS**—Speaking. Active Listening. Writing. Reading Comprehension. Instructing.

**GOE**—**Interest Area:** 09. Business Detail. **Work Group:** 09.05. Customer Service. **Other Job Titles in This Work Group:** Bill and Account Collectors; Cashiers; Counter and Rental Clerks; Customer Service Representatives; Customer Service Representatives, Utilities; Gaming Cage Workers; Gaming Change Persons and Booth Cashiers; New Accounts Clerks; Order Clerks; Receptionists and Information Clerks; Tellers; Travel Clerks. **PERSONALITY TYPE**—Conventional. Conventional occupations frequently involve following set procedures and routines. These occupations can include working with data and details more than with ideas. Usually there is a clear line of authority to follow.

**EDUCATION/TRAINING PROGRAM(S)**—Receptionist. **RELATED KNOWLEDGE/COURSES**—**English Language:** Knowledge of the structure and content of the English language, including the meaning and spelling of words, rules of composition, and grammar. **Mathematics:** Knowledge of arithmetic, algebra, geometry, calculus, statistics, and their applications. **Customer and Personal Service:** Knowledge of principles and processes for providing customer and personal services. This includes customer needs assessment, meeting quality standards for services, and evaluation of customer satisfaction. **Education and Training:** Knowledge of principles and methods for curriculum and training design, teaching and instruction for individuals and groups, and the measurement of training effects. **Economics and Accounting:** Knowledge of economic and accounting principles and practices, the financial markets, banking, and the analysis and reporting of financial data.

# Advertising Sales Agents

▲ Growth: 26.3%

▲ Annual Job Openings: 25,000

▲ Annual Earnings: $44,960

▲ Education/Training Required: Moderate-term on-the-job training

▲ Self-Employed: 3.9%

▲ Part-Time: 22.3%

**Sell or solicit advertising, including graphic art, advertising space in publications, custom-made signs, or TV and radio advertising time. May obtain leases for outdoor advertising sites or persuade retailer to use sales promotion display items.** Advises customer in advantages of various types of programming and methods of composing layouts and designs for signs and displays. Draws up contract covering arrangements for designing, fabricating, erecting, and maintaining sign or display. Sells signs to be made according to customers' specifications, utilizing knowledge of lettering, color harmony, and sign making processes. Visits advertisers to point out advantages of publication. Exhibits prepared layouts with mats and copy with headings. Calls on prospects and presents outlines of various programs or commercial announcements. Prepares list of prospects for classified and display space for publication from leads in other papers and from old accounts. Arranges for and accompanies prospect to commercial taping sessions. Delivers advertising or illustration proofs to customer for approval. Collects payments due. Writes copy as part of layout. Computes job costs. Plans and sketches layouts to meet customer needs. Prepares promotional plans, sales literature, and sales contracts, using computer. Calls on advertisers and sales promotion people to obtain information concerning prospects for current advertising and sales promotion. Obtains pertinent information concerning prospect's past and current advertising for use in sales presentation. Informs customer of types of artwork available by providing samples. **SKILLS**—Speaking. Persuasion. Writing. Reading Comprehension. Active Listening.

**GOE**—Interest Area: 10. Sales and Marketing. **Work Group:** 10.02. Sales Technology. **Other Job Titles in This Work Group:** Insurance Sales Agents; Sales Agents, Financial Services; Sales Agents, Securities and Commodities; Sales Representatives, Agricultural; Sales Representatives, Chemical and Pharmaceutical; Sales Representatives, Electrical/Electronic; Sales Representatives, Instruments; Sales Representatives, Mechanical Equipment and Supplies; Sales Representatives, Medical; Sales Representatives, Services, All Other; Sales Representatives, Wholesale and Manufacturing, Technical and Scientific Products; Securities, Commodities, and Financial Services Sales Agents. **PERSONALITY TYPE**—Enterprising. Enterprising occupations frequently involve starting up and carrying out projects. These occupations can involve leading people and making many decisions. They sometimes require risk taking and often deal with business.

**EDUCATION/TRAINING PROGRAM(S)**—Advertising. **RELATED KNOWLEDGE/COURSES**—**Sales and Marketing:** Knowledge of principles and methods for showing, promoting, and selling products or services. This includes marketing strategy and tactics, product demonstration, sales techniques, and sales control systems. **English Language:** Knowledge of the structure and content of the English language, including the meaning and spelling of words, rules of composition, and grammar. **Communications and Media:** Knowledge of media production, communication, and dissemination techniques and methods. This includes alternative ways to inform and entertain via written, oral, and visual media. **Fine Arts:** Knowledge of the theory and techniques required to compose, produce, and perform works of music, dance, visual arts, drama, and sculpture. **Mathematics:** Knowledge of arithmetic, algebra, geometry, calculus, statistics, and their applications.

# Air Traffic Controllers

- ▲ Growth: 7.2%
- ▲ Annual Job Openings: 2,000
- ▲ Annual Earnings: $79,460
- ▲ Education/Training Required: Long-term on-the-job training
- ▲ Self-Employed: 0%
- ▲ Part-Time: 11.7%

Control air traffic on and within vicinity of airport and movement of air traffic between altitude sectors and control centers according to established procedures and policies. Authorize, regulate, and control commercial airline flights according to government or company regulations to expedite and ensure flight safety. Communicates with, relays flight plans to, and coordinates movement of air traffic between control centers. Determines timing of and procedure for flight vector changes in sector. Issues landing and take-off authorizations and instructions, and communicates other information to aircraft. Controls air traffic at and within vicinity of airport. Recommends flight path changes to planes traveling in storms or fog or in emergency situations. Relays air traffic information, such as altitude, expected time of arrival, and course of aircraft to control centers. Transfers control of departing flights to traffic control center and accepts control of arriving flights from air traffic control center. Analyzes factors such as weather reports, fuel requirements, and maps to determine flights and air routes. Directs radio searches for aircraft and alerts control centers emergency facilities of flight difficulties. Inspects, adjusts, and controls radio equipment and airport lights. Completes daily activity report and keeps record of messages from aircraft. Reviews records and reports for clarity and completeness and maintains records and reports. **SKILLS**—Operation and Control. Active Listening. Critical Thinking. Operation Monitoring. Coordination.

**GOE—Interest Area:** 07. Transportation. **Work Group:** 07.02. Vehicle Expediting and Coordinating. **Other Job Titles in This Work Group:** Airfield Operations Specialists; Railroad Brake, Signal, and Switch Operators; Traffic Technicians. **PERSONALITY TYPE**—Conventional. Conventional occupations frequently involve following set procedures and routines. These occupations can include working with data and details more than with ideas. Usually there is a clear line of authority to follow.

**EDUCATION/TRAINING PROGRAM(S)**—Air Traffic Controller. **RELATED KNOWLEDGE/ COURSES—Transportation:** Knowledge of principles and methods for moving people or goods by air, rail, sea, or road, including the relative costs and benefits. **Telecommunications:** Knowledge of transmission, broadcasting, switching, control, and operation of telecommunications systems. **English Language:** Knowledge of the structure and content of the English language, including the meaning and spelling of words, rules of composition, and grammar. **Physics:** Knowledge and prediction of physical principles and laws and their interrelationships and applications to understanding fluid, material, and atmospheric dynamics and mechanical, electrical, atomic, and sub-atomic structures and processes. **Computers and Electronics:** Knowledge of circuit boards, processors, chips, electronic equipment, and computer hardware and software, including applications and programming. **Mathematics:** Knowledge of arithmetic, algebra, geometry, calculus, statistics, and their applications.

# Aircraft Mechanics and Service Technicians

- ▲ Growth: 16.7%
- ▲ Annual Job Openings: 11,000
- ▲ Annual Earnings: $40,550
- ▲ Education/Training Required: Post-secondary vocational training
- ▲ Self-Employed: 1.8%
- ▲ Part-Time: 2.3%

**Diagnose, adjust, repair, or overhaul aircraft engines and assemblies, such as hydraulic and pneumatic systems.** SKILLS—No data available.

GOE—**Interest Area:** 05. Mechanics, Installers, and Repairers. **Work Group:** 05.03. Mechanical Work. **Other Job Titles in This Work Group:** Aircraft Body and Bonded Structure Repairers; Aircraft Engine Specialists; Airframe-and-Power-Plant Mechanics; Automotive Body and Related Repairers; Automotive Glass Installers and Repairers; Automotive Master Mechanics; Automotive Service Technicians and Mechanics; Automotive Specialty Technicians; Bicycle Repairers; Bridge and Lock Tenders; Bus and Truck Mechanics and Diesel Engine Specialists; Camera and Photographic Equipment Repairers; Coin, Vending, and Amusement Machine Servicers and Repairers; Control and Valve Installers and Repairers, Except Mechanical Door; Farm Equipment Mechanics; Gas Appliance Repairers; Hand and Portable Power Tool Repairers; Heating and Air Conditioning Mechanics; Heating, Air Conditioning, and Refrigeration Mechanics and Installers; Helpers—Electricians; Helpers—Installation, Maintenance, and Repair Workers; Industrial Machinery Mechanics; Keyboard Instrument Repairers and Tuners; Locksmiths and Safe Repairers; Maintenance and Repair Workers, General; Maintenance Workers, Machinery; Mechanical Door Repairers; Medical Appliance Technicians; Medical Equipment Repairers; Meter Mechanics; Millwrights; Mobile Heavy Equipment Mechanics, Except Engines; Motorboat Mechanics; Motorcycle Mechanics; Musical Instrument Repairers and Tuners; Ophthalmic Laboratory Technicians; Optical Instrument Assemblers; Outdoor Power Equipment and Other Small Engine Mechanics; Painters, Transportation Equipment; Percussion Instrument Repairers and Tuners; Precision Instrument and Equipment Repairers, All Other; others. **PERSONALITY TYPE**—No data available.

**EDUCATION/TRAINING PROGRAM(S)**—Aircraft Mechanic/Technician, Airframe; Aircraft Mechanic/Technician, Powerplant. **RELATED KNOWLEDGE/COURSES**—No data available.

# Aircraft Rigging Assemblers

- ▲ Growth: 14.2%
- ▲ Annual Job Openings: 2,000
- ▲ Annual Earnings: $38,150
- ▲ Education/Training Required: Long-term on-the-job training
- ▲ Self-Employed: 0%
- ▲ Part-Time: 3.4%

**Fabricate and assemble aircraft tubing or cable components or assemblies.** Sets up and operates machines and systems to crimp, cut, bend, form, swage, flare, bead, burr, and straighten tubing according to specifications. Assembles and attaches fittings onto cable and tubing components, using hand tools. Measures, cuts, and inspects cable and tubing, using master template, measuring instruments, and cable cutter or saw. Welds tubing and fittings and solders cable ends, using tack-welder, induction brazing chamber, or other equipment. Fabricates cable templates. Verifies dimensions of cable assembly and position of fittings, using measuring instruments, and repairs and reworks defective assemblies. Marks identifying information on tubing or cable assemblies, using electro-chemical etching device, label, rubber stamp, or other methods. Cleans, lubricates, and coats tubing and cable assemblies. Tests tubing and cable assemblies for defects, using pressure testing equipment and proofloading machines. Selects and installs accessories in swaging machine, using hand tools. Reads and interprets blueprints, work orders, data charts, and specifications to determine operations, type, quantity, dimensions, configuration, and finish of tubing, cable and fittings. Marks location of cutouts, holes, and trim lines of parts and relationship of parts, using measuring instruments. Forms loops or splices in cables, using clamps and fittings, or reweaves cable strands. Swages fittings onto cable, using swaging machine. **SKILLS**—Installation. Equipment Selection. Reading Comprehension. Operation and Control. Mathematics.

GOE—**Interest Area:** 08. Industrial Production. **Work Group:** 08.02. Production Technology. **Other Job Titles in This Work Group:** Aircraft Structure Assemblers, Precision; Aircraft Structure, Surfaces, Rigging, and Systems Assemblers; Aircraft Systems Assemblers, Precision; Bench Workers, Jewelry; Bindery Machine Setters and Set-Up Operators; Bindery Workers; Bookbinders; Buffing and Polishing Set-Up Operators; Casting Machine Set-Up Operators; Coating, Painting, and Spraying Machine Setters and Set-Up Operators; Coating, Painting, and Spraying Machine Setters, Operators, and Tenders; Combination Machine Tool Setters and Set-Up Operators, Metal and Plastic; Cutting, Punching, and Press Machine Setters, Operators, and Tenders, Metal and Plastic; Dental Laboratory Technicians; Drilling and Boring Machine Tool Setters, Operators, and Tenders, Metal and Plastic; Electrical and Electronic Equipment Assemblers; Electrical and Electronic Inspectors and Testers; Electromechanical Equip-

ment Assemblers; Engine and Other Machine Assemblers; Extruding and Drawing Machine Setters, Operators, and Tenders, Metal and Plastic; Extruding, Forming, Pressing, and Compacting Machine Setters and Set-Up Operators; Extruding, Forming, Pressing, and Compacting Machine Setters, Operators, and Tenders; Forging Machine Setters, Operators, and Tenders, Metal and Plastic; Foundry Mold and Coremakers; Gem and Diamond Workers; Grinding, Honing, Lapping, and Deburring Machine Set-Up Operators; Grinding, Lapping, Polishing, and Buffing Machine Tool Setters, Operators, and Tenders, Metal and Plastic; Heat Treating Equipment Setters, Operators, and Tenders, Metal and Plastic; others. **PERSONALITY TYPE**—Realistic. Realistic occupations frequently involve work activities that include practical, hands-on problems and solutions. They often deal with plants, animals, and real-world materials like wood, tools, and machinery. Many of the occupations require working outside and do not involve a lot of paperwork or working closely with others.

**EDUCATION/TRAINING PROGRAM(S)**—Aircraft Mechanic/Technician, Airframe; Aircraft Mechanic/Technician, Powerplant; Aviation Systems and Avionics Maintenance Technologist/Technician. **RELATED KNOWLEDGE/COURSES**—**Engineering and Technology:** Knowledge of the practical application of engineering science and technology. This includes applying principles, techniques, procedures, and equipment to the design and production of various goods and services. **Principles of Mechanical Devices:** Knowledge of machines and tools, including their designs, uses, repair, and maintenance. **Production and Processing:** Knowledge of raw materials, production processes, quality control, costs, and other techniques for maximizing the effective manufacture and distribution of goods. **Building and Construction:** Knowledge of materials, methods, and tools involved in the construction or repair of houses, buildings, or other structures such as highways and roads. **Design:** Knowledge of design techniques, tools, and principles involved in production of precision technical plans, blueprints, drawings, and models.

# Aircraft Structure Assemblers, Precision

- ▲ Growth: 14.2%
- ▲ Annual Job Openings: 2,000
- ▲ Annual Earnings: $38,150
- ▲ Education/Training Required: Long-term on-the-job training
- ▲ Self-Employed: 0%
- ▲ Part-Time: 3.4%

**Assemble tail, wing, fuselage, or other structural section of aircraft, space vehicles, and missiles from parts, subassemblies, and components and install functional units, parts, or equipment, such as landing gear, control surfaces, doors, and floorboards.** Installs units, parts, equipment, and components in structural assembly according to blueprints and specifications, using hand tools and power tools. Bolts, screws, or rivets accessories to fasten, support, or hang components and subassemblies. Drills holes in structure and subassemblies and attaches brackets, hinges, or clips to secure installation or to fasten subassemblies. Locates and marks reference points and holes for installation of parts and components, using jigs, templates, and measuring instruments. Inspects and tests installed units, parts, and equipment for fit, performance, and compliance with standards, using measuring instruments and test equipment. Positions and aligns subassemblies in jigs or fixtures, using measuring instruments, following blueprint lines and index points. Cuts, trims, and files parts, and verifies fitting tolerances to prepare for installation. Aligns structural assemblies. **SKILLS**—Installation. Equipment Selection. Quality Control Analysis. Mathematics. Troubleshooting.

**GOE—Interest Area:** 08. Industrial Production. **Work Group:** 08.02. Production Technology. **Other Job Titles in This Work Group:** Aircraft Rigging Assemblers; Aircraft Structure, Surfaces, Rigging, and Systems Assemblers; Aircraft Systems Assemblers, Precision; Bench Workers, Jewelry; Bindery Machine Setters and Set-Up Operators; Bindery Workers; Bookbinders; Buffing and Polishing Set-Up Operators; Casting Machine Set-Up Operators; Coating, Painting, and Spraying Machine Setters and Set-Up Operators; Coating, Painting, and Spraying Machine Setters, Operators, and Tenders; Combination Machine Tool Setters and Set-Up Operators, Metal and Plastic; Cutting, Punching, and Press Machine Setters, Operators, and Tenders, Metal and Plastic; Dental Laboratory Technicians; Drilling and Boring Machine Tool Setters, Operators, and Tenders, Metal and Plastic; Electrical and Electronic Equipment Assemblers; Electrical and Electronic Inspectors and Testers; Electromechanical Equipment Assemblers; Engine and Other Machine Assemblers; Extruding and Drawing Machine Setters, Operators, and Tenders, Metal and Plastic; Extruding, Forming, Pressing, and Compacting Machine Setters and Set-Up Operators; Extruding, Forming, Pressing, and Compacting Machine Setters, Operators, and Tenders; Forging Machine Setters, Operators, and Tenders, Metal and Plastic; Foundry Mold and Coremakers; Gem and Diamond Workers; Grinding, Honing, Lapping, and Deburring Machine Set-Up Operators; Grinding, Lapping, Polishing, and Buffing Machine Tool Setters, Operators, and Tenders, Metal and Plastic; Heat Treating Equipment Setters, Operators, and Tenders, Metal and Plastic; others. **PERSONALITY TYPE**—Realistic. Realistic occupations frequently involve work activities that include practical, hands-on problems and solutions. They often deal with plants, animals, and real-world materials like wood, tools, and machinery. Many of the occupations require working outside and do not involve a lot of paperwork or working closely with others.

**EDUCATION/TRAINING PROGRAM(S)**—Aircraft Mechanic/Technician, Airframe; Aircraft Mechanic/Technician, Powerplant; Aviation Systems and Avionics Maintenance Technologist/Technician. **RELATED KNOWLEDGE/COURSES**—**Principles of Mechanical Devices:** Knowledge of machines and tools, including their designs, uses, repair, and maintenance.

Engineering and Technology: Knowledge of the practical application of engineering science and technology. This includes applying principles, techniques, procedures, and equipment to the design and production of various goods and services. **Production and Processing:** Knowledge of raw materials, production processes, quality control, costs, and other techniques for maximizing the effective manufacture and distribution of goods. **Building and Construction:** Knowledge of materials, methods, and tools involved in the construction or repair of houses, buildings, or other structures such as highways and roads. **Design:** Knowledge of design techniques, tools, and principles involved in production of precision technical plans, blueprints, drawings, and models.

# Aircraft Systems Assemblers, Precision

- ▲ Growth: 14.2%
- ▲ Annual Job Openings: 2,000
- ▲ Annual Earnings: $38,150
- ▲ Education/Training Required: Long-term on-the-job training
- ▲ Self-Employed: 0%
- ▲ Part-Time: 3.4%

**Lay out, assemble, install, and test aircraft systems, such as armament, environmental control, plumbing, and hydraulic.** Aligns, fits, and assembles system components, such as armament, structural, and mechanical components, using jigs, fixtures, measuring instruments, hand tools, and power tools. Measures, drills, files, cuts, bends, and smoothes materials to ensure fit and clearance of parts. Reads and interprets blueprints, illustrations, and specifications to determine layout, sequence of operations, or identity and relationship of parts. Tests systems and assemblies for functional performance and adjusts, repairs, or replaces malfunctioning units or parts. Installs mechanical linkages and actuators and verifies tension of cables, using tensiometer. Examines parts for defects and for conformance to specifications, using precision measuring instruments. Cleans, oils, assembles, and attaches system components to aircraft, using hand tools, power tools, and measuring instruments. Reworks, replaces, realigns, and adjusts parts and assemblies according to specifications. Assembles and installs parts, fittings, and assemblies on aircraft, using layout tools, hand tools, power tools, and fasteners. Lays out location of parts and assemblies according to specifications. **SKILLS**—Equipment Maintenance. Installation. Troubleshooting. Quality Control Analysis. Repairing.

**GOE—Interest Area:** 08. Industrial Production. **Work Group:** 08.02. Production Technology. **Other Job Titles in This Work Group:** Aircraft Rigging Assemblers; Aircraft Structure Assemblers, Precision; Aircraft Structure, Surfaces, Rigging, and Systems Assemblers; Bench Workers, Jewelry; Bindery Machine Setters and Set-Up Operators; Bindery Workers; Bookbinders; Buffing and Polishing Set-Up Operators; Casting Machine Set-Up Operators; Coating, Painting, and Spraying Machine Setters and Set-Up Operators; Coating, Painting, and Spraying Machine Setters, Operators, and Tenders; Combination Machine Tool Setters and Set-Up Operators, Metal and Plastic; Cutting, Punching, and Press Machine Setters, Operators, and Tenders, Metal and Plastic; Dental Laboratory Technicians; Drilling and Boring Machine Tool Setters, Operators, and Tenders, Metal and Plastic; Electrical and Electronic Equipment Assemblers; Electrical and Electronic Inspectors and Testers; Electromechanical Equipment Assemblers; Engine and Other Machine Assemblers; Extruding and Drawing Machine Setters, Operators, and Tenders, Metal and Plastic; Extruding, Forming, Pressing, and Compacting Machine Setters and Set-Up Operators; Extruding, Forming, Pressing, and Compacting Machine Setters, Operators, and Tenders; Forging Machine Setters, Operators, and Tenders, Metal and Plastic; Foundry Mold and Coremakers; Gem and Diamond

Workers; Grinding, Honing, Lapping, and Deburring Machine Set-Up Operators; Grinding, Lapping, Polishing, and Buffing Machine Tool Setters, Operators, and Tenders, Metal and Plastic; Heat Treating Equipment Setters, Operators, and Tenders, Metal and Plastic; others. **PERSONALITY TYPE**—Realistic. Realistic occupations frequently involve work activities that include practical, hands-on problems and solutions. They often deal with plants, animals, and real-world materials like wood, tools, and machinery. Many of the occupations require working outside and do not involve a lot of paperwork or working closely with others.

**EDUCATION/TRAINING PROGRAM(S)**—Aircraft Mechanic/Technician, Airframe; Aircraft Mechanic/Technician, Powerplant; Aviation Systems and Avionics Maintenance Technologist/Technician. **RELATED KNOWLEDGE/COURSES**—Principles

**of Mechanical Devices:** Knowledge of machines and tools, including their designs, uses, repair, and maintenance. **Engineering and Technology:** Knowledge of the practical application of engineering science and technology. This includes applying principles, techniques, procedures, and equipment to the design and production of various goods and services. **Production and Processing:** Knowledge of raw materials, production processes, quality control, costs, and other techniques for maximizing the effective manufacture and distribution of goods. **Design:** Knowledge of design techniques, tools, and principles involved in production of precision technical plans, blueprints, drawings, and models. **Building and Construction:** Knowledge of materials, methods, and tools involved in the construction or repair of houses, buildings, or other structures such as highways and roads.

# Amusement and Recreation Attendants

- ▲ Growth: 32.4%
- ▲ Annual Job Openings: 62,000
- ▲ Annual Earnings: $15,480
- ▲ Education/Training Required: Short-term on-the-job training
- ▲ Self-Employed: 3%
- ▲ Part-Time: 48.8%

**Perform variety of attending duties at amusement or recreation facility. May schedule use of recreation facilities, maintain and provide equipment to participants of sporting events or recreational pursuits, or operate amusement concessions and rides.** Schedules use of recreation facilities, such as golf courses, tennis courts, bowling alleys, and softball diamonds. Operates, drives, or explains use of mechanical riding devices or other automatic equipment in amusement parks, carnivals, or recreation areas. Receives, retrieves, replaces, and stores sports equipment and supplies, arranges items in designated areas, and erects or removes equipment. Sells tickets and collects fees from customers, and collects or punches tickets. Rents, sells, and issues sports equipment and supplies, such as bowling shoes, golf balls, swimming suits, and beach chairs. Provides information about facilities, entertainment options, and

rules and regulations. Directs patrons of establishment to rides, seats, or attractions, or escorts patrons on tours of points of interest. Records details of attendance, sales, receipts, reservations, and repair activities. Inspects, repairs, adjusts, tests, fuels, and oils sporting and recreation equipment, game machines, and amusement rides. Cleans sporting equipment, vehicles, rides, booths, facilities, and grounds. Attends amusement booth in parks, carnivals, or stadiums and awards prizes to winning players. Sells and serves refreshments to customers. Announces and describes amusement park attractions to patrons to entice customers to games and other entertainment. Provides entertainment services, such as guessing patron's weight, conducting games, explaining use of arcade game machines, and photographing patrons. Launches, moors, and demonstrates use of boats, such as rowboats, canoes, and motorboats, or caddies for golfers. Monitors activities to ensure adherence to rules and safety procedures to protect environment and maintain order, and ejects unruly patrons. Attends animals, performing such tasks as harnessing, saddling, feeding, watering, and grooming, and drives horse-drawn vehicle for entertainment or advertising purposes. Assists patrons on and off amusement rides, boats, or ski lifts and in mounting and riding animals, and fastens or directs patrons to fasten safety devices. **SKILLS**—Active Listening. Operation and Control. Service Orientation. Repairing.

**GOE—Interest Area:** 11. Recreation, Travel, and Other Personal Services. **Work Group:** 11.02. Recreational Services. **Other Job Titles in This Work Group:** Entertainment Attendants and Related Workers, All Other; Gaming and Sports Book Writers and Runners; Gaming Dealers; Gaming Service Workers, All Other; Motion Picture Projectionists; Recreation Workers; Slot Key Persons; Tour Guides and Escorts; Travel Guides; Ushers, Lobby Attendants, and Ticket Takers. **PERSONALITY TYPE**—Realistic. Realistic occupations frequently involve work activities that include practical, hands-on problems and solutions. They often deal with plants, animals, and real-world materials like wood,

tools, and machinery. Many of the occupations require working outside and do not involve a lot of paperwork or working closely with others.

**EDUCATION/TRAINING PROGRAM(S)**—No data available. **RELATED KNOWLEDGE/ COURSES—Customer and Personal Service:** Knowledge of principles and processes for providing customer and personal services. This includes customer needs assessment, meeting quality standards for services, and evaluation of customer satisfaction. **Sales and Marketing:** Knowledge of principles and methods for showing, promoting, and selling products or services. This includes marketing strategy and tactics, product demonstration, sales techniques, and sales control systems. **Public Safety and Security:** Knowledge of relevant equipment, policies, procedures, and strategies to promote effective local, state, or national security operations for the protection of people, data, property, and institutions. **Principles of Mechanical Devices:** Knowledge of machines and tools, including their designs, uses, repair, and maintenance. **Mathematics:** Knowledge of arithmetic, algebra, geometry, calculus, statistics, and their applications.

# Appraisers, Real Estate

- ▲ Growth: 18%
- ▲ Annual Job Openings: 6,000
- ▲ Annual Earnings: $41,700
- ▲ Education/Training Required: Post-secondary vocational training
- ▲ Self-Employed: 2.3%
- ▲ Part-Time: 16.6%

**Appraise real property to determine its value for purchase, sales, investment, mortgage, or loan purposes.** Considers such factors as depreciation, value comparison of similar property, and income potential when computing final estimation of property value. Inspects property for construction, condition, and functional design and takes property measurements. Interviews persons familiar with property and immediate surroundings, such as contractors, homeowners, and other realtors to obtain pertinent information. Considers

location and trends or impending changes that could influence future value of property. Prepares written report, utilizing data collected, and submits report to corroborate value established. Photographs interiors and exteriors of property to assist in estimating property value, to substantiate finding, and to complete appraisal report. Searches public records for transactions, such as sales, leases, and assessments. **SKILLS**—Writing. Reading Comprehension. Mathematics. Active Listening. Speaking.

**GOE—Interest Area:** 13. General Management and Support. **Work Group:** 13.02. Management Support. **Other Job Titles in This Work Group:** Accountants; Accountants and Auditors; Appraisers and Assessors of Real Estate; Assessors; Auditors; Budget Analysts; Claims Adjusters, Examiners, and Investigators; Claims Examiners, Property and Casualty Insurance; Compensation, Benefits, and Job Analysis Specialists; Cost Estimators; Credit Analysts; Employment Interviewers, Private or Public Employment Service; Employment, Recruitment, and Placement Specialists; Financial Analysts; Human Resources, Training, and Labor Relations Specialists, All Other; Insurance Adjusters, Examiners, and Investigators; Insurance Appraisers, Auto Damage; Insurance Underwriters; Loan Counselors; Loan Officers; Logisticians; Management Analysts; Market Research Analysts; Personnel Recruiters; Purchasing Agents and Buyers, Farm Products; Purchasing Agents, Except Wholesale, Retail, and Farm Products; Tax Examiners, Collectors, and Revenue Agents; Training and Development Specialists; Wholesale and Retail Buyers, Except Farm Products. **PERSONALITY TYPE—**Enterprising. Enterprising occupations frequently involve starting up and carrying out projects. These occupations can involve leading people and making many decisions. They sometimes require risk taking and often deal with business.

**EDUCATION/TRAINING PROGRAM(S)—**Real Estate. **RELATED KNOWLEDGE/COURSES—Mathematics:** Knowledge of arithmetic, algebra, geometry, calculus, statistics, and their applications. **Building and Construction:** Knowledge of materials, methods, and tools involved in the construction or repair of houses, buildings, or other structures such as highways and roads. **Economics and Accounting:** Knowledge of economic and accounting principles and practices, the financial markets, banking, and the analysis and reporting of financial data. **English Language:** Knowledge of the structure and content of the English language, including the meaning and spelling of words, rules of composition, and grammar. **Clerical Studies:** Knowledge of administrative and clerical procedures and systems such as word processing, managing files and records, stenography and transcription, designing forms, and other office procedures and terminology.

# Architectural Drafters

- ▲ Growth: 20.8%
- ▲ Annual Job Openings: 12,000
- ▲ Annual Earnings: $37,100
- ▲ Education/Training Required: Postsecondary vocational training
- ▲ Self-Employed: 4.6%
- ▲ Part-Time: 7.9%

**Prepare detailed drawings of architectural designs and plans for buildings and structures according to specifications provided by architect.** Draws rough and detailed scale plans, to scale, for foundations, buildings, and structures, according to specifications. Prepares colored drawings of landscape and interior designs for presentation to client. Develops diagrams for construction, fabrication, and installation of equipment, structures, components, and systems, using field documents and specifications. Lays out and plans interior room arrangements for commercial buildings and draws charts, forms, and records, using computer assisted equipment. Lays out schematics and wiring diagrams used to erect, install, and repair establishment cable and electrical systems, using computer equipment. Drafts and corrects topographical maps to represent geological stratigraphy, mineral deposits, and pipeline systems, using survey data and aerial photographs. Builds landscape models, using data provided by landscape architect. Calculates heat loss and gain of buildings and structures to determine required equipment specifications, following standard procedures. Traces copies of plans and drawings, using transparent paper or cloth, ink, pencil, and standard drafting instruments for reproduction purposes. **SKILLS**—Mathematics. Programming. Reading Comprehension. Active Learning. Operations Analysis.

**GOE—Interest Area:** 02. Science, Math, and Engineering. **Work Group:** 02.08. Engineering Technology. **Other Job Titles in This Work Group:** Aerospace Engineering and Operations Technicians; Architectural and Civil Drafters; Calibration and Instrumentation Technicians; Cartographers and Photogrammetrists; Civil Drafters; Civil Engineering Technicians; Construction and Building Inspectors; Drafters, All Other; Electrical and Electronic Engineering Technicians; Electrical and Electronics Drafters; Electrical Drafters; Electrical Engineering Technicians; Electro-Mechanical Technicians; Electronic Drafters; Electronics Engineering Technicians; Engineering Technicians, Except Drafters, All Other; Environmental Engineering Technicians; Industrial Engineering Technicians; Mapping Technicians; Mechanical Drafters; Mechanical Engineering Technicians; Numerical Tool and Process Control Programmers; Pressure Vessel Inspectors; Surveying and Mapping Technicians; Surveying Technicians; Surveyors. **PERSONALITY TYPE**—Realistic. Realistic occupations frequently involve work activities that include practical, hands-on problems and solutions. They often deal with plants, animals, and real-world materials like wood, tools, and machinery. Many of the occupations require working outside and do not involve a lot of paperwork or working closely with others.

**EDUCATION/TRAINING PROGRAM(S)**—Architectural Drafting; Civil/Structural Drafting. **RELATED KNOWLEDGE/COURSES—Design:** Knowledge of design techniques, tools, and principles involved in production of precision technical plans, blueprints, drawings, and models. **Mathematics:** Knowledge of arithmetic, algebra, geometry, calculus, statistics, and their applications. **Engineering and Technology:** Knowledge of the practical application of engineering science and technology. This includes applying principles, techniques, procedures, and equipment to the design and production of various goods and services. **Computers and Electronics:** Knowledge of circuit boards, processors, chips, electronic equipment, and computer hardware and software, including applications and programming. **Physics:** Knowledge and prediction of physical principles and laws and their interrelationships and applications to understanding fluid, material, and atmospheric dynamics and mechanical, electrical, atomic, and sub-atomic structures and processes.

# Athletes and Sports Competitors

▲ Growth: 22.5%

▲ Annual Job Openings: 3,000

▲ Annual Earnings: $62,960

▲ Education/Training Required: Long-term on-the-job training

▲ Self-Employed: 27.2%

▲ Part-Time: 25.3%

**Compete in athletic events.** Participates in athletic events and competitive sports, according to established rules and regulations. Plays professional sport and is identified according to sport played, such as football, basketball, baseball, hockey, or boxing. Represents team or professional sports club, speaking to groups involved in activities, such as sports clinics and fundraisers. Exercises and practices under direction of athletic trainer or professional coach to prepare and train for competitive events. **SKILLS**—Monitoring. Coordination. Active Learning. Speaking. Active Listening. Learning Strategies. Social Perceptiveness.

**GOE—Interest Area:** 01. Arts, Entertainment, and Media. **Work Group:** 01.10. Sports: Coaching, Instructing, Officiating, and Performing. **Other Job Titles in This Work Group:** Coaches and Scouts; Fitness Trainers and Aerobics Instructors; Umpires, Referees, and Other Sports Officials. **PERSONALITY TYPE—**

Enterprising. Enterprising occupations frequently involve starting up and carrying out projects. These occupations can involve leading people and making many decisions. They sometimes require risk taking and often deal with business.

EDUCATION/TRAINING PROGRAM(S)—Health and Physical Education, General. **RELATED KNOWLEDGE/COURSES—Biology:** Knowledge of plant and animal organisms and their tissues, cells, functions, interdependencies, and interactions with each other and the environment. **Physics:** Knowledge and prediction of physical principles and laws and their interrelationships and applications to understanding fluid, material, and atmospheric dynamics and mechanical, electrical, atomic, and sub-atomic structures and processes. **Psychology:** Knowledge of human behavior and performance; individual differences in ability, personality, and interests; learning and motivation; psychological research methods; and the assessment and treatment of behavioral and affective disorders. **Communications and Media:** Knowledge of media production, communication, and dissemination techniques and methods. This includes alternative ways to inform and entertain via written, oral, and visual media. **Education and Training:** Knowledge of principles and methods for curriculum and training design, teaching and instruction for individuals and groups, and the measurement of training effects.

# Audio-Visual Collections Specialists

- ▲ Growth: 13.6%
- ▲ Annual Job Openings: 2,000
- ▲ Annual Earnings: $35,590
- ▲ Education/Training Required: Moderate-term on-the-job training
- ▲ Self-Employed: 0%
- ▲ Part-Time: 11.7%

**Prepare, plan, and operate audio-visual teaching aids for use in education. May record, catalogue, and file audio-visual materials.** Plans and develops preproduction ideas into outlines, scripts, continuity, storyboards, and graphics, or directs assistants to develop ideas. Sets up, adjusts, and operates equipment, such as cameras, sound mixers, and recorders, during production. Constructs and positions properties, sets, lighting equipment, and other equipment. Determines format, approach, content, level, and medium to meet objectives most effectively within budgetary constraints, utilizing research, knowledge, and training. Executes, or directs assistants to execute, rough and finished graphics and graphic designs. Directs and coordinates activities of assistants and other personnel during production. Conducts training sessions on selection, use, and design of audiovisual materials and operation of presentation equipment. Performs narration or presents announcements. Develops manuals, texts, workbooks, or related materials for use in conjunction with production materials. Develops production ideas based on assignment or generates own ideas based on objectives and interest. Locates and secures settings, properties, effects, and other production necessities. **SKILLS—** Writing. Learning Strategies. Speaking. Reading Comprehension. Instructing.

**GOE—Interest Area:** 12. Education and Social Service. **Work Group:** 12.03. Educational Services. **Other Job Titles in This Work Group:** Adult Literacy, Remedial Education, and GED Teachers and Instructors; Agricultural Sciences Teachers, Postsecondary; Anthropology and Archeology Teachers, Postsecondary; Architecture Teachers, Postsecondary; Archivists; Area, Ethnic, and Cultural Studies Teachers, Postsecondary; Art, Drama, and Music Teachers, Postsecondary; Atmospheric, Earth, Marine, and Space Sciences Teachers, Postsecondary; Biological Science Teachers, Postsecondary; Business Teachers, Postsecondary; Chemistry Teachers, Postsecondary; Child Care Workers; Communications Teachers, Postsecondary; Computer Science Teachers, Postsecondary; Criminal Justice and Law Enforcement Teachers, Postsecondary; Curators; Economics Teachers, Postsecondary; Education Teachers, Postsecondary; Educational Psychologists; Educational, Vocational, and School Counselors; Elementary School Teachers, Except Special Education; Engineering Teachers, Postsecondary; English Language and Literature Teachers, Postsecondary; Environmental Science Teachers, Postsecondary; Farm and Home Management Advisors; Foreign Language and Literature Teachers, Postsecondary; Forestry and Conservation Science Teachers, Postsecondary; Geography Teachers, Postsecondary; Graduate Teaching Assistants; Health Specialties Teachers, Postsecondary; History Teachers, Postsecondary; Home Economics Teachers, Postsecondary; Kindergarten Teachers, Except Special Education; Law Teachers, Postsecondary; Librarians; Library Assistants, Clerical; Library Science Teachers, Postsecondary; others. **PERSONALITY TYPE**—Conventional. Conventional occupations frequently involve following set procedures and routines. These occupations can include working with data and details more than with ideas. Usually there is a clear line of authority to follow.

**EDUCATION/TRAINING PROGRAM(S)**—Educational/Instructional Media Technologist/Technician. **RELATED KNOWLEDGE/COURSES**—**Communications and Media:** Knowledge of media production, communication, and dissemination techniques and methods. This includes alternative ways to inform and entertain via written, oral, and visual media. **Education and Training:** Knowledge of principles and methods for curriculum and training design, teaching and instruction for individuals and groups, and the measurement of training effects. **Telecommunications:** Knowledge of transmission, broadcasting, switching, control, and operation of telecommunications systems. **English Language:** Knowledge of the structure and content of the English language, including the meaning and spelling of words, rules of composition, and grammar. **Computers and Electronics:** Knowledge of circuit boards, processors, chips, electronic equipment, and computer hardware and software, including applications and programming.

# Automatic Teller Machine Servicers

- ▲ Growth: 14.2%
- ▲ Annual Job Openings: 24,000
- ▲ Annual Earnings: $32,860
- ▲ Education/Training Required: Postsecondary vocational training
- ▲ Self-Employed: 14.8%
- ▲ Part-Time: 6.5%

**Collect deposits and replenish automatic teller machines with cash and supplies.** Removes money canisters from ATM and replenishes machine supplies, such as deposit envelopes, receipt paper, and cash. Counts cash and items deposited by customers and compares to transactions indicated on transaction tape from ATM. Records transaction information on form or log and notifies designated personnel of discrepancies. Tests machine functions and balances machine cash account, using electronic keypad. Corrects malfunctions, such as jammed cash or paper, or calls repair personnel when

ATM needs repair. **SKILLS**—Mathematics. Writing. Critical Thinking. Troubleshooting.

**GOE—Interest Area:** 09. Business Detail. **Work Group:** 09.09. Clerical Machine Operation. **Other Job Titles in This Work Group:** Billing, Posting, and Calculating Machine Operators; Computer Operators; Data Entry Keyers; Duplicating Machine Operators; Mail Clerks and Mail Machine Operators, Except Postal Service; Mail Machine Operators, Preparation and Handling; Office Machine Operators, Except Computer; Postal Service Clerks; Typesetting and Composing Machine

Operators and Tenders; Word Processors and Typists. **PERSONALITY TYPE**—Realistic. Realistic occupations frequently involve work activities that include practical, hands-on problems and solutions. They often deal with plants, animals, and real-world materials like wood, tools, and machinery. Many of the occupations require working outside and do not involve a lot of paperwork or working closely with others.

**EDUCATION/TRAINING PROGRAM(S)**—Building/Property Maintenance and Manager; Business Machine Repairer; Computer Installer and Repairer; Computer Maintenance Technologist/Technician. **RELATED KNOWLEDGE/COURSES**—**Mathematics:** Knowledge of arithmetic, algebra, geometry, calculus, statistics, and their applications. **Computers and Elec-** **tronics:** Knowledge of circuit boards, processors, chips, electronic equipment, and computer hardware and software, including applications and programming. **Clerical Studies:** Knowledge of administrative and clerical procedures and systems such as word processing, managing files and records, stenography and transcription, designing forms, and other office procedures and terminology. **Geography:** Knowledge of principles and methods for describing the features of land, sea, and air masses, including their physical characteristics, locations, interrelationships, and distribution of plant, animal, and human life. **Telecommunications:** Knowledge of transmission, broadcasting, switching, control, and operation of telecommunications systems.

# Automotive Body and Related Repairers

- ▲ Growth: 10.2%
- ▲ Annual Job Openings: 18,000
- ▲ Annual Earnings: $33,710
- ▲ Education/Training Required: Long-term on-the-job training
- ▲ Self-Employed: 13.4%
- ▲ Part-Time: 8.6%

**Repair and refinish automotive vehicle bodies and straighten vehicle frames.** Positions dolly block against surface of dented area and beats opposite surface to remove dents, using hammer. Straightens bent automobile or other vehicle frames, using pneumatic frame-straightening machine. Paints and sands repaired surface, using paint spraygun and motorized sander. Removes damaged fenders and panels, using wrenches and cutting torch, and installs replacement parts, using wrenches or welding equipment. Fits and secures windows, vinyl roof, and metal trim to vehicle body, using caulking gun, adhesive brush, and mallet. Cuts opening in vehicle body for installation of customized windows, using templates and power shears or chisel. Fills depressions with body filler and files, grinds, and sands repaired surfaces, using power tools and hand tools. Measures and marks vinyl material and cuts material to size for roof installation, using rule, straightedge, and hand shears. Adjusts or aligns headlights, wheels, and brake system. Reads specifications or confers with customer to determine custom modifications to alter appearance of vehicle. Removes upholstery, accessories, electrical window-and-seat-operating equipment, and trim to gain access to vehicle body and fenders. Cuts and tapes plastic separating film to outside repair area to avoid damaging surrounding surfaces during repair procedure. Examines vehicle to determine extent and type of damage. Peels separating film from repair area and washes repaired surface with water. Mixes polyester resin and hardener to be used in restoring damaged area. Soaks fiberglass matting in resin mixture and applies layers matting over repair area to specified thickness. Cuts away damaged fiberglass from automobile body, using air grinder. Cleans work area, using air hose to remove damaged material and to remove discarded fiberglass strips used in repair procedures. **SKILLS**—Repairing. Installation. Technology Design. Quality Control Analysis. Mathematics.

GOE—**Interest Area:** 05. Mechanics, Installers, and Repairers. **Work Group:** 05.03. Mechanical Work. **Other Job Titles in This Work Group:** Aircraft Body and Bonded Structure Repairers; Aircraft Engine Specialists; Aircraft Mechanics and Service Technicians; Airframe-and-Power-Plant Mechanics; Automotive Glass Installers and Repairers; Automotive Master Mechanics; Automotive Service Technicians and Mechanics; Automotive Specialty Technicians; Bicycle Repairers; Bridge and Lock Tenders; Bus and Truck Mechanics and Diesel Engine Specialists; Camera and Photographic Equipment Repairers; Coin, Vending, and Amusement Machine Servicers and Repairers; Control and Valve Installers and Repairers, Except Mechanical Door; Farm Equipment Mechanics; Gas Appliance Repairers; Hand and Portable Power Tool Repairers; Heating and Air Conditioning Mechanics; Heating, Air Conditioning, and Refrigeration Mechanics and Installers; Helpers—Electricians; Helpers—Installation, Maintenance, and Repair Workers; Industrial Machinery Mechanics; Keyboard Instrument Repairers and Tuners; Locksmiths and Safe Repairers; Maintenance and Repair Workers, General; Maintenance Workers, Machinery; Mechanical Door Repairers; Medical Appliance Technicians; Medical Equipment Repairers; Meter Mechanics; Millwrights; Mobile Heavy Equipment Mechanics, Except Engines; Motorboat Mechanics; Motorcycle Mechanics; Musical Instrument Repairers and Tuners; Ophthalmic Laboratory Technicians; Optical Instrument Assemblers; Outdoor Power Equipment and Other Small Engine Mechanics; Painters, Transportation Equipment; Percussion Instrument Repairers and Tuners; Precision Instrument and Equipment Repairers, All Other; others. **PERSONALITY TYPE**—Realistic.

Realistic occupations frequently involve work activities that include practical, hands-on problems and solutions. They often deal with plants, animals, and real-world materials like wood, tools, and machinery. Many of the occupations require working outside and do not involve a lot of paperwork or working closely with others.

**EDUCATION/TRAINING PROGRAM(S)**—Auto/Automotive Body Repairer. **RELATED KNOWLEDGE/COURSES**—**Principles of Mechanical Devices:** Knowledge of machines and tools, including their designs, uses, repair, and maintenance. **Engineering and Technology:** Knowledge of the practical application of engineering science and technology. This includes applying principles, techniques, procedures, and equipment to the design and production of various goods and services. **Building and Construction:** Knowledge of materials, methods, and tools involved in the construction or repair of houses, buildings, or other structures such as highways and roads. **Design:** Knowledge of design techniques, tools, and principles involved in production of precision technical plans, blueprints, drawings, and models. **Customer and Personal Service:** Knowledge of principles and processes for providing customer and personal services. This includes customer needs assessment, meeting quality standards for services, and evaluation of customer satisfaction. **Physics:** Knowledge and prediction of physical principles and laws and their interrelationships and applications to understanding fluid, material, and atmospheric dynamics and mechanical, electrical, atomic, and sub-atomic structures and processes. **Mathematics:** Knowledge of arithmetic, algebra, geometry, calculus, statistics, and their applications.

# Automotive Master Mechanics

- ▲ Growth: 18%
- ▲ Annual Job Openings: 104,000
- ▲ Annual Earnings: $30,780
- ▲ Education/Training Required: Post-secondary vocational training
- ▲ Self-Employed: 17.9%
- ▲ Part-Time: 6.8%

Repair automobiles, trucks, buses, and other vehicles. Master mechanics repair virtually any part on the vehicle or specialize in the transmission system. Repairs and overhauls defective automotive units, such as engines, transmissions, or differentials. Installs and repairs accessories, such as radios, heaters, mirrors, and windshield wipers. Repairs damaged automobile bodies. Rebuilds parts, such as crankshafts and cylinder blocks. Aligns front end. Examines vehicles and discusses extent of damage or malfunction with customer. Replaces and adjusts headlights. Repairs radiator leaks. Repairs or replaces shock absorbers. Repairs or replaces parts, such as pistons, rods, gears, valves, and bearings. Repairs manual and automatic transmissions. Repairs, relines, replaces, and adjusts brakes. Rewires ignition system, lights, and instrument panel. Overhauls or replaces carburetors, blowers, generators, distributors, starts, and pumps. **SKILLS**—Repairing. Troubleshooting. Equipment Maintenance. Installation. Critical Thinking.

**GOE—Interest Area:** 05. Mechanics, Installers, and Repairers. **Work Group:** 05.03. Mechanical Work. **Other Job Titles in This Work Group:** Aircraft Body and Bonded Structure Repairers; Aircraft Engine Specialists; Aircraft Mechanics and Service Technicians; Airframe-and-Power-Plant Mechanics; Automotive Body and Related Repairers; Automotive Glass Installers and Repairers; Automotive Service Technicians and Mechanics; Automotive Specialty Technicians; Bicycle Repairers; Bridge and Lock Tenders; Bus and Truck Mechanics and Diesel Engine Specialists; Camera and Photographic Equipment Repairers; Coin, Vending, and Amusement Machine Servicers and Repairers; Control and Valve Installers and Repairers, Except Mechanical Door; Farm Equipment Mechanics; Gas Appliance Repairers; Hand and Portable Power Tool Repairers; Heating and Air Conditioning Mechanics; Heating, Air Conditioning, and Refrigeration Mechanics and Installers; Helpers—Electricians; Helpers—Installation, Maintenance, and Repair Workers; Industrial Machinery Mechanics; Keyboard Instrument Repairers and Tuners; Locksmiths and Safe Repairers; Maintenance and Repair Workers, General; Maintenance Workers, Machinery; Mechanical Door Repairers; Medical Appliance Technicians; Medical Equipment Repairers; Meter Mechanics; Millwrights; Mobile Heavy Equipment Mechanics, Except Engines; Motorboat Mechanics; Motorcycle Mechanics; Musical Instrument Repairers and Tuners; Ophthalmic Laboratory Technicians; Optical Instrument Assemblers; Outdoor Power Equipment and Other Small Engine Mechanics; Painters, Transportation Equipment; Percussion Instrument Repairers and Tuners; others. **PERSONALITY TYPE**—Realistic. Realistic occupations frequently involve work activities that include practical, hands-on problems and solutions. They often deal with plants, animals, and real-world materials like wood, tools, and machinery. Many of the occupations require working outside and do not involve a lot of paperwork or working closely with others.

**EDUCATION/TRAINING PROGRAM(S)**—Auto/Automotive Mechanic/Technician; Automotive Engineering Technologist/Technician. **RELATED KNOWLEDGE/COURSES—Principles of Mechanical Devices:** Knowledge of machines and tools, including their designs, uses, repair, and maintenance. **Computers and Electronics:** Knowledge of circuit boards, processors, chips, electronic equipment, and computer hardware and software, including applications and programming. **Engineering and Technology:** Knowledge of the practical application of engineering science and technology. This includes applying principles, techniques, procedures, and equipment to the design and production of various goods and services. **Customer and Personal Service:** Knowledge of principles and processes for providing customer and personal services. This includes customer needs assessment, meeting quality standards for services, and evaluation of customer satisfaction. **Physics:** Knowledge and prediction of physical principles and laws and their interrelationships and applications to understanding fluid, material, and atmospheric dynamics and mechanical, electrical, atomic, and sub-atomic structures and processes.

# Automotive Specialty Technicians

- ▲ Growth: 18%
- ▲ Annual Job Openings: 104,000
- ▲ Annual Earnings: $30,780
- ▲ Education/Training Required: Post-secondary vocational training
- ▲ Self-Employed: 17.9%
- ▲ Part-Time: 6.8%

**Repair only one system or component on a vehicle, such as brakes, suspension, or radiator.** Repairs, installs, and adjusts hydraulic and electromagnetic automatic lift mechanisms used to raise and lower automobile windows, seats, and tops. Repairs, overhauls, and adjusts automobile brake systems. Rebuilds, repairs, and tests automotive injection units. Aligns and repairs wheels, axles, frames, torsion bars, and steering mechanisms of automobiles. Examines vehicle, compiles estimate of repair costs, and secures customer approval to perform repairs. Tunes automobile engines and tests electronic computer components. Inspects, tests, repairs, and replaces automotive cooling systems and fuel tanks. Inspects and tests new vehicles for damage, records findings, and makes repairs. Repairs and replaces defective balljoint suspension, brake shoes, and wheel bearings. Repairs, replaces, and adjusts defective carburetor parts and gasoline filters. Converts vehicle fuel systems from gasoline to butane gas operations and repairs and services operating butane fuel units. Installs and repairs automotive air-conditioning units. Repairs and rebuilds clutch systems. Repairs and replaces automobile leaf springs. Removes and replaces defective mufflers and tailpipes from automobiles. Repairs and aligns defective wheels of automobiles. **SKILLS**—Installation. Repairing. Troubleshooting. Equipment Maintenance. Quality Control Analysis.

**GOE—Interest Area:** 05. Mechanics, Installers, and Repairers. **Work Group:** 05.03. Mechanical Work. **Other Job Titles in This Work Group:** Aircraft Body and Bonded Structure Repairers; Aircraft Engine Specialists; Aircraft Mechanics and Service Technicians; Airframe-and-Power-Plant Mechanics; Automotive Body and Related Repairers; Automotive Glass Installers and Repairers; Automotive Master Mechanics; Automotive Service Technicians and Mechanics; Bicycle Repairers; Bridge and Lock Tenders; Bus and Truck Mechanics and Diesel Engine Specialists; Camera and Photographic Equipment Repairers; Coin, Vending, and Amusement Machine Servicers and Repairers; Control and Valve Installers and Repairers, Except Mechanical Door; Farm Equipment Mechanics; Gas Appliance Repairers; Hand and Portable Power Tool Repairers; Heating and Air Conditioning Mechanics; Heating, Air Conditioning, and Refrigeration Mechanics and Installers; Helpers—Electricians; Helpers—Installation, Maintenance, and Repair Workers; Industrial Machinery Mechanics; Keyboard Instrument Repairers and Tuners; Locksmiths and Safe Repairers; Maintenance and Repair Workers, General; Maintenance Workers, Machinery; Mechanical Door Repairers; Medical Appliance Technicians; Medical Equipment Repairers; Meter Mechanics; Millwrights; Mobile Heavy Equipment Mechanics, Except Engines; Motorboat Mechanics; Motorcycle Mechanics; Musical Instrument Repairers and Tuners; Ophthalmic Laboratory Technicians; Optical Instrument Assemblers; Outdoor Power Equipment and Other Small Engine Mechanics; Painters, Transportation Equipment; Percussion Instrument Repairers and Tuners; Precision Instrument and Equipment Repairers, All Other; others. **PERSONALITY TYPE**—Realistic. Realistic occupations frequently involve work activities that include practical, hands-on problems and solutions. They often deal with plants, animals, and real-world materials like wood, tools, and machinery. Many of the occupations require working outside and do not involve a lot of paperwork or working closely with others.

**EDUCATION/TRAINING PROGRAM(S)**—Auto/Automotive Mechanic/Technician; Automotive Engineering Technologist/Technician. **RELATED**

KNOWLEDGE/COURSES—**Principles of Mechanical Devices:** Knowledge of machines and tools, including their designs, uses, repair, and maintenance. **Computers and Electronics:** Knowledge of circuit boards, processors, chips, electronic equipment, and computer hardware and software, including applications and programming. **Engineering and Technology:** Knowledge of the practical application of engineering science and technology. This includes applying principles, techniques, procedures, and equipment to the design and production of various goods and services. **Customer and Personal Service:** Knowledge of principles and processes for providing customer and personal services. This includes customer needs assessment, meeting quality standards for services, and evaluation of customer satisfaction. **Physics:** Knowledge and prediction of physical principles and laws and their interrelationships and applications to understanding fluid, material, and atmospheric dynamics and mechanical, electrical, atomic, and sub-atomic structures and processes.

# Aviation Inspectors

▲ Growth: 11.3%
▲ Annual Job Openings: 3,000
▲ Annual Earnings: $44,200
▲ Education/Training Required: Work experience in a related occupation
▲ Self-Employed: 9%
▲ Part-Time: 2.9%

**Inspect aircraft, maintenance procedures, air navigational aids, air traffic controls, and communications equipment to ensure conformance with Federal safety regulations.** Inspects aircraft and components to identify damage or defects and to determine structural and mechanical airworthiness, using hand tools and test instruments. Examines maintenance record and flight log to determine if service and maintenance checks and overhauls were performed at prescribed intervals. Examines access plates and doors for security. Starts aircraft and observes gauges, meters, and other instruments to detect evidence of malfunction. Conducts flight test program to test equipment, instruments, and systems under various conditions, including adverse weather, using both manual and automatic controls. Recommends purchase, repair, or modification of equipment. Schedules and coordinates inflight testing program with ground crews and air traffic control to assure ground tracking, equipment monitoring, and related services. Prepares reports to document flight activities and inspection findings. Approves or disapproves issuance of certificate of airworthiness. Investigates air accidents to determine cause. Analyzes training program and conducts examinations to assure competency of persons operating, installing, and repairing equipment. SKILLS—Reading Comprehension. Writing. Quality Control Analysis. Operation Monitoring. Critical Thinking.

GOE—**Interest Area:** 04. Law, Law Enforcement, and Public Safety. **Work Group:** 04.04. Public Safety. **Other Job Titles in This Work Group:** Agricultural Inspectors; Compliance Officers, Except Agriculture, Construction, Health and Safety, and Transportation; Emergency Medical Technicians and Paramedics; Environmental Compliance Inspectors; Equal Opportunity Representatives and Officers; Financial Examiners; Fire Fighters; Fire Inspectors; Fire Inspectors and Investigators; Forest Fire Fighters; Forest Fire Inspectors and Prevention Specialists; Government Property Inspectors and Investigators; Licensing Examiners and Inspectors; Marine Cargo Inspectors; Municipal Fire Fighters; Nuclear Monitoring Technicians; Occupational Health and Safety Specialists; Occupational Health and Safety Technicians; Public Transportation Inspectors. **PERSONALITY TYPE**—Realistic. Realistic occupations frequently involve work activities that include practical, hands-on problems and solutions. They often deal with plants, animals, and real-world materials like wood, tools, and machinery. Many of the occupations require working outside and do not involve a lot of paperwork or working closely with others.

EDUCATION/TRAINING PROGRAM(S)—Operations Management and Supervision. **RELATED KNOWLEDGE/COURSES—Engineering and Technology:** Knowledge of the practical application of engineering science and technology. This includes applying principles, techniques, procedures, and equipment to the design and production of various goods and services. **Public Safety and Security:** Knowledge of relevant equipment, policies, procedures, and strategies to promote effective local, state, or national security operations for the protection of people, data, property, and institutions. **Principles of Mechanical Devices:** Knowledge of machines and tools, including their designs, uses, repair, and maintenance. **English Language:** Knowledge of the structure and content of the English language, including the meaning and spelling of words, rules of composition, and grammar. **Law and Government:** Knowledge of laws, legal codes, court procedures, precedents, government regulations, executive orders, agency rules, and the democratic political process.

# Avionics Technicians

- ▲ Growth: 9.8%
- ▲ Annual Job Openings: 2,000
- ▲ Annual Earnings: $41,600
- ▲ Education/Training Required: Post-secondary vocational training
- ▲ Self-Employed: 0%
- ▲ Part-Time: 6.2%

**Install, inspect, test, adjust, or repair avionics equipment, such as radar, radio, navigation, and missile control systems in aircraft or space vehicles.** Assembles components, such as switches, electrical controls, and junction boxes, using hand tools and soldering iron. Connects components to assemblies, such as radio systems, instruments, magnetos, inverters, and in-flight refueling systems, using hand tools and soldering iron. Tests components or assemblies, using circuit tester, oscilloscope, and voltmeter. Lays out installation of assemblies and systems in aircraft according to blueprints and wiring diagrams, using scribe, scale, and protractor. Sets up and operates ground support and test equipment to perform functional flight test of electrical and electronic systems. Fabricates parts and test aids as required. Interprets flight test data to diagnose malfunctions and systemic performance problems. Installs electrical and electronic components, assemblies, and systems in aircraft, using hand tools, power tools, and soldering iron. Adjusts, repairs, or replaces malfunctioning components or assemblies, using hand tools and soldering iron. **SKILLS—Troubleshooting. Repairing.** Mathematics. Installation. Operation Monitoring. Operation and Control. Equipment Maintenance.

GOE—**Interest Area:** 05. Mechanics, Installers, and Repairers. **Work Group:** 05.02. Electrical and Electronic Systems. **Other Job Titles in This Work Group:** Battery Repairers; Central Office and PBX Installers and Repairers; Communication Equipment Mechanics, Installers, and Repairers; Computer, Automated Teller, and Office Machine Repairers; Data Processing Equipment Repairers; Electric Home Appliance and Power Tool Repairers; Electric Meter Installers and Repairers; Electric Motor and Switch Assemblers and Repairers; Electric Motor, Power Tool, and Related Repairers; Electrical and Electronics Installers and Repairers, Transportation Equipment; Electrical and Electronics Repairers, Commercial and Industrial Equipment; Electrical and Electronics Repairers, Powerhouse, Substation, and Relay; Electrical Parts Reconditioners; Electrical Power-Line Installers and Repairers; Electronic Equipment Installers and Repairers, Motor Vehicles; Electronic Home Entertainment Equipment Installers and Repairers; Elevator Installers and Repairers; Frame Wirers, Central Office; Home Appliance Installers; Home Appliance Repairers; Office Machine and Cash Register Servicers; Radio Mechanics; Signal and Track Switch Repairers; Station Installers and Repairers, Telephone; Telecommunications Equipment Installers and Repairers, Except Line Installers; Telecommunications Facility Examiners; Telecommunications Line Installers and Repairers; Transformer Repairers. **PERSONALITY TYPE**—Realistic. Realistic occupations frequently involve work activities that include practical, hands-on problems and solutions. They often deal with plants, animals, and real-world materials like wood, tools, and machinery. Many of the occupations require working outside and do not involve a lot of paperwork or working closely with others.

**EDUCATION/TRAINING PROGRAM(S)**—Aircraft Mechanic/Technician, Airframe; Aviation Systems and Avionics Maintenance Technologist/Technician; Business Machine Repairer; Computer Installer and

Repairer; Computer Maintenance Technologist/Technician; Industrial Electronics Installer and Repairer. **RELATED KNOWLEDGE/COURSES—Computers and Electronics:** Knowledge of circuit boards, processors, chips, electronic equipment, and computer hardware and software, including applications and programming. **Engineering and Technology:** Knowledge of the practical application of engineering science and technology. This includes applying principles, techniques, procedures, and equipment to the design and production of various goods and services. **Design:** Knowledge of design techniques, tools, and principles involved in production of precision technical plans, blueprints, drawings, and models. **Principles of Mechanical Devices:** Knowledge of machines and tools, including their designs, uses, repair, and maintenance. **Physics:** Knowledge and prediction of physical principles and laws and their interrelationships and applications to understanding fluid, material, and atmospheric dynamics and mechanical, electrical, atomic, and sub-atomic structures and processes.

# Bakers, Bread and Pastry

- ▲ Growth: 16.8%
- ▲ Annual Job Openings: 25,000
- ▲ Annual Earnings: $21,050
- ▲ Education/Training Required: Long-term on-the-job training
- ▲ Self-Employed: 4.4%
- ▲ Part-Time: 38.5%

**Mix and bake ingredients according to recipes to produce small quantities of breads, pastries, and other baked goods for consumption on premises or for sale as specialty baked goods.** Weighs and measures ingredients, using measuring cups and spoons. Mixes ingredients to form dough or batter by hand or using electric mixer. Rolls and shapes dough, using rolling pin, and cuts dough in uniform portions with knife, divider, cookie cutter. Molds dough in desired shapes, places dough in greased or floured pans, and trims overlapping edges with knife. Mixes and cooks pie fillings, pours fillings into pie shells, and tops filling with meringue or cream. Checks production schedule to determine variety and quantity of goods to bake. Spreads or

sprinkles toppings on loaves or specialties and places dough in oven, using long-handled paddle (peel). Covers filling with top crust, places pies in oven, and adjust drafts or thermostatic controls to regulate oven temperatures. Mixes ingredients to make icings, decorates cakes and pastries, and blends colors for icings, shaped ornaments, and statuaries. Cuts, peels, and prepares fruit for pie fillings. **SKILLS**—Mathematics. Monitoring. Coordination.

**GOE—Interest Area:** 11. Recreation, Travel, and Other Personal Services. **Work Group:** 11.05. Food and Beverage Services. **Other Job Titles in This Work Group:** Bakers; Bartenders; Butchers and Meat Cutters; Chefs and Head Cooks; Combined Food Preparation and

Serving Workers, Including Fast Food; Cooks, All Other; Cooks, Fast Food; Cooks, Institution and Cafeteria; Cooks, Restaurant; Cooks, Short Order; Counter Attendants, Cafeteria, Food Concession, and Coffee Shop; Dining Room and Cafeteria Attendants and Bartender Helpers; Dishwashers; Food Preparation and Serving Related Workers, All Other; Food Preparation Workers; Food Servers, Nonrestaurant; Hosts and Hostesses, Restaurant, Lounge, and Coffee Shop; Waiters and Waitresses. **PERSONALITY TYPE**—Realistic. Realistic occupations frequently involve work activities that include practical, hands-on problems and solutions. They often deal with plants, animals, and real-world materials like wood, tools, and machinery. Many of the occupations require working outside and do not involve a lot of paperwork or working closely with others.

# Bakers, Manufacturing

Mix and bake ingredients according to recipes to produce breads, pastries, and other baked goods. Goods are produced in large quantities for sale through establishments such as grocery stores. Generally, high-volume production equipment is used. Measures flour and other ingredients to prepare batters, dough, fillings, and icings, using scale and graduated containers. Places dough in pans, molds, or on sheets and bakes dough in oven or on grill. Dumps ingredients into mixing-machine bowl or steam kettle to mix or cook ingredients according to specific instructions. Decorates cakes. Applies glace, icing, or other topping to baked goods, using spatula or brush. Rolls, cuts, and shapes dough to form sweet rolls, pie crusts, tarts, cookies, and related products prior to baking. Observes color of products being baked and adjusts oven temperature. Develops new recipes for cakes and icings. **SKILLS**—Mathematics. Monitoring. Equipment Selection.

**EDUCATION/TRAINING PROGRAM(S)**—Baker/Pastry Chef. **RELATED KNOWLEDGE/COURSES**—**Food Production:** Knowledge of techniques and equipment for planting, growing, and harvesting food products (both plant and animal) for consumption, including storage/handling techniques. **Customer and Personal Service:** Knowledge of principles and processes for providing customer and personal services. This includes customer needs assessment, meeting quality standards for services, and evaluation of customer satisfaction. **Production and Processing:** Knowledge of raw materials, production processes, quality control, costs, and other techniques for maximizing the effective manufacture and distribution of goods. **Mathematics:** Knowledge of arithmetic, algebra, geometry, calculus, statistics, and their applications.

- ▲ Growth: 16.8%
- ▲ Annual Job Openings: 25,000
- ▲ Annual Earnings: $21,050
- ▲ Education/Training Required: Long-term on-the-job training
- ▲ Self-Employed: 4.4%
- ▲ Part-Time: 22%

**GOE—Interest Area:** 08. Industrial Production. **Work Group:** 08.03. Production Work. **Other Job Titles in This Work Group:** Bindery Machine Operators and Tenders; Brazers; Cementing and Gluing Machine Operators and Tenders; Chemical Equipment Controllers and Operators; Chemical Equipment Operators and Tenders; Chemical Equipment Tenders; Cleaning, Washing, and Metal Pickling Equipment Operators and Tenders; Coating, Painting, and Spraying Machine Operators and Tenders; Coil Winders, Tapers, and Finishers; Combination Machine Tool Operators and Tenders, Metal and Plastic; Computer-Controlled Machine Tool Operators, Metal and Plastic; Cooling and Freezing Equipment Operators and Tenders; Crushing, Grinding, and Polishing Machine Setters, Operators, and Tenders; Cutters and Trimmers, Hand; Cutting and Slicing Machine Operators and Tenders; Cutting and Slicing Machine Setters, Operators, and Tenders; Design Printing Machine Setters and Set-Up Operators;

Electrolytic Plating and Coating Machine Operators and Tenders, Metal and Plastic; Electrolytic Plating and Coating Machine Setters and Set-Up Operators, Metal and Plastic; Electrotypers and Stereotypers; Embossing Machine Set-Up Operators; Engraver Set-Up Operators; Extruding and Forming Machine Operators and Tenders, Synthetic or Glass Fibers; Extruding and Forming Machine Setters, Operators, and Tenders, Synthetic and Glass Fibers; Extruding, Forming, Pressing, and Compacting Machine Operators and Tenders; Fabric and Apparel Patternmakers; Fiber Product Cutting Machine Setters and Set-Up Operators; Fiberglass Laminators and Fabricators; Film Laboratory Technicians; others. **PERSONALITY TYPE**—Realistic. Realistic occupations frequently involve work activities that include practical, hands-on problems and solutions. They often deal with plants, animals, and real-world materials like wood, tools, and machinery. Many of the occupations require working outside and do not involve a lot of paperwork or working closely with others.

**EDUCATION/TRAINING PROGRAM(S)**—Baker/Pastry Chef. **RELATED KNOWLEDGE/COURSES—Production and Processing:** Knowledge of raw materials, production processes, quality control, costs, and other techniques for maximizing the effective manufacture and distribution of goods. **Food Production:** Knowledge of techniques and equipment for planting, growing, and harvesting food products (both plant and animal) for consumption, including storage/handling techniques. **Mathematics:** Knowledge of arithmetic, algebra, geometry, calculus, statistics, and their applications.

# Bartenders

- ▲ Growth: 13.4%
- ▲ Annual Job Openings: 84,000
- ▲ Annual Earnings: $16,150
- ▲ Education/Training Required: Short-term on-the-job training
- ▲ Self-Employed: 1.3%
- ▲ Part-Time: 43.1%

**Mix and serve drinks to patrons, directly or through waitstaff.** Mixes ingredients, such as liquor, soda, water, sugar, and bitters, to prepare cocktails and other drinks. Arranges bottles and glasses to make attractive display. Slices and pits fruit for garnishing drinks. Orders or requisitions liquors and supplies. Prepares appetizers, such as pickles, cheese, and cold meats. Cleans glasses, utensils, and bar equipment. Collects money for drinks served. Serves wine and draft or bottled beer. **SKILLS**—Service Orientation. Writing.

**GOE—Interest Area:** 11. Recreation, Travel, and Other Personal Services. **Work Group:** 11.05. Food and Beverage Services. **Other Job Titles in This Work Group:** Bakers; Bakers, Bread and Pastry; Butchers and Meat Cutters; Chefs and Head Cooks; Combined Food Preparation and Serving Workers, Including Fast Food; Cooks, All Other; Cooks, Fast Food; Cooks, Institution and Cafeteria; Cooks, Restaurant; Cooks, Short Order; Counter Attendants, Cafeteria, Food Concession, and Coffee Shop; Dining Room and Cafeteria Attendants and Bartender Helpers; Dishwashers; Food Preparation and Serving Related Workers, All Other; Food Preparation Workers; Food Servers, Nonrestaurant; Hosts and Hostesses, Restaurant, Lounge, and Coffee Shop; Waiters and Waitresses. **PERSONALITY TYPE**—Enterprising. Enterprising occupations frequently involve starting up and carrying out projects. These occupations can involve leading people and making many decisions. They sometimes require risk taking and often deal with business.

**EDUCATION/TRAINING PROGRAM(S)**—Bartender/Mixologist. **RELATED KNOWLEDGE/COURSES—Customer and Personal Service:** Knowledge of principles and processes for providing customer and personal services. This includes customer needs assessment, meeting quality standards for services, and evaluation of customer satisfaction. **Sales and Marketing:** Knowledge of principles and methods for showing, promoting, and selling products or services. This includes marketing strategy and tactics, product demonstration, sales techniques, and sales control systems. **Law and Government:** Knowledge of laws, legal codes, court procedures, precedents, government regulations, executive orders, agency rules, and the democratic political process. **Mathematics:** Knowledge of arithmetic, algebra, geometry, calculus, statistics, and their applications. **English Language:** Knowledge of the structure and content of the English language, including the meaning and spelling of words, rules of composition, and grammar.

# Bill and Account Collectors

▲ Growth: 25.3%
▲ Annual Job Openings: 71,000
▲ Annual Earnings: $26,670
▲ Education/Training Required: Short-term on-the-job training
▲ Self-Employed: 0.6%
▲ Part-Time: 12.7%

**Locate and notify customers of delinquent accounts by mail, telephone, or personal visit to solicit payment. Duties include receiving payment and posting amount to customer's account; preparing statements to credit department if customer fails to respond; initiating repossession proceedings or service disconnection; keeping records of collection and status of accounts.** Mails form letters to customers to encourage payment of delinquent accounts. Receives payments and posts amount paid to customer account, using computer or paper records. Confers with customer by telephone or in person to determine reason for overdue payment and review terms of sales, service, or credit contract. Drives vehicle to visit customer, return merchandise to creditor, or deliver bills. Sorts and files correspondence and performs miscellaneous clerical duties. Traces delinquent customer to new address by inquiring at post office or questioning neighbors. Records information about financial status of customer and status of collection efforts. Notifies credit department, orders merchandise repossession or service disconnection, or turns over account to attorney if customer fails to respond. Persuades customer to pay amount due on credit account, damage claim, or nonpayable check or negotiates extension of credit. **SKILLS**—Active Listening. Speaking. Persuasion. Writing. Reading Comprehension.

**GOE—Interest Area:** 09. Business Detail. **Work Group:** 09.05. Customer Service. **Other Job Titles in This Work Group:** Adjustment Clerks; Cashiers; Counter and Rental Clerks; Customer Service Representatives; Customer Service Representatives, Utilities; Gaming Cage Workers; Gaming Change Persons and Booth Cashiers; New Accounts Clerks; Order Clerks; Receptionists and Information Clerks; Tellers; Travel Clerks. **PERSONALITY TYPE**—Conventional. Conventional occupations frequently involve following set procedures and routines. These occupations can include working with data and details more than with ideas. Usually there is a clear line of authority to follow.

**EDUCATION/TRAINING PROGRAM(S)**—Banking and Financial Support Services. **RELATED KNOWLEDGE/COURSES—Clerical Studies:** Knowledge of administrative and clerical procedures and systems such as word processing, managing files and records, stenography and transcription, designing forms, and other office procedures and terminology. **Mathematics:** Knowledge of arithmetic, algebra, geometry, calculus, statistics, and their applications. **Economics and Accounting:** Knowledge of economic and accounting principles and practices, the financial markets, banking, and the analysis and reporting of financial data. **English Language:** Knowledge of the structure and content of the English language, including the meaning and spelling of words, rules of composition, and grammar. **Computers and Electronics:** Knowledge of circuit boards, processors, chips, electronic equipment, and computer hardware and software, including applications and programming.

# Billing, Cost, and Rate Clerks

- ▲ Growth: 8.5%
- ▲ Annual Job Openings: 69,000
- ▲ Annual Earnings: $25,480
- ▲ Education/Training Required: Short-term on-the-job training
- ▲ Self-Employed: 0.3%
- ▲ Part-Time: 13.8%

**Compile data, compute fees and charges, and prepare invoices for billing purposes. Duties include computing costs and calculating rates for goods, services, and shipment of goods; posting data; and keeping other relevant records. May involve use of computer or typewriter, calculator, and adding and bookkeeping machines.** Computes amounts due from such documents as purchase orders, sales tickets, and charge slips. Compiles and computes credit terms, discounts, and purchase prices for billing documents. Keeps records of invoices and support documents. Consults manuals which include rates, rules, regulations, and government tax and tariff information. Verifies compiled data from vendor invoices to ensure accuracy and revises billing data when errors are found. Resolves discrepancies on accounting records. Updates manuals when rates, rules, or regulations are amended. Estimates market value of product or services. Answers mail and telephone inquiries regarding rates, routing, and procedures. Types billing documents, shipping labels, credit memorandums, and credit forms, using typewriter or computer. Compiles cost factor reports, such as labor, production, storage, and equipment. **SKILLS—**Mathematics. Reading Comprehension. Active Listening. Writing. Speaking.

**GOE—Interest Area:** 09. Business Detail. **Work Group:** 09.03. Bookkeeping, Auditing, and Accounting. **Other Job Titles in This Work Group:** Billing and Posting Clerks and Machine Operators; Bookkeeping, Account-

ing, and Auditing Clerks; Brokerage Clerks; Payroll and Timekeeping Clerks; Statement Clerks; Tax Preparers. **PERSONALITY TYPE—**Conventional. Conventional occupations frequently involve following set procedures and routines. These occupations can include working with data and details more than with ideas. Usually there is a clear line of authority to follow.

**EDUCATION/TRAINING PROGRAM(S)—**Accounting Technician. **RELATED KNOWLEDGE/ COURSES—Clerical Studies:** Knowledge of administrative and clerical procedures and systems such as word processing, managing files and records, stenography and transcription, designing forms, and other office procedures and terminology. **Mathematics:** Knowledge of arithmetic, algebra, geometry, calculus, statistics, and their applications. **Economics and Accounting:** Knowledge of economic and accounting principles and practices, the financial markets, banking, and the analysis and reporting of financial data. **English Language:** Knowledge of the structure and content of the English language, including the meaning and spelling of words, rules of composition, and grammar. **Customer and Personal Service:** Knowledge of principles and processes for providing customer and personal services. This includes customer needs assessment, meeting quality standards for services, and evaluation of customer satisfaction.

# Billing, Posting, and Calculating Machine Operators

- ▲ Growth: 8.5%
- ▲ Annual Job Openings: 69,000
- ▲ Annual Earnings: $25,480
- ▲ Education/Training Required: Short-term on-the-job training
- ▲ Self-Employed: 0.3%
- ▲ Part-Time: 12.8%

Operate machines that automatically perform mathematical processes, such as addition, subtraction, multiplication, and division, to calculate and record billing, accounting, statistical, and other numerical data. Duties include operating special billing machines to prepare statements, bills, and invoices and operating bookkeeping machines to copy and post data, make computations, and compile records of transactions. Calculates accounting and other numerical data, such as amounts customers owe, sales totals, and inventory data, using calculating machine. Observes operation of sorter to note document machine cannot read and manually records amount, using keyboard. Manually sorts and lists items for proof or collection. Cleans machines, such as encoding or sorting machines, and replaces ribbons, film, and tape. Bundles sorted documents to prepare those drawn on other banks for collection. Transfers data from machine, such as encoding machine, to computer. Posts totals to records and prepares bill or invoice to be sent to customers, using billing machine. Sorts and microfilms transaction documents, such as checks, using sorting machine. Compares machine totals to records for errors and encodes correct amount or prepares correction record if error is found. Transcribes data from office records, using specified forms, billing machine, and transcribing machine. Encodes and adds amounts of transaction documents, such as checks or money orders, using encoding machine. **SKILLS**—Mathematics. Operation and Control. Reading Comprehension.

**GOE**—**Interest Area:** 09. Business Detail. **Work Group:** 09.09. Clerical Machine Operation. **Other Job Titles**

in This Work Group: Automatic Teller Machine Servicers; Computer Operators; Data Entry Keyers; Duplicating Machine Operators; Mail Clerks and Mail Machine Operators, Except Postal Service; Mail Machine Operators, Preparation and Handling; Office Machine Operators, Except Computer; Postal Service Clerks; Typesetting and Composing Machine Operators and Tenders; Word Processors and Typists. **PERSONALITY TYPE**—Conventional. Conventional occupations frequently involve following set procedures and routines. These occupations can include working with data and details more than with ideas. Usually there is a clear line of authority to follow.

**EDUCATION/TRAINING PROGRAM(S)**—Accounting Technician. **RELATED KNOWLEDGE/COURSES**—**Clerical Studies:** Knowledge of administrative and clerical procedures and systems such as word processing, managing files and records, stenography and transcription, designing forms, and other office procedures and terminology. **Mathematics:** Knowledge of arithmetic, algebra, geometry, calculus, statistics, and their applications. **Computers and Electronics:** Knowledge of circuit boards, processors, chips, electronic equipment, and computer hardware and software, including applications and programming. **Economics and Accounting:** Knowledge of economic and accounting principles and practices, the financial markets, banking, and the analysis and reporting of financial data. **English Language:** Knowledge of the structure and content of the English language, including the meaning and spelling of words, rules of composition, and grammar.

# Biological Technicians

- ▲ Growth: 26.4%
- ▲ Annual Job Openings: 7,000
- ▲ Annual Earnings: $32,970
- ▲ Education/Training Required: Associate's degree
- ▲ Self-Employed: 0%
- ▲ Part-Time: 11.7%

**Assist biological and medical scientists in laboratories. Set up, operate, and maintain laboratory instruments and equipment, monitor experiments, make observations, and calculate and record results. May analyze organic substances, such as blood, food, and drugs.** Sets up laboratory and field equipment to assist research workers. Cleans and maintains laboratory and field equipment and work areas. Examines animals and specimens to determine presence of disease or other problems. Pricks animals and collects blood samples for testing, using hand-held devices. Plants seeds in specified area and counts plants that grow in order to determine germination rate of seeds. Waters and feeds rations to livestock and laboratory animals. Adjusts testing equipment and prepares culture media, following standard procedures. Measures or weighs ingredients used in testing or as animal feed. Records production and test data for evaluation by personnel. **SKILLS**—Mathematics. Reading Comprehension. Science. Equipment Selection.

**GOE—Interest Area:** 02. Science, Math, and Engineering. **Work Group:** 02.05. Laboratory Technology. **Other Job Titles in This Work Group:** Chemical Technicians; Environmental Science and Protection Technicians, Including Health; Geological and Petroleum Technicians; Geological Data Technicians; Geological Sample Test Technicians; Nuclear Equipment Operation Technicians; Nuclear Technicians; Photographers, Scientific.

**PERSONALITY TYPE**—Realistic. Realistic occupations frequently involve work activities that include practical, hands-on problems and solutions. They often deal with plants, animals, and real-world materials like wood, tools, and machinery. Many of the occupations require working outside and do not involve a lot of paperwork or working closely with others.

**EDUCATION/TRAINING PROGRAM(S)**—Biological Technologist/Technician. **RELATED KNOWLEDGE/COURSES**—**Biology:** Knowledge of plant and animal organisms and their tissues, cells, functions, interdependencies, and interactions with each other and the environment. **Mathematics:** Knowledge of arithmetic, algebra, geometry, calculus, statistics, and their applications. **Food Production:** Knowledge of techniques and equipment for planting, growing, and harvesting food products (both plant and animal) for consumption, including storage/handling techniques. **Clerical Studies:** Knowledge of administrative and clerical procedures and systems such as word processing, managing files and records, stenography and transcription, designing forms, and other office procedures and terminology. **Medicine and Dentistry:** Knowledge of the information and techniques needed to diagnose and treat human injuries, diseases, and deformities. This includes symptoms, treatment alternatives, drug properties and interactions, and preventive health-care measures.

# Boat Builders and Shipwrights

▲ Growth: 8.2%
▲ Annual Job Openings: 161,000
▲ Annual Earnings: $35,100
▲ Education/Training Required: Long-term on-the-job training
▲ Self-Employed: 28.6%
▲ Part-Time: 8.1%

**Construct and repair ships or boats according to blueprints.** Cuts and forms parts, such as keel, ribs, sidings, and support structures and blocks, using woodworking hand tools and power tools. Constructs and shapes wooden frames, structures, and other parts according to blueprint specifications, using hand tools, power tools, and measuring instruments. Attaches metal parts, such as fittings, plates, and bulkheads, to ship, using brace and bits, augers, and wrenches. Establishes dimensional reference points on layout and hull to make template of parts and locate machinery and equipment. Smoothes and finishes ship surfaces, using power sander, broadax, adz, and paint, and waxes and buffs surface to specified finish. Cuts out defect, using power tools and hand tools, and fits and secures replacement part, using caulking gun, adhesive, or hand tools. Assembles and installs hull timbers and other structures in ship, using adhesive, measuring instruments, and hand tools or power tools. Measures and marks dimensional lines on lumber, following template and using scriber. Consults with customer or supervisor and reads blueprint to determine necessary repairs. Attaches hoist to sections of hull and directs hoist operator to align parts over blocks according to layout of boat. Marks outline of boat on building dock, shipway, or mold loft according to blueprint specifications, using measuring instruments and crayon. Inspects boat to determine location and extent of defect. Positions and secures support structures on construction area. **SKILLS**—Mathematics. Equipment Selection. Operations Analysis. Repairing. Installation.

**GOE—Interest Area:** 06. Construction, Mining, and Drilling. **Work Group:** 06.02. Construction. **Other Job Titles in This Work Group:** Boilermakers; Brattice Builders; Brickmasons and Blockmasons; Carpenters; Carpet Installers; Ceiling Tile Installers; Cement Masons and Concrete Finishers; Commercial Divers; Construction Carpenters; Drywall and Ceiling Tile Installers; Drywall Installers; Electricians; Explosives Workers, Ordnance Handling Experts, and Blasters; Fence Erectors; Floor Layers, Except Carpet, Wood, and Hard Tiles; Floor Sanders and Finishers; Glaziers; Grader, Bulldozer, and Scraper Operators; Hazardous Materials Removal Workers; Insulation Workers, Floor, Ceiling, and Wall; Insulation Workers, Mechanical; Manufactured Building and Mobile Home Installers; Operating Engineers; Operating Engineers and Other Construction Equipment Operators; Painters, Construction and Maintenance; Paperhangers; Paving, Surfacing, and Tamping Equipment Operators; Pile-Driver Operators; Pipe Fitters; Pipelayers; Pipelaying Fitters; Plasterers and Stucco Masons; Plumbers; Plumbers, Pipefitters, and Steamfitters; Rail-Track Laying and Maintenance Equipment Operators; Refractory Materials Repairers, Except Brickmasons; Reinforcing Iron and Rebar Workers; Riggers; Roofers; Rough Carpenters; Security and Fire Alarm Systems Installers; Segmental Pavers; Sheet Metal Workers; Ship Carpenters and Joiners; Stone Cutters and Carvers; Stonemasons; Structural Iron and Steel Workers; Tapers; Terrazzo Workers and Finishers; Tile and Marble Setters. **PERSONALITY TYPE**—Realistic. Realistic occupations frequently involve work activities that include practical, hands-on problems and solutions. They often deal with plants, animals, and real-world materials like wood, tools, and machinery. Many of the occupations require working outside and do not involve a lot of paperwork or working closely with others.

**EDUCATION/TRAINING PROGRAM(S)**—Carpenter; Marine Maintenance and Ship Repairer. **RE-**

LATED KNOWLEDGE/COURSES—**Building and Construction:** Knowledge of materials, methods, and tools involved in the construction or repair of houses, buildings, or other structures such as highways and roads. **Principles of Mechanical Devices:** Knowledge of machines and tools, including their designs, uses, repair, and maintenance. **Design:** Knowledge of design techniques, tools, and principles involved in production of precision technical plans, blueprints, drawings, and models. **Engineering and Technology:** Knowledge of the practical application of engineering science and technology. This includes applying principles, techniques, procedures, and equipment to the design and production of various goods and services. **Production and Processing:** Knowledge of raw materials, production processes, quality control, costs, and other techniques for maximizing the effective manufacture and distribution of goods.

# Bookkeeping, Accounting, and Auditing Clerks

- ▲ Growth: 2%
- ▲ Annual Job Openings: 298,000
- ▲ Annual Earnings: $26,950
- ▲ Education/Training Required: Moderate-term on-the-job training
- ▲ Self-Employed: 10.1%
- ▲ Part-Time: 32.8%

Compute, classify, and record numerical data to keep financial records complete. Perform any combination of routine calculating, posting, and verifying duties to obtain primary financial data for use in maintaining accounting records. May also check the accuracy of figures, calculations, and postings pertaining to business transactions recorded by other workers. Records financial transactions and other account information to update and maintain accounting records. Evaluates records for accuracy of balances, postings, calculations, and other records pertaining to business or operating transactions and reconciles or notes discrepancies. Processes negotiable instruments such as checks and vouchers. Compiles reports and tables to show statistics related to cash receipts, expenditures, accounts payable and receivable, and profit and loss. Performs financial calculations such as amounts due, balances, discounts, equity, and principal. Debits or credits accounts. Complies with federal, state, and company policies, procedures, and regulations. Verifies balances and entries, calculations, and postings recorded by other workers. **SKILLS**—Reading Comprehension. Mathematics. Active Listening. Writing. Speaking. Management of Financial Resources.

**GOE—Interest Area:** 09. Business Detail. **Work Group:** 09.03. Bookkeeping, Auditing, and Accounting. **Other Job Titles in This Work Group:** Billing and Posting Clerks and Machine Operators; Billing, Cost, and Rate Clerks; Brokerage Clerks; Payroll and Timekeeping Clerks; Statement Clerks; Tax Preparers. **PERSONALITY TYPE**—Conventional. Conventional occupations frequently involve following set procedures and routines. These occupations can include working with data and details more than with ideas. Usually there is a clear line of authority to follow.

**EDUCATION/TRAINING PROGRAM(S)**—Accounting Technician; Accounting, Other. **RELATED KNOWLEDGE/COURSES—Economics and Accounting:** Knowledge of economic and accounting principles and practices, the financial markets, banking, and the analysis and reporting of financial data. **Clerical Studies:** Knowledge of administrative and clerical procedures and systems such as word processing, managing files and records, stenography and transcription, designing forms, and other office procedures and terminology. **Mathematics:** Knowledge of arithmetic, algebra, geometry, calculus, statistics, and their applications. **English Language:** Knowledge of the structure and content of the English language, including the meaning and spelling of words, rules of composition, and grammar. **Computers and Electronics:** Knowledge of circuit boards, processors, chips, electronic equipment, and computer hardware and software, including applications and programming.

# Brattice Builders

- ▲ Growth: 8.2%
- ▲ Annual Job Openings: 161,000
- ▲ Annual Earnings: $35,100
- ▲ Education/Training Required: Long-term on-the-job training
- ▲ Self-Employed: 28.6%
- ▲ Part-Time: 8.1%

**Build doors or brattices (ventilation walls or partitions) in underground passageways to control the proper circulation of air through the passageways and to the working places.** Installs rigid and flexible air ducts to transport air to work areas. Drills and blasts obstructing boulders to reopen ventilation shafts. Erects partitions to support roof in areas unsuited to timbering or bolting. **SKILLS**—Installation. Equipment Selection. Coordination. Quality Control Analysis. Technology Design. Operations Analysis.

**GOE—Interest Area:** 06. Construction, Mining, and Drilling. **Work Group:** 06.02. Construction. **Other Job Titles in This Work Group:** Boat Builders and Shipwrights; Boilermakers; Brickmasons and Blockmasons; Carpenters; Carpet Installers; Ceiling Tile Installers; Cement Masons and Concrete Finishers; Commercial Divers; Construction Carpenters; Drywall and Ceiling Tile Installers; Drywall Installers; Electricians; Explosives Workers, Ordnance Handling Experts, and Blasters; Fence Erectors; Floor Layers, Except Carpet, Wood, and Hard Tiles; Floor Sanders and Finishers; Glaziers; Grader, Bulldozer, and Scraper Operators; Hazardous Materials Removal Workers; Insulation Workers, Floor, Ceiling, and Wall; Insulation Workers, Mechanical; Manufactured Building and Mobile Home Installers; Operating Engineers; Operating Engineers and Other Construction Equipment Operators; Painters, Construction and Maintenance; Paperhangers; Paving, Surfacing, and Tamping Equipment Operators; Pile-Driver Operators; Pipe Fitters; Pipelayers; Pipelaying Fitters; Plasterers and Stucco Masons; Plumbers; Plumbers, Pipefitters, and Steamfitters; Rail-Track Laying and Maintenance Equipment Operators; Refractory Materials Repairers, Except Brickmasons; Reinforcing Iron and Rebar Workers; Riggers; Roofers; Rough Carpenters; Security and Fire Alarm Systems Installers; Segmental Pavers; Sheet Metal Workers; Ship Carpenters and Joiners; Stone Cutters and Carvers; Stonemasons; Structural Iron and Steel Workers; Tapers; Terrazzo Workers and Finishers; Tile and Marble Setters. **PERSONALITY TYPE**—Realistic. Realistic occupations frequently involve work activities that include practical, hands-on problems and solutions. They often deal with plants, animals, and real-world materials like wood, tools, and machinery. Many of the occupations require working outside and do not involve a lot of paperwork or working closely with others.

**EDUCATION/TRAINING PROGRAM(S)**—Carpenter; Marine Maintenance and Ship Repairer. **RELATED KNOWLEDGE/COURSES**—**Building and Construction:** Knowledge of materials, methods, and tools involved in the construction or repair of houses, buildings, or other structures such as highways and roads. **Principles of Mechanical Devices:** Knowledge of machines and tools, including their designs, uses, repair, and maintenance. **Physics:** Knowledge and prediction of physical principles and laws and their interrelationships and applications to understanding fluid, material, and atmospheric dynamics and mechanical, electrical, atomic, and sub-atomic structures and processes. **Engineering and Technology:** Knowledge of the practical application of engineering science and technology. This includes applying principles, techniques, procedures, and equipment to the design and production of various goods and services.

# Brazers

- ▲ Growth: 19.3%
- ▲ Annual Job Openings: 51,000
- ▲ Annual Earnings: $29,080
- ▲ Education/Training Required: Post-secondary vocational training
- ▲ Self-Employed: 5.8%
- ▲ Part-Time: 8.6%

**Braze together components to assemble fabricated metal parts, using torch or welding machine and flux.** Guides torch and rod along joint of workpieces to heat to brazing temperature, melt braze alloy, and bond workpieces together. Cuts carbon electrodes to specified size and shape, using cutoff saw. Removes workpiece from fixture, using tongs, and cools workpiece, using air or water. Cleans joints of workpieces, using wire brush or by dipping them into cleaning solution. Examines seam and rebrazes defective joints or broken parts. Connects hoses from torch to regulator valves and cylinders of oxygen and specified fuel gas, acetylene or natural. Turns valves to start flow of gases, lights flame, and adjusts valves to obtain desired color and size of flame. Brushes flux onto joint of workpiece or dips braze rod into flux to prevent oxidation of metal. Aligns and secures workpieces in fixtures, jigs, or vise, using rule, square, or template. Melts and separates brazed joints to remove and straighten damaged or misaligned components, using hand torch or furnace. Selects torch tip, flux, and brazing alloy from data charts or work order. Adjusts electric current and timing cycle of resistance welding machine to heat metal to bonding temperature. **SKILLS**—Operation and Control. Equipment Selection. Operation Monitoring. Installation. Monitoring.

**GOE—Interest Area:** 08. Industrial Production. **Work Group:** 08.03. Production Work. **Other Job Titles in This Work Group:** Bakers, Manufacturing; Bindery Machine Operators and Tenders; Cementing and Gluing Machine Operators and Tenders; Chemical Equipment Controllers and Operators; Chemical Equipment Operators and Tenders; Chemical Equipment Tenders; Cleaning, Washing, and Metal Pickling Equipment Operators and Tenders; Coating, Painting, and Spraying Machine Operators and Tenders; Coil Winders, Tapers, and Finishers; Combination Machine Tool Operators and Tenders, Metal and Plastic; Computer-Controlled Machine Tool Operators, Metal and Plastic; Cooling and Freezing Equipment Operators and Tenders; Crushing, Grinding, and Polishing Machine Setters, Operators, and Tenders; Cutters and Trimmers, Hand; Cutting and Slicing Machine Operators and Tenders; Cutting and Slicing Machine Setters, Operators, and Tenders; Design Printing Machine Setters and Set-Up Operators; Electrolytic Plating and Coating Machine Operators and Tenders, Metal and Plastic; Electrolytic Plating and Coating Machine Setters and Set-Up Operators, Metal and Plastic; Electrotypers and Stereotypers; Embossing Machine Set-Up Operators; Engraver Set-Up Operators; Extruding and Forming Machine Operators and Tenders, Synthetic or Glass Fibers; Extruding and Forming Machine Setters, Operators, and Tenders, Synthetic and Glass Fibers; Extruding, Forming, Pressing, and Compacting Machine Operators and Tenders; Fabric and Apparel Patternmakers; Fiber Product Cutting Machine Setters and Set-Up Operators; Fiberglass Laminators and Fabricators; others. **PERSONALITY TYPE**—Realistic. Realistic occupations frequently involve work activities that include practical, hands-on problems and solutions. They often deal with plants, animals, and real-world materials like wood, tools, and machinery. Many of the occupations require working outside and do not involve a lot of paperwork or working closely with others.

**EDUCATION/TRAINING PROGRAM(S)**—Welder/Welding Technologist. **RELATED KNOWLEDGE/COURSES—Engineering and Technology:** Knowledge of the practical application of engineering science and technology. This includes applying principles, techniques, procedures, and equipment to the design and production of various goods and services. **Principles of Mechanical Devices:** Knowledge of machines and tools, including their designs, uses, repair, and maintenance. **Production and Processing:** Knowledge of raw materials, production processes, quality control, costs, and other techniques for maximizing the effective manufacture and distribution of goods. **Building and Construction:** Knowledge of materials, methods, and tools involved in the construction or repair of houses, buildings, or other structures such as highways and roads. **Chemistry:** Knowledge of the chemical composition, structure, and properties of substances and of the chemical processes and transformations that they undergo. This includes uses of chemicals and their interactions, danger signs, production techniques, and disposal methods.

# Brickmasons and Blockmasons

▲ Growth: 12.5%

▲ Annual Job Openings: 18,000

▲ Annual Earnings: $41,140

▲ Education/Training Required: Long-term on-the-job training

▲ Self-Employed: 28.3%

▲ Part-Time: 8.7%

**Lay and bind building materials, such as brick, structural tile, concrete block, cinder block, glass block, and terra-cotta block, with mortar and other substances to construct or repair walls, partitions, arches, sewers, and other structures.** Lays and aligns bricks, blocks, or tiles to build or repair structures or high temperature equipment, such as cupola, kilns, ovens, or furnaces. Applies and smoothes mortar or other mixture over work surface and removes excess, using trowel and hand tools. Examines brickwork or structure to determine need for repair. Measures distance from reference points and marks guidelines to lay out work, using plumb bobs and levels. Breaks or cuts bricks, tiles, or blocks to size, using edge of trowel, hammer, or power saw. Removes burned or damaged brick or mortar, using sledgehammer, crowbar, chipping gun, or chisel. Sprays or spreads refractory material over brickwork to protect against deterioration. Cleans working surface to remove scale, dust, soot, or chips of brick and mortar, using broom, wire brush, or scraper. Fastens or fuses brick or other building material to structure with wire clamps, anchor holes, torch, or cement. Mixes specified amount of sand, clay, dirt, or mortar powder with water to form refractory mixture. Calculates angles and courses and determines vertical and horizontal alignment of courses. **SKILLS**—Mathematics. Equipment Selection. Repairing. Coordination.

**GOE—Interest Area:** 06. Construction, Mining, and Drilling. **Work Group:** 06.02. Construction. **Other Job Titles in This Work Group:** Boat Builders and Shipwrights; Boilermakers; Brattice Builders; Carpenters; Carpet Installers; Ceiling Tile Installers; Cement Masons and Concrete Finishers; Commercial Divers; Construction Carpenters; Drywall and Ceiling Tile Installers; Drywall Installers; Electricians; Explosives Workers, Ordnance Handling Experts, and Blasters; Fence Erectors; Floor Layers, Except Carpet, Wood, and Hard Tiles; Floor Sanders and Finishers; Glaziers; Grader, Bulldozer, and Scraper Operators; Hazardous Materials Removal Workers; Insulation Workers, Floor, Ceiling, and Wall; Insulation Workers, Mechanical; Manufactured Building and Mobile Home Installers; Operating Engineers; Operating Engineers and Other Construction Equipment Operators; Painters, Construction and Maintenance; Paperhangers; Paving, Surfacing, and Tamping Equipment Operators; Pile-Driver Operators; Pipe Fitters; Pipelayers; Pipelaying Fitters; Plasterers and Stucco Masons; Plumbers; Plumbers, Pipefitters, and Steamfitters; Rail-Track Laying and

Maintenance Equipment Operators; Refractory Materials Repairers, Except Brickmasons; Reinforcing Iron and Rebar Workers; Riggers; Roofers; Rough Carpenters; Security and Fire Alarm Systems Installers; Segmental Pavers; Sheet Metal Workers; Ship Carpenters and Joiners; Stone Cutters and Carvers; Stonemasons; Structural Iron and Steel Workers; Tapers; Terrazzo Workers and Finishers; Tile and Marble Setters. **PERSONALITY TYPE**—Realistic. Realistic occupations frequently involve work activities that include practical, hands-on problems and solutions. They often deal with plants, animals, and real-world materials like wood, tools, and machinery. Many of the occupations require working outside and do not involve a lot of paperwork or working closely with others.

**EDUCATION/TRAINING PROGRAM(S)**—Mason and Tile Setter. **RELATED KNOWLEDGE/COURSES**—**Building and Construction:** Knowledge of materials, methods, and tools involved in the construction or repair of houses, buildings, or other structures such as highways and roads. **Principles of Mechanical Devices:** Knowledge of machines and tools, including their designs, uses, repair, and maintenance. **Mathematics:** Knowledge of arithmetic, algebra, geometry, calculus, statistics, and their applications. **Physics:** Knowledge and prediction of physical principles and laws and their interrelationships and applications to understanding fluid, material, and atmospheric dynamics and mechanical, electrical, atomic, and sub-atomic structures and processes.

# Bus and Truck Mechanics and Diesel Engine Specialists

- ▲ Growth: 14.2%
- ▲ Annual Job Openings: 20,000
- ▲ Annual Earnings: $33,210
- ▲ Education/Training Required: Post-secondary vocational training
- ▲ Self-Employed: 3.9%
- ▲ Part-Time: 2.9%

**Diagnose, adjust, repair, or overhaul trucks, buses, and all types of diesel engines. Includes mechanics working primarily with automobile diesel engines.** Inspects defective equipment and diagnoses malfunctions, using test instruments such as motor analyzers, chassis charts, and pressure gauges. Reads job orders and observes and listens to operating equipment to ensure conformance to specifications or to determine malfunctions. Adjusts brakes, aligns wheels, tightens bolts and screws, and reassembles equipment. Operates valve-grinding machine to grind and reset valves. Examines and adjusts protective guards, loose bolts, and specified safety devices. Changes oil, checks batteries, repairs tires and tubes, and lubricates equipment and machinery. Attaches test instruments to equipment and reads dials and gauges to diagnose malfunctions. Reconditions and replaces parts, pistons, bearings, gears, and valves. Inspects and verifies dimensions and clearances of parts to ensure conformance to factory specifications. Inspects, repairs, and maintains automotive and mechanical equipment and machinery, such as pumps and compressors. Disassembles and overhauls internal combustion engines, pumps, generators, transmissions, clutches, and rear ends. **SKILLS**—Repairing. Troubleshooting. Equipment Maintenance. Installation. Quality Control Analysis.

**GOE**—**Interest Area:** 05. Mechanics, Installers, and Repairers. **Work Group:** 05.03. Mechanical Work. **Other Job Titles in This Work Group:** Aircraft Body and Bonded Structure Repairers; Aircraft Engine Specialists; Aircraft Mechanics and Service Technicians; Airframe-and-Power-Plant Mechanics; Automotive Body and Related Repairers; Automotive Glass Installers and Repairers; Automotive Master Mechanics; Automotive Service Technicians and Mechanics; Automotive Specialty Technicians; Bicycle Repairers; Bridge and Lock Tenders; Camera and Photographic Equipment Repairers; Coin, Vending, and Amusement Machine Servicers and Repairers; Control and Valve

Installers and Repairers, Except Mechanical Door; Farm Equipment Mechanics; Gas Appliance Repairers; Hand and Portable Power Tool Repairers; Heating and Air Conditioning Mechanics; Heating, Air Conditioning, and Refrigeration Mechanics and Installers; Helpers—Electricians; Helpers—Installation, Maintenance, and Repair Workers; Industrial Machinery Mechanics; Keyboard Instrument Repairers and Tuners; Locksmiths and Safe Repairers; Maintenance and Repair Workers, General; Maintenance Workers, Machinery; Mechanical Door Repairers; Medical Appliance Technicians; Medical Equipment Repairers; Meter Mechanics; Millwrights; Mobile Heavy Equipment Mechanics, Except Engines; Motorboat Mechanics; Motorcycle Mechanics; Musical Instrument Repairers and Tuners; Ophthalmic Laboratory Technicians; Optical Instrument Assemblers; Outdoor Power Equipment and Other Small Engine Mechanics; Painters, Transportation Equipment; Percussion Instrument Repairers and Tuners; Precision Instrument and Equipment Repairers, All Other; others. **PERSONALITY TYPE**—Realistic. Realistic occupations frequently involve work activities that include practical, hands-on problems and solutions. They often deal with plants, animals, and real-world

materials like wood, tools, and machinery. Many of the occupations require working outside and do not involve a lot of paperwork or working closely with others.

**EDUCATION/TRAINING PROGRAM(S)**—Diesel Engine Mechanic and Repairer; Vehicle and Mobile Equipment Mechanics and Repairers, Other. **RELATED KNOWLEDGE/COURSES—Principles of Mechanical Devices:** Knowledge of machines and tools, including their designs, uses, repair, and maintenance. **Engineering and Technology:** Knowledge of the practical application of engineering science and technology. This includes applying principles, techniques, procedures, and equipment to the design and production of various goods and services. **Public Safety and Security:** Knowledge of relevant equipment, policies, procedures, and strategies to promote effective local, state, or national security operations for the protection of people, data, property, and institutions. **Physics:** Knowledge and prediction of physical principles and laws and their interrelationships and applications to understanding fluid, material, and atmospheric dynamics and mechanical, electrical, atomic, and sub-atomic structures and processes.

# Bus Drivers, School

▲ Growth: 11.6%

▲ Annual Job Openings: 63,000

▲ Annual Earnings: $21,430

▲ Education/Training Required: Short-term on-the-job training

▲ Self-Employed: 0.9%

▲ Part-Time: 43.3%

**Transport students or special clients, such as the elderly or persons with disabilities. Ensure adherence to safety rules. May assist passengers in boarding or exiting.** Drives bus to transport pupils over specified routes. Reports delays or accidents. Regulates heating, lighting, and ventilating systems for passenger comfort. Complies with local traffic regulations. Maintains order among pupils during trip. Inspects bus and checks gas, oil, and water levels. Makes minor repairs to bus. **SKILLS**—Operation and Control. Operation Monitoring. Repairing.

**GOE—Interest Area:** 07. Transportation. **Work Group:** 07.07. Other Services Requiring Driving. **Other Job Titles in This Work Group:** Ambulance Drivers and Attendants, Except Emergency Medical Technicians; Bus Drivers, Transit and Intercity; Driver/Sales Workers; Parking Lot Attendants; Taxi Drivers and Chauffeurs. **PERSONALITY TYPE**—Realistic. Realistic occupations frequently involve work activities that include practical, hands-on problems and solutions. They often deal with plants, animals, and real-world materials like wood, tools, and machinery. Many of the occupations require working outside and do not involve a lot of paperwork or working closely with others.

**EDUCATION/TRAINING PROGRAM(S)**—Truck, Bus and Other Commercial Vehicle Operator. **RELATED KNOWLEDGE/COURSES—Transportation:** Knowledge of principles and methods for moving people or goods by air, rail, sea, or road, including the relative costs and benefits. **Public Safety and Security:** Knowledge of relevant equipment, policies, procedures, and strategies to promote effective local, state, or national security operations for the protection of people, data, property, and institutions. **Customer and Personal Service:** Knowledge of principles and processes for providing customer and personal services. This includes customer needs assessment, meeting quality standards for services, and evaluation of customer satisfaction. **Geography:** Knowledge of principles and methods for describing the features of land, sea, and air masses, including their physical characteristics, locations, interrelationships, and distribution of plant, animal, and human life. **Law and Government:** Knowledge of laws, legal codes, court procedures, precedents, government regulations, executive orders, agency rules, and the democratic political process.

# Bus Drivers, Transit and Intercity

- ▲ Growth: 17.4%
- ▲ Annual Job Openings: 24,000
- ▲ Annual Earnings: $27,250
- ▲ Education/Training Required: Moderate-term on-the-job training
- ▲ Self-Employed: 0.8%
- ▲ Part-Time: 43.3%

**Drive bus or motor coach, including regular route operations, charters, and private carriage. May assist passengers with baggage. May collect fares or tickets.** Drives vehicle over specified route or to specified destination according to time schedule to transport passengers, complying with traffic regulations. Assists passengers with baggage and collects tickets or cash fares. Parks vehicle at loading area for passengers to board. Loads and unloads baggage in baggage compartment. Advises passengers to be seated and orderly while on vehicle. Inspects vehicle and checks gas, oil, and water before departure. Makes minor repairs to vehicle and changes tires. Reports delays or accidents. Records cash receipts and ticket fares. Regulates heating, lighting, and ventilating systems for passenger comfort. **SKILLS**—Operation and Control. Repairing. Operation Monitoring. Service Orientation. Time Management.

**GOE—Interest Area:** 07. Transportation. **Work Group:** 07.07. Other Services Requiring Driving. **Other Job Titles in This Work Group:** Ambulance Drivers and Attendants, Except Emergency Medical Technicians; Bus Drivers, School; Driver/Sales Workers; Parking Lot Attendants; Taxi Drivers and Chauffeurs. **PERSONALITY TYPE**—Realistic. Realistic occupations frequently involve work activities that include practical, hands-on problems and solutions. They often deal with plants, animals, and real-world materials like wood, tools, and machinery. Many of the occupations require working outside and do not involve a lot of paperwork or working closely with others.

**EDUCATION/TRAINING PROGRAM(S)**—Truck, Bus and Other Commercial Vehicle Operator. **RELATED KNOWLEDGE/COURSES—Transportation:** Knowledge of principles and methods for moving people or goods by air, rail, sea, or road, including the relative costs and benefits. **Geography:** Knowledge of principles and methods for describing the features of land, sea, and air masses, including their physical characteristics, locations, interrelationships, and distribution of plant, animal, and human life. **Principles of Mechanical Devices:** Knowledge of machines and tools, including their designs, uses, repair, and maintenance.

**Public Safety and Security:** Knowledge of relevant equipment, policies, procedures, and strategies to promote effective local, state, or national security operations for the protection of people, data, property, and institutions. **Customer and Personal Service:** Knowledge of principles and processes for providing customer and personal services. This includes customer needs assessment, meeting quality standards for services, and evaluation of customer satisfaction.

# Calibration and Instrumentation Technicians

- ▲ Growth: 10.8%
- ▲ Annual Job Openings: 22,000
- ▲ Annual Earnings: $41,210
- ▲ Education/Training Required: Associate's degree
- ▲ Self-Employed: 2.7%
- ▲ Part-Time: 3.1%

**Develop, test, calibrate, operate, and repair electrical, mechanical, electromechanical, electrohydraulic, or electronic measuring and recording instruments, apparatus, and equipment.** Plans sequence of testing and calibration program for instruments and equipment according to blueprints, schematics, technical manuals, and other specifications. Performs preventative and corrective maintenance of test apparatus and peripheral equipment. Confers with engineers, supervisor, and other technical workers to assist with equipment installation, maintenance, and repair techniques. Analyzes and converts test data, using mathematical formulas, and reports results and proposed modifications. Sets up test equipment and conducts tests on performance and reliability of mechanical, structural, or electromechanical equipment. Selects sensing, telemetering, and recording instrumentation and circuitry. Disassembles and reassembles instruments and equipment, using hand tools, and inspects instruments and equipment for defects. Sketches plans for developing jigs, fixtures, instruments, and related nonstandard apparatus. Modifies performance and operation of component parts and circuitry to specifications, using test equipment and precision instruments. **SKILLS**—Technology Design. Equipment Selection. Quality Control Analysis. Equipment Maintenance. Active Listening. Mathematics.

**GOE—Interest Area:** 02. Science, Math, and Engineering. **Work Group:** 02.08. Engineering Technology. **Other Job Titles in This Work Group:** Aerospace Engineering and Operations Technicians; Architectural and Civil Drafters; Architectural Drafters; Cartographers and Photogrammetrists; Civil Drafters; Civil Engineering Technicians; Construction and Building Inspectors; Drafters, All Other; Electrical and Electronic Engineering Technicians; Electrical and Electronics Drafters; Electrical Drafters; Electrical Engineering Technicians; Electro-Mechanical Technicians; Electronic Drafters; Electronics Engineering Technicians; Engineering Technicians, Except Drafters, All Other; Environmental Engineering Technicians; Industrial Engineering Technicians; Mapping Technicians; Mechanical Drafters; Mechanical Engineering Technicians; Numerical Tool and Process Control Programmers; Pressure Vessel Inspectors; Surveying and Mapping Technicians; Surveying Technicians; Surveyors. **PERSONALITY TYPE**—Realistic. Realistic occupations frequently involve work activities that include practical, hands-on problems and solutions. They often deal with plants, animals, and real-world materials like wood, tools, and machinery. Many of the occupations require working outside and do not involve a lot of paperwork or working closely with others.

**EDUCATION/TRAINING PROGRAM(S)**—Computer Engineering Technologist/Technician; Electrical and Electronic Engineering-Related Technologist/Technician; Electrical, Electronic and Communications Engineering Technologist/Technician. **RELATED KNOWLEDGE/COURSES**—**Design:** Knowledge of design techniques, tools, and principles involved in production of precision technical plans, blueprints, drawings, and models. **Mathematics:** Knowledge of arithmetic, algebra, geometry, calculus, statistics, and their applications. **Principles of Mechanical Devices:** Knowledge of machines and tools, including their designs, uses, repair, and maintenance. **Engineering and Technology:** Knowledge of the practical application of engineering science and technology. This includes applying principles, techniques, procedures, and equipment to the design and production of various goods and services. **Computers and Electronics:** Knowledge of circuit boards, processors, chips, electronic equipment, and computer hardware and software, including applications and programming.

# Camera Operators, Television, Video, and Motion Picture

- ▲ Growth: 25.8%
- ▲ Annual Job Openings: 3,000
- ▲ Annual Earnings: $33,860
- ▲ Education/Training Required: Moderate-term on-the-job training
- ▲ Self-Employed: 24.4%
- ▲ Part-Time: 23.1%

**Operate television, video, or motion picture camera to photograph images or scenes for various purposes, such as TV broadcasts, advertising, video production, or motion pictures.** Sets up cameras, optical printers, and related equipment to produce photographs and special effects. Adjusts position and controls of camera, printer, and related equipment to produce desired effects, using precision measuring instruments. Selects cameras, accessories, equipment, and film stock to use during filming, using knowledge of filming techniques, requirements, and computations. Reads work order to determine specifications and location of subject material. Views film to resolve problems of exposure control, subject and camera movement, changes in subject distance, and related variables. Observes set or location for potential problems and to determine filming and lighting requirements. Analyzes specifications to determine work procedures, sequence of operations, and machine setup. Reads charts and computes ratios to determine variables, such as lighting, shutter angles, filter factors, and camera distance. Instructs camera operators regarding camera setup, angles, distances, movement, and other variables and cues for starting and stopping filming. Exposes frames of film in sequential order and regulates exposures and aperture to obtain special effects. Confers with director and electrician regarding interpretation of scene, desired effects, and film-ing and lighting requirements. **SKILLS**—Operation and Control. Technology Design. Mathematics. Equipment Selection. Reading Comprehension.

**GOE—Interest Area:** 01. Arts, Entertainment, and Media. **Work Group:** 01.08. Media Technology. **Other Job Titles in This Work Group:** Audio and Video Equipment Technicians; Broadcast Technicians; Film and Video Editors; Media and Communication Equipment Workers, All Other; Photographers; Professional Photographers; Radio Operators; Sound Engineering Technicians. **PERSONALITY TYPE**—Artistic. Artistic occupations frequently involve working with forms, designs, and patterns. They often require self-expression, and the work can be done without following a clear set of rules.

**EDUCATION/TRAINING PROGRAM(S)**—Communications Technologists/Technicians, Other; Film-Video Making/Cinematography and Production; Radio and Television Broadcasting Technologist/Technician. **RELATED KNOWLEDGE/COURSES—Fine Arts:** Knowledge of the theory and techniques required to compose, produce, and perform works of music, dance, visual arts, drama, and sculpture. **Telecommunications:** Knowledge of transmission, broadcasting, switching, control, and operation of telecommunications systems. **Physics:** Knowledge and prediction of physical principles and laws and their interrelationships and applications to understanding fluid, material, and atmospheric dynamics and mechanical, electrical, atomic, and sub-atomic structures and processes. **Mathematics:** Knowledge of arithmetic, algebra, geometry, calculus, statistics, and their applications. **Communications and Media:** Knowledge of media production, communication, and dissemination techniques and methods. This includes alternative ways to inform and entertain via written, oral, and visual media.

# Cardiovascular Technologists and Technicians

▲ Growth: 34.9%
▲ Annual Job Openings: 3,000
▲ Annual Earnings: $34,960
▲ Education/Training Required: Associate's degree
▲ Self-Employed: 0%
▲ Part-Time: 22.9%

**Conduct tests on pulmonary or cardiovascular systems of patients for diagnostic purposes. May conduct or assist in electrocardiograms, cardiac catheterizations, pulmonary-functions, lung capacity, and similar tests.** Operates diagnostic imaging equipment to produce contrast-enhanced radiographs of heart and cardiovascular system. Injects contrast medium into blood vessels of patient. Conducts electrocardiogram, phonocardiogram, echocardiogram, stress testing, and other cardiovascular tests, using specialized electronic test equipment, recording devices, and laboratory instruments. Operates monitor to measure and record functions of cardiovascular and pulmonary systems as part of cardiac catheterization team. Observes gauges, recorder, and video screens of data analysis system during imaging of cardiovascular system. Conducts tests of pulmonary system, using spirometer and other respiratory testing equipment. Activates fluoroscope and camera to produce images used to guide catheter through cardiovascular system. Records variations in action of heart muscle, using electrocardiograph. Prepares and positions patients for testing. Records test results and other data into patient records. Reviews test results with physician. Explains testing procedures to patient to obtain cooperation and reduce anxiety. Adjusts equipment and controls according to physicians' orders or established protocol. Alerts physician to abnormalities or changes in patient responses. Enters factors such as amount and quality of radiation beam and filming sequence into computer. Assesses cardiac physiology and calculates valve areas from blood flow velocity measurements. Compares measurements of heart wall thickness and chamber sizes to standard norms to identify abnormalities. Observes ultrasound display screen and listens to signals to acquire data for measurement of blood flow velocities. Records analyses of heart and related structures, using ultrasound equipment. **SKILLS**—Reading Comprehension. Mathematics. Operation Monitoring. Active Listening. Operation and Control. Writing. Science.

**GOE—Interest Area:** 14. Medical and Health Services. **Work Group:** 14.05. Medical Technology. **Other Job Titles in This Work Group:** Diagnostic Medical Sonographers; Health Technologists and Technicians, All Other; Medical and Clinical Laboratory Technicians; Medical and Clinical Laboratory Technologists; Medical Equipment Preparers; Nuclear Medicine Technologists; Orthotists and Prosthetists; Radiologic Technicians; Radiologic Technologists; Radiologic Technologists and Technicians. **PERSONALITY TYPE**—Investigative. Investigative occupations frequently involve working with ideas and require an extensive amount of thinking. These occupations can involve searching for facts and figuring out problems mentally.

**EDUCATION/TRAINING PROGRAM(S)**—Cardiovascular Technologist/Technician; Electrocardiograph Technologist/Technician; Perfusion Technologist/Technician. **RELATED KNOWLEDGE/COURSES**—**Medicine and Dentistry:** Knowledge of the information and techniques needed to diagnose and treat human injuries, diseases, and deformities. This includes symptoms, treatment alternatives, drug properties and interactions, and preventive health-care measures. **Computers and Electronics:** Knowledge of circuit boards, processors, chips, electronic equipment, and computer hardware and software, including applications and programming. **Biology:** Knowledge of plant and animal organisms and their tissues, cells, functions, interdependencies, and interactions with each other and the environment. **Mathematics:** Knowledge of arithmetic, algebra, geometry, calculus, statistics, and their applications. **English Language:** Knowledge of the structure and content of the English language, including the meaning and spelling of words, rules of composition, and grammar.

# Carpenter Assemblers and Repairers

- ▲ Growth: 8.2%
- ▲ Annual Job Openings: 161,000
- ▲ Annual Earnings: $35,100
- ▲ Education/Training Required: Long-term on-the-job training
- ▲ Self-Employed: 28.6%
- ▲ Part-Time: 8.1%

**Perform a variety of tasks requiring a limited knowledge of carpentry, such as applying siding and weatherboard to building exteriors or assembling and erecting prefabricated buildings.** Measures and marks location of studs, leaders, and receptacle openings, using tape measure, template, and marker. Cuts sidings and moldings, sections of weatherboard, openings in sheetrock, and lumber, using hand tools and power tools. Lays out and aligns materials on worktable or in assembly jig according to specified instructions. Removes surface defects, using knife, scraper, wet sponge, electric iron, and sanding tools. Trims overlapping edges of wood and weatherboard, using portable router or power saw and hand tools. Installs prefabricated windows and doors; insulation; wall, ceiling, and floor panels; or siding, using adhesives, hoists, hand tools, and power tools. Aligns and fastens materials together, using hand tools and power tools, to form building or bracing. Repairs or replaces defective locks, hinges, cranks, and pieces of wood, using glue, hand tools, and power tools. Applies stain, paint, or crayons to defects and filter to touch up the repaired area. Directs crane operator in positioning floor, wall, ceiling, and roof panel on house foundation. Moves panel or roof section to other work stations or to storage or shipping area, using electric hoist. Studies blueprints, specification sheets, and drawings to determine style and type of window or wall panel required. Fills cracks, seams, depressions, and nail holes with filler. Examines wood surfaces for defects, such as nicks, cracks, or blisters. Measures cut materials to determine conformance to specifications, using tape measure. Realigns windows and screens to fit casements and oils moving parts. **SKILLS**—Repairing. Installation. Operation and Control.

**GOE—Interest Area:** 06. Construction, Mining, and Drilling. **Work Group:** 06.04. Hands-on Work in Construction, Extraction, and Maintenance. **Other Job Titles in This Work Group:** Construction Laborers; Grips and Set-Up Workers, Motion Picture Sets, Studios, and Stages; Helpers, Construction Trades, All Other; Helpers—Brickmasons, Blockmasons, Stonemasons, and Tile and Marble Setters; Helpers—Carpenters; Helpers—Extraction Workers; Helpers—Painters, Paperhangers, Plasterers, and Stucco Masons; Helpers—Pipelayers, Plumbers, Pipefitters, and Steamfitters; Helpers—Roofers; Highway Maintenance Workers; Septic Tank Servicers and Sewer Pipe Cleaners. **PERSONALITY TYPE**—Realistic. Realistic occupations frequently involve work activities that include practical, hands-on problems and solutions. They often deal with plants, animals, and real-world materials like wood, tools, and machinery. Many of the occupations require

C

working outside and do not involve a lot of paperwork or working closely with others.

**EDUCATION/TRAINING PROGRAM(S)**—Carpenter; Marine Maintenance and Ship Repairer. **RELATED KNOWLEDGE/COURSES**—**Building and Construction:** Knowledge of materials, methods, and tools involved in the construction or repair of houses, buildings, or other structures such as highways and roads. **Engineering and Technology:** Knowledge of the practical application of engineering science and technology. This includes applying principles, techniques, procedures, and equipment to the design and production of various goods and services. **Principles of Mechanical Devices:** Knowledge of machines and tools, including their designs, uses, repair, and maintenance. **Design:** Knowledge of design techniques, tools, and principles involved in production of precision technical plans, blueprints, drawings, and models. **Mathematics:** Knowledge of arithmetic, algebra, geometry, calculus, statistics, and their applications.

# Carpet Installers

▲ Growth: 10.5%

▲ Annual Job Openings: 7,000

▲ Annual Earnings: $33,030

▲ Education/Training Required: Moderate-term on-the-job training

▲ Self-Employed: 48.5%

▲ Part-Time: 13.2%

**Lay and install carpet from rolls or blocks on floors. Install padding and trim flooring materials.** Stretches carpet to ensure smooth surface and presses carpet in place over tack strips. Installs carpet on some floors using adhesive, following prescribed method. Measures and cuts carpeting to size according to floor sketches, using carpet knife. Studies floor sketches to determine area to be carpeted and amount of material needed to complete job. Joins edges of carpet that meet at openings, using tape with glue and heated carpet iron. Cuts and trims carpet to fit along wall edges, openings, and projections. Cuts carpet padding to size and installs padding, following prescribed method. Sews sections of carpeting together by hand when necessary. Moves furniture from area to be carpeted and removes old carpet and padding. Fastens metal treads across door openings or where carpet meets flooring to hold carpet in place. Nails tack strips around area to be carpeted or uses old strips to attach edges of new carpet. **SKILLS**—Mathematics. Installation.

**GOE**—**Interest Area:** 06. Construction, Mining, and Drilling. **Work Group:** 06.02. Construction. **Other Job Titles in This Work Group:** Boat Builders and Shipwrights; Boilermakers; Brattice Builders; Brickmasons and Blockmasons; Carpenters; Ceiling Tile Installers; Cement Masons and Concrete Finishers; Commercial Divers; Construction Carpenters; Drywall and Ceiling Tile Installers; Drywall Installers; Electricians; Explosives Workers, Ordnance Handling Experts, and Blasters; Fence Erectors; Floor Layers, Except Carpet, Wood, and Hard Tiles; Floor Sanders and Finishers; Glaziers; Grader, Bulldozer, and Scraper Operators; Hazardous Materials Removal Workers; Insulation Workers, Floor, Ceiling, and Wall; Insulation Workers, Mechanical; Manufactured Building and Mobile Home Installers; Operating Engineers; Operating Engineers and Other Construction Equipment Operators; Painters, Construction and Maintenance; Paperhangers; Paving, Surfacing, and Tamping Equipment Operators; Pile-Driver Operators; Pipe Fitters; Pipelayers; Pipelaying Fitters; Plasterers and Stucco Masons; Plumbers; Plumbers, Pipefitters, and Steamfitters; Rail-Track Laying and Maintenance Equipment Operators; Refractory Materials Repairers, Except Brickmasons; Reinforcing Iron and Rebar Workers; Riggers; Roofers; Rough Carpenters; Security and Fire Alarm Systems Installers; Segmental Pavers; Sheet Metal Workers; Ship Carpenters and Joiners; Stone Cutters and Carvers; Stonemasons;

Structural Iron and Steel Workers; Tapers; Terrazzo Workers and Finishers; Tile and Marble Setters. **PERSONALITY TYPE**—Realistic. Realistic occupations frequently involve work activities that include practical, hands-on problems and solutions. They often deal with plants, animals, and real-world materials like wood, tools, and machinery. Many of the occupations require working outside and do not involve a lot of paperwork or working closely with others.

**EDUCATION/TRAINING PROGRAM(S)**—Construction Trades, Other. **RELATED KNOWLEDGE/ COURSES**—**Building and Construction:** Knowledge of materials, methods, and tools involved in the construction or repair of houses, buildings, or other structures such as highways and roads. **Design:** Knowledge of design techniques, tools, and principles involved in production of precision technical plans, blueprints, drawings, and models. **Principles of Mechanical Devices:** Knowledge of machines and tools, including their designs, uses, repair, and maintenance. **Mathematics:** Knowledge of arithmetic, algebra, geometry, calculus, statistics, and their applications. **Transportation:** Knowledge of principles and methods for moving people or goods by air, rail, sea, or road, including the relative costs and benefits.

# Cartoonists

- ▲ Growth: 13.4%
- ▲ Annual Job Openings: 4,000
- ▲ Annual Earnings: $35,770
- ▲ Education/Training Required: Long-term on-the-job training
- ▲ Self-Employed: 56.7%
- ▲ Part-Time: 24%

**Create original artwork using any of a wide variety of mediums and techniques, such as painting and sculpture.** Sketches and submits cartoon or animation for approval. Develops personal ideas for cartoons, comic strips, or animations or reads written material to develop ideas. Makes changes and corrections to cartoon, comic strip, or animation as necessary. Creates and prepares sketches and model drawings of characters, providing details from memory, live models, manufactured products, or reference material. Renders sequential drawings of characters or other subject material which, when photographed and projected at specific speed, become animated. Develops color patterns and moods and paints background layouts to dramatize action for animated cartoon scenes. Discusses ideas for cartoons, comic strips, or animations with editor or publisher's representative. Labels each section with designated colors when colors are used. **SKILLS**—Active Listening. Reading Comprehension. Writing.

**GOE**—**Interest Area:** 01. Arts, Entertainment, and Media. **Work Group:** 01.04. Visual Arts. **Other Job Titles in This Work Group:** Commercial and Industrial Designers; Designers, All Other; Exhibit Designers; Fashion Designers; Fine Artists, Including Painters, Sculptors, and Illustrators; Floral Designers; Graphic Designers; Interior Designers; Merchandise Displayers and Window Trimmers; Multi-Media Artists and Animators; Painters and Illustrators; Sculptors; Set and Exhibit Designers; Set Designers; Sketch Artists. **PERSONALITY TYPE**—Artistic. Artistic occupations frequently involve working with forms, designs, and patterns. They often require self-expression, and the work can be done without following a clear set of rules.

**EDUCATION/TRAINING PROGRAM(S)**—Art, General; Ceramics Arts and Ceramics; Drawing; Fine Arts and Art Studies, Other; Fine/Studio Arts; Intermedia; Medical Illustrating; Painting; Printmaking; Sculpture. **RELATED KNOWLEDGE/COURSES**— **Fine Arts:** Knowledge of the theory and techniques required to compose, produce, and perform works of music, dance, visual arts, drama, and sculpture. **Communications and Media:** Knowledge of media production, communication, and dissemination techniques and methods. This includes alternative ways to inform and entertain via written, oral, and visual media. **Design:** Knowledge of design techniques, tools, and principles involved in production of precision technical plans, blueprints, drawings, and models. **English Language:** Knowledge of the structure and content of the English language, including the meaning and spelling of words, rules of composition, and grammar. **Telecom-** **munications:** Knowledge of transmission, broadcasting, switching, control, and operation of telecommunications systems. **Sales and Marketing:** Knowledge of principles and methods for showing, promoting, and selling products or services. This includes marketing strategy and tactics, product demonstration, sales techniques, and sales control systems.

# Cashiers

- ▲ Growth: 14.2%
- ▲ Annual Job Openings: 1,125,000
- ▲ Annual Earnings: $15,730
- ▲ Education/Training Required: Short-term on-the-job training
- ▲ Self-Employed: 0.4%
- ▲ Part-Time: 57.2%

**Receive and disburse money in establishments other than financial institutions. Usually involves use of electronic scanners, cash registers, or related equipment. Often involved in processing credit or debit card transactions and validating checks.** Receives sales slip, cash, check, voucher, or charge payments and issues receipts, refunds, credits, or change due to customer. Learns prices, stocks shelves, marks prices, weighs items, issues trading stamps, and redeems food stamps and coupons. Monitors checkout stations, issues and removes cash as needed, and assigns workers to reduce customer delay. Resolves customer complaints. Compiles and maintains non-monetary reports and records. Bags, boxes, or wraps merchandise. Answers questions and provides information to customers. Sorts, counts, and wraps currency and coins. Operates cash register or electronic scanner. Cashes checks. Keeps periodic balance sheet of amount and number of transactions. Sells tickets and other items to customer. Computes and records totals of transactions. **SKILLS**—Active Listening. Mathematics. Reading Comprehension. Service Orientation. Writing. Speaking.

**GOE**—**Interest Area:** 09. Business Detail. **Work Group:** 09.05. Customer Service. **Other Job Titles in This Work Group:** Adjustment Clerks; Bill and Account Collectors; Counter and Rental Clerks; Customer Ser- vice Representatives; Customer Service Representatives, Utilities; Gaming Cage Workers; Gaming Change Per- sons and Booth Cashiers; New Accounts Clerks; Order Clerks; Receptionists and Information Clerks; Tellers; Travel Clerks. **PERSONALITY TYPE**—Conventional. Conventional occupations frequently involve follow- ing set procedures and routines. These occupations can include working with data and details more than with ideas. Usually there is a clear line of authority to follow.

**EDUCATION/TRAINING PROGRAM(S)**—Food Products Retailing and Wholesaling Operations; Gen- eral Retailing Operations. **RELATED KNOWLEDGE/ COURSES**—**Customer and Personal Service:** Knowl- edge of principles and processes for providing customer and personal services. This includes customer needs as- sessment, meeting quality standards for services, and evaluation of customer satisfaction. **Clerical Studies:** Knowledge of administrative and clerical procedures and systems such as word processing, managing files and records, stenography and transcription, designing forms, and other office procedures and terminology. **Math- ematics:** Knowledge of arithmetic, algebra, geometry, calculus, statistics, and their applications. **Computers and Electronics:** Knowledge of circuit boards, proces- sors, chips, electronic equipment, and computer hard- ware and software, including applications and programming. **English Language:** Knowledge of the structure and content of the English language, including the meaning and spelling of words, rules of composition, and grammar.

# Casting Machine Set-Up Operators

- ▲ Growth: 9.8%
- ▲ Annual Job Openings: 38,000
- ▲ Annual Earnings: $23,630
- ▲ Education/Training Required: Moderate-term on-the-job training
- ▲ Self-Employed: 0%
- ▲ Part-Time: 5.5%

**Set up and operate machines to cast and assemble printing type.** Sets up matrices in assembly stick by hand according to specifications. Positions composing stick to length of line specified in casting instructions. Places reel of controller paper on holder, threads around reels, and attaches to winding roll. Forwards galley to appropriate personnel for proofing. Removes and stores assembly stick, controller reel, and matrix case. Inserts and locks galley or matrix case into place on machine. Stops machine when galley is full or when strip is completed. Starts machine and monitors operation for proper functioning. **SKILLS**—Operation and Control. Operation Monitoring.

**GOE**—**Interest Area:** 08. Industrial Production. **Work Group:** 08.02. Production Technology. **Other Job Titles in This Work Group:** Aircraft Rigging Assemblers; Aircraft Structure Assemblers, Precision; Aircraft Structure, Surfaces, Rigging, and Systems Assemblers; Aircraft Systems Assemblers, Precision; Bench Workers, Jewelry; Bindery Machine Setters and Set-Up Operators; Bindery Workers; Bookbinders; Buffing and Polishing Set-Up Operators; Coating, Painting, and Spraying Machine Setters and Set-Up Operators; Coating, Painting, and Spraying Machine Setters, Operators, and Tenders; Combination Machine Tool Setters and Set-Up Operators, Metal and Plastic; Cutting, Punching, and Press Machine Setters, Operators, and Tenders, Metal and Plastic; Dental Laboratory Technicians; Drilling and Boring Machine Tool Setters, Operators, and Tenders, Metal and Plastic; Electrical and Electronic Equipment Assemblers; Electrical and Electronic Inspectors and Testers; Electromechanical Equipment Assemblers; Engine and Other Machine Assemblers; Extruding and Drawing Machine Setters, Operators, and Tenders, Metal and Plastic; Extruding, Forming, Pressing, and Compacting Machine Setters and Set-Up Operators; Extruding, Forming, Pressing, and Compacting Machine Setters, Operators, and Tenders; Forging Machine Setters, Operators, and Tenders, Metal and Plastic; Foundry Mold and Coremakers; Gem and Diamond Workers; Grinding, Honing, Lapping, and Deburring Machine Set-Up Operators; Grinding, Lapping, Polishing, and Buffing Machine Tool Setters, Operators, and Tenders, Metal and Plastic; Heat Treating Equipment Setters, Operators, and Tenders, Metal and Plastic; others. **PERSONALITY TYPE**—Realistic. Realistic occupations frequently involve work activities that include practical, hands-on problems and solutions. They often deal with plants, animals, and real-world materials like wood, tools, and machinery. Many of the occupations require working outside and do not involve a lot of paperwork or working closely with others.

**EDUCATION/TRAINING PROGRAM(S)**—Aviation Systems and Avionics Maintenance Technologist/Technician; Dental Laboratory Technician; Machinist/Machine Technologist; Precision Metal Workers, Other. **RELATED KNOWLEDGE/COURSES**—**Principles of Mechanical Devices:** Knowledge of machines and tools, including their designs, uses, repair, and maintenance. **Production and Processing:** Knowledge of raw materials, production processes, quality control, costs, and other techniques for maximizing the effective manufacture and distribution of goods. **Engineering and Technology:** Knowledge of the practical application of engineering science and technology. This includes applying principles, techniques, procedures, and equipment to the design and production of various goods and services. **English Language:** Knowledge of the struc- ture and content of the English language, including the meaning and spelling of words, rules of composition, and grammar.

# Ceiling Tile Installers

- ▲ Growth: 9.4%
- ▲ Annual Job Openings: 19,000
- ▲ Annual Earnings: $35,580
- ▲ Education/Training Required: Moderate-term on-the-job training
- ▲ Self-Employed: 20.4%
- ▲ Part-Time: 8.1%

**Apply plasterboard or other wallboard to ceilings or interior walls of buildings. Apply or mount acoustical tiles or blocks, strips, or sheets of shock-absorbing materials to ceilings and walls of buildings to reduce or reflect sound. Materials may be of decorative quality. Includes lathers who fasten wooden, metal, or rockboard lath to walls, ceilings, or partitions of buildings to provide support base for plaster, fire-proofing, or acoustical material.** Applies acoustical tiles or shock-absorbing materials to ceilings and walls of buildings to reduce or reflect sound and to decorate rooms. Washes concrete surfaces with washing soda and zinc sulfate solution before mounting tile to increase adhesive qualities of surfaces. Inspects furrings, mechanical mountings, and masonry surface for plumbness and level, using spirit or water level. Hangs dry lines (stretched string) to wall molding to guide positioning of main runners. Nails or screws molding to wall to support and seals joint between ceiling tile and wall. Scribes and cuts edges of tile to fit wall where wall molding is not specified. Nails channels or wood furring strips to surfaces to provide mounting for tile. Measures and marks surface to lay out work according to blueprints and drawings. Cuts tiles for fixture and borders, using keyhole saw, and inserts tiles into supporting framework. Applies cement to back of tile and presses tile into place, aligning with layout marks and joints of previously laid tile. **SKILLS**—Mathematics.

**GOE—Interest Area:** 06. Construction, Mining, and Drilling. **Work Group:** 06.02. Construction. **Other Job**

**Titles in This Work Group:** Boat Builders and Shipwrights; Boilermakers; Brattice Builders; Brickmasons and Blockmasons; Carpenters; Carpet Installers; Cement Masons and Concrete Finishers; Commercial Divers; Construction Carpenters; Drywall and Ceiling Tile Installers; Drywall Installers; Electricians; Explosives Workers, Ordnance Handling Experts, and Blasters; Fence Erectors; Floor Layers, Except Carpet, Wood, and Hard Tiles; Floor Sanders and Finishers; Glaziers; Grader, Bulldozer, and Scraper Operators; Hazardous Materials Removal Workers; Insulation Workers, Floor, Ceiling, and Wall; Insulation Workers, Mechanical; Manufactured Building and Mobile Home Installers; Operating Engineers; Operating Engineers and Other Construction Equipment Operators; Painters, Construction and Maintenance; Paperhangers; Paving, Surfacing, and Tamping Equipment Operators; Pile-Driver Operators; Pipe Fitters; Pipelayers; Pipelaying Fitters; Plasterers and Stucco Masons; Plumbers; Plumbers, Pipefitters, and Steamfitters; Rail-Track Laying and Maintenance Equipment Operators; Refractory Materials Repairers, Except Brickmasons; Reinforcing Iron and Rebar Workers; Riggers; Roofers; Rough Carpenters; Security and Fire Alarm Systems Installers; Segmental Pavers; Sheet Metal Workers; Ship Carpenters and Joiners; Stone Cutters and Carvers; Stonemasons; Structural Iron and Steel Workers; Tapers; Terrazzo Workers and Finishers; Tile and Marble Setters. **PERSONALITY TYPE**—Realistic. Realistic occupations frequently involve work activities that include practical, hands-on problems and solutions. They often deal with plants, animals, and real-world materials like wood, tools, and machinery. Many of the occupations require working outside and do not involve a lot of paperwork or working closely with others.

EDUCATION/TRAINING PROGRAM(S)—No data available. RELATED KNOWLEDGE/ COURSES—Building and Construction: Knowledge of materials, methods, and tools involved in the construction or repair of houses, buildings, or other structures such as highways and roads. Mathematics: Knowledge of arithmetic, algebra, geometry, calculus,

statistics, and their applications. Design: Knowledge of design techniques, tools, and principles involved in production of precision technical plans, blueprints, drawings, and models. Principles of Mechanical Devices: Knowledge of machines and tools, including their designs, uses, repair, and maintenance. Engineering and Technology: Knowledge of the practical application of engineering science and technology. This includes applying principles, techniques, procedures, and equipment to the design and production of various goods and services.

# Central Office and PBX Installers and Repairers

▲ Growth: -3.1%
▲ Annual Job Openings: 9,000
▲ Annual Earnings: $42,520
▲ Education/Training Required: Postsecondary vocational training
▲ Self-Employed: 6.2%
▲ Part-Time: 3.4%

Test, analyze, and repair telephone or telegraph circuits and equipment at a central office location using test meters and hand tools. Analyze and repair defects in communications equipment on customers' premises using circuit diagrams, polarity probes, meters, and a telephone test set. May install equipment. Tests circuits and components of malfunctioning telecommunication equipment to isolate source of malfunction, using test instruments and circuit diagrams. Analyzes test readings, computer printouts, and trouble reports to determine method of repair. Tests and adjusts installed equipment to ensure circuit continuity and operational performance, using test instruments. Connects wires to equipment, using hand tools, soldering iron, or wire wrap gun. Installs preassembled or partially assembled switching equipment, switchboards, wiring frames, and power apparatus according to floor plans. Retests repaired equipment to ensure that malfunction has been corrected. Repairs or replaces defective components, such as switches, relays, amplifiers, and circuit boards, using hand tools and soldering iron. Removes and remakes connections on wire distributing frame to change circuit layout, following diagrams. Routes cables and trunklines from entry points to speci-

fied equipment, following diagrams. Enters codes to correct programming of electronic switching systems. SKILLS—Repairing. Installation. Troubleshooting. Mathematics. Equipment Selection.

GOE—Interest Area: 05. Mechanics, Installers, and Repairers. Work Group: 05.02. Electrical and Electronic Systems. Other Job Titles in This Work Group: Avionics Technicians; Battery Repairers; Communication Equipment Mechanics, Installers, and Repairers; Computer, Automated Teller, and Office Machine Repairers; Data Processing Equipment Repairers; Electric Home Appliance and Power Tool Repairers; Electric Meter Installers and Repairers; Electric Motor and Switch Assemblers and Repairers; Electric Motor, Power Tool, and Related Repairers; Electrical and Electronics Installers and Repairers, Transportation Equipment; Electrical and Electronics Repairers, Commercial and Industrial Equipment; Electrical and Electronics Repairers, Powerhouse, Substation, and Relay; Electrical Parts Reconditioners; Electrical Power-Line Installers and Repairers; Electronic Equipment Installers and Repairers, Motor Vehicles; Electronic Home Entertainment Equipment Installers and Repairers; Elevator

Installers and Repairers; Frame Wirers, Central Office; Home Appliance Installers; Home Appliance Repairers; Office Machine and Cash Register Servicers; Radio Mechanics; Signal and Track Switch Repairers; Station Installers and Repairers, Telephone; Telecommunications Equipment Installers and Repairers, Except Line Installers; Telecommunications Facility Examiners; Telecommunications Line Installers and Repairers; Transformer Repairers. **PERSONALITY TYPE**—Realistic. Realistic occupations frequently involve work activities that include practical, hands-on problems and solutions. They often deal with plants, animals, and real-world materials like wood, tools, and machinery. Many of the occupations require working outside and do not involve a lot of paperwork or working closely with others.

**EDUCATION/TRAINING PROGRAM(S)**—Communication Systems Installer and Repairer. **RELATED**

**KNOWLEDGE/COURSES**—**Computers and Electronics:** Knowledge of circuit boards, processors, chips, electronic equipment, and computer hardware and software, including applications and programming. **Telecommunications:** Knowledge of transmission, broadcasting, switching, control, and operation of telecommunications systems. **Engineering and Technology:** Knowledge of the practical application of engineering science and technology. This includes applying principles, techniques, procedures, and equipment to the design and production of various goods and services. **Design:** Knowledge of design techniques, tools, and principles involved in production of precision technical plans, blueprints, drawings, and models. **Principles of Mechanical Devices:** Knowledge of machines and tools, including their designs, uses, repair, and maintenance.

# Chefs and Head Cooks

- ▲ Growth: 9%
- ▲ Annual Job Openings: 35,000
- ▲ Annual Earnings: $28,550
- ▲ Education/Training Required: Postsecondary vocational training
- ▲ Self-Employed: 1.3%
- ▲ Part-Time: 8.5%

**Direct the preparation, seasoning, and cooking of salads, soups, fish, meats, vegetables, desserts, or other foods. May plan and price menu items, order supplies, and keep records and accounts. May participate in cooking.** Supervises and coordinates activities of cooks and workers engaged in food preparation. Observes workers and work procedures to ensure compliance with established standards. Evaluates and solves procedural problems to ensure safe and efficient operations. Records production and operational data on specified forms. Inspects supplies, equipment, and work areas to ensure conformance to established standards. Collaborates with specified personnel and plans and develops recipes and menus. Determines production schedules and worker-time requirements to ensure timely delivery of services. Estimates amounts and costs and requisitions supplies and equipment to ensure effi-

cient operation. Helps cooks and workers cook and prepare food on demand. Trains and otherwise instructs cooks and workers in proper food preparation procedures. **SKILLS**—Coordination. Instructing. Management of Financial Resources. Management of Material Resources. Management of Personnel Resources.

**GOE**—**Interest Area:** 11. Recreation, Travel, and Other Personal Services. **Work Group:** 11.05. Food and Beverage Services. **Other Job Titles in This Work Group:** Bakers; Bakers, Bread and Pastry; Bartenders; Butchers and Meat Cutters; Combined Food Preparation and Serving Workers, Including Fast Food; Cooks, All Other; Cooks, Fast Food; Cooks, Institution and Cafeteria; Cooks, Restaurant; Cooks, Short Order; Counter Attendants, Cafeteria, Food Concession, and Coffee Shop; Dining Room and Cafeteria Attendants and Bartender Helpers; Dishwashers; Food Preparation and

Serving Related Workers, All Other; Food Preparation Workers; Food Servers, Nonrestaurant; Hosts and Hostesses, Restaurant, Lounge, and Coffee Shop; Waiters and Waitresses. **PERSONALITY TYPE**—Enterprising. Enterprising occupations frequently involve starting up and carrying out projects. These occupations can involve leading people and making many decisions. They sometimes require risk taking and often deal with business.

**EDUCATION/TRAINING PROGRAM(S)**—Culinary Arts/Chef Training; Food Caterer; Recreation Products/Services Marketing Operations. **RELATED KNOWLEDGE/COURSES—Administration and Management:** Knowledge of business and management principles involved in strategic planning, resource allocation, human resources modeling, leadership tech-nique, production methods, and coordination of people and resources. **Personnel and Human Resources:** Knowledge of principles and procedures for personnel recruitment, selection, training, compensation and benefits, labor relations and negotiation, and personnel information systems. **Economics and Accounting:** Knowledge of economic and accounting principles and practices, the financial markets, banking, and the analysis and reporting of financial data. **Education and Training:** Knowledge of principles and methods for curriculum and training design, teaching and instruction for individuals and groups, and the measurement of training effects. **Mathematics:** Knowledge of arithmetic, algebra, geometry, calculus, statistics, and their applications.

# Chemical Equipment Controllers and Operators

- ▲ Growth: 14.9%
- ▲ Annual Job Openings: 9,000
- ▲ Annual Earnings: $36,310
- ▲ Education/Training Required: Moderate-term on-the-job training
- ▲ Self-Employed: 0%
- ▲ Part-Time: 0.3%

**Control or operate equipment to control chemical changes or reactions in the processing of industrial or consumer products. Typical equipment used: reaction kettles, catalytic converters, continuous or batch treating equipment, saturator tanks, electrolytic cells, reactor vessels, recovery units, and fermentation chambers.** Sets and adjusts indicating, controlling, or timing devices, such as gauging instruments, thermostat, gas analyzers, or recording calorimeter. Moves controls to adjust feed and flow of liquids and gases through equipment in specified sequence. Adjusts controls to regulate temperature, pressure, and time of prescribed reaction according to knowledge of equipment and process. Opens valves or operates pumps to admit or drain specified amounts of materials, impurities, or treating agents to or from equipment. Starts pumps, agitators, reactors, blowers, or automatic feed of materials. Monitors gauges, recording instruments, flowmeters, or product to regulate or maintain specified conditions. Mixes chemicals according to proportion tables or prescribed formulas. Records operational data, such as temperature, pressure, ingredients used, processing time, or test results, in operating log. Flushes or cleans equipment, using steamhose or mechanical reamer. Draws samples of product and sends to laboratory for analysis. Tests sample for specific gravity, chemical characteristics, pH level, concentration, or viscosity. Patrols and inspects equipment or unit to detect leaks and malfunctions. Weighs or measures specified amounts of materials. Reads plant specifications to ascertain product, ingredient, and prescribed modifications of plant procedures. Dumps or scoops prescribed solid, granular, or powdered materials into equipment. Adds treating or neutralizing agent to product and pumps product through filter or centrifuge to remove impurities or precipitate product. Directs activities of workers assisting in control or verification of process or in unloading materials. Makes minor repairs and lubricates and maintains equipment, using hand tools. Operates or tends auxiliary equipment, such as heaters, scrubbers, filters, or driers, to prepare or further process materials. **SKILLS—** Operation Monitoring. Operation and Control. Science. Reading Comprehension. Quality Control Analysis.

**GOE—Interest Area:** 08. Industrial Production. **Work Group:** 08.03. Production Work. **Other Job Titles in This Work Group:** Bakers, Manufacturing; Bindery Machine Operators and Tenders; Brazers; Cementing and Gluing Machine Operators and Tenders; Chemical Equipment Operators and Tenders; Chemical Equipment Tenders; Cleaning, Washing, and Metal Pickling Equipment Operators and Tenders; Coating, Painting, and Spraying Machine Operators and Tenders; Coil Winders, Tapers, and Finishers; Combination Machine Tool Operators and Tenders, Metal and Plastic; Computer-Controlled Machine Tool Operators, Metal and Plastic; Cooling and Freezing Equipment Operators and Tenders; Crushing, Grinding, and Polishing Machine Setters, Operators, and Tenders; Cutters and Trimmers, Hand; Cutting and Slicing Machine Operators and Tenders; Cutting and Slicing Machine Setters, Operators, and Tenders; Design Printing Machine Setters and Set-Up Operators; Electrolytic Plating and Coating Machine Operators and Tenders, Metal and Plastic; Electrolytic Plating and Coating Machine Setters and Set-Up Operators, Metal and Plastic; Electrotypers and Stereotypers; Embossing Machine Set-Up Operators; Engraver Set-Up Operators; Extruding and Forming Machine Operators and Tenders, Synthetic or Glass Fibers; Extruding and Forming Machine Setters, Operators, and Tenders, Synthetic and Glass Fibers; Extruding, Forming, Pressing, and Compacting Machine

Operators and Tenders; Fabric and Apparel Patternmakers; Fiber Product Cutting Machine Setters and Set-Up Operators; Fiberglass Laminators and Fabricators; Film Laboratory Technicians; Fitters, Structural Metal—Precision; others. **PERSONALITY TYPE—** Realistic. Realistic occupations frequently involve work activities that include practical, hands-on problems and solutions. They often deal with plants, animals, and real-world materials like wood, tools, and machinery. Many of the occupations require working outside and do not involve a lot of paperwork or working closely with others.

**EDUCATION/TRAINING PROGRAM(S)—** Chemical Technologist/Technician. **RELATED KNOWLEDGE/COURSES—Chemistry:** Knowledge of the chemical composition, structure, and properties of substances and of the chemical processes and transformations that they undergo. This includes uses of chemicals and their interactions, danger signs, production techniques, and disposal methods. **Principles of Mechanical Devices:** Knowledge of machines and tools, including their designs, uses, repair, and maintenance. **Mathematics:** Knowledge of arithmetic, algebra, geometry, calculus, statistics, and their applications. **Engineering and Technology:** Knowledge of the practical application of engineering science and technology. This includes applying principles, techniques, procedures, and equipment to the design and production of various goods and services. **Public Safety and Security:** Knowledge of relevant equipment, policies, procedures, and strategies to promote effective local, state, or national security operations for the protection of people, data, property, and institutions. **English Language:** Knowledge of the structure and content of the English language, including the meaning and spelling of words, rules of composition, and grammar.

# Chemical Equipment Tenders

▲ Growth: 14.9%

▲ Annual Job Openings: 9,000

▲ Annual Earnings: $36,310

▲ Education/Training Required: Moderate-term on-the-job training

▲ Self-Employed: 0%

▲ Part-Time: 0.3%

**Tend equipment in which a chemical change or reaction takes place in the processing of industrial or consumer products. Typical equipment used: devulcanizers, batch stills, fermenting tanks, steam-jacketed kettles, and reactor vessels.** Starts pumps and agitators, turns valves, or moves controls of processing equipment to admit, transfer, filter, or mix chemicals. Inventories supplies received and consumed. Assists other workers in preparing and maintaining equipment. Observes safety precautions to prevent fires and explosions. Notifies maintenance engineer of equipment malfunction. Records data in log from instruments and gauges concerning temperature, pressure, materials used, treating time, and shift production. Tests samples to determine specific gravity, composition, or acidity, using chemical test equipment such as hydrometer or pH meter. Replaces filtering media or makes minor repairs to equipment, using hand tools. Loads specified amounts of chemicals into processing equipment. Patrols work area to detect leaks and equipment malfunctions and monitor operating conditions. Weighs, measures, or mixes prescribed quantities of materials. Draws sample of products for analysis to aid in process adjustments and maintain production standards. Drains equipment and pumps water or other solution through to flush and clean tanks or equipment. Observes gauges, meters, and panel lights to monitor operating conditions, such as temperature or pressure. Adjusts valves or controls to maintain system within specified operating conditions. **SKILLS**—Operation Monitoring. Operation and Control. Science. Quality Control Analysis. Equipment Maintenance.

**GOE—Interest Area:** 08. Industrial Production. **Work Group:** 08.03. Production Work. **Other Job Titles in This Work Group:** Bakers, Manufacturing; Bindery Machine Operators and Tenders; Brazers; Cementing and Gluing Machine Operators and Tenders; Chemical Equipment Controllers and Operators; Chemical Equipment Operators and Tenders; Cleaning, Washing, and Metal Pickling Equipment Operators and Tenders; Coating, Painting, and Spraying Machine Operators and Tenders; Coil Winders, Tapers, and Finishers; Combination Machine Tool Operators and Tenders, Metal and Plastic; Computer-Controlled Machine Tool Operators, Metal and Plastic; Cooling and Freezing Equipment Operators and Tenders; Crushing, Grinding, and Polishing Machine Setters, Operators, and Tenders; Cutters and Trimmers, Hand; Cutting and Slicing Machine Operators and Tenders; Cutting and Slicing Machine Setters, Operators, and Tenders; Design Printing Machine Setters and Set-Up Operators; Electrolytic Plating and Coating Machine Operators and Tenders, Metal and Plastic; Electrolytic Plating and Coating Machine Setters and Set-Up Operators, Metal and Plastic; Electrotypers and Stereotypers; Embossing Machine Set-Up Operators; Engraver Set-Up Operators; Extruding and Forming Machine Operators and Tenders, Synthetic or Glass Fibers; Extruding and Forming Machine Setters, Operators, and Tenders, Synthetic and Glass Fibers; Extruding, Forming, Pressing, and Compacting Machine Operators and Tenders; Fabric and Apparel Patternmakers; Fiber Product Cutting Machine Setters and Set-Up Operators; Fiberglass Laminators and Fabricators; Film Laboratory Technicians; others. **PERSONALITY TYPE**—Realistic. Realistic occupations frequently involve work activities that include practical, hands-on problems and solutions. They often deal with plants, animals, and real-world materials like wood, tools, and machinery. Many of the occupations require working outside and do not involve a lot of paperwork or working closely with others.

**EDUCATION/TRAINING PROGRAM(S)**—Chemical Technologist/Technician. **RELATED KNOWLEDGE/COURSES**—**Chemistry:** Knowledge of the chemical composition, structure, and properties of substances and of the chemical processes and transformations that they undergo. This includes uses of chemicals and their interactions, danger signs, production techniques, and disposal methods. **Principles of Mechanical Devices:** Knowledge of machines and tools, including their designs, uses, repair, and maintenance. **Mathematics:** Knowledge of arithmetic, algebra, geometry, calculus, statistics, and their applications. **Public Safety and Security:** Knowledge of relevant equipment, policies, procedures, and strategies to promote effective local, state, or national security operations for the protection of people, data, property, and institutions. **Production and Processing:** Knowledge of raw materials, production processes, quality control, costs, and other techniques for maximizing the effective manufacture and distribution of goods.

# Chemical Technicians

- ▲ Growth: 15%
- ▲ Annual Job Openings: 13,000
- ▲ Annual Earnings: $37,080
- ▲ Education/Training Required: Associate's degree
- ▲ Self-Employed: 0%
- ▲ Part-Time: 11.7%

Conduct chemical and physical laboratory tests to assist scientists in making qualitative and quantitative analyses of solids, liquids, and gaseous materials for purposes such as research and development of new products or processes, quality control, maintenance of environmental standards, and other work involving experimental, theoretical, or practical application of chemistry and related sciences. Tests and analyzes chemical and physical properties of liquids, solids, gases, radioactive and biological materials, and products such as perfumes. Documents results of tests and analyses and writes technical reports or prepares graphs and charts. Directs other workers in compounding and distilling chemicals. Reviews process paperwork for products to ensure compliance to standards and specifications. Cleans and sterilizes laboratory equipment. Prepares chemical solutions for products and processes, following standardized formulas, or creates experimental formulas. Sets up and calibrates laboratory equipment and instruments used for testing, process control, product development, and research. **SKILLS**—Science. Reading Comprehension. Mathematics. Critical Thinking. Active Listening. Writing.

**GOE—Interest Area:** 02. Science, Math, and Engineering. **Work Group:** 02.05. Laboratory Technology. **Other Job Titles in This Work Group:** Biological Technicians; Environmental Science and Protection Technicians, Including Health; Geological and Petroleum Technicians; Geological Data Technicians; Geological Sample Test Technicians; Nuclear Equipment Operation Technicians; Nuclear Technicians; Photographers, Scientific. **PERSONALITY TYPE**—Realistic. Realistic occupations frequently involve work activities that include practical, hands-on problems and solutions. They often deal with plants, animals, and real-world materials like wood, tools, and machinery. Many of the occupations require working outside and do not involve a lot of paperwork or working closely with others.

**EDUCATION/TRAINING PROGRAM(S)**—Chemical Technologist/Technician; Food Sciences and Technology. **RELATED KNOWLEDGE/COURSES**—**Chemistry:** Knowledge of the chemical composition, structure, and properties of substances and of the chemical processes and transformations that they undergo. This includes uses of chemicals and their interactions, danger signs, production techniques, and disposal methods. **Mathematics:** Knowledge of arithmetic, algebra, geometry, calculus, statistics, and their applications. **English Language:** Knowledge of the structure and content of the English language, including the meaning and spelling of words, rules of composition, and grammar. **Physics:** Knowledge and prediction of physical principles and laws and their interrelationships and applications to understanding fluid, material, and atmospheric dynamics and mechanical, electrical, atomic, and sub-atomic structures and processes. **Engineering and Technology:** Knowledge of the practical application of engineering science and technology. This includes applying principles, techniques, procedures, and equipment to the design and production of various goods and services.

# Child Care Workers

- ▲ Growth: 10.6%
- ▲ Annual Job Openings: 370,000
- ▲ Annual Earnings: $16,350
- ▲ Education/Training Required: Short-term on-the-job training
- ▲ Self-Employed: 39.4%
- ▲ Part-Time: 43.4%

**Attend to children at schools, businesses, private households, and child care institutions. Perform a variety of tasks, such as dressing, feeding, bathing, and overseeing play.** Cares for children in institutional setting, such as group homes, nursery schools, private businesses, or schools for the handicapped. Monitors children on life-support equipment to detect malfunctioning of equipment and calls for medical assistance when needed. Wheels handicapped children to classes or other areas of facility while secure in equipment, such as chairs and slings. Reads to children and teaches them simple painting, drawing, handwork, and songs. Assists in preparing food for children and serves meals and refreshments to children and regulates rest periods. Instructs children regarding desirable health and personal habits, such as eating, resting, and toilet habits. Organizes and participates in recreational activities, such as games. Places or hoists children into baths or pools. Disciplines children and recommends or initiates other measures to control behavior, such as caring for own clothing and picking up toys and books. **SKILLS**—Learning Strategies. Reading Comprehension. Monitoring. Service Orientation. Social Perceptiveness. Active Listening.

**GOE—Interest Area:** 12. Education and Social Service. **Work Group:** 12.03. Educational Services. **Other Job Titles in This Work Group:** Adult Literacy, Remedial Education, and GED Teachers and Instructors; Agricultural Sciences Teachers, Postsecondary; Anthropology and Archeology Teachers, Postsecondary; Architecture Teachers, Postsecondary; Archivists; Area, Ethnic, and Cultural Studies Teachers, Postsecondary; Art, Drama, and Music Teachers, Postsecondary; Atmospheric, Earth, Marine, and Space Sciences Teachers, Postsecondary; Audio-Visual Collections Specialists; Biological Science Teachers, Postsecondary; Business Teachers, Postsecondary; Chemistry Teachers, Postsecondary; Communications Teachers, Postsecondary; Computer Science Teachers, Postsecondary; Criminal Justice and Law Enforcement Teachers, Postsecondary; Curators; Economics Teachers, Postsecondary; Education Teachers, Postsecondary; Educational Psychologists; Educational, Vocational, and School Counselors; Elementary School Teachers, Except Special Education; Engineering Teachers, Postsecondary; English Language and Literature Teachers, Postsecondary; Environmental Science Teachers, Postsecondary; Farm and Home Management Advisors; Foreign Language and Literature Teachers, Postsecondary; Forestry and Conservation Science Teachers, Postsecondary; Geography Teachers, Postsecondary; Graduate Teaching Assistants; Health Specialties Teachers, Postsecondary; History Teachers, Postsecondary; Home Economics Teachers, Postsecondary; Kindergarten Teachers, Except Special Education; Law Teachers, Postsecondary; Librarians; Library Assistants, Clerical; Library Science Teachers, Postsecondary; others. **PERSONALITY TYPE**—Social. Social occupations frequently involve working with, communicating with, and teaching people. These occupations often involve helping or providing service to others.

**EDUCATION/TRAINING PROGRAM(S)**—Child Care and Guidance Workers and Managers, General; Child Care and Guidance Workers and Managers, Other; Child Care Provider/Assistant. **RELATED KNOWLEDGE/COURSES—Customer and Personal Service:** Knowledge of principles and processes for providing customer and personal services. This includes customer needs assessment, meeting quality standards for services, and evaluation of customer satisfaction. **Psychology:** Knowledge of human behavior and performance; individual differences in ability, personality, and interests; learning and motivation; psychological research methods; and the assessment and treatment of behavioral and affective disorders. **Education and Training:** Knowledge of principles and methods for curriculum and training design, teaching and instruction for individuals and groups, and the measurement of training effects. **English Language:** Knowledge of the struc- ture and content of the English language, including the meaning and spelling of words, rules of composition, and grammar. **Administration and Management:** Knowledge of business and management principles involved in strategic planning, resource allocation, human resources modeling, leadership technique, production methods, and coordination of people and resources.

# Child Support, Missing Persons, and Unemployment Insurance Fraud Investigators

▲ Growth: 16.4%
▲ Annual Job Openings: 4,000
▲ Annual Earnings: $49,830
▲ Education/Training Required: Work experience in a related occupation
▲ Self-Employed: 0%
▲ Part-Time: 6.5%

**Conduct investigations to locate, arrest, and return fugitives and persons wanted for non-payment of support payments and unemployment insurance fraud and to locate missing persons.** Serves warrants and makes arrests to return persons sought in connection with crimes or for non-payment of child support. Computes amount of child support payments. Testifies in court to present evidence regarding cases. Examines medical and dental x rays, fingerprints, and other information to identify bodies held in morgue. Examines case file to determine that divorce decree and court-ordered judgment for payment are in order. Completes reports to document information acquired during criminal and child support cases and actions taken. Monitors child support payments awarded by court to ensure compliance and enforcement of child support laws. Determines types of court jurisdiction, according to facts and circumstances surrounding case, and files court action. Confers with prosecuting attorney to prepare court case and with court clerk to obtain arrest warrant and schedule court date. Interviews client to obtain information, such as relocation of absent parent, amount of child support awarded, and names of witnesses. Interviews and discusses case with parent charged with nonpayment of support to resolve issues in lieu of filing court proceedings. Reviews files and criminal records to develop possible leads, such as previous addresses and aliases. Prepares file indicating data, such as wage records of accused, witnesses, and blood test results. Obtains extradition papers to bring about return of fugitive. Contacts employers, neighbors, relatives, and law enforcement agencies to locate person sought and verify information gathered about case. **SKILLS**—Active Listening. Speaking. Reading Comprehension. Critical Thinking. Writing.

**GOE—Interest Area:** 04. Law, Law Enforcement, and Public Safety. **Work Group:** 04.03. Law Enforcement. **Other Job Titles in This Work Group:** Animal Control Workers; Bailiffs; Correctional Officers and Jailers; Criminal Investigators and Special Agents; Crossing Guards; Detectives and Criminal Investigators; Fire Investigators; Fish and Game Wardens; Forensic Science Technicians; Gaming Surveillance Officers and Gaming Investigators; Highway Patrol Pilots; Immigration and Customs Inspectors; Lifeguards, Ski Patrol, and Other Recreational Protective Service Workers; Parking Enforcement Workers; Police and Sheriff's Patrol Officers; Police Detectives; Police Identification and Records Officers; Police Patrol Officers; Private Detectives and Investigators; Security Guards; Sheriffs and Deputy Sheriffs; Transit and Railroad Police. **PERSONALITY TYPE**—Enterprising. Enterprising occupations frequently involve starting up and carrying out projects.

These occupations can involve leading people and making many decisions. They sometimes require risk taking and often deal with business.

**EDUCATION/TRAINING PROGRAM(S)**—Law Enforcement/Police Science. **RELATED KNOWLEDGE/COURSES**—**Law and Government:** Knowledge of laws, legal codes, court procedures, precedents, government regulations, executive orders, agency rules, and the democratic political process. **Public Safety and Security:** Knowledge of relevant equipment, policies, procedures, and strategies to promote effective local, state, or national security operations for the protection of people, data, property, and institutions. **Economics and Accounting:** Knowledge of economic and accounting principles and practices, the financial markets, banking, and the analysis and reporting of financial data. **English Language:** Knowledge of the structure and content of the English language, including the meaning and spelling of words, rules of composition, and grammar. **Mathematics:** Knowledge of arithmetic, algebra, geometry, calculus, statistics, and their applications.

# Civil Drafters

- ▲ Growth: 20.8%
- ▲ Annual Job Openings: 12,000
- ▲ Annual Earnings: $37,100
- ▲ Education/Training Required: Post-secondary vocational training
- ▲ Self-Employed: 4.6%
- ▲ Part-Time: 7.9%

**Prepare drawings and topographical and relief maps used in civil engineering projects, such as highways, bridges, pipelines, flood control projects, and water and sewerage control systems.** Draws maps, diagrams, and profiles, using cross-sections and surveys, to represent elevations, topographical contours, subsurface formations, and structures. Accompanies field survey crew to locate grading markers or to collect data required to revise construction drawings. Correlates, interprets, and modifies data obtained from topographical surveys, well logs, and geophysical prospecting reports. Finishes and duplicates drawings according to required mediums and specifications for reproduction, using blueprinting, photographing, or other duplicating methods. Identifies symbols located on topographical surveys to denote geological and geophysical formations or oil field installations. Calculates excavation tonnage and prepares graphs and fill-hauling diagrams used in earth-moving operations. Computes and represents characteristics and dimensions of borehole, such as depth, degree, and direction of inclination. Reviews rough sketches, drawings, specifications, and other engineering data received from civil engineer. Plots boreholes for oil and gas wells from photographic subsurface survey recordings and other data, using computer assisted drafting equipment. Drafts plans and detailed drawings for structures, installations, and construction projects, such as highways, sewage disposal systems, and dikes. **SKILLS**—Mathematics. Reading Comprehension. Operations Analysis. Active Learning. Complex Problem Solving. Critical Thinking.

**GOE—Interest Area:** 02. Science, Math, and Engineering. **Work Group:** 02.08. Engineering Technology. **Other Job Titles in This Work Group:** Aerospace Engineering and Operations Technicians; Architectural and Civil Drafters; Architectural Drafters; Calibration and Instrumentation Technicians; Cartographers and Photogrammetrists; Civil Engineering Technicians; Construction and Building Inspectors; Drafters, All Other; Electrical and Electronic Engineering Technicians; Electrical and Electronics Drafters; Electrical Drafters; Electrical Engineering Technicians; Electro-Mechanical Technicians; Electronic Drafters; Electronics Engineering Technicians; Engineering Technicians, Except Drafters, All Other; Environmental Engineering Technicians; Industrial Engineering Technicians; Mapping Technicians; Mechanical Drafters; Mechanical Engineering

Technicians; Numerical Tool and Process Control Programmers; Pressure Vessel Inspectors; Surveying and Mapping Technicians; Surveying Technicians; Surveyors. **PERSONALITY TYPE**—Realistic. Realistic occupations frequently involve work activities that include practical, hands-on problems and solutions. They often deal with plants, animals, and real-world materials like wood, tools, and machinery. Many of the occupations require working outside and do not involve a lot of paperwork or working closely with others.

**EDUCATION/TRAINING PROGRAM(S)**—Architectural Drafting; Civil/Structural Drafting. **RELATED KNOWLEDGE/COURSES**—**Design:** Knowledge of design techniques, tools, and principles involved in production of precision technical plans, blueprints, drawings, and models. **Mathematics:** Knowledge of arithmetic, algebra, geometry, calculus, statistics, and their applications. **Engineering and Technology:** Knowledge of the practical application of engineering science and technology. This includes applying principles, techniques, procedures, and equipment to the design and production of various goods and services. **Computers and Electronics:** Knowledge of circuit boards, processors, chips, electronic equipment, and computer hardware and software, including applications and programming. **Physics:** Knowledge and prediction of physical principles and laws and their interrelationships and applications to understanding fluid, material, and atmospheric dynamics and mechanical, electrical, atomic, and sub-atomic structures and processes.

# Claims Examiners, Property and Casualty Insurance

- ▲ Growth: 15.1%
- ▲ Annual Job Openings: 25,000
- ▲ Annual Earnings: $44,000
- ▲ Education/Training Required: Long-term on-the-job training
- ▲ Self-Employed: 2.3%
- ▲ Part-Time: 7.3%

Review settled insurance claims to determine that payments and settlements have been made in accordance with company practices and procedures. Report overpayments, underpayments, and other irregularities. Confer with legal counsel on claims requiring litigation. Analyzes data used in settling claim to determine its validity in payment of claims. Reports overpayments, underpayments, and other irregularities. Confers with legal counsel on claims requiring litigation. **SKILLS**—Reading Comprehension. Mathematics. Writing. Critical Thinking. Active Listening. Judgment and Decision Making. Monitoring.

**GOE**—**Interest Area:** 13. General Management and Support. **Work Group:** 13.02. Management Support. **Other Job Titles in This Work Group:** Accountants; Accountants and Auditors; Appraisers and Assessors of Real Estate; Appraisers, Real Estate; Assessors; Auditors; Budget Analysts; Claims Adjusters, Examiners, and Investigators; Compensation, Benefits, and Job Analysis Specialists; Cost Estimators; Credit Analysts; Employment Interviewers, Private or Public Employment Service; Employment, Recruitment, and Placement Specialists; Financial Analysts; Human Resources, Training, and Labor Relations Specialists, All Other; Insurance Adjusters, Examiners, and Investigators; Insurance Appraisers, Auto Damage; Insurance Underwriters; Loan Counselors; Loan Officers; Logisticians; Management Analysts; Market Research Analysts; Personnel Recruiters; Purchasing Agents and Buyers, Farm Products; Purchasing Agents, Except Wholesale, Retail, and Farm Products; Tax Examiners, Collectors, and Revenue Agents; Training and Development Specialists; Wholesale and Retail Buyers, Except Farm Products. **PERSONALITY TYPE**—Conventional. Conventional occupations frequently involve following set procedures and routines. These occupations can include working with data and details more than with ideas. Usually there is a clear line of authority to follow.

EDUCATION/TRAINING PROGRAM(S)—Human Resources Management; Insurance and Risk Management; Insurance Marketing Operations; Labor/Personnel Relations and Studies; Purchasing, Procurement and Contracts Management. **RELATED KNOWLEDGE/COURSES—Mathematics:** Knowledge of arithmetic, algebra, geometry, calculus, statistics, and their applications. **Law and Government:** Knowledge of laws, legal codes, court procedures, precedents, government regulations, executive orders, agency rules, and the democratic political process. **English Language:** Knowledge of the structure and content of the English language, including the meaning and spelling of words, rules of composition, and grammar. **Computers and Electronics:** Knowledge of cir-

cuit boards, processors, chips, electronic equipment, and computer hardware and software, including applications and programming. **Economics and Accounting:** Knowledge of economic and accounting principles and practices, the financial markets, banking, and the analysis and reporting of financial data. **Administration and Management:** Knowledge of business and management principles involved in strategic planning, resource allocation, human resources modeling, leadership technique, production methods, and coordination of people and resources. **Communications and Media:** Knowledge of media production, communication, and dissemination techniques and methods. This includes alternative ways to inform and entertain via written, oral, and visual media.

# Cleaners of Vehicles and Equipment

- ▲ Growth: 18.8%
- ▲ Annual Job Openings: 86,000
- ▲ Annual Earnings: $17,380
- ▲ Education/Training Required: Short-term on-the-job training
- ▲ Self-Employed: 6%
- ▲ Part-Time: 22.9%

**Wash or otherwise clean vehicles, machinery, and other equipment. Use such materials as water, cleaning agents, brushes, cloths, and hoses.** Scrubs, scrapes, or sprays machine parts, equipment, or vehicles, using scrapers, brushes, cleaners, disinfectants, insecticides, acid, and abrasives. Monitors operation of cleaning machines and stops machine or notifies supervisor when malfunctions occur. Maintains inventories of supplies. Records production and operational data on specified forms. Collects and tests samples of cleaning solutions and vapors. Transports materials, equipment, or supplies to and from work area, using carts or hoists. Lubricates machinery, vehicles, and equipment and performs minor repairs and adjustments, using hand tools. Applies paints, dyes, polishes, reconditioners, and masking materials to vehicles to preserve, protect, or restore color and condition. Examines and inspects parts, equipment, and vehicles for cleanliness, damage, and compliance with standards or regulations. Places

objects on drying racks or dyes surfaces, using cloth, squeegees, or air compressors. Disassembles and reassembles machines or equipment or removes and reattaches vehicle parts and trim, using hand tools. Connects hoses and lines to pumps and other equipment. Mixes cleaning solutions and abrasive compositions and other compounds according to formula. Pre-soaks or rinses machine parts, equipment, or vehicles by immersing objects in cleaning solutions or water, manually or using hoists. Turns valves or handles on equipment to regulate pressure and flow of water, air, steam, or abrasives from sprayer nozzles. Turns valves or disconnects hoses to eliminate water, cleaning solutions, or vapors from machinery or tanks. Sweeps, shovels, or vacuums loose debris and salvageable scrap into containers and removes from work area. Presses buttons to activate cleaning equipment or machines. **SKILLS—Operation and Control. Equipment Selection. Monitoring. Reading Comprehension.**

GOE—**Interest Area:** 11. Recreation, Travel, and Other Personal Services. **Work Group:** 11.08. Other Personal Services. **Other Job Titles in This Work Group:** Cooks, Private Household; Embalmers; Funeral Attendants; Personal and Home Care Aides; Personal Care and Service Workers, All Other. **PERSONALITY TYPE**—Realistic. Realistic occupations frequently involve work activities that include practical, hands-on problems and solutions. They often deal with plants, animals, and real-world materials like wood, tools, and machinery. Many of the occupations require working outside and do not involve a lot of paperwork or working closely with others.

**EDUCATION/TRAINING PROGRAM(S)**—No data available. **RELATED KNOWLEDGE/ COURSES**—**Principles of Mechanical Devices:** Knowledge of machines and tools, including their de-

signs, uses, repair, and maintenance. **Chemistry:** Knowledge of the chemical composition, structure, and properties of substances and of the chemical processes and transformations that they undergo. This includes uses of chemicals and their interactions, danger signs, production techniques, and disposal methods. **Mathematics:** Knowledge of arithmetic, algebra, geometry, calculus, statistics, and their applications. **Clerical Studies:** Knowledge of administrative and clerical procedures and systems such as word processing, managing files and records, stenography and transcription, designing forms, and other office procedures and terminology. **Engineering and Technology:** Knowledge of the practical application of engineering science and technology. This includes applying principles, techniques, procedures, and equipment to the design and production of various goods and services.

# Coaches and Scouts

▲ Growth: 17.6%
▲ Annual Job Openings: 19,000
▲ Annual Earnings: $33,470
▲ Education/Training Required: Long-term on-the-job training
▲ Self-Employed: 30%
▲ Part-Time: 25.3%

**Instruct or coach groups or individuals in the fundamentals of sports. Demonstrate techniques and methods of participation. May evaluate athletes' strengths and weaknesses as possible recruits or to improve the athletes' technique to prepare them for competition. Those required to hold teaching degrees should be reported in the appropriate teaching category.** Analyzes athletes' performance and reviews game statistics or records to determine fitness and potential for professional sports. Evaluates team and opposition capabilities to develop and plan game strategy. Evaluates athletes' skills and discusses or recommends acquisition, trade, or position assignment of players. Negotiates with professional athletes or representatives to obtain services and arrange contracts. Prepares scouting reports detailing information such as selection or rejection of athletes and locations identified for future recruitment.

Instructs athletes, individually or in groups, demonstrating sport techniques and game strategies. Plans and directs physical conditioning program for athletes to achieve maximum athletic performance. Observes athletes to determine areas of deficiency and need for individual or team improvement. **SKILLS**—Instructing. Negotiation. Writing. Management of Personnel Resources. Judgment and Decision Making. Reading Comprehension. Time Management.

GOE—**Interest Area:** 01. Arts, Entertainment, and Media. **Work Group:** 01.10. Sports: Coaching, Instructing, Officiating, and Performing. **Other Job Titles in This Work Group:** Athletes and Sports Competitors; Fitness Trainers and Aerobics Instructors; Umpires, Referees, and Other Sports Officials. **PERSONALITY TYPE**—Enterprising. Enterprising occupations frequently involve starting up and carrying out projects.

These occupations can involve leading people and making many decisions. They sometimes require risk taking and often deal with business.

**EDUCATION/TRAINING PROGRAM(S)**—Health and Physical Education, General; Physical Education Teaching and Coaching; Sport and Fitness Administration/Management. **RELATED KNOWLEDGE/ COURSES—Education and Training:** Knowledge of principles and methods for curriculum and training design, teaching and instruction for individuals and groups, and the measurement of training effects. **Psychology:** Knowledge of human behavior and performance; individual differences in ability, personality, and interests; learning and motivation; psychological re-search methods; and the assessment and treatment of behavioral and affective disorders. **English Language:** Knowledge of the structure and content of the English language, including the meaning and spelling of words, rules of composition, and grammar. **Sales and Marketing:** Knowledge of principles and methods for showing, promoting, and selling products or services. This includes marketing strategy and tactics, product demonstration, sales techniques, and sales control systems. **Administration and Management:** Knowledge of business and management principles involved in strategic planning, resource allocation, human resources modeling, leadership technique, production methods, and coordination of people and resources.

# Coating, Painting, and Spraying Machine Operators and Tenders

- ▲ Growth: 11.9%
- ▲ Annual Job Openings: 18,000
- ▲ Annual Earnings: $25,140
- ▲ Education/Training Required: Moderate-term on-the-job training
- ▲ Self-Employed: 7.4%
- ▲ Part-Time: 5.7%

**Coating Machine Operators and Tenders: Operate or tend machines to coat any of a wide variety of items: Coating food products with sugar, chocolate, or butter; coat paper and paper products with chemical solutions, wax, or glazes; or coat fabric with rubber or plastic. Painting and Spraying Machine Operators and Tenders: Operate or tend machines to spray or paint decorative, protective, or other coating or finish, such as adhesive, lacquer, paint, stain, latex, preservative, oil, or other solutions. May apply coating or finish to any of a wide variety of items or materials, such as wood and wood products, ceramics, and glass. Includes workers who apply coating or finish to materials preparatory to further processing or to consumer use.** Observes machine operation and gauges to detect defects or deviations from standards. Fills hopper, reservoir, trough, or pan with material used to coat, paint, or spray, using conveyor or pail. Measures and mixes specified quantities of substances to create coatings, paints, or sprays. Threads or feeds item or product through or around machine rollers and dryers. Examines, measures, weighs, or tests sample product to ensure conformance to specifications. Cleans machine, equipment, and work area, using water, solvents, and other cleaning aids. Records production data. Transfers completed item or product from machine to drying or storage area, using handcart, handtruck, or crane. Places item or product on feedrack, spindle, or reel strand to coat, paint, or spray, using hands, hoist, or trucklift. Aligns or fastens machine parts such as rollers, guides, brushes, and blades to secure roll, using hand tools. Attaches specified hose or nozzle to machine, using wrench and pliers. Starts and stops operation of machine, using lever or button. Turns dial, handwheel, valve, or switch to control and adjust temperature, speed, and flow of product or machine. **SKILLS**—Operation and Control. Operation Monitoring. Mathematics.

**GOE—Interest Area:** 08. Industrial Production. **Work Group:** 08.03. Production Work. **Other Job Titles in This Work Group:** Bakers, Manufacturing; Bindery Machine Operators and Tenders; Brazers; Cementing and Gluing Machine Operators and Tenders; Chemical Equipment Controllers and Operators; Chemical Equipment Operators and Tenders; Chemical Equipment Tenders; Cleaning, Washing, and Metal Pickling Equipment Operators and Tenders; Coil Winders, Tapers, and Finishers; Combination Machine Tool Operators and Tenders, Metal and Plastic; Computer-Controlled Machine Tool Operators, Metal and Plastic; Cooling and Freezing Equipment Operators and Tenders; Crushing, Grinding, and Polishing Machine Setters, Operators, and Tenders; Cutters and Trimmers, Hand; Cutting and Slicing Machine Operators and Tenders; Cutting and Slicing Machine Setters, Operators, and Tenders; Design Printing Machine Setters and Set-Up Operators; Electrolytic Plating and Coating Machine Operators and Tenders, Metal and Plastic; Electrolytic Plating and Coating Machine Setters and Set-Up Operators, Metal and Plastic; Electrotypers and Stereotypers; Embossing Machine Set-Up Operators; Engraver Set-Up Operators; Extruding and Forming Machine Operators and Tenders, Synthetic or Glass Fibers; Extruding and Forming Machine Setters, Operators, and Tenders, Synthetic and Glass Fibers; Extruding, Forming, Pressing, and Compacting Machine Operators and Tenders; Fabric and Apparel Patternmakers; Fiber Product Cutting Machine Setters and Set-Up Operators; Fiberglass Laminators and Fabricators; Film Laboratory Technicians; Fitters, Structural Metal—Precision; others. **PERSONALITY TYPE**—Realistic. Realistic occupations frequently in-

volve work activities that include practical, hands-on problems and solutions. They often deal with plants, animals, and real-world materials like wood, tools, and machinery. Many of the occupations require working outside and do not involve a lot of paperwork or working closely with others.

**EDUCATION/TRAINING PROGRAM(S)**—Industrial Machinery Maintenance and Repairer; Machinist/Machine Technologist; Precision Metal Workers, Other; Precision Production Trades, Other. **RELATED KNOWLEDGE/COURSES—Production and Processing:** Knowledge of raw materials, production processes, quality control, costs, and other techniques for maximizing the effective manufacture and distribution of goods. **Principles of Mechanical Devices:** Knowledge of machines and tools, including their designs, uses, repair, and maintenance. **Engineering and Technology:** Knowledge of the practical application of engineering science and technology. This includes applying principles, techniques, procedures, and equipment to the design and production of various goods and services. **Chemistry:** Knowledge of the chemical composition, structure, and properties of substances and of the chemical processes and transformations that they undergo. This includes uses of chemicals and their interactions, danger signs, production techniques, and disposal methods. **Mathematics:** Knowledge of arithmetic, algebra, geometry, calculus, statistics, and their applications.

# Coating, Painting, and Spraying Machine Setters and Set-Up Operators

- ▲ Growth: 11.9%
- ▲ Annual Job Openings: 18,000
- ▲ Annual Earnings: $25,140
- ▲ Education/Training Required: Moderate-term on-the-job training
- ▲ Self-Employed: 7.4%
- ▲ Part-Time: 5.7%

Set up or set up and operate machines to coat or paint any of a wide variety of products, such as food products, glassware, and cloth, ceramic, metal, plastic, paper, and wood products, with lacquer, silver and copper solution, rubber, paint, varnish, glaze, enamel, oil, or

rust-proofing materials. Sets up and operates machines to paint or coat products with such materials as silver and copper solution, rubber, paint, glaze, oil, or rust-proofing materials. Removes materials, parts, or workpieces from painting or coating machines, using hand tools. Records operational data on specified forms. Cleans and maintains coating and painting machines, using hand tools. Measures thickness and quality of coating, using micrometer. Examines and tests solutions, paints, products, and workpieces to ensure specifications are met. Observes and adjusts loaded workpiece or machine, according to specifications. Selects and loads materials, parts, and workpieces on machine, using hand tools. Starts pumps to mix solutions and to activate coating or painting machines. Operates auxiliary machines or equipment used on the coating or painting process. Weighs or measures chemicals, coatings, or paints and adds to machine. Turns valves and adjusts controls to regulate speed of conveyor, temperature, air pressure and circulation, and flow or spray of coating or paint. **SKILLS**—Equipment Selection. Operation and Control. Operation Monitoring. Quality Control Analysis.

**GOE**—**Interest Area:** 08. Industrial Production. **Work Group:** 08.02. Production Technology. **Other Job Titles in This Work Group:** Aircraft Rigging Assemblers; Aircraft Structure Assemblers, Precision; Aircraft Structure, Surfaces, Rigging, and Systems Assemblers; Aircraft Systems Assemblers, Precision; Bench Workers, Jewelry; Bindery Machine Setters and Set-Up Operators; Bindery Workers; Bookbinders; Buffing and Polishing Set-Up Operators; Casting Machine Set-Up Operators; Coating, Painting, and Spraying Machine Setters, Operators, and Tenders; Combination Machine Tool Setters and Set-Up Operators, Metal and Plastic; Cutting, Punching, and Press Machine Setters, Operators, and Tenders, Metal and Plastic; Dental Laboratory Technicians; Drilling and Boring Machine Tool Setters, Operators, and Tenders, Metal and Plastic; Electrical and Electronic Equipment Assemblers; Electrical and Electronic Inspectors and Testers; Electromechanical Equipment Assemblers; Engine and Other Machine Assemblers; Extruding and Drawing Machine Setters, Operators, and Tenders, Metal and Plastic; Extruding, Forming, Pressing, and Compacting Machine Setters

and Set-Up Operators; Extruding, Forming, Pressing, and Compacting Machine Setters, Operators, and Tenders; Forging Machine Setters, Operators, and Tenders, Metal and Plastic; Foundry Mold and Coremakers; Gem and Diamond Workers; Grinding, Honing, Lapping, and Deburring Machine Set-Up Operators; Grinding, Lapping, Polishing, and Buffing Machine Tool Setters, Operators, and Tenders, Metal and Plastic; Heat Treating Equipment Setters, Operators, and Tenders, Metal and Plastic; Heat Treating, Annealing, and Tempering Machine Operators and Tenders, Metal and Plastic; others. **PERSONALITY TYPE**—Realistic. Realistic occupations frequently involve work activities that include practical, hands-on problems and solutions. They often deal with plants, animals, and real-world materials like wood, tools, and machinery. Many of the occupations require working outside and do not involve a lot of paperwork or working closely with others.

**EDUCATION/TRAINING PROGRAM(S)**—Industrial Machinery Maintenance and Repairer; Machinist/Machine Technologist; Precision Metal Workers, Other; Precision Production Trades, Other. **RELATED KNOWLEDGE/COURSES**—**Principles of Mechanical Devices:** Knowledge of machines and tools, including their designs, uses, repair, and maintenance. **Production and Processing:** Knowledge of raw materials, production processes, quality control, costs, and other techniques for maximizing the effective manufacture and distribution of goods. **Chemistry:** Knowledge of the chemical composition, structure, and properties of substances and of the chemical processes and transformations that they undergo. This includes uses of chemicals and their interactions, danger signs, production techniques, and disposal methods. **Mathematics:** Knowledge of arithmetic, algebra, geometry, calculus, statistics, and their applications. **Clerical Studies:** Knowledge of administrative and clerical procedures and systems such as word processing, managing files and records, stenography and transcription, designing forms, and other office procedures and terminology.

# Combination Machine Tool Operators and Tenders, Metal and Plastic

▲ Growth: 14.7%
▲ Annual Job Openings: 21,000
▲ Annual Earnings: $29,350
▲ Education/Training Required: Moderate-term on-the-job training
▲ Self-Employed: 0%
▲ Part-Time: 2.3%

Operate or tend more than one type of cutting or forming machine tool which has been previously set up. Includes such machine tools as band saws, press brakes, slitting machines, drills, lathes, and boring machines. Activates and tends or operates machines to cut, shape, thread, bore, drill, tap, bend, or mill metal or non-metallic material. Positions, adjusts, and secures workpiece against stops, on arbor, or in chuck, fixture, or automatic feeding mechanism manually or using hoist. Aligns layout marks with die or blade. Inspects workpiece for defects and measures workpiece, using rule, template, or other measuring instruments to determine accuracy of machine operation. Performs minor machine maintenance, such as oiling or cleaning machines, dies, or workpieces or adding coolant to machine reservoir. Removes burrs, sharp edges, rust, or scale from workpiece, using file, hand grinder, wire brush, or power tools. Installs machine components, such as chucks, boring bars, or cutting tools, according to specifications, using hand tools. Sets machine stops or guides to specified length as indicated by scale, rule or template. Adjusts machine components and changes worn accessories, such as cutting tools and brushes, using hand tools. Extracts or lifts jammed pieces from machine, using fingers, wire hooks, or lift bar. Reads job specifications to determine machine adjustments and material requirements. Observes machine operation to detect workpiece defects or machine malfunction. **SKILLS**—Operation and Control. Operation Monitoring. Quality Control Analysis. Equipment Maintenance. Equipment Selection. Installation. Reading Comprehension.

**GOE—Interest Area:** 08. Industrial Production. **Work Group:** 08.03. Production Work. **Other Job Titles in This Work Group:** Bakers, Manufacturing; Bindery Machine Operators and Tenders; Brazers; Cementing and Gluing Machine Operators and Tenders; Chemical Equipment Controllers and Operators; Chemical Equipment Operators and Tenders; Chemical Equipment Tenders; Cleaning, Washing, and Metal Pickling Equipment Operators and Tenders; Coating, Painting, and Spraying Machine Operators and Tenders; Coil Winders, Tapers, and Finishers; Computer-Controlled Machine Tool Operators, Metal and Plastic; Cooling and Freezing Equipment Operators and Tenders; Crushing, Grinding, and Polishing Machine Setters, Operators, and Tenders; Cutters and Trimmers, Hand; Cutting and Slicing Machine Operators and Tenders; Cutting and Slicing Machine Setters, Operators, and Tenders; Design Printing Machine Setters and Set-Up Operators; Electrolytic Plating and Coating Machine Operators and Tenders, Metal and Plastic; Electrolytic Plating and Coating Machine Setters and Set-Up Operators, Metal and Plastic; Electrotypers and Stereotypers; Embossing Machine Set-Up Operators; Engraver Set-Up Operators; Extruding and Forming Machine Operators and Tenders, Synthetic or Glass Fibers; Extruding and Forming Machine Setters, Operators, and Tenders, Synthetic and Glass Fibers; Extruding, Forming, Pressing, and Compacting Machine Operators and Tenders; Fabric and Apparel Patternmakers; Fiber Product Cutting Machine Setters and Set-Up Operators; Fiberglass Laminators and Fabricators; Film Laboratory Technicians; Fitters, Structural Metal—Precision; others. **PERSONALITY TYPE**—Realistic. Realistic occupations frequently involve work activities that include practical, hands-on problems and solutions. They often deal with plants, animals, and real-world materials like wood, tools, and machinery. Many of the occupations require working outside and do not involve a lot of paperwork or working closely with others.

EDUCATION/TRAINING PROGRAM(S)—Machine Shop Assistant; Machinist/Machine Technologist. **RELATED KNOWLEDGE/COURSES—Production and Processing:** Knowledge of raw materials, production processes, quality control, costs, and other techniques for maximizing the effective manufacture and distribution of goods. **Principles of Mechanical Devices:** Knowledge of machines and tools, including their designs, uses, repair, and maintenance. **Mathematics:** Knowledge of arithmetic, algebra, geometry, calculus, statistics, and their applications. **Engineering and Tech-**

**nology:** Knowledge of the practical application of engineering science and technology. This includes applying principles, techniques, procedures, and equipment to the design and production of various goods and services. **Design:** Knowledge of design techniques, tools, and principles involved in production of precision technical plans, blueprints, drawings, and models. **Building and Construction:** Knowledge of materials, methods, and tools involved in the construction or repair of houses, buildings, or other structures such as highways and roads.

# Combination Machine Tool Setters and Set-Up Operators, Metal and Plastic

- ▲ Growth: 14.7%
- ▲ Annual Job Openings: 21,000
- ▲ Annual Earnings: $29,350
- ▲ Education/Training Required: Moderate-term on-the-job training
- ▲ Self-Employed: 0%
- ▲ Part-Time: 2.3%

**Set up or set up and operate more than one type of cutting or forming machine tool, such as gear hobbers, lathes, press brakes, shearing, and boring machines.** Sets up and operates lathes, cutters, borers, millers, grinders, presses, drills, and auxiliary machines to make metallic and plastic workpieces. Computes data, such as gear dimensions and machine settings, applying knowledge of shop mathematics. Instructs operators or other workers in machine setup and operation. Records operational data such as pressure readings, length of stroke, feeds, and speeds. Makes minor electrical and mechanical repairs and adjustments to machines and notifies supervisor when major service is required. Lifts, positions, and secures workpieces in holding devices, using hoists and hand tools. Inspects first-run workpieces and verifies conformance to specifications to check accuracy of machine setup. Measures and marks reference points and cutting lines on workpiece, using traced templates, compasses, and rules. Moves controls or mounts gears, cams, or templates in machine to set feed rate and cutting speed, depth, and angle. Selects, installs, and adjusts alignment of drills, cutters, dies, guides, and holding devices, using template, measuring instruments, and hand tools. Starts machine and

turns handwheels or valves to engage feeding, cooling, and lubricating mechanisms. Reads blueprint or job order to determine product specifications and tooling instructions and to plan operational sequences. Monitors machine operation and moves controls to align and adjust position of workpieces and action of cutting tools. **SKILLS**—Quality Control Analysis. Operation and Control. Mathematics. Operation Monitoring. Equipment Maintenance. Instructing.

**GOE—Interest Area:** 08. Industrial Production. **Work Group:** 08.02. Production Technology. **Other Job Titles in This Work Group:** Aircraft Rigging Assemblers; Aircraft Structure Assemblers, Precision; Aircraft Structure, Surfaces, Rigging, and Systems Assemblers; Aircraft Systems Assemblers, Precision; Bench Workers, Jewelry; Bindery Machine Setters and Set-Up Operators; Bindery Workers; Bookbinders; Buffing and Polishing Set-Up Operators; Casting Machine Set-Up Operators; Coating, Painting, and Spraying Machine Setters and Set-Up Operators; Coating, Painting, and Spraying Machine Setters, Operators, and Tenders; Cutting, Punching, and Press Machine Setters, Operators, and Tenders, Metal and Plastic; Dental Laboratory Technicians; Drilling and Boring Machine Tool Setters,

Operators, and Tenders, Metal and Plastic; Electrical and Electronic Equipment Assemblers; Electrical and Electronic Inspectors and Testers; Electromechanical Equipment Assemblers; Engine and Other Machine Assemblers; Extruding and Drawing Machine Setters, Operators, and Tenders, Metal and Plastic; Extruding, Forming, Pressing, and Compacting Machine Setters and Set-Up Operators; Extruding, Forming, Pressing, and Compacting Machine Setters, Operators, and Tenders; Forging Machine Setters, Operators, and Tenders, Metal and Plastic; Foundry Mold and Coremakers; Gem and Diamond Workers; Grinding, Honing, Lapping, and Deburring Machine Set-Up Operators; Grinding, Lapping, Polishing, and Buffing Machine Tool Setters, Operators, and Tenders, Metal and Plastic; Heat Treating Equipment Setters, Operators, and Tenders, Metal and Plastic; Heat Treating, Annealing, and Tempering Machine Operators and Tenders, Metal and Plastic; others. **PERSONALITY TYPE**—Realistic. Realistic occupations frequently involve work activities that include practical, hands-on problems and solutions. They often deal with plants, animals, and real-world materials like wood, tools, and machinery. Many of the occupations require working outside and do not involve a lot of paperwork or working closely with others.

**EDUCATION/TRAINING PROGRAM(S)**—Machine Shop Assistant; Machinist/Machine Technologist. **RELATED KNOWLEDGE/COURSES—Principles of Mechanical Devices:** Knowledge of machines and tools, including their designs, uses, repair, and maintenance. **Design:** Knowledge of design techniques, tools, and principles involved in production of precision technical plans, blueprints, drawings, and models. **Mathematics:** Knowledge of arithmetic, algebra, geometry, calculus, statistics, and their applications. **Engineering and Technology:** Knowledge of the practical application of engineering science and technology. This includes applying principles, techniques, procedures, and equipment to the design and production of various goods and services. **Production and Processing:** Knowledge of raw materials, production processes, quality control, costs, and other techniques for maximizing the effective manufacture and distribution of goods.

# Combined Food Preparation and Serving Workers, Including Fast Food

- ▲ Growth: 30.5%
- ▲ Annual Job Openings: 737,000
- ▲ Annual Earnings: $14,240
- ▲ Education/Training Required: Short-term on-the-job training
- ▲ Self-Employed: 0.1%
- ▲ Part-Time: 57.4%

**Perform duties which combine both food preparation and food service.** Selects food items from serving or storage areas and places food and beverage items on serving tray or in takeout bag. Notifies kitchen personnel of shortages or special orders. Receives payment. Requests and records customer order and computes bill. Makes and serves hot and cold beverages or desserts. Cooks or re-heats food items, such as french fries. **SKILLS**—Mathematics. Speaking.

**GOE—Interest Area:** 11. Recreation, Travel, and Other Personal Services. **Work Group:** 11.05. Food and Beverage Services. **Other Job Titles in This Work Group:** Bakers; Bakers, Bread and Pastry; Bartenders; Butchers and Meat Cutters; Chefs and Head Cooks; Cooks, All Other; Cooks, Fast Food; Cooks, Institution and Cafeteria; Cooks, Restaurant; Cooks, Short Order; Counter Attendants, Cafeteria, Food Concession, and Coffee Shop; Dining Room and Cafeteria Attendants and Bartender Helpers; Dishwashers; Food Preparation and Serving Related Workers, All Other; Food Preparation Workers; Food Servers, Nonrestaurant; Hosts and Hostesses, Restaurant, Lounge, and Coffee Shop; Waiters and Waitresses. **PERSONALITY TYPE**—Realistic. Realistic occupations frequently involve work activities that include practical, hands-on problems and solutions. They often deal with plants, animals, and real-world materials like wood, tools, and machinery. Many of the occupations require working outside and do not involve a lot of paperwork or working closely with others.

**EDUCATION/TRAINING PROGRAM(S)—** Kitchen Personnel/Cook and Assistant Training. **RELATED KNOWLEDGE/COURSES—Customer and Personal Service:** Knowledge of principles and processes for providing customer and personal services. This includes customer needs assessment, meeting quality standards for services, and evaluation of customer satisfaction. **Mathematics:** Knowledge of arithmetic, algebra, geometry, calculus, statistics, and their appli-

cations. **Sales and Marketing:** Knowledge of principles and methods for showing, promoting, and selling products or services. This includes marketing strategy and tactics, product demonstration, sales techniques, and sales control systems. **English Language:** Knowledge of the structure and content of the English language, including the meaning and spelling of words, rules of composition, and grammar. **Clerical Studies:** Knowledge of administrative and clerical procedures and systems such as word processing, managing files and records, stenography and transcription, designing forms, and other office procedures and terminology.

# Commercial Pilots

▲ Growth: 26.9%
▲ Annual Job Openings: 1,000
▲ Annual Earnings: $51,370
▲ Education/Training Required: Post-secondary vocational training
▲ Self-Employed: 9.5%
▲ Part-Time: 23.3%

**Pilot and navigate the flight of small fixed or rotary winged aircraft, primarily for the transport of cargo and passengers. Requires Commercial Rating.** Starts engines, operates controls, and pilots airplane to transport passengers, mail, or freight, adhering to flight plan and regulations and procedures. Obtains and reviews data, such as load weight, fuel supply, weather conditions, and flight schedule. Plots flight pattern and files flight plan with appropriate officials. Orders changes in fuel supply, load, route, or schedule to ensure safety of flight. Conducts preflight checks and reads gauges to verify that fluids and pressure are at prescribed levels. Operates radio equipment and contacts control tower for takeoff, clearance, arrival instructions, and other information. Coordinates flight activities with ground crew and air-traffic control and informs crew members of flight and test procedures. Holds commercial pilot's license issued by Federal Aviation Administration. Conducts in-flight tests and evaluations, at specified altitudes, in all types of weather to determine receptivity and other characteristics of equipment and systems. Logs information, such as flight time, altitude

flown, and fuel consumption. Plans and formulates flight activities and test schedules and prepares flight evaluation reports. Gives training and instruction in aircraft operations for students and other pilots. **SKILLS—**Operation and Control. Operation Monitoring. Instructing. Coordination. Judgment and Decision Making.

**GOE—Interest Area:** 07. Transportation. **Work Group:** 07.03. Air Vehicle Operation. **Other Job Titles in This Work Group:** Airline Pilots, Copilots, and Flight Engineers. **PERSONALITY TYPE—**Realistic. Realistic occupations frequently involve work activities that include practical, hands-on problems and solutions. They often deal with plants, animals, and real-world materials like wood, tools, and machinery. Many of the occupations require working outside and do not involve a lot of paperwork or working closely with others.

**EDUCATION/TRAINING PROGRAM(S)—**Aircraft Pilot (Private); Aircraft Pilot and Navigator (Professional). **RELATED KNOWLEDGE/COURSES— Transportation:** Knowledge of principles and methods

C

for moving people or goods by air, rail, sea, or road, including the relative costs and benefits. **Physics:** Knowledge and prediction of physical principles and laws and their interrelationships and applications to understanding fluid, material, and atmospheric dynamics and mechanical, electrical, atomic, and sub-atomic structures and processes. **Geography:** Knowledge of principles and methods for describing the features of land, sea, and air masses, including their physical characteristics, locations, interrelationships, and distribution of plant, animal, and human life. **Public Safety and Security:** Knowledge of relevant equipment, policies, procedures, and strategies to promote effective local, state, or national security operations for the protection of people, data, property, and institutions. **Mathematics:** Knowledge of arithmetic, algebra, geometry, calculus, statistics, and their applications. **Telecommunications:** Knowledge of transmission, broadcasting, switching, control, and operation of telecommunications systems.

# Communication Equipment Mechanics, Installers, and Repairers

▲ Growth: -3.1%
▲ Annual Job Openings: 9,000
▲ Annual Earnings: $42,520
▲ Education/Training Required: Post-secondary vocational training
▲ Self-Employed: 6.2%
▲ Part-Time: 24.3%

**Install, maintain, test, and repair communication cables and equipment.** Examines and tests malfunctioning equipment to determine defects, using blueprints and electrical measuring instruments. Tests installed equipment for conformance to specifications, using test equipment. Assembles and installs communication equipment, such as data communication lines and equipment, computer systems, and antennas and towers, using hand tools. Repairs, replaces, or adjusts defective components. Disassembles equipment to adjust, repair, or replace parts, using hand tools. Evaluates quality of performance of installed equipment by observance and using test equipment. Digs holes or trenches. Answers customers' inquiries or complaints. Cleans and maintains tools, test equipment, and motor vehicle. Communicates with base, using telephone or two-way radio to receive instructions or technical advice or to report unauthorized use of equipment. Demonstrates equipment and instructs customer in use of equipment. Determines viability of site through observation and discusses site location and construction requirements with customer. Measures distance from landmarks to identify exact installation site. Climbs poles and ladders; constructs pole, roof mounts, or reinforcements; and mixes concrete to enable equipment installation. Plans layout and installation of data communications equipment. Reviews work orders, building permits, manufacturer's instructions, and ordinances to move, change, install, repair, or remove communication equipment. Adjusts or modifies equipment in accordance with customer request or to enhance performance of equipment. Performs routine maintenance on equipment, which includes adjustment, repair, and painting. Measures, cuts, splices, connects, solders, and installs wires and cables. **SKILLS**—Repairing. Troubleshooting. Installation. Quality Control Analysis. Equipment Maintenance.

**GOE—Interest Area:** 05. Mechanics, Installers, and Repairers. **Work Group:** 05.02. Electrical and Electronic Systems. **Other Job Titles in This Work Group:** Avionics Technicians; Battery Repairers; Central Office and PBX Installers and Repairers; Computer, Automated Teller, and Office Machine Repairers; Data Processing Equipment Repairers; Electric Home Appliance and Power Tool Repairers; Electric Meter Installers and Repairers; Electric Motor and Switch Assemblers and Repairers; Electric Motor, Power Tool, and Related Repairers; Electrical and Electronics Installers and Repairers, Transportation Equipment; Electrical and Electronics Repairers, Commercial and Industrial Equipment; Electrical and Electronics Repairers, Powerhouse, Substation, and Relay; Electrical Parts Reconditioners; Electrical Power-Line Installers and Repairers; Electronic Equipment Installers and Repairers, Motor Vehicles; Electronic Home Entertainment Equipment Installers and Repairers; Elevator Installers and Repairers; Frame Wirers, Central Office; Home Appliance Installers; Home Appliance Repairers; Office Machine and Cash Register Servicers; Radio Mechanics; Signal and Track Switch Repairers; Station Installers and Repairers, Telephone; Telecommunications Equipment Installers and Repairers, Except Line Installers; Telecommunications Facility Examiners; Telecommunications Line Installers and Repairers; Transformer Repairers. **PERSONALITY TYPE**—Realistic. Realistic occupations frequently involve work activities that include practical, hands-on problems and solutions. They often deal with plants, animals, and real-world materials like wood, tools, and machinery. Many of the occupations require working outside and do not involve a lot of paperwork or working closely with others.

**EDUCATION/TRAINING PROGRAM(S)**—Communication Systems Installer and Repairer. **RELATED KNOWLEDGE/COURSES**—**Telecommunications:** Knowledge of transmission, broadcasting, switching, control, and operation of telecommunications systems. **Computers and Electronics:** Knowledge of circuit boards, processors, chips, electronic equipment, and computer hardware and software, including applications and programming. **Principles of Mechanical Devices:** Knowledge of machines and tools, including their designs, uses, repair, and maintenance. **Design:** Knowledge of design techniques, tools, and principles involved in production of precision technical plans, blueprints, drawings, and models. **Mathematics:** Knowledge of arithmetic, algebra, geometry, calculus, statistics, and their applications.

# Construction and Building Inspectors

- ▲ Growth: 15%
- ▲ Annual Job Openings: 2,000
- ▲ Annual Earnings: $39,730
- ▲ Education/Training Required: Work experience in a related occupation
- ▲ Self-Employed: 6.2%
- ▲ Part-Time: 2.9%

Inspect structures using engineering skills to determine structural soundness and compliance with specifications, building codes, and other regulations. Inspections may be general in nature or may be limited to a specific area, such as electrical systems or plumbing. Inspects bridges, dams, highways, building, wiring, plumbing, electrical circuits, sewer, heating system, and foundation for conformance to specifications and codes. Approves and signs plans that meet required specifications. Issues violation notices, stop-work orders, and permits for construction and occupancy. Reviews complaints, obtains evidence, and testifies in court that construction does not conform to code. Evaluates premises for cleanliness, including garbage disposal and lack of vermin infestation. Computes estimates of work completed and approves payment for contractors. Maintains daily logs, inventory, and inspection and construction records and prepares reports. Confers with owners, violators, and authorities to explain regulations and recommend alterations in construction or specifications. Records and notifies owners, violators, and authorities of violations of construction specifications and building codes. Measures dimensions and verifies level, alignment, and elevation of structures and fixtures to ensure compliance to building plans and codes. Reviews and interprets plans, blueprints, specifications, and construction methods to ensure compliance to legal requirements. **SKILLS**—Speaking. Quality Control Analysis. Active Listening. Critical Thinking. Active Learning. Writing. Reading Comprehension.

GOE—**Interest Area:** 02. Science, Math, and Engineering. **Work Group:** 02.08. Engineering Technology. **Other Job Titles in This Work Group:** Aerospace Engineering and Operations Technicians; Architectural and Civil Drafters; Architectural Drafters; Calibration and Instrumentation Technicians; Cartographers and Photogrammetrists; Civil Drafters; Civil Engineering Technicians; Drafters, All Other; Electrical and Electronic Engineering Technicians; Electrical and Electronics Drafters; Electrical Drafters; Electrical Engineering Technicians; Electro-Mechanical Technicians; Electronic Drafters; Electronics Engineering Technicians; Engineering Technicians, Except Drafters, All Other; Environmental Engineering Technicians; Industrial Engineering Technicians; Mapping Technicians; Mechanical Drafters; Mechanical Engineering Technicians; Numerical Tool and Process Control Programmers; Pressure Vessel Inspectors; Surveying and Mapping Technicians; Surveying Technicians; Surveyors. **PERSONALITY TYPE**—Conventional. Conventional occupations frequently involve following set procedures and routines. These occupations can include working with data and details more than with ideas. Usually there is a clear line of authority to follow.

**EDUCATION/TRAINING PROGRAM(S)**—Construction/Building Inspector. **RELATED KNOWLEDGE/COURSES**—**Building and Construction:** Knowledge of materials, methods, and tools involved in the construction or repair of houses, buildings, or other structures such as highways and roads. **Public Safety and Security:** Knowledge of relevant equipment, policies, procedures, and strategies to promote effective local, state, or national security operations for the protection of people, data, property, and institutions. **Mathematics:** Knowledge of arithmetic, algebra, geometry, calculus, statistics, and their applications. **Principles of Mechanical Devices:** Knowledge of machines and tools, including their designs, uses, repair, and maintenance. **Design:** Knowledge of design techniques, tools, and principles involved in production of precision technical plans, blueprints, drawings, and models.

# Construction Carpenters

- ▲ Growth: 8.2%
- ▲ Annual Job Openings: 161,000
- ▲ Annual Earnings: $35,100
- ▲ Education/Training Required: Long-term on-the-job training
- ▲ Self-Employed: 28.6%
- ▲ Part-Time: 8.1%

**Construct, erect, install, and repair structures and fixtures of wood, plywood, and wallboard, using carpenter's hand tools and power tools.** Shapes or cuts materials to specified measurements, using hand tools, machines, or power saw. Assembles and fastens materials, using hand tools and wood screws, nails, dowel pins, or glue, to make framework or props. Installs structures and fixtures, such as windows, frames, floorings, and trim, or hardware, using carpenter's hand and power tools. Builds or repairs cabinets, doors, frameworks, floors, and other wooden fixtures used in buildings, using woodworking machines, carpenter's hand tools, and power tools. Removes damaged or defective parts or sections of structure and repairs or replaces, using hand tools. Verifies trueness of structure, using plumb bob and level. Prepares layout according to blueprint or oral instructions, using rule, framing square, and calipers. Estimates amount and kind of lumber or other materials required and selects and orders them. Inspects ceiling or floor tile, wall coverings, siding, glass, or woodwork to detect broken or damaged structures. Studies specifications in blueprints, sketches, or building plans to determine materials required and dimensions of structure to be fabricated. Measures and marks cutting lines on materials, using ruler, pencil, chalk, and marking gauge. Finishes surfaces of woodworking or wallboard in houses and buildings, using paint, hand tools, and paneling. Fills cracks and other defects in plaster or plasterboard and sands patch, using patching plaster, trowel, and sanding tool. **SKILLS**—Repairing. Installation. Mathematics. Management of Material Resources. Reading Comprehension. Equipment Selection.

**GOE—Interest Area:** 06. Construction, Mining, and Drilling. **Work Group:** 06.02. Construction. **Other Job Titles in This Work Group:** Boat Builders and Shipwrights; Boilermakers; Brattice Builders; Brickmasons and Blockmasons; Carpenters; Carpet Installers; Ceiling Tile Installers; Cement Masons and Concrete Finishers; Commercial Divers; Drywall and Ceiling Tile Installers; Drywall Installers; Electricians; Explosives Workers, Ordnance Handling Experts, and Blasters; Fence Erectors; Floor Layers, Except Carpet, Wood, and Hard Tiles; Floor Sanders and Finishers; Glaziers; Grader, Bulldozer, and Scraper Operators; Hazardous Materials Removal Workers; Insulation Workers, Floor, Ceiling, and Wall; Insulation Workers, Mechanical; Manufactured Building and Mobile Home Installers; Operating Engineers; Operating Engineers and Other Construction Equipment Operators; Painters, Construction and Maintenance; Paperhangers; Paving, Surfacing, and Tamping Equipment Operators; Pile-Driver Operators; Pipe Fitters; Pipelayers; Pipelaying Fitters; Plasterers and Stucco Masons; Plumbers; Plumbers, Pipefitters, and Steamfitters; Rail-Track Laying and Maintenance Equipment Operators; Refractory Materials Repairers, Except Brickmasons; Reinforcing Iron and Rebar Workers; Riggers; Roofers; Rough Carpenters; Security and Fire Alarm Systems Installers; Segmental Pavers; Sheet Metal Workers; Ship Carpenters and Joiners; Stone Cutters and Carvers; Stonemasons; Structural Iron and Steel Workers; Tapers; Terrazzo Workers and Finishers; Tile and Marble Setters. **PERSONALITY TYPE**—Realistic. Realistic occupations frequently involve work activities that include practical, hands-on problems and solutions. They often deal with plants, animals, and real-world materials like wood, tools, and machinery. Many of the occupations require working outside and do not involve a lot of paperwork or working closely with others.

**EDUCATION/TRAINING PROGRAM(S)**—Carpenter; Marine Maintenance and Ship Repairer. **RELATED KNOWLEDGE/COURSES**—**Building and Construction:** Knowledge of materials, methods, and tools involved in the construction or repair of houses, buildings, or other structures such as highways and roads. **Design:** Knowledge of design techniques, tools, and principles involved in production of precision technical plans, blueprints, drawings, and models. **Principles of Mechanical Devices:** Knowledge of machines and tools, including their designs, uses, repair, and maintenance. **Engineering and Technology:** Knowledge of the practical application of engineering science and technology. This includes applying principles, techniques, procedures, and equipment to the design and production of various goods and services. **Mathematics:** Knowledge of arithmetic, algebra, geometry, calculus, statistics, and their applications.

# Construction Laborers

- ▲ Growth: 17%
- ▲ Annual Job Openings: 236,000
- ▲ Annual Earnings: $26,940
- ▲ Education/Training Required: Moderate-term on-the-job training
- ▲ Self-Employed: 0%
- ▲ Part-Time: 8.5%

Perform tasks involving physical labor at building, highway, and heavy construction projects, tunnel and shaft excavations, and demolition sites. May operate hand and power tools of all types: air hammers, earth tampers, cement mixers, small mechanical hoists, surveying and measuring equipment, and a variety of other equipment and instruments. May clean and prepare sites, dig trenches, set braces to support the sides of excavations, erect scaffolding, clean up rubble and debris, and remove asbestos, lead, and other hazardous waste materials. May assist other craft workers. Tends pumps, compressors, and generators to provide power for tools, machinery, and equipment or to heat and move materials such as asphalt. Lubricates, cleans, and repairs machinery, equipment, and tools. Mixes ingredients to create compounds used to cover or clean surfaces. Loads and unloads trucks and hauls and hoists materials. Erects and disassembles scaffolding, shoring, braces, and other temporary structures. Builds and positions forms for pouring concrete and dismantles forms after use, using saws, hammers, nails, or bolts. Measures, marks, and records openings and distances to lay out area to be graded or to erect building structures. Smooth and finishes freshly poured cement or concrete, using float, trowel, screed, or powered cement-finishing tool. Applies caulking compounds by hand or with caulking gun to seal crevices. Positions, joins, aligns, and seals structural components, such as concrete wall sections and pipes. Digs ditches and levels earth to grade specifications, using pick and shovel. Signals equipment operators to facilitate alignment, movement, and adjustment of machinery, equipment, and materials. Grinds, scrapes, sands, or polishes surfaces, such as concrete, marble, terrazzo, or wood flooring, using abrasive tools or machines. Mixes concrete, using portable mixer. Razes buildings and salvages useful materials. Sprays materials such as water, sand, steam, vinyl, paint, or stucco through hose to clean, coat, or seal surfaces. Tends machine that pumps concrete, grout, cement, sand, plaster, or stucco through spray gun for application to ceilings and walls. Mops, brushes, or spreads paints, cleaning solutions, or other compounds over surfaces to clean or provide protection. Cleans construction site to eliminate possible hazards. **SKILLS**—Equipment Maintenance. Mathematics.

**GOE—Interest Area:** 06. Construction, Mining, and Drilling. **Work Group:** 06.04. Hands-on Work in Construction, Extraction, and Maintenance. **Other Job Titles in This Work Group:** Carpenter Assemblers and Repairers; Grips and Set-Up Workers, Motion Picture Sets, Studios, and Stages; Helpers, Construction Trades, All Other; Helpers—Brickmasons, Blockmasons, Stonemasons, and Tile and Marble Setters; Helpers—Carpenters; Helpers—Extraction Workers; Helpers—Painters, Paperhangers, Plasterers, and Stucco Masons; Helpers—Pipelayers, Plumbers, Pipefitters, and Steamfitters; Helpers—Roofers; Highway Maintenance Workers; Septic Tank Servicers and Sewer Pipe Cleaners. **PERSONALITY TYPE**—Realistic. Realistic occupations frequently involve work activities that include practical, hands-on problems and solutions. They often deal with plants, animals, and real-world materials like wood, tools, and machinery. Many of the occupations require working outside and do not involve a lot of paperwork or working closely with others.

**EDUCATION/TRAINING PROGRAM(S)**—No data available. **RELATED KNOWLEDGE/ COURSES—Building and Construction:** Knowledge of materials, methods, and tools involved in the construction or repair of houses, buildings, or other structures such as highways and roads. **Principles of Mechanical Devices:** Knowledge of machines and tools, including their designs, uses, repair, and maintenance. **Engineering and Technology:** Knowledge of the practical application of engineering science and technology. This includes applying principles, techniques, procedures, and equipment to the design and production of various goods and services. **Mathematics:** Knowledge of arithmetic, algebra, geometry, calculus, statistics, and their applications. **Design:** Knowledge of design techniques, tools, and principles involved in production of precision technical plans, blueprints, drawings, and models.

# Cooks, Restaurant

- ▲ Growth: 21.7%
- ▲ Annual Job Openings: 158,000
- ▲ Annual Earnings: $18,880
- ▲ Education/Training Required: Long-term on-the-job training
- ▲ Self-Employed: 1.5%
- ▲ Part-Time: 38.5%

**Prepare, season, and cook soups, meats, vegetables, desserts, or other foodstuffs in restaurants. May order supplies, keep records and accounts, price items on menu, or plan menu.** Weighs, measures, and mixes ingredients according to recipe or personal judgment, using various kitchen utensils and equipment. Bakes, roasts, broils, and steams meats, fish, vegetables, and other foods. Observes and tests food to determine that it is cooked by tasting, smelling, or piercing, and turns or stirs food if necessary. Seasons and cooks food according to recipes or personal judgment and experience. Washes, peels, cuts, and seeds fruits and vegetables to prepare fruits and vegetables for use. Plans items on menu. Butchers and dresses animals, fowl, or shellfish or cuts and bones meat prior to cooking. Estimates food consumption and requisitions or purchases supplies or procures food from storage. Carves and trims meats, such as beef, veal, ham, pork, and lamb, for hot or cold service or for sandwiches. Portions, arranges, and garnishes food, and serves food to waiter or patron. Inspects food preparation and serving areas to ensure observance of safe, sanitary food-handling practices. Bakes bread, rolls, cakes, and pastry. Regulates temperature of ovens, broilers, grills, and roasters. **SKILLS—**Active Learning. Speaking. Coordination. Monitoring. Learning Strategies.

**GOE—Interest Area:** 11. Recreation, Travel, and Other Personal Services. **Work Group:** 11.05. Food and Beverage Services. **Other Job Titles in This Work Group:** Bakers; Bakers, Bread and Pastry; Bartenders; Butchers and Meat Cutters; Chefs and Head Cooks; Combined Food Preparation and Serving Workers, Including Fast Food; Cooks, All Other; Cooks, Fast Food; Cooks, Institution and Cafeteria; Cooks, Short Order; Counter Attendants, Cafeteria, Food Concession, and Coffee Shop; Dining Room and Cafeteria Attendants and Bartender Helpers; Dishwashers; Food Preparation and Serving Related Workers, All Other; Food Preparation Workers; Food Servers, Nonrestaurant; Hosts and Hostesses, Restaurant, Lounge, and Coffee Shop; Waiters and Waitresses. **PERSONALITY TYPE—**Realistic. Realistic occupations frequently involve work activities that include practical, hands-on problems and solutions. They often deal with plants, animals, and real-world materials like wood, tools, and machinery. Many of the occupations require working outside and do not involve a lot of paperwork or working closely with others.

**EDUCATION/TRAINING PROGRAM(S)—**Culinary Arts/Chef Training. **RELATED KNOWLEDGE/ COURSES—Customer and Personal Service:** Knowledge of principles and processes for providing customer and personal services. This includes customer needs assessment, meeting quality standards for services, and evaluation of customer satisfaction. **Mathematics:** Knowledge of arithmetic, algebra, geometry, calculus, statistics, and their applications. **Public Safety and Security:** Knowledge of relevant equipment, policies, procedures, and strategies to promote effective local, state, or national security operations for the protection of people, data, property, and institutions. **Education and Training:** Knowledge of principles and methods for curriculum and training design, teaching and instruction for individuals and groups, and the measurement of training effects. **Personnel and Human Resources:** Knowledge of principles and procedures for personnel recruitment, selection, training, compensation and benefits, labor relations and negotiation, and personnel information systems. **Production and Processing:** Knowledge of raw materials, production processes, quality control, costs, and other techniques for maximizing the effective manufacture and distribution of goods. **Food Production:** Knowledge of techniques and equipment for planting, growing, and harvesting food products (both plant and animal) for consumption, including storage/handling techniques.

# Coroners

▲ Growth: 8.9%

▲ Annual Job Openings: 9,000

▲ Annual Earnings: $44,140

▲ Education/Training Required: Long-term on-the-job training

▲ Self-Employed: 0%

▲ Part-Time: 2.9%

**Direct activities such as autopsies, pathological and toxicological analyses, and inquests relating to the investigation of deaths occurring within a legal jurisdiction to determine cause of death or to fix responsibility for accidental, violent, or unexplained deaths.** Directs activities of physicians and technologists conducting autopsies and pathological and toxicological analyses to determine cause of death. Directs activities of workers involved in preparing documents for permanent records. Testifies at inquests, hearings, and court trials. Confers with officials of public health and law enforcement agencies to coordinate interdepartmental activities. Directs investigations into circumstances of deaths to fix responsibility for accidental, violent, or unexplained death. Coordinates activities for disposition of unclaimed corpse and personal effects of deceased. Provides information concerning death circumstance to relatives of deceased. **SKILLS**—Science. Reading Comprehension. Speaking. Critical Thinking. Writing.

**GOE—Interest Area:** 14. Medical and Health Services. **Work Group:** 14.01. Managerial Work in Medical and Health Services. **Other Job Titles in This Work Group:** Medical and Health Services Managers. **PERSONALITY TYPE**—Investigative. Investigative occupations frequently involve working with ideas and require an extensive amount of thinking. These occupations can involve searching for facts and figuring out problems mentally.

**EDUCATION/TRAINING PROGRAM(S)**—Business Administration and Management, General; Construction/Building Technologist/Technician; Logistics and Materials Management; Material Engineering; Mechanical Engineering; Operations Management and Supervision; Purchasing, Procurement and Contracts Management; Systems Engineering. **RELATED KNOWLEDGE/COURSES**—Biology: Knowledge of plant and animal organisms and their tissues, cells, functions, interdependencies, and interactions with each other and the environment. **Medicine and Dentistry:** Knowledge of the information and techniques needed to diagnose and treat human injuries, diseases, and deformities. This includes symptoms, treatment alternatives, drug properties and interactions, and preventive health-care measures. **English Language:** Knowledge of the structure and content of the English language, including the meaning and spelling of words, rules of composition, and grammar. **Administration and Management:** Knowledge of business and management principles involved in strategic planning, resource allocation, human resources modeling, leadership technique, production methods, and coordination of people and resources. **Law and Government:** Knowledge of laws, legal codes, court procedures, precedents, government regulations, executive orders, agency rules, and the democratic political process.

# Correctional Officers and Jailers

- ▲ Growth: 32.4%
- ▲ Annual Job Openings: 30,000
- ▲ Annual Earnings: $32,680
- ▲ Education/Training Required: Moderate-term on-the-job training
- ▲ Self-Employed: 0%
- ▲ Part-Time: 1.5%

Guard inmates in penal or rehabilitative institution in accordance with established regulations and procedures. May guard prisoners in transit between jail, courtroom, prison, or other point. Includes deputy sheriffs and police who spend the majority of their time guarding prisoners in correctional institutions. Monitors conduct of prisoners, according to established policies, regulations, and procedures, to prevent escape or violence. Takes prisoner into custody and escorts to locations within and outside of facility, such as visiting room, courtroom, or airport. Uses weapons, handcuffs, and physical force to maintain discipline and order among prisoners. Records information, such as prisoner identification, charges, and incidences of inmate disturbance. Guards facility entrance to screen visitors. Searches prisoners, cells, and vehicles for weapons, valuables, or drugs. Inspects locks, window bars, grills, doors, and gates at correctional facility to prevent escape. Serves meals and distributes commissary items to prisoners. **SKILLS**—Social Perceptiveness. Active Listening. Speaking. Reading Comprehension. Coordination.

**GOE—Interest Area:** 04. Law, Law Enforcement, and Public Safety. **Work Group:** 04.03. Law Enforcement. **Other Job Titles in This Work Group:** Animal Control Workers; Bailiffs; Child Support, Missing Persons, and Unemployment Insurance Fraud Investigators; Criminal Investigators and Special Agents; Crossing Guards; Detectives and Criminal Investigators; Fire Investigators; Fish and Game Wardens; Forensic Science Technicians; Gaming Surveillance Officers and Gaming Investigators; Highway Patrol Pilots; Immigration and Customs Inspectors; Lifeguards, Ski Patrol, and Other Recreational Protective Service Workers; Parking Enforcement Workers; Police and Sheriff's Pa-

trol Officers; Police Detectives; Police Identification and Records Officers; Police Patrol Officers; Private Detectives and Investigators; Security Guards; Sheriffs and Deputy Sheriffs; Transit and Railroad Police. **PERSONALITY TYPE**—Realistic. Realistic occupations frequently involve work activities that include practical, hands-on problems and solutions. They often deal with plants, animals, and real-world materials like wood, tools, and machinery. Many of the occupations require working outside and do not involve a lot of paperwork or working closely with others.

**EDUCATION/TRAINING PROGRAM(S)**—Corrections/Correctional Administration; Criminal Justice and Corrections, Other. **RELATED KNOWLEDGE/COURSES**—**Public Safety and Security:** Knowledge of relevant equipment, policies, procedures, and strategies to promote effective local, state, or national security operations for the protection of people, data, property, and institutions. **Medicine and Dentistry:** Knowledge of the information and techniques needed to diagnose and treat human injuries, diseases, and deformities. This includes symptoms, treatment alternatives, drug properties and interactions, and preventive health-care measures. **English Language:** Knowledge of the structure and content of the English language, including the meaning and spelling of words, rules of composition, and grammar. **Law and Government:** Knowledge of laws, legal codes, court procedures, precedents, government regulations, executive orders, agency rules, and the democratic political process. **Sociology and Anthropology:** Knowledge of group behavior and dynamics, societal trends and influences, human migrations, ethnicity, cultures, and their history and origins. **Psychology:** Knowledge of human behavior and performance; individual differences in ability, personality, and interests; learning and motivation; psychological research methods; and the assessment and treatment of behavioral and affective disorders.

# Costume Attendants

▲ Growth: 19.1%

▲ Annual Job Openings: 8,000

▲ Annual Earnings: $24,790

▲ Education/Training Required: Short-term on-the-job training

▲ Self-Employed: 0%

▲ Part-Time: 40.1%

**Select, fit, and take care of costumes for cast members, and aid entertainers.** Inventories stock to determine types and condition of costuming available and selects costumes based on historical analysis and studies. Examines costume fit on cast member and sketches or writes notes for alterations. Repairs, alters, cleans, presses, and refits costume prior to performance and cleans and stores costume following performance. Analyzes or reviews analysis of script to determine locale of story, period, number of characters, and costumes required per character. Studies books, pictures, and examples of period clothing to determine styles worn during specific period in history. Assists cast in donning costumes or assigns cast dresser to assist specific cast members with costume changes. Purchases or rents costumes and other wardrobe accessories from vendor. Arranges or directs cast dresser to arrange costumes on clothing racks in sequence of appearance. Designs and constructs costume or sends it to tailor for construction or major repairs and alterations. **SKILLS**—Reading Comprehension. Speaking. Writing. Active Learning. Monitoring. Active Listening.

**GOE**—**Interest Area:** 01. Arts, Entertainment, and Media. **Work Group:** 01.09. Modeling and Personal Appearance. **Other Job Titles in This Work Group:** Makeup Artists, Theatrical and Performance; Models. **PERSONALITY TYPE**—Artistic. Artistic occupations frequently involve working with forms, designs, and patterns. They often require self-expression, and the work can be done without following a clear set of rules.

**EDUCATION/TRAINING PROGRAM(S)**—No data available. **RELATED KNOWLEDGE/ COURSES**—**Design:** Knowledge of design techniques, tools, and principles involved in production of precision technical plans, blueprints, drawings, and models. **Fine Arts:** Knowledge of the theory and techniques required to compose, produce, and perform works of music, dance, visual arts, drama, and sculpture. **English Language:** Knowledge of the structure and content of the English language, including the meaning and spelling of words, rules of composition, and grammar. **Customer and Personal Service:** Knowledge of principles and processes for providing customer and personal services. This includes customer needs assessment, meeting quality standards for services, and evaluation of customer satisfaction. **History and Archeology:** Knowledge of historical events and their causes, indicators, and effects on civilizations and cultures. **Geography:** Knowledge of principles and methods for describing the features of land, sea, and air masses, including their physical characteristics, locations, interrelationships, and distribution of plant, animal, and human life. **Sociology and Anthropology:** Knowledge of group behavior and dynamics, societal trends and influences, human migrations, ethnicity, cultures, and their history and origins.

# Counter and Rental Clerks

- ▲ Growth: 19.4%
- ▲ Annual Job Openings: 150,000
- ▲ Annual Earnings: $18,670
- ▲ Education/Training Required: Short-term on-the-job training
- ▲ Self-Employed: 2.4%
- ▲ Part-Time: 50.8%

**Receive orders for repairs, rentals, and services. May describe available options, compute cost, and accept payment.** Rents item or arranges for provision of service to customer. Receives, examines, and tags articles to be altered, cleaned, stored, or repaired. Collects deposit or payment or records credit charges. Recommends to customer items offered by rental facility that meet customer needs. Inspects and adjusts rental items to meet needs of customer. Greets customers of agency that rents items, such as apparel, tools, and conveyances, or that provides services, such as rug cleaning. Reserves items for requested time and keeps record of items rented. Answers telephone and receives orders by phone. Explains rental fees and provides information about rented items, such as operation or description. Computes charges based on rental rate. Prepares rental forms, obtaining customer signature and other information, such as required licenses. **SKILLS**—Service Orientation. Reading Comprehension. Active Listening. Mathematics. Writing.

**GOE**—**Interest Area:** 09. Business Detail. **Work Group:** 09.05. Customer Service. **Other Job Titles in This Work Group:** Adjustment Clerks; Bill and Account Collectors; Cashiers; Customer Service Representatives; Customer Service Representatives, Utilities; Gaming Cage Workers; Gaming Change Persons and Booth Cashiers; New Accounts Clerks; Order Clerks; Receptionists and Information Clerks; Tellers; Travel Clerks.

**PERSONALITY TYPE**—Conventional. Conventional occupations frequently involve following set procedures and routines. These occupations can include working with data and details more than with ideas. Usually there is a clear line of authority to follow.

**EDUCATION/TRAINING PROGRAM(S)**—General Selling Skills and Sales Operations; Vehicle and Petroleum Products Marketing Operations, Other. **RELATED KNOWLEDGE/COURSES**—**Customer and Personal Service:** Knowledge of principles and processes for providing customer and personal services. This includes customer needs assessment, meeting quality standards for services, and evaluation of customer satisfaction. **Clerical Studies:** Knowledge of administrative and clerical procedures and systems such as word processing, managing files and records, stenography and transcription, designing forms, and other office procedures and terminology. **English Language:** Knowledge of the structure and content of the English language, including the meaning and spelling of words, rules of composition, and grammar. **Sales and Marketing:** Knowledge of principles and methods for showing, promoting, and selling products or services. This includes marketing strategy and tactics, product demonstration, sales techniques, and sales control systems. **Mathematics:** Knowledge of arithmetic, algebra, geometry, calculus, statistics, and their applications.

# Counter Attendants, Cafeteria, Food Concession, and Coffee Shop

▲ Growth: 14.4%
▲ Annual Job Openings: 216,000
▲ Annual Earnings: $15,030
▲ Education/Training Required: Short-term on-the-job training
▲ Self-Employed: 0.6%
▲ Part-Time: 62.9%

**Serve food to diners at counter or from a steam table.** Serves food, beverages, or desserts to customers in variety of settings, such as take-out counter of restaurant or lunchroom. Serves salads, vegetables, meat, breads, and cocktails, ladles soups and sauces, portions desserts, and fills beverage cups and glasses. Orders items to replace stocks. Scrubs and polishes counters, steam tables, and other equipment; cleans glasses, dishes, and fountain equipment; and polishes metalwork on fountain. Adds relishes and garnishes according to instructions. Carves meat. Prepares sandwiches, salads, and other short-order items. Accepts payment for food, using cash register or adding machine to total check. Wraps menu items, such as sandwiches, hot entrees, and desserts. Brews coffee and tea and fills containers with requested beverages. Prepares and serves soft drinks and ice cream dishes, such as sundaes, using memorized formulas and methods of following directions. Replenishes foods at serving stations. Serves sandwiches, salads, beverages, desserts, and candies to employees in industrial establishment. Writes items ordered on tickets, totals orders, passes orders to cook, and gives ticket stubs to customers to identify filled orders. Calls order to kitchen and picks up and serves order when it is ready. **SKILLS—** Writing.

**GOE—Interest Area:** 11. Recreation, Travel, and Other Personal Services. **Work Group:** 11.05. Food and Beverage Services. **Other Job Titles in This Work Group:** Bakers; Bakers, Bread and Pastry; Bartenders; Butchers and Meat Cutters; Chefs and Head Cooks; Combined Food Preparation and Serving Workers, Including Fast Food; Cooks, All Other; Cooks, Fast Food; Cooks, Institution and Cafeteria; Cooks, Restaurant; Cooks, Short Order; Dining Room and Cafeteria Attendants and Bartender Helpers; Dishwashers; Food Preparation and Serving Related Workers, All Other; Food Preparation Workers; Food Servers, Nonrestaurant; Hosts and Hostesses, Restaurant, Lounge, and Coffee Shop; Waiters and Waitresses. **PERSONALITY TYPE—**Social. Social occupations frequently involve working with, communicating with, and teaching people. These occupations often involve helping or providing service to others.

**EDUCATION/TRAINING PROGRAM(S)—** Waiter/ Waitress and Dining Room Manager. **RELATED KNOWLEDGE/COURSES—Customer and Personal Service:** Knowledge of principles and processes for providing customer and personal services. This includes customer needs assessment, meeting quality standards for services, and evaluation of customer satisfaction. **English Language:** Knowledge of the structure and content of the English language, including the meaning and spelling of words, rules of composition, and grammar. **Mathematics:** Knowledge of arithmetic, algebra, geometry, calculus, statistics, and their applications. **Sales and Marketing:** Knowledge of principles and methods for showing, promoting, and selling products or services. This includes marketing strategy and tactics, product demonstration, sales techniques, and sales control systems.

# Court Clerks

- ▲ Growth: 12%
- ▲ Annual Job Openings: 14,000
- ▲ Annual Earnings: $27,780
- ▲ Education/Training Required: Short-term on-the-job training
- ▲ Self-Employed: 0%
- ▲ Part-Time: 16%

**Perform clerical duties in court of law; prepare docket of cases to be called; secure information for judges; and contact witnesses, attorneys, and litigants to obtain information for court.** Prepares docket or calendar of cases to be called, using typewriter or computer. Administers oath to witnesses. Collects court fees or fines and records amounts collected. Records case disposition, court orders, and arrangement for payment of court fees. Records minutes of court proceedings, using stenotype machine or shorthand, and transcribes testimony, using typewriter or computer. Notifies district attorney's office of cases prosecuted by district attorney. Explains procedures or forms to parties in case. Examines legal documents submitted to court for adherence to law or court procedures. Instructs parties when to appear in court. Prepares case folders and posts, files, or routes documents. Secures information for judges and contacts witnesses, attorneys, and litigants to obtain information for court. **SKILLS**—Reading Comprehension. Active Listening. Writing. Speaking. Time Management.

**GOE—Interest Area:** 09. Business Detail. **Work Group:** 09.02. Administrative Detail. **Other Job Titles in This Work Group:** Claims Takers, Unemployment Benefits; Court, Municipal, and License Clerks; Eligibility Interviewers, Government Programs; Executive Secretaries and Administrative Assistants; Interviewers, Except Eligibility and Loan; Legal Secretaries; License Clerks; Loan Interviewers and Clerks; Medical Secretaries; Municipal Clerks; Secretaries, Except Legal, Medical, and Executive; Welfare Eligibility Workers and Interviewers. **PERSONALITY TYPE**—Conventional. Conventional occupations frequently involve following set procedures and routines. These occupations can include working with data and details more than with ideas. Usually there is a clear line of authority to follow.

**EDUCATION/TRAINING PROGRAM(S)**—General Office/Clerical and Typing Services. **RELATED KNOWLEDGE/COURSES—Clerical Studies:** Knowledge of administrative and clerical procedures and systems such as word processing, managing files and records, stenography and transcription, designing forms, and other office procedures and terminology. **Law and Government:** Knowledge of laws, legal codes, court procedures, precedents, government regulations, executive orders, agency rules, and the democratic political process. **English Language:** Knowledge of the structure and content of the English language, including the meaning and spelling of words, rules of composition, and grammar. **Computers and Electronics:** Knowledge of circuit boards, processors, chips, electronic equipment, and computer hardware and software, including applications and programming. **Mathematics:** Knowledge of arithmetic, algebra, geometry, calculus, statistics, and their applications.

# Crane and Tower Operators

▲ Growth: 8.6%

▲ Annual Job Openings: 5,000

▲ Annual Earnings: $35,340

▲ Education/Training Required: Moderate-term on-the-job training

▲ Self-Employed: 0%

▲ Part-Time: 0.2%

**Operate mechanical boom and cable or tower and cable equipment to lift and move materials, machines, or products in many directions.** Operates cranes, cherry pickers, or other moving equipment to lift and move loads, such as machinery or bulk materials. Inspects cables and grappling devices for wear and installs or replaces cables. Inspects bundle packaging for conformance to customer requirements and removes and batches packaging tickets. Weighs bundles, using floor scale, and records weight for company records. Directs helpers engaged in placing blocking and outrigging under crane when lifting loads. Directs truck drivers backing vehicles into loading bays and covers, uncovers, and secures loads for delivery. Loads and unloads bundles from trucks and moves containers to storage bins, using moving equipment. Inspects and compares load weights with lifting capacity to ensure against overload. Cleans, lubricates, and maintains mechanisms, such as cables, pulleys, and grappling devices. Reviews daily truck-delivery schedule to ascertain orders, sequence of deliveries, and special loading instructions. Inspects and adjusts crane mechanisms and accessory equipment to prevent malfunctions and wear. **SKILLS**—Operation and Control. Repairing. Equipment Selection. Coordination. Installation. Equipment Maintenance. Operation Monitoring.

**GOE—Interest Area:** 08. Industrial Production. **Work Group:** 08.07. Hands-on Work: Loading, Moving, Hoisting, and Conveying. **Other Job Titles in This Work Group:** Conveyor Operators and Tenders; Dragline Operators; Excavating and Loading Machine and Dragline Operators; Freight, Stock, and Material Movers, Hand; Hoist and Winch Operators; Industrial Truck and Tractor Operators; Irradiated-Fuel Handlers; Laborers and Freight, Stock, and Material Movers, Hand; Machine Feeders and Offbearers; Material Moving Workers, All Other; Packers and Packagers, Hand; Pump Operators, Except Wellhead Pumpers; Refuse and Recyclable Material Collectors; Tank Car, Truck, and Ship Loaders. **PERSONALITY TYPE**—Realistic. Realistic occupations frequently involve work activities that include practical, hands-on problems and solutions. They often deal with plants, animals, and real-world materials like wood, tools, and machinery. Many of the occupations require working outside and do not involve a lot of paperwork or working closely with others.

**EDUCATION/TRAINING PROGRAM(S)**—Construction Equipment Operator. **RELATED KNOWLEDGE/COURSES**—**Principles of Mechanical Devices:** Knowledge of machines and tools, including their designs, uses, repair, and maintenance. **Engineering and Technology:** Knowledge of the practical application of engineering science and technology. This includes applying principles, techniques, procedures, and equipment to the design and production of various goods and services. **Transportation:** Knowledge of principles and methods for moving people or goods by air, rail, sea, or road, including the relative costs and benefits. **Physics:** Knowledge and prediction of physical principles and laws and their interrelationships and applications to understanding fluid, material, and atmospheric dynamics and mechanical, electrical, atomic, and sub-atomic structures and processes. **Clerical Studies:** Knowledge of administrative and clerical procedures and systems such as word processing, managing files and records, stenography and transcription, designing forms, and other office procedures and terminology.

# Criminal Investigators and Special Agents

- ▲ Growth: 16.4%
- ▲ Annual Job Openings: 4,000
- ▲ Annual Earnings: $49,830
- ▲ Education/Training Required: Work experience in a related occupation
- ▲ Self-Employed: 0%
- ▲ Part-Time: 1.5%

**Investigate alleged or suspected criminal violations of Federal, state, or local laws to determine if evidence is sufficient to recommend prosecution.** Obtains and verifies evidence or establishes facts by interviewing, observing, and interrogating suspects and witnesses and analyzing records. Analyzes charge, complaint, or allegation of law violation to identify issues involved and types of evidence needed. Assists in determining scope, timing, and direction of investigation. Examines records to detect links in chain of evidence or information. Obtains and uses search and arrest warrants. Develops and uses informants to get leads to information. Testifies before grand juries. Serves subpoenas or other official papers. Photographs, fingerprints, and measures height and weight of arrested suspects, noting physical characteristics, and posts data on record for filing. Reports critical information to and coordinates activities with other offices or agencies when applicable. Presents findings in reports. Maintains surveillance and performs undercover assignments. Compares crime scene fingerprints with those of suspect or fingerprint files to identify perpetrator, using computer. Searches for evidence, dusts surfaces to reveal latent fingerprints, and collects and records evidence and documents, using cameras and investigative equipment. **SKILLS**—Speaking. Active Listening. Social Perceptiveness. Critical Thinking. Writing. Reading Comprehension.

**GOE**—**Interest Area:** 04. Law, Law Enforcement, and Public Safety. **Work Group:** 04.03. Law Enforcement. **Other Job Titles in This Work Group:** Animal Control Workers; Bailiffs; Child Support, Missing Persons, and Unemployment Insurance Fraud Investigators; Correctional Officers and Jailers; Crossing Guards; Detectives and Criminal Investigators; Fire Investigators; Fish and Game Wardens; Forensic Science Technicians; Gaming Surveillance Officers and Gaming Investigators; Highway Patrol Pilots; Immigration and Customs Inspectors; Lifeguards, Ski Patrol, and Other Recreational Protective Service Workers; Parking Enforcement Workers; Police and Sheriff's Patrol Officers; Police Detectives; Police Identification and Records Officers; Police Patrol Officers; Private Detectives and Investigators; Security Guards; Sheriffs and Deputy Sheriffs; Transit and Railroad Police. **PERSONALITY TYPE**—Enterprising. Enterprising occupations frequently involve starting up and carrying out projects. These occupations can involve leading people and making many decisions. They sometimes require risk taking and often deal with business.

**EDUCATION/TRAINING PROGRAM(S)**—Law Enforcement/Police Science. **RELATED KNOWLEDGE/COURSES**—**Public Safety and Security:** Knowledge of relevant equipment, policies, procedures, and strategies to promote effective local, state, or national security operations for the protection of people, data, property, and institutions. **Law and Government:** Knowledge of laws, legal codes, court procedures, precedents, government regulations, executive orders, agency rules, and the democratic political process. **Sociology and Anthropology:** Knowledge of group behavior and dynamics, societal trends and influences, human migrations, ethnicity, cultures, and their history and origins. **Telecommunications:** Knowledge of transmission, broadcasting, switching, control, and operation of telecommunications systems. **English Language:** Knowledge of the structure and content of the English language, including the meaning and spelling of words, rules of composition, and grammar. **Psychology:** Knowledge of human behavior and performance; individual differences in ability, personality, and interests; learning and motivation; psychological research methods; and the assessment and treatment of behavioral and affective disorders.

# Customer Service Representatives, Utilities

▲ Growth: 32.4%
▲ Annual Job Openings: 359,000
▲ Annual Earnings: $26,530
▲ Education/Training Required: Moderate-term on-the-job training
▲ Self-Employed: 0.2%
▲ Part-Time: 12.8%

**Interview applicants for water, gas, electric, or telephone service. Talk with customer by phone or in person and receive orders for installation, turn-on, discontinuance, or change in services.** Confers with customer by phone or in person to receive orders for installation, turn-on, discontinuance, or change in service. Completes contract forms, prepares change of address records, and issues discontinuance orders, using computer. Determines charges for service requested and collects deposits. Solicits sale of new or additional utility services. Resolves billing or service complaints and refers grievances to designated departments for investigation. **SKILLS**—Active Listening. Speaking. Service Orientation. Writing. Mathematics. Reading Comprehension.

**GOE**—**Interest Area:** 09. Business Detail. **Work Group:** 09.05. Customer Service. **Other Job Titles in This Work Group:** Adjustment Clerks; Bill and Account Collectors; Cashiers; Counter and Rental Clerks; Customer Service Representatives; Gaming Cage Workers; Gaming Change Persons and Booth Cashiers; New Accounts Clerks; Order Clerks; Receptionists and Information Clerks; Tellers; Travel Clerks. **PERSONALITY TYPE**—Conventional. Conventional occupations frequently involve following set procedures and routines. These occupations can include working with data and details more than with ideas. Usually there is a clear line of authority to follow.

**EDUCATION/TRAINING PROGRAM(S)**—Receptionist. **RELATED KNOWLEDGE/COURSES**—**Customer and Personal Service:** Knowledge of principles and processes for providing customer and personal services. This includes customer needs assessment, meeting quality standards for services, and evaluation of customer satisfaction. **English Language:** Knowledge of the structure and content of the English language, including the meaning and spelling of words, rules of composition, and grammar. **Sales and Marketing:** Knowledge of principles and methods for showing, promoting, and selling products or services. This includes marketing strategy and tactics, product demonstration, sales techniques, and sales control systems. **Mathematics:** Knowledge of arithmetic, algebra, geometry, calculus, statistics, and their applications. **Telecommunications:** Knowledge of transmission, broadcasting, switching, control, and operation of telecommunications systems.

# Data Processing Equipment Repairers

▲ Growth: 14.2%
▲ Annual Job Openings: 24,000
▲ Annual Earnings: $32,860
▲ Education/Training Required: Post-secondary vocational training
▲ Self-Employed: 14.8%
▲ Part-Time: 6.9%

Repair, maintain, and install computer hardware such as peripheral equipment and word processing systems. Replaces defective components and wiring. Tests faulty equipment and applies knowledge of functional operation of electronic units and systems to diagnose cause of malfunction. Aligns, adjusts, and calibrates equipment according to specifications. Calibrates testing instruments. Adjusts mechanical parts, using hand tools and soldering iron. Converses with equipment operators to ascertain problems with equipment before breakdown or cause of breakdown. Tests electronic components and circuits to locate defects, using oscilloscopes, signal generators, ammeters, and voltmeters. Maintains records of repairs, calibrations, and tests. Enters information into computer to copy program from one electronic component to another or to draw, modify, or store schematics. **SKILLS**—Installation. Repairing. Troubleshooting. Reading Comprehension. Quality Control Analysis. Science. Equipment Maintenance.

**GOE—Interest Area:** 05. Mechanics, Installers, and Repairers. **Work Group:** 05.02. Electrical and Electronic Systems. **Other Job Titles in This Work Group:** Avionics Technicians; Battery Repairers; Central Office and PBX Installers and Repairers; Communication Equipment Mechanics, Installers, and Repairers; Computer, Automated Teller, and Office Machine Repairers; Electric Home Appliance and Power Tool Repairers; Electric Meter Installers and Repairers; Electric Motor and Switch Assemblers and Repairers; Electric Motor, Power Tool, and Related Repairers; Electrical and Electronics Installers and Repairers, Transportation Equipment; Electrical and Electronics Repairers, Commercial and Industrial Equipment; Electrical and Electronics Repairers, Powerhouse, Substation, and Relay; Electrical Parts Reconditioners; Electrical Power-Line Installers and Repairers; Electronic Equipment Installers and Repairers, Motor Vehicles; Electronic Home Entertainment Equipment Installers and Repairers; Elevator Installers and Repairers; Frame Wirers, Central Office; Home Appliance Installers; Home Appliance Repairers; Office Machine and Cash Register Servicers; Radio Mechanics; Signal and Track Switch Repairers; Station Installers and Repairers, Telephone; Telecommunications Equipment Installers and Repairers, Except Line Installers; Telecommunications Facility Examiners; Telecommunications Line Installers and Repairers; Transformer Repairers. **PERSONALITY TYPE**—Realistic. Realistic occupations frequently involve work activities that include practical, hands-on problems and solutions. They often deal with plants, animals, and real-world materials like wood, tools, and machinery. Many of the occupations require working outside and do not involve a lot of paperwork or working closely with others.

**EDUCATION/TRAINING PROGRAM(S)**—Building/Property Maintenance and Manager; Business Machine Repairer; Computer Installer and Repairer; Computer Maintenance Technologist/Technician. **RELATED KNOWLEDGE/COURSES—Computers and Electronics:** Knowledge of circuit boards, processors, chips, electronic equipment, and computer hardware and software, including applications and programming. **Principles of Mechanical Devices:** Knowledge of machines and tools, including their designs, uses, repair, and maintenance. **Telecommunications:** Knowledge of transmission, broadcasting, switching, control, and operation of telecommunications systems. **Mathematics:** Knowledge of arithmetic, algebra, geometry, calculus, statistics, and their applications. **Design:** Knowledge of design techniques, tools, and principles involved in production of precision technical plans, blueprints, drawings, and models.

# Demonstrators and Product Promoters

▲ Growth: 24.9%

▲ Annual Job Openings: 34,000

▲ Annual Earnings: $24,460

▲ Education/Training Required: Moderate-term on-the-job training

▲ Self-Employed: 5.5%

▲ Part-Time: 40.2%

Demonstrate merchandise and answer questions for the purpose of creating public interest in buying the product. May sell demonstrated merchandise. Demonstrates and explains products, methods, or services to persuade customers to purchase products or utilize services available and answers questions. Visits homes, community organizations, stores, and schools to demonstrate products or services. Attends trade, traveling, promotional, educational, or amusement exhibit to answer visitors' questions and to protect exhibit against theft or damage. Sets up and arranges display to attract attention of prospective customers. Suggests product improvements to employer and product to purchase to customer. Gives product samples or token gifts to customers and distributes handbills, brochures, or gift certificates to passers-by. Answers telephone and written requests from customers for information about product use and writes articles and pamphlets on product. Lectures and shows slides to users of company product. Advises customers on homemaking problems related to products or services offered by company. Wears costume or sign boards and walks in public to attract attention to advertise merchandise, services, or belief. Contacts businesses and civic establishments and arranges to exhibit and sell merchandise made by disadvantaged persons. Instructs customers in alteration of products. Develops list of prospective clients from sources such as newspaper items, company records, local merchants, and customers. Solicits new organization membership. Trains demonstrators to present company's products or services. Conducts guided tours of plant where product is made. Prepares reports of services rendered and visits made. Drives truck and trailer to transport exhibit. Collects fees or accepts donations.

SKILLS—Speaking. Persuasion. Social Perceptiveness. Learning Strategies. Active Learning. Writing.

GOE—Interest Area: 10. Sales and Marketing. Work Group: 10.04. Personal Soliciting. Other Job Titles in This Work Group: Door-To-Door Sales Workers, News and Street Vendors, and Related Workers; Telemarketers. PERSONALITY TYPE—Enterprising. Enterprising occupations frequently involve starting up and carrying out projects. These occupations can involve leading people and making many decisions. They sometimes require risk taking and often deal with business.

EDUCATION/TRAINING PROGRAM(S)—General Retailing Operations. RELATED KNOWLEDGE/COURSES—Sales and Marketing: Knowledge of principles and methods for showing, promoting, and selling products or services. This includes marketing strategy and tactics, product demonstration, sales techniques, and sales control systems. Communications and Media: Knowledge of media production, communication, and dissemination techniques and methods. This includes alternative ways to inform and entertain via written, oral, and visual media. English Language: Knowledge of the structure and content of the English language, including the meaning and spelling of words, rules of composition, and grammar. Education and Training: Knowledge of principles and methods for curriculum and training design, teaching and instruction for individuals and groups, and the measurement of training effects. Customer and Personal Service: Knowledge of principles and processes for providing customer and personal services. This includes customer needs assessment, meeting quality standards for services, and evaluation of customer satisfaction.

# Dental Assistants

- ▲ Growth: 37.2%
- ▲ Annual Job Openings: 16,000
- ▲ Annual Earnings: $26,740
- ▲ Education/Training Required: Moderate-term on-the-job training
- ▲ Self-Employed: 0%
- ▲ Part-Time: 39.7%

Assist dentist, set up patient and equipment, and keep records. Prepares patient, sterilizes and disinfects instruments, sets up instrument trays, prepares materials, and assists dentist during dental procedures. Takes and records medical and dental histories and vital signs of patients. Assists dentist in management of medical and dental emergencies. Provides postoperative instructions prescribed by dentist. Applies protective coating of fluoride to teeth. Exposes dental diagnostic X rays. Records treatment information in patient records. Makes preliminary impressions for study casts and occlusal registrations for mounting study casts. Fabricates temporary restorations and custom impressions from preliminary impressions. Cleans teeth, using dental instruments. Schedules appointments, prepares bills and receives payment for dental services, completes insurance forms, and maintains records, manually or using computer. Instructs patients in oral hygiene and plaque control programs. Cleans and polishes removable appliances. Pours, trims, and polishes study casts. **SKILLS**—Reading Comprehension. Active Listening. Speaking. Writing. Service Orientation. Mathematics.

**GOE**—**Interest Area:** 14. Medical and Health Services. **Work Group:** 14.03. Dentistry. **Other Job Titles in This Work Group:** Dental Hygienists; Dentists, All Other Specialists; Dentists, General; Oral and Maxil-

lofacial Surgeons; Orthodontists; Prosthodontists. **PERSONALITY TYPE**—Social. Social occupations frequently involve working with, communicating with, and teaching people. These occupations often involve helping or providing service to others.

**EDUCATION/TRAINING PROGRAM(S)**—Dental Assistant. **RELATED KNOWLEDGE/COURSES**—**Medicine and Dentistry:** Knowledge of the information and techniques needed to diagnose and treat human injuries, diseases, and deformities. This includes symptoms, treatment alternatives, drug properties and interactions, and preventive health-care measures. **Clerical Studies:** Knowledge of administrative and clerical procedures and systems such as word processing, managing files and records, stenography and transcription, designing forms, and other office procedures and terminology. **English Language:** Knowledge of the structure and content of the English language, including the meaning and spelling of words, rules of composition, and grammar. **Customer and Personal Service:** Knowledge of principles and processes for providing customer and personal services. This includes customer needs assessment, meeting quality standards for services, and evaluation of customer satisfaction. **Mathematics:** Knowledge of arithmetic, algebra, geometry, calculus, statistics, and their applications.

# Dental Hygienists

- ▲ Growth: 37.1%
- ▲ Annual Job Openings: 5,000
- ▲ Annual Earnings: $51,980
- ▲ Education/Training Required: Associate's degree
- ▲ Self-Employed: 0.7%
- ▲ Part-Time: 22.9%

**Clean teeth and examine oral areas, head, and neck for signs of oral disease. May educate patients on oral hygiene, take and develop X rays, or apply fluoride or sealants.** Cleans calcareous deposits, accretions, and stains from teeth and beneath margins of gums, using dental instruments. Charts conditions of decay and disease for diagnosis and treatment by dentist. Examines gums, using probes, to locate periodontal recessed gums

and signs of gum disease. Administers local anesthetic agents. Exposes and develops X-ray film. Applies fluorides and other cavity-preventing agents to arrest dental decay. Removes sutures and dressings. Makes impressions for study casts. Places, carves, and finishes amalgam restorations. Feels and visually examines gums for sores and signs of disease. Feels lymph nodes under patient's chin to detect swelling or tenderness that could indicate presence of oral cancer. Places and removes rubber dams, matrices, and temporary restorations. Removes excess cement from coronal surfaces of teeth. Conducts dental health clinics for community groups to augment services of dentist. Provides clinical services and health education to improve and maintain oral health of school children. **SKILLS**—Reading Comprehension. Active Learning. Speaking. Critical Thinking. Service Orientation. Science.

**GOE—Interest Area:** 14. Medical and Health Services. **Work Group:** 14.03. Dentistry. **Other Job Titles in This Work Group:** Dental Assistants; Dentists, All Other Specialists; Dentists, General; Oral and Maxillofacial Surgeons; Orthodontists; Prosthodontists. **PERSONALITY TYPE**—Social. Social occupations frequently involve working with, communicating with, and teaching people. These occupations often involve helping or providing service to others.

**EDUCATION/TRAINING PROGRAM(S)**—Dental Hygienist. **RELATED KNOWLEDGE/COURSES**—

**Medicine and Dentistry:** Knowledge of the information and techniques needed to diagnose and treat human injuries, diseases, and deformities. This includes symptoms, treatment alternatives, drug properties and interactions, and preventive health-care measures. **Biology:** Knowledge of plant and animal organisms and their tissues, cells, functions, interdependencies, and interactions with each other and the environment. **Education and Training:** Knowledge of principles and methods for curriculum and training design, teaching and instruction for individuals and groups, and the measurement of training effects. **English Language:** Knowledge of the structure and content of the English language, including the meaning and spelling of words, rules of composition, and grammar. **Customer and Personal Service:** Knowledge of principles and processes for providing customer and personal services. This includes customer needs assessment, meeting quality standards for services, and evaluation of customer satisfaction.

# Design Printing Machine Setters and Set-Up Operators

▲ Growth: 5.5%
▲ Annual Job Openings: 24,000
▲ Annual Earnings: $30,090
▲ Education/Training Required: Moderate-term on-the-job training
▲ Self-Employed: 2.6%
▲ Part-Time: 3.3%

**Set up or set up and operate machines to print designs on materials.** Installs printing plates, cylinders, or rollers on machine, using hand tools and gauges. Measures and records amount of product produced. Repairs or replaces worn or broken parts, using hand tools. Cleans and lubricates equipment. Inspects product to detect defects. Mixes colors of paint according to formulas. Adjusts and changes gears, using hand tools. Fills reservoirs with paint or ink. Adjusts feed guides, gauges, and rollers, using hand tools. Monitors machines and gauges to ensure and maintain standards. **SKILLS**—Operation and Control. Operation Monitoring. Equipment Maintenance. Repairing. Equipment Selection.

**GOE—Interest Area:** 08. Industrial Production. **Work Group:** 08.03. Production Work. **Other Job Titles in This Work Group:** Bakers, Manufacturing; Bindery Machine Operators and Tenders; Brazers; Cementing and Gluing Machine Operators and Tenders; Chemical Equipment Controllers and Operators; Chemical Equipment Operators and Tenders; Chemical Equipment Tenders; Cleaning, Washing, and Metal Pickling Equipment Operators and Tenders; Coating, Painting, and Spraying Machine Operators and Tenders; Coil Winders, Tapers, and Finishers; Combination Machine Tool Operators and Tenders, Metal and Plastic; Computer-Controlled Machine Tool Operators, Metal and Plastic; Cooling and Freezing Equipment Operators and

Tenders; Crushing, Grinding, and Polishing Machine Setters, Operators, and Tenders; Cutters and Trimmers, Hand; Cutting and Slicing Machine Operators and Tenders; Cutting and Slicing Machine Setters, Operators, and Tenders; Electrolytic Plating and Coating Machine Operators and Tenders, Metal and Plastic; Electrolytic Plating and Coating Machine Setters and Set-Up Operators, Metal and Plastic; Electrotypers and Stereotypers; Embossing Machine Set-Up Operators; Engraver Set-Up Operators; Extruding and Forming Machine Operators and Tenders, Synthetic or Glass Fibers; Extruding and Forming Machine Setters, Operators, and Tenders, Synthetic and Glass Fibers; Extruding, Forming, Pressing, and Compacting Machine Operators and Tenders; Fabric and Apparel Patternmakers; Fiber Product Cutting Machine Setters and Set-Up Operators; Fiberglass Laminators and Fabricators; Film Laboratory Technicians; Fitters, Structural Metal—Precision; others. **PERSONALITY TYPE—** Realistic. Realistic occupations frequently involve work activities that include practical, hands-on problems and solutions. They often deal with plants, animals, and real-world materials like wood, tools, and machinery. Many of the occupations require working outside and do not involve a lot of paperwork or working closely with others.

**EDUCATION/TRAINING PROGRAM(S)**—Graphic and Printing Equipment Operator, General; Graphic and Printing Equipment Operators, Other; Printing Press Operator. **RELATED KNOWLEDGE/COURSES**— **Principles of Mechanical Devices:** Knowledge of machines and tools, including their designs, uses, repair, and maintenance. **Production and Processing:** Knowledge of raw materials, production processes, quality control, costs, and other techniques for maximizing the effective manufacture and distribution of goods. **Engineering and Technology:** Knowledge of the practical application of engineering science and technology. This includes applying principles, techniques, procedures, and equipment to the design and production of various goods and services. **Mathematics:** Knowledge of arithmetic, algebra, geometry, calculus, statistics, and their applications.

# Desktop Publishers

- ▲ Growth: 66.7%
- ▲ Annual Job Openings: 5,000
- ▲ Annual Earnings: $32,700
- ▲ Education/Training Required: Post-secondary vocational training
- ▲ Self-Employed: 2.6%
- ▲ Part-Time: 19.4%

**Format typescript and graphic elements using computer software to produce publication-ready material.** Views monitors for visual representation of work in progress and for instructions and feedback throughout process. Activates options, such as masking, pixel (picture element) editing, airbrushing, or image retouching. Saves completed work on floppy disks or magnetic tape. Studies layout or other instructions to determine work to be done and sequence of operations. Creates special effects, such as vignettes, mosaics, and image combining. Loads floppy disks or tapes containing information into system. Enters digitized data into electronic prepress system computer memory, using scanner, camera, keyboard, or mouse. Enters data, such as coordinates of images and color specifications, into system to retouch and make color corrections. Enters data, such as background color, shapes, and coordinates of images, and retrieves data from system memory. Activates options, such as masking or text processing. **SKILLS**— Equipment Selection. Operation and Control. Reading Comprehension. Operations Analysis. Monitoring.

**GOE—Interest Area:** 01. Arts, Entertainment, and Media. **Work Group:** 01.07. Graphic Arts. **Other Job Titles in This Work Group:** Camera Operators; Dot Etchers; Electronic Masking System Operators; Engravers, Hand; Engravers/Carvers; Etchers; Etchers and Engravers; Etchers, Hand; Pantograph Engravers; Paste-Up Workers; Photoengravers; Precision Etchers and Engravers, Hand or Machine. **PERSONALITY TYPE**—Realistic. Realistic occupations frequently involve work activities that include practical, hands-on problems and solutions. They often deal with plants, animals, and real-world materials like wood, tools, and machinery. Many of the occupations require working outside and do not involve a lot of paperwork or working closely with others.

**EDUCATION/TRAINING PROGRAM(S)**—Desktop Publishing Equipment Operator. **RELATED KNOWLEDGE/COURSES**—**Computers and Electronics:** Knowledge of circuit boards, processors, chips, electronic equipment, and computer hardware and software, including applications and programming. **Cleri-**

cal **Studies:** Knowledge of administrative and clerical procedures and systems such as word processing, managing files and records, stenography and transcription, designing forms, and other office procedures and terminology. **Communications and Media:** Knowledge of media production, communication, and dissemination techniques and methods. This includes alternative ways to inform and entertain via written, oral, and visual media. **English Language:** Knowledge of the structure and content of the English language, including the meaning and spelling of words, rules of composition, and grammar. **Production and Processing:** Knowledge of raw materials, production processes, quality control, costs, and other techniques for maximizing the effective manufacture and distribution of goods. **Design:** Knowledge of design techniques, tools, and principles involved in production of precision technical plans, blueprints, drawings, and models.

# Dispatchers, Except Police, Fire, and Ambulance

▲ Growth: 22.2%

▲ Annual Job Openings: 8,000

▲ Annual Earnings: $30,410

▲ Education/Training Required: Moderate-term on-the-job training

▲ Self-Employed: 0%

▲ Part-Time: 8.6%

Schedule and dispatch workers, work crews, equipment, or service vehicles for conveyance of materials, freight, or passengers or for normal installation, service, or emergency repairs rendered outside the place of business. Duties may include using radio, telephone, or computer to transmit assignments and compiling statistics and reports on work progress. Routes or assigns workers or equipment to appropriate location, according to customer request, specifications, or needs. Confers with customer or supervising personnel regarding questions, problems, and requests for service or equipment. Orders supplies and equipment, and issues to personnel. Records and maintains files and records regarding customer requests, work or services performed, charges, expenses, inventory, and other dispatch information. Determines types or amount of equipment, vehicles, materials, or personnel required, according to

work order or specifications. Receives or prepares work orders according to customer request or specifications. Relays work orders, messages, and information to or from work crews, supervisors, and field inspectors, using telephone or two-way radio. **SKILLS**—Active Listening. Time Management. Equipment Selection. Coordination. Speaking.

**GOE**—Interest Area: 09. Business Detail. **Work Group:** 09.06. Communications. **Other Job Titles in This Work Group:** Central Office Operators; Communications Equipment Operators, All Other; Directory Assistance Operators; Police, Fire, and Ambulance Dispatchers; Switchboard Operators, Including Answering Service; Telephone Operators. **PERSONALITY TYPE**—Conventional. Conventional occupations frequently involve following set procedures and routines.

These occupations can include working with data and details more than with ideas. Usually there is a clear line of authority to follow.

**EDUCATION/TRAINING PROGRAM(S)**—Stationary Energy Sources Installer and Operator; Water Transportation Workers, Other. **RELATED KNOWLEDGE/COURSES**—**Telecommunications:** Knowledge of transmission, broadcasting, switching, control, and operation of telecommunications systems. **Transportation:** Knowledge of principles and methods for moving people or goods by air, rail, sea, or road, including the relative costs and benefits. **Customer and**

**Personal Service:** Knowledge of principles and processes for providing customer and personal services. This includes customer needs assessment, meeting quality standards for services, and evaluation of customer satisfaction. **Clerical Studies:** Knowledge of administrative and clerical procedures and systems such as word processing, managing files and records, stenography and transcription, designing forms, and other office procedures and terminology. **English Language:** Knowledge of the structure and content of the English language, including the meaning and spelling of words, rules of composition, and grammar.

# Dragline Operators

- ▲ Growth: 14.8%
- ▲ Annual Job Openings: 5,000
- ▲ Annual Earnings: $33,480
- ▲ Education/Training Required: Moderate-term on-the-job training
- ▲ Self-Employed: 8.3%
- ▲ Part-Time: 12.8%

**Operate power-driven crane equipment with dragline bucket to excavate or move sand, gravel, mud, or other materials.** Moves controls to position boom, lower and drag bucket through material, and release material at unloading point. Directs workers engaged in placing blocks and outriggers to prevent capsizing of machine when lifting heavy loads. Drives machine to work site. **SKILLS**—Operation and Control. Coordination. Speaking.

**GOE**—**Interest Area:** 08. Industrial Production. **Work Group:** 08.07. Hands-on Work: Loading, Moving, Hoisting, and Conveying. **Other Job Titles in This Work Group:** Conveyor Operators and Tenders; Crane and Tower Operators; Excavating and Loading Machine and Dragline Operators; Freight, Stock, and Material Movers, Hand; Hoist and Winch Operators; Industrial Truck and Tractor Operators; Irradiated-Fuel Handlers; Laborers and Freight, Stock, and Material Movers, Hand; Machine Feeders and Offbearers; Material Moving Workers, All Other; Packers and Packagers, Hand; Pump Operators, Except Wellhead Pumpers; Refuse and Recyclable Material Collectors; Tank Car, Truck, and

Ship Loaders. **PERSONALITY TYPE**—Realistic. Realistic occupations frequently involve work activities that include practical, hands-on problems and solutions. They often deal with plants, animals, and real-world materials like wood, tools, and machinery. Many of the occupations require working outside and do not involve a lot of paperwork or working closely with others.

**EDUCATION/TRAINING PROGRAM(S)**—Construction Equipment Operator. **RELATED KNOWLEDGE/COURSES**—**Principles of Mechanical Devices:** Knowledge of machines and tools, including their designs, uses, repair, and maintenance. **Building and Construction:** Knowledge of materials, methods, and tools involved in the construction or repair of houses, buildings, or other structures such as highways and roads. **Engineering and Technology:** Knowledge of the practical application of engineering science and technology. This includes applying principles, techniques, procedures, and equipment to the design and production of various goods and services. **Transportation:** Knowledge of principles and methods for moving people or goods by air, rail, sea, or road, including

D

the relative costs and benefits. **Public Safety and Security:** Knowledge of relevant equipment, policies, procedures, and strategies to promote effective local, state, or national security operations for the protection of people, data, property, and institutions. **Geography:** Knowledge of principles and methods for describing the features of land, sea, and air masses, including their physical characteristics, locations, interrelationships, and distribution of plant, animal, and human life. **Physics:** Knowledge and prediction of physical principles and laws and their interrelationships and applications to understanding fluid, material, and atmospheric dynamics and mechanical, electrical, atomic, and sub-atomic structures and processes.

# Drywall Installers

- ▲ Growth: 9.4%
- ▲ Annual Job Openings: 19,000
- ▲ Annual Earnings: $35,580
- ▲ Education/Training Required: Moderate-term on-the-job training
- ▲ Self-Employed: 20.4%
- ▲ Part-Time: 8.4%

**Apply plasterboard or other wallboard to ceilings and interior walls of buildings.** Trims rough edges from wallboard to maintain even joints, using knife. Fits and fastens wallboard or sheetrock into specified position, using hand tools, portable power tools, or adhesive. Measures and marks cutting lines on framing, drywall, and trim, using tape measure, straightedge or square, and marking devices. Installs blanket insulation between studs and tacks plastic moisture barrier over insulation. Removes plaster, drywall, or paneling, using crowbar and hammer. Assembles and installs metal framing and decorative trim for windows, doorways, and bents. Reads blueprints and other specifications to determine method of installation, work procedures, and material and tool requirements. Lays out reference lines and points, computes position of framing and furring channels, and marks position, using chalkline. Suspends angle iron grid and channel iron from ceiling, using wire. Installs horizontal and vertical metal or wooden studs for attachment of wallboard on interior walls, using hand tools. Cuts metal or wood framing, angle and channel iron, and trim to size, using cutting tools. Cuts openings into board for electrical outlets, windows, vents, or fixtures, using keyhole saw or other cutting tools. **SKILLS**—Installation. Equipment Selection. Mathematics. Judgment and Decision Making.

**GOE—Interest Area:** 06. Construction, Mining, and Drilling. **Work Group:** 06.02. Construction. **Other Job Titles in This Work Group:** Boat Builders and Shipwrights; Boilermakers; Brattice Builders; Brickmasons and Blockmasons; Carpenters; Carpet Installers; Ceiling Tile Installers; Cement Masons and Concrete Finishers; Commercial Divers; Construction Carpenters; Drywall and Ceiling Tile Installers; Electricians; Explosives Workers, Ordnance Handling Experts, and Blasters; Fence Erectors; Floor Layers, Except Carpet, Wood, and Hard Tiles; Floor Sanders and Finishers; Glaziers; Grader, Bulldozer, and Scraper Operators; Hazardous Materials Removal Workers; Insulation Workers, Floor, Ceiling, and Wall; Insulation Workers, Mechanical; Manufactured Building and Mobile Home Installers; Operating Engineers; Operating Engineers and Other Construction Equipment Operators; Painters, Construction and Maintenance; Paperhangers; Paving, Surfacing, and Tamping Equipment Operators; Pile-Driver Operators; Pipe Fitters; Pipelayers; Pipelaying Fitters; Plasterers and Stucco Masons; Plumbers; Plumbers, Pipefitters, and Steamfitters; Rail-Track Laying and Maintenance Equipment Operators; Refractory Materials Repairers, Except Brickmasons; Reinforcing Iron and Rebar Workers; Riggers; Roofers; Rough Carpenters; Security and Fire Alarm Systems Installers; Segmental Pavers; Sheet Metal Workers; Ship Carpenters and Joiners; Stone Cutters and Carvers; Stonemasons; Structural Iron and Steel Workers; Tapers; Terrazzo Workers and Finishers; Tile and Marble Setters. **PERSONALITY TYPE**—Realistic. Realistic occupations frequently involve work activities that include practical, hands-on problems and solutions. They often deal with plants, animals, and real-world materials like wood, tools, and machinery. Many of the occupations require working outside and do not involve a lot of paperwork or working closely with others.

**EDUCATION/TRAINING PROGRAM(S)**—No data available. **RELATED KNOWLEDGE/COURSES**—**Building and Construction:** Knowledge of materials, methods, and tools involved in the construction or repair of houses, buildings, or other structures such as highways and roads. **Design:** Knowledge of design techniques, tools, and principles involved in production of precision technical plans, blueprints, drawings, and models. **Principles of Mechanical Devices:** Knowledge of machines and tools, including their designs, uses, repair, and maintenance. **Engineering and Technology:** Knowledge of the practical application of engineering science and technology. This includes applying principles, techniques, procedures, and equipment to the design and production of various goods and services. **Mathematics:** Knowledge of arithmetic, algebra, geometry, calculus, statistics, and their applications.

# Electrical and Electronics Repairers, Commercial and Industrial Equipment

- ▲ Growth: 9.2%
- ▲ Annual Job Openings: 10,000
- ▲ Annual Earnings: $37,190
- ▲ Education/Training Required: Post-secondary vocational training
- ▲ Self-Employed: 0%
- ▲ Part-Time: 2.6%

**Repair, test, adjust, or install electronic equipment, such as industrial controls, transmitters, and antennas.** Analyzes technical requirements of customer desiring to utilize electronic equipment and performs installation and maintenance duties. Calibrates testing instruments and installed or repaired equipment to prescribed specifications. Consults with customer, supervisor, and engineers to plan layout of equipment and to resolve problems in system operation and maintenance. Enters information into computer to copy program or to draw, modify, or store schematics, applying knowledge of software package used. Maintains records of repairs, calibrations, and tests. Converses with equipment operators to ascertain whether mechanical or human error contributed to equipment breakdown. Studies blueprints, schematics, manuals, and other specifications to determine installation procedures. Operates equipment to demonstrate use of equipment and to analyze malfunctions. Determines feasibility of using standardized equipment and develops specifications for equipment required to perform additional functions. Inspects components of equipment for defects, such as loose connections and frayed wire, and for accuracy of assembly and installation. Tests faulty equipment, using test equipment and applying knowledge of functional operation of electronic unit and systems to diagnose malfunction. Advises management regarding customer satisfaction, product performance, and suggestions for product improvements. Signs overhaul documents for equipment replaced or repaired. Installs equipment in industrial or military establishments and in aircraft and missiles. Replaces or repairs defective components, using hand tools and technical documents. Adjusts defective components, using hand tools and technical documents. **SKILLS**—Equipment Maintenance. Troubleshooting. Installation. Repairing. Reading Comprehension.

**GOE**—**Interest Area:** 05. Mechanics, Installers, and Repairers. **Work Group:** 05.02. Electrical and Electronic Systems. **Other Job Titles in This Work Group:**

Avionics Technicians; Battery Repairers; Central Office and PBX Installers and Repairers; Communication Equipment Mechanics, Installers, and Repairers; Computer, Automated Teller, and Office Machine Repairers; Data Processing Equipment Repairers; Electric Home Appliance and Power Tool Repairers; Electric Meter Installers and Repairers; Electric Motor and Switch Assemblers and Repairers; Electric Motor, Power Tool, and Related Repairers; Electrical and Electronics Installers and Repairers, Transportation Equipment; Electrical and Electronics Repairers, Powerhouse, Substation, and Relay; Electrical Parts Reconditioners; Electrical Power-Line Installers and Repairers; Electronic Equipment Installers and Repairers, Motor Vehicles; Electronic Home Entertainment Equipment Installers and Repairers; Elevator Installers and Repairers; Frame Wirers, Central Office; Home Appliance Installers; Home Appliance Repairers; Office Machine and Cash Register Servicers; Radio Mechanics; Signal and Track Switch Repairers; Station Installers and Repairers, Telephone; Telecommunications Equipment Installers and Repairers, Except Line Installers; Telecommunications Facility Examiners; Telecommunications Line Installers and Repairers; Transformer Repairers. **PERSONALITY TYPE**—Realistic. Realistic occupations frequently involve work activities that include practical, hands-on problems and solutions. They often deal with plants, animals, and real-world materials like wood,

tools, and machinery. Many of the occupations require working outside and do not involve a lot of paperwork or working closely with others.

**EDUCATION/TRAINING PROGRAM(S)**—Computer Installer and Repairer; Computer Maintenance Technologist/Technician; Industrial Electronics Installer and Repairer. **RELATED KNOWLEDGE/COURSES**—**Computers and Electronics:** Knowledge of circuit boards, processors, chips, electronic equipment, and computer hardware and software, including applications and programming. **Telecommunications:** Knowledge of transmission, broadcasting, switching, control, and operation of telecommunications systems. **Design:** Knowledge of design techniques, tools, and principles involved in production of precision technical plans, blueprints, drawings, and models. **Engineering and Technology:** Knowledge of the practical application of engineering science and technology. This includes applying principles, techniques, procedures, and equipment to the design and production of various goods and services. **Mathematics:** Knowledge of arithmetic, algebra, geometry, calculus, statistics, and their applications. **Physics:** Knowledge and prediction of physical principles and laws and their interrelationships and applications to understanding fluid, material, and atmospheric dynamics and mechanical, electrical, atomic, and sub-atomic structures and processes.

# Electrical Drafters

- ▲ Growth: 23.3%
- ▲ Annual Job Openings: 5,000
- ▲ Annual Earnings: $40,420
- ▲ Education/Training Required: Postsecondary vocational training
- ▲ Self-Employed: 4.9%
- ▲ Part-Time: 7.9%

**Develop specifications and instructions for installation of voltage transformers, overhead or underground cables, and related electrical equipment used to conduct electrical energy from transmission lines or high-voltage distribution lines to consumers.** Drafts working drawing, wiring diagrams, wiring connections, or cross section of underground cables as required for instruc-

tions to installation crew. Takes measurements, such as distances to be spanned by wire and cable, which affect installation and arrangement of equipment. Reviews completed construction drawings and cost estimates for accuracy and conformity to standards and regulations. Draws master sketch showing relation of proposed installation to existing facilities. Drafts sketches to scale.

Studies work order request to determine type of service, such as lighting or power, demanded by installation. Estimates labor and material costs for installation of electrical equipment and distribution systems. Confers with engineering staff and other personnel to resolve problems. Visits site of proposed installation and draws rough sketch of location. **SKILLS**—Operations Analysis. Judgment and Decision Making. Mathematics. Equipment Selection. Management of Personnel Resources. Reading Comprehension.

**GOE**—**Interest Area:** 02. Science, Math, and Engineering. **Work Group:** 02.08. Engineering Technology. **Other Job Titles in This Work Group:** Aerospace Engineering and Operations Technicians; Architectural and Civil Drafters; Architectural Drafters; Calibration and Instrumentation Technicians; Cartographers and Photogrammetrists; Civil Drafters; Civil Engineering Technicians; Construction and Building Inspectors; Drafters, All Other; Electrical and Electronic Engineering Technicians; Electrical and Electronics Drafters; Electrical Engineering Technicians; Electro-Mechanical Technicians; Electronic Drafters; Electronics Engineering Technicians; Engineering Technicians, Except Drafters, All Other; Environmental Engineering Technicians; Industrial Engineering Technicians; Mapping Technicians; Mechanical Drafters; Mechanical Engineering Technicians; Numerical Tool and Process Control Programmers; Pressure Vessel Inspectors; Surveying and Mapping Technicians; Surveying Technicians; Surveyors. **PERSONALITY TYPE**—Conventional. Conventional occupations frequently involve following set procedures and routines. These occupations can include working with data and details more than with ideas. Usually there is a clear line of authority to follow.

**EDUCATION/TRAINING PROGRAM(S)**—Electrical/Electronics Drafting. **RELATED KNOWLEDGE/COURSES**—**Design:** Knowledge of design techniques, tools, and principles involved in production of precision technical plans, blueprints, drawings, and models. **Engineering and Technology:** Knowledge of the practical application of engineering science and technology. This includes applying principles, techniques, procedures, and equipment to the design and production of various goods and services. **Mathematics:** Knowledge of arithmetic, algebra, geometry, calculus, statistics, and their applications. **Administration and Management:** Knowledge of business and management principles involved in strategic planning, resource allocation, human resources modeling, leadership technique, production methods, and coordination of people and resources. **Building and Construction:** Knowledge of materials, methods, and tools involved in the construction or repair of houses, buildings, or other structures such as highways and roads.

# Electrical Engineering Technicians

- ▲ Growth: 10.8%
- ▲ Annual Job Openings: 22,000
- ▲ Annual Earnings: $41,210
- ▲ Education/Training Required: Associate's degree
- ▲ Self-Employed: 2.7%
- ▲ Part-Time: 3.1%

**Apply electrical theory and related knowledge to test and modify developmental or operational electrical machinery and electrical control equipment and circuitry in industrial or commercial plants and laboratories. Usually work under direction of engineering staff.** Sets up and operates test equipment to evaluate performance of developmental parts, assemblies, or systems under simulated operating conditions. Maintains and repairs testing equipment. Plans method and sequence of operations for testing and developing experimental electronic and electrical equipment. Assembles electrical and electronic systems and prototypes according to engineering data and knowledge of electrical principles, using hand tools and measuring instruments. Analyzes and interprets test information. Collaborates with electrical engineer and other personnel to solve developmental problems. Draws diagrams and writes engineering specifications to clarify design details and functional criteria of experimental electronics units. Modifies electrical prototypes, parts, assemblies, and systems to correct functional deviations. **SKILLS**—Technology Design. Active Learning. Troubleshooting. Operations Analysis. Reading Comprehension. Equipment Selection.

**GOE**—**Interest Area:** 02. Science, Math, and Engineering. **Work Group:** 02.08. Engineering Technology. **Other Job Titles in This Work Group:** Aerospace Engineering and Operations Technicians; Architectural and Civil Drafters; Architectural Drafters; Calibration and Instrumentation Technicians; Cartographers and Photogrammetrists; Civil Drafters; Civil Engineering Technicians; Construction and Building Inspectors; Drafters, All Other; Electrical and Electronic Engineering Technicians; Electrical and Electronics Drafters; Electrical Drafters; Electro-Mechanical Technicians; Electronic Drafters; Electronics Engineering Technicians; Engineering Technicians, Except Drafters, All Other; Environmental Engineering Technicians; Industrial Engineering Technicians; Mapping Technicians; Mechanical Drafters; Mechanical Engineering Technicians; Numerical Tool and Process Control Programmers; Pressure Vessel Inspectors; Surveying and Mapping Technicians; Surveying Technicians; Surveyors. **PERSONALITY TYPE**—Realistic. Realistic occupations frequently involve work activities that include practical, hands-on problems and solutions. They often deal with plants, animals, and real-world materials like wood, tools, and machinery. Many of the occupations require working outside and do not involve a lot of paperwork or working closely with others.

**EDUCATION/TRAINING PROGRAM(S)**—Computer Engineering Technologist/Technician; Electrical and Electronic Engineering-Related Technologist/Technician; Electrical, Electronic and Communications Engineering Technologist/Technician. **RELATED KNOWLEDGE/COURSES**—**Engineering and Technology:** Knowledge of the practical application of engineering science and technology. This includes applying principles, techniques, procedures, and equipment to the design and production of various goods and services. **Mathematics:** Knowledge of arithmetic, algebra, geometry, calculus, statistics, and their applications. **Design:** Knowledge of design techniques, tools, and principles involved in production of precision technical plans, blueprints, drawings, and models. **Computers and Electronics:** Knowledge of circuit boards, processors, chips, electronic equipment, and computer hardware and software, including applications and programming. **Physics:** Knowledge and prediction of physical principles and laws and their interrelationships and applications to understanding fluid, material, and atmospheric dynamics and mechanical, electrical, atomic, and sub-atomic structures and processes.

# Electrical Power-Line Installers and Repairers

- ▲ Growth: 9.3%
- ▲ Annual Job Openings: 5,000
- ▲ Annual Earnings: $44,490
- ▲ Education/Training Required: Long-term on-the-job training
- ▲ Self-Employed: 0%
- ▲ Part-Time: 1%

**Install or repair cables or wires used in electrical power or distribution systems. May erect poles and light or heavy duty transmission towers.** Repairs electrical power cables and auxiliary equipment for electrical power lines. Drives conveyance equipped with tools and materials to job site. Works on energized lines to avoid interruption of service. Covers conductors with insulating or fireproofing materials. Installs watt-hour meters and connects service drops between power line and consumer. Tests conductors to identify corresponding conductors and to prevent incorrect connections, according to electrical diagrams and specifications. Cleans, tins, and splices corresponding conductors by twisting ends together or by joining ends with metal clamps and soldering connection. Cuts and peels lead sheath and insulation from defective or newly installed cables and conducts prior to splicing. Replaces and straightens poles and attaches crossarms, insulators, and auxiliary equipment to wood poles preparatory to erection. Splices, solders, and insulates conductors and wiring to join sections of power line and to connect transformers and electrical accessories. Tests electric power lines and auxiliary equipment, using direct reading and testing instruments to identify cause of disturbances. Strings wire conductors and cable between erected poles and adjusts slack, using winch. Opens switches or clamps grounding device to de-energize disturbed or fallen lines to facilitate repairs or to remove electrical hazards. Climbs poles and removes and installs hardware, wires, and other equipment. Splices cables together or to overhead transmission line, customer service line, or street light line. Installs and repairs conduits, cables, wires, and auxiliary equipment following blueprints. **SKILLS**—Installation. Troubleshooting. Repairing. Equipment Maintenance. Quality Control Analysis.

**GOE—Interest Area:** 05. Mechanics, Installers, and Repairers. **Work Group:** 05.02. Electrical and Electronic Systems. **Other Job Titles in This Work Group:** Avionics Technicians; Battery Repairers; Central Office and PBX Installers and Repairers; Communication Equipment Mechanics, Installers, and Repairers; Computer, Automated Teller, and Office Machine Repairers; Data Processing Equipment Repairers; Electric Home Appliance and Power Tool Repairers; Electric Meter Installers and Repairers; Electric Motor and Switch Assemblers and Repairers; Electric Motor, Power Tool, and Related Repairers; Electrical and Electronics Installers and Repairers, Transportation Equipment; Electrical and Electronics Repairers, Commercial and Industrial Equipment; Electrical and Electronics Repairers, Powerhouse, Substation, and Relay; Electrical Parts Reconditioners; Electronic Equipment Installers

and Repairers, Motor Vehicles; Electronic Home Entertainment Equipment Installers and Repairers; Elevator Installers and Repairers; Frame Wirers, Central Office; Home Appliance Installers; Home Appliance Repairers; Office Machine and Cash Register Servicers; Radio Mechanics; Signal and Track Switch Repairers; Station Installers and Repairers, Telephone; Telecommunications Equipment Installers and Repairers, Except Line Installers; Telecommunications Facility Examiners; Telecommunications Line Installers and Repairers; Transformer Repairers. **PERSONALITY TYPE**—Realistic. Realistic occupations frequently involve work activities that include practical, hands-on problems and solutions. They often deal with plants, animals, and real-world materials like wood, tools, and machinery. Many of the occupations require working outside and do not involve a lot of paperwork or working closely with others.

**EDUCATION/TRAINING PROGRAM(S)**—Electrical and Power Transmission Installer, General; Electrical and Power Transmission Installer, Other; Lineworker. **RELATED KNOWLEDGE/COURSES—Principles of Mechanical Devices:** Knowledge of machines and tools, including their designs, uses, repair, and maintenance. **Building and Construction:** Knowledge of materials, methods, and tools involved in the construction or repair of houses, buildings, or other structures such as highways and roads. **Transportation:** Knowledge of principles and methods for moving people or goods by air, rail, sea, or road, including the relative costs and benefits. **Public Safety and Security:** Knowledge of relevant equipment, policies, procedures, and strategies to promote effective local, state, or national security operations for the protection of people, data, property, and institutions. **Engineering and Technology:** Knowledge of the practical application of engineering science and technology. This includes applying principles, techniques, procedures, and equipment to the design and production of various goods and services. **Design:** Knowledge of design techniques, tools, and principles involved in production of precision technical plans, blueprints, drawings, and models.

# Electricians

▲ Growth: 17.3%

▲ Annual Job Openings: 66,000

▲ Annual Earnings: $42,210

▲ Education/Training Required: Long-term on-the-job training

▲ Self-Employed: 8%

▲ Part-Time: 4.4%

**Install, maintain, and repair electrical wiring, equipment, and fixtures. Ensure that work is in accordance with relevant codes. May install or service street lights, intercom systems, or electrical control systems.** Installs electrical wiring, equipment, apparatus, and fixtures, using hand tools and power tools. Tests electrical systems and continuity of circuits in electrical wiring, equipment, and fixtures, using testing devices such as ohmmeters, voltmeters, and oscilloscopes. Readies and assembles electrical wiring, equipment, and fixtures, using specifications and hand tools. Climbs ladder to install, maintain, or repair electrical wiring, equipment, and fixtures. Possesses electrician's license or identification card to meet governmental regulations. Drives vehicle, operates flood lights, and places flares during power failure or emergency. Directs and trains workers to install, maintain, or repair electrical wiring, equipment, and fixtures. Constructs and fabricates parts, using hand tools and specifications. Prepares sketches of location of wiring and equipment or follows blueprints to determine location of equipment and conformance to safety codes. Diagnoses malfunctioning systems, apparatus, and components, using test equipment and hand tools. Inspects systems and electrical parts to detect hazards, defects, and need for adjustments or repair. Maintains and repairs or replaces wiring, equipment and fixtures, using hand tools. Plans layout and installation of electrical wiring, equipment, and fixtures consistent with specifications and local codes. **SKILLS**—Installation. Repairing. Equipment Selection. Troubleshooting. Mathematics.

**GOE—Interest Area:** 06. Construction, Mining, and Drilling. **Work Group:** 06.02. Construction. **Other Job Titles in This Work Group:** Boat Builders and Shipwrights; Boilermakers; Brattice Builders; Brickmasons and Blockmasons; Carpenters; Carpet Installers; Ceiling Tile Installers; Cement Masons and Concrete Finishers; Commercial Divers; Construction Carpenters; Drywall and Ceiling Tile Installers; Drywall Installers; Explosives Workers, Ordnance Handling Experts, and Blasters; Fence Erectors; Floor Layers, Except Carpet, Wood, and Hard Tiles; Floor Sanders and Finishers; Glaziers; Grader, Bulldozer, and Scraper Operators; Hazardous Materials Removal Workers; Insulation Workers, Floor, Ceiling, and Wall; Insulation Workers, Mechanical; Manufactured Building and Mobile Home Installers; Operating Engineers; Operating Engineers and Other Construction Equipment Operators; Painters, Construction and Maintenance; Paperhangers; Paving, Surfacing, and Tamping Equipment Operators; Pile-Driver Operators; Pipe Fitters; Pipelayers; Pipelaying Fitters; Plasterers and Stucco Masons; Plumbers; Plumbers, Pipefitters, and Steamfitters; Rail-Track Laying and Maintenance Equipment Operators; Refractory Materials Repairers, Except Brickmasons; Reinforcing Iron and Rebar Workers; Riggers; Roofers; Rough Carpenters; Security and Fire Alarm Systems Installers; Segmental Pavers; Sheet Metal Workers; Ship Carpenters and Joiners; Stone Cutters and Carvers; Stonemasons; Structural Iron and Steel Workers; Tapers; Terrazzo Workers and Finishers; Tile and Marble Setters. **PERSONALITY TYPE**—Realistic. Realistic occupations frequently involve work activities that include practical, hands-on problems and solutions. They often deal with plants, animals, and real-world materials like wood, tools, and machinery. Many of the occupations require working outside and do not involve a lot of paperwork or working closely with others.

**EDUCATION/TRAINING PROGRAM(S)**—Electrician; Marine Maintenance and Ship Repairer.

RELATED KNOWLEDGE/COURSES—Design: Knowledge of design techniques, tools, and principles involved in production of precision technical plans, blueprints, drawings, and models. **Engineering and Technology:** Knowledge of the practical application of engineering science and technology. This includes applying principles, techniques, procedures, and equipment to the design and production of various goods and services. **Computers and Electronics:** Knowledge of circuit boards, processors, chips, electronic equipment, and computer hardware and software, including applications and programming. **Building and Construction:** Knowledge of materials, methods, and tools involved in the construction or repair of houses, buildings, or other structures such as highways and roads. **Principles of Mechanical Devices:** Knowledge of machines and tools, including their designs, uses, repair, and maintenance. **Physics:** Knowledge and prediction of physical principles and laws and their interrelationships and applications to understanding fluid, material, and atmospheric dynamics and mechanical, electrical, atomic, and sub-atomic structures and processes. **Education and Training:** Knowledge of principles and methods for curriculum and training design, teaching and instruction for individuals and groups, and the measurement of training effects.

# Electro-Mechanical Technicians

- ▲ Growth: 14.5%
- ▲ Annual Job Openings: 4,000
- ▲ Annual Earnings: $38,630
- ▲ Education/Training Required: Associate's degree
- ▲ Self-Employed: 0%
- ▲ Part-Time: 3.8%

**Operate, test, and maintain unmanned, automated, servo-mechanical, or electromechanical equipment. May operate unmanned submarines, aircraft, or other equipment at worksites, such as oil rigs, deep ocean exploration, or hazardous waste removal. May assist engineers in testing and designing robotics equipment.** Operates metalworking machines to fabricate housings, jigs, fittings, and fixtures. Aligns, fits, and assembles component parts, using hand tools, power tools, fixtures, templates, and microscope. Installs electrical and electronic parts and hardware in housing or assembly, using soldering equipment and hand tools. Tests performance of electromechanical assembly, using test instruments such as oscilloscope, electronic voltmeter, and bridge. Analyzes and records test results and prepares written documentation. Reads blueprints, schematics, diagrams, and technical orders to determine method and sequence of assembly. Inspects parts for surface defects. Verifies dimensions and clearances of parts to ensure conformance to specifications, using precision measuring instruments. Repairs, reworks, and calibrates assemblies to meet operational specifications and tolerances. **SKILLS**—Troubleshooting. Repairing. Quality Control Analysis. Equipment Maintenance. Operation and Control.

**GOE—Interest Area:** 02. Science, Math, and Engineering. **Work Group:** 02.08. Engineering Technology. **Other Job Titles in This Work Group:** Aerospace Engineering and Operations Technicians; Architectural and Civil Drafters; Architectural Drafters; Calibration and Instrumentation Technicians; Cartographers and Photogrammetrists; Civil Drafters; Civil Engineering Technicians; Construction and Building Inspectors; Drafters, All Other; Electrical and Electronic Engineering Technicians; Electrical and Electronics Drafters; Electrical Drafters; Electrical Engineering Technicians; Electronic Drafters; Electronics Engineering Technicians; Engineering Technicians, Except Drafters, All Other; Environmental Engineering Technicians; Industrial Engineering Technicians; Mapping Technicians; Mechanical Drafters; Mechanical Engineering Technicians; Numerical Tool and Process Control Programmers; Pressure Vessel Inspectors; Surveying and Mapping

Technicians; Surveying Technicians; Surveyors. **PER-SONALITY TYPE**—Realistic. Realistic occupations frequently involve work activities that include practical, hands-on problems and solutions. They often deal with plants, animals, and real-world materials like wood, tools, and machinery. Many of the occupations require working outside and do not involve a lot of paperwork or working closely with others.

**EDUCATION/TRAINING PROGRAM(S)**—Computer Engineering Technologist/Technician; Electrical and Electronic Engineering-Related Technologist/Technician; Electrical, Electronic and Communications Engineering Technologist/Technician; Electromechanical Instrumentation and Maintenance Technologist/Technician; Electromechanical Technologist/Technician; Engineering-Related Technologist/Technician, General; Engineering-Related Technologists/Technicians, Other; Mechanical Engineering/Mechanical Technologist/Technician; Robotics Technologist/Technician; Solar Technologist/Technician. **RELATED KNOWLEDGE/COURSES**—**Principles of Mechanical Devices:** Knowledge of machines and tools, including their designs, uses, repair, and maintenance. **Engineering and Technology:** Knowledge of the practical application of engineering science and technology. This includes applying principles, techniques, procedures, and equipment to the design and production of various goods and services. **Production and Processing:** Knowledge of raw materials, production processes, quality control, costs, and other techniques for maximizing the effective manufacture and distribution of goods. **Computers and Electronics:** Knowledge of circuit boards, processors, chips, electronic equipment, and computer hardware and software, including applications and programming. **Design:** Knowledge of design techniques, tools, and principles involved in production of precision technical plans, blueprints, drawings, and models.

# Electronic Drafters

- ▲ Growth: 23.3%
- ▲ Annual Job Openings: 5,000
- ▲ Annual Earnings: $40,420
- ▲ Education/Training Required: Post-secondary vocational training
- ▲ Self-Employed: 4.9%
- ▲ Part-Time: 7.9%

**Draw wiring diagrams, circuit board assembly diagrams, schematics, and layout drawings used for manufacture, installation, and repair of electronic equipment.** Drafts detail and assembly drawings and designs of electromechanical equipment and related data processing systems. Plots electrical test points on layout sheet, using pencil, and draws schematics to wire test fixture heads to frame. Creates master layout of design components and circuitry and printed circuit boards according to specifications, utilizing computer-assisted equipment. Consults with engineers to discuss and interpret design concepts and determine requirements of detailed working drawings. Compares logic element configuration on display screen with engineering schematics and calculates figures to convert, redesign, and modify element. Copies drawings of printed circuit board fabrication, using print machine or blueprinting procedure. Generates computer tapes of final layout design to produce layered photo masks and photo plotting design onto film. Examines and verifies master layout for electrical and mechanical accuracy. Supervises and coordinates work activities of workers engaged in drafting, designing layouts, assembling, and testing printed circuit boards. Locates files relating to specified design projection database library, loads program into computer, and records completed job data. Reviews work orders and procedural manuals and confers with vendors and design staff to resolve problems and modify design. Keys and programs specified commands and engineering specifications into computer system to change functions and test final layout. Compiles data, computes quantities, and prepares cost estimates to determine equipment needs and requisitions materials as required. Selects drill size to drill test head, according to test design and specifications, and submits guide layout to designated department. Reviews blueprints to determine customer requirements and consults with assembler regarding schematics, wiring procedures, and conductor paths. Examines electronic schematics and analyzes logic diagrams and design documents to plan layout of printed circuit board components and circuitry. **SKILLS**—Mathematics. Operations Analysis. Reading Comprehension. Technology Design. Programming.

**GOE**—**Interest Area:** 02. Science, Math, and Engineering. **Work Group:** 02.08. Engineering Technology. **Other Job Titles in This Work Group:** Aerospace Engineering and Operations Technicians; Architectural and Civil Drafters; Architectural Drafters; Calibration and Instrumentation Technicians; Cartographers and Photogrammetrists; Civil Drafters; Civil Engineering Technicians; Construction and Building Inspectors; Drafters, All Other; Electrical and Electronic Engineering Technicians; Electrical and Electronics Drafters; Electrical Drafters; Electrical Engineering Technicians; Electro-Mechanical Technicians; Electronics Engineering Technicians; Engineering Technicians, Except Drafters, All Other; Environmental Engineering Technicians; Industrial Engineering Technicians; Mapping Technicians; Mechanical Drafters; Mechanical Engineering Technicians; Numerical Tool and Process Control Programmers; Pressure Vessel Inspectors; Surveying and Mapping Technicians; Surveying Technicians; Survey-

ors. **PERSONALITY TYPE**—Realistic. Realistic occupations frequently involve work activities that include practical, hands-on problems and solutions. They often deal with plants, animals, and real-world materials like wood, tools, and machinery. Many of the occupations require working outside and do not involve a lot of paperwork or working closely with others.

**EDUCATION/TRAINING PROGRAM(S)**—Electrical/Electronics Drafting. **RELATED KNOWLEDGE/COURSES**—**Design:** Knowledge of design techniques, tools, and principles involved in production of precision technical plans, blueprints, drawings, and models. **Computers and Electronics:** Knowledge of circuit boards, processors, chips, electronic equipment, and computer hardware and software, including applications and programming. **Mathematics:** Knowledge of arithmetic, algebra, geometry, calculus, statistics, and their applications. **Engineering and Technology:** Knowledge of the practical application of engineering science and technology. This includes applying principles, techniques, procedures, and equipment to the design and production of various goods and services. **English Language:** Knowledge of the structure and content of the English language, including the meaning and spelling of words, rules of composition, and grammar. **Administration and Management:** Knowledge of business and management principles involved in strategic planning, resource allocation, human resources modeling, leadership technique, production methods, and coordination of people and resources.

# Electronics Engineering Technicians

- ▲ Growth: 10.8%
- ▲ Annual Job Openings: 22,000
- ▲ Annual Earnings: $41,210
- ▲ Education/Training Required: Associate's degree
- ▲ Self-Employed: 2.7%
- ▲ Part-Time: 3.1%

Lay out, build, test, troubleshoot, repair, and modify developmental and production electronic components, parts, equipment, and systems, such as computer equipment, missile control instrumentation, electron tubes, test equipment, and machine tool numerical controls, applying principles and theories of electronics, **electrical circuitry, engineering mathematics, electronic and electrical testing, and physics. Usually work under direction of engineering staff.** Reads blueprints, wiring diagrams, schematic drawings, and engineering instructions for assembling electronics units, applying knowledge of electronic theory and components. Assembles circuitry or electronic components, according to engineering instructions, technical manuals, and knowledge of electronics using hand tools and power tools. Tests electronics unit, using standard test equipment, to evaluate performance and determine needs for adjustments. Adjusts and replaces defective or improperly functioning circuitry and electronics components, using hand tools and soldering iron. Assists engineers in development of testing techniques, laboratory equipment, and circuitry or installation specifications, by writing reports and recording data. Designs basic circuitry and sketches for design documentation, as directed by engineers, using drafting instruments and computer aided design equipment. Fabricates parts, such as coils, terminal boards, and chassis, using bench lathes, drills, or other machine tools. **SKILLS**—Mathematics. Active Learning. Operations Analysis. Troubleshooting. Technology Design. Critical Thinking. Installation.

**GOE—Interest Area:** 02. Science, Math, and Engineering. **Work Group:** 02.08. Engineering Technology. **Other Job Titles in This Work Group:** Aerospace Engineering and Operations Technicians; Architectural and Civil Drafters; Architectural Drafters; Calibration and Instrumentation Technicians; Cartographers and Photogrammetrists; Civil Drafters; Civil Engineering Technicians; Construction and Building Inspectors; Drafters, All Other; Electrical and Electronic Engineering Technicians; Electrical and Electronics Drafters; Electrical Drafters; Electrical Engineering Technicians; Electro-Mechanical Technicians; Electronic Drafters; Engineer-

ing Technicians, Except Drafters, All Other; Environmental Engineering Technicians; Industrial Engineering Technicians; Mapping Technicians; Mechanical Drafters; Mechanical Engineering Technicians; Numerical Tool and Process Control Programmers; Pressure Vessel Inspectors; Surveying and Mapping Technicians; Surveying Technicians; Surveyors. **PERSONALITY TYPE**—Realistic. Realistic occupations frequently involve work activities that include practical, hands-on problems and solutions. They often deal with plants, animals, and real-world materials like wood, tools, and machinery. Many of the occupations require working outside and do not involve a lot of paperwork or working closely with others.

**EDUCATION/TRAINING PROGRAM(S)**—Computer Engineering Technologist/Technician; Electrical and Electronic Engineering-Related Technologist/Technician; Electrical, Electronic and Communications Engineering Technologist/Technician. **RELATED KNOWLEDGE/COURSES—Computers and Electronics:** Knowledge of circuit boards, processors, chips, electronic equipment, and computer hardware and software, including applications and programming. **Engineering and Technology:** Knowledge of the practical application of engineering science and technology. This includes applying principles, techniques, procedures, and equipment to the design and production of various goods and services. **Design:** Knowledge of design techniques, tools, and principles involved in production of precision technical plans, blueprints, drawings, and models. **Mathematics:** Knowledge of arithmetic, algebra, geometry, calculus, statistics, and their applications. **English Language:** Knowledge of the structure and content of the English language, including the meaning and spelling of words, rules of composition, and grammar.

# Elevator Installers and Repairers

▲ Growth: 17.2%

▲ Annual Job Openings: 2,000

▲ Annual Earnings: $46,240

▲ Education/Training Required: Long-term on-the-job training

▲ Self-Employed: 0%

▲ Part-Time: 7.5%

**Assemble, install, repair, or maintain electric or hydraulic freight or passenger elevators, escalators, or dumbwaiters.** Studies blueprints to determine layout of framework and foundations. Cuts prefabricated sections of framework, rails, and other components to specified dimensions. Locates malfunction in brakes, motor, switches, and signal and control systems, using test equipment. Connects electrical wiring to control panels and electric motors. Installs safety and control devices, cables, drives, rails, motors, and elevator cars. Disassembles defective unit and repairs or replaces parts, such as locks, gears, cables, and electric wiring. Completes service reports to verify conformance to prescribed standards. Inspects wiring connections, control panel hookups, door installation, and alignment and clearance of car hoistway. Lubricates bearings and other parts to minimize friction. Operates elevator to determine power demand and tests power consumption to detect overload factors. Adjusts safety controls, counterweights, and mechanism of doors. **SKILLS**—Installation. Repairing. Troubleshooting. Equipment Maintenance. Quality Control Analysis.

**GOE**—**Interest Area:** 05. Mechanics, Installers, and Repairers. **Work Group:** 05.02. Electrical and Electronic Systems. **Other Job Titles in This Work Group:** Avionics Technicians; Battery Repairers; Central Office and PBX Installers and Repairers; Communication Equipment Mechanics, Installers, and Repairers; Computer, Automated Teller, and Office Machine Repairers; Data Processing Equipment Repairers; Electric Home Appliance and Power Tool Repairers; Electric Meter Installers and Repairers; Electric Motor and Switch Assemblers and Repairers; Electric Motor, Power Tool, and Related Repairers; Electrical and Electronics Installers and Repairers, Transportation Equipment; Electrical and Electronics Repairers, Commercial and Industrial Equipment; Electrical and Electronics Repairers, Powerhouse, Substation, and Relay; Electrical Parts Reconditioners; Electrical Power-Line Installers and Repairers; Electronic Equipment Installers and Repairers, Motor Vehicles; Electronic Home Entertainment Equipment Installers and Repairers; Frame Wirers, Central Office; Home Appliance Installers; Home Appliance Repairers; Office Machine and Cash Register Servicers; Radio Mechanics; Signal and Track Switch Repairers; Station Installers and Repairers, Telephone; Telecommunications Equipment Installers and Repairers, Except Line Installers; Telecommunications Facility Examiners; Telecommunications Line Installers and Repairers; Transformer Repairers. **PERSONALITY TYPE**—Realistic. Realistic occupations frequently involve work activities that include practical, hands-on problems and solutions. They often deal with plants, animals, and real-world materials like wood, tools, and machinery. Many of the occupations require working outside and do not involve a lot of paperwork or working closely with others.

**EDUCATION/TRAINING PROGRAM(S)**—Industrial Machinery Maintenance and Repairer. **RELATED KNOWLEDGE/COURSES**—**Principles of Mechanical Devices:** Knowledge of machines and tools, including their designs, uses, repair, and maintenance. **Building and Construction:** Knowledge of materials, methods, and tools involved in the construction or repair of houses, buildings, or other structures such as highways and roads. **Engineering and Technology:** Knowledge of the practical application of engineering science and technology. This includes applying principles, techniques, procedures, and equipment to the design and production of various goods and services. **Public Safety and Security:** Knowledge of relevant equipment, policies, procedures, and strategies to promote effective local, state, or national security operations for the protection of people, data, property, and institutions. **Mathematics:** Knowledge of arithmetic, algebra, geometry, calculus, statistics, and their applications.

# Embossing Machine Set-Up Operators

▲ Growth: 5.5%
▲ Annual Job Openings: 24,000
▲ Annual Earnings: $30,090
▲ Education/Training Required: Moderate-term on-the-job training
▲ Self-Employed: 2.6%
▲ Part-Time: 5.5%

**Set up and operate embossing machines.** Sets guides to hold cover in position and adjusts table height to obtain correct depth of impression. Positions, installs, and locks embossed plate in chase and locks chase in bed of press. Makes impression of embossing to desired depth in composition on platen, trims off excess, and allows composition to harden. Stamps embossing design on workpiece, using heated work tools. Starts machine to lower ram and impress cardboard. Sets sheets singly in gauge pins and starts press. Scrapes high spots on counter die to prevent from puncturing paper. Removes and stacks embossed covers. Cuts surface of cardboard leaving design or letters, using hand tools. Mixes embossing composition to putty-like consistency, spreads glue on paten, and applies thin pad of composition over glue. **SKILLS**—Operation and Control. Repairing. Equipment Selection.

**GOE**—**Interest Area:** 08. Industrial Production. **Work Group:** 08.03. Production Work. **Other Job Titles in This Work Group:** Bakers, Manufacturing; Bindery Machine Operators and Tenders; Brazers; Cementing and Gluing Machine Operators and Tenders; Chemical Equipment Controllers and Operators; Chemical Equipment Operators and Tenders; Chemical Equipment Tenders; Cleaning, Washing, and Metal Pickling Equipment Operators and Tenders; Coating, Painting, and Spraying Machine Operators and Tenders; Coil Winders, Tapers, and Finishers; Combination Machine Tool Operators and Tenders, Metal and Plastic; Computer-Controlled Machine Tool Operators, Metal and Plastic; Cooling and Freezing Equipment Operators and Tenders; Crushing, Grinding, and Polishing Machine Setters, Operators, and Tenders; Cutters and Trimmers, Hand; Cutting and Slicing Machine Operators and Tenders; Cutting and Slicing Machine Setters, Opera-

tors, and Tenders; Design Printing Machine Setters and Set-Up Operators; Electrolytic Plating and Coating Machine Operators and Tenders, Metal and Plastic; Electrolytic Plating and Coating Machine Setters and Set-Up Operators, Metal and Plastic; Electrotypers and Stereotypers; Engraver Set-Up Operators; Extruding and Forming Machine Operators and Tenders, Synthetic or Glass Fibers; Extruding and Forming Machine Setters, Operators, and Tenders, Synthetic and Glass Fibers; Extruding, Forming, Pressing, and Compacting Machine Operators and Tenders; Fabric and Apparel Patternmakers; Fiber Product Cutting Machine Setters and Set-Up Operators; Fiberglass Laminators and Fabricators; Film Laboratory Technicians; others. **PERSONALITY TYPE**—Realistic. Realistic occupations frequently involve work activities that include practical, hands-on problems and solutions. They often deal with plants, animals, and real-world materials like wood, tools, and machinery. Many of the occupations require working outside and do not involve a lot of paperwork or working closely with others.

**EDUCATION/TRAINING PROGRAM(S)**—Graphic and Printing Equipment Operator, General; Graphic and Printing Equipment Operators, Other; Printing Press Operator. **RELATED KNOWLEDGE/COURSES**—**Production and Processing:** Knowledge of raw materials, production processes, quality control, costs, and other techniques for maximizing the effective manufacture and distribution of goods. **Principles of Mechanical Devices:** Knowledge of machines and tools, including their designs, uses, repair, and maintenance. **English Language:** Knowledge of the structure and content of the English language, including the meaning and spelling of words, rules of composition, and grammar. **Chemistry:** Knowledge of the chemical composition, structure, and properties of substances and of the chemical processes and transformations that they undergo. This includes uses of

# Emergency Medical Technicians and Paramedics

chemicals and their interactions, danger signs, production techniques, and disposal methods.

> ▲ Growth: 31.3%
> ▲ Annual Job Openings: 19,000
> ▲ Annual Earnings: $24,740
> ▲ Education/Training Required: Post-secondary vocational training
> ▲ Self-Employed: 0%
> ▲ Part-Time: 22.9%

**Assess injuries, administer emergency medical care, and extricate trapped individuals. Transport injured or sick persons to medical facilities.** Administers first-aid treatment and life support care to sick or injured persons in prehospital setting. Assesses nature and extent of illness or injury to establish and prioritize medical procedures. Observes, records, and reports patient's condition and reactions to drugs and treatment to physician. Communicates with treatment center personnel to arrange reception of victims and to receive instructions for further treatment. Assists treatment center personnel to obtain information relating to circumstances of emergency. Maintains vehicles and medical and communication equipment and replenishes first-aid equipment and supplies. Drives mobile intensive care unit to specified location, following instructions from emergency medical dispatcher. Assists treatment center personnel to obtain and record victim's vital statistics and to administer emergency treatment. Monitors patient's condition, using electrocardiograph. Assists in removal and transport of victims to treatment center. **SKILLS**—Coordination. Service Orientation. Active Listening. Judgment and Decision Making. Social Perceptiveness.

**GOE—Interest Area:** 04. Law, Law Enforcement, and Public Safety. **Work Group:** 04.04. Public Safety. **Other Job Titles in This Work Group:** Agricultural Inspectors; Aviation Inspectors; Compliance Officers, Except Agriculture, Construction, Health and Safety, and Transportation; Environmental Compliance Inspectors; Equal Opportunity Representatives and Officers; Financial Examiners; Fire Fighters; Fire Inspectors; Fire

Inspectors and Investigators; Forest Fire Fighters; Forest Fire Inspectors and Prevention Specialists; Government Property Inspectors and Investigators; Licensing Examiners and Inspectors; Marine Cargo Inspectors; Municipal Fire Fighters; Nuclear Monitoring Technicians; Occupational Health and Safety Specialists; Occupational Health and Safety Technicians; Public Transportation Inspectors. **PERSONALITY TYPE**—Social. Social occupations frequently involve working with, communicating with, and teaching people. These occupations often involve helping or providing service to others.

**EDUCATION/TRAINING PROGRAM(S)**—Emergency Medical Technologist/Technician. **RELATED KNOWLEDGE/COURSES**—**Medicine and Dentistry:** Knowledge of the information and techniques needed to diagnose and treat human injuries, diseases, and deformities. This includes symptoms, treatment alternatives, drug properties and interactions, and preventive health-care measures. **Therapy and Counseling:** Knowledge of principles, methods, and procedures for diagnosis, treatment, and rehabilitation of physical and mental dysfunctions and for career counseling and guidance. **Biology:** Knowledge of plant and animal organisms and their tissues, cells, functions, interdependencies, and interactions with each other and the environment. **Transportation:** Knowledge of principles and methods for moving people or goods by air, rail, sea, or road, including the relative costs and benefits. **Telecommunications:** Knowledge of transmission, broadcasting, switching, control, and operation of telecommunications systems.

E

# Engraver Set-Up Operators

▲ Growth: 5.5%

▲ Annual Job Openings: 24,000

▲ Annual Earnings: $30,090

▲ Education/Training Required: Moderate-term on-the-job training

▲ Self-Employed: 2.6%

▲ Part-Time: 5.5%

**Set up and operate machines to transfer printing designs.** Positions machine mechanisms and depresses levers to apply marks on roller. Aligns plate with markings on machine table and tacks to table. Turns screws to align machine components. Determines ground setting according to weight of fabric, type of design, and colors in design. Examines marks on roller to verify alignment and detect defects. Records ground setting, length of roller, width of engraving, and circumference of roller on production sheet. Measures depth of engraving and weighs diamond points, using gauges and scales. Inserts mandrel through roller and lifts into position on machine. Adjusts and tightens levers in position, using hand tools. **SKILLS**—Operation and Control.

**GOE—Interest Area:** 08. Industrial Production. **Work Group:** 08.03. Production Work. **Other Job Titles in This Work Group:** Bakers, Manufacturing; Bindery Machine Operators and Tenders; Brazers; Cementing and Gluing Machine Operators and Tenders; Chemical Equipment Controllers and Operators; Chemical Equipment Operators and Tenders; Chemical Equipment Tenders; Cleaning, Washing, and Metal Pickling Equipment Operators and Tenders; Coating, Painting, and Spraying Machine Operators and Tenders; Coil Winders, Tapers, and Finishers; Combination Machine Tool Operators and Tenders, Metal and Plastic; Computer-Controlled Machine Tool Operators, Metal and Plastic; Cooling and Freezing Equipment Operators and Tenders; Crushing, Grinding, and Polishing Machine Setters, Operators, and Tenders; Cutters and Trimmers, Hand; Cutting and Slicing Machine Operators and Tenders; Cutting and Slicing Machine Setters, Operators, and Tenders; Design Printing Machine Setters and Set-Up Operators; Electrolytic Plating and Coating Machine Operators and Tenders, Metal and Plastic;

Electrolytic Plating and Coating Machine Setters and Set-Up Operators, Metal and Plastic; Electrotypers and Stereotypers; Embossing Machine Set-Up Operators; Extruding and Forming Machine Operators and Tenders, Synthetic or Glass Fibers; Extruding and Forming Machine Setters, Operators, and Tenders, Synthetic and Glass Fibers; Extruding, Forming, Pressing, and Compacting Machine Operators and Tenders; Fabric and Apparel Patternmakers; Fiber Product Cutting Machine Setters and Set-Up Operators; Fiberglass Laminators and Fabricators; Film Laboratory Technicians; others. **PERSONALITY TYPE**—Realistic. Realistic occupations frequently involve work activities that include practical, hands-on problems and solutions. They often deal with plants, animals, and real-world materials like wood, tools, and machinery. Many of the occupations require working outside and do not involve a lot of paperwork or working closely with others.

**EDUCATION/TRAINING PROGRAM(S)**—Graphic and Printing Equipment Operator, General; Graphic and Printing Equipment Operators, Other; Printing Press Operator. **RELATED KNOWLEDGE/COURSES**—**Production and Processing:** Knowledge of raw materials, production processes, quality control, costs, and other techniques for maximizing the effective manufacture and distribution of goods. **Principles of Mechanical Devices:** Knowledge of machines and tools, including their designs, uses, repair, and maintenance. **Mathematics:** Knowledge of arithmetic, algebra, geometry, calculus, statistics, and their applications. **Engineering and Technology:** Knowledge of the practical application of engineering science and technology. This includes applying principles, techniques, procedures, and equipment to the design and production of various goods and services. **Clerical Studies:** Knowledge of administrative and clerical procedures and systems such as word processing, managing files and records, stenography and transcription, designing forms, and other office procedures and terminology.

# Environmental Compliance Inspectors

- ▲ Growth: 8.9%
- ▲ Annual Job Openings: 9,000
- ▲ Annual Earnings: $44,140
- ▲ Education/Training Required: Long-term on-the-job training
- ▲ Self-Employed: 0%
- ▲ Part-Time: 2.9%

**Inspect and investigate sources of pollution to protect the public and environment and ensure conformance with Federal, state, and local regulations and ordinances.** Inspects solid waste disposal and treatment facilities, wastewater treatment facilities, or other water courses or sites for conformance with regulations. Inspects establishments to ensure that handling, storage, and disposal of fertilizers, pesticides, and other hazardous chemicals conform with regulations. Conducts field tests and collects samples for laboratory analysis. Examines permits, licenses, applications, and records to ensure compliance with licensing requirements. Reviews and evaluates applications for registration of products containing dangerous materials or pollution control discharge permits. Assists in development of spill prevention programs and hazardous waste rules and regulations and recommends corrective action in event of hazardous spill. Prepares, organizes, and maintains records to document activities, recommend action, provide reference materials, and prepare technical and evidentiary reports. Evaluates label information for accuracy and conformance to regulatory requirements. Studies laws and statutes to determine nature of code violation and type of action to be taken. Advises individuals and groups concerning pollution control regulations, inspection and investigation findings and encourages voluntary action to correct problems or issues citations for violations. Conducts research on hazardous waste management projects to determine magnitude of disposal problem, treatment, and disposal alternatives and costs. Interviews individuals to determine nature of suspected violations and to obtain evidence of violation. Investigates complaints and suspected violations concerning illegal dumping, pollution, pesticides, product quality, or labeling laws. **SKILLS**—Reading Comprehension. Critical Thinking. Speaking. Science. Writing.

**GOE—Interest Area:** 04. Law, Law Enforcement, and Public Safety. **Work Group:** 04.04. Public Safety. **Other Job Titles in This Work Group:** Agricultural Inspectors; Aviation Inspectors; Compliance Officers, Except Agriculture, Construction, Health and Safety, and Transportation; Emergency Medical Technicians and Paramedics; Equal Opportunity Representatives and Officers; Financial Examiners; Fire Fighters; Fire Inspectors; Fire Inspectors and Investigators; Forest Fire Fighters; Forest Fire Inspectors and Prevention Specialists; Government Property Inspectors and Investigators; Licensing Examiners and Inspectors; Marine Cargo Inspectors; Municipal Fire Fighters; Nuclear Monitoring Technicians; Occupational Health and Safety Specialists; Occupational Health and Safety Technicians; Public Transportation Inspectors. **PERSONALITY TYPE**—Investigative. Investigative occupations frequently involve working with ideas and require an extensive amount of thinking. These occupations can involve searching for facts and figuring out problems mentally.

**EDUCATION/TRAINING PROGRAM(S)**—Business Administration and Management, General; Construction/Building Technologist/Technician; Logistics and Materials Management; Material Engineering; Mechanical Engineering; Operations Management and Supervision; Purchasing, Procurement and Contracts Management; Systems Engineering. **RELATED**

KNOWLEDGE/COURSES—**Chemistry:** Knowledge of the chemical composition, structure, and properties of substances and of the chemical processes and transformations that they undergo. This includes uses of chemicals and their interactions, danger signs, production techniques, and disposal methods. **Public Safety and Security:** Knowledge of relevant equipment, policies, procedures, and strategies to promote effective local, state, or national security operations for the protection of people, data, property, and institutions. **Law and Government:** Knowledge of laws, legal codes, court procedures, precedents, government regulations, executive orders, agency rules, and the democratic political process. **Mathematics:** Knowledge of arithmetic, algebra, geometry, calculus, statistics, and their applications. **Production and Processing:** Knowledge of raw materials, production processes, quality control, costs, and other techniques for maximizing the effective manufacture and distribution of goods. **English Language:** Knowledge of the structure and content of the English language, including the meaning and spelling of words, rules of composition, and grammar.

# Environmental Science and Protection Technicians, Including Health

- ▲ Growth: 24.5%
- ▲ Annual Job Openings: 3,000
- ▲ Annual Earnings: $35,830
- ▲ Education/Training Required: Associate's degree
- ▲ Self-Employed: 3.7%
- ▲ Part-Time: 11.7%

**Perform laboratory and field tests to monitor the environment and investigate sources of pollution, including those that affect health. Under direction of an environmental scientist or specialist, may collect samples of gases, soil, water, and other materials for testing and take corrective actions as assigned.** Collects samples of gases, soils, water, industrial wastewater, and asbestos products to conduct tests on pollutant levels. Discusses test results and analyses with customers. Calibrates microscopes and test instruments. Develops procedures and directs activities of workers in laboratory. Records test data and prepares reports, summaries, and charts that interpret test results and recommend changes. Sets up equipment or station to monitor and collect pollutants from sites, such as smoke stacks, manufacturing plants, or mechanical equipment. Determines amounts and kinds of chemicals to use in destroying harmful organisms and removing impurities from purification systems. Conducts standardized tests to ensure materials and supplies used throughout power supply system meet processing and safety specifications. Examines and analyzes material for presence and concentration of contaminants such as asbestos in environment, using variety of microscopes. Weighs, analyzes, and measures collected sample particles, such as lead, coal dust, or rock, to determine concentration of pollutants. Prepares samples or photomicrographs for testing and analysis. Calculates amount of pollutant in samples or computes air pollution or gas flow in industrial processes, using chemical and mathematical formulas. Performs chemical and physical laboratory and field tests on collected samples to assess compliance with pollution standards, using test instruments. **SKILLS—** Science. Mathematics. Reading Comprehension. Writing. Critical Thinking.

**GOE—Interest Area:** 02. Science, Math, and Engineering. **Work Group:** 02.05. Laboratory Technology. **Other Job Titles in This Work Group:** Biological Technicians; Chemical Technicians; Geological and Petroleum Technicians; Geological Data Technicians; Geological Sample Test Technicians; Nuclear Equipment Operation Technicians; Nuclear Technicians; Photographers, Scientific. **PERSONALITY TYPE—**Investigative. Investigative occupations frequently involve working with ideas and require an extensive amount of thinking. These occupations can involve searching for facts and figuring out problems mentally.

**EDUCATION/TRAINING PROGRAM(S)**—Aeronautical and Aerospace Engineering Technologist/Technician; Architectural Engineering Technologist/Technician; Chemical Technologist/Technician; Communications Technologists/Technicians, Other; Energy Management and Systems Technologist/Technician; Engineering-Related Technologist/Technician, General; Engineering-Related Technologists/Technicians, Other; Environmental and Pollution Control Technologist/Technician; Environmental Control Technologists/Technicians, Other; Environmental Science/Studies; Hydraulic Technologist/Technician; Industrial Production Technologists/Technicians, Other; Laser and Optical Technologist/Technician; Mechanical Engineering-Related Technologists/Technicians, Other; Metallurgical Technologist/Technician; Mining and Petroleum Technologists/Technicians, Other; Mining Technologist/Technician; Physical Science Technologists/Technicians, Other; Plastics Technologist/Technician; Radio and Television Broadcasting Technologist/

Technician; Science Technologists/Technicians, Other; Solar Technologist/Technician. **RELATED KNOWLEDGE/COURSES**—**Chemistry:** Knowledge of the chemical composition, structure, and properties of substances and of the chemical processes and transformations that they undergo. This includes uses of chemicals and their interactions, danger signs, production techniques, and disposal methods. **Mathematics:** Knowledge of arithmetic, algebra, geometry, calculus, statistics, and their applications. **Public Safety and Security:** Knowledge of relevant equipment, policies, procedures, and strategies to promote effective local, state, or national security operations for the protection of people, data, property, and institutions. **English Language:** Knowledge of the structure and content of the English language, including the meaning and spelling of words, rules of composition, and grammar. **Computers and Electronics:** Knowledge of circuit boards, processors, chips, electronic equipment, and computer hardware and software, including applications and programming.

# Equal Opportunity Representatives and Officers

- ▲ Growth: 8.9%
- ▲ Annual Job Openings: 9,000
- ▲ Annual Earnings: $44,140
- ▲ Education/Training Required: Long-term on-the-job training
- ▲ Self-Employed: 0%
- ▲ Part-Time: 2.9%

**Monitor and evaluate compliance with equal opportunity laws, guidelines, and policies to ensure that employment practices and contracting arrangements give equal opportunity without regard to race, religion, color, national origin, sex, age, or disability.** Interprets civil rights laws and equal opportunity governmental regulations for individuals and employers. Studies equal opportunity complaints to clarify issues. Consults with community representatives to develop technical assistance agreements in accordance with governmental regulations. Reviews contracts to determine company actions required to meet governmental equal opportunity provisions. Acts as representative between minority placement agencies and employers. Develops guidelines for nondiscriminatory employment practices for use by

employers. Confers with management or other personnel to resolve or settle equal opportunity issues and disputes. Conducts surveys and evaluates findings to determine existence of systematic discrimination. Prepares report of findings and recommendations for corrective action. Investigates employment practices and alleged violations of law to document and correct discriminatory factors. **SKILLS**—Reading Comprehension. Speaking. Writing. Active Listening. Critical Thinking.

**GOE**—**Interest Area:** 04. Law, Law Enforcement, and Public Safety. **Work Group:** 04.04. Public Safety. **Other Job Titles in This Work Group:** Agricultural Inspectors; Aviation Inspectors; Compliance Officers, Except

Agriculture, Construction, Health and Safety, and Transportation; Emergency Medical Technicians and Paramedics; Environmental Compliance Inspectors; Financial Examiners; Fire Fighters; Fire Inspectors; Fire Inspectors and Investigators; Forest Fire Fighters; Forest Fire Inspectors and Prevention Specialists; Government Property Inspectors and Investigators; Licensing Examiners and Inspectors; Marine Cargo Inspectors; Municipal Fire Fighters; Nuclear Monitoring Technicians; Occupational Health and Safety Specialists; Occupational Health and Safety Technicians; Public Transportation Inspectors. **PERSONALITY TYPE—**Social. Social occupations frequently involve working with, communicating with, and teaching people. These occupations often involve helping or providing service to others.

**EDUCATION/TRAINING PROGRAM(S)—**Business Administration and Management, General; Construction/Building Technologist/Technician; Logistics and Materials Management; Material Engineering;

Mechanical Engineering; Operations Management and Supervision; Purchasing, Procurement and Contracts Management; Systems Engineering. **RELATED KNOWLEDGE/COURSES—Personnel and Human Resources:** Knowledge of principles and procedures for personnel recruitment, selection, training, compensation and benefits, labor relations and negotiation, and personnel information systems. **Law and Government:** Knowledge of laws, legal codes, court procedures, precedents, government regulations, executive orders, agency rules, and the democratic political process. **English Language:** Knowledge of the structure and content of the English language, including the meaning and spelling of words, rules of composition, and grammar. **Mathematics:** Knowledge of arithmetic, algebra, geometry, calculus, statistics, and their applications. **Communications and Media:** Knowledge of media production, communication, and dissemination techniques and methods. This includes alternative ways to inform and entertain via written, oral, and visual media.

# Excavating and Loading Machine Operators

- ▲ Growth: 14.8%
- ▲ Annual Job Openings: 5,000
- ▲ Annual Earnings: $33,480
- ▲ Education/Training Required: Moderate-term on-the-job training
- ▲ Self-Employed: 8.3%
- ▲ Part-Time: 4.9%

**Operate machinery equipped with scoops, shovels, or buckets to excavate and load loose materials.** Operates power machinery, such as powered-shovel, stripping-shovel, scraper loader (mucking machine), or back-hoe (trench-excavating machine) to excavate and load material. Observes hand signals, grade stakes, and other markings when operating machines. Receives written or oral instructions to move or excavate material. Measures and verifies levels of rock or gravel, base, and other excavated material. Lubricates and repairs machinery and replaces parts, such as gears, bearings, and bucket teeth. Directs ground workers engaged in activities, such as moving stakes or markers. **SKILLS—**Operation and Control. Operation Monitoring. Repair-

ing. Equipment Selection. Coordination. Equipment Maintenance.

**GOE—Interest Area:** 06. Construction, Mining, and Drilling. **Work Group:** 06.03. Mining and Drilling. **Other Job Titles in This Work Group:** Construction Drillers; Continuous Mining Machine Operators; Derrick Operators, Oil and Gas; Earth Drillers, Except Oil and Gas; Loading Machine Operators, Underground Mining; Mine Cutting and Channeling Machine Operators; Mining Machine Operators, All Other; Rock Splitters, Quarry; Roof Bolters, Mining; Rotary Drill Operators, Oil and Gas; Roustabouts, Oil and Gas; Service Unit Operators, Oil, Gas, and Mining; Shuttle Car Operators; Well and Core Drill Operators. **PER-**

SONALITY TYPE—Realistic. Realistic occupations frequently involve work activities that include practical, hands-on problems and solutions. They often deal with plants, animals, and real-world materials like wood, tools, and machinery. Many of the occupations require working outside and do not involve a lot of paperwork or working closely with others.

EDUCATION/TRAINING PROGRAM(S)—Construction Equipment Operator. RELATED KNOWLEDGE/COURSES—Principles of Mechanical Devices: Knowledge of machines and tools, including their designs, uses, repair, and maintenance. Engineering and Technology: Knowledge of the practical application of engineering science and technology. This includes applying principles, techniques, procedures, and equipment to the design and production of various goods and services. Physics: Knowledge and prediction of physical principles and laws and their interrelationships and applications to understanding fluid, material, and atmospheric dynamics and mechanical, electrical, atomic, and sub-atomic structures and processes. Mathematics: Knowledge of arithmetic, algebra, geometry, calculus, statistics, and their applications. English Language: Knowledge of the structure and content of the English language, including the meaning and spelling of words, rules of composition, and grammar.

# Executive Secretaries and Administrative Assistants

- ▲ Growth: 11.5%
- ▲ Annual Job Openings: 185,000
- ▲ Annual Earnings: $32,520
- ▲ Education/Training Required: Moderate-term on-the-job training
- ▲ Self-Employed: 2.3%
- ▲ Part-Time: 7.7%

Provide high-level administrative support by conducting research, preparing statistical reports, handling information requests, and performing clerical functions such as preparing correspondence, receiving visitors, arranging conference calls, and scheduling meetings. May also train and supervise lower-level clerical staff. Coordinates and directs office services, such as records and budget preparation, personnel, and housekeeping, to aid executives. Prepares records and reports, such as recommendations for solutions of administrative problems and annual reports. Files and retrieves corporation documents, records, and reports. Analyzes operating practices and procedures to create new or revise existing methods. Studies management methods to improve workflow, simplify reporting procedures, or implement cost reductions. Reads and answers correspondence. Plans conferences. Interprets administrative and operating policies and procedures for employees. SKILLS—Reading Comprehension. Coordination. Writing. Active Listening. Speaking. Mathematics. Monitoring.

GOE—Interest Area: 09. Business Detail. Work Group: 09.02. Administrative Detail. Other Job Titles in This Work Group: Claims Takers, Unemployment Benefits; Court Clerks; Court, Municipal, and License Clerks; Eligibility Interviewers, Government Programs; Interviewers, Except Eligibility and Loan; Legal Secretaries; License Clerks; Loan Interviewers and Clerks; Medical Secretaries; Municipal Clerks; Secretaries, Except Legal, Medical, and Executive; Welfare Eligibility Workers and Interviewers. PERSONALITY TYPE—Conventional. Conventional occupations frequently involve following set procedures and routines. These occupations can include working with data and details more than with ideas. Usually there is a clear line of authority to follow.

EDUCATION/TRAINING PROGRAM(S)—Administrative Assistant/Secretarial Science, General; Executive Assistant/Secretary. RELATED KNOWLEDGE/COURSES—Clerical Studies: Knowledge of administrative and clerical procedures and systems such as word processing, managing files and records, stenography and transcription, designing forms, and other office procedures and terminology. **Administration and Management:** Knowledge of business and management principles involved in strategic planning, resource allocation, human resources modeling, leadership technique, production methods, and coordination of people and resources. **Computers and Electronics:** Knowledge of circuit boards, processors, chips, electronic equipment, and computer hardware and software, including appli-

cations and programming. **English Language:** Knowledge of the structure and content of the English language, including the meaning and spelling of words, rules of composition, and grammar. **Mathematics:** Knowledge of arithmetic, algebra, geometry, calculus, statistics, and their applications. **Economics and Accounting:** Knowledge of economic and accounting principles and practices, the financial markets, banking, and the analysis and reporting of financial data.

# Extruding and Drawing Machine Setters, Operators, and Tenders, Metal and Plastic

- ▲ Growth: 13.5%
- ▲ Annual Job Openings: 23,000
- ▲ Annual Earnings: $25,030
- ▲ Education/Training Required: Moderate-term on-the-job training
- ▲ Self-Employed: 0%
- ▲ Part-Time: 2.7%

**Set up, operate, or tend machines to extrude or draw thermoplastic or metal materials into tubes, rods, hoses, wire, bars, or structural shapes.** Installs dies, machine screws, and sizing rings on machine extruding thermoplastic or metal materials. Starts machine and sets controls to regulate vacuum, air pressure, sizing rings, and temperature and synchronizes speed of extrusion. Loads machine hopper with mixed materials, using auger, or stuffs rolls of plastic dough into machine cylinders. Operates shearing mechanism to cut rods to specified length. Studies specifications, determines setup procedures, and selects machine dies and parts. Adjusts controls to draw or press metal into specified shape and diameter. Selects nozzles, spacers, and wire guides according to diameter and length of rod. Weighs and mixes pelletized, granular, or powdered thermoplastic materials and coloring pigments. Reels extruded product into rolls of specified length and weight. Tests physical properties of product with testing devices, such as acid-bath tester, burst tester, and impact tester. Measures extruded articles for conformance to specifications and adjusts controls to obtain product of specified dimensions. Examines extruded product for defects, such as wrinkles, bubbles, and splits. Replaces worn dies when products vary from specifications. **SKILLS**—Quality Control Analysis. Operation

and Control. Operation Monitoring. Equipment Maintenance. Equipment Selection.

**GOE—Interest Area:** 08. Industrial Production. **Work Group:** 08.02. Production Technology. **Other Job Titles in This Work Group:** Aircraft Rigging Assemblers; Aircraft Structure Assemblers, Precision; Aircraft Structure, Surfaces, Rigging, and Systems Assemblers; Aircraft Systems Assemblers, Precision; Bench Workers, Jewelry; Bindery Machine Setters and Set-Up Operators; Bindery Workers; Bookbinders; Buffing and Polishing Set-Up Operators; Casting Machine Set-Up Operators; Coating, Painting, and Spraying Machine Setters and Set-Up Operators; Coating, Painting, and Spraying Machine Setters, Operators, and Tenders; Combination Machine Tool Setters and Set-Up Operators, Metal and Plastic; Cutting, Punching, and Press Machine Setters, Operators, and Tenders, Metal and Plastic; Dental Laboratory Technicians; Drilling and Boring Machine Tool Setters, Operators, and Tenders, Metal and Plastic; Electrical and Electronic Equipment Assemblers; Electrical and Electronic Inspectors and Testers; Electromechanical Equipment Assemblers; Engine and Other Machine Assemblers; Extruding, Forming, Pressing, and Compacting Machine Setters and Set-Up Operators; Extruding, Forming, Pressing, and Compacting Machine Setters, Operators, and Tenders; Forging Machine

Setters, Operators, and Tenders, Metal and Plastic; Foundry Mold and Coremakers; Gem and Diamond Workers; Grinding, Honing, Lapping, and Deburring Machine Set-Up Operators; Grinding, Lapping, Polishing, and Buffing Machine Tool Setters, Operators, and Tenders, Metal and Plastic; Heat Treating Equipment Setters, Operators, and Tenders, Metal and Plastic; Heat Treating, Annealing, and Tempering Machine Operators and Tenders, Metal and Plastic; others. **PERSONALITY TYPE**—Realistic. Realistic occupations frequently involve work activities that include practical, hands-on problems and solutions. They often deal with plants, animals, and real-world materials like wood, tools, and machinery. Many of the occupations require working outside and do not involve a lot of paperwork or working closely with others.

**EDUCATION/TRAINING PROGRAM(S)**—Machinist/Machine Technologist. **RELATED KNOWLEDGE/COURSES**—**Production and Processing:** Knowledge of raw materials, production processes, quality control, costs, and other techniques for maximizing the effective manufacture and distribution of goods. **Principles of Mechanical Devices:** Knowledge of machines and tools, including their designs, uses, repair, and maintenance. **Engineering and Technology:** Knowledge of the practical application of engineering science and technology. This includes applying principles, techniques, procedures, and equipment to the design and production of various goods and services. **Mathematics:** Knowledge of arithmetic, algebra, geometry, calculus, statistics, and their applications.

# Fire Inspectors

- ▲ Growth: 15.1%
- ▲ Annual Job Openings: 1,000
- ▲ Annual Earnings: $42,800
- ▲ Education/Training Required: Work experience in a related occupation
- ▲ Self-Employed: 0%
- ▲ Part-Time: 1.9%

**Inspect buildings and equipment to detect fire hazards and enforce state and local regulations.** Inspects interiors and exteriors of buildings to detect hazardous conditions or violations of fire codes. Tests equipment, such as gasoline storage tanks, air compressors, and fire-extinguishing and fire protection equipment, to ensure conformance to fire and safety codes. Discusses violations and unsafe conditions with facility representative, makes recommendations, and instructs in fire safety practices. Prepares reports, such as inspections performed, code violations, and recommendations for eliminating fire hazards. Gives first aid in emergencies. Collects fees for permits and licenses. Issues permits and summons and enforces fire codes. **SKILLS**—Writing. Critical Thinking. Reading Comprehension. Judgment and Decision Making. Speaking.

**GOE—Interest Area:** 04. Law, Law Enforcement, and Public Safety. **Work Group:** 04.04. Public Safety. **Other**

**Job Titles in This Work Group:** Agricultural Inspectors; Aviation Inspectors; Compliance Officers, Except Agriculture, Construction, Health and Safety, and Transportation; Emergency Medical Technicians and Paramedics; Environmental Compliance Inspectors; Equal Opportunity Representatives and Officers; Financial Examiners; Fire Fighters; Fire Inspectors and Investigators; Forest Fire Fighters; Forest Fire Inspectors and Prevention Specialists; Government Property Inspectors and Investigators; Licensing Examiners and Inspectors; Marine Cargo Inspectors; Municipal Fire Fighters; Nuclear Monitoring Technicians; Occupational Health and Safety Specialists; Occupational Health and Safety Technicians; Public Transportation Inspectors. **PERSONALITY TYPE**—Conventional. Conventional occupations frequently involve following set procedures and routines. These occupations can include working with data and details more than with ideas. Usually there is a clear line of authority to follow.

EDUCATION/TRAINING PROGRAM(S)—Fire Protection and Safety Technologist/Technician; Fire Science/Firefighting. **RELATED KNOWLEDGE/ COURSES—Public Safety and Security:** Knowledge of relevant equipment, policies, procedures, and strategies to promote effective local, state, or national security operations for the protection of people, data, property, and institutions. **Law and Government:** Knowledge of laws, legal codes, court procedures, precedents, government regulations, executive orders, agency rules, and the democratic political process. **English Language:** Knowledge of the structure and content of the English language, including the meaning and spelling of words, rules of composition, and grammar. **Building and Construction:** Knowledge of materials, methods, and tools involved in the construction or repair of houses, buildings, or other structures such as highways and roads. **Engineering and Technology:** Knowledge of the practical application of engineering science and technology. This includes applying principles, techniques, procedures, and equipment to the design and production of various goods and services.

# Fire Inspectors and Investigators

▲ Growth: 15.1%
▲ Annual Job Openings: 1,000
▲ Annual Earnings: $42,800
▲ Education/Training Required: Work experience in a related occupation
▲ Self-Employed: 0%
▲ Part-Time: 1.9%

Inspect buildings to detect fire hazards and enforce local ordinances and state laws. Investigate and gather facts to determine cause of fires and explosions. **SKILLS**—No data available.

**GOE—Interest Area:** 04. Law, Law Enforcement, and Public Safety. **Work Group:** 04.04. Public Safety. **Other Job Titles in This Work Group:** Agricultural Inspectors; Aviation Inspectors; Compliance Officers, Except Agriculture, Construction, Health and Safety, and Transportation; Emergency Medical Technicians and Paramedics; Environmental Compliance Inspectors; Equal Opportunity Representatives and Officers; Financial Examiners; Fire Fighters; Fire Inspectors; Forest Fire Fighters; Forest Fire Inspectors and Prevention Specialists; Government Property Inspectors and Investigators; Licensing Examiners and Inspectors; Marine Cargo Inspectors; Municipal Fire Fighters; Nuclear Monitoring Technicians; Occupational Health and Safety Specialists; Occupational Health and Safety Technicians; Public Transportation Inspectors. **PERSONALITY TYPE**—No data available.

EDUCATION/TRAINING PROGRAM(S)—Fire Protection and Safety Technologist/Technician; Fire Science/Firefighting. **RELATED KNOWLEDGE/ COURSES**—No data available.

# First-Line Supervisors and Manager/Supervisors— Construction Trades Workers

▲ Growth: 16.5%
▲ Annual Job Openings: 43,000
▲ Annual Earnings: $47,740
▲ Education/Training Required: Work experience in a related occupation
▲ Self-Employed: 37.4%
▲ Part-Time: 2.3%

Directly supervise and coordinate activities of construction trades workers and their helpers. **Manager/Supervisors are generally found in smaller establishments, where they perform both supervisory and management functions such as accounting, marketing, and personnel work and may also engage in the same construction trades work as the workers they supervise.** Supervises and coordinates activities of construction trades workers. Directs and leads workers engaged in construction activities. Assigns work to employees, using material and worker requirements data. Confers with staff and worker to ensure production and personnel problems are resolved. Suggests and initiates personnel actions, such as promotions, transfers, and hires. Analyzes and resolves worker problems and recommends motivational plans. Examines and inspects work progress, equipment, and construction sites to verify safety and ensure that specifications are met. Estimates material and worker requirements to complete job. Reads specifications, such as blueprints and data, to determine construction requirements. Analyzes and plans installation and construction of equipment and structures. Locates, measures, and marks location and placement of structures and equipment. Records information, such as personnel, production, and operational data, on specified forms and reports. Trains workers in construction methods and operation of equipment. Recommends measures to improve production methods and equipment performance to increase efficiency and safety. Assists workers engaged in construction activities, using hand tools and equipment. **SKILLS—** Management of Personnel Resources. Coordination. Time Management. Equipment Selection. Instructing.

**GOE—Interest Area:** 06. Construction, Mining, and Drilling. **Work Group:** 06.01. Managerial Work in Construction, Mining, and Drilling. **Other Job Titles in This Work Group:** Construction Managers; First-Line Supervisors and Manager/Supervisors—Extractive Workers; First-Line Supervisors/Managers of Construction Trades and Extraction Workers. **PERSONALITY TYPE—**Enterprising. Enterprising occupations frequently involve starting up and carrying out projects. These occupations can involve leading people and making many decisions. They sometimes require risk taking and often deal with business.

**EDUCATION/TRAINING PROGRAM(S)—**No data available. **RELATED KNOWLEDGE/ COURSES—Building and Construction:** Knowledge of materials, methods, and tools involved in the construction or repair of houses, buildings, or other structures such as highways and roads. **Administration and Management:** Knowledge of business and management principles involved in strategic planning, resource allocation, human resources modeling, leadership technique, production methods, and coordination of people and resources. **Personnel and Human Resources:** Knowledge of principles and procedures for personnel recruitment, selection, training, compensation and benefits, labor relations and negotiation, and personnel information systems. **Design:** Knowledge of design techniques, tools, and principles involved in production of precision technical plans, blueprints, drawings, and models. **English Language:** Knowledge of the structure and content of the English language, including the meaning and spelling of words, rules of composition, and grammar. **Engineering and Technology:** Knowledge of the practical application of engineering science and technology. This includes applying principles, techniques, procedures, and equipment to the design and production of various goods and services.

# First-Line Supervisors and Manager/Supervisors— Extractive Workers

- ▲ Growth: 16.5%
- ▲ Annual Job Openings: 43,000
- ▲ Annual Earnings: $47,740
- ▲ Education/Training Required: Work experience in a related occupation
- ▲ Self-Employed: 37.4%
- ▲ Part-Time: 2.3%

Directly supervise and coordinate activities of extractive workers and their helpers. **Manager/Supervisors are generally found in smaller establishments, where they perform both supervisory and management functions, such as accounting, marketing, and personnel work, and may also engage in the same extractive work as the workers they supervise.** Supervises and coordinates activities of workers engaged in the extraction of geological materials. Directs and leads workers engaged in extraction of geological materials. Assigns work to employees, using material and worker requirements data. Confers with staff and workers to ensure production personnel problems are resolved. Analyzes and resolves worker problems and recommends motivational plans. Analyzes and plans extraction process of geological materials. Trains workers in construction methods and operation of equipment. Examines and inspects equipment, site, and materials to verify specifications are met. Recommends measures to improve production methods and equipment performance to increase efficiency and safety. Suggests and initiates personnel actions, such as promotions, transfers, and hires. Records information, such as personnel, production, and operational data, on specified forms. Assists workers engaged in extraction activities, using hand tools and equipment. Locates, measures, and marks materials and site location, using measuring and marking equipment. Orders materials, supplies, and repair of equipment and machinery. **SKILLS**—Management of Personnel Resources. Coordination. Instructing. Monitoring. Speaking. Time Management. Judgment and Decision Making.

**GOE—Interest Area:** 06. Construction, Mining, and Drilling. **Work Group:** 06.01. Managerial Work in Construction, Mining, and Drilling. **Other Job Titles in This Work Group:** Construction Managers; First-Line Supervisors and Manager/Supervisors—Construction Trades Workers; First-Line Supervisors/Managers of Construction Trades and Extraction Workers. **PERSONALITY TYPE**—Enterprising. Enterprising occupations frequently involve starting up and carrying out projects. These occupations can involve leading people and making many decisions. They sometimes require risk taking and often deal with business.

**EDUCATION/TRAINING PROGRAM(S)**—No data available. **RELATED KNOWLEDGE/COURSES**—**Administration and Management:** Knowledge of business and management principles involved in strategic planning, resource allocation, human resources modeling, leadership technique, production methods, and coordination of people and resources. **Personnel and Human Resources:** Knowledge of principles and procedures for personnel recruitment, selection, training, compensation and benefits, labor relations and negotiation, and personnel information systems. **English Language:** Knowledge of the structure and content of the English language, including the meaning and spelling of words, rules of composition, and grammar. **Engineering and Technology:** Knowledge of the practical application of engineering science and technology. This includes applying principles, techniques, procedures, and equipment to the design and production of various goods and services. **Education and Training:** Knowledge of principles and methods for curriculum and training design, teaching and instruction for individuals and groups, and the measurement of training effects.

# First-Line Supervisors and Manager/Supervisors— Landscaping Workers

▲ Growth: 20.1%

▲ Annual Job Openings: 10,000

▲ Annual Earnings: $33,720

▲ Education/Training Required: Work experience in a related occupation

▲ Self-Employed: 37.8%

▲ Part-Time: 25.6%

Directly supervise and coordinate activities of landscaping workers. Manager/Supervisors are generally found in smaller establishments, where they perform both supervisory and management functions, such as accounting, marketing, and personnel work, and may also engage in the same landscaping work as the workers they supervise. Directs workers in maintenance and repair of driveways, walkways, benches, graves, and mausoleums. Observes ongoing work to ascertain if work is being performed according to instructions and will be completed on time. Determines work priority and crew and equipment requirements and assigns workers tasks, such as planting, fertilizing, irrigating, and mowing. Directs and assists workers engaged in maintenance and repair of equipment, such as power mower and backhoe, using hand tools and power tools. Confers with manager to develop plans and schedules for maintenance and improvement of grounds. Keeps employee time records and records daily work performed. Interviews, hires, and discharges workers. Assists workers in performing work when completion is critical. Tours grounds, such as park, botanical garden, cemetery, or golf course, to inspect conditions. Trains workers in tasks, such as transplanting and pruning trees and shrubs, finishing cement, using equipment, and caring for turf. Mixes and prepares spray and dust solutions and directs application of fertilizer, insecticide, and fungicide. **SKILLS**—Coordination. Management of Personnel Resources. Speaking. Instructing. Time Management.

**GOE**—Interest Area: 03. Plants and Animals. **Work Group:** 03.01. Managerial Work in Plants and Animals. **Other Job Titles in This Work Group:** Agricultural Crop Farm Managers; Farm Labor Contractors; Farmers and Ranchers; First-Line Supervisors and Manager/Supervisors—Agricultural Crop Workers; First-Line Supervisors and Manager/Supervisors—Animal Care Workers, Except Livestock; First-Line Supervisors and Manager/Supervisors—Animal Husbandry Workers; First-Line Supervisors and Manager/Supervisors—Fish-ery Workers; First-Line Supervisors and Manager/Supervisors—Horticultural Workers; First-Line Supervisors and Manager/Supervisors—Logging Workers; First-Line Supervisors/Managers of Farming, Fishing, and Forestry Workers; First-Line Supervisors/Managers of Landscaping, Lawn Service, and Groundskeeping Workers; Fish Hatchery Managers; Lawn Service Managers; Nursery and Greenhouse Managers. **PERSONALITY TYPE**—Realistic. Realistic occupations frequently involve work activities that include practical, hands-on problems and solutions. They often deal with plants, animals, and real-world materials like wood, tools, and machinery. Many of the occupations require working outside and do not involve a lot of paperwork or working closely with others.

**EDUCATION/TRAINING PROGRAM(S)**—Landscaping Operations and Management; Ornamental Horticulture Operations and Management; Recreation Products/Services Marketing Operations; Turf Management. **RELATED KNOWLEDGE/COURSES**—**Administration and Management:** Knowledge of business and management principles involved in strategic planning, resource allocation, human resources modeling, leadership technique, production methods, and coordination of people and resources. **Personnel and Human Resources:** Knowledge of principles and procedures for personnel recruitment, selection, training, compensation and benefits, labor relations and negotiation, and personnel information systems. **Chemistry:** Knowledge of the chemical composition, structure, and properties of substances and of the chemical processes and transformations that they undergo. This includes uses of chemicals and their interactions, danger signs, production techniques, and disposal methods. **Biology:** Knowledge of plant and animal organisms and their tissues, cells, functions, interdependencies, and interactions with each other and the environment. **Principles of Mechanical Devices:** Knowledge of machines and tools, including their designs, uses, repair, and maintenance.

# First-Line Supervisors, Administrative Support

▲ Growth: 9.4%

▲ Annual Job Openings: 146,000

▲ Annual Earnings: $39,410

▲ Education/Training Required: Work experience in a related occupation

▲ Self-Employed: 0%

▲ Part-Time: 3.3%

**Supervise and coordinate activities of workers involved in providing administrative support.** Supervises and coordinates activities of workers engaged in clerical or administrative support activities. Plans, prepares, and revises work schedules and duty assignments according to budget allotments, customer needs, problems, workloads, and statistical forecasts. Verifies completeness and accuracy of subordinates' work, computations, and records. Interviews, selects, and discharges employees. Oversees, coordinates, or performs activities associated with shipping, receiving, distribution, and transportation. Evaluates subordinate job performance and conformance to regulations and recommends appropriate personnel action. Consults with supervisor and other personnel to resolve problems, such as equipment performance, output quality, and work schedules. Trains employees in work and safety procedures and company policies. Computes figures, such as balances, totals, and commissions. Analyzes financial activities of establishment or department and assists in planning budget. Inspects equipment for defects and notifies maintenance personnel or outside service contractors for repairs. Plans layout of stockroom, warehouse, or other storage areas, considering turnover, size, weight, and related factors pertaining to items stored. Compiles reports and information required by management or governmental agencies. Identifies and resolves discrepancies or errors. Maintains records of such matters as inventory, personnel, orders, supplies, and machine maintenance. Examines procedures and recommends changes to save time, labor, and other costs and to improve quality control and operating efficiency. Participates in work of subordinates to facilitate productivity or overcome difficult aspects of work. Requisitions supplies. Reviews records and reports pertaining to such activities as production, operation, payroll, customer accounts, and shipping. **SKILLS**—Monitoring. Active Listening. Time Management. Management of Personnel Resources. Coordination. Reading Comprehension. Speaking.

**GOE—Interest Area:** 09. Business Detail. **Work Group:** 09.01. Managerial Work in Business Detail. **Other Job Titles in This Work Group:** Administrative Services Managers; First-Line Supervisors, Customer Service; First-Line Supervisors/Managers of Office and Administrative Support Workers. **PERSONALITY TYPE—** Enterprising. Enterprising occupations frequently involve starting up and carrying out projects. These occupations can involve leading people and making many decisions. They sometimes require risk taking and often deal with business.

**EDUCATION/TRAINING PROGRAM(S)**—Office Supervision and Management. **RELATED KNOWLEDGE/COURSES**—**Administration and Management:** Knowledge of business and management principles involved in strategic planning, resource allocation, human resources modeling, leadership technique, production methods, and coordination of people and resources. **Clerical Studies:** Knowledge of administrative and clerical procedures and systems such as word processing, managing files and records, stenography and transcription, designing forms, and other office procedures and terminology. **English Language:** Knowledge of the structure and content of the English language, including the meaning and spelling of words, rules of composition, and grammar. **Personnel and Human Resources:** Knowledge of principles and procedures for personnel recruitment, selection, training, compensation and benefits, labor relations and negotiation, and personnel information systems. **Education and**

Training: Knowledge of principles and methods for curriculum and training design, teaching and instruction for individuals and groups, and the measurement of training effects. Mathematics: Knowledge of arithmetic, algebra, geometry, calculus, statistics, and their applications.

# First-Line Supervisors, Customer Service

- ▲ Growth: 9.4%
- ▲ Annual Job Openings: 146,000
- ▲ Annual Earnings: $39,410
- ▲ Education/Training Required: Work experience in a related occupation
- ▲ Self-Employed: 0%
- ▲ Part-Time: 3.3%

**Supervise and coordinate activities of workers involved in providing customer service.** Supervises and coordinates activities of workers engaged in customer service activities. Plans, prepares, and devises work schedules according to budgets and workloads. Observes and evaluates workers' performance. Issues instructions and assigns duties to workers. Trains and instructs employees. Hires and discharges workers. Communicates with other departments and management to resolve problems and expedite work. Interprets and communicates work procedures and company policies to staff. Helps workers in resolving problems and completing work. Resolves complaints and answers questions of customers regarding services and procedures. Reviews and checks work of subordinates, such as reports, records, and applications, for accuracy and content and corrects errors. Prepares, maintains, and submits reports and records, such as budgets and operational and personnel reports. Makes recommendations to management concerning staff and improvement of procedures. Plans and develops improved procedures. Requisitions or purchases supplies. SKILLS—Management of Personnel Resources. Coordination. Monitoring. Critical Thinking. Speaking.

GOE—Interest Area: 09. Business Detail. Work Group: 09.01. Managerial Work in Business Detail. Other Job Titles in This Work Group: Administrative Services Managers; First-Line Supervisors, Administrative Support; First-Line Supervisors/Managers of Office and Administrative Support Workers. PERSONALITY TYPE—Enterprising. Enterprising occupations frequently involve starting up and carrying out projects. These occupations can involve leading people and making many decisions. They sometimes require risk taking and often deal with business.

EDUCATION/TRAINING PROGRAM(S)—Office Supervision and Management. RELATED KNOWLEDGE/COURSES—Administration and Management: Knowledge of business and management principles involved in strategic planning, resource allocation, human resources modeling, leadership technique, production methods, and coordination of people and resources. Customer and Personal Service: Knowledge of principles and processes for providing customer and personal services. This includes customer needs assessment, meeting quality standards for services, and evaluation of customer satisfaction. Personnel and Human Resources: Knowledge of principles and procedures for personnel recruitment, selection, training, compensation and benefits, labor relations and negotiation, and personnel information systems. Clerical Studies: Knowledge of administrative and clerical procedures and systems such as word processing, managing files and records, stenography and transcription, designing forms, and other office procedures and terminology. Education and Training: Knowledge of principles and methods for curriculum and training design, teaching and instruction for individuals and groups, and the measurement of training effects. English Language: Knowledge of the structure and content of the English language, including the meaning and spelling of words, rules of composition, and grammar.

# First-Line Supervisors/ Managers of Food Preparation and Serving Workers

- ▲ Growth: 12.7%
- ▲ Annual Job Openings: 136,000
- ▲ Annual Earnings: $24,600
- ▲ Education/Training Required: Work experience in a related occupation
- ▲ Self-Employed: 5.7%
- ▲ Part-Time: 8.5%

**Supervise workers engaged in preparing and serving food.** Supervises and coordinates activities of workers engaged in preparing and serving food and other related duties. Observes and evaluates workers and work procedures to ensure quality standards and service. Assigns duties, responsibilities, and work stations to employees, following work requirements. Collaborates with specified personnel to plan menus, serving arrangements, and other related details. Recommends measures to improve work procedures and worker performance to increase quality of services and job safety. Purchases or requisitions supplies and equipment to ensure quality and timely delivery of services. Initiates personnel actions, such as hires and discharges, to ensure proper staffing. Analyzes operational problems, such as theft and wastage, and establishes controls. Schedules parties and reservations and greets and escorts guests to seating arrangements. Receives, issues, and takes inventory of supplies and equipment and reports shortages to designated personnel. Resolves customer complaints regarding food service. Records production and operational data on specified forms. Trains workers in proper food preparation and service procedures. Inspects supplies, equipment, and work areas to ensure efficient service and conformance to standards. Specifies food portions and courses, production and time sequences, and work station and equipment arrangements. **SKILLS**—Management of Personnel Resources. Coordination. Speaking. Time Management. Active Listening.

**GOE—Interest Area:** 11. Recreation, Travel, and Other Personal Services. **Work Group:** 11.01. Managerial Work in Recreation, Travel, and Other Personal Services. **Other Job Titles in This Work Group:** Aircraft Cargo Handling Supervisors; First-Line Supervisors/ Managers of Housekeeping and Janitorial Workers; First-Line Supervisors/Managers of Personal Service Workers; Food Service Managers; Gaming Managers; Gaming Supervisors; Housekeeping Supervisors; Janitorial Supervisors; Lodging Managers; Meeting and Convention Planners. **PERSONALITY TYPE**—Enterprising. Enterprising occupations frequently involve starting up and carrying out projects. These occupations can involve leading people and making many decisions. They sometimes require risk taking and often deal with business.

**EDUCATION/TRAINING PROGRAM(S)**—Food Sales Operations; Recreation Products/Services Marketing Operations. **RELATED KNOWLEDGE/ COURSES—Administration and Management:** Knowledge of business and management principles involved in strategic planning, resource allocation, human resources modeling, leadership technique, production methods, and coordination of people and resources. **Customer and Personal Service:** Knowledge of principles and processes for providing customer and personal services. This includes customer needs assessment, meeting quality standards for services, and evaluation of customer satisfaction. **Personnel and Human Resources:** Knowledge of principles and procedures for personnel recruitment, selection, training, compensation and benefits, labor relations and negotiation, and personnel information systems. **English Language:** Knowledge of the structure and content of the English language, including the meaning and spelling of words, rules of composition, and grammar. **Clerical Studies:** Knowledge of administrative and clerical procedures and systems such as word processing, managing files and records, stenography and transcription, designing forms, and other office procedures and terminology. **Education and Training:** Knowledge of principles and methods for curriculum and training design, teaching and instruction for individuals and groups, and the measurement of training effects. **Production and Processing:** Knowledge of raw materials, production processes, quality control, costs, and other techniques for maximizing the effective manufacture and distribution of goods.

# First-Line Supervisors/ Managers of Helpers, Laborers, and Material Movers, Hand

▲ Growth: 18.9%
▲ Annual Job Openings: 14,000
▲ Annual Earnings: $36,910
▲ Education/Training Required: Work experience in a related occupation
▲ Self-Employed: 3.6%
▲ Part-Time: 2.3%

**Supervise and coordinate the activities of helpers, laborers, or material movers.** Supervises and coordinates activities of workers performing assigned tasks. Verifies materials loaded or unloaded against work order and schedules times of shipment and mode of transportation. Inspects equipment for wear and completed work for conformance to standards. Informs designated employee or department of items loaded or reports loading deficiencies. Resolves customer complaints. Quotes prices to customers. Inventories and orders supplies. Examines freight to determine sequence of loading and equipment to determine compliance with specifications. Records information, such as daily receipts, employee time and wage data, description of freight, and inspection results. Determines work sequence and equipment needed according to work order, shipping records, and experience. Observes work procedures to ensure quality of work. Trains and instructs workers. Assigns duties and work schedules. **SKILLS**—Instructing. Social Perceptiveness. Critical Thinking. Speaking. Management of Personnel Resources. Coordination. Learning Strategies.

**GOE—Interest Area:** 08. Industrial Production. **Work Group:** 08.01. Managerial Work in Industrial Production. **Other Job Titles in This Work Group:** First-Line Supervisors/Managers of Production and Operating Workers; Industrial Production Managers. **PERSON-** ALITY TYPE—Enterprising. Enterprising occupations frequently involve starting up and carrying out projects. These occupations can involve leading people and making many decisions. They sometimes require risk taking and often deal with business.

**EDUCATION/TRAINING PROGRAM(S)**—Operations Management and Supervision. **RELATED KNOWLEDGE/COURSES—Production and Processing:** Knowledge of raw materials, production processes, quality control, costs, and other techniques for maximizing the effective manufacture and distribution of goods. **Administration and Management:** Knowledge of business and management principles involved in strategic planning, resource allocation, human resources modeling, leadership technique, production methods, and coordination of people and resources. **Personnel and Human Resources:** Knowledge of principles and procedures for personnel recruitment, selection, training, compensation and benefits, labor relations and negotiation, and personnel information systems. **Mathematics:** Knowledge of arithmetic, algebra, geometry, calculus, statistics, and their applications. **Economics and Accounting:** Knowledge of economic and accounting principles and practices, the financial markets, banking, and the analysis and reporting of financial data.

# First-Line Supervisors/ Managers of Mechanics, Installers, and Repairers

▲ Growth: 16%
▲ Annual Job Openings: 38,000
▲ Annual Earnings: $46,560
▲ Education/Training Required: Work experience in a related occupation
▲ Self-Employed: 3.7%
▲ Part-Time: 2.3%

**Supervise and coordinate the activities of mechanics, installers, and repairers.** Assigns workers to perform activities, such as service appliances, repair and maintain vehicles, and install machinery and equipment. Confers with personnel, such as management, engineering, quality control, customers, and workers' representatives, to coordinate work activities and resolve problems. Recommends or initiates personnel actions, such as employment, performance evaluations, promotions, transfers, discharges, and disciplinary measures. Directs, coordinates, and assists in performance of workers' activities, such as engine tune-up, hydroelectric turbine repair, or circuit breaker installation. Examines object, system, or facilities, such as telephone, air-conditioning, or industrial plant, and analyzes information to determine installation, service, or repair needed. Monitors operations and inspects, tests, and measures completed work, using devices such as hand tools, gauges, and specifications to verify conformance to standards. Computes estimates and actual costs of factors, such as materials, labor, and outside contractors, and prepares budgets. Patrols work area and examines tools and equipment to detect unsafe conditions or violations of safety rules. Recommends measures, such as procedural changes, service manual revisions, and equipment purchases, to improve work performance and minimize operating costs. Trains workers in methods, procedures, and use of equipment and work aids, such as blueprints, hand tools, and test equipment. Completes and maintains reports, such as time and production records, inventories, and test results. Requisitions materials and supplies, such as tools, equipment, and replacement parts, for work activities. Establishes or adjusts work methods and procedures to meet production schedules, using knowledge of capacities of machines, equipment, and personnel. Interprets specifications, blueprints, and job orders and constructs templates and lays out reference points for workers. **SKILLS**—Coordination. Management of Personnel Resources. Reading Comprehension. Active Listening. Management of Material Resources. Management of Financial Resources. Time Management.

**GOE**—**Interest Area:** 05. Mechanics, Installers, and Repairers. **Work Group:** 05.01. Managerial Work in Mechanics, Installers, and Repairers. **Other Job Titles in This Work Group:** No other jobs in this work group. **PERSONALITY TYPE**—Enterprising. Enterprising occupations frequently involve starting up and carrying out projects. These occupations can involve leading people and making many decisions. They sometimes require risk taking and often deal with business.

**EDUCATION/TRAINING PROGRAM(S)**—Operations Management and Supervision. **RELATED KNOWLEDGE/COURSES**—**Principles of Mechanical Devices:** Knowledge of machines and tools, including their designs, uses, repair, and maintenance. **Administration and Management:** Knowledge of business and management principles involved in strategic planning, resource allocation, human resources modeling, leadership technique, production methods, and coordination of people and resources. **Personnel and Human Resources:** Knowledge of principles and procedures for personnel recruitment, selection, training, compensation and benefits, labor relations and negotiation, and personnel information systems. **English Language:** Knowledge of the structure and content of the English language, including the meaning and spelling of words, rules of composition, and grammar. **Engineering and Technology:** Knowledge of the practical application of engineering science and technology. This includes applying principles, techniques, procedures, and equipment to the design and production of various goods and services.

# First-Line Supervisors/ Managers of Non-Retail Sales Workers

▲ Growth: 5.8%

▲ Annual Job Openings: 41,000

▲ Annual Earnings: $56,850

▲ Education/Training Required: Work experience in a related occupation

▲ Self-Employed: 27%

▲ Part-Time: 8.2%

**Directly supervise and coordinate activities of sales workers other than retail sales workers. May perform duties such as budgeting, accounting, and personnel work in addition to supervisory duties.** Directs and supervises employees engaged in sales, inventory-taking, reconciling cash receipts, or performing specific service such as pumping gasoline for customers. Plans and prepares work schedules and assigns employees to specific duties. Hires, trains, and evaluates personnel in sales or marketing establishment. Coordinates sales promotion activities and prepares merchandise displays and advertising copy. Listens to and resolves customer complaints regarding service, product, or personnel. Examines merchandise to ensure that it is correctly priced or displayed or functions as advertised. Inventories stock and reorders when inventories drop to specified level. Examines products purchased for resale or received for storage to determine condition of product or item. Prepares rental or lease agreement, specifying charges and payment procedures, for use of machinery, tools, or other such items. Formulates pricing policies on merchandise according to requirements for profitability of store operations. Keeps records pertaining to purchases, sales, and requisitions. Assists sales staff in completing complicated and difficult sales. Prepares sales and inventory reports for management and budget departments. Confers with company officials to develop methods and procedures to increase sales, expand markets, and promote business. **SKILLS**—Active Listening. Coordination. Speaking. Management of Personnel Resources. Mathematics. Reading Comprehension.

**GOE—Interest Area:** 10. Sales and Marketing. **Work Group:** 10.01. Managerial Work in Sales and Marketing. **Other Job Titles in This Work Group:** Advertising and Promotions Managers; First-Line Supervisors/Managers of Retail Sales Workers; Marketing Managers; Sales Managers. **PERSONALITY TYPE**—Enterprising. Enterprising occupations frequently involve starting up and carrying out projects. These occupations can involve leading people and making many decisions. They sometimes require risk taking and often deal with business.

**EDUCATION/TRAINING PROGRAM(S)**—Business and Personal Services Marketing Operations, Other; Business Services Marketing Operations; General Retailing and Wholesaling Operations and Skills, Other; General Retailing Operations; Home Products Marketing Operations; Office Products Marketing Operations. **RELATED KNOWLEDGE/COURSES—Administration and Management:** Knowledge of business and management principles involved in strategic planning, resource allocation, human resources modeling, leadership technique, production methods, and coordination of people and resources. **Personnel and Human Resources:** Knowledge of principles and procedures for personnel recruitment, selection, training, compensation and benefits, labor relations and negotiation, and personnel information systems. **Mathematics:** Knowledge of arithmetic, algebra, geometry, calculus, statistics, and their applications. **Sales and Marketing:** Knowledge of principles and methods for showing, promoting, and selling products or services. This includes marketing strategy and tactics, product demonstration, sales techniques, and sales control systems. **Economics and Accounting:** Knowledge of economic and accounting principles and practices, the financial markets, banking, and the analysis and reporting of financial data.

# First-Line Supervisors/ Managers of Personal Service Workers

▲ Growth: 15.1%

▲ Annual Job Openings: 8,000

▲ Annual Earnings: $30,350

▲ Education/Training Required: Work experience in a related occupation

▲ Self-Employed: 31.1%

▲ Part-Time: 8.5%

**Supervise and coordinate activities of personal service workers, such as supervisors of flight attendants, hairdressers, or caddies.** Supervises and coordinates activities of workers engaged in lodging and personal services. Observes and evaluates workers' appearance and performance to ensure quality service and compliance with specifications. Trains workers in proper operational procedures and functions and explains company policy. Analyzes and records personnel and operational data and writes activity reports. Collaborates with personnel to plan and develop programs of events, schedules of activities, and menus. Resolves customer complaints regarding worker performance and services rendered. Assigns work schedules, following work requirements, to ensure quality and timely delivery of services. Inspects work areas and operating equipment to ensure conformance to established standards. Furnishes customers with information on events and activities. Informs workers about interests of specific groups. Requisitions supplies, equipment, and designated services to ensure quality and timely service and efficient operations. **SKILLS**—Coordination. Service Orientation. Active Listening. Speaking. Time Management.

**GOE—Interest Area:** 11. Recreation, Travel, and Other Personal Services. **Work Group:** 11.01. Managerial Work in Recreation, Travel, and Other Personal Services. **Other Job Titles in This Work Group:** Aircraft Cargo Handling Supervisors; First-Line Supervisors/ Managers of Food Preparation and Serving Workers; First-Line Supervisors/Managers of Housekeeping and Janitorial Workers; Food Service Managers; Gaming Managers; Gaming Supervisors; Housekeeping Supervisors; Janitorial Supervisors; Lodging Managers; Meeting and Convention Planners. **PERSONALITY TYPE**—Enterprising. Enterprising occupations frequently involve starting up and carrying out projects. These occupations can involve leading people and making many decisions. They sometimes require risk taking and often deal with business.

**EDUCATION/TRAINING PROGRAM(S)**—Recreation Products/Services Marketing Operations. **RELATED KNOWLEDGE/COURSES—Administration and Management:** Knowledge of business and management principles involved in strategic planning, resource allocation, human resources modeling, leadership technique, production methods, and coordination of people and resources. **Customer and Personal Service:** Knowledge of principles and processes for providing customer and personal services. This includes customer needs assessment, meeting quality standards for services, and evaluation of customer satisfaction. **Personnel and Human Resources:** Knowledge of principles and procedures for personnel recruitment, selection, training, compensation and benefits, labor relations and negotiation, and personnel information systems. **English Language:** Knowledge of the structure and content of the English language, including the meaning and spelling of words, rules of composition, and grammar. **Education and Training:** Knowledge of principles and methods for curriculum and training design, teaching and instruction for individuals and groups, and the measurement of training effects.

# First-Line Supervisors/ Managers of Police and Detectives

▲ Growth: 13.1%
▲ Annual Job Openings: 9,000
▲ Annual Earnings: $57,900
▲ Education/Training Required: Work experience in a related occupation
▲ Self-Employed: 0%
▲ Part-Time: 0%

**Supervise and coordinate activities of members of police force.** Prepares work schedules, assigns duties, and develops and revises departmental procedures. Supervises and coordinates investigation of criminal cases. Disciplines staff for violation of department rules and regulations. Investigates and resolves personnel problems within organization. Assists subordinates in performing job duties. Directs collection, preparation, and handling of evidence and personal property of prisoners. Monitors and evaluates job performance of subordinates. Investigates charges of misconduct against staff. Cooperates with court personnel and officials from other law enforcement agencies and testifies in court. Prepares news releases and responds to police correspondence. Reviews contents of written orders to ensure adherence to legal requirements. Directs release or transfer of prisoners. Requisitions and issues department equipment and supplies. Inspects facilities, supplies, vehicles, and equipment to ensure conformance to standards. Prepares budgets and manages expenditures of department funds. Trains staff. Prepares reports and directs preparation, handling, and maintenance of departmental records. Meets with civic, educational, and community groups to develop community programs and events and addresses groups concerning law enforcement subjects. Conducts raids and orders detention of witnesses and suspects for questioning. **SKILLS—** Management of Personnel Resources. Judgment and Decision Making. Coordination. Time Management. Management of Financial Resources. Social Perceptiveness.

**GOE—Interest Area:** 04. Law, Law Enforcement, and Public Safety. **Work Group:** 04.01. Managerial Work in Law, Law Enforcement, and Public Safety. **Other Job Titles in This Work Group:** Emergency Management Specialists; First-Line Supervisors/Managers of Correctional Officers; First-Line Supervisors/Managers of Fire Fighting and Prevention Workers; First-Line Supervisors/Managers, Protective Service Workers, All Other; Forest Fire Fighting and Prevention Supervisors; Municipal Fire Fighting and Prevention Supervisors. **PERSONALITY TYPE—**Enterprising. Enterprising occupations frequently involve starting up and carrying out projects. These occupations can involve leading people and making many decisions. They sometimes require risk taking and often deal with business.

**EDUCATION/TRAINING PROGRAM(S)—**Corrections/Correctional Administration; Criminal Justice Studies; Criminal Justice/Law Enforcement Administration; Law Enforcement/Police Science. **RELATED KNOWLEDGE/COURSES—Public Safety and Security:** Knowledge of relevant equipment, policies, procedures, and strategies to promote effective local, state, or national security operations for the protection of people, data, property, and institutions. **Administration and Management:** Knowledge of business and management principles involved in strategic planning, resource allocation, human resources modeling, leadership technique, production methods, and coordination of people and resources. **Law and Government:** Knowledge of laws, legal codes, court procedures, precedents, government regulations, executive orders, agency rules, and the democratic political process. **Personnel and Human Resources:** Knowledge of principles and procedures for personnel recruitment, selection, training, compensation and benefits, labor relations and negotiation, and personnel information systems. **English Language:** Knowledge of the structure and content of the English language, including the meaning and spelling of words, rules of composition, and grammar.

# First-Line Supervisors/ Managers of Production and Operating Workers

▲ Growth: 1%
▲ Annual Job Openings: 71,000
▲ Annual Earnings: $43,020
▲ Education/Training Required: Work experience in a related occupation
▲ Self-Employed: 3.6%
▲ Part-Time: 2.3%

**Supervise and coordinate the activities of production and operating workers, such as inspectors, precision workers, machine setters and operators, assemblers, fabricators, and plant and system operators.** Directs and coordinates the activities of employees engaged in production or processing of goods. Plans and establishes work schedules, assignments, and production sequences to meet production goals. Calculates labor and equipment requirements and production specifications, using standard formulas. Determines standards, production, and rates based on company policy, equipment and labor availability, and workload. Reviews operations and accounting records or reports to determine the feasibility of production estimates and evaluate current production. Confers with management or subordinates to resolve worker problems, complaints, or grievances. Confers with other supervisors to coordinate operations and activities within departments or between departments. Reads and analyzes charts, work orders, or production schedules to determine production requirements. Maintains operations data, such as time, production, and cost records, and prepares management reports. Recommends or implements measures to motivate employees and improve production methods, equipment performance, product quality, or efficiency. Requisitions materials, supplies, equipment parts, or repair services. Interprets specifications, blueprints, job orders, and company policies and procedures for workers. Inspects materials, products, or equipment to detect defects or malfunctions. Demonstrates equipment operations or work procedures to new employees or assigns employees to experienced workers for training. Monitors or patrols work area and enforces safety or sanitation regulations. Monitor gauges, dials, and other indicators to ensure operators conform to production or processing standards. Sets up and adjusts machines and equipment. **SKILLS**—Coordination. Management of Personnel Resources. Mathematics. Management of Material Resources. Writing. Reading Comprehension.

**GOE—Interest Area:** 08. Industrial Production. **Work Group:** 08.01. Managerial Work in Industrial Production. **Other Job Titles in This Work Group:** First-Line Supervisors/Managers of Helpers, Laborers, and Material Movers, Hand; Industrial Production Managers. **PERSONALITY TYPE**—Enterprising. Enterprising occupations frequently involve starting up and carrying out projects. These occupations can involve leading people and making many decisions. They sometimes require risk taking and often deal with business.

**EDUCATION/TRAINING PROGRAM(S)**—Operations Management and Supervision. **RELATED KNOWLEDGE/COURSES—Production and Processing:** Knowledge of raw materials, production processes, quality control, costs, and other techniques for maximizing the effective manufacture and distribution of goods. **Administration and Management:** Knowledge of business and management principles involved in strategic planning, resource allocation, human resources modeling, leadership technique, production methods, and coordination of people and resources. **Personnel and Human Resources:** Knowledge of principles and procedures for personnel recruitment, selection, training, compensation and benefits, labor relations and negotiation, and personnel information systems. **Education and Training:** Knowledge of principles and methods for curriculum and training design, teaching and instruction for individuals and groups, and the measurement of training effects. **Mathematics:** Knowledge of arithmetic, algebra, geometry, calculus, statistics, and their applications.

# First-Line Supervisors/ Managers of Retail Sales Workers

- ▲ Growth: 8.1%
- ▲ Annual Job Openings: 206,000
- ▲ Annual Earnings: $32,170
- ▲ Education/Training Required: Work experience in a related occupation
- ▲ Self-Employed: 38.7%
- ▲ Part-Time: 8.2%

**Directly supervise sales workers in a retail establishment or department. Duties may include management functions, such as purchasing, budgeting, accounting, and personnel work, in addition to supervisory duties.** Directs and supervises employees engaged in sales, inventory-taking, reconciling cash receipts, or performing specific service such as pumping gasoline for customers. Plans and prepares work schedules and assigns employees to specific duties. Hires, trains, and evaluates personnel in sales or marketing establishment. Prepares sales and inventory reports for management and budget departments. Confers with company officials to develop methods and procedures to increase sales, expand markets, and promote business. Coordinates sales promotion activities and prepares merchandise displays and advertising copy. Assists sales staff in completing complicated and difficult sales. Keeps records pertaining to purchases, sales, and requisitions. Formulates pricing policies on merchandise according to requirements for profitability of store operations. Examines products purchased for resale or received for storage to determine condition of product or item. Prepares rental or lease agreement, specifying charges and payment procedures, for use of machinery, tools, or other such items. Inventories stock and reorders when inventories drop to specified level. Examines merchandise to ensure that it is correctly priced or displayed or functions as advertised. Listens to and resolves customer complaints regarding service, product, or personnel. Keeps records of employees' work schedules and time cards. **SKILLS**—Speaking. Coordination. Active Listening. Mathematics. Management of Personnel Resources. Reading Comprehension.

**GOE—Interest Area:** 10. Sales and Marketing. **Work Group:** 10.01. Managerial Work in Sales and Market-

ing. **Other Job Titles in This Work Group:** Advertising and Promotions Managers; First-Line Supervisors/Managers of Non-Retail Sales Workers; Marketing Managers; Sales Managers. **PERSONALITY TYPE**—Enterprising. Enterprising occupations frequently involve starting up and carrying out projects. These occupations can involve leading people and making many decisions. They sometimes require risk taking and often deal with business.

**EDUCATION/TRAINING PROGRAM(S)**—Business and Personal Services Marketing Operations, Other; Business Services Marketing Operations; Food Products Retailing and Wholesaling Operations; General Retailing and Wholesaling Operations and Skills, Other; General Retailing Operations; General Selling Skills and Sales Operations; Home Products Marketing Operations; Office Products Marketing Operations. **RELATED KNOWLEDGE/COURSES**—**Administration and Management:** Knowledge of business and management principles involved in strategic planning, resource allocation, human resources modeling, leadership technique, production methods, and coordination of people and resources. **Personnel and Human Resources:** Knowledge of principles and procedures for personnel recruitment, selection, training, compensation and benefits, labor relations and negotiation, and personnel information systems. **Mathematics:** Knowledge of arithmetic, algebra, geometry, calculus, statistics, and their applications. **Sales and Marketing:** Knowledge of principles and methods for showing, promoting, and selling products or services. This includes marketing strategy and tactics, product demonstration, sales techniques, and sales control systems. **Economics and Accounting:** Knowledge of economic and accounting principles and practices, the financial markets, banking, and the analysis and reporting of financial data.

## First-Line Supervisors/ Managers of Transportation and Material-Moving Machine and Vehicle Operators

▲ Growth: 19.9%

▲ Annual Job Openings: 17,000

▲ Annual Earnings: $43,120

▲ Education/Training Required: Work experience in a related occupation

▲ Self-Employed: 3.8%

▲ Part-Time: 2.3%

**Directly supervise and coordinate activities of transportation and material-moving machine and vehicle operators and helpers.** Reviews orders, production schedules, and shipping/receiving notices to determine work sequence and material shipping dates, type, volume, and destinations. Plans and establishes transportation routes, work schedules, and assignments and allocates equipment to meet transportation, operations, or production goals. Directs workers in transportation or related services, such as pumping, moving, storing, and loading/unloading of materials or people. Maintains or verifies time, transportation, financial, inventory, and personnel records. Explains and demonstrates work tasks to new workers or assigns workers to experienced workers for further training. Resolves worker problems or assists workers in solving problems. Computes and estimates cash, payroll, transportation, personnel, and storage requirements, using calculator. Requisitions needed personnel, supplies, equipment, parts, or repair services. Recommends and implements measures to improve worker motivation, equipment performance, work methods, and customer services. Prepares, compiles, and submits reports on work activities, operations, production, and work-related accidents. Inspects or tests materials, stock, vehicles, equipment, and facilities to locate defects, meet maintenance or production specifications, and verify safety standards. Interprets transportation and tariff regulations, shipping orders, safety regulations, and company policies and procedures for workers. Recommends or implements personnel actions, such as hiring, firing, and performance evaluations. Receives telephone or radio reports of emergencies and dispatches personnel and vehicle in response to request. Confers with customers, supervisors, contractors, and other personnel to exchange information and resolve problems. Assists workers in performing tasks, such as coupling railroad cars or loading vehicles. Repairs or schedules repair and preventive maintenance of vehicles and other equipment. Examines, measures, and weighs cargo or materials to determine specific handling requirements. Drives vehicles or operates machines or equipment. **SKILLS**—Reading Comprehension. Coordination. Management of Financial Resources. Management of Personnel Resources. Active Listening. Speaking.

**GOE—Interest Area:** 07. Transportation. **Work Group:** 07.01. Managerial Work in Transportation. **Other Job Titles in This Work Group:** Railroad Conductors and Yardmasters; Transportation Managers. **PERSONALITY TYPE**—Enterprising. Enterprising occupations frequently involve starting up and carrying out projects. These occupations can involve leading people and making many decisions. They sometimes require risk taking and often deal with business.

**EDUCATION/TRAINING PROGRAM(S)**—Logistics and Materials Management. **RELATED KNOWLEDGE/COURSES—Transportation:** Knowledge of principles and methods for moving people or goods by air, rail, sea, or road, including the relative costs and benefits. **Administration and Management:** Knowledge of business and management principles involved in strategic planning, resource allocation, human resources modeling, leadership technique, production methods, and coordination of people and resources. **Personnel and Human Resources:** Knowledge of principles and procedures for personnel recruitment, selection, training, compensation and benefits, labor relations and negotiation, and personnel information systems. **Mathematics:** Knowledge of arithmetic, algebra, geometry, calculus, statistics, and their applications. **Economics and Accounting:** Knowledge of economic and accounting principles and practices, the financial markets, banking, and the analysis and reporting of financial data.

# Fitness Trainers and Aerobics Instructors

▲ Growth: 40.3%
▲ Annual Job Openings: 19,000
▲ Annual Earnings: $28,750
▲ Education/Training Required: Post-secondary vocational training
▲ Self-Employed: 5.7%
▲ Part-Time: 42.5%

Instruct or coach groups or individuals in exercise activities and the fundamentals of sports. Demonstrate techniques and methods of participation. Observe participants and inform them of corrective measures necessary to improve their skills. Those required to hold teaching degrees should be reported in the appropriate teaching category. Organizes and conducts competitions and tournaments. Selects, stores, orders, issues, and inventories equipment, materials, and supplies. Advises participants in use of heat or ultraviolet treatments and hot baths. Teaches individual and team sports to participants, utilizing knowledge of sports techniques and of physical capabilities of participants. Explains and enforces safety rules and regulations. Teaches and demonstrates use of gymnastic and training apparatus, such as trampolines and weights. Plans physical education program to promote development of participant physical attributes and social skills. Organizes, leads, instructs, and referees indoor and outdoor games, such as volleyball, baseball, and basketball. **SKILLS—** Instructing. Coordination. Learning Strategies. Speaking. Monitoring.

**GOE—Interest Area:** 01. Arts, Entertainment, and Media. **Work Group:** 01.10. Sports: Coaching, Instructing, Officiating, and Performing. **Other Job Titles in This Work Group:** Athletes and Sports Competitors; Coaches and Scouts; Umpires, Referees, and Other Sports Officials. **PERSONALITY TYPE—Social.** Social occupations frequently involve working with, communicating with, and teaching people. These occupations often involve helping or providing service to others.

**EDUCATION/TRAINING PROGRAM(S)—Adult** and Continuing Teacher Education; Dietician Assistant; Health and Physical Education, General; Health and Physical Education/Fitness, Other; Hospitality and Recreation Marketing Operations, General; Hospitality and Recreation Marketing Operations, Other; Parks, Recreation and Leisure Facilities Management; Parks, Recreation and Leisure Studies; Parks, Recreation, Leisure and Fitness Studies, Other; Physical Education Teaching and Coaching; Sport and Fitness Administration/Management. **RELATED KNOWLEDGE/ COURSES—Education and Training:** Knowledge of principles and methods for curriculum and training design, teaching and instruction for individuals and groups, and the measurement of training effects. **Psychology:** Knowledge of human behavior and performance; individual differences in ability, personality, and interests; learning and motivation; psychological research methods; and the assessment and treatment of behavioral and affective disorders. **Customer and Personal Service:** Knowledge of principles and processes for providing customer and personal services. This includes customer needs assessment, meeting quality standards for services, and evaluation of customer satisfaction. **Biology:** Knowledge of plant and animal organisms and their tissues, cells, functions, interdependencies, and interactions with each other and the environment. **English Language:** Knowledge of the structure and content of the English language, including the meaning and spelling of words, rules of composition, and grammar.

# Fitters, Structural Metal—Precision

▲ Growth: 19.5%

▲ Annual Job Openings: 20,000

▲ Annual Earnings: $28,490

▲ Education/Training Required: Moderate-term on-the-job training

▲ Self-Employed: 0%

▲ Part-Time: 3.4%

**Lay out, position, align, and fit together fabricated parts of structural metal products preparatory to welding or riveting.** Aligns parts, using jack, turnbuckles, wedges, drift pins, pry bars, and hammer. Moves parts into position manually or by hoist or crane. Marks reference points onto floor or face block and transposes them to workpiece, using measuring devices, squares, chalk, and soapstone. Gives directions to welder to build up low spots or short pieces with weld. Heat treats parts with acetylene torch. Straightens warped or bent parts, using sledge, hand torch, straightening press, or bulldozer. Locates reference points, using transit, and erects ladders and scaffolding to fit together large assemblies. Removes high spots and cuts bevels, using hand files, portable grinders, and cutting torch. Sets up face block, jigs, and fixtures. Examines blueprints and plans sequence of operation, applying knowledge of geometry, effects of heat, weld shrinkage, machining, and metal thickness. Tack welds fitted parts together. Positions or tightens braces, jacks, clamps, ropes, or bolt straps or bolts parts in positions for welding or riveting. **SKILLS**—Mathematics. Equipment Selection. Reading Comprehension. Critical Thinking. Coordination. Judgment and Decision Making.

**GOE—Interest Area:** 08. Industrial Production. **Work Group:** 08.03. Production Work. **Other Job Titles in This Work Group:** Bakers, Manufacturing; Bindery Machine Operators and Tenders; Brazers; Cementing and Gluing Machine Operators and Tenders; Chemical Equipment Controllers and Operators; Chemical Equipment Operators and Tenders; Chemical Equipment Tenders; Cleaning, Washing, and Metal Pickling Equipment Operators and Tenders; Coating, Painting, and Spraying Machine Operators and Tenders; Coil Winders, Tapers, and Finishers; Combination Machine Tool Operators and Tenders, Metal and Plastic;

Computer-Controlled Machine Tool Operators, Metal and Plastic; Cooling and Freezing Equipment Operators and Tenders; Crushing, Grinding, and Polishing Machine Setters, Operators, and Tenders; Cutters and Trimmers, Hand; Cutting and Slicing Machine Operators and Tenders; Cutting and Slicing Machine Setters, Operators, and Tenders; Design Printing Machine Setters and Set-Up Operators; Electrolytic Plating and Coating Machine Operators and Tenders, Metal and Plastic; Electrolytic Plating and Coating Machine Setters and Set-Up Operators, Metal and Plastic; Electrotypers and Stereotypers; Embossing Machine Set-Up Operators; Engraver Set-Up Operators; Extruding and Forming Machine Operators and Tenders, Synthetic or Glass Fibers; Extruding and Forming Machine Setters, Operators, and Tenders, Synthetic and Glass Fibers; Extruding, Forming, Pressing, and Compacting Machine Operators and Tenders; Fabric and Apparel Patternmakers; Fiber Product Cutting Machine Setters and Set-Up Operators; Fiberglass Laminators and Fabricators; others. **PERSONALITY TYPE**—Realistic. Realistic occupations frequently involve work activities that include practical, hands-on problems and solutions. They often deal with plants, animals, and real-world materials like wood, tools, and machinery. Many of the occupations require working outside and do not involve a lot of paperwork or working closely with others.

**EDUCATION/TRAINING PROGRAM(S)**—Machine Shop Assistant; Marine Maintenance and Ship Repairer. **RELATED KNOWLEDGE/COURSES**—**Building and Construction:** Knowledge of materials, methods, and tools involved in the construction or repair of houses, buildings, or other structures such as highways and roads. **Principles of Mechanical Devices:** Knowledge of machines and tools, including their designs, uses, repair, and maintenance. **Mathematics:** Knowledge of arithmetic, algebra, geometry, calculus, statistics, and their applications. **Engineering and Technology:** Knowledge of the practical application of engineering science and technology. This includes applying principles, techniques, procedures, and equipment to the design and production of various goods and services. **Physics:** Knowledge and prediction of physical principles and laws and their interrelationships and applications to understanding fluid, material, and atmospheric dynamics and mechanical, electrical, atomic, and sub-atomic structures and processes.

# Flight Attendants

- ▲ Growth: 18.4%
- ▲ Annual Job Openings: 8,000
- ▲ Annual Earnings: $45,220
- ▲ Education/Training Required: Long-term on-the-job training
- ▲ Self-Employed: 0%
- ▲ Part-Time: 45.7%

**Provide personal services to ensure the safety and comfort of airline passengers during flight. Greet passengers, verify tickets, explain use of safety equipment, and serve food or beverages.** Greets passengers, verifies tickets, records destinations, and directs passengers to assigned seats. Explains use of safety equipment to passengers. Serves prepared meals and beverages. Walks aisle of plane to verify that passengers have complied with Federal regulations prior to take off. Collects money for meals and beverages. Prepares reports showing place of departure and destination, passenger ticket numbers, meal and beverage inventories, and lost and found articles. Administers first aid to passengers in distress when needed. Assists passengers to store carry-on luggage in overhead, garment, or under-seat storage. SKILLS— Service Orientation. Social Perceptiveness. Reading Comprehension. Active Listening. Coordination.

**GOE—Interest Area:** 11. Recreation, Travel, and Other Personal Services. **Work Group:** 11.03. Transportation and Lodging Services. **Other Job Titles in This Work Group:** Baggage Porters and Bellhops; Concierges; Hotel, Motel, and Resort Desk Clerks; Reservation and Transportation Ticket Agents; Reservation and Transportation Ticket Agents and Travel Clerks; Transportation Attendants, Except Flight Attendants and Baggage Porters. **PERSONALITY TYPE**—Enterprising. Enterprising occupations frequently involve starting up and carrying out projects. These occupations can involve leading people and making many decisions. They sometimes require risk taking and often deal with business.

EDUCATION/TRAINING PROGRAM(S)—Flight Attendant. **RELATED KNOWLEDGE/COURSES**— **Customer and Personal Service:** Knowledge of principles and processes for providing customer and personal services. This includes customer needs assessment, meeting quality standards for services, and evaluation of customer satisfaction. **Public Safety and Security:** Knowledge of relevant equipment, policies, procedures, and strategies to promote effective local, state, or national security operations for the protection of people, data, property, and institutions. **Medicine and Dentistry:** Knowledge of the information and techniques needed to diagnose and treat human injuries, diseases, and deformities. This includes symptoms, treatment alternatives, drug properties and interactions, and preventive health-care measures. **English Language:** Knowledge of the structure and content of the English language, including the meaning and spelling of words, rules of composition, and grammar. **Transportation:** Knowledge of principles and methods for moving people or goods by air, rail, sea, or road, including the relative costs and benefits. **Law and Government:** Knowledge of laws, legal codes, court procedures, precedents, government regulations, executive orders, agency rules, and the democratic political process.

# Food Preparation Workers

▲ Growth: 16.9%
▲ Annual Job Openings: 231,000
▲ Annual Earnings: $16,180
▲ Education/Training Required: Short-term on-the-job training
▲ Self-Employed: 0.5%
▲ Part-Time: 57.4%

**Perform a variety of food preparation duties other than cooking, such as preparing cold foods and shellfish, slicing meat, and brewing coffee or tea.** Cleans, portions, cuts, or peels various foods to prepare for cooking or serving. Stores food in designated containers and storage areas to prevent spoilage. Cleans and maintains work areas, equipment, and utensils. Butchers and cleans fowl, fish, poultry, and shellfish to prepare for cooking or serving. Requisitions, stores, and distributes food supplies, equipment, and utensils. Distributes food to waiters and waitresses to serve to customers. Carries food supplies, equipment, and utensils to and from storage and work areas. Portions and arranges food on serving dishes, trays, carts, or conveyor belts. Cleans, cuts, slices, or disjoints meats and poultry to prepare for cooking. Prepares and serves variety of beverages, such as coffee, tea, and soft drinks. Prepares variety of foods according to customers' orders or instructions of superior, following approved procedures. **SKILLS**—Service Orientation.

**GOE—Interest Area:** 11. Recreation, Travel, and Other Personal Services. **Work Group:** 11.05. Food and Beverage Services. **Other Job Titles in This Work Group:** Bakers; Bakers, Bread and Pastry; Bartenders; Butchers and Meat Cutters; Chefs and Head Cooks; Combined Food Preparation and Serving Workers, Including Fast Food; Cooks, All Other; Cooks, Fast Food; Cooks, Institution and Cafeteria; Cooks, Restaurant; Cooks, Short Order; Counter Attendants, Cafeteria, Food Concession, and Coffee Shop; Dining Room and Cafeteria Attendants and Bartender Helpers; Dishwashers; Food Preparation and Serving Related Workers, All Other;

Food Servers, Nonrestaurant; Hosts and Hostesses, Restaurant, Lounge, and Coffee Shop; Waiters and Waitresses. **PERSONALITY TYPE**—Realistic. Realistic occupations frequently involve work activities that include practical, hands-on problems and solutions. They often deal with plants, animals, and real-world materials like wood, tools, and machinery. Many of the occupations require working outside and do not involve a lot of paperwork or working closely with others.

**EDUCATION/TRAINING PROGRAM(S)**—Food Caterer; Kitchen Personnel/Cook and Assistant Training. **RELATED KNOWLEDGE/COURSES—Customer and Personal Service:** Knowledge of principles and processes for providing customer and personal services. This includes customer needs assessment, meeting quality standards for services, and evaluation of customer satisfaction. **Food Production:** Knowledge of techniques and equipment for planting, growing, and harvesting food products (both plant and animal) for consumption, including storage/handling techniques. **Public Safety and Security:** Knowledge of relevant equipment, policies, procedures, and strategies to promote effective local, state, or national security operations for the protection of people, data, property, and institutions. **Principles of Mechanical Devices:** Knowledge of machines and tools, including their designs, uses, repair, and maintenance. **Chemistry:** Knowledge of the chemical composition, structure, and properties of substances and of the chemical processes and transformations that they undergo. This includes uses of chemicals and their interactions, danger signs, production techniques, and disposal methods.

# Food Servers, Nonrestaurant

- ▲ Growth: 16.4%
- ▲ Annual Job Openings: 85,000
- ▲ Annual Earnings: $16,170
- ▲ Education/Training Required: Short-term on-the-job training
- ▲ Self-Employed: 0.2%
- ▲ Part-Time: 58.2%

**Serve food to patrons outside of a restaurant environment, such as in hotels, hospital rooms, or cars.** Prepares and delivers food trays. Washes dishes and cleans work area, tables, cabinets, and ovens, and sweeps service area with broom. Restocks service counter with items such as ice, napkins, and straws. Totals and presents check to customer and accepts payment for service. Records amount and types of special food items served to customers. Prepares fountain drinks, such as sodas, milkshakes, and malted milks. Prepares food items, such as sandwiches, salads, soups, and beverages, and places items, such as eating utensils, napkins, and condiments, on trays. Reads orders to determine items to place on food tray. Examines filled tray for completeness. Takes order and relays order to kitchen or serving counter to be filled. Carries silverware, linen, and food on tray or uses cart. Removes tray and stacks dishes for return to kitchen. Pushes carts to rooms and serves trays to patients or guests. Apportions and places food servings on plates and trays according to order or instructions. **SKILLS**—Service Orientation. Speaking.

**GOE—Interest Area:** 11. Recreation, Travel, and Other Personal Services. **Work Group:** 11.05. Food and Beverage Services. **Other Job Titles in This Work Group:** Bakers; Bakers, Bread and Pastry; Bartenders; Butchers and Meat Cutters; Chefs and Head Cooks; Combined Food Preparation and Serving Workers, Including Fast Food; Cooks, All Other; Cooks, Fast Food; Cooks, Institution and Cafeteria; Cooks, Restaurant; Cooks, Short Order; Counter Attendants, Cafeteria, Food Concession, and Coffee Shop; Dining Room and Cafeteria Attendants and Bartender Helpers; Dishwashers; Food Preparation and Serving Related Workers, All Other; Food Preparation Workers; Hosts and Hostesses, Restaurant, Lounge, and Coffee Shop; Waiters and Waitresses. **PERSONALITY TYPE**—Social. Social occupations frequently involve working with, communicating with, and teaching people. These occupations often involve helping or providing service to others.

**EDUCATION/TRAINING PROGRAM(S)**—Waiter/Waitress and Dining Room Manager. **RELATED KNOWLEDGE/COURSES—Customer and Personal Service:** Knowledge of principles and processes for providing customer and personal services. This includes customer needs assessment, meeting quality standards for services, and evaluation of customer satisfaction. **Mathematics:** Knowledge of arithmetic, algebra, geometry, calculus, statistics, and their applications. **English Language:** Knowledge of the structure and content of the English language, including the meaning and spelling of words, rules of composition, and grammar. **Sales and Marketing:** Knowledge of principles and methods for showing, promoting, and selling products or services. This includes marketing strategy and tactics, product demonstration, sales techniques, and sales control systems.

# Food Service Managers

▲ Growth: 15%

▲ Annual Job Openings: 55,000

▲ Annual Earnings: $34,350

▲ Education/Training Required: Work experience in a related occupation

▲ Self-Employed: 33.8%

▲ Part-Time: 8.5%

**Plan, direct, or coordinate activities of an organization or department that serves food and beverages.** Monitors compliance with health and fire regulations regarding food preparation and serving and building maintenance in lodging and dining facility. Coordinates assignments of cooking personnel to ensure economical use of food and timely preparation. Estimates food, liquor, wine, and other beverage consumption to anticipate amount to be purchased or requisitioned. Organizes and directs worker training programs, resolves personnel problems, hires new staff, and evaluates employee performance in dining and lodging facilities. Plans menus and food utilization based on anticipated number of guests, nutritional value, palatability, popularity, and costs. Monitors food preparation and methods, size of portions, and garnishing and presentation of food to ensure food is prepared and presented in accepted manner. Investigates and resolves complaints regarding food quality, service, or accommodations. Creates specialty dishes and develops recipes to be used in dining facility. Tests cooked food by tasting and smelling to ensure palatability and flavor conformity. Keeps records required by government agencies regarding sanitation and regarding food subsidies where indicated. Establishes and enforces nutrition standards for dining establishment based on accepted industry standards. Reviews menus and analyzes recipes to determine labor and overhead costs and assigns prices to menu items. Monitors budget and payroll records and reviews financial transactions to ensure expenditures are authorized and budgeted. **SKILLS**—Coordination. Management of Personnel Resources. Speaking. Monitoring. Time Management.

**GOE**—**Interest Area:** 11. Recreation, Travel, and Other Personal Services. **Work Group:** 11.01. Managerial Work in Recreation, Travel, and Other Personal Services. **Other Job Titles in This Work Group:** Aircraft Cargo Handling Supervisors; First-Line Supervisors/ Managers of Food Preparation and Serving Workers; First-Line Supervisors/Managers of Housekeeping and Janitorial Workers; First-Line Supervisors/Managers of Personal Service Workers; Gaming Managers; Gaming Supervisors; Housekeeping Supervisors; Janitorial Supervisors; Lodging Managers; Meeting and Convention Planners. **PERSONALITY TYPE**—Enterprising. Enterprising occupations frequently involve starting up and carrying out projects. These occupations can involve leading people and making many decisions. They sometimes require risk taking and often deal with business.

**EDUCATION/TRAINING PROGRAM(S)**—Food and Beverage/Restaurant Operations Manager; Food Sales Operations; Hospitality/Administration Management; Hotel/Motel and Restaurant Management. **RELATED KNOWLEDGE/COURSES**—**Administration and Management:** Knowledge of business and management principles involved in strategic planning, resource allocation, human resources modeling, leadership technique, production methods, and coordination of people and resources. **Customer and Personal Service:** Knowledge of principles and processes for providing customer and personal services. This includes customer needs assessment, meeting quality standards for services, and evaluation of customer satisfaction. **Economics and Accounting:** Knowledge of economic and accounting principles and practices, the financial markets, banking, and the analysis and reporting of financial data. **Education and Training:** Knowledge of principles and methods for curriculum and training design, teaching and instruction for individuals and groups, and the measurement of training effects. **Mathematics:** Knowledge of arithmetic, algebra, geometry, calculus, statistics, and their applications. **Personnel and Human Resources:** Knowledge of principles and procedures for personnel recruitment, selection, training, compensation and benefits, labor relations and negotiation, and personnel information systems. **Public Safety and Security:** Knowledge of relevant equipment, policies, procedures, and strategies to promote effective local, state, or national security operations for the protection of people, data, property, and institutions.

# Forest Fire Fighters

- ▲ Growth: 8.9%
- ▲ Annual Job Openings: 12,000
- ▲ Annual Earnings: $35,260
- ▲ Education/Training Required: Long-term on-the-job training
- ▲ Self-Employed: 0%
- ▲ Part-Time: 2%

**Control and suppress fires in forests or vacant public land.** Fells trees, cuts and clears brush, and digs trenches to contain fire, using ax, chain saw, or shovel. Extinguishes flames and embers to suppress fire, using shovel or engine or hand-driven water or chemical pumps. Ascertains best method for attacking fire and communicates plan to airplane or base camp, using two-way radio. Patrols burned area after fire to watch for hot spots that may restart fire. Packs parachutes. Parachutes from aircraft and guides direction of fall toward clear landing area near scene of fire. Orients self in relation to fire, using compass and map, and collects supplies and equipment dropped by parachute. Works as member of fire fighting crew. **SKILLS**—Service Orientation. Coordination. Critical Thinking. Monitoring. Speaking.

**GOE—Interest Area:** 04. Law, Law Enforcement, and Public Safety. **Work Group:** 04.04. Public Safety. **Other Job Titles in This Work Group:** Agricultural Inspectors; Aviation Inspectors; Compliance Officers, Except Agriculture, Construction, Health and Safety, and Transportation; Emergency Medical Technicians and Paramedics; Environmental Compliance Inspectors; Equal Opportunity Representatives and Officers; Financial Examiners; Fire Fighters; Fire Inspectors; Fire Inspectors and Investigators; Forest Fire Inspectors and Prevention Specialists; Government Property Inspectors and Investigators; Licensing Examiners and Inspectors; Marine Cargo Inspectors; Municipal Fire Fighters; Nuclear Monitoring Technicians; Occupational Health and Safety Specialists; Occupational Health and Safety Technicians; Public Transportation Inspectors. **PERSONALITY TYPE**—Realistic. Realistic occupations frequently involve work activities that include practical, hands-on problems and solutions. They often deal with plants, animals, and real-world materials like wood, tools, and machinery. Many of the occupations require working outside and do not involve a lot of paperwork or working closely with others.

**EDUCATION/TRAINING PROGRAM(S)**—Fire Protection, Other; Fire Science/Firefighting. **RELATED KNOWLEDGE/COURSES—Public Safety and Security:** Knowledge of relevant equipment, policies, procedures, and strategies to promote effective local, state, or national security operations for the protection of people, data, property, and institutions. **Transportation:** Knowledge of principles and methods for moving people or goods by air, rail, sea, or road, including the relative costs and benefits. **Telecommunications:** Knowledge of transmission, broadcasting, switching, control, and operation of telecommunications systems. **Engineering and Technology:** Knowledge of the practical application of engineering science and technology. This includes applying principles, techniques, procedures, and equipment to the design and production of various goods and services. **English Language:** Knowledge of the structure and content of the English language, including the meaning and spelling of words, rules of composition, and grammar. **Computers and Electronics:** Knowledge of circuit boards, processors, chips, electronic equipment, and computer hardware and software, including applications and programming.

# Forest Fire Fighting and Prevention Supervisors

▲ Growth: 7.2%
▲ Annual Job Openings: 5,000
▲ Annual Earnings: $52,990
▲ Education/Training Required: Work experience in a related occupation
▲ Self-Employed: 0%
▲ Part-Time: 2.1%

**Supervise fire fighters who control and suppress fires in forests or vacant public land.** Dispatches crews according to reported size, location, and condition of forest fires. Trains workers in parachute jumping, fire suppression, aerial observation, and radio communication. Parachutes to major fire locations and directs fire containment and suppression activities. Maintains radio communication with crews at fire scene to inform crew and base of changing conditions and learn of casualties. Observes fire and crews from air to determine force requirements and note changing conditions. Directs loading of fire suppression equipment into aircraft and parachuting of equipment to crews on ground. **SKILLS**—Coordination. Management of Personnel Resources. Judgment and Decision Making. Monitoring. Service Orientation. Instructing.

**GOE—Interest Area:** 04. Law, Law Enforcement, and Public Safety. **Work Group:** 04.01. Managerial Work in Law, Law Enforcement, and Public Safety. **Other Job Titles in This Work Group:** Emergency Management Specialists; First-Line Supervisors/Managers of Correctional Officers; First-Line Supervisors/Managers of Fire Fighting and Prevention Workers; First-Line Supervisors/Managers of Police and Detectives; First-Line Supervisors/Managers, Protective Service Workers, All Other; Municipal Fire Fighting and Prevention Supervisors. **PERSONALITY TYPE**—Realistic. Realistic occupations frequently involve work activities that include practical, hands-on problems and solutions. They often deal with plants, animals, and real-world materials like wood, tools, and machinery. Many of the occupations require working outside and do not involve a lot of paperwork or working closely with others.

**EDUCATION/TRAINING PROGRAM(S)**—Fire Protection and Safety Technologist/Technician; Fire Services Administration. **RELATED KNOWLEDGE/COURSES—Public Safety and Security:** Knowledge of relevant equipment, policies, procedures, and strategies to promote effective local, state, or national security operations for the protection of people, data, property, and institutions. **Transportation:** Knowledge of principles and methods for moving people or goods by air, rail, sea, or road, including the relative costs and benefits. **Administration and Management:** Knowledge of business and management principles involved in strategic planning, resource allocation, human resources modeling, leadership technique, production methods, and coordination of people and resources. **Education and Training:** Knowledge of principles and methods for curriculum and training design, teaching and instruction for individuals and groups, and the measurement of training effects. **Telecommunications:** Knowledge of transmission, broadcasting, switching, control, and operation of telecommunications systems.

# Freight Inspectors

- ▲ Growth: 11.3%
- ▲ Annual Job Openings: 3,000
- ▲ Annual Earnings: $44,200
- ▲ Education/Training Required: Work experience in a related occupation
- ▲ Self-Employed: 9%
- ▲ Part-Time: 5.5%

**Inspect freight for proper storage according to specifications.** Inspects shipment to ascertain that freight is securely braced and blocked. Observes loading of freight to ensure that crews comply with procedures. Monitors temperature and humidity of freight storage area. Records freight condition and handling and notifies crews to reload freight or insert additional bracing or packing. Measures height and width of loads that will pass over bridges or through tunnels. Notifies workers of special treatment required for shipments. Prepares and submits report after trip. Posts warning signs on vehicles containing explosives or inflammatory or radioactive materials. **SKILLS**—Reading Comprehension. Writing. Mathematics. Monitoring. Active Listening.

**GOE**—**Interest Area:** 07. Transportation. **Work Group:** 07.08. Support Work. **Other Job Titles in This Work Group:** Railroad Yard Workers; Stevedores, Except Equipment Operators; Train Crew Members; Transportation Inspectors. **PERSONALITY TYPE**—Conventional. Conventional occupations frequently involve following set procedures and routines. These occupations can include working with data and details more than with ideas. Usually there is a clear line of authority to follow.

**EDUCATION/TRAINING PROGRAM(S)**—Operations Management and Supervision. **RELATED KNOWLEDGE/COURSES**—**Transportation:** Knowledge of principles and methods for moving people or goods by air, rail, sea, or road, including the relative costs and benefits. **English Language:** Knowledge of the structure and content of the English language, including the meaning and spelling of words, rules of composition, and grammar. **Public Safety and Security:** Knowledge of relevant equipment, policies, procedures, and strategies to promote effective local, state, or national security operations for the protection of people, data, property, and institutions. **Production and Processing:** Knowledge of raw materials, production processes, quality control, costs, and other techniques for maximizing the effective manufacture and distribution of goods. **Mathematics:** Knowledge of arithmetic, algebra, geometry, calculus, statistics, and their applications. **Clerical Studies:** Knowledge of administrative and clerical procedures and systems such as word processing, managing files and records, stenography and transcription, designing forms, and other office procedures and terminology.

# Freight, Stock, and Material Movers, Hand

- ▲ Growth: 13.9%
- ▲ Annual Job Openings: 519,000
- ▲ Annual Earnings: $20,460
- ▲ Education/Training Required: Short-term on-the-job training
- ▲ Self-Employed: 1.1%
- ▲ Part-Time: 38.4%

**Load, unload, and move materials at plant, yard, or other work site.** Loads and unloads materials to and from designated storage areas, such as racks and shelves, or vehicles, such as trucks. Stacks or piles materials, such as lumber, boards, or pallets. Bundles and bands material, such as fodder and tobacco leaves, using banding machines. Sorts and stores items according to specifications. Assembles product containers and crates, using hand tools and precut lumber. Adjusts or replaces equipment parts, such as rollers, belts, plugs and caps, using hand tools. Records number of units handled and moved, using daily production sheet or work tickets. Attaches identifying tags or marks information on containers. Cleans work area, using brooms, rags, and cleaning compounds. Installs protective devices, such as bracing, padding or strapping, to prevent shifting or damage to items being transported. Reads work orders or receives and listens to oral instructions to determine work assignment. Shovels materials, such as gravel, ice, or spilled concrete, into containers or bins or onto conveyors. Directs spouts and positions receptacles, such as bins, carts, and containers, to receive loads. Transports receptacles to and from designated areas by hand or using dollies, hand trucks, and wheelbarrows. Secures lifting attachments to materials and conveys load to destination, using crane or hoist. **SKILLS**—Equipment Selection. Active Listening. Installation.

**GOE—Interest Area:** 08. Industrial Production. **Work Group:** 08.07. Hands-on Work: Loading, Moving, Hoisting, and Conveying. **Other Job Titles in This Work Group:** Conveyor Operators and Tenders; Crane and Tower Operators; Dragline Operators; Excavating and Loading Machine and Dragline Operators; Hoist and Winch Operators; Industrial Truck and Tractor Operators; Irradiated-Fuel Handlers; Laborers and Freight, Stock, and Material Movers, Hand; Machine Feeders and Offbearers; Material Moving Workers, All Other; Packers and Packagers, Hand; Pump Operators, Except Wellhead Pumpers; Refuse and Recyclable Material Collectors; Tank Car, Truck, and Ship Loaders. **PERSONALITY TYPE**—Realistic. Realistic occupations frequently involve work activities that include practical, hands-on problems and solutions. They often deal with plants, animals, and real-world materials like wood, tools, and machinery. Many of the occupations require working outside and do not involve a lot of paperwork or working closely with others.

**EDUCATION/TRAINING PROGRAM(S)**—No data available. **RELATED KNOWLEDGE/COURSES**—**Production and Processing:** Knowledge of raw materials, production processes, quality control, costs, and other techniques for maximizing the effective manufacture and distribution of goods. **Principles of Mechanical Devices:** Knowledge of machines and tools, including their designs, uses, repair, and maintenance. **Engineering and Technology:** Knowledge of the practical application of engineering science and technology. This includes applying principles, techniques, procedures, and equipment to the design and production of various goods and services. **Clerical Studies:** Knowledge of administrative and clerical procedures and systems such as word processing, managing files and records, stenography and transcription, designing forms, and other office procedures and terminology. **Physics:** Knowledge and prediction of physical principles and laws and their interrelationships and applications to understanding fluid, material, and atmospheric dynamics and mechanical, electrical, atomic, and sub-atomic structures and processes.

# Gaming Dealers

- ▲ Growth: 32.4%
- ▲ Annual Job Openings: 28,000
- ▲ Annual Earnings: $15,550
- ▲ Education/Training Required: Post-secondary vocational training
- ▲ Self-Employed: 0%
- ▲ Part-Time: 48.8%

**Operate table games. Stand or sit behind table and operate games of chance by dispensing the appropriate number of cards or blocks to players or operating other gaming equipment. Compare the house's hand against players' hands and pay off or collect players' money or chips.** Conducts gambling table or game, such as dice, roulette, cards, or keno, and ensures that game rules are followed. Exchanges paper currency for playing chips or coin money and collects game fees or wagers. Verifies, computes, and pays out winnings. Participates in game for gambling establishment to provide minimum complement of players at table. Prepares collection report for submission to supervisor. Seats patrons at gaming tables. Sells food, beverages, and tobacco to players. **SKILLS**—Service Orientation. Monitoring.

**GOE**—**Interest Area:** 11. Recreation, Travel, and Other Personal Services. **Work Group:** 11.02. Recreational Services. **Other Job Titles in This Work Group:** Amusement and Recreation Attendants; Entertainment Attendants and Related Workers, All Other; Gaming and Sports Book Writers and Runners; Gaming Service Workers, All Other; Motion Picture Projectionists; Recreation Workers; Slot Key Persons; Tour Guides and Escorts; Travel Guides; Ushers, Lobby Attendants, and Ticket Takers. **PERSONALITY TYPE**—Enterprising. Enterprising occupations frequently involve starting up and carrying out projects. These occupations can involve leading people and making many decisions. They sometimes require risk taking and often deal with business.

**EDUCATION/TRAINING PROGRAM(S)**—Card Dealer. **RELATED KNOWLEDGE/COURSES**—**Customer and Personal Service:** Knowledge of principles and processes for providing customer and personal services. This includes customer needs assessment, meeting quality standards for services, and evaluation of customer satisfaction. **Mathematics:** Knowledge of arithmetic, algebra, geometry, calculus, statistics, and their applications. **Sales and Marketing:** Knowledge of principles and methods for showing, promoting, and selling products or services. This includes marketing strategy and tactics, product demonstration, sales techniques, and sales control systems. **English Language:** Knowledge of the structure and content of the English language, including the meaning and spelling of words, rules of composition, and grammar. **Law and Government:** Knowledge of laws, legal codes, court procedures, precedents, government regulations, executive orders, agency rules, and the democratic political process. **Education and Training:** Knowledge of principles and methods for curriculum and training design, teaching and instruction for individuals and groups, and the measurement of training effects.

# Glaziers

- ▲ Growth: 14.8%
- ▲ Annual Job Openings: 6,000
- ▲ Annual Earnings: $32,360
- ▲ Education/Training Required: Long-term on-the-job training
- ▲ Self-Employed: 2.1%
- ▲ Part-Time: 8.4%

**Install glass in windows, skylights, storefronts, and display cases or on surfaces such as building fronts, interior walls, ceilings, and tabletops.** Assembles, fits, and attaches metal-framed glass enclosures for showers or bathtubs to framing around bath enclosure. Measures mirror and dimensions of area to be covered and determines plumb of walls or ceilings, using plumb-line and level. Attaches mounting strips and moldings to surface and applies mastic cement, putty, or screws to secure mirrors into position. Covers mirrors with protective material to prevent damage. Drives truck to installation site and unloads mirrors, equipment, and tools. Moves furniture to clear work site and covers floors and furnishings with drop cloths. Loads and arranges mirrors on truck, following sequence of deliveries. Measures, cuts, fits, and presses anti-glare adhesive film to glass or sprays glass with tinting solution to prevent light glare. Fastens glass panes into wood sash and spreads and smoothes putty around edge of pane with knife to seal joints. Installs pre-assembled framework for windows or doors designed to be fitted with glass panels, including stained glass windows, using hand tools. Marks outline or pattern on glass, cuts glass, and breaks off excess glass by hand or with notched tool. Sets glass doors into frame and bolts metal hinges, handles, locks, and other hardware onto glass doors. Attaches backing and leveling devices to wall surface, using nails and screws, and cuts mounting strips and moldings to required lengths. **SKILLS**—Mathematics. Installation. Coordination. Equipment Selection. Technology Design.

**GOE**—**Interest Area:** 06. Construction, Mining, and Drilling. **Work Group:** 06.02. Construction. **Other Job Titles in This Work Group:** Boat Builders and Shipwrights; Boilermakers; Brattice Builders; Brickmasons and Blockmasons; Carpenters; Carpet Installers; Ceiling Tile Installers; Cement Masons and Concrete Finishers; Commercial Divers; Construction Carpenters; Drywall and Ceiling Tile Installers; Drywall Installers; Electricians; Explosives Workers, Ordnance Handling Experts, and Blasters; Fence Erectors; Floor Layers, Except Carpet, Wood, and Hard Tiles; Floor Sanders and Finishers; Grader, Bulldozer, and Scraper Operators; Hazardous Materials Removal Workers; Insulation Workers, Floor, Ceiling, and Wall; Insulation Workers, Mechanical; Manufactured Building and Mobile Home Installers; Operating Engineers; Operating Engineers and Other Construction Equipment Operators; Painters, Construction and Maintenance; Paperhangers; Paving, Surfacing, and Tamping Equipment Operators; Pile-Driver Operators; Pipe Fitters; Pipelayers; Pipelaying Fitters; Plasterers and Stucco Masons; Plumbers; Plumbers, Pipefitters, and Steamfitters; Rail-Track Laying and Maintenance Equipment Operators; Refractory Materials Repairers, Except Brickmasons; Reinforcing Iron and Rebar Workers; Riggers; Roofers; Rough Carpenters; Security and Fire Alarm Systems Installers; Segmental Pavers; Sheet Metal Workers; Ship Carpenters and Joiners; Stone Cutters and Carvers; Stonemasons; Structural Iron and Steel Workers; Tapers; Terrazzo Workers and Finishers; Tile and Marble Setters. **PERSONALITY TYPE**—Realistic. Realistic occupations frequently involve work activities that include practical, hands-on problems and solutions. They often deal with plants, animals, and real-world materials like wood, tools, and machinery. Many of the occupations require working outside and do not involve a lot of paperwork or working closely with others.

**EDUCATION/TRAINING PROGRAM(S)**—No data available. **RELATED KNOWLEDGE/COURSES**—**Building and Construction:** Knowledge of materials, methods, and tools involved in the construction or repair of houses, buildings, or other structures such as highways and roads. **Engineering and Technology:** Knowledge of the practical application of engineering science and technology. This includes applying principles, techniques, procedures, and equipment to the design and production of various goods and services. **Transportation:** Knowledge of principles and methods for moving people or goods by air, rail, sea, or road, including the relative costs and benefits. **Principles of Mechanical Devices:** Knowledge of machines and tools, including their designs, uses, repair, and maintenance. **Design:** Knowledge of design techniques, tools, and principles involved in production of precision technical plans, blueprints, drawings, and models.

# Government Property Inspectors and Investigators

- ▲ Growth: 8.9%
- ▲ Annual Job Openings: 9,000
- ▲ Annual Earnings: $44,140
- ▲ Education/Training Required: Long-term on-the-job training
- ▲ Self-Employed: 0%
- ▲ Part-Time: 2.9%

**Investigate or inspect government property to ensure compliance with contract agreements and government regulations.** Investigates regulated activities to detect violation of law relating to such activities as revenue collection, employment practices, or fraudulent benefit claims. Inspects manufactured or processed products to ensure compliance with contract specifications and legal requirements. Examines records, reports, and documents to establish facts and detect discrepancies. Investigates character of applicant for special license or permit and misuses of license or permit. Inspects government-owned equipment and materials in hands of private contractors to prevent waste, damage, theft, and other irregularities. Locates and interviews plaintiffs, witnesses, or representatives of business or government to gather facts relevant to inspection or alleged violation. Submits samples of product to government laboratory for testing as indicated by departmental procedures. Testifies in court or at administrative proceedings concerning findings of investigation. Prepares correspondence, reports of inspections or investigations, and recommendations for administrative or legal authorities. **SKILLS**—Speaking. Reading Comprehension. Writing. Critical Thinking. Judgment and Decision Making.

**GOE—Interest Area:** 04. Law, Law Enforcement, and Public Safety. **Work Group:** 04.04. Public Safety. **Other Job Titles in This Work Group:** Agricultural Inspectors; Aviation Inspectors; Compliance Officers, Except Agriculture, Construction, Health and Safety, and Transportation; Emergency Medical Technicians and Paramedics; Environmental Compliance Inspectors; Equal Opportunity Representatives and Officers; Financial Examiners; Fire Fighters; Fire Inspectors; Fire Inspectors and Investigators; Forest Fire Fighters; Forest Fire Inspec-

tors and Prevention Specialists; Licensing Examiners and Inspectors; Marine Cargo Inspectors; Municipal Fire Fighters; Nuclear Monitoring Technicians; Occupational Health and Safety Specialists; Occupational Health and Safety Technicians; Public Transportation Inspectors. **PERSONALITY TYPE**—Enterprising. Enterprising occupations frequently involve starting up and carrying out projects. These occupations can involve leading people and making many decisions. They sometimes require risk taking and often deal with business.

**EDUCATION/TRAINING PROGRAM(S)**—Business Administration and Management, General; Construction/Building Technologist/Technician; Logistics and Materials Management; Material Engineering; Mechanical Engineering; Operations Management and Supervision; Purchasing, Procurement and Contracts Management; Systems Engineering. **RELATED KNOWLEDGE/COURSES—Law and Government:** Knowledge of laws, legal codes, court procedures, precedents, government regulations, executive orders, agency rules, and the democratic political process. **English Language:** Knowledge of the structure and content of the English language, including the meaning and spelling of words, rules of composition, and grammar. **Mathematics:** Knowledge of arithmetic, algebra, geometry, calculus, statistics, and their applications. **Public Safety and Security:** Knowledge of relevant equipment, policies, procedures, and strategies to promote effective local, state, or national security operations for the protection of people, data, property, and institutions. **Personnel and Human Resources:** Knowledge of principles and procedures for personnel recruitment, selection, training, compensation and benefits, labor relations and negotiation, and personnel information systems.

# Grader, Bulldozer, and Scraper Operators

- ▲ Growth: 6.9%
- ▲ Annual Job Openings: 25,000
- ▲ Annual Earnings: $36,170
- ▲ Education/Training Required: Moderate-term on-the-job training
- ▲ Self-Employed: 6.6%
- ▲ Part-Time: 5%

**Operate machines or vehicles equipped with blades to remove, distribute, level, or grade earth.** Starts engine, moves throttle, switches, and levers, and depresses pedals to operate machines, equipment, and attachments. Drives equipment in successive passes over working area to achieve specified result, such as grading terrain or removing, dumping, or spreading earth and rock. Aligns machine, cutterhead, or depth gauge marker with reference stakes and guidelines on ground or positions equipment following hand signals of assistant. Fastens bulldozer blade or other attachment to tractor, using hitches. Greases, oils, and performs minor repairs on tractor, using grease gun, oil cans, and hand tools. Signals operator to guide movement of tractor-drawn machine. Connects hydraulic hoses, belts, mechanical linkage, or power takeoff shaft to tractor. **SKILLS**—Operation and Control. Equipment Selection. Operation Monitoring.

**GOE—Interest Area:** 06. Construction, Mining, and Drilling. **Work Group:** 06.02. Construction. **Other Job Titles in This Work Group:** Boat Builders and Shipwrights; Boilermakers; Brattice Builders; Brickmasons and Blockmasons; Carpenters; Carpet Installers; Ceiling Tile Installers; Cement Masons and Concrete Finishers; Commercial Divers; Construction Carpenters; Drywall and Ceiling Tile Installers; Drywall Installers; Electricians; Explosives Workers, Ordnance Handling Experts, and Blasters; Fence Erectors; Floor Layers, Except Carpet, Wood, and Hard Tiles; Floor Sanders and Finishers; Glaziers; Hazardous Materials Removal Workers; Insulation Workers, Floor, Ceiling, and Wall; Insulation Workers, Mechanical; Manufactured Building and Mobile Home Installers; Operating Engineers; Operating Engineers and Other Construction Equipment Operators; Painters, Construction and Maintenance; Paperhangers; Paving, Surfacing, and Tamping Equipment Operators; Pile-Driver Operators; Pipe Fitters; Pipelayers; Pipelaying Fitters; Plasterers and Stucco Masons; Plumbers; Plumbers, Pipefitters, and Steamfitters; Rail-Track Laying and Maintenance Equipment Operators; Refractory Materials Repairers, Except Brickmasons; Reinforcing Iron and Rebar Workers; Riggers; Roofers; Rough Carpenters; Security and Fire Alarm Systems Installers; Segmental Pavers; Sheet Metal Workers; Ship Carpenters and Joiners; Stone Cutters and Carvers; Stonemasons; Structural Iron and Steel Workers; Tapers; Terrazzo Workers and Finishers; Tile and Marble Setters. **PERSONALITY TYPE**—Realistic. Realistic occupations frequently involve work activities that include practical, hands-on problems and solutions. They often deal with plants, animals, and real-world materials like wood, tools, and machinery. Many of the occupations require working outside and do not involve a lot of paperwork or working closely with others.

**EDUCATION/TRAINING PROGRAM(S)**—Construction Equipment Operator. **RELATED KNOWLEDGE/COURSES—Principles of Mechanical Devices:** Knowledge of machines and tools, including their designs, uses, repair, and maintenance. **Transportation:** Knowledge of principles and methods for moving people or goods by air, rail, sea, or road, including the relative costs and benefits. **Physics:** Knowledge and prediction of physical principles and laws and their interrelationships and applications to understanding fluid, material, and atmospheric dynamics and mechanical, electrical, atomic, and sub-atomic structures and processes. **Engineering and Technology:** Knowledge of the practical application of engineering science and technology. This includes applying principles, techniques, procedures, and equipment to the design and production of various goods and services. **Building and Construction:** Knowledge of materials, methods, and tools involved in the construction or repair of houses, buildings, or other structures such as highways and roads.

# Grips and Set-Up Workers, Motion Picture Sets, Studios, and Stages

▲ Growth: 13.9%
▲ Annual Job Openings: 519,000
▲ Annual Earnings: $20,460
▲ Education/Training Required: Short-term on-the-job training
▲ Self-Employed: 1.1%
▲ Part-Time: 16.2%

**Arrange equipment; raise and lower scenery; move dollies, cranes, and booms; and perform other duties for motion-picture, recording, or television industry.** Arranges equipment preparatory to sessions and performances following work order specifications and handles props during performances. Rigs and dismantles stage or set equipment, such as frames, scaffolding, platforms, or backdrops, using carpenter's hand tools. Adjusts controls to raise and lower scenery and stage curtain during performance, following cues. Adjusts controls to guide, position, and move equipment, such as cranes, booms, and cameras. Erects canvas covers to protect equipment from weather. Reads work orders and follows oral instructions to determine specified material and equipment to be moved and its relocation. Connects electrical equipment to power source and tests equipment before performance. Orders equipment and maintains equipment storage areas. Sews and repairs items using materials and hand tools such as canvas and sewing machines. Produces special lighting and sound effects during performances, using various machines and devices. **SKILLS**—Monitoring. Operation and Control. Coordination. Active Listening. Reading Comprehension.

**GOE**—**Interest Area:** 06. Construction, Mining, and Drilling. **Work Group:** 06.04. Hands-on Work in Construction, Extraction, and Maintenance. **Other Job Titles in This Work Group:** Carpenter Assemblers and Repairers; Construction Laborers; Helpers, Construction Trades, All Other; Helpers—Brickmasons, Blockmasons, Stonemasons, and Tile and Marble Setters; Helpers—Carpenters; Helpers—Extraction Workers; Helpers—Painters, Paperhangers, Plasterers, and Stucco Masons; Helpers—Pipelayers, Plumbers, Pipefitters, and Steamfitters; Helpers—Roofers; Highway Maintenance Workers; Septic Tank Servicers and Sewer Pipe Cleaners. **PERSONALITY TYPE**—Realistic. Realistic occupations frequently involve work activities that include practical, hands-on problems and solutions. They often deal with plants, animals, and real-world materials like wood, tools, and machinery. Many of the occupations require working outside and do not involve a lot of paperwork or working closely with others.

**EDUCATION/TRAINING PROGRAM(S)**—No data available. **RELATED KNOWLEDGE/COURSES**—**Building and Construction:** Knowledge of materials, methods, and tools involved in the construction or repair of houses, buildings, or other structures such as highways and roads. **Engineering and Technology:** Knowledge of the practical application of engineering science and technology. This includes applying principles, techniques, procedures, and equipment to the design and production of various goods and services. **Principles of Mechanical Devices:** Knowledge of machines and tools, including their designs, uses, repair, and maintenance. **Fine Arts:** Knowledge of the theory and techniques required to compose, produce, and perform works of music, dance, visual arts, drama, and sculpture. **Design:** Knowledge of design techniques, tools, and principles involved in production of precision technical plans, blueprints, drawings, and models. **English Language:** Knowledge of the structure and content of the English language, including the meaning and spelling of words, rules of composition, and grammar.

# Hairdressers, Hairstylists, and Cosmetologists

- ▲ Growth: 13%
- ▲ Annual Job Openings: 78,000
- ▲ Annual Earnings: $20,710
- ▲ Education/Training Required: Post-secondary vocational training
- ▲ Self-Employed: 48.5%
- ▲ Part-Time: 36.5%

**Provide beauty services, such as shampooing, cutting, coloring, and styling hair and massaging and treating scalp. May also apply makeup, dress wigs, perform hair removal, and provide nail and skin care services.** Cuts, trims and shapes hair or hairpieces, using clippers, scissors, trimmers and razors. Bleaches, dyes, or tints hair, using applicator or brush. Combs, brushes, and sprays hair or wigs to set style. Analyzes patron's hair and other physical features or reads makeup instructions to determine and recommend beauty treatment. Administers therapeutic medication and advises patron to seek medical treatment for chronic or contagious scalp conditions. Shapes and colors eyebrows or eyelashes and removes facial hair, using depilatory cream and tweezers. Updates and maintains customer information records, such as beauty services provided. Cleans, shapes, and polishes fingernails and toenails, using files and nail polish. Recommends and applies cosmetics, lotions, and creams to patron to soften and lubricate skin and enhance and restore natural appearance. Massages and treats scalp for hygienic and remedial purposes, using hands, fingers, or vibrating equipment. Attaches wig or hairpiece to model head and dresses wigs and hairpieces according to instructions, samples, sketches or photographs. Applies water and setting or waving solutions to hair and winds hair on curlers or rollers. Shampoos, rinses, and dries hair and scalp or hairpieces with water, liquid soap, or other solutions. **SKILLS**—Service Orientation. Active Listening.

**GOE**—**Interest Area:** 11. Recreation, Travel, and Other Personal Services. **Work Group:** 11.04. Barber and Beauty Services. **Other Job Titles in This Work Group:** Barbers; Manicurists and Pedicurists; Shampooers; Skin Care Specialists. **PERSONALITY TYPE**—Enterprising. Enterprising occupations frequently involve starting up and carrying out projects. These occupations can involve leading people and making many decisions. They sometimes require risk taking and often deal with business.

**EDUCATION/TRAINING PROGRAM(S)**—Barber/Hairstylist; Cosmetic Services, General; Cosmetic Services, Other; Cosmetologist; Electrolysis Technician; Make-Up Artist. **RELATED KNOWLEDGE/COURSES**—**Customer and Personal Service:** Knowledge of principles and processes for providing customer and personal services. This includes customer needs assessment, meeting quality standards for services, and evaluation of customer satisfaction. **Clerical Studies:** Knowledge of administrative and clerical procedures and systems such as word processing, managing files and records, stenography and transcription, designing forms, and other office procedures and terminology. **Sales and Marketing:** Knowledge of principles and methods for showing, promoting, and selling products or services. This includes marketing strategy and tactics, product demonstration, sales techniques, and sales control systems. **English Language:** Knowledge of the structure and content of the English language, including the meaning and spelling of words, rules of composition, and grammar. **Medicine and Dentistry:** Knowledge of the information and techniques needed to diagnose and treat human injuries, diseases, and deformities. This includes symptoms, treatment alternatives, drug properties and interactions, and preventive health-care measures. **Mathematics:** Knowledge of arithmetic, algebra, geometry, calculus, statistics, and their applications.

# Heat Treating, Annealing, and Tempering Machine Operators and Tenders, Metal and Plastic

- ▲ Growth: 13.4%
- ▲ Annual Job Openings: 9,000
- ▲ Annual Earnings: $28,020
- ▲ Education/Training Required: Moderate-term on-the-job training
- ▲ Self-Employed: 0%
- ▲ Part-Time: 1.9%

**Operate or tend machines, such as furnaces, baths, flame-hardening machines, and electronic induction machines, to harden, anneal, and heat-treat metal products or metal parts.** Sets automatic controls, observes gauges, and operates gas or electric furnace used to harden, temper, or anneal metal parts. Loads parts into containers, closes furnace door, and inserts parts into furnace when specified temperature is reached. Covers parts with charcoal before inserting in furnace to prevent discoloration caused by rapid heating. Cleans oxides and scale from parts or fittings, using steam spray or immersing parts in chemical and water baths. Signals forklift operator to deposit or extract containers of parts into and from furnaces and quenching rinse tanks. Tests parts for hardness, using hardness testing equipment, and stamps heat treatment identification mark on part, using hammer and punch. Examines parts to ensure metal shade and color conform to specifications, utilizing knowledge of metal heat-treating. Removes parts from furnace after specified time and air dries or cools parts in water or oil brine or other baths. Reduces heat and allows parts to cool in furnace. Positions part in fixture, presses buttons to light burners, and tends flame-hardening machine, according to procedures, to case-harden metal part. Adjusts speed and operates continuous furnace through which parts are passed by means of reels and conveyors. Sets up and operates die-quenching machine to prevent parts from warping. Reads production schedule to determine processing sequence and furnace temperature requirements for objects to be heat treated. Activates and tends electric furnace that anneals base sections of hardened parts for subsequent machining. **SKILLS**—Operation Monitoring. Quality Control Analysis. Operation and Control. Equipment Selection. Reading Comprehension.

**GOE—Interest Area:** 08. Industrial Production. **Work Group:** 08.02. Production Technology. **Other Job Titles in This Work Group:** Aircraft Rigging Assemblers; Aircraft Structure Assemblers, Precision; Aircraft Structure, Surfaces, Rigging, and Systems Assemblers; Aircraft Systems Assemblers, Precision; Bench Workers, Jewelry; Bindery Machine Setters and Set-Up Operators; Bindery Workers; Bookbinders; Buffing and Polishing Set-Up Operators; Casting Machine Set-Up Operators; Coating, Painting, and Spraying Machine Setters and Set-Up Operators; Coating, Painting, and Spraying Machine Setters, Operators, and Tenders; Combination Machine Tool Setters and Set-Up Operators, Metal and Plastic; Cutting, Punching, and Press Machine Setters, Operators, and Tenders, Metal and Plastic; Dental Laboratory Technicians; Drilling and Boring Machine Tool Setters, Operators, and Tenders, Metal and Plastic; Electrical and Electronic Equipment Assemblers; Electrical and Electronic Inspectors and Testers; Electromechanical Equipment Assemblers; Engine and Other Machine Assemblers; Extruding and Drawing Machine Setters, Operators, and Tenders, Metal and Plastic; Extruding, Forming, Pressing, and Compacting Machine Setters and Set-Up Operators; Extruding, Forming, Pressing, and Compacting Machine Setters, Operators, and Tenders; Forging Machine Setters, Operators, and Tenders, Metal and Plastic; Foundry Mold and Coremakers; Gem and Diamond Workers; Grinding, Honing, Lapping, and Deburring Machine Set-Up Operators; Grinding, Lapping, Polishing, and Buffing Machine Tool Setters, Operators, and Tenders, Metal and Plastic; Heat Treating Equipment Setters, Operators, and Tenders, Metal and Plastic; others. **PERSONALITY TYPE**—Realistic. Realistic occupations frequently involve work activities that include practical, hands-on problems and solutions. They often deal with plants, animals, and real-world materials like wood, tools, and machinery. Many of the occupations require working outside and do not involve a lot of paperwork or working closely with others.

EDUCATION/TRAINING PROGRAM(S)—Machine Shop Assistant. **RELATED KNOWLEDGE/ COURSES—Production and Processing:** Knowledge of raw materials, production processes, quality control, costs, and other techniques for maximizing the effective manufacture and distribution of goods. **Principles of Mechanical Devices:** Knowledge of machines and tools, including their designs, uses, repair, and maintenance. **Physics:** Knowledge and prediction of physical principles and laws and their interrelationships and applications to understanding fluid, material, and atmospheric dynamics and mechanical, electrical, atomic, and sub-atomic structures and processes. **Mathematics:** Knowledge of arithmetic, algebra, geometry, calculus, statistics, and their applications. **Chemistry:** Knowledge of the chemical composition, structure, and properties of substances and of the chemical processes and transformations that they undergo. This includes uses of chemicals and their interactions, danger signs, production techniques, and disposal methods.

# Heaters, Metal and Plastic

▲ Growth: 13.4%

▲ Annual Job Openings: 9,000

▲ Annual Earnings: $28,020

▲ Education/Training Required: Moderate-term on-the-job training

▲ Self-Employed: 0%

▲ Part-Time: 1.9%

**Operate or tend heating equipment, such as soaking pits, reheating furnaces, and heating and vacuum equipment, to heat metal sheets, blooms, billets, bars, plate, and rods to a specified temperature for rolling or processing or to heat and cure preformed plastic parts.** Ignites furnace with torch and turns valve to regulate flow of fuel and air to burners. Inserts vacuum tube into bag and seals bag around tube with tape. Positions plastic sheet and mold in plastic bag, heats material under lamps, and forces confrontation of sheet to mold by vacuum pressure. Removes material from furnace, using crane, or signals crane operator to transfer to next station. Assists workers in repairing, replacing, cleaning, lubricating, or adjusting furnace equipment, using hand tools. Records time and production data. Signals coworker to charge steel into furnace. Impregnates fabric with plastic resins and cuts fabric into strips. Pushes cart to curing oven or places part in autoclave. Removes part and cuts away plastic bag. Positions part in plastic bag and seals bag with iron. Removes stock from furnace, using cold rod, tongs or chain hoist, and places stock on conveyor for transport to work area. Positions stock in furnace, using tongs, chain hoist, or pry bar. Places part on cart, connects vacuum line to tube, and smoothes bag around part to ensure vacuum. Adjusts controls to synchronize speed of feed and take-off conveyors of furnace. Starts conveyors and opens furnace doors to load stock or signals crane operator to uncover soaking pits and lower ingots into them. Adjusts controls to maintain temperature and heating time, using thermal instruments and charts, dials and gauges of furnace, and color of stock. Sets oven controls or turns air-pressure valve or autoclave. **SKILLS—Equipment Maintenance. Operation and Control. Repairing. Operation Monitoring.**

**GOE—Interest Area:** 08. Industrial Production. **Work Group:** 08.03. Production Work. **Other Job Titles in This Work Group:** Bakers, Manufacturing; Bindery Machine Operators and Tenders; Brazers; Cementing and Gluing Machine Operators and Tenders; Chemical Equipment Controllers and Operators; Chemical Equipment Operators and Tenders; Chemical Equipment Tenders; Cleaning, Washing, and Metal Pickling Equipment Operators and Tenders; Coating, Painting, and Spraying Machine Operators and Tenders; Coil Winders, Tapers, and Finishers; Combination Machine Tool Operators and Tenders, Metal and Plastic; Computer-Controlled Machine Tool Operators, Metal and Plastic; Cooling and Freezing Equipment Operators and Tenders; Crushing, Grinding, and Polishing Machine Setters, Operators, and Tenders; Cutters and Trimmers, Hand; Cutting and Slicing Machine Operators and Tenders; Cutting and Slicing Machine Setters, Operators, and Tenders; Design Printing Machine Setters and Set-Up Operators; Electrolytic Plating and Coating Machine Operators and Tenders, Metal and Plastic; Electrolytic Plating and Coating Machine Setters and Set-Up Operators, Metal and Plastic; Electrotypers and Stereotypers; Embossing Machine Set-Up Operators; Engraver Set-Up Operators; Extruding and Forming Machine Operators and Tenders, Synthetic or Glass Fibers; Extruding and Forming Machine Setters, Operators, and Tenders, Synthetic and Glass Fibers; Extruding, Forming, Pressing, and Compacting Machine Operators and Tenders; Fabric and Apparel Patternmakers; Fiber Product Cutting Machine Setters and Set-Up Operators; Fiberglass Laminators and Fabricators; others. **PERSONALITY TYPE**—Realistic. Realistic occupations frequently involve work activities that include practical, hands-on problems and solutions.

They often deal with plants, animals, and real-world materials like wood, tools, and machinery. Many of the occupations require working outside and do not involve a lot of paperwork or working closely with others.

**EDUCATION/TRAINING PROGRAM(S)**—Machine Shop Assistant. **RELATED KNOWLEDGE/COURSES—Production and Processing:** Knowledge of raw materials, production processes, quality control, costs, and other techniques for maximizing the effective manufacture and distribution of goods. **Principles of Mechanical Devices:** Knowledge of machines and tools, including their designs, uses, repair, and maintenance. **Physics:** Knowledge and prediction of physical principles and laws and their interrelationships and applications to understanding fluid, material, and atmospheric dynamics and mechanical, electrical, atomic, and sub-atomic structures and processes. **Engineering and Technology:** Knowledge of the practical application of engineering science and technology. This includes applying principles, techniques, procedures, and equipment to the design and production of various goods and services. **Mathematics:** Knowledge of arithmetic, algebra, geometry, calculus, statistics, and their applications.

# Heating and Air Conditioning Mechanics

- ▲ Growth: 22.3%
- ▲ Annual Job Openings: 21,000
- ▲ Annual Earnings: $34,180
- ▲ Education/Training Required: Long-term on-the-job training
- ▲ Self-Employed: 20%
- ▲ Part-Time: 4.9%

**Install, service, and repair heating and air conditioning systems in residences and commercial establishments.** Installs, connects, and adjusts thermostats, humidistats, and timers, using hand tools. Repairs or replaces defective equipment, components, or wiring. Joins pipes or tubing to equipment and to fuel, water, or refrigerant source to form complete circuit. Fabricates, assembles, and installs duct work and chassis parts, using portable metal-working tools and welding equip-

ment. Tests electrical circuits and components for continuity, using electrical test equipment. Disassembles system and cleans and oils parts. Assembles, positions, and mounts heating or cooling equipment, following blueprints. Tests pipe or tubing joints and connections for leaks, using pressure gauge or soap-and-water solution. Installs auxiliary components to heating-cooling equipment, such as expansion and discharge valves, air ducts, pipes, blowers, dampers, flues, and stokers, following blueprints. Adjusts system controls to setting recommended by manufacturer to balance system, using hand tools. Inspects and tests system to verify system compliance with plans and specifications and to detect malfunctions. Discusses heating-cooling system malfunctions with users to isolate problems or to verify malfunctions have been corrected. Inspects inoperative equipment to locate source of trouble. Studies blueprints to determine configuration of heating or cooling equipment components. Wraps pipes in insulation and secures it in place with cement or wire bands. Lays out and connects electrical wiring between controls and equipment according to wiring diagram, using electrician's hand tools. Reassembles equipment and starts unit to test operation. Measures, cuts, threads, and bends pipe or tubing, using pipefitter's tools. Cuts and drills holes in floors, walls, and roof to install equipment, using power saws and drills. **SKILLS**—Installation. Troubleshooting. Repairing. Equipment Maintenance. Quality Control Analysis.

**GOE—Interest Area:** 05. Mechanics, Installers, and Repairers. **Work Group:** 05.03. Mechanical Work. **Other Job Titles in This Work Group:** Aircraft Body and Bonded Structure Repairers; Aircraft Engine Specialists; Aircraft Mechanics and Service Technicians; Airframe-and-Power-Plant Mechanics; Automotive Body and Related Repairers; Automotive Glass Installers and Repairers; Automotive Master Mechanics; Automotive Service Technicians and Mechanics; Automotive Specialty Technicians; Bicycle Repairers; Bridge and Lock Tenders; Bus and Truck Mechanics and Diesel Engine Specialists; Camera and Photographic Equipment Repairers; Coin, Vending, and Amusement Machine Servicers and Repairers; Control and Valve Installers and Repairers, Except Mechanical Door; Farm Equipment Mechanics; Gas Appliance Repairers; Hand and Portable Power Tool Repairers; Heating, Air Conditioning, and Refrigeration Mechanics and Installers; Helpers—Electricians; Helpers—Installation, Maintenance, and Repair Workers; Industrial Machinery Mechanics; Keyboard Instrument Repairers and Tuners; Locksmiths and Safe Repairers; Maintenance and Repair Workers, General; Maintenance Workers, Machinery; Mechanical Door Repairers; Medical Appliance Technicians; Medical Equipment Repairers; Meter Mechanics; Millwrights; Mobile Heavy Equipment Mechanics, Except Engines; Motorboat Mechanics; Motorcycle Mechanics; Musical Instrument Repairers and Tuners; Ophthalmic Laboratory Technicians; Optical Instrument Assemblers; Outdoor Power Equipment and Other Small Engine Mechanics; Painters, Transportation Equipment; Percussion Instrument Repairers and Tuners; Precision Instrument and Equipment Repairers, All Other; others. **PERSONALITY TYPE**—Realistic. Realistic occupations frequently involve work activities that include practical, hands-on problems and solutions. They often deal with plants, animals, and real-world materials like wood, tools, and machinery. Many of the occupations require working outside and do not involve a lot of paperwork or working closely with others.

**EDUCATION/TRAINING PROGRAM(S)**—Heating, Air Conditioning and Refrigeration Mechanic and Rep; Heating, Air Conditioning and Refrigeration Technologist/Technician. **RELATED KNOWLEDGE/COURSES—Principles of Mechanical Devices:** Knowledge of machines and tools, including their designs, uses, repair, and maintenance. **Design:** Knowledge of design techniques, tools, and principles involved in production of precision technical plans, blueprints, drawings, and models. **Building and Construction:** Knowledge of materials, methods, and tools involved in the construction or repair of houses, buildings, or other structures such as highways and roads. **Engineering and Technology:** Knowledge of the practical application of engineering science and technology. This includes applying principles, techniques, procedures, and equipment to the design and production of various goods and services. **Customer and Personal Service:** Knowledge of principles and processes for providing customer and personal services. This includes customer needs assessment, meeting quality standards for services, and evaluation of customer satisfaction. **English Language:** Knowledge of the structure and content of the English language, including the meaning and spelling of words, rules of composition, and grammar.

# Heating Equipment Setters and Set-Up Operators, Metal and Plastic

▲ Growth: 13.4%
▲ Annual Job Openings: 9,000
▲ Annual Earnings: $28,020
▲ Education/Training Required: Moderate-term on-the-job training
▲ Self-Employed: 0%
▲ Part-Time: 1.9%

**Set up or set up and operate heating equipment, such as heat-treating furnaces, flame-hardening machines, and induction machines, that anneal or heat-treat metal objects.** Mounts fixtures and industrial coil on machine and workpieces in fixture, using hand tools. Starts conveyors and dial feeder plates and turns set-screws in nozzles to direct flames which anneal specific area of object. Reads work order to determine processing specifications. Crushes random samples between fingers to determine hardness. Instructs new workers in machine operation. Replaces worn dial-feed, burner, and conveyor parts, using hand tools. Visually examines or tests objects, using hardness testing equipment, to determine flame temperature and degree of hardness. Estimates flame temperature and heating cycle based on degree of hardness required and metal to be treated. Sets frequency of current and automatic timer. Lights gas burners and adjusts flow of gas and coolant water. **SKILLS**—Operation Monitoring. Operation and Control. Equipment Maintenance. Quality Control Analysis. Mathematics.

**GOE—Interest Area:** 08. Industrial Production. **Work Group:** 08.02. Production Technology. **Other Job Titles in This Work Group:** Aircraft Rigging Assemblers; Aircraft Structure Assemblers, Precision; Aircraft Structure, Surfaces, Rigging, and Systems Assemblers; Aircraft Systems Assemblers, Precision; Bench Workers, Jewelry; Bindery Machine Setters and Set-Up Operators; Bindery Workers; Bookbinders; Buffing and Polishing Set-Up Operators; Casting Machine Set-Up Operators; Coating, Painting, and Spraying Machine Setters and Set-Up Operators; Coating, Painting, and Spraying Machine Setters, Operators, and Tenders; Combination Machine Tool Setters and Set-Up Operators, Metal and Plastic; Cutting, Punching, and Press Machine Setters, Operators, and Tenders, Metal and Plastic; Dental Laboratory Technicians; Drilling and Boring Machine Tool Setters, Operators, and Tenders, Metal and Plastic; Electrical and Electronic Equipment Assemblers; Electrical and Electronic Inspectors and Testers; Electromechanical Equipment Assemblers; Engine and Other Machine Assemblers; Extruding and Drawing Machine Setters, Operators, and Tenders, Metal and Plastic; Extruding, Forming, Pressing, and Compacting Machine Setters and Set-Up Operators; Extruding, Forming, Pressing, and Compacting Machine Setters, Operators, and Tenders; Forging Machine Setters, Operators, and Tenders, Metal and Plastic; Foundry Mold and Coremakers; Gem and Diamond Workers; Grinding, Honing, Lapping, and Deburring Machine Set-Up Operators; Grinding, Lapping, Polishing, and Buffing Machine Tool Setters, Operators, and Tenders, Metal and Plastic; Heat Treating Equipment Setters, Operators, and Tenders, Metal and Plastic; others. **PERSONALITY TYPE**—Realistic. Realistic occupations frequently involve work activities that include practical, hands-on problems and solutions. They often deal with plants, animals, and real-world materials like wood, tools, and machinery. Many of the occupations require working outside and do not involve a lot of paperwork or working closely with others.

**EDUCATION/TRAINING PROGRAM(S)**—Machine Shop Assistant. **RELATED KNOWLEDGE/COURSES—Principles of Mechanical Devices:** Knowledge of machines and tools, including their designs, uses, repair, and maintenance. **Production and Processing:** Knowledge of raw materials, production processes, quality control, costs, and other techniques for maximizing the effective manufacture and distribution of goods. **Physics:** Knowledge and prediction of physical principles and laws and their interrelationships and applications to understanding fluid, material, and atmospheric dynamics and mechanical, electrical, atomic, and sub-atomic structures and processes. **Education and Training:** Knowledge of principles and methods for curriculum and training design, teaching and instruction for individuals and groups, and the measurement of training effects. **English Language:**

Knowledge of the structure and content of the English language, including the meaning and spelling of words, rules of composition, and grammar. **Engineering and Technology:** Knowledge of the practical application of engineering science and technology. This includes applying principles, techniques, procedures, and equipment to the design and production of various goods and services.

# Helpers—Brickmasons, Blockmasons, Stonemasons, and Tile and Marble Setters

- ▲ Growth: 14.1%
- ▲ Annual Job Openings: 14,000
- ▲ Annual Earnings: $25,780
- ▲ Education/Training Required: Short-term on-the-job training
- ▲ Self-Employed: 0.5%
- ▲ Part-Time: 16%

Help brickmasons, blockmasons, stonemasons, or tile and marble setters by performing duties of lesser skill. Duties include using, supplying, or holding materials or tools and cleaning work area and equipment. Assists in the preparation, installation, repair, or rebuilding of tile, brick, or stone surfaces. Applies caulk, sealants, or other agents to installed surface. Removes excess grout and residue from tile or brick joints with wet sponge or trowel. Applies grout between joints of bricks or tiles, using grouting trowel. Removes damaged tile, brick, or mortar and prepares installation surfaces, using pliers, chipping hammers, chisels, drills, and metal wire anchors. Cleans installation surfaces, equipment, tools, work site, and storage areas, using water, chemical solutions, oxygen lance, or polishing machines. Corrects surface imperfections or fills chipped, cracked, or broken bricks or tiles, using fillers, adhesives, and grouting materials. Modifies material moving, mixing, grouting, grinding, polishing, or cleaning procedures according to the type of installation or materials required. Manually or machine-mixes mortar, plaster, and grout according to standard formulae. Cuts materials to specified size for installation, using power saw or tile cutter. Arranges and stores materials, machines, tools and equipment. Erects scaffolding or other installation structures. Moves or positions marble slabs and ingot covers, using crane, hoist, or dolly. Selects materials for installation, following numbered sequence or drawings. Transports materials, tools, and machines to installation site, manually or using conveyance equipment. **SKILLS—Installation.**

**GOE—Interest Area:** 06. Construction, Mining, and Drilling. **Work Group:** 06.04. Hands-on Work in Construction, Extraction, and Maintenance. **Other Job Titles in This Work Group:** Carpenter Assemblers and Repairers; Construction Laborers; Grips and Set-Up Workers, Motion Picture Sets, Studios, and Stages; Helpers, Construction Trades, All Other; Helpers—Carpenters; Helpers—Extraction Workers; Helpers—Painters, Paperhangers, Plasterers, and Stucco Masons; Helpers—Pipelayers, Plumbers, Pipefitters, and Steamfitters; Helpers—Roofers; Highway Maintenance Workers; Septic Tank Servicers and Sewer Pipe Cleaners. **PERSONALITY TYPE—Realistic.** Realistic occupations frequently involve work activities that include practical, hands-on problems and solutions. They often deal with plants, animals, and real-world materials like wood, tools, and machinery. Many of the occupations require working outside and do not involve a lot of paperwork or working closely with others.

**EDUCATION/TRAINING PROGRAM(S)—**Mason and Tile Setter. **RELATED KNOWLEDGE/COURSES—Building and Construction:** Knowledge of materials, methods, and tools involved in the construction or repair of houses, buildings, or other structures such as highways and roads. **Principles of Mechanical Devices:** Knowledge of machines and tools, including their designs, uses, repair, and maintenance. **Design:** Knowledge of design techniques, tools, and principles involved in production of precision technical plans, blueprints, drawings, and models. **Mathematics:** Knowledge of arithmetic, algebra, geometry,

calculus, statistics, and their applications. **English Language:** Knowledge of the structure and content of the English language, including the meaning and spelling of words, rules of composition, and grammar. **Physics:** Knowledge and prediction of physical principles and laws and their interrelationships and applications to understanding fluid, material, and atmospheric dynamics and mechanical, electrical, atomic, and sub-atomic structures and processes.

# Helpers—Electricians

- ▲ Growth: 13.3%
- ▲ Annual Job Openings: 27,000
- ▲ Annual Earnings: $22,740
- ▲ Education/Training Required: Short-term on-the-job training
- ▲ Self-Employed: 0.4%
- ▲ Part-Time: 16%

**Help electricians by performing duties of lesser skill. Duties include using, supplying, or holding materials or tools and cleaning work area and equipment.** Maintains tools and equipment, washes parts, and keeps supplies and parts in order. Threads conduit ends, connects couplings, and fabricates and secures conduit support brackets, using hand tools. Disassembles defective electrical equipment, replaces defective or worn parts, and reassembles equipment, using hand tools. Strings transmission lines or cables through ducts or conduits, underground, through equipment, or to towers. Examines electrical units for loose connections and broken insulation and tightens connections, using hand tools. Traces out short circuits in wiring, using test meter. Rigs scaffolds, hoists, and shoring, erects barricades, and digs trenches. Solders electrical connections, using soldering iron. Bolts component parts together to form tower assemblies, using hand tools. Drills holes for wiring, using power drill, and pulls or pushes wiring through opening. Raises, lowers, or positions equipment, tools, and materials for installation or use, using hoist, handline, or block and tackle. Breaks up concrete to facilitate installation or repair of equipment, using air hammer. Trims trees and clears undergrowth along right-of-way. Measures, cuts, and bends wire and conduit, using measuring instruments and hand tools. Strips

insulation from wire ends, using wire-stripping pliers, and attaches wires to terminals for subsequent soldering. Transports tools, materials, equipment, and supplies to work site, manually or using hand truck or by driving truck. **SKILLS**—Equipment Maintenance.

**GOE—Interest Area:** 05. Mechanics, Installers, and Repairers. **Work Group:** 05.03. Mechanical Work. **Other Job Titles in This Work Group:** Aircraft Body and Bonded Structure Repairers; Aircraft Engine Specialists; Aircraft Mechanics and Service Technicians; Airframe-and-Power-Plant Mechanics; Automotive Body and Related Repairers; Automotive Glass Installers and Repairers; Automotive Master Mechanics; Automotive Service Technicians and Mechanics; Automotive Specialty Technicians; Bicycle Repairers; Bridge and Lock Tenders; Bus and Truck Mechanics and Diesel Engine Specialists; Camera and Photographic Equipment Repairers; Coin, Vending, and Amusement Machine Servicers and Repairers; Control and Valve Installers and Repairers, Except Mechanical Door; Farm Equipment Mechanics; Gas Appliance Repairers; Hand and Portable Power Tool Repairers; Heating and Air Conditioning Mechanics; Heating, Air Conditioning, and Refrigeration Mechanics and Installers; Helpers—Installation, Maintenance, and Repair Workers; Industrial Machinery Mechanics; Keyboard Instrument Repairers and Tuners; Locksmiths and Safe Repairers; Maintenance and Repair Workers, General; Maintenance Workers, Machinery; Mechanical Door Repairers; Medical Appliance Technicians; Medical Equipment Repairers; Meter Mechanics; Millwrights; Mobile Heavy Equipment Mechanics, Except Engines; Motorboat Mechanics; Motorcycle Mechanics; Musical Instrument Repairers and Tuners; Ophthalmic Laboratory Technicians; Optical Instrument Assemblers; Outdoor Power Equipment and Other Small Engine Mechanics; Painters, Transportation Equipment; Percussion Instrument Repairers and Tuners; others. **PERSONALITY TYPE**—Realistic. Realistic occupations frequently involve work activities that include practical, hands-on problems and solutions. They often deal with plants, animals, and real-world materials like wood, tools, and machinery. Many of the occupations require working outside and do not involve a lot of paperwork or working closely with others.

**EDUCATION/TRAINING PROGRAM(S)**—Electrician. **RELATED KNOWLEDGE/COURSES**—**Engineering and Technology:** Knowledge of the practical application of engineering science and technology. This includes applying principles, techniques, procedures, and equipment to the design and production of various goods and services. **Principles of Mechanical Devices:** Knowledge of machines and tools, including their designs, uses, repair, and maintenance. **Computers and Electronics:** Knowledge of circuit boards, processors, chips, electronic equipment, and computer hardware and software, including applications and programming. **Public Safety and Security:** Knowledge of relevant equipment, policies, procedures, and strategies to promote effective local, state, or national security operations for the protection of people, data, property, and institutions. **Building and Construction:** Knowledge of materials, methods, and tools involved in the construction or repair of houses, buildings, or other structures such as highways and roads.

# Helpers—Installation, Maintenance, and Repair Workers

- ▲ Growth: 18.5%
- ▲ Annual Job Openings: 35,000
- ▲ Annual Earnings: $22,620
- ▲ Education/Training Required: Short-term on-the-job training
- ▲ Self-Employed: 0%
- ▲ Part-Time: 16.2%

**Help installation, maintenance, and repair workers in maintenance, parts replacement, and repair of vehicles, industrial machinery, and electrical and electronic equipment. Perform duties, such as furnishing tools, materials, and supplies to other workers; cleaning work area, machines, and tools; and holding materials or tools for other workers.** Helps mechanics and repairers maintain and repair vehicles, industrial machinery, and electrical and electronic equipment. Tends and observes equipment and machinery to verify efficient and safe operation. Builds or erects and maintains physical structures, using hand tools or power tools. Examines and tests machinery, equipment, components, and parts for defects and to ensure proper functioning. Positions vehicles, machinery, equipment, physical structures, and other objects for assembly or installation, using hand tools, power tools, and moving equipment. Applies protective materials to equipment, components, and parts to prevent defects and corrosion. Cleans or lubricates vehicles, machinery, equipment, instruments, tools, work areas, and other objects, using hand tools, power tools, and cleaning equipment. Assembles and disassembles machinery, equipment, components, and other parts, using hand tools and power tools. Installs or replaces machinery, equipment, and new or replacement parts and instruments, using hand tools or power tools. Adjusts and connects or disconnects wiring, piping, tubing, and other parts, using hand tools or power tools. Transfers equipment, tools, parts, and other objects to and from work stations and other areas, using hand tools, power tools, and moving equipment. Furnishes tools, parts, equipment, and supplies to other workers. **SKILLS**—Equipment Maintenance. Repairing. Installation. Operation and Control. Quality Control Analysis.

**GOE—Interest Area:** 05. Mechanics, Installers, and Repairers. **Work Group:** 05.03. Mechanical Work. **Other Job Titles in This Work Group:** Aircraft Body and Bonded Structure Repairers; Aircraft Engine Specialists; Aircraft Mechanics and Service Technicians; Airframe-and-Power-Plant Mechanics; Automotive Body and Related Repairers; Automotive Glass Installers and Repairers; Automotive Master Mechanics; Automotive Service Technicians and Mechanics; Automotive Specialty Technicians; Bicycle Repairers; Bridge and Lock Tenders; Bus and Truck Mechanics and Diesel Engine Specialists; Camera and Photographic Equipment Repairers; Coin, Vending, and Amusement Machine Servicers and Repairers; Control and Valve Installers and Repairers, Except Mechanical Door; Farm Equipment Mechanics; Gas Appliance Repairers; Hand and Portable Power Tool Repairers; Heating and Air Conditioning Mechanics; Heating, Air Conditioning, and Refrigeration Mechanics and Installers; Helpers—Electricians; Industrial Machinery Mechanics; Keyboard Instrument Repairers and Tuners; Locksmiths and Safe Repairers; Maintenance and Repair Workers, General; Maintenance Workers, Machinery; Mechanical Door Repairers; Medical Appliance Technicians; Medical Equipment Repairers; Meter Mechanics; Millwrights; Mobile Heavy Equipment Mechanics, Except Engines; Motorboat Mechanics; Motorcycle Mechanics; Musical Instrument Repairers and Tuners; Ophthalmic Laboratory Technicians; Optical Instrument Assemblers;

Outdoor Power Equipment and Other Small Engine Mechanics; Painters, Transportation Equipment; Percussion Instrument Repairers and Tuners; Precision Instrument and Equipment Repairers, All Other; others. **PERSONALITY TYPE**—Realistic. Realistic occupations frequently involve work activities that include practical, hands-on problems and solutions. They often deal with plants, animals, and real-world materials like wood, tools, and machinery. Many of the occupations require working outside and do not involve a lot of paperwork or working closely with others.

**EDUCATION/TRAINING PROGRAM(S)**—Industrial Machinery Maintenance and Repairer. **RELATED KNOWLEDGE/COURSES—Principles of Mechanical Devices:** Knowledge of machines and tools, including their designs, uses, repair, and maintenance. **Engineering and Technology:** Knowledge of the practical application of engineering science and technology. This includes applying principles, techniques, procedures, and equipment to the design and production of various goods and services. **Building and Construction:** Knowledge of materials, methods, and tools involved in the construction or repair of houses, buildings, or other structures such as highways and roads. **Computers and Electronics:** Knowledge of circuit boards, processors, chips, electronic equipment, and computer hardware and software, including applications and programming. **English Language:** Knowledge of the structure and content of the English language, including the meaning and spelling of words, rules of composition, and grammar. **Production and Processing:** Knowledge of raw materials, production processes, quality control, costs, and other techniques for maximizing the effective manufacture and distribution of goods.

# Highway Patrol Pilots

▲ Growth: 23.2%
▲ Annual Job Openings: 21,000
▲ Annual Earnings: $40,590
▲ Education/Training Required: Long-term on-the-job training
▲ Self-Employed: 0%
▲ Part-Time: 1.5%

**Pilot aircraft to patrol highway and enforce traffic laws.** Pilots airplane to maintain order, respond to emergencies, enforce traffic and criminal laws, and apprehend criminals. Investigates traffic accidents and other accidents to determine causes and to determine if crime were committed. Arrests perpetrator of criminal act or submits citation or warning to violator of motor vehicle ordinance. Informs ground personnel where to re-route traffic in case of emergencies. Informs ground personnel of traffic congestion or unsafe driving conditions to ensure traffic flow and reduce incidence of accidents. Reviews facts to determine if criminal act or statute violation involved. Expedites processing of prisoners, prepares and maintains records of prisoner bookings, and maintains record of prisoner status during booking and pre-trial process. Prepares reports to document activities. Relays complaint and emergency request information to appropriate agency dispatcher. Evaluates complaint and emergency request information to determine response requirements. Renders aid to accident victims and other persons requiring first aid for physical injuries. Testifies in court to present evidence or act as witness in traffic and criminal cases. Records facts, photographs and diagrams crime or accident scene, and interviews witnesses to gather information for possible use in legal action or safety programs. **SKILLS—** Operation and Control. Social Perceptiveness. Active Listening. Reading Comprehension. Judgment and Decision Making. Critical Thinking.

**GOE—Interest Area:** 04. Law, Law Enforcement, and Public Safety. **Work Group:** 04.03. Law Enforcement. **Other Job Titles in This Work Group:** Animal Control Workers; Bailiffs; Child Support, Missing Persons, and Unemployment Insurance Fraud Investigators; Correctional Officers and Jailers; Criminal Investigators and Special Agents; Crossing Guards; Detectives and Criminal Investigators; Fire Investigators; Fish and Game Wardens; Forensic Science Technicians; Gaming Surveillance Officers and Gaming Investigators; Immigration and Customs Inspectors; Lifeguards, Ski Patrol, and Other Recreational Protective Service Workers; Parking Enforcement Workers; Police and Sheriff's Patrol Officers; Police Detectives; Police Identification and Records Officers; Police Patrol Officers; Private Detectives and Investigators; Security Guards; Sheriffs and Deputy Sheriffs; Transit and Railroad Police. **PERSONALITY TYPE**—Realistic. Realistic occupations frequently involve work activities that include practical, hands-on problems and solutions. They often deal with plants, animals, and real-world materials like wood, tools, and machinery. Many of the occupations require working outside and do not involve a lot of paperwork or working closely with others.

**EDUCATION/TRAINING PROGRAM(S)**—Law Enforcement/Police Science. **RELATED KNOWLEDGE/COURSES—Transportation:** Knowledge of principles and methods for moving people or goods by air, rail, sea, or road, including the relative costs and benefits. **Public Safety and Security:** Knowledge of relevant equipment, policies, procedures, and strategies to promote effective local, state, or national security operations for the protection of people, data, property, and institutions. **Law and Government:** Knowledge of laws, legal codes, court procedures, precedents, government regulations, executive orders, agency rules, and the democratic political process. **Telecommunications:** Knowledge of transmission, broadcasting, switching, control, and operation of telecommunications systems. **Geography:** Knowledge of principles and methods for describing the features of land, sea, and air masses, including their physical characteristics, locations, interrelationships, and distribution of plant, animal, and human life.

# Home Health Aides

- ▲ Growth: 47.3%
- ▲ Annual Job Openings: 120,000
- ▲ Annual Earnings: $18,110
- ▲ Education/Training Required: Short-term on-the-job training
- ▲ Self-Employed: 3.5%
- ▲ Part-Time: 26.4%

**Provide routine personal health care, such as bathing, dressing, or grooming, to elderly, convalescent, or disabled persons in the home of patients or in a residential care facility.** Changes bed linens, washes and irons patient's laundry, and cleans patient's quarters. Assists patients into and out of bed, automobiles, or wheelchair, to lavatory, and up and down stairs. Administers prescribed oral medication under written direction of physician or as directed by home care nurse and aide. Massages patient and applies preparations and treatment, such as liniment or alcohol rubs and heat-lamp stimulation. Performs variety of miscellaneous duties as requested, such as obtaining household supplies and running errands. Entertains patient, reads aloud, and plays cards and other games with patient. Maintains records of services performed and of apparent condition of patient. Purchases, prepares, and serves food for patient and other members of family, following special prescribed diets. **SKILLS**—Service Orientation. Reading Comprehension. Social Perceptiveness. Critical Thinking. Monitoring. Speaking. Active Listening.

**GOE—Interest Area:** 14. Medical and Health Services. **Work Group:** 14.07. Patient Care and Assistance. **Other Job Titles in This Work Group:** Licensed Practical and Licensed Vocational Nurses; Nursing Aides, Orderlies, and Attendants; Psychiatric Aides; Psychiatric Technicians. **PERSONALITY TYPE**—Social. Social occupations frequently involve working with, communicating with, and teaching people. These occupations often involve helping or providing service to others.

**EDUCATION/TRAINING PROGRAM(S)**—Home Health Aide. **RELATED KNOWLEDGE/ COURSES—Customer and Personal Service:** Knowledge of principles and processes for providing customer and personal services. This includes customer needs assessment, meeting quality standards for services, and evaluation of customer satisfaction. **Medicine and Dentistry:** Knowledge of the information and techniques needed to diagnose and treat human injuries, diseases, and deformities. This includes symptoms, treatment alternatives, drug properties and interactions, and preventive health-care measures. **Psychology:** Knowledge of human behavior and performance; individual differences in ability, personality, and interests; learning and motivation; psychological research methods; and the assessment and treatment of behavioral and affective disorders. **Therapy and Counseling:** Knowledge of principles, methods, and procedures for diagnosis, treatment, and rehabilitation of physical and mental dysfunctions and for career counseling and guidance. **Clerical Studies:** Knowledge of administrative and clerical procedures and systems such as word processing, managing files and records, stenography and transcription, designing forms, and other office procedures and terminology.

# Hotel, Motel, and Resort Desk Clerks

▲ Growth: 33.4%

▲ Annual Job Openings: 73,000

▲ Annual Earnings: $17,100

▲ Education/Training Required: Short-term on-the-job training

▲ Self-Employed: 0%

▲ Part-Time: 25.8%

**Accommodate hotel, motel, and resort patrons by registering and assigning rooms to guests, issuing room keys, transmitting and receiving messages, keeping records of occupied rooms and guests' accounts, making and confirming reservations, and presenting statements to and collecting payments from departing guests.** Greets, registers, and assigns rooms to guests of hotel or motel. Makes and confirms reservations. Transmits and receives messages, using telephone or telephone switchboard. Date-stamps, sorts, and racks incoming mail and messages. Deposits guests' valuables in hotel safe or safe-deposit box. Answers inquiries pertaining to hotel services; registration of guests; and shopping, dining, entertainment, and travel directions. Issues room key and escort instructions to bellhop. Posts charges, such as room, food, liquor, or telephone, to ledger, manually or using computer. Computes bill, collects payment, and makes change for guests. Keeps records of room availability and guests' accounts, manually or using computer. **SKILLS**—Service Orientation. Active Listening. Reading Comprehension. Coordination. Speaking.

**GOE—Interest Area:** 11. Recreation, Travel, and Other Personal Services. **Work Group:** 11.03. Transportation and Lodging Services. **Other Job Titles in This Work Group:** Baggage Porters and Bellhops; Concierges; Flight Attendants; Reservation and Transportation Ticket Agents; Reservation and Transportation Ticket Agents and Travel Clerks; Transportation Attendants, Except Flight Attendants and Baggage Porters. **PERSONALITY TYPE**—Conventional. Conventional occupations frequently involve following set procedures and routines. These occupations can include working with data and details more than with ideas. Usually there is a clear line of authority to follow.

**EDUCATION/TRAINING PROGRAM(S)**—Hotel/Motel Services Marketing Operations. **RELATED KNOWLEDGE/COURSES—Customer and Personal Service:** Knowledge of principles and processes for providing customer and personal services. This includes customer needs assessment, meeting quality standards for services, and evaluation of customer satisfaction. **Clerical Studies:** Knowledge of administrative and clerical procedures and systems such as word processing, managing files and records, stenography and transcription, designing forms, and other office procedures and terminology. **English Language:** Knowledge of the structure and content of the English language, including the meaning and spelling of words, rules of composition, and grammar. **Mathematics:** Knowledge of arithmetic, algebra, geometry, calculus, statistics, and their applications. **Computers and Electronics:** Knowledge of circuit boards, processors, chips, electronic equipment, and computer hardware and software, including applications and programming.

# Housekeeping Supervisors

- ▲ Growth: 14.2%
- ▲ Annual Job Openings: 18,000
- ▲ Annual Earnings: $27,830
- ▲ Education/Training Required: Work experience in a related occupation
- ▲ Self-Employed: 0.8%
- ▲ Part-Time: 6.4%

Supervise work activities of cleaning personnel to ensure clean, orderly, and attractive rooms in hotels, hospitals, educational institutions, and similar establishments. Assign duties, inspect work, and investigate complaints regarding housekeeping service and equipment and take corrective action. May purchase housekeeping supplies and equipment, take periodic inventories, screen applicants, train new employees, and recommend dismissals. Assigns workers their duties and inspects work for conformance to prescribed standards of cleanliness. Investigates complaints regarding housekeeping service and equipment and takes corrective action. Obtains list of rooms to be cleaned immediately and list of prospective check-outs or discharges to prepare work assignments. Coordinates work activities among departments. Conducts orientation training and in-service training to explain policies and work procedures and to demonstrate use and maintenance of equipment. Inventories stock to ensure adequate supplies. Evaluates records to forecast department personnel requirements. Makes recommendations to improve service and ensure more efficient operation. Prepares reports concerning room occupancy, payroll, and department expenses. Selects and purchases new furnishings. Performs cleaning duties in cases of emergency or staff shortage. Examines building to determine need for repairs or replacement of furniture or equipment and makes recommendations to management. Attends staff meetings to discuss company policies and patrons' complaints. Issues supplies and equipment to workers. Establishes standards and procedures for work of housekeeping staff. Advises manager, desk clerk, or admitting personnel of rooms ready for occupancy. Records data regarding work assignments, personnel actions, and time cards and prepares periodic reports.

Screens job applicants, hires new employees, and recommends promotions, transfers, and dismissals. **SKILLS**—Time Management. Speaking. Management of Personnel Resources. Coordination. Reading Comprehension.

**GOE—Interest Area:** 11. Recreation, Travel, and Other Personal Services. **Work Group:** 11.01. Managerial Work in Recreation, Travel, and Other Personal Services. **Other Job Titles in This Work Group:** Aircraft Cargo Handling Supervisors; First-Line Supervisors/Managers of Food Preparation and Serving Workers; First-Line Supervisors/Managers of Housekeeping and Janitorial Workers; First-Line Supervisors/Managers of Personal Service Workers; Food Service Managers; Gaming Managers; Gaming Supervisors; Janitorial Supervisors; Lodging Managers; Meeting and Convention Planners. **PERSONALITY TYPE**—Enterprising. Enterprising occupations frequently involve starting up and carrying out projects. These occupations can involve leading people and making many decisions. They sometimes require risk taking and often deal with business.

**EDUCATION/TRAINING PROGRAM(S)**—Executive Housekeeper. **RELATED KNOWLEDGE/COURSES—Customer and Personal Service:** Knowledge of principles and processes for providing customer and personal services. This includes customer needs assessment, meeting quality standards for services, and evaluation of customer satisfaction. **Personnel and Human Resources:** Knowledge of principles and procedures for personnel recruitment, selection, training, compensation and benefits, labor relations and negotiation, and personnel information systems. **Administration and Management:** Knowledge of business and management principles involved in strategic planning, resource allocation, human resources modeling, leadership technique, production methods, and coordination of people and resources. **Education and Training:** Knowledge of principles and methods for curriculum and training design, teaching and instruction for indi-

viduals and groups, and the measurement of training effects. **English Language:** Knowledge of the structure and content of the English language, including the meaning and spelling of words, rules of composition, and grammar.

# Human Resources Assistants, Except Payroll and Timekeeping

▲ Growth: 19.3%
▲ Annual Job Openings: 25,000
▲ Annual Earnings: $29,400
▲ Education/Training Required: Short-term on-the-job training
▲ Self-Employed: 0%
▲ Part-Time: 6.3%

**Compile and keep personnel records. Record data for each employee, such as address, weekly earnings, absences, amount of sales or production, supervisory reports on ability, and date of and reason for termination. Compile and type reports from employment records. File employment records. Search employee files and furnish information to authorized persons.** Examines employee files to answer inquiries and provide information for personnel actions. Prepares listing of vacancies and notifies eligible workers of position availability. Requests information from law enforcement officials, previous employers, and other references to determine applicant's employment acceptability. Selects applicants having specified job requirements and refers to employing official. Explains company insurance policies and options to employees and files claim and cancellation forms. Communicates with employees or applicants to explain company personnel policies and procedures. Administers and scores employee aptitude, skills, personality, and interests tests. Answers questions regarding examinations, eligibility, salaries, benefits, and other pertinent information. Records employee data, such as address, rate of pay, absences, and benefits, using personal computer. Maintains and updates employee records to document personnel actions and changes in employee status. Processes and reviews employment application to evaluate qualifications or eligibility of applicant. Interviews applicants to obtain and verify information. Compiles and types reports from employment records. **SKILLS**—Reading Comprehension. Speaking. Active

Listening. Equipment Selection. Writing.

**GOE—Interest Area:** 09. Business Detail. **Work Group:** 09.07. Records Processing. **Other Job Titles in This Work Group:** Correspondence Clerks; Court Reporters; Credit Authorizers; Credit Authorizers, Checkers, and Clerks; Credit Checkers; File Clerks; Information and Record Clerks, All Other; Insurance Claims and Policy Processing Clerks; Insurance Claims Clerks; Insurance Policy Processing Clerks; Medical Records and Health Information Technicians; Medical Transcriptionists; Office Clerks, General; Procurement Clerks; Proofreaders and Copy Markers. **PERSONALITY TYPE**—Conventional. Conventional occupations frequently involve following set procedures and routines. These occupations can include working with data and details more than with ideas. Usually there is a clear line of authority to follow.

**EDUCATION/TRAINING PROGRAM(S)**—General Office/Clerical and Typing Services. **RELATED KNOWLEDGE/COURSES—Clerical Studies:** Knowledge of administrative and clerical procedures and systems such as word processing, managing files and records, stenography and transcription, designing forms, and other office procedures and terminology. **Personnel and Human Resources:** Knowledge of principles and procedures for personnel recruitment, selection, training, compensation and benefits, labor relations and negotiation, and personnel information systems. **English Language:** Knowledge of the structure and content of the English language, including the meaning and spelling of words, rules of composition, and grammar. **Mathematics:** Knowledge of arithmetic, algebra, geometry, calculus, statistics, and their applications.

**Computers and Electronics:** Knowledge of circuit boards, processors, chips, electronic equipment, and computer hardware and software, including applications and programming.

# Immigration and Customs Inspectors

- ▲ Growth: 16.4%
- ▲ Annual Job Openings: 4,000
- ▲ Annual Earnings: $49,830
- ▲ Education/Training Required: Work experience in a related occupation
- ▲ Self-Employed: 0%
- ▲ Part-Time: 2.9%

**Investigate and inspect persons, common carriers, goods, and merchandise arriving in or departing from the United States or between states to detect violations of immigration and customs laws and regulations.** Inspects cargo, baggage, personal articles, and common carriers entering or leaving U.S. for compliance with revenue laws and U.S. Customs Service regulations. Testifies in administrative and judicial proceedings. Collects samples of merchandise for examination, appraising, or testing and requests laboratory analyses. Institutes civil and criminal prosecutions and assists other governmental agencies with regulation violation issues. Issues or denies permits. Interprets and explains laws and regulations to others. Determines duty and taxes to be paid, investigates applications for duty refunds, or petitions for remission or mitigation of penalties. Examines, classifies, weighs, measures, and appraises merchandise to enforce regulations of U.S. Customs Service and prevent illegal importing and exporting. Determines investigative and seizure techniques to be used and seizes contraband, undeclared merchandise, vehicles, and air or sea craft carrying smuggled merchandise. Arrests, detains, paroles, or arranges for deportation of persons in violation of customs or immigration laws. Reviews private and public records and documents to establish, assemble, and verify facts and secure legal evidence. Keeps records and writes reports of activities, findings, transactions, violations, discrepancies, and decisions. Examines visas and passports and interviews persons to determine eligibility for admission, residence, and travel in U.S. **SKILLS**—Writing.

Speaking. Reading Comprehension. Judgment and Decision Making. Active Listening.

**GOE—Interest Area:** 04. Law, Law Enforcement, and Public Safety. **Work Group:** 04.03. Law Enforcement. **Other Job Titles in This Work Group:** Animal Control Workers; Bailiffs; Child Support, Missing Persons, and Unemployment Insurance Fraud Investigators; Correctional Officers and Jailers; Criminal Investigators and Special Agents; Crossing Guards; Detectives and Criminal Investigators; Fire Investigators; Fish and Game Wardens; Forensic Science Technicians; Gaming Surveillance Officers and Gaming Investigators; Highway Patrol Pilots; Lifeguards, Ski Patrol, and Other Recreational Protective Service Workers; Parking Enforcement Workers; Police and Sheriff's Patrol Officers; Police Detectives; Police Identification and Records Officers; Police Patrol Officers; Private Detectives and Investigators; Security Guards; Sheriffs and Deputy Sheriffs; Transit and Railroad Police. **PERSONALITY TYPE**—Conventional. Conventional occupations frequently involve following set procedures and routines. These occupations can include working with data and details more than with ideas. Usually there is a clear line of authority to follow.

**EDUCATION/TRAINING PROGRAM(S)**—Law Enforcement/Police Science. **RELATED KNOWLEDGE/COURSES—Law and Government:** Knowledge of laws, legal codes, court procedures, precedents, government regulations, executive orders, agency rules, and the democratic political process. **English Language:**

Knowledge of the structure and content of the English language, including the meaning and spelling of words, rules of composition, and grammar. **Public Safety and Security:** Knowledge of relevant equipment, policies, procedures, and strategies to promote effective local, state, or national security operations for the protection of people, data, property, and institutions. **Communi-** **cations and Media:** Knowledge of media production, communication, and dissemination techniques and methods. This includes alternative ways to inform and entertain via written, oral, and visual media. **Mathematics:** Knowledge of arithmetic, algebra, geometry, calculus, statistics, and their applications.

# Industrial Truck and Tractor Operators

- ▲ Growth: 11.3%
- ▲ Annual Job Openings: 91,000
- ▲ Annual Earnings: $26,090
- ▲ Education/Training Required: Short-term on-the-job training
- ▲ Self-Employed: 0.3%
- ▲ Part-Time: 3%

**Operate industrial trucks or tractors equipped to move materials around a warehouse, storage yard, factory, construction site, or similar location.** Moves controls to drive gasoline- or electric-powered trucks, cars, or tractors and transport materials between loading, processing, and storage areas. Moves levers and controls to operate lifting devices, such as forklifts, lift beams and swivel-hooks, hoists, and elevating platforms, to load, unload, transport, and stack material. Positions lifting device under, over, or around loaded pallets, skids, and boxes and secures material or products for transport to designated areas. Hooks tow trucks to trailer hitches and fastens attachments, such as graders, plows, rollers, and winch cables, to tractor, using hitchpins. Turns valves and opens chutes to dump, spray, or release materials from dump cars or storage bins into hoppers. Performs routine maintenance on vehicles and auxiliary equipment, such as cleaning, lubricating, recharging batteries, fueling, or replacing liquefied-gas tank. Manually loads or unloads materials onto or off pallets, skids, platforms, cars, or lifting devices. Operates or tends automatic stacking, loading, packaging, or cutting machines. Weighs materials or products and records weight and other production data on tags or labels. Signals workers to discharge, dump, or level materials. **SKILLS**—Operation and Control. Equipment Selection. Operation Monitoring. Troubleshooting. Coordination. Repairing.

GOE—**Interest Area:** 08. Industrial Production. **Work Group:** 08.07. Hands-on Work: Loading, Moving, Hoisting, and Conveying. **Other Job Titles in This Work Group:** Conveyor Operators and Tenders; Crane and Tower Operators; Dragline Operators; Excavating and Loading Machine and Dragline Operators; Freight, Stock, and Material Movers, Hand; Hoist and Winch Operators; Irradiated-Fuel Handlers; Laborers and Freight, Stock, and Material Movers, Hand; Machine Feeders and Offbearers; Material Moving Workers, All Other; Packers and Packagers, Hand; Pump Operators, Except Wellhead Pumpers; Refuse and Recyclable Material Collectors; Tank Car, Truck, and Ship Loaders. **PERSONALITY TYPE**—Realistic. Realistic occupations frequently involve work activities that include practical, hands-on problems and solutions. They often deal with plants, animals, and real-world materials like wood, tools, and machinery. Many of the occupations require working outside and do not involve a lot of paperwork or working closely with others.

**EDUCATION/TRAINING PROGRAM(S)**—No data available. **RELATED KNOWLEDGE/ COURSES**—**Transportation:** Knowledge of principles and methods for moving people or goods by air, rail, sea, or road, including the relative costs and benefits. **Principles of Mechanical Devices:** Knowledge of machines and tools, including their designs, uses, repair, and maintenance. **Mathematics:** Knowledge of arithmetic, algebra, geometry, calculus, statistics, and their applications. **Production and Processing:** Knowledge of raw materials, production processes, quality control, costs, and other techniques for maximizing the effective manufacture and distribution of goods. **Physics:** Knowledge and prediction of physical principles and laws and their interrelationships and applications to understanding fluid, material, and atmospheric dynamics and mechanical, electrical, atomic, and sub-atomic structures and processes. **Clerical Studies:** Knowledge of administrative and clerical procedures and systems such as word processing, managing files and records, stenography and transcription, designing forms, and other office procedures and terminology.

# Insurance Adjusters, Examiners, and Investigators

- ▲ Growth: 15.1%
- ▲ Annual Job Openings: 25,000
- ▲ Annual Earnings: $44,000
- ▲ Education/Training Required: Long-term on-the-job training
- ▲ Self-Employed: 2.3%
- ▲ Part-Time: 7.3%

**Investigate, analyze, and determine the extent of insurance company's liability concerning personal, casualty, or property loss or damages and attempt to effect settlement with claimants. Correspond with or interview medical specialists, agents, witnesses, or claimants to compile information. Calculate benefit payments and approve payment of claims within a certain monetary limit.** Investigates and assesses damage to property. Interviews or corresponds with claimant and witnesses, consults police and hospital records, and inspects property damage to determine extent of liability. Interviews or corresponds with agents and claimants to correct errors or omissions and to investigate questionable entries. Analyzes information gathered by investigation and reports findings and recommendations. Collects evidence to support contested claims in court. Communicates with former associates to verify employment record and to obtain background information regarding persons or businesses applying for credit. Obtains credit information from banks and other credit services. Refers questionable claims to investigator or claims adjuster for investigation or settlement. Prepares report of findings of investigation. Examines claims form and other records to determine insurance coverage. Examines titles to property to determine validity and acts as company agent in transactions with property owners. Negotiates claim settlements and recommends litigation when settlement cannot be negotiated. **SKILLS**—Active Listening. Writing. Reading Comprehension. Critical Thinking. Speaking.

**GOE—Interest Area:** 13. General Management and Support. **Work Group:** 13.02. Management Support. **Other Job Titles in This Work Group:** Accountants; Accountants and Auditors; Appraisers and Assessors of Real Estate; Appraisers, Real Estate; Assessors; Auditors; Budget Analysts; Claims Adjusters, Examiners, and Investigators; Claims Examiners, Property and Casualty Insurance; Compensation, Benefits, and Job Analysis Specialists; Cost Estimators; Credit Analysts; Employment Interviewers, Private or Public Employment Service; Employment, Recruitment, and Placement Specialists; Financial Analysts; Human Resources, Training, and Labor Relations Specialists, All Other; Insurance Appraisers, Auto Damage; Insurance Underwriters; Loan Counselors; Loan Officers; Logisticians; Management Analysts; Market Research Analysts; Personnel Recruiters; Purchasing Agents and Buyers, Farm Products; Purchasing Agents, Except Wholesale, Retail, and Farm Products; Tax Examiners, Collectors, and Revenue Agents; Training and Development Specialists; Wholesale and Retail Buyers, Except Farm Products. **PERSONALITY TYPE**—Enterprising.

Enterprising occupations frequently involve starting up and carrying out projects. These occupations can involve leading people and making many decisions. They sometimes require risk taking and often deal with business.

**EDUCATION/TRAINING PROGRAM(S)**—Human Resources Management; Insurance and Risk Management; Insurance Marketing Operations; Labor/Personnel Relations and Studies; Purchasing, Procurement and Contracts Management. **RELATED KNOWLEDGE/COURSES**—**Mathematics:** Knowledge of arithmetic, algebra, geometry, calculus, statistics, and their applications. **Law and Government:** Knowledge of laws, legal codes, court procedures, precedents, government regulations, executive orders, agency rules, and the democratic political process. **Economics and Accounting:** Knowledge of economic and accounting principles and practices, the financial markets, banking, and the analysis and reporting of financial data. **Public Safety and Security:** Knowledge of relevant equipment, policies, procedures, and strategies to promote effective local, state, or national security operations for the protection of people, data, property, and institutions. **English Language:** Knowledge of the structure and content of the English language, including the meaning and spelling of words, rules of composition, and grammar.

# Interpreters and Translators

▲ Growth: 23.8%
▲ Annual Job Openings: 3,000
▲ Annual Earnings: $33,550
▲ Education/Training Required: Long-term on-the-job training
▲ Self-Employed: 21.5%
▲ Part-Time: 20.6%

**Translate or interpret written, oral, or sign language text into another language for others.** Translates approximate or exact message of speaker into specified language orally or by using hand signs for hearing impaired. Listens to statements of speaker to ascertain meaning and to remember what is said, using electronic audio system. Translates responses from second language to first. Reads written material, such as legal documents, scientific works, or news reports, and rewrites material into specified language, according to established rules of grammar. Receives information on subject to be discussed prior to interpreting session. **SKILLS**—Active Listening. Writing. Reading Comprehension. Speaking. Service Orientation.

**GOE—Interest Area:** 01. Arts, Entertainment, and Media. **Work Group:** 01.03. News, Broadcasting and Public Relations. **Other Job Titles in This Work Group:** Broadcast News Analysts; Caption Writers; Public Relations Specialists; Reporters and Correspondents. **PERSONALITY TYPE**—Artistic. Artistic occupations frequently involve working with forms, designs, and patterns. They often require self-expression, and the work can be done without following a clear set of rules.

**EDUCATION/TRAINING PROGRAM(S)**—Education of the Deaf and Hearing Impaired; Foreign Language Interpretation and Translation; Sign Language Interpreter. **RELATED KNOWLEDGE/COURSES**—**Foreign Language:** Knowledge of the structure and content of a foreign (non-English) language, including the meaning and spelling of words, rules of composition and grammar, and pronunciation. **English Language:** Knowledge of the structure and content of the English language, including the meaning and spelling of words, rules of composition, and grammar. **Communications and Media:** Knowledge of media production, communication, and dissemination techniques and methods. This includes alternative ways to inform and entertain via written, oral, and visual media. **Sociology and Anthropology:** Knowledge of group behavior and dynamics, societal trends and influences, human migrations, ethnicity, cultures, and their history and origins. **Customer and Personal Service:** Knowledge of principles and processes for providing customer and personal services. This includes customer needs assessment, meeting quality standards for services, and evaluation of customer satisfaction.

# Interviewers, Except Eligibility and Loan

- ▲ Growth: 33.4%
- ▲ Annual Job Openings: 53,000
- ▲ Annual Earnings: $22,360
- ▲ Education/Training Required: Short-term on-the-job training
- ▲ Self-Employed: 0%
- ▲ Part-Time: 32.5%

**Interview persons by telephone, mail, in person, or by other means for the purpose of completing forms, applications, or questionnaires. Ask specific questions, record answers, and assist persons with completing form. May sort, classify, and file forms.** Contacts persons at home, place of business, or field location by telephone, by mail, or in person. Explains reason for questioning and other specified information. Compiles and sorts data from interview and reviews to correct errors. Asks questions to obtain various specified information, such as person's name, address, age, religion, and state of residency. Assists person in filling out application or questionnaire. Records results and data from interview or survey, using computer or specified form. **SKILLS**—Speaking. Active Listening. Reading Comprehension. Social Perceptiveness.

**GOE—Interest Area:** 09. Business Detail. **Work Group:** 09.02. Administrative Detail. **Other Job Titles in This Work Group:** Claims Takers, Unemployment Benefits; Court Clerks; Court, Municipal, and License Clerks; Eligibility Interviewers, Government Programs; Executive Secretaries and Administrative Assistants; Legal Secretaries; License Clerks; Loan Interviewers and Clerks; Medical Secretaries; Municipal Clerks; Secretaries, Except Legal, Medical, and Executive; Welfare Eligibility Workers and Interviewers. **PERSONALITY TYPE**—Conventional. Conventional occupations fre-

quently involve following set procedures and routines. These occupations can include working with data and details more than with ideas. Usually there is a clear line of authority to follow.

**EDUCATION/TRAINING PROGRAM(S)**—Human Resources Management; Receptionist. **RELATED KNOWLEDGE/COURSES—Clerical Studies:** Knowledge of administrative and clerical procedures and systems such as word processing, managing files and records, stenography and transcription, designing forms, and other office procedures and terminology. **Computers and Electronics:** Knowledge of circuit boards, processors, chips, electronic equipment, and computer hardware and software, including applications and programming. **English Language:** Knowledge of the structure and content of the English language, including the meaning and spelling of words, rules of composition, and grammar. **Telecommunications:** Knowledge of transmission, broadcasting, switching, control, and operation of telecommunications systems. **Mathematics:** Knowledge of arithmetic, algebra, geometry, calculus, statistics, and their applications. **Personnel and Human Resources:** Knowledge of principles and procedures for personnel recruitment, selection, training, compensation and benefits, labor relations and negotiation, and personnel information systems.

# Irradiated-Fuel Handlers

▲ Growth: 32.8%

▲ Annual Job Openings: 9,000

▲ Annual Earnings: $31,630

▲ Education/Training Required: Moderate-term on-the-job training

▲ Self-Employed: 0%

▲ Part-Time: 5.2%

**Package, store, and convey irradiated fuels and wastes, using hoists, mechanical arms, shovels, and industrial truck.** Operates machines and equipment to package, store, or transport loads of waste materials. Follows prescribed safety procedures and complies with federal laws regulating waste disposal methods. Cleans contaminated equipment for reuse, using detergents and solvents, sandblasters, filter pumps, and steam cleaners. Records number of containers stored at disposal site and specifies amount and type of equipment and waste disposed. Mixes and pours concrete into forms to encase waste material for disposal. Drives truck to convey contaminated waste to designated sea or ground location. Loads and unloads materials into containers and onto trucks, using hoists or forklift. **SKILLS**—Reading Comprehension. Operation and Control.

**GOE**—**Interest Area:** 08. Industrial Production. **Work Group:** 08.07. Hands-on Work: Loading, Moving, Hoisting, and Conveying. **Other Job Titles in This Work Group:** Conveyor Operators and Tenders; Crane and Tower Operators; Dragline Operators; Excavating and Loading Machine and Dragline Operators; Freight, Stock, and Material Movers, Hand; Hoist and Winch Operators; Industrial Truck and Tractor Operators; Laborers and Freight, Stock, and Material Movers, Hand; Machine Feeders and Offbearers; Material Moving Workers, All Other; Packers and Packagers, Hand; Pump Operators, Except Wellhead Pumpers; Refuse and Recyclable Material Collectors; Tank Car, Truck, and Ship Loaders. **PERSONALITY TYPE**—Realistic. Realistic occupations frequently involve work activities that include practical, hands-on problems and solutions. They often deal with plants, animals, and real-world materials like wood, tools, and machinery. Many of the occupations require working outside and do not involve a lot of paperwork or working closely with others.

**EDUCATION/TRAINING PROGRAM(S)**—Construction Trades, Other. **RELATED KNOWLEDGE/COURSES**—**Production and Processing:** Knowledge of raw materials, production processes, quality control, costs, and other techniques for maximizing the effective manufacture and distribution of goods. **Transportation:** Knowledge of principles and methods for moving people or goods by air, rail, sea, or road, including the relative costs and benefits. **Chemistry:** Knowledge of the chemical composition, structure, and properties of substances and of the chemical processes and transformations that they undergo. This includes uses of chemicals and their interactions, danger signs, production techniques, and disposal methods. **Public Safety and Security:** Knowledge of relevant equipment, policies, procedures, and strategies to promote effective local, state, or national security operations for the protection of people, data, property, and institutions. **Law and Government:** Knowledge of laws, legal codes, court procedures, precedents, government regulations, executive orders, agency rules, and the democratic political process.

# Janitorial Supervisors

- ▲ Growth: 14.2%
- ▲ Annual Job Openings: 18,000
- ▲ Annual Earnings: $27,830
- ▲ Education/Training Required: Work experience in a related occupation
- ▲ Self-Employed: 0.8%
- ▲ Part-Time: 6.4%

**Supervise work activities of janitorial personnel in commercial and industrial establishments. Assign duties, inspect work, and investigate complaints regarding janitorial services and take corrective action. May purchase janitorial supplies and equipment, take periodic inventories, screen applicants, train new employees, and recommend dismissals.** Supervises and coordinates activities of workers engaged in janitorial services. Assigns janitorial work to employees, following material and work requirements. Inspects work performed to ensure conformance to specifications and established standards. Records personnel data on specified forms. Recommends personnel actions, such as hires and discharges, to ensure proper staffing. Confers with staff to resolve production and personnel problems. Trains workers in janitorial methods and procedures and proper operation of equipment. Issues janitorial supplies and equipment to workers to ensure quality and timely delivery of services. **SKILLS**—Coordination. Time Management. Management of Personnel Resources. Speaking. Social Perceptiveness. Writing.

**GOE—Interest Area:** 11. Recreation, Travel, and Other Personal Services. **Work Group:** 11.01. Managerial Work in Recreation, Travel, and Other Personal Services. **Other Job Titles in This Work Group:** Aircraft Cargo Handling Supervisors; First-Line Supervisors/Managers of Food Preparation and Serving Workers; First-Line Supervisors/Managers of Housekeeping and Janitorial Workers; First-Line Supervisors/Managers of Personal Service Workers; Food Service Managers; Gaming Managers; Gaming Supervisors; Housekeeping Supervisors; Lodging Managers; Meeting and Convention Planners. **PERSONALITY TYPE**—Enterprising. Enterprising occupations frequently involve starting up and

carrying out projects. These occupations can involve leading people and making many decisions. They sometimes require risk taking and often deal with business.

**EDUCATION/TRAINING PROGRAM(S)**—Executive Housekeeper. **RELATED KNOWLEDGE/COURSES**—**Administration and Management:** Knowledge of business and management principles involved in strategic planning, resource allocation, human resources modeling, leadership technique, production methods, and coordination of people and resources. **Personnel and Human Resources:** Knowledge of principles and procedures for personnel recruitment, selection, training, compensation and benefits, labor relations and negotiation, and personnel information systems. **Education and Training:** Knowledge of principles and methods for curriculum and training design, teaching and instruction for individuals and groups, and the measurement of training effects. **Customer and Personal Service:** Knowledge of principles and processes for providing customer and personal services. This includes customer needs assessment, meeting quality standards for services, and evaluation of customer satisfaction. **Chemistry:** Knowledge of the chemical composition, structure, and properties of substances and of the chemical processes and transformations that they undergo. This includes uses of chemicals and their interactions, danger signs, production techniques, and disposal methods. **English Language:** Knowledge of the structure and content of the English language, including the meaning and spelling of words, rules of composition, and grammar. **Principles of Mechanical Devices:** Knowledge of machines and tools, including their designs, uses, repair, and maintenance.

# Janitors and Cleaners, Except Maids and Housekeeping Cleaners

▲ Growth: 13.5%

▲ Annual Job Openings: 507,000

▲ Annual Earnings: $19,080

▲ Education/Training Required: Short-term on-the-job training

▲ Self-Employed: 4.7%

▲ Part-Time: 32.3%

**Keep buildings in clean and orderly condition. Perform heavy cleaning duties, such as cleaning floors, shampooing rugs, washing walls and glass, and removing rubbish. Duties may include tending furnace and boiler, performing routine maintenance activities, notifying management of need for repairs, and cleaning snow or debris from sidewalk.** Sweeps, mops, scrubs, and vacuums floors of buildings, using cleaning solutions, tools and equipment. Cleans or polishes walls, ceilings, windows, plant equipment, and building fixtures, using steam cleaning equipment, scrapers, brooms, and variety of hand and power tools. Gathers and empties trash. Notifies management personnel concerning need for major repairs or additions to building operating systems. Dusts furniture, walls, machines, and equipment. Moves items between departments manually or using hand truck. Sets up, arranges, and removes decorations, tables, chairs, ladders, and scaffolding for events such as banquets and social functions. Requisitions supplies and equipment used in cleaning and maintenance duties. Sprays insecticides and fumigants to prevent insect and rodent infestation. Cleans laboratory equipment, such as glassware and metal instruments, using solvents, brushes, rags, and power cleaning equipment. Mows and trims lawns and shrubbery, using mowers and hand and power trimmers, and clears debris from grounds. Mixes water and detergents or acids in container to prepare cleaning solutions according to specifications. Drives vehicles, such as van, industrial truck, or industrial vacuum cleaner. Cleans chimneys, flues, and connecting pipes, using power and hand tools. Cleans and restores building interiors damaged by fire, smoke, or water, using commercial cleaning equipment. Services and repairs cleaning and maintenance equipment and machinery and performs minor routine painting, plumbing, electrical, and related activities. Removes snow from sidewalks, driveways, and parking areas, using snowplow, snowblower, and snow shovel, and spreads snow-melting chemicals. Tends, cleans, adjusts, and services furnaces, air conditioners, boilers, and other building heating and cooling systems. Applies waxes or sealers to wood or concrete floors. **SKILLS—Equipment Maintenance. Repairing. Equipment Selection. Troubleshooting. Operation and Control.**

**GOE—Interest Area:** 11. Recreation, Travel, and Other Personal Services. **Work Group:** 11.07. Cleaning and Building Services. **Other Job Titles in This Work Group:** Building Cleaning Workers, All Other; Locker Room, Coatroom, and Dressing Room Attendants; Maids and Housekeeping Cleaners. **PERSONALITY TYPE—Realistic.** Realistic occupations frequently involve work activities that include practical, hands-on problems and solutions. They often deal with plants, animals, and real-world materials like wood, tools, and machinery. Many of the occupations require working outside and do not involve a lot of paperwork or working closely with others.

**EDUCATION/TRAINING PROGRAM(S)—**Custodial, Housekeeping and Home Services Workers and Manage; Custodian/Caretaker. **RELATED KNOWLEDGE/COURSES—Principles of Mechanical Devices:** Knowledge of machines and tools, including their designs, uses, repair, and maintenance. **Chemistry:** Knowledge of the chemical composition, structure, and properties of substances and of the chemical processes and transformations that they undergo. This includes uses of chemicals and their interactions, danger signs, production techniques, and disposal methods. **Cus-**

tomer and Personal Service: Knowledge of principles and processes for providing customer and personal services. This includes customer needs assessment, meeting quality standards for services, and evaluation of customer satisfaction. **Building and Construction:**

# Landscaping and Groundskeeping Workers

▲ Growth: 29%
▲ Annual Job Openings: 193,000
▲ Annual Earnings: $20,030
▲ Education/Training Required: Short-term on-the-job training
▲ Self-Employed: 12.8%
▲ Part-Time: 28.5%

**Landscape or maintain grounds of property using hand or power tools or equipment. Workers typically perform a variety of tasks, which may include any combination of the following: sod laying, mowing, trimming, planting, watering, fertilizing, digging, raking, sprinkler installation, and installation of mortarless segmental concrete masonry wall units.** Mows lawns, using power mower. Trims and picks flowers and cleans flower beds. Hauls or spreads topsoil and spreads straw over seeded soil to hold soil in place. Applies herbicides, fungicides, fertilizers, and pesticides, using spreaders or spray equipment. Decorates garden with stones and plants. Waters lawns, trees, and plants, using portable sprinkler system, hose, or watering can. Digs holes for plants, mixes fertilizer or lime with dirt in holes, inserts plants, and fills holes with dirt. Attaches wires from planted trees to support stakes. Shovels snow from walks and driveways. Builds forms and mixes and pours cement to form garden borders. Maintains tools and equipment. Seeds and fertilizes lawns. **SKILLS**—Operation and Control. Installation. Mathematics.

**GOE**—**Interest Area:** 03. Plants and Animals. **Work Group:** 03.03. Hands-on Work in Plants and Animals. **Other Job Titles in This Work Group:** Agricultural Equipment Operators; Fallers; Farmworkers and Laborers, Crop, Nursery, and Greenhouse; Farmworkers, Farm and Ranch Animals; Fishers and Related Fishing Workers; Forest and Conservation Technicians; Forest and Conservation Workers; General Farmworkers; Grounds

Knowledge of materials, methods, and tools involved in the construction or repair of houses, buildings, or other structures such as highways and roads. **Mathematics:** Knowledge of arithmetic, algebra, geometry, calculus, statistics, and their applications.

Maintenance Workers, All Other; Hunters and Trappers; Logging Equipment Operators; Logging Tractor Operators; Logging Workers, All Other; Nursery Workers; Pest Control Workers; Pesticide Handlers, Sprayers, and Applicators, Vegetation; Tree Trimmers and Pruners. **PERSONALITY TYPE**—Realistic. Realistic occupations frequently involve work activities that include practical, hands-on problems and solutions. They often deal with plants, animals, and real-world materials like wood, tools, and machinery. Many of the occupations require working outside and do not involve a lot of paperwork or working closely with others.

**EDUCATION/TRAINING PROGRAM(S)**—Landscaping Operations and Management. **RELATED KNOWLEDGE/COURSES**—**Chemistry:** Knowledge of the chemical composition, structure, and properties of substances and of the chemical processes and transformations that they undergo. This includes uses of chemicals and their interactions, danger signs, production techniques, and disposal methods. **Principles of Mechanical Devices:** Knowledge of machines and tools, including their designs, uses, repair, and maintenance. **Building and Construction:** Knowledge of materials, methods, and tools involved in the construction or repair of houses, buildings, or other structures such as highways and roads. **Biology:** Knowledge of plant and animal organisms and their tissues, cells, functions, interdependencies, and interactions with each other and the environment.

# Lawn Service Managers

▲ Growth: 20.1%

▲ Annual Job Openings: 10,000

▲ Annual Earnings: $33,720

▲ Education/Training Required: Work experience in a related occupation

▲ Self-Employed: 37.8%

▲ Part-Time: 24.5%

**Plan, direct, and coordinate activities of workers engaged in pruning trees and shrubs, cultivating lawns, and applying pesticides and other chemicals according to service contract specifications.** Supervises workers who provide grounds-keeping services on a contract basis. Investigates customer complaints. Prepares work activity and personnel reports. Suggests changes in work procedures and orders corrective work done. Spot-checks completed work to improve quality of service and to ensure contract compliance. Schedules work for crew according to weather conditions, availability of equipment, and seasonal limitations. Reviews contracts to ascertain service, machine, and workforce requirements for job. Prepares service cost estimates for customers. Answers customers' questions about groundskeeping care requirements. **SKILLS**—Time Management. Management of Personnel Resources. Coordination. Speaking. Mathematics.

**GOE—Interest Area:** 03. Plants and Animals. **Work Group:** 03.01. Managerial Work in Plants and Animals. **Other Job Titles in This Work Group:** Agricultural Crop Farm Managers; Farm Labor Contractors; Farmers and Ranchers; First-Line Supervisors and Manager/Supervisors—Agricultural Crop Workers; First-Line Supervisors and Manager/Supervisors—Animal Care Workers, Except Livestock; First-Line Supervisors and Manager/Supervisors—Animal Husbandry Workers; First-Line Supervisors and Manager/Supervisors—Fishery Workers; First-Line Supervisors and Manager/Supervisors—Horticultural Workers; First-Line Supervisors and Manager/Supervisors—Landscaping Workers; First-Line Supervisors and Manager/Supervisors—Logging Workers; First-Line Supervisors/Managers of Farming, Fishing, and Forestry Workers; First-Line Supervisors/Managers of Landscaping, Lawn Service, and Groundskeeping Workers; Fish Hatchery Managers; Nursery and Greenhouse Managers. **PERSONALITY TYPE**—Enterprising. Enterprising occupations frequently involve starting up and carrying out projects. These occupations can involve leading people and making many decisions. They sometimes require risk taking and often deal with business.

**EDUCATION/TRAINING PROGRAM(S)**—Landscaping Operations and Management; Ornamental Horticulture Operations and Management; Recreation Products/Services Marketing Operations; Turf Management. **RELATED KNOWLEDGE/COURSES—Administration and Management:** Knowledge of business and management principles involved in strategic planning, resource allocation, human resources modeling, leadership technique, production methods, and coordination of people and resources. **Customer and Personal Service:** Knowledge of principles and processes for providing customer and personal services. This includes customer needs assessment, meeting quality standards for services, and evaluation of customer satisfaction. **Personnel and Human Resources:** Knowledge of principles and procedures for personnel recruitment, selection, training, compensation and benefits, labor relations and negotiation, and personnel information systems. **Economics and Accounting:** Knowledge of economic and accounting principles and practices, the financial markets, banking, and the analysis and reporting of financial data. **English Language:** Knowledge of the structure and content of the English language, including the meaning and spelling of words, rules of composition, and grammar.

# Legal Secretaries

- ▲ Growth: 20.3%
- ▲ Annual Job Openings: 36,000
- ▲ Annual Earnings: $35,370
- ▲ Education/Training Required: Post-secondary vocational training
- ▲ Self-Employed: 2.5%
- ▲ Part-Time: 19.8%

Perform secretarial duties utilizing legal terminology, procedures, and documents. Prepare legal papers and correspondence, such as summonses, complaints, motions, and subpoenas. May also assist with legal research. Prepares and processes legal documents and papers, such as summonses, subpoenas, complaints, appeals, motions, and pretrial agreements. Reviews legal publications and performs database searches to identify laws and court decisions relevant to pending cases. Submits articles and information from searches to attorneys for review and approval for use. Assists attorneys in collecting information such as employment, medical, and other records. Organizes and maintains law libraries and document and case files. Completes various forms, such as accident reports, trial and courtroom requests, and applications for clients. Mails, faxes, or arranges for delivery of legal correspondence to clients, witnesses, and court officials. Attends legal meetings, such as client interviews, hearings, or depositions, and takes notes. Drafts and types office memos. Receives and places telephone calls. Schedules and makes appointments. Makes photocopies of correspondence, documents, and other printed matter. **SKILLS**—Reading Comprehension. Writing. Active Listening. Critical Thinking. Active Learning.

**GOE—Interest Area:** 09. Business Detail. **Work Group:** 09.02. Administrative Detail. **Other Job Titles in This Work Group:** Claims Takers, Unemployment Benefits; Court Clerks; Court, Municipal, and License Clerks; Eligibility Interviewers, Government Programs; Executive Secretaries and Administrative Assistants; Interviewers, Except Eligibility and Loan; License Clerks; Loan Interviewers and Clerks; Medical Secretaries; Municipal Clerks; Secretaries, Except Legal, Medical, and Executive; Welfare Eligibility Workers and Interviewers. **PERSONALITY TYPE**—Conventional. Conventional occupations frequently involve following set procedures and routines. These occupations can include working with data and details more than with ideas. Usually there is a clear line of authority to follow.

**EDUCATION/TRAINING PROGRAM(S)**—Legal Administrative Assistant/Secretary. **RELATED KNOWLEDGE/COURSES—Clerical Studies:** Knowledge of administrative and clerical procedures and systems such as word processing, managing files and records, stenography and transcription, designing forms, and other office procedures and terminology. **Law and Government:** Knowledge of laws, legal codes, court procedures, precedents, government regulations, executive orders, agency rules, and the democratic political process. **English Language:** Knowledge of the structure and content of the English language, including the meaning and spelling of words, rules of composition, and grammar. **Computers and Electronics:** Knowledge of circuit boards, processors, chips, electronic equipment, and computer hardware and software, including applications and programming. **Telecommunications:** Knowledge of transmission, broadcasting, switching, control, and operation of telecommunications systems. **Communications and Media:** Knowledge of media production, communication, and dissemination techniques and methods. This includes alternative ways to inform and entertain via written, oral, and visual media.

# Letterpress Setters and Set-Up Operators

▲ Growth: 5.5%
▲ Annual Job Openings: 24,000
▲ Annual Earnings: $30,090
▲ Education/Training Required: Moderate-term on-the-job training
▲ Self-Employed: 2.6%
▲ Part-Time: 3.3%

Set up or set up and operate direct relief letterpresses, either sheet or roll (web) fed, to produce single or multicolor printed material, such as newspapers, books, and periodicals. Dismantles and reassembles printing unit or parts, using hand tools, to repair, clean, maintain, or adjust press. Operates specially equipped presses and auxiliary equipment, such as cutting, folding, numbering, and pasting devices. Reads work orders and job specifications to select ink and paper stock. Records and maintains production logsheet. Directs and monitors activities of apprentices and feeding or stacking workers. Inspects printed materials for irregularities such as off-level areas, variations in ink volume, register slippage, and poor color register. Moves controls to set or adjust ink flow, tension rollers, paper guides, and feed controls. Positions and installs printing plates, cylinder packing, die, and type forms in press according to specifications, using hand tools. Loads, positions, and adjusts unprinted materials on holding fixtures or in feeding mechanism of press. Pushes buttons or moves controls to start printing press and control operation. Mixes colors or inks and fills reservoirs. Monitors feeding and printing operations to maintain specified operating levels and detect malfunctions. **SKILLS**—Operation and Control. Operation Monitoring. Installation. Equipment Selection. Equipment Maintenance.

**GOE—Interest Area:** 08. Industrial Production. **Work Group:** 08.03. Production Work. **Other Job Titles in This Work Group:** Bakers, Manufacturing; Bindery Machine Operators and Tenders; Brazers; Cementing and Gluing Machine Operators and Tenders; Chemical Equipment Controllers and Operators; Chemical Equipment Operators and Tenders; Chemical Equipment Tenders; Cleaning, Washing, and Metal Pickling Equipment Operators and Tenders; Coating, Painting, and Spraying Machine Operators and Tenders; Coil Winders, Tapers, and Finishers; Combination Machine Tool Operators and Tenders, Metal and Plastic; Computer-Controlled Machine Tool Operators, Metal and Plastic; Cooling and Freezing Equipment Operators and Tenders; Crushing, Grinding, and Polishing Machine Setters, Operators, and Tenders; Cutters and Trimmers, Hand; Cutting and Slicing Machine Operators and Tenders; Cutting and Slicing Machine Setters, Operators, and Tenders; Design Printing Machine Setters and Set-Up Operators; Electrolytic Plating and Coating Machine Operators and Tenders, Metal and Plastic; Electrolytic Plating and Coating Machine Setters and Set-Up Operators, Metal and Plastic; Electrotypers and Stereotypers; Embossing Machine Set-Up Operators; Engraver Set-Up Operators; Extruding and Forming Machine Operators and Tenders, Synthetic or Glass Fibers; Extruding and Forming Machine Setters, Operators, and Tenders, Synthetic and Glass Fibers; Extruding, Forming, Pressing, and Compacting Machine Operators and Tenders; Fabric and Apparel Patternmakers; Fiber Product Cutting Machine Setters and Set-Up Operators; Fiberglass Laminators and Fabricators; others. **PERSONALITY TYPE**—Realistic. Realistic occupations frequently involve work activities that include practical, hands-on problems and solutions. They often deal with plants, animals, and real-world materials like wood, tools, and machinery. Many of the occupations require working outside and do not involve a lot of paperwork or working closely with others.

**EDUCATION/TRAINING PROGRAM(S)**—Graphic and Printing Equipment Operator, General; Graphic and Printing Equipment Operators, Other; Printing Press Operator. **RELATED KNOWLEDGE/**

COURSES—**Production and Processing:** Knowledge of raw materials, production processes, quality control, costs, and other techniques for maximizing the effective manufacture and distribution of goods. **Principles of Mechanical Devices:** Knowledge of machines and tools, including their designs, uses, repair, and maintenance. **English Language:** Knowledge of the structure and content of the English language, including the meaning and spelling of words, rules of composition, and grammar. **Engineering and Technology:** Knowledge of the practical application of engineering science and technology.

This includes applying principles, techniques, procedures, and equipment to the design and production of various goods and services. **Clerical Studies:** Knowledge of administrative and clerical procedures and systems such as word processing, managing files and records, stenography and transcription, designing forms, and other office procedures and terminology. **Communications and Media:** Knowledge of media production, communication, and dissemination techniques and methods. This includes alternative ways to inform and entertain via written, oral, and visual media.

# Library Assistants, Clerical

- ▲ Growth: 19.7%
- ▲ Annual Job Openings: 26,000
- ▲ Annual Earnings: $19,380
- ▲ Education/Training Required: Short-term on-the-job training
- ▲ Self-Employed: 0%
- ▲ Part-Time: 61.7%

**Compile records, sort and shelve books, and issue and receive library materials such as pictures, cards, slides and microfilm. Locate library materials for loan and replace material in shelving area, stacks, or files according to identification number and title. Register patrons to permit them to borrow books, periodicals, and other library materials.** Issues borrower's identification card according to established procedures. Drives bookmobile to specified locations following library services schedule and to garage for preventive maintenance and repairs. Locates library materials for patrons, such as books, periodicals, tape cassettes, Braille volumes, and pictures. Classifies and catalogs items according to contents and purpose. Sorts books, publications, and other items according to procedure and returns them to shelves, files, or other designated storage area. Issues books to patrons and records or scans information on borrower's card. Maintains records of items received, stored, issued, and returned and files catalog cards according to system used. Delivers and retrieves items to and from departments by hand or push cart. Repairs books, using mending tape and paste and brush, and places plastic covers on new books. Prepares address labels for books to be mailed, overdue notices, and duty schedules, using com-puter or typewriter. Operates and maintains audio-visual equipment and explains use of reference equipment to patrons. Places books in mailing container, affixes address label, and secures container with straps for mailing to blind library patrons. Selects substitute titles, following criteria such as age, education, and interest when requested materials are unavailable. Inspects returned books for damage, verifies due date, and computes and receives overdue fines. Reviews records, such as microfilm and issue cards, to determine title of overdue materials and to identify borrower. Prepares, stores, and retrieves classification and catalog information, lecture notes, or other documents related to document stored, using computer. Answers routine inquiries and refers patrons who need professional assistance to librarian. **SKILLS**—Reading Comprehension. Active Listening. Service Orientation. Writing. Speaking.

**GOE**—**Interest Area:** 12. Education and Social Service. **Work Group:** 12.03. Educational Services. **Other Job Titles in This Work Group:** Adult Literacy, Remedial Education, and GED Teachers and Instructors; Agricultural Sciences Teachers, Postsecondary; Anthropology and Archeology Teachers, Postsecondary; Architecture Teachers, Postsecondary; Archivists; Area,

Ethnic, and Cultural Studies Teachers, Postsecondary; Art, Drama, and Music Teachers, Postsecondary; Atmospheric, Earth, Marine, and Space Sciences Teachers, Postsecondary; Audio-Visual Collections Specialists; Biological Science Teachers, Postsecondary; Business Teachers, Postsecondary; Chemistry Teachers, Postsecondary; Child Care Workers; Communications Teachers, Postsecondary; Computer Science Teachers, Postsecondary; Criminal Justice and Law Enforcement Teachers, Postsecondary; Curators; Economics Teachers, Postsecondary; Education Teachers, Postsecondary; Educational Psychologists; Educational, Vocational, and School Counselors; Elementary School Teachers, Except Special Education; Engineering Teachers, Postsecondary; English Language and Literature Teachers, Postsecondary; Environmental Science Teachers, Postsecondary; Farm and Home Management Advisors; Foreign Language and Literature Teachers, Postsecondary; Forestry and Conservation Science Teachers, Postsecondary; Geography Teachers, Postsecondary; Graduate Teaching Assistants; Health Specialties Teachers, Postsecondary; History Teachers, Postsecondary; Home Economics Teachers, Postsecondary; Kindergarten Teachers, Except Special Education; Law Teachers, Postsecondary; Librarians; Library Science Teachers, Postsecondary; others. **PERSONALITY TYPE**—Conventional. Conventional occupations frequently involve following set procedures and routines. These occupations can include working with data and details more than with ideas. Usually there is a clear line of authority to follow.

**EDUCATION/TRAINING PROGRAM(S)**—Curriculum and Instruction; Educational/Instructional Media Design; Library Assistant. **RELATED KNOWLEDGE/COURSES—Clerical Studies:** Knowledge of administrative and clerical procedures and systems such as word processing, managing files and records, stenography and transcription, designing forms, and other office procedures and terminology. **English Language:** Knowledge of the structure and content of the English language, including the meaning and spelling of words, rules of composition, and grammar. **Customer and Personal Service:** Knowledge of principles and processes for providing customer and personal services. This includes customer needs assessment, meeting quality standards for services, and evaluation of customer satisfaction. **Computers and Electronics:** Knowledge of circuit boards, processors, chips, electronic equipment, and computer hardware and software, including applications and programming. **Communications and Media:** Knowledge of media production, communication, and dissemination techniques and methods. This includes alternative ways to inform and entertain via written, oral, and visual media.

# Library Technicians

- ▲ Growth: 19.5%
- ▲ Annual Job Openings: 29,000
- ▲ Annual Earnings: $24,230
- ▲ Education/Training Required: Short-term on-the-job training
- ▲ Self-Employed: 0%
- ▲ Part-Time: 11.7%

Assist librarians by helping readers in the use of library catalogs, databases, and indexes to locate books and other materials and by answering questions that require only brief consultation of standard reference. Compile records; sort and shelve books; remove or repair damaged books; register patrons; check materials in and out of the circulation process. Replace materials in shelving area (stacks) or files. Includes bookmobile drivers who operate bookmobiles or light trucks that pull trailers to specific locations on a predetermined schedule and assist with providing services in mobile libraries. Assists patrons in operating equipment and obtaining library materials and services and explains use of reference tools. Reviews subject matter of materials to be classified and selects classification numbers and headings according to classification system. Files catalog cards according to system used. Verifies bibliographical data, including author, title, publisher, publication date, and edition, on computer terminal. Processes print and non-print library materials and classifies and catalogs materials. Issues identification card to borrowers and checks materials in and out. Compiles and maintains records relating to circulation, materials, and equipment. Composes explanatory summaries of contents of books or other reference materials. Designs posters and special displays to promote use of library facilities or specific reading program at library. Prepares order slips for materials, follows up on orders, and compiles lists of materials acquired or withdrawn. Directs activities of library clerks and aides. **SKILLS**—Reading Comprehension. Active Listening. Writing. Service Orientation. Speaking.

**GOE—Interest Area:** 12. Education and Social Service. **Work Group:** 12.03. Educational Services. **Other Job Titles in This Work Group:** Adult Literacy, Remedial Education, and GED Teachers and Instructors; Agricultural Sciences Teachers, Postsecondary; Anthropology and Archeology Teachers, Postsecondary; Architecture Teachers, Postsecondary; Archivists; Area, Ethnic, and Cultural Studies Teachers, Postsecondary; Art, Drama, and Music Teachers, Postsecondary; Atmospheric, Earth, Marine, and Space Sciences Teachers, Postsecondary; Audio-Visual Collections Specialists; Biological Science Teachers, Postsecondary; Business Teachers, Postsecondary; Chemistry Teachers, Postsecondary; Child Care Workers; Communications Teachers, Postsecondary; Computer Science Teachers, Postsecondary; Criminal Justice and Law Enforcement Teachers, Postsecondary; Curators; Economics Teachers, Postsecondary; Education Teachers, Postsecondary; Educational Psychologists; Educational, Vocational, and School Counselors; Elementary School Teachers, Except Special Education; Engineering Teachers, Postsecondary; English Language and Literature Teachers, Postsecondary; Environmental Science Teachers, Postsecondary; Farm and Home Management Advisors; Foreign Language and Literature Teachers, Postsecondary; Forestry and Conservation Science Teachers, Postsecondary; Geography Teachers, Postsecondary; Graduate Teaching Assistants; Health Specialties Teachers, Postsecondary; History Teachers, Postsecondary; Home Economics Teachers, Postsecondary; Kindergarten Teachers, Except Special Education; Law Teachers, Postsecondary; Librarians; Library Assistants, Clerical; others. **PERSONALITY TYPE**—Conventional. Conventional occupations frequently involve following set procedures and routines. These occupations can include working with data and details more than with ideas. Usually there is a clear line of authority to follow.

**EDUCATION/TRAINING PROGRAM(S)**—Library Assistant. **RELATED KNOWLEDGE/ COURSES**—**Clerical Studies:** Knowledge of administrative and clerical procedures and systems such as word processing, managing files and records, stenography and transcription, designing forms, and other office procedures and terminology. **Customer and Personal Service:** Knowledge of principles and processes for providing customer and personal services. This includes customer needs assessment, meeting quality standards for services, and evaluation of customer satisfaction. **English Language:** Knowledge of the structure and content of the English language, including the meaning and spelling of words, rules of composition, and grammar. **Computers and Electronics:** Knowledge of circuit boards, processors, chips, electronic equipment, and computer hardware and software, including applications and programming. **Mathematics:** Knowledge of arithmetic, algebra, geometry, calculus, statistics, and their applications. **Communications and Media:** Knowledge of media production, communication, and dissemination techniques and methods. This includes alternative ways to inform and entertain via written, oral, and visual media.

# Licensed Practical and Licensed Vocational Nurses

▲ Growth: 20.3%

▲ Annual Job Openings: 58,000

▲ Annual Earnings: $30,470

▲ Education/Training Required: Post-secondary vocational training

▲ Self-Employed: 0.2%

▲ Part-Time: 22.1%

Care for ill, injured, convalescent, or disabled persons in hospitals, nursing homes, clinics, private homes, group homes, and similar institutions. May work under the supervision of a registered nurse. Licensing required. Administers specified medication, orally or by subcutaneous or intramuscular injection, and notes time and amount on patients' charts. Provides medical treatment and personal care to patients in private home settings. Takes and records patients' vital signs. Dresses wounds and gives enemas, douches, alcohol rubs, and massages. Applies compresses, ice bags, and hot water bottles. Observes patients and reports adverse reactions to medication or treatment to medical personnel in charge. Bathes, dresses, and assists patients in walking and turning. Assembles and uses such equipment as catheters, tracheotomy tubes, and oxygen suppliers. Collects samples, such as urine, blood, and sputum, from patients for testing and performs routine laboratory tests on samples. Sterilizes equipment and supplies, using germicides, sterilizer, or autoclave. Records food and fluid intake and output. Prepares or examines food trays for prescribed diet and feeds patients. Assists in delivery, care, and feeding of infants. Cleans rooms, makes beds, and answers patients' calls. Washes and dresses bodies of deceased persons. Inventories and requisitions supplies. **SKILLS**—Service Orientation. Reading Comprehension. Social Perceptiveness. Critical Thinking. Active Listening.

**GOE**—**Interest Area:** 14. Medical and Health Services. **Work Group:** 14.07. Patient Care and Assistance. **Other Job Titles in This Work Group:** Home Health Aides; Nursing Aides, Orderlies, and Attendants; Psychiatric Aides; Psychiatric Technicians. **PERSONALITY**

**TYPE**—Social. Social occupations frequently involve working with, communicating with, and teaching people. These occupations often involve helping or providing service to others.

**EDUCATION/TRAINING PROGRAM(S)**—Practical Nurse (L.P.N. Training). **RELATED KNOWLEDGE/COURSES**—**Medicine and Dentistry:** Knowledge of the information and techniques needed to diagnose and treat human injuries, diseases, and deformities. This includes symptoms, treatment alternatives, drug properties and interactions, and preventive health-care measures. **Customer and Personal Service:** Knowledge of principles and processes for providing customer and personal services. This includes customer needs assessment, meeting quality standards for services, and evaluation of customer satisfaction. **Biology:** Knowledge of plant and animal organisms and their tissues, cells, functions, interdependencies, and interactions with each other and the environment. **Psychology:** Knowledge of human behavior and performance; individual differences in ability, personality, and interests; learning and motivation; psychological research methods; and the assessment and treatment of behavioral and affective disorders. **Clerical Studies:** Knowledge of administrative and clerical procedures and systems such as word processing, managing files and records, stenography and transcription, designing forms, and other office procedures and terminology. **Chemistry:** Knowledge of the chemical composition, structure, and properties of substances and of the chemical processes and transformations that they undergo. This includes uses of chemicals and their interactions, danger signs, production techniques, and disposal methods.

# Licensing Examiners and Inspectors

- ▲ Growth: 8.9%
- ▲ Annual Job Openings: 9,000
- ▲ Annual Earnings: $44,140
- ▲ Education/Training Required: Long-term on-the-job training
- ▲ Self-Employed: 0%
- ▲ Part-Time: 2.9%

**Examine, evaluate, and investigate eligibility for, conformity with, or liability under licenses or permits.** Evaluates applications, records, and documents to determine relevant eligibility information or liability incurred. Prepares reports of activities, evaluations, recommendations, and decisions. Provides information and answers questions of individuals or groups concerning licensing, permit, or passport regulations. Warns violators of infractions or penalties. Prepares correspondence to inform concerned parties of decisions made and appeal rights. Confers with officials or technical or professional specialists and interviews individuals to obtain information or clarify facts. Determines eligibility or liability and approves or disallows application or license. Scores tests and rates ability of applicant through observation of equipment operation and control. Visits establishments to determine that valid licenses and permits are displayed and that licensing standards are being upheld. Issues licenses to individuals meeting standards. Administers oral, written, road, or flight test to determine applicant's eligibility for licensing. **SKILLS**—Reading Comprehension. Speaking. Active Listening. Monitoring. Writing.

**GOE—Interest Area:** 04. Law, Law Enforcement, and Public Safety. **Work Group:** 04.04. Public Safety. **Other Job Titles in This Work Group:** Agricultural Inspectors; Aviation Inspectors; Compliance Officers, Except Agriculture, Construction, Health and Safety, and Transportation; Emergency Medical Technicians and Paramedics; Environmental Compliance Inspectors; Equal Opportunity Representatives and Officers; Financial Examiners; Fire Fighters; Fire Inspectors; Fire Inspectors and Investigators; Forest Fire Fighters; Forest Fire Inspectors and Prevention Specialists; Government Property Inspectors and Investigators; Marine Cargo Inspectors; Municipal Fire Fighters; Nuclear Monitoring Technicians; Occupational Health and Safety Specialists; Occupational Health and Safety Technicians; Public Transportation Inspectors. **PERSONALITY TYPE**—Conventional. Conventional occupations frequently involve following set procedures and routines. These occupations can include working with data and details more than with ideas. Usually there is a clear line of authority to follow.

**EDUCATION/TRAINING PROGRAM(S)**—Business Administration and Management, General; Construction/Building Technologist/Technician; Logistics and Materials Management; Material Engineering; Mechanical Engineering; Operations Management and Supervision; Purchasing, Procurement and Contracts Management; Systems Engineering. **RELATED KNOWLEDGE/COURSES**—**English Language:** Knowledge of the structure and content of the English language, including the meaning and spelling of words, rules of composition, and grammar. **Law and Government:** Knowledge of laws, legal codes, court procedures, precedents, government regulations, executive orders, agency rules, and the democratic political process. **Clerical Studies:** Knowledge of administrative and clerical procedures and systems such as word processing, managing files and records, stenography and transcription, designing forms, and other office procedures and terminology. **Communications and Media:** Knowledge of media production, communication, and dissemination techniques and methods. This includes alternative ways to inform and entertain via written, oral, and visual media. **Mathematics:** Knowledge of arithmetic, algebra, geometry, calculus, statistics, and their applications.

# Lodging Managers

- ▲ Growth: 9.3%
- ▲ Annual Job Openings: 8,000
- ▲ Annual Earnings: $34,800
- ▲ Education/Training Required: Work experience in a related occupation
- ▲ Self-Employed: 51.5%
- ▲ Part-Time: 8.5%

**Plan, direct, or coordinate activities of an organization or department that provides lodging and other accommodations.** Coordinates front-office activities of hotel or motel and resolves problems. Inspects guest rooms, public areas, and grounds for cleanliness and appearance. Observes and monitors performance to ensure efficient operations and adherence to facility's policies and procedures. Arranges telephone answering service, delivers mail and packages, and answers questions regarding locations for eating and entertainment. Greets and registers guests. Collects payment and records data pertaining to funds and expenditures. Shows, rents, or assigns accommodations. Confers and cooperates with other department heads to ensure coordination of hotel activities. Interviews and hires applicants. Assigns duties to workers and schedules shifts. Receives and processes advance registration payments, sends out letters of confirmation, and returns checks when registration cannot be accepted. Purchases supplies and arranges for outside services, such as deliveries, laundry, maintenance and repair, and trash collection. Answers inquiries pertaining to hotel policies and services and resolves occupants' complaints. Manages and maintains temporary or permanent lodging facilities. **SKILLS—**Coordination. Service Orientation. Time Management. Management of Personnel Resources. Management of Material Resources.

**GOE—Interest Area:** 11. Recreation, Travel, and Other Personal Services. **Work Group:** 11.01. Managerial Work in Recreation, Travel, and Other Personal Services. **Other Job Titles in This Work Group:** Aircraft Cargo Handling Supervisors; First-Line Supervisors/Managers of Food Preparation and Serving Workers; First-Line Supervisors/Managers of Housekeeping and Janitorial Workers; First-Line Supervisors/Managers of Personal Service Workers; Food Service Managers; Gaming Managers; Gaming Supervisors; Housekeeping Supervisors; Janitorial Supervisors; Meeting and Convention Planners. **PERSONALITY TYPE—**Enterprising. Enterprising occupations frequently involve starting up and carrying out projects. These occupations can involve leading people and making many decisions. They sometimes require risk taking and often deal with business.

**EDUCATION/TRAINING PROGRAM(S)—**Food and Beverage/Restaurant Operations Manager; Hospitality/Administration Management; Hotel/Motel and Restaurant Management. **RELATED KNOWLEDGE/COURSES—Administration and Management:** Knowledge of business and management principles involved in strategic planning, resource allocation, human resources modeling, leadership technique, production methods, and coordination of people and resources. **Customer and Personal Service:** Knowledge of principles and processes for providing customer and personal services. This includes customer needs assessment, meeting quality standards for services, and evaluation of customer satisfaction. **Personnel and Human Resources:** Knowledge of principles and procedures for personnel recruitment, selection, training, compensation and benefits, labor relations and negotiation, and personnel information systems. **Economics and Accounting:** Knowledge of economic and accounting principles and practices, the financial markets, banking, and the analysis and reporting of financial data. **English Language:** Knowledge of the structure and content of the English language, including the meaning and spelling of words, rules of composition, and grammar. **Clerical Studies:** Knowledge of administrative and clerical procedures and systems such as word processing, managing files and records, stenography and transcription, designing forms, and other office procedures and terminology. **Public Safety and Security:** Knowledge of relevant equipment, policies, procedures, and strategies to promote effective local, state, or national security operations for the protection of people, data, property, and institutions.

# Machinists

▲ Growth: 9.1%
▲ Annual Job Openings: 28,000
▲ Annual Earnings: $31,610
▲ Education/Training Required: Long-term on-the-job training
▲ Self-Employed: 1.4%
▲ Part-Time: 2.1%

**Set up and operate a variety of machine tools to produce precision parts and instruments. Includes precision instrument makers who fabricate, modify, or repair mechanical instruments. May also fabricate and modify parts to make or repair machine tools or maintain industrial machines, applying knowledge of mechanics, shop mathematics, metal properties, layout, and machining procedures.** Studies sample parts, blueprints, drawings, and engineering information to determine methods and sequence of operations to fabricate product. Operates metalworking machine tools, such as lathe, milling machine, shaper, or grinder, to machine parts to specifications. Assembles parts into completed units, using jigs, fixtures, hand tools, and power tools. Fabricates, assembles, and modifies tooling, such as jigs, fixtures, templates, and molds or dies, to produce parts and assemblies. Lays out and verifies dimensions of parts, using precision measuring and marking instruments and knowledge of trigonometry. Calculates and sets controls to regulate machining or enters commands to retrieve, input, or edit computerized machine control media. Selects, aligns, and secures holding fixtures, cutting tools, attachments, accessories, and materials onto machines. Measures, examines, and tests completed units to detect defects and ensure conformance to specifications. Installs repaired part into equipment and operates equipment to verify operational efficiency. Operates brazing, heat-treating, and welding equipment to cut, solder, and braze metal. Dismantles machine or equipment, using hand tools and power tools, to examine parts for defect or to remove defective parts. Cleans, lubricates, and maintains machines, tools, and equipment to remove grease, rust, stains, and foreign matter. Observes and listens to operating machines or equipment to diagnose machine malfunction and determine need for adjustment or repair. Cuts and shapes sheet metal and heats and bends metal to specified shape. Installs experimental parts and assemblies, such as hydraulic systems, electrical wiring, lubricants, and batteries, into machines and mechanisms. Establishes work procedures for fabricating new structural products, using variety of metalworking machines. Confers with engineering, supervisory, and manufacturing personnel to exchange technical information. Designs fixtures, tooling, and experimental parts to meet special engineering needs. Tests experimental models under simulated operating conditions for such purposes as development, standardization, and feasibility of design. Evaluates experimental procedures and recommends changes or modifications for efficiency and adaptability to setup and production. **SKILLS—** Installation. Mathematics. Equipment Selection. Quality Control Analysis. Critical Thinking. Operations Analysis.

**GOE—Interest Area:** 08. Industrial Production. **Work Group:** 08.04. Metal and Plastics Machining Technology. **Other Job Titles in This Work Group:** Lay-Out Workers, Metal and Plastic; Metal Workers and Plastic Workers, All Other; Model Makers, Metal and Plastic; Patternmakers, Metal and Plastic; Tool and Die Makers; Tool Grinders, Filers, and Sharpeners. **PERSONALITY TYPE—**Realistic. Realistic occupations frequently involve work activities that include practical, hands-on problems and solutions. They often deal with plants, animals, and real-world materials like wood, tools, and machinery. Many of the occupations require working outside and do not involve a lot of paperwork or working closely with others.

**EDUCATION/TRAINING PROGRAM(S)**—Machine Shop Assistant; Machinist/Machine Technologist. **RELATED KNOWLEDGE/COURSES—Principles of Mechanical Devices:** Knowledge of machines and tools, including their designs, uses, repair, and maintenance. **Design:** Knowledge of design techniques, tools,

and principles involved in production of precision technical plans, blueprints, drawings, and models. **Engineering and Technology:** Knowledge of the practical application of engineering science and technology. This includes applying principles, techniques, procedures, and equipment to the design and production of various goods and services. **Mathematics:** Knowledge of arithmetic, algebra, geometry, calculus, statistics, and their applications. **Production and Processing:** Knowledge of raw materials, production processes, quality control, costs, and other techniques for maximizing the effective manufacture and distribution of goods.

# Maintenance and Repair Workers, General

▲ Growth: 4.7%
▲ Annual Job Openings: 103,000
▲ Annual Earnings: $29,420
▲ Education/Training Required: Long-term on-the-job training
▲ Self-Employed: 0.4%
▲ Part-Time: 9.3%

**Perform work involving the skills of two or more maintenance or craft occupations to keep machines, mechanical equipment, or the structure of an establishment in repair. Duties may involve pipe fitting; boiler making; insulating; welding; machining; carpentry; repairing electrical or mechanical equipment; installing, aligning, and balancing new equipment; and repairing buildings, floors, or stairs.** Inspects and tests machinery and equipment to diagnose machine malfunctions. Paints and repairs woodwork and plaster. Estimates costs of repairs. Records repairs made and costs. Fabricates and repairs counters, benches, partitions, and other wooden structures, such as sheds and outbuildings. Operates cutting torch or welding equipment to cut or join metal parts. Sets up and operates machine tools to repair or fabricate machine parts, jigs and fixtures, and tools. Lays brick to repair and maintain physical structure of establishment. Assembles, installs, and/or repairs plumbing. Installs new or repaired parts. Installs and/or repairs wiring and electrical and electronic components. Assembles, installs, and/or repairs pipe systems and hydraulic and pneumatic equipment. Installs machinery and equipment. Cleans and

lubricates shafts, bearings, gears, and other parts of machinery. Dismantles and reassembles defective machines and equipment. **SKILLS**—Repairing. Installation. Equipment Maintenance. Troubleshooting. Equipment Selection.

**GOE—Interest Area:** 05. Mechanics, Installers, and Repairers. **Work Group:** 05.03. Mechanical Work. **Other Job Titles in This Work Group:** Aircraft Body and Bonded Structure Repairers; Aircraft Engine Specialists; Aircraft Mechanics and Service Technicians; Airframe-and-Power-Plant Mechanics; Automotive Body and Related Repairers; Automotive Glass Installers and Repairers; Automotive Master Mechanics; Automotive Service Technicians and Mechanics; Automotive Specialty Technicians; Bicycle Repairers; Bridge and Lock Tenders; Bus and Truck Mechanics and Diesel Engine Specialists; Camera and Photographic Equipment Repairers; Coin, Vending, and Amusement Machine Servicers and Repairers; Control and Valve Installers and Repairers, Except Mechanical Door; Farm Equipment Mechanics; Gas Appliance Repairers; Hand and Portable Power Tool Repairers; Heating and Air Conditioning Mechanics; Heating, Air Conditioning, and Refrigeration Mechanics and Installers; Helpers—Electricians; Helpers—Installation, Maintenance, and Repair Workers; Industrial Machinery Mechanics; Keyboard Instrument Repairers and Tuners; Locksmiths and Safe Repairers; Maintenance Workers, Machinery; Mechanical Door Repairers; Medical Appliance Technicians; Medical Equipment Repairers; Meter Mechanics; Millwrights; Mobile Heavy Equipment Mechanics, Except Engines; Motorboat Mechanics; Motorcycle Mechanics; Musical Instrument Repairers and Tuners; Ophthalmic Laboratory Technicians; Optical Instrument Assemblers; Outdoor Power Equipment and Other Small Engine Mechanics; Painters, Transportation Equipment; Percussion Instrument Repairers and Tuners; Precision Instrument and Equipment Repairers, All Other; others. **PERSONALITY TYPE**—Realistic. Realistic occupations frequently involve work activities that include practical, hands-on problems and solutions. They often deal with plants, animals, and real-world materials like wood, tools, and machinery. Many of the occupations require working outside and do not involve a lot of paperwork or working closely with others.

**EDUCATION/TRAINING PROGRAM(S)**—Building/Property Maintenance and Manager. **RELATED**

**KNOWLEDGE/COURSES—Building and Construction:** Knowledge of materials, methods, and tools involved in the construction or repair of houses, buildings, or other structures such as highways and roads. **Principles of Mechanical Devices:** Knowledge of machines and tools, including their designs, uses, repair, and maintenance. **Engineering and Technology:** Knowledge of the practical application of engineering science and technology. This includes applying principles, techniques, procedures, and equipment to the design and production of various goods and services. **Public Safety and Security:** Knowledge of relevant equipment, policies, procedures, and strategies to promote effective local, state, or national security operations for the protection of people, data, property, and institutions. **Computers and Electronics:** Knowledge of circuit boards, processors, chips, electronic equipment, and computer hardware and software, including applications and programming. **Physics:** Knowledge and prediction of physical principles and laws and their interrelationships and applications to understanding fluid, material, and atmospheric dynamics and mechanical, electrical, atomic, and sub-atomic structures and processes. **Mathematics:** Knowledge of arithmetic, algebra, geometry, calculus, statistics, and their applications.

# Marine Cargo Inspectors

▲ Growth: 11.3%

▲ Annual Job Openings: 3,000

▲ Annual Earnings: $44,200

▲ Education/Training Required: Work experience in a related occupation

▲ Self-Employed: 9%

▲ Part-Time: 2.9%

**Inspect cargoes of seagoing vessels to certify compliance with health and safety regulations in cargo handling and stowage.** Inspects loaded cargo in holds and cargo handling devices to determine compliance with regulations and need for maintenance. Reads vessel documents to ascertain cargo capabilities according to design and cargo regulations. Calculates gross and net tonnage, hold capacities, volume of stored fuel and water, cargo weight, and ship stability factors, using mathematical formulas. Determines type of license and safety equipment required and computes applicable tolls and wharfage fees. Examines blueprints of ship and takes physical measurements to determine capacity and depth of vessel in water, using measuring instruments. Writes certificates of admeasurement, listing details such as design, length, depth, and breadth of vessel, and method of propulsion. Issues certificate of compliance when violations are not detected or recommends remedial procedures to correct deficiencies. Times roll of ship, using stopwatch. Analyzes data, formulates recommendations, and writes reports of findings. Advises crew in techniques of stowing dangerous and heavy cargo according to knowledge of hazardous cargo. **SKILLS**— Mathematics. Reading Comprehension. Active Listening. Writing. Speaking. Critical Thinking.

**GOE**—**Interest Area:** 04. Law, Law Enforcement, and Public Safety. **Work Group:** 04.04. Public Safety. **Other Job Titles in This Work Group:** Agricultural Inspectors; Aviation Inspectors; Compliance Officers, Except Agriculture, Construction, Health and Safety, and Transportation; Emergency Medical Technicians and Paramedics; Environmental Compliance Inspectors; Equal Opportunity Representatives and Officers; Financial Examiners; Fire Fighters; Fire Inspectors; Fire Inspectors and Investigators; Forest Fire Fighters; Forest Fire Inspectors and Prevention Specialists; Government Property Inspectors and Investigators; Licensing Examiners and Inspectors; Municipal Fire Fighters; Nuclear Monitoring Technicians; Occupational Health and Safety Specialists; Occupational Health and Safety Technicians; Public Transportation Inspectors. **PERSON-**

ALITY TYPE**—Conventional. Conventional occupations frequently involve following set procedures and routines. These occupations can include working with data and details more than with ideas. Usually there is a clear line of authority to follow.

**EDUCATION/TRAINING PROGRAM(S)**—Operations Management and Supervision. **RELATED KNOWLEDGE/COURSES**—**Mathematics:** Knowledge of arithmetic, algebra, geometry, calculus, statistics, and their applications. **Public Safety and Security:** Knowledge of relevant equipment, policies, procedures, and strategies to promote effective local, state, or national security operations for the protection of people, data, property, and institutions. **English Language:** Knowledge of the structure and content of the English language, including the meaning and spelling of words, rules of composition, and grammar. **Transportation:** Knowledge of principles and methods for moving people or goods by air, rail, sea, or road, including the relative costs and benefits. **Design:** Knowledge of design techniques, tools, and principles involved in production of precision technical plans, blueprints, drawings, and models.

# Marking and Identification Printing Machine Setters and Set-Up Operators

- ▲ Growth: 5.5%
- ▲ Annual Job Openings: 24,000
- ▲ Annual Earnings: $30,090
- ▲ Education/Training Required: Moderate-term on-the-job training
- ▲ Self-Employed: 2.6%
- ▲ Part-Time: 3.3%

**Set up or set up and operate machines to print trademarks, labels, or multicolored identification symbols on materials.** Adjusts machine as needed, using hand tools. Selects printing plates, dies, or type according to work order. Mounts printing plates, dies, or type onto machine. Fills reservoirs with ink or specified coloring agents. Monitors printing process to detect machine malfunctions. Cleans machine and equipment, using solvent and rags. Examines product to detect defects. Sets rate of flow of coloring agent and speed and spacing of materials to achieve desired product. Mounts

materials to be printed onto feed mechanisms and threads materials through guides on machine. **SKILLS**—Operation and Control. Operation Monitoring. Equipment Selection. Equipment Maintenance.

**GOE**—**Interest Area:** 08. Industrial Production. **Work Group:** 08.03. Production Work. **Other Job Titles in This Work Group:** Bakers, Manufacturing; Bindery Machine Operators and Tenders; Brazers; Cementing and Gluing Machine Operators and Tenders; Chemical Equipment Controllers and Operators; Chemical Equipment Operators and Tenders; Chemical Equipment Tenders; Cleaning, Washing, and Metal Pickling Equipment Operators and Tenders; Coating, Painting, and Spraying Machine Operators and Tenders; Coil Winders, Tapers, and Finishers; Combination Machine Tool Operators and Tenders, Metal and Plastic; Computer-Controlled Machine Tool Operators, Metal and Plastic; Cooling and Freezing Equipment Operators and Tenders; Crushing, Grinding, and Polishing Machine Setters, Operators, and Tenders; Cutters and Trimmers, Hand; Cutting and Slicing Machine Operators and Tenders; Cutting and Slicing Machine Setters, Operators, and Tenders; Design Printing Machine Setters and Set-Up Operators; Electrolytic Plating and Coating Machine Operators and Tenders, Metal and Plastic; Electrolytic Plating and Coating Machine Setters and Set-Up Operators, Metal and Plastic; Electrotypers and Stereotypers; Embossing Machine Set-Up Operators; Engraver Set-Up Operators; Extruding and Forming Machine Operators and Tenders, Synthetic or Glass Fibers; Extruding and Forming Machine Setters, Operators, and Tenders, Synthetic and Glass Fibers; Extruding, Forming, Pressing, and Compacting Machine Operators and Tenders; Fabric and Apparel Patternmakers; Fiber Product Cutting Machine Setters and Set-Up Operators; Fiberglass Laminators and Fabricators; others. **PERSONALITY TYPE**—Realistic. Realistic occupations frequently involve work activities that include practical, hands-on problems and solutions.

They often deal with plants, animals, and real-world materials like wood, tools, and machinery. Many of the occupations require working outside and do not involve a lot of paperwork or working closely with others.

**EDUCATION/TRAINING PROGRAM(S)**— Graphic and Printing Equipment Operator, General; Graphic and Printing Equipment Operators, Other; Printing Press Operator. **RELATED KNOWLEDGE/ COURSES—English Language:** Knowledge of the structure and content of the English language, including the meaning and spelling of words, rules of composition, and grammar. **Principles of Mechanical Devices:** Knowledge of machines and tools, including their designs, uses, repair, and maintenance. **Production and Processing:** Knowledge of raw materials, production processes, quality control, costs, and other techniques for maximizing the effective manufacture and distribution of goods. **Communications and Media:** Knowledge of media production, communication, and dissemination techniques and methods. This includes alternative ways to inform and entertain via written, oral, and visual media. **Chemistry:** Knowledge of the chemical composition, structure, and properties of substances and of the chemical processes and transformations that they undergo. This includes uses of chemicals and their interactions, danger signs, production techniques, and disposal methods.

# Marking Clerks

- ▲ Growth: 8.5%
- ▲ Annual Job Openings: 467,000
- ▲ Annual Earnings: $20,650
- ▲ Education/Training Required: Short-term on-the-job training
- ▲ Self-Employed: 0.2%
- ▲ Part-Time: 16.8%

**Print and attach price tickets to articles of merchandise using one or several methods, such as marking price on tickets by hand or using ticket-printing machine.** Marks selling price by hand on boxes containing merchandise or on price tickets. Performs other clerical tasks during periods between auction sales. Keeps records of production, returned goods, and related trans-

actions. Records number and types of articles marked and packs articles in boxes. Pins, pastes, sews, ties, or staples tickets, tags, or labels to article, using tagging mechanism. Records price, buyer, and grade of product on tickets attached to products auctioned. Indicates price, size, style, color, and inspection results on tags, tickets, and labels, using rubber stamp or writing instrument. Compares printed price tickets with entries on purchase order to verify accuracy and notifies supervisor of discrepancies. Prints information on tickets, using ticket-printing machine. **SKILLS**—Mathematics.

**GOE—Interest Area:** 09. Business Detail. **Work Group:** 09.08. Records and Materials Processing. **Other Job Titles in This Work Group:** Cargo and Freight Agents; Couriers and Messengers; Mail Clerks, Except Mail Machine Operators and Postal Service; Order Fillers, Wholesale and Retail Sales; Postal Service Mail Carriers; Postal Service Mail Sorters, Processors, and Processing Machine Operators; Shipping, Receiving, and Traffic Clerks; Stock Clerks and Order Fillers; Stock Clerks—Stockroom, Warehouse, or Storage Yard; Weighers, Measurers, Checkers, and Samplers, Recordkeeping. **PERSONALITY TYPE**—Conventional. Conventional occupations frequently involve following set procedures and routines. These occupations can include working with data and details more than with ideas. Usually there is a clear line of authority to follow.

**EDUCATION/TRAINING PROGRAM(S)**—Food Products Retailing and Wholesaling Operations; General Retailing Operations; Home and Office Products Marketing Operations, Other. **RELATED KNOWLEDGE/COURSES—Clerical Studies:** Knowledge of administrative and clerical procedures and systems such as word processing, managing files and records, stenography and transcription, designing forms, and other office procedures and terminology. **Mathematics:** Knowledge of arithmetic, algebra, geometry, calculus, statistics, and their applications. **Production and Processing:** Knowledge of raw materials, production processes, quality control, costs, and other techniques for maximizing the effective manufacture and distribution of goods.

# Mechanical Drafters

- ▲ Growth: 15.4%
- ▲ Annual Job Openings: 8,000
- ▲ Annual Earnings: $40,330
- ▲ Education/Training Required: Post-secondary vocational training
- ▲ Self-Employed: 4.7%
- ▲ Part-Time: 7.9%

**Prepare detailed working diagrams of machinery and mechanical devices, including dimensions, fastening methods, and other engineering information.** Develops detailed design drawings and specifications for mechanical equipment, dies/tools, and controls, according to engineering sketches and design proposals. Designs scale or full-size blueprints of specialty items, such as furniture and automobile body or chassis components. Lays out and draws schematic, orthographic, or angle views to depict functional relationships of components, assemblies, systems, and machines. Draws freehand sketches of designs and traces finished drawings onto designated paper for reproduction of blueprints. Shades or colors drawings to clarify and emphasize details and dimensions and eliminate background, using ink, crayon, airbrush, and overlays. Reviews and analyzes specifications, sketches, engineering drawings, ideas, and related design data to determine factors affecting component designs. Modifies and revises designs to correct operating deficiencies or to reduce production problems. Measures machine set-up and parts during production to ensure compliance with design specifications, using precision measuring instruments. Directs work activities of detailer and confers with staff and supervisors to resolve design or other problems. Coordinates and works in conjunction with other workers to design, lay out, or detail components and systems. Confers with customer representatives to review schematics and answer questions pertaining to installation of systems. Compiles and analyzes test data to determine effect of machine design on various factors, such as temperature and pressure. Observes set-up and gauges during programmed machine or equipment trial run to verify conformance of signals and systems to specifications. Computes mathematical formulas to develop and design detailed specifications for components or machinery, using computer-assisted equipment. Positions instructions and comments onto drawings and illustrates and describes installation and maintenance details. Lays out, draws, and reproduces illustrations for reference manuals and technical publications to describe operation and maintenance of mechanical systems. **SKILLS**—Mathematics. Operations Analysis. Critical Thinking. Technology Design. Quality Control Analysis.

**GOE**—**Interest Area:** 02. Science, Math, and Engineering. **Work Group:** 02.08. Engineering Technology. **Other Job Titles in This Work Group:** Aerospace Engineering and Operations Technicians; Architectural and Civil Drafters; Architectural Drafters; Calibration and Instrumentation Technicians; Cartographers and Photogrammetrists; Civil Drafters; Civil Engineering Technicians; Construction and Building Inspectors; Drafters, All Other; Electrical and Electronic Engineering Technicians; Electrical and Electronics Drafters; Electrical Drafters; Electrical Engineering Technicians; Electro-Mechanical Technicians; Electronic Drafters; Electronics Engineering Technicians; Engineering Technicians, Except Drafters, All Other; Environmental Engineering Technicians; Industrial Engineering Technicians; Mapping Technicians; Mechanical Engineering Tech-

nicians; Numerical Tool and Process Control Programmers; Pressure Vessel Inspectors; Surveying and Mapping Technicians; Surveying Technicians; Surveyors. **PERSONALITY TYPE**—Realistic. Realistic occupations frequently involve work activities that include practical, hands-on problems and solutions. They often deal with plants, animals, and real-world materials like wood, tools, and machinery. Many of the occupations require working outside and do not involve a lot of paperwork or working closely with others.

**EDUCATION/TRAINING PROGRAM(S)**—Mechanical Drafting. **RELATED KNOWLEDGE/COURSES**—**Design:** Knowledge of design techniques, tools, and principles involved in production of precision technical plans, blueprints, drawings, and models. **Engineering and Technology:** Knowledge of the practical application of engineering science and technology. This includes applying principles, techniques, procedures, and equipment to the design and production of various goods and services. **Mathematics:** Knowledge of arithmetic, algebra, geometry, calculus, statistics, and their applications. **English Language:** Knowledge of the structure and content of the English language, including the meaning and spelling of words, rules of composition, and grammar. **Computers and Electronics:** Knowledge of circuit boards, processors, chips, electronic equipment, and computer hardware and software, including applications and programming.

# Medical and Clinical Laboratory Technicians

- ▲ Growth: 19%
- ▲ Annual Job Openings: 19,000
- ▲ Annual Earnings: $28,970
- ▲ Education/Training Required: Associate's degree
- ▲ Self-Employed: 0.7%
- ▲ Part-Time: 19.5%

**Perform routine medical laboratory tests for the diagnosis, treatment, and prevention of disease. May work under the supervision of a medical technologist.** Conducts quantitative and qualitative chemical analyses of body fluids, such as blood, urine, and spinal fluid. Conducts blood tests for transfusion purposes. Tests vac-

cines for sterility and virus inactivity. Draws blood from patient, observing principles of asepsis to obtain blood sample. Prepares standard volumetric solutions and reagents used in testing. Inoculates fertilized eggs, broths, or other bacteriological media with organisms. Incubates bacteria for specified period and prepares vaccines and serums by standard laboratory methods. Performs blood counts, using microscope. **SKILLS**—Science. Reading Comprehension. Quality Control Analysis. Mathematics. Equipment Selection.

**GOE**—**Interest Area:** 14. Medical and Health Services. **Work Group:** 14.05. Medical Technology. **Other Job Titles in This Work Group:** Cardiovascular Technologists and Technicians; Diagnostic Medical Sonographers; Health Technologists and Technicians, All Other; Medical and Clinical Laboratory Technologists; Medical Equipment Preparers; Nuclear Medicine Technologists; Orthotists and Prosthetists; Radiologic Technicians; Radiologic Technologists; Radiologic Technologists and Technicians. **PERSONALITY TYPE**—Realistic. Realistic occupations frequently involve work activities that include practical, hands-on problems and solutions. They often deal with plants, animals, and real-world materials like wood, tools, and machinery. Many of the occupations require working outside and do not involve a lot of paperwork or working closely with others.

**EDUCATION/TRAINING PROGRAM(S)**—Blood Bank Technologist/Technician; Hematology Technologist/Technician; Medical Laboratory Assistant; Medical Laboratory Technician. **RELATED KNOWLEDGE/COURSES**—**Chemistry:** Knowledge of the chemical composition, structure, and properties of substances and of the chemical processes and transformations that they undergo. This includes uses of chemicals and their interactions, danger signs, production techniques, and disposal methods. **Biology:** Knowledge of plant and animal organisms and their tissues, cells, functions, interdependencies, and interactions with each other and the environment. **Medicine and Dentistry:** Knowledge of the information and techniques needed to diagnose and treat human injuries, diseases, and deformities. This includes symptoms, treatment alternatives, drug properties and interactions, and preventive health-care measures. **Mathematics:** Knowledge of arithmetic, algebra, geometry, calculus, statistics, and their applications. **Public Safety and Security:** Knowledge of relevant equipment, policies, procedures, and strategies to promote effective local, state, or national security operations for the protection of people, data, property, and institutions.

# Medical Assistants

- ▲ Growth: 57%
- ▲ Annual Job Openings: 18,700
- ▲ Annual Earnings: $23,840
- ▲ Education/Training Required: Moderate-term on-the-job training
- ▲ Self-Employed: 1.9%
- ▲ Part-Time: 22.9%

**Perform administrative and certain clinical duties under the direction of physician. Administrative duties may include scheduling appointments, maintaining medical records, billing, and coding for insurance purposes. Clinical duties may include taking and recording vital signs and medical histories, preparing patients for examination, drawing blood, and administering medications as directed by physician.** Prepares treatment rooms for examination of patients. Hands instruments and materials to physician. Schedules appointments. Maintains medical records. Contacts medical facility or department to schedule patients for tests. Lifts and turns patients. Gives physiotherapy treatments, such as diathermy, galvanics, and hydrotherapy. Receives payment for bills. Performs routine laboratory tests. Gives injections or treatments to patients. Operates X-ray, electrocardiograph (EKG), and other equipment to administer routine diagnostic tests. Completes insurance forms. Computes and mails monthly statements to patients and records transactions. Cleans and sterilizes instruments. Inventories and orders medical supplies and materials. Interviews patients, measures vital signs, weight, and height, and records information. **SKILLS**—Reading Comprehension. Active Listening. Service Orientation. Speaking. Writing.

**GOE**—**Interest Area:** 14. Medical and Health Services. **Work Group:** 14.02. Medicine and Surgery. **Other Job Titles in This Work Group:** Anesthesiologists; Family and General Practitioners; Internists, General; Obstetricians and Gynecologists; Pediatricians, General; Pharmacists; Pharmacy Aides; Pharmacy Technicians; Physician Assistants; Physicians and Surgeons, All Other; Psychiatrists; Registered Nurses; Surgeons; Surgical Technologists. **PERSONALITY TYPE**—Social. Social occupations frequently involve working with, communicating with, and teaching people. These occupations often involve helping or providing service to others.

**EDUCATION/TRAINING PROGRAM(S)**—Health and Medical Assistants, Other; Medical Assistant; Medical Office Management; Ophthalmic Medical Assistant;

Orthoptics. **RELATED KNOWLEDGE/COURSES**—**Medicine and Dentistry:** Knowledge of the information and techniques needed to diagnose and treat human injuries, diseases, and deformities. This includes symptoms, treatment alternatives, drug properties and interactions, and preventive health-care measures. **Clerical Studies:** Knowledge of administrative and clerical procedures and systems such as word processing, managing files and records, stenography and transcription, designing forms, and other office procedures and terminology. **Biology:** Knowledge of plant and animal organisms and their tissues, cells, functions, interdependencies, and interactions with each other and the environment. **English Language:** Knowledge of the structure and content of the English language, including the meaning and spelling of words, rules of composition, and grammar. **Therapy and Counseling:** Knowledge of principles, methods, and procedures for diagnosis, treatment, and rehabilitation of physical and mental dysfunctions and for career counseling and guidance.

# Medical Equipment Repairers

- ▲ Growth: 14.9%
- ▲ Annual Job Openings: 3,000
- ▲ Annual Earnings: $37,470
- ▲ Education/Training Required: Moderate-term on-the-job training
- ▲ Self-Employed: 27.2%
- ▲ Part-Time: 9.3%

**Test, adjust, or repair biomedical or electromedical equipment.** Inspects and tests malfunctioning medical and related equipment, using test and analysis instruments and following manufacturers' specifications. Demonstrates and explains correct operation of equipment to medical personnel. Consults with medical or research staff to ensure that equipment functions properly and safely. Logs records of maintenance and repair work and approved updates of equipment as required by manufacturer. Cleans and lubricates equipment, using solvents, rags, and lubricants. Disassembles malfunctioning equipment and removes defective components. Safety-tests medical equipment and facility's structural environment to ensure patient and staff safety from electrical or mechanical hazards. Solders loose connections,

using soldering iron. Installs medical, dental, and related technical equipment in medical and research facilities. Maintains various equipment and apparatus, such as patient monitors, electrocardiographs, X-ray units, defibrillators, electrosurgical units, anesthesia apparatus, pacemakers, and sterilizers. Calibrates and adjusts components and equipment, using hand tools, power tools, and measuring devices and following manufacturers' manuals and troubleshooting techniques. Repairs and replaces defective parts, such as motors, clutches, tubes, transformers, resistors, condensers, and switches, using hand tools. **SKILLS**—Installation. Repairing. Equipment Maintenance. Troubleshooting. Instructing.

GOE—**Interest Area:** 05. Mechanics, Installers, and Repairers. **Work Group:** 05.03. Mechanical Work. **Other Job Titles in This Work Group:** Aircraft Body and Bonded Structure Repairers; Aircraft Engine Specialists; Aircraft Mechanics and Service Technicians; Airframe-and-Power-Plant Mechanics; Automotive Body and Related Repairers; Automotive Glass Installers and Repairers; Automotive Master Mechanics; Automotive Service Technicians and Mechanics; Automotive Specialty Technicians; Bicycle Repairers; Bridge and Lock Tenders; Bus and Truck Mechanics and Diesel Engine Specialists; Camera and Photographic Equipment Repairers; Coin, Vending, and Amusement Machine Servicers and Repairers; Control and Valve Installers and Repairers, Except Mechanical Door; Farm Equipment Mechanics; Gas Appliance Repairers; Hand and Portable Power Tool Repairers; Heating and Air Conditioning Mechanics; Heating, Air Conditioning, and Refrigeration Mechanics and Installers; Helpers—Electricians; Helpers—Installation, Maintenance, and Repair Workers; Industrial Machinery Mechanics; Keyboard Instrument Repairers and Tuners; Locksmiths and Safe Repairers; Maintenance and Repair Workers, General; Maintenance Workers, Machinery; Mechanical Door Repairers; Medical Appliance Technicians; Meter Mechanics; Millwrights; Mobile Heavy Equipment Mechanics, Except Engines; Motorboat Mechanics; Motorcycle Mechanics; Musical Instrument Repairers and Tuners; Ophthalmic Laboratory Technicians; Optical Instrument Assemblers; Outdoor Power Equipment and Other Small Engine Mechanics; Painters, Transportation Equipment; Percussion Instrument Repairers and Tuners; others. **PERSONALITY TYPE**—Realistic. Realistic occupations frequently involve work activities that include practical, hands-on problems and solutions. They often deal with plants, animals, and real-world materials like wood, tools, and machinery. Many of the occupations require working outside and do not involve a lot of paperwork or working closely with others.

**EDUCATION/TRAINING PROGRAM(S)**—Biomedical Engineering-Related Technologist/Technician. **RELATED KNOWLEDGE/COURSES—Principles of Mechanical Devices:** Knowledge of machines and tools, including their designs, uses, repair, and maintenance. **Engineering and Technology:** Knowledge of the practical application of engineering science and technology. This includes applying principles, techniques, procedures, and equipment to the design and production of various goods and services. **Computers and Electronics:** Knowledge of circuit boards, processors, chips, electronic equipment, and computer hardware and software, including applications and programming. **Mathematics:** Knowledge of arithmetic, algebra, geometry, calculus, statistics, and their applications. **Design:** Knowledge of design techniques, tools, and principles involved in production of precision technical plans, blueprints, drawings, and models.

# Medical Records and Health Information Technicians

- ▲ Growth: 49%
- ▲ Annual Job Openings: 14,000
- ▲ Annual Earnings: $24,430
- ▲ Education/Training Required: Associate's degree
- ▲ Self-Employed: 0%
- ▲ Part-Time: 22.9%

**Compile, process, and maintain medical records of hospital and clinic patients in a manner consistent with medical, administrative, ethical, legal, and regulatory requirements of the health care system. Process, maintain, compile, and report patient information for health requirements and standards.** Compiles and maintains medical records of patients to document condition and treatment and to provide data for research studies. Maintains variety of health record indexes and storage and retrieval systems. Enters data, such as demographic characteristics, history and extent of disease, diagnostic procedures, and treatment into computer.

Prepares statistical reports, narrative reports, and graphic presentations of tumor registry data for use by hospital staff, researchers, and other users. Assists in special studies or research as needed. Contacts discharged patients and their families and physicians to maintain registry with follow-up information, such as quality of life and length of survival of cancer patients. Reviews records for completeness and to abstract and code data, using standard classification systems, and to identify and compile patient data. Compiles medical care and census data for statistical reports on diseases treated, surgery performed, and use of hospital beds. **SKILLS**—Reading Comprehension. Writing. Speaking. Active Listening. Mathematics.

**GOE**—**Interest Area:** 09. Business Detail. **Work Group:** 09.07. Records Processing. **Other Job Titles in This Work Group:** Correspondence Clerks; Court Reporters; Credit Authorizers; Credit Authorizers, Checkers, and Clerks; Credit Checkers; File Clerks; Human Resources Assistants, Except Payroll and Timekeeping; Information and Record Clerks, All Other; Insurance Claims and Policy Processing Clerks; Insurance Claims Clerks; Insurance Policy Processing Clerks; Medical Transcriptionists; Office Clerks, General; Procurement Clerks; Proofreaders and Copy Markers. **PERSONAL-ITY TYPE**—Conventional. Conventional occupations frequently involve following set procedures and routines. These occupations can include working with data and details more than with ideas. Usually there is a clear line of authority to follow.

**EDUCATION/TRAINING PROGRAM(S)**—Medical Records Technologist/Technician. **RELATED KNOWLEDGE/COURSES**—**Clerical Studies:** Knowledge of administrative and clerical procedures and systems such as word processing, managing files and records, stenography and transcription, designing forms, and other office procedures and terminology. **Computers and Electronics:** Knowledge of circuit boards, processors, chips, electronic equipment, and computer hardware and software, including applications and programming. **Mathematics:** Knowledge of arithmetic, algebra, geometry, calculus, statistics, and their applications. **English Language:** Knowledge of the structure and content of the English language, including the meaning and spelling of words, rules of composition, and grammar. **Medicine and Dentistry:** Knowledge of the information and techniques needed to diagnose and treat human injuries, diseases, and deformities. This includes symptoms, treatment alternatives, drug properties and interactions, and preventive health-care measures.

# Medical Secretaries

- ▲ Growth: 19%
- ▲ Annual Job Openings: 40,000
- ▲ Annual Earnings: $24,460
- ▲ Education/Training Required: Post-secondary vocational training
- ▲ Self-Employed: 2%
- ▲ Part-Time: 19.8%

**Perform secretarial duties utilizing specific knowledge of medical terminology and hospital, clinic, or laboratory procedures. Duties include scheduling appointments, billing patients, and compiling and recording medical charts, reports, and correspondence.** Compiles and records medical charts, reports, and correspondence, using typewriter or personal computer. Transcribes recorded messages and practitioner's diagnosis and recommendations into patient's medical record. Transmits correspondence and medical records by mail, e-mail, or fax. Greets visitors, ascertains purpose of visits, and directs to appropriate staff. Routes messages and documents such as laboratory results to appropriate staff. Prepares and transmits patients' bills. Maintains medical records and correspondence files. Answers telephone and directs call to appropriate staff. Schedules patient diagnostic appointments and medical consultations. Takes dictation in shorthand. **SKILLS**—

Active Listening. Reading Comprehension. Writing. Speaking. Coordination.

**GOE—Interest Area:** 09. Business Detail. **Work Group:** 09.02. Administrative Detail. **Other Job Titles in This Work Group:** Claims Takers, Unemployment Benefits; Court Clerks; Court, Municipal, and License Clerks; Eligibility Interviewers, Government Programs; Executive Secretaries and Administrative Assistants; Interviewers, Except Eligibility and Loan; Legal Secretaries; License Clerks; Loan Interviewers and Clerks; Municipal Clerks; Secretaries, Except Legal, Medical, and Executive; Welfare Eligibility Workers and Interviewers. **PERSONALITY TYPE**—Conventional. Conventional occupations frequently involve following set procedures and routines. These occupations can include working with data and details more than with ideas. Usually there is a clear line of authority to follow.

# Metal Fabricators, Structural Metal Products

▲ Growth: 19.5%
▲ Annual Job Openings: 20,000
▲ Annual Earnings: $28,490
▲ Education/Training Required: Moderate-term on-the-job training
▲ Self-Employed: 0%
▲ Part-Time: 2.3%

**EDUCATION/TRAINING PROGRAM(S)**—Medical Administrative Assistant/Secretary. **RELATED KNOWLEDGE/COURSES—Clerical Studies:** Knowledge of administrative and clerical procedures and systems such as word processing, managing files and records, stenography and transcription, designing forms, and other office procedures and terminology. **Computers and Electronics:** Knowledge of circuit boards, processors, chips, electronic equipment, and computer hardware and software, including applications and programming. **English Language:** Knowledge of the structure and content of the English language, including the meaning and spelling of words, rules of composition, and grammar. **Mathematics:** Knowledge of arithmetic, algebra, geometry, calculus, statistics, and their applications. **Customer and Personal Service:** Knowledge of principles and processes for providing customer and personal services. This includes customer needs assessment, meeting quality standards for services, and evaluation of customer satisfaction.

**Fabricate and assemble structural metal products, such as frameworks or shells for machinery, ovens, tanks, and stacks and metal parts for buildings and bridges, according to job order or blueprints.** Develops layout and plans sequence of operations for fabricating and assembling structural metal products, applying trigonometry and knowledge of metal. Locates and marks bending and cutting lines onto workpiece, allowing for stock thickness and machine and welding shrinkage. Hammers, chips, and grinds workpiece to cut, bend, and straighten metal. Verifies conformance of workpiece to specifications, using square, ruler, and measuring tape. Preheats workpieces to render them malleable, using hand torch or furnace. Positions, aligns, fits, and welds together parts, using jigs, welding torch, and hand tools. Sets up and operates fabricating machines, such as brakes, rolls, shears, flame cutters, and drill presses. Sets up and operates machine tools associated with fabricating shops, such as radial drill, end mill, and edge planer. Designs and constructs templates and fixtures, using hand tools. **SKILLS—Mathematics.** Operation and Control. Equipment Selection. Quality Control Analysis. Operations Analysis.

**GOE—Interest Area:** 08. Industrial Production. **Work Group:** 08.03. Production Work. **Other Job Titles in This Work Group:** Bakers, Manufacturing; Bindery Machine Operators and Tenders; Brazers; Cementing and Gluing Machine Operators and Tenders; Chemical Equipment Controllers and Operators; Chemical Equipment Operators and Tenders; Chemical Equipment Tenders; Cleaning, Washing, and Metal Pickling

Equipment Operators and Tenders; Coating, Painting, and Spraying Machine Operators and Tenders; Coil Winders, Tapers, and Finishers; Combination Machine Tool Operators and Tenders, Metal and Plastic; Computer-Controlled Machine Tool Operators, Metal and Plastic; Cooling and Freezing Equipment Operators and Tenders; Crushing, Grinding, and Polishing Machine Setters, Operators, and Tenders; Cutters and Trimmers, Hand; Cutting and Slicing Machine Operators and Tenders; Cutting and Slicing Machine Setters, Operators, and Tenders; Design Printing Machine Setters and Set-Up Operators; Electrolytic Plating and Coating Machine Operators and Tenders, Metal and Plastic; Electrolytic Plating and Coating Machine Setters and Set-Up Operators, Metal and Plastic; Electrotypers and Stereotypers; Embossing Machine Set-Up Operators; Engraver Set-Up Operators; Extruding and Forming Machine Operators and Tenders, Synthetic or Glass Fibers; Extruding and Forming Machine Setters, Operators, and Tenders, Synthetic and Glass Fibers; Extruding, Forming, Pressing, and Compacting Machine Operators and Tenders; Fabric and Apparel Patternmakers; Fiber Product Cutting Machine Setters and Set-Up Operators; Fiberglass Laminators and Fabricators; others. **PERSONALITY TYPE**—Realistic. Realistic occupations frequently involve work activities that include practical, hands-on problems and solutions. They often deal with plants, animals, and real-world materials like wood, tools, and machinery. Many of the occupations require working outside and do not involve a lot of paperwork or working closely with others.

**EDUCATION/TRAINING PROGRAM(S)**—Machine Shop Assistant; Marine Maintenance and Ship Repairer. **RELATED KNOWLEDGE/COURSES**—**Principles of Mechanical Devices:** Knowledge of machines and tools, including their designs, uses, repair, and maintenance. **Building and Construction:** Knowledge of materials, methods, and tools involved in the construction or repair of houses, buildings, or other structures such as highways and roads. **Design:** Knowledge of design techniques, tools, and principles involved in production of precision technical plans, blueprints, drawings, and models. **Production and Processing:** Knowledge of raw materials, production processes, quality control, costs, and other techniques for maximizing the effective manufacture and distribution of goods. **Engineering and Technology:** Knowledge of the practical application of engineering science and technology. This includes applying principles, techniques, procedures, and equipment to the design and production of various goods and services.

# Metal Molding, Coremaking, and Casting Machine Operators and Tenders

- ▲ Growth: 9.8%
- ▲ Annual Job Openings: 38,000
- ▲ Annual Earnings: $23,630
- ▲ Education/Training Required: Moderate-term on-the-job training
- ▲ Self-Employed: 0%
- ▲ Part-Time: 2.6%

**Operate or tend metal molding, casting, or coremaking machines to mold or cast metal products, such as pipes, brake drums, rods, and metal parts, such as automobile trim, carburetor housings, and motor parts. Machines include centrifugal casting machines, vacuum casting machines, turnover draw-type coremaking machines, conveyor-screw coremaking machines, and die casting machines.** Starts and operates furnace, oven, or diecasting, coremaking, metal molding, or rotating machines to pour metal or create molds and casts. Removes casting from mold, mold from press, or core from core box, using tongs, pliers, or hydraulic ram or by inversion. Pours or loads metal or sand into melting pot, furnace, mold, core box, or hopper, using shovel, ladle, or machine. Inspects metal casts and molds for cracks, bubbles, or other defects and measures castings to ensure specifications met. Cleans, glues, and racks cores, ingots, or finished products for storage. Cuts spouts and pouring holes in molds and sizes hardened cores, using saws. Signals or directs other workers to load conveyor, spray molds, or remove ingots. Requisitions molds and supplies and inventories and records finished products. Weighs metals and powders and computes amounts of materials necessary to produce mixture of specified content. Smoothes and cleans inner surface of mold, using brush, scraper, airhose, or grinding wheel, and fills imperfections with refractory material. Sprays, smokes, or coats molds with compounds to lubricate or insulate mold, using acetylene torches or sprayers. Skims or pours dross, slag, or impurities from molten metal, using ladle, rake, hoe, spatula, or spoon. Assembles shell halves, patterns, and foundry flasks and reinforces core boxes, using glue, clamps, wire, bolts, rams, or machines. Repairs or replaces damaged molds, pipes, belts, chains, or other equipment, using hand tools, hand-powered press, or jib crane. Fills core boxes and mold patterns with sand or powders, using ramming tools or pneumatic hammers, and removes excess. Observes and records data from pyrometers, lights, and gauges to monitor molding process and adjust furnace temperature. Positions, aligns, and secures molds or core boxes in holding devices or under pouring spouts and tubes, using hand tools. Positions ladles or pourers and adjusts controls to regulate the flow of metal, sand, or coolant into mold. **SKILLS**—Operation and Control. Operation Monitoring. Quality Control Analysis. Equipment Maintenance. Repairing.

**GOE—Interest Area:** 08. Industrial Production. **Work Group:** 08.02. Production Technology. **Other Job Titles in This Work Group:** Aircraft Rigging Assemblers; Aircraft Structure Assemblers, Precision; Aircraft Structure, Surfaces, Rigging, and Systems Assemblers; Aircraft Systems Assemblers, Precision; Bench Workers, Jewelry; Bindery Machine Setters and Set-Up Operators; Bindery Workers; Bookbinders; Buffing and Polishing Set-Up Operators; Casting Machine Set-Up Operators; Coating, Painting, and Spraying Machine Setters and Set-Up Operators; Coating, Painting, and Spraying Machine Setters, Operators, and Tenders; Combination Machine Tool Setters and Set-Up Operators, Metal and Plastic; Cutting, Punching, and Press Machine Setters, Operators, and Tenders, Metal and Plastic; Dental Laboratory Technicians; Drilling and Boring Machine Tool Setters, Operators, and Tenders, Metal and Plastic; Elec-

trical and Electronic Equipment Assemblers; Electrical and Electronic Inspectors and Testers; Electromechanical Equipment Assemblers; Engine and Other Machine Assemblers; Extruding and Drawing Machine Setters, Operators, and Tenders, Metal and Plastic; Extruding, Forming, Pressing, and Compacting Machine Setters and Set-Up Operators; Extruding, Forming, Pressing, and Compacting Machine Setters, Operators, and Tenders; Forging Machine Setters, Operators, and Tenders, Metal and Plastic; Foundry Mold and Coremakers; Gem and Diamond Workers; Grinding, Honing, Lapping, and Deburring Machine Set-Up Operators; Grinding, Lapping, Polishing, and Buffing Machine Tool Setters, Operators, and Tenders, Metal and Plastic; Heat Treating Equipment Setters, Operators, and Tenders, Metal and Plastic; others. **PERSONALITY TYPE**—Realistic. Realistic occupations frequently involve work activities that include practical, hands-on problems and solutions. They often deal with plants, animals, and real-world materials like wood, tools, and machinery. Many of the occupations require working outside and do not involve a lot of paperwork or working closely with others.

**EDUCATION/TRAINING PROGRAM(S)**—Aviation Systems and Avionics Maintenance Technologist/ Technician; Dental Laboratory Technician; Machinist/ Machine Technologist; Precision Metal Workers, Other. **RELATED KNOWLEDGE/COURSES—Principles of Mechanical Devices:** Knowledge of machines and tools, including their designs, uses, repair, and maintenance. **Production and Processing:** Knowledge of raw materials, production processes, quality control, costs, and other techniques for maximizing the effective manufacture and distribution of goods. **Building and Construction:** Knowledge of materials, methods, and tools involved in the construction or repair of houses, buildings, or other structures such as highways and roads. **Mathematics:** Knowledge of arithmetic, algebra, geometry, calculus, statistics, and their applications. **Engineering and Technology:** Knowledge of the practical application of engineering science and technology. This includes applying principles, techniques, procedures, and equipment to the design and production of various goods and services.

# Metal Molding, Coremaking, and Casting Machine Setters and Set-Up Operators

▲ Growth: 9.8%
▲ Annual Job Openings: 38,000
▲ Annual Earnings: $23,630
▲ Education/Training Required: Moderate-term on-the-job training
▲ Self-Employed: 0%
▲ Part-Time: 2.6%

Set up or set up and operate metal casting, molding, and coremaking machines to mold or cast metal parts and products, such as tubes, rods, automobile trim, carburetor housings, and motor parts. Machines include die casting and continuous casting machines and roll-over, squeeze, and shell molding machines. Moves controls to start, set, or adjust casting, molding, or pressing machines. Cleans and lubricates casting machine and dies, using airhose and brushes. Inspects castings and core slots for defects, using fixed gauges. Repairs or replaces worn or defective machine parts and dies. Obtains and moves specified pattern to work station, manually or using hoist, and secures pattern to machine, using wrenches. Removes castings from dies and dips castings in water to cool, using pliers or tongs. Preheats die sections with torch or electric heater. Pours molten metal into cold-chamber machine or cylinders, using hand ladle. Connects water hose to cooling system of die, using hand tools. Loads metal ingots or aluminum bars into melting furnace and transfers molten metal to reservoir of die casting machine. Stacks and mounts rotor core laminations over keyed mandrel of casting machine and removes and stamps rotor with identifying data. Lines cylinder pot with asbestos strips and disk to prevent chilling. Loads die sections into machine, using equipment such as chain fall or hoist, and secures in position, using hand tools. **SKILLS**—Equipment Selection. Operation Monitoring. Operation and Control. Equipment Maintenance. Quality Control Analysis.

**GOE—Interest Area:** 08. Industrial Production. **Work Group:** 08.02. Production Technology. **Other Job Titles in This Work Group:** Aircraft Rigging Assemblers; Aircraft Structure Assemblers, Precision; Aircraft Structure, Surfaces, Rigging, and Systems Assemblers; Aircraft Systems Assemblers, Precision; Bench Workers, Jewelry; Bindery Machine Setters and Set-Up Operators; Bindery Workers; Bookbinders; Buffing and Polishing Set-Up Operators; Casting Machine Set-Up Operators; Coating, Painting, and Spraying Machine Setters and Set-Up Operators; Coating, Painting, and Spraying Machine Setters, Operators, and Tenders; Combination Machine Tool Setters and Set-Up Operators, Metal and Plastic; Cutting, Punching, and Press Machine Setters, Operators, and Tenders, Metal and Plastic; Dental Laboratory Technicians; Drilling and Boring Machine Tool Setters, Operators, and Tenders, Metal and Plastic; Electrical and Electronic Equipment Assemblers; Electrical and Electronic Inspectors and Testers; Electromechanical Equipment Assemblers; Engine and Other Machine Assemblers; Extruding and Drawing Machine Setters, Operators, and Tenders, Metal and Plastic; Extruding, Forming, Pressing, and Compacting Machine Setters and Set-Up Operators; Extruding, Forming, Pressing, and Compacting Machine Setters, Operators, and Tenders; Forging Machine Setters, Operators, and Tenders, Metal and Plastic; Foundry Mold and Coremakers; Gem and Diamond Workers; Grinding, Honing, Lapping, and Deburring Machine Set-Up Operators; Grinding, Lapping, Polishing, and Buffing Machine Tool Setters, Operators, and Tenders, Metal and Plastic; Heat Treating Equipment Setters, Operators, and Tenders, Metal and Plastic; others. **PERSONALITY TYPE**—Realistic. Realistic occupations frequently involve work activities that include practical, hands-on problems and solutions. They often deal with plants, animals, and real-world materials like wood, tools, and machinery. Many of the occupations require working outside and do not involve a lot of paperwork or working closely with others.

EDUCATION/TRAINING PROGRAM(S)—Aviation Systems and Avionics Maintenance Technologist/Technician; Dental Laboratory Technician; Machinist/Machine Technologist; Precision Metal Workers, Other. RELATED KNOWLEDGE/COURSES—**Production and Processing:** Knowledge of raw materials, production processes, quality control, costs, and other techniques for maximizing the effective manufacture and distribution of goods. **Principles of Mechanical Devices:** Knowledge of machines and tools, including their designs, uses, repair, and maintenance. **Engineering and Technology:** Knowledge of the practical application of engineering science and technology. This includes applying principles, techniques, procedures, and equipment to the design and production of various goods and services. **Physics:** Knowledge and prediction of physical principles and laws and their interrelationships and applications to understanding fluid, material, and atmospheric dynamics and mechanical, electrical, atomic, and sub-atomic structures and processes.

# Mobile Heavy Equipment Mechanics, Except Engines

- ▲ Growth: 14%
- ▲ Annual Job Openings: 11,000
- ▲ Annual Earnings: $34,790
- ▲ Education/Training Required: Post-secondary vocational training
- ▲ Self-Employed: 3.6%
- ▲ Part-Time: 2.4%

**Diagnose, adjust, repair, or overhaul mobile mechanical, hydraulic, and pneumatic equipment, such as cranes, bulldozers, graders, and conveyors, used in construction, logging, and surface mining.** Repairs and replaces damaged or worn parts. Adjusts, maintains, and repairs or replaces engines and subassemblies, including transmissions and crawler heads, using hand tools, jacks, and cranes. Dismantles and reassembles heavy equipment, using hoists and hand tools. Overhauls and tests machines or equipment to ensure operating efficiency. Examines parts for damage or excessive wear, using micrometers and gauges. Operates and inspects machines or heavy equipment to diagnose defects. Welds or cuts metal and welds broken parts and structural members, using electric or gas welder. Immerses parts in tanks of solvent or sprays parts with grease solvent to clean parts. Directs workers engaged in cleaning parts and assisting with assembly or disassembly of equipment. **SKILLS**—Repairing. Equipment Maintenance. Troubleshooting. Quality Control Analysis. Operation and Control.

**GOE—Interest Area:** 05. Mechanics, Installers, and Repairers. **Work Group:** 05.03. Mechanical Work. **Other Job Titles in This Work Group:** Aircraft Body and Bonded Structure Repairers; Aircraft Engine Specialists; Aircraft Mechanics and Service Technicians; Airframe-and-Power-Plant Mechanics; Automotive Body and Related Repairers; Automotive Glass Installers and Repairers; Automotive Master Mechanics; Automotive Service Technicians and Mechanics; Automotive Specialty Technicians; Bicycle Repairers; Bridge and Lock Tenders; Bus and Truck Mechanics and Diesel Engine Specialists; Camera and Photographic Equipment Repairers; Coin, Vending, and Amusement Machine Servicers and Repairers; Control and Valve Installers and Repairers, Except Mechanical Door; Farm Equipment Mechanics; Gas Appliance Repairers; Hand and Portable Power Tool Repairers; Heating and Air Conditioning Mechanics; Heating, Air Conditioning, and Refrigeration Mechanics and Installers; Helpers—Electricians; Helpers—Installation, Maintenance, and Repair Workers; Industrial Machinery Mechanics; Keyboard Instrument Repairers and Tuners; Locksmiths and Safe Repairers; Maintenance and Repair Workers, General; Maintenance Workers, Machinery; Mechanical Door Repairers; Medical Appliance Technicians; Medical Equipment Repairers; Meter Mechanics; Millwrights; Motorboat Mechanics; Motorcycle Mechanics; Musical Instrument Repairers and Tuners; Ophthalmic

Laboratory Technicians; Optical Instrument Assemblers; Outdoor Power Equipment and Other Small Engine Mechanics; Painters, Transportation Equipment; Percussion Instrument Repairers and Tuners; Precision Instrument and Equipment Repairers, All Other; others. **PERSONALITY TYPE**—Realistic. Realistic occupations frequently involve work activities that include practical, hands-on problems and solutions. They often deal with plants, animals, and real-world materials like wood, tools, and machinery. Many of the occupations require working outside and do not involve a lot of paperwork or working closely with others.

**EDUCATION/TRAINING PROGRAM(S)**—Heavy Equipment Maintenance and Repairer. **RELATED KNOWLEDGE/COURSES**—**Principles of Mechanical Devices:** Knowledge of machines and tools, including their designs, uses, repair, and maintenance. **Engineering and Technology:** Knowledge of the practical application of engineering science and technology. This includes applying principles, techniques, procedures, and equipment to the design and production of various goods and services. **English Language:** Knowledge of the structure and content of the English language, including the meaning and spelling of words, rules of composition, and grammar. **Production and Processing:** Knowledge of raw materials, production processes, quality control, costs, and other techniques for maximizing the effective manufacture and distribution of goods. **Physics:** Knowledge and prediction of physical principles and laws and their interrelationships and applications to understanding fluid, material, and atmospheric dynamics and mechanical, electrical, atomic, and sub-atomic structures and processes.

# Motor Vehicle Inspectors

▲ Growth: 11.3%

▲ Annual Job Openings: 3,000

▲ Annual Earnings: $44,200

▲ Education/Training Required: Work experience in a related occupation

▲ Self-Employed: 9%

▲ Part-Time: 5.5%

**Inspect automotive vehicles to ensure compliance with governmental regulations and safety standards.** Inspects truck accessories, air lines, and electric circuits, and reports needed repairs. Examines vehicles for damage and drives vehicles to detect malfunctions. Tests vehicle components for wear, damage, or improper adjustment, using mechanical or electrical devices. Applies inspection sticker to vehicles that pass inspection and rejection sticker to vehicles that fail. Prepares report on each vehicle for follow-up action by owner or police. Prepares and keeps record of vehicles delivered. Positions trailer and drives car onto truck trailer. Notifies authorities of owners having illegal equipment installed on vehicle. Services vehicles with fuel and water. **SKILLS**—Quality Control Analysis. Troubleshooting. Science. Writing. Reading Comprehension.

**GOE—Interest Area:** 08. Industrial Production. **Work Group:** 08.02. Production Technology. **Other Job Titles in This Work Group:** Aircraft Rigging Assemblers; Aircraft Structure Assemblers, Precision; Aircraft Structure, Surfaces, Rigging, and Systems Assemblers; Aircraft Systems Assemblers, Precision; Bench Workers, Jewelry; Bindery Machine Setters and Set-Up Operators; Bindery Workers; Bookbinders; Buffing and Polishing Set-Up Operators; Casting Machine Set-Up Operators; Coating, Painting, and Spraying Machine Setters and Set-Up Operators; Coating, Painting, and Spraying Machine Setters, Operators, and Tenders; Combination Machine Tool Setters and Set-Up Operators, Metal and Plastic; Cutting, Punching, and Press Machine Setters, Operators, and Tenders, Metal and Plastic; Dental Laboratory Technicians; Drilling and Boring Machine Tool Setters, Operators, and Tenders, Metal and Plastic; Electrical and Electronic Equipment Assemblers; Electrical and Electronic Inspectors and Testers; Electromechanical Equipment Assemblers; Engine and Other Machine Assemblers;

Extruding and Drawing Machine Setters, Operators, and Tenders, Metal and Plastic; Extruding, Forming, Pressing, and Compacting Machine Setters and Set-Up Operators; Extruding, Forming, Pressing, and Compacting Machine Setters, Operators, and Tenders; Forging Machine Setters, Operators, and Tenders, Metal and Plastic; Foundry Mold and Coremakers; Gem and Diamond Workers; Grinding, Honing, Lapping, and Deburring Machine Set-Up Operators; Grinding, Lapping, Polishing, and Buffing Machine Tool Setters, Operators, and Tenders, Metal and Plastic; Heat Treating Equipment Setters, Operators, and Tenders, Metal and Plastic; others. **PERSONALITY TYPE**—Realistic. Realistic occupations frequently involve work activities that include practical, hands-on problems and solutions. They often deal with plants, animals, and real-world materials like wood, tools, and machinery. Many of the occupations require working outside and do not involve a lot of paperwork or working closely with others.

**EDUCATION/TRAINING PROGRAM(S)**—Operations Management and Supervision. **RELATED KNOWLEDGE/COURSES**—**Public Safety and Security:** Knowledge of relevant equipment, policies, procedures, and strategies to promote effective local, state, or national security operations for the protection of people, data, property, and institutions. **Principles of Mechanical Devices:** Knowledge of machines and tools, including their designs, uses, repair, and maintenance. **English Language:** Knowledge of the structure and content of the English language, including the meaning and spelling of words, rules of composition, and grammar. **Transportation:** Knowledge of principles and methods for moving people or goods by air, rail, sea, or road, including the relative costs and benefits. **Computers and Electronics:** Knowledge of circuit boards, processors, chips, electronic equipment, and computer hardware and software, including applications and programming.

# Municipal Clerks

- ▲ Growth: 12%
- ▲ Annual Job Openings: 14,000
- ▲ Annual Earnings: $27,780
- ▲ Education/Training Required: Short-term on-the-job training
- ▲ Self-Employed: 0%
- ▲ Part-Time: 16%

**Draft agendas and bylaws for town or city council, record minutes of council meetings, answer official correspondence, keep fiscal records and accounts, and prepare reports on civic needs.** Prepares agendas and bylaws for town council. Prepares reports on civic needs. Keeps fiscal records and accounts. Records minutes of council meetings. Answers official correspondence. **SKILLS**—Writing. Active Listening. Reading Comprehension. Critical Thinking. Mathematics.

**GOE—Interest Area:** 09. Business Detail. **Work Group:** 09.02. Administrative Detail. **Other Job Titles in This Work Group:** Claims Takers, Unemployment Benefits; Court Clerks; Court, Municipal, and License Clerks; Eligibility Interviewers, Government Programs; Executive Secretaries and Administrative Assistants; Interviewers, Except Eligibility and Loan; Legal Secretaries; License Clerks; Loan Interviewers and Clerks; Medical Secretaries; Secretaries, Except Legal, Medical, and Executive; Welfare Eligibility Workers and Interviewers. **PERSONALITY TYPE**—Conventional. Conventional occupations frequently involve following set procedures and routines. These occupations can include working with data and details more than with ideas. Usually there is a clear line of authority to follow.

**EDUCATION/TRAINING PROGRAM(S)**—General Office/Clerical and Typing Services. **RELATED KNOWLEDGE/COURSES**—**Clerical Studies:** Knowledge of administrative and clerical procedures and systems such as word processing, managing files and records, stenography and transcription, designing forms, and other office procedures and terminology. **Economics and Accounting:** Knowledge of economic and accounting principles and practices, the financial markets, banking, and the analysis and reporting of financial data. **English Language:** Knowledge of the structure and content of the English language, including the meaning and spelling of words, rules of composition, and grammar. **Mathematics:** Knowledge of arithmetic, algebra, geometry, calculus, statistics, and their applications. **Administration and Management:** Knowledge of business and management principles involved in strategic planning, resource allocation, human resources modeling, leadership technique, production methods, and coordination of people and resources.

# Municipal Fire Fighters

- ▲ Growth: 8.9%
- ▲ Annual Job Openings: 12,000
- ▲ Annual Earnings: $35,260
- ▲ Education/Training Required: Long-term on-the-job training
- ▲ Self-Employed: 0%
- ▲ Part-Time: 2%

**Control and extinguish municipal fires, protect life and property, and conduct rescue efforts.** Positions and climbs ladders to gain access to upper levels of buildings or to rescue individuals from burning structures. Assesses fire and situation, reports to superior, and receives instructions, using two-way radio. Inspects buildings for fire hazards and compliance with fire prevention ordinances. Participates in courses in hydraulics, pump operation, and firefighting techniques. Participates in fire drills and demonstrations of firefighting techniques. Maintains firefighting equipment and apparatus, vehicles, hydrants, and fire station. Drives and operates firefighting vehicles and equipment. Establishes firelines to prevent unauthorized persons from entering area. Responds to fire alarms and other emergency calls. Creates openings in buildings for ventilation or entrance using ax, chisel, crowbar, electric saw, or core cutter. Protects property from water and smoke, using waterproof salvage covers, smoke ejectors, and deodorants. Administers first aid and cardiopulmonary resuscitation to injured persons and those overcome by fire and smoke. Sprays foam onto runway, extinguishes fire, and rescues aircraft crew and passengers in air-crash emergency. Selects hose nozzle, depending on type of fire, and directs stream of water or chemicals onto fire. **SKILLS**—Service Orientation. Coordination. Critical Thinking. Judgment and Decision Making. Active Listening.

**GOE—Interest Area:** 04. Law, Law Enforcement, and Public Safety. **Work Group:** 04.04. Public Safety. **Other Job Titles in This Work Group:** Agricultural Inspectors; Aviation Inspectors; Compliance Officers, Except Agriculture, Construction, Health and Safety, and Transportation; Emergency Medical Technicians and Paramedics; Environmental Compliance Inspectors; Equal Opportunity Representatives and Officers; Financial Examiners; Fire Fighters; Fire Inspectors; Fire Inspectors and Investigators; Forest Fire Fighters; Forest Fire Inspectors and Prevention Specialists; Government Property Inspectors and Investigators; Licensing Examiners and Inspectors; Marine Cargo Inspectors; Nuclear Monitoring Technicians; Occupational Health and Safety Specialists; Occupational Health and Safety Technicians; Public Transportation Inspectors. **PERSONALITY TYPE**—Realistic. Realistic occupations frequently involve work activities that include practical, hands-on problems and solutions. They often deal with plants, animals, and real-world materials like wood, tools, and machinery. Many of the occupations require working outside and do not involve a lot of paperwork or working closely with others.

**EDUCATION/TRAINING PROGRAM(S)**—Fire Protection, Other; Fire Science/Firefighting. **RELATED KNOWLEDGE/COURSES**—**Public Safety and Security:** Knowledge of relevant equipment, policies, procedures, and strategies to promote effective local, state, or national security operations for the protection of people, data, property, and institutions. **Medicine and Dentistry:** Knowledge of the information and techniques needed to diagnose and treat human injuries, diseases, and deformities. This includes symptoms, treatment alternatives, drug properties and interactions, and preventive health-care measures. **Transportation:** Knowledge of principles and methods for moving people or goods by air, rail, sea, or road, including the relative costs and benefits. **Therapy and Counseling:** Knowledge of principles, methods, and procedures for diagnosis, treatment, and rehabilitation of physical and mental dysfunctions and for career counseling and guidance. **Principles of Mechanical Devices:** Knowledge of machines and tools, including their designs, uses, repair, and maintenance.

# Municipal Fire Fighting and Prevention Supervisors

- ▲ Growth: 7.2%
- ▲ Annual Job Openings: 5,000
- ▲ Annual Earnings: $52,990
- ▲ Education/Training Required: Work experience in a related occupation
- ▲ Self-Employed: 0%
- ▲ Part-Time: 2.1%

**Supervise fire fighters who control and extinguish municipal fires, protect life and property, and conduct rescue efforts.** Coordinates and supervises firefighting and rescue activities and reports events to supervisor, using two-way radio. Assesses nature and extent of fire, condition of building, danger to adjacent buildings, and water supply to determine crew or company requirements. Directs investigation of cases of suspected arson, hazards, and false alarms. Inspects fire stations, equipment, and records to ensure efficiency and enforcement of departmental regulations. Directs building inspections to ensure compliance with fire and safety regulations. Trains subordinates in use of equipment, methods of extinguishing fires, and rescue operations. Evaluates efficiency and performance of employees and recommends awards for service. Keeps equipment and personnel records. Compiles report of fire call, listing location, type, probable cause, estimated damage, and disposition. Studies and interprets fire safety codes to establish procedures for issuing permits regulating storage or use of hazardous or flammable substances. Writes and submits proposal for new equipment or modification of existing equipment. Orders and directs fire drills for occupants of buildings. Oversees review of new building plans to ensure compliance with laws, ordinances, and administrative rules for pub-lic fire safety. Confers with civic representatives and plans talks and demonstrations of fire safety to direct fire prevention information program. **SKILLS**—Coordination. Active Listening. Service Orientation. Reading Comprehension. Management of Personnel Resources. Critical Thinking. Judgment and Decision Making.

**GOE—Interest Area:** 04. Law, Law Enforcement, and Public Safety. **Work Group:** 04.01. Managerial Work in Law, Law Enforcement, and Public Safety. **Other Job Titles in This Work Group:** Emergency Management Specialists; First-Line Supervisors/Managers of Correctional Officers; First-Line Supervisors/Managers of Fire Fighting and Prevention Workers; First-Line Supervisors/Managers of Police and Detectives; First-Line Supervisors/Managers, Protective Service Workers, All Other; Forest Fire Fighting and Prevention Supervisors. **PERSONALITY TYPE**—Realistic. Realistic occupations frequently involve work activities that include practical, hands-on problems and solutions. They often deal with plants, animals, and real-world materials like wood, tools, and machinery. Many of the occupations require working outside and do not involve a lot of paperwork or working closely with others.

**EDUCATION/TRAINING PROGRAM(S)**—Fire Protection and Safety Technologist/Technician; Fire

Services Administration. **RELATED KNOWLEDGE/ COURSES—Public Safety and Security:** Knowledge of relevant equipment, policies, procedures, and strategies to promote effective local, state, or national security operations for the protection of people, data, property, and institutions. **Education and Training:** Knowledge of principles and methods for curriculum and training design, teaching and instruction for individuals and groups, and the measurement of training effects. **Principles of Mechanical Devices:** Knowledge of machines and tools, including their designs, uses, repair, and maintenance. **Personnel and Human Resources:** Knowledge of principles and procedures for personnel recruitment, selection, training, compensation and benefits, labor relations and negotiation, and personnel information systems. **Administration and Management:** Knowledge of business and management principles involved in strategic planning, resource allocation, human resources modeling, leadership technique, production methods, and coordination of people and resources. **Transportation:** Knowledge of principles and methods for moving people or goods by air, rail, sea, or road, including the relative costs and benefits.

# Musicians, Instrumental

- ▲ Growth: 20.1%
- ▲ Annual Job Openings: 33,000
- ▲ Annual Earnings: $44,520
- ▲ Education/Training Required: Long-term on-the-job training
- ▲ Self-Employed: 45.4%
- ▲ Part-Time: 53.5%

**Play one or more musical instruments in recital, in accompaniment, or as members of an orchestra, band, or other musical group.** Plays musical instrument as soloist or as member of musical group, such as orchestra or band, to entertain audience. Practices performance on musical instrument to maintain and improve skills. Transposes music to play in alternate key or to fit individual style or purposes. Directs band/orchestra. Teaches music for specific instruments. Composes new musical scores. Memorizes musical scores. Improvises music during performance. Plays from memory or by following score. Studies and rehearses music to learn and interpret score. **SKILLS—Coordination.** Active Learning. Instructing. Monitoring. Learning Strategies.

**GOE—Interest Area:** 01. Arts, Entertainment, and Media. **Work Group:** 01.05. Performing Arts. **Other Job Titles in This Work Group:** Actors; Choreographers; Composers; Dancers; Directors—Stage, Motion Pictures, Television, and Radio; Music Arrangers and Orchestrators; Music Directors; Music Directors and Composers; Musicians and Singers; Public Address System and Other Announcers; Radio and Television Announcers; Singers; Talent Directors. **PERSONALITY TYPE—Artistic.** Artistic occupations frequently involve working with forms, designs, and patterns. They often require self-expression, and the work can be done without following a clear set of rules.

**EDUCATION/TRAINING PROGRAM(S)—Music - General Performance; Music - Piano and Organ Performance; Music - Voice and Choral/Opera Performance; Music, General; Music, Other. RELATED KNOWLEDGE/COURSES—Fine Arts:** Knowledge of the theory and techniques required to compose, produce, and perform works of music, dance, visual arts, drama, and sculpture. **Education and Training:** Knowledge of principles and methods for curriculum and training design, teaching and instruction for individuals and groups, and the measurement of training effects. **Mathematics:** Knowledge of arithmetic, algebra, geometry, calculus, statistics, and their applications. **English Language:** Knowledge of the structure and content of the English language, including the meaning and spelling of words, rules of composition, and grammar. **Psychology:** Knowledge of human behavior and performance;

individual differences in ability, personality, and interests; learning and motivation; psychological research methods; and the assessment and treatment of behavioral and affective disorders.

# Nonfarm Animal Caretakers

▲ Growth: 21.6%

▲ Annual Job Openings: 20,000

▲ Annual Earnings: $17,600

▲ Education/Training Required: Short-term on-the-job training

▲ Self-Employed: 28.6%

▲ Part-Time: 38.1%

Feed, water, groom, bathe, exercise, or otherwise care for pets and other nonfarm animals, such as dogs, cats, ornamental fish or birds, zoo animals, and mice. Work in settings such as kennels, animal shelters, zoos, circuses, and aquariums. May keep records of feedings, treatments, and animals received or discharged. May clean, disinfect, and repair cages, pens, or fish tanks. Feeds and waters animal according to schedules and feeding instructions. Mixes food, liquid formulas, medications, or food supplements according to instructions, prescriptions, and knowledge of animal species. Adjusts controls to regulate specified temperature and humidity of animal quarters, nursery, or exhibit area. Cleans and disinfects animal quarters, such as pens, stables, cages, and yards, and surgical or other equipment, such as saddles and bridles. Washes, brushes, clips, trims, and grooms animals. Examines and observes animals for signs of illness, disease, or injury and provides treatment or informs veterinarian. Exercises animals to maintain their fitness and health or trains animals to perform certain tasks. Anesthetizes and inoculates animals according to instructions. Repairs fences, cages, or pens. Installs equipment in animal care facility, such as infrared lights, feeding devices, or cribs. Observes and cautions children petting and feeding animals in designated area. Responds to questions from patrons and provides information about animals, such as behavior, habitat, breeding habits, or facility activities. Saddles and shoes animals. Orders, unloads, and stores feed and supplies. Records information about animals, such as weight, size, physical condition, diet, medications, and food intake. Transfers animals between enclosures for breeding, birthing, shipping, or rearranging exhibits. **SKILLS**—Service Orientation. Mathematics. Active Listening. Speaking. Equipment Maintenance. Equipment Selection.

**GOE—Interest Area:** 03. Plants and Animals. **Work Group:** 03.02. Animal Care and Training. **Other Job Titles in This Work Group:** Animal Breeders; Animal Trainers; Veterinarians; Veterinary Assistants and Laboratory Animal Caretakers; Veterinary Technologists and Technicians. **PERSONALITY TYPE**—Realistic. Realistic occupations frequently involve work activities that include practical, hands-on problems and solutions. They often deal with plants, animals, and real-world materials like wood, tools, and machinery. Many of the occupations require working outside and do not involve a lot of paperwork or working closely with others.

**EDUCATION/TRAINING PROGRAM(S)**—Agricultural Supplies Retailing and Wholesaling. **RELATED KNOWLEDGE/COURSES**—**Biology:** Knowledge of plant and animal organisms and their tissues, cells, functions, interdependencies, and interactions with each other and the environment. **Medicine and Dentistry:** Knowledge of the information and techniques needed to diagnose and treat human injuries, diseases, and deformities. This includes symptoms, treatment alternatives, drug properties and interactions, and preventive health-care measures. **Building and Construction:** Knowledge of materials, methods, and tools involved in the construction or repair of houses, buildings, or other structures such as highways and roads. **Principles of Mechanical Devices:** Knowledge of machines and tools, including their designs, uses, repair, and maintenance. **English Language:** Knowledge of the structure and content of the English language, including the meaning and spelling of words, rules of composition, and grammar.

# Nuclear Equipment Operation Technicians

- ▲ Growth: 20.7%
- ▲ Annual Job Openings: Fewer than 500
- ▲ Annual Earnings: $61,970
- ▲ Education/Training Required: Associate's degree
- ▲ Self-Employed: 0%
- ▲ Part-Time: 11.7%

**Operate equipment used for the release, control, and utilization of nuclear energy to assist scientists in laboratory and production activities.** Sets control panel switches and activates equipment, such as nuclear reactor, particle accelerator, or gamma radiation equipment, according to specifications. Adjusts controls of equipment to control particle beam, chain reaction, or radiation according to specifications. Installs instrumentation leads in reactor core to measure operating temperature and pressure according to mockups, blueprints, and diagrams. Controls laboratory compounding equipment enclosed in protective hot cell to prepare radioisotopes and other radioactive materials. Sets up and operates machines to saw fuel elements to size or to cut and polish test pieces, following blueprints and other specifications. Tests physical, chemical, or metallurgical properties of experimental materials according to standardized procedures, using test equipment and measuring instruments. Modifies, devises, and maintains equipment used in operations. Disassembles, cleans, and decontaminates hot cells and reactor parts during maintenance shutdown, using slave manipulators, crane, and hand tools. Writes summary of activities or records experiment data in log for further analysis by engineers, scientists, or customers or for future reference. Communicates with maintenance personnel to ensure readiness of support systems and to warn of radiation hazards. Withdraws radioactive sample for analysis, fills container with prescribed quantity of material for shipment, or removes spent fuel elements. Transfers experimental materials to and from specified containers and to tube, chamber, or tunnel, using slave manipulators or extension tools. Positions fuel elements in reactor or environmental chamber according to specified configuration, using slave manipulators or extension tools. Reviews experiment schedule to determine specifications, such as subatomic particle parameters, radiation time, dosage, and gamma intensity. Monitors instruments, gauges, and recording devices in control room during operation of equipment under direction of nuclear experimenter. Calculates equipment operating factors, such as radiation time, dosage, temperature, and pressure, using standard formulas and conversion tables. **SKILLS**—Mathematics. Science. Installation. Operation and Control. Reading Comprehension.

**GOE—Interest Area:** 02. Science, Math, and Engineering. **Work Group:** 02.05. Laboratory Technology. **Other Job Titles in This Work Group:** Biological Technicians; Chemical Technicians; Environmental Science and Protection Technicians, Including Health; Geological and Petroleum Technicians; Geological Data Technicians; Geological Sample Test Technicians; Nuclear Technicians; Photographers, Scientific. **PERSONALITY TYPE**—Realistic. Realistic occupations frequently involve work activities that include practical, hands-on problems and solutions. They often deal with plants, animals, and real-world materials like wood, tools, and machinery. Many of the occupations require working outside and do not involve a lot of paperwork or working closely with others.

**EDUCATION/TRAINING PROGRAM(S)**—Industrial Radiologic Technologist/Technician; Nuclear and Industrial Radiologic Technologists/Technicians, Other; Nuclear/Nuclear Power Technologist/Technician. **RELATED KNOWLEDGE/COURSES—Engineering**

and Technology: Knowledge of the practical application of engineering science and technology. This includes applying principles, techniques, procedures, and equipment to the design and production of various goods and services. Physics: Knowledge and prediction of physical principles and laws and their interrelationships and applications to understanding fluid, material, and atmospheric dynamics and mechanical, electrical, atomic, and sub-atomic structures and processes. Public Safety and Security: Knowledge of relevant equipment, policies, procedures, and strategies to promote effective local, state, or national security operations for the protection of people, data, property, and institutions. Mathematics: Knowledge of arithmetic, algebra, geometry, calculus, statistics, and their applications. Chemistry: Knowledge of the chemical composition, structure, and properties of substances and of the chemical processes and transformations that they undergo. This includes uses of chemicals and their interactions, danger signs, production techniques, and disposal methods.

# Nuclear Medicine Technologists

▲ Growth: 22.4%
▲ Annual Job Openings: 1,000
▲ Annual Earnings: $44,850
▲ Education/Training Required: Associate's degree
▲ Self-Employed: 0%
▲ Part-Time: 17.5%

**Prepare, administer, and measure radioactive isotopes in therapeutic, diagnostic, and tracer studies utilizing a variety of radioisotope equipment. Prepare stock solutions of radioactive materials and calculate doses to be administered by radiologists. Subject patients to radiation. Execute blood volume, red cell survival, and fat absorption studies following standard laboratory techniques.** Administers radiopharmaceuticals or radiation to patient to detect or treat diseases, using radio-isotope equipment, under direction of physician. Measures glandular activity, blood volume, red cell survival, and radioactivity of patient, using scanners, Geiger counters, scintillometers, and other laboratory equipment. Maintains and calibrates radioisotope and laboratory equipment. Disposes of radioactive materials and stores radiopharmaceuticals, following radiation safety procedures. Develops treatment procedures for nuclear medicine treatment programs. Positions radiation fields, radiation beams, and patient to develop most effective treatment of patient's disease, using computer. Calculates, measures, prepares, and records radiation dosage or radiopharmaceuticals, using computer and following physician's prescription and X rays. **SKILLS—** Reading Comprehension. Mathematics. Instructing. Science. Speaking. Active Listening.

GOE—Interest Area: 14. Medical and Health Services. Work Group: 14.05. Medical Technology. Other Job Titles in This Work Group: Cardiovascular Technologists and Technicians; Diagnostic Medical Sonographers; Health Technologists and Technicians, All Other; Medical and Clinical Laboratory Technicians; Medical and Clinical Laboratory Technologists; Medical Equipment Preparers; Orthotists and Prosthetists; Radiologic Technicians; Radiologic Technologists; Radiologic Technologists and Technicians. PERSONALITY TYPE—Investigative. Investigative occupations frequently involve working with ideas and require an extensive amount of thinking. These occupations can involve searching for facts and figuring out problems mentally.

EDUCATION/TRAINING PROGRAM(S)— Nuclear Medical Technologist/Technician. RELATED KNOWLEDGE/COURSES—Medicine and Dentistry: Knowledge of the information and techniques needed to diagnose and treat human injuries, diseases, and deformities. This includes symptoms, treatment alternatives, drug properties and interactions, and preventive health-care measures. Biology: Knowledge of plant and animal organisms and their tissues, cells, functions, interdependencies, and interactions with each other and the environment. **Computers and Electronics:** Knowledge of circuit boards, processors, chips, electronic equipment, and computer hardware and software, including applications and programming. **Mathematics:** Knowledge of arithmetic, algebra, geometry, calculus, statistics, and their applications. **Chemistry:** Knowledge of the chemical composition, structure, and properties of substances and of the chemical processes and transformations that they undergo. This includes uses of chemicals and their interactions, danger signs, production techniques, and disposal methods.

# Nuclear Monitoring Technicians

▲ Growth: 20.7%

▲ Annual Job Openings: Fewer than 500

▲ Annual Earnings: $61,970

▲ Education/Training Required: Associate's degree

▲ Self-Employed: 0%

▲ Part-Time: 11.7%

**Collect and test samples to monitor results of nuclear experiments and contamination of humans, facilities, and environment.** Measures intensity and identifies type of radiation in work areas, equipment, and materials, using radiation detectors and other instruments. Calculates safe radiation exposure time for personnel, using plant contamination readings and prescribed safe levels of radiation. Scans photographic emulsions exposed to direct radiation to compute track properties from standard formulas, using microscope with scales and protractors. Calibrates and maintains chemical instrumentation sensing elements and sampling system equipment, using calibrations instruments and hand tools. Prepares reports on contamination tests, material and equipment decontaminated, and methods used in decontamination process. Instructs personnel in radiation safety procedures and demonstrates use of protective clothing and equipment. Places radioactive waste, such as sweepings and broken sample bottles, into containers for disposal. Decontaminates objects by cleaning with soap or solvents or by abrading, using wire brush, buffing wheel, or sandblasting machine. Enters data into computer to record characteristics of nuclear events and locating coordinates of particles. Weighs and mixes decontamination chemical solutions in tank and immerses objects in solution for specified time, using hoist. Determines or recommends radioactive decontamination procedures according to size and nature of equipment and degree of contamination. Confers with scientist directing project to determine significant events to watch for during test. Informs supervisors to take action when individual exposures or area radiation levels approach maximum permissible limits. Monitors personnel for length and intensity of exposure to radiation for health and safety purposes. Observes projected photographs to locate particle tracks and events and compiles lists of events from particle detectors. Assists in setting up equipment that automatically detects area radiation deviations and tests detection equipment to ensure accuracy. Collects samples of air, water, gases, and solids to determine radioactivity levels of contamination. **SKILLS**—Science. Mathematics. Reading Comprehension. Speaking. Operation Monitoring. Critical Thinking. Writing.

**GOE—Interest Area:** 04. Law, Law Enforcement, and Public Safety. **Work Group:** 04.04. Public Safety. **Other Job Titles in This Work Group:** Agricultural Inspectors; Aviation Inspectors; Compliance Officers, Except Agriculture, Construction, Health and Safety, and Transportation; Emergency Medical Technicians and Paramedics; Environmental Compliance Inspectors; Equal Opportunity Representatives and Officers; Financial Examiners; Fire Fighters; Fire Inspectors; Fire Inspectors and Investigators; Forest Fire Fighters; Forest Fire Inspectors and Prevention Specialists; Government Property Inspectors and Investigators; Licensing Examiners and Inspectors; Marine Cargo Inspectors; Municipal Fire Fighters; Occupational Health and Safety Specialists; Occupational Health and Safety Technicians; Public Transportation Inspectors. **PERSONALITY TYPE**—Realistic. Realistic occupations frequently involve work activities that include practical, hands-on problems and solutions. They often deal with plants, animals, and real-world materials like wood, tools, and machinery. Many of the occupations require working outside and do not involve a lot of paperwork or working closely with others.

**EDUCATION/TRAINING PROGRAM(S)**—Industrial Radiologic Technologist/Technician; Nuclear and Industrial Radiologic Technologists/Technicians, Other; Nuclear/Nuclear Power Technologist/Technician. **RELATED KNOWLEDGE/COURSES**—**Physics:** Knowledge and prediction of physical principles and laws and their interrelationships and applications to understanding fluid, material, and atmospheric dynamics and mechanical, electrical, atomic, and sub-atomic structures and processes. **Mathematics:** Knowledge of arithmetic, algebra, geometry, calculus, statistics, and their applications. **Public Safety and Security:** Knowledge of relevant equipment, policies, procedures, and strategies to promote effective local, state, or national security operations for the protection of people, data, property, and institutions. **Chemistry:** Knowledge of the chemical composition, structure, and properties of substances and of the chemical processes and transformations that they undergo. This includes uses of chemicals and their interactions, danger signs, production techniques, and disposal methods. **Education and Training:** Knowledge of principles and methods for curriculum and training design, teaching and instruction for individuals and groups, and the measurement of training effects.

# Numerical Control Machine Tool Operators and Tenders, Metal and Plastic

- ▲ Growth: 19.7%
- ▲ Annual Job Openings: 15,000
- ▲ Annual Earnings: $28,780
- ▲ Education/Training Required: Long-term on-the-job training
- ▲ Self-Employed: 0%
- ▲ Part-Time: 2.3%

Set up and operate numerical control (magnetic- or punched-tape-controlled) machine tools that automatically mill, drill, broach, and ream metal and plastic parts. May adjust machine feed and speed, change cutting tools, or adjust machine controls when automatic programming is faulty or if machine malfunctions. Selects, measures, assembles, and sets machine tools, such as drill bits and milling or cutting tools, using precision gauges and instruments. Mounts, installs, aligns, and secures tools, attachments, fixtures, and workpiece on machine, using hand tools and precision measuring instruments. Determines specifications or procedures for tooling setup, machine operation, workpiece dimensions, or numerical control sequences, using blueprints, instructions, and machine knowledge. Calculates and sets machine controls to position tools, synchronize tape and tool, or regulate cutting depth, speed, feed, or coolant flow. Lays out and marks areas of part to be shot-peened and fills hopper with shot. Positions and secures workpiece on machine bed, indexing table, fixture, or dispensing or holding device. Loads control media, such as tape, card, or disk, in machine controller or enters commands to retrieve programmed instructions. Starts automatic operation of numerical control machine to machine parts or test setup, workpiece dimensions, or programming. Confers with supervisor or programmer to resolve machine malfunctions and production errors and obtains approval to continue production. Maintains machines and removes and replaces broken or worn machine tools, using hand tools. Examines electronic components for defects and completeness of laser-beam trimming, using microscope. Operates lathe, drill-press, jig-boring machine, or other machines manually or semiautomatically. Measures dimensions of finished workpiece to ensure conformance to specifications, using precision measuring instruments, templates, and fixtures. Lifts workpiece to machine manually, with hoist or crane, or with tweezers. Enters commands or manually adjusts machine controls to correct malfunctions or tolerances. Stops machine to remove finished workpiece or change tooling, setup, or workpiece placement according to required machining sequence. Monitors machine operation and control panel displays to detect malfunctions and compare readings to specifications. Cleans machine, tooling, and parts, using solvent or solution and rag. **SKILLS**—Operation and Control. Mathematics. Operation Monitoring. Equipment Maintenance. Equipment Selection.

**GOE**—**Interest Area:** 08. Industrial Production. **Work Group:** 08.03. Production Work. **Other Job Titles in This Work Group:** Bakers, Manufacturing; Bindery Machine Operators and Tenders; Brazers; Cementing and Gluing Machine Operators and Tenders; Chemical Equipment Controllers and Operators; Chemical Equipment Operators and Tenders; Chemical Equipment Tenders; Cleaning, Washing, and Metal Pickling Equipment Operators and Tenders; Coating, Painting, and Spraying Machine Operators and Tenders; Coil Winders, Tapers, and Finishers; Combination Machine Tool Operators and Tenders, Metal and Plastic; Computer-Controlled Machine Tool Operators, Metal and Plastic; Cooling and Freezing Equipment Operators and Tenders; Crushing, Grinding, and Polishing Machine Setters, Operators, and Tenders; Cutters and Trimmers, Hand; Cutting and Slicing Machine Operators and Tenders; Cutting and Slicing Machine Setters, Operators, and Tenders; Design Printing Machine Setters and Set-Up Operators; Electrolytic Plating and Coating Machine Operators and Tenders, Metal and Plastic; Electrolytic Plating and Coating Machine Setters and Set-Up Operators, Metal and Plastic; Electrotypers and Stereotypers; Embossing Machine Set-Up Operators; Engraver Set-Up Operators; Extruding and Forming Machine Operators and Tenders, Synthetic or Glass Fibers; Extruding and Forming Machine Setters, Operators, and Tenders, Synthetic and Glass Fibers; Extruding, Forming, Pressing, and Compacting Machine Operators and Tenders; Fabric and Apparel Patternmakers; Fiber Product Cutting Machine Setters and Set-Up Operators; Fiberglass Laminators and Fabricators; others. **PERSONALITY TYPE**—Realistic. Realistic occupations frequently involve work activities that include practical, hands-on problems and solutions. They often deal with plants, animals, and real-world materials like wood, tools, and machinery. Many of the occupations require working outside and do not involve a lot of paperwork or working closely with others.

**EDUCATION/TRAINING PROGRAM(S)**—Machine Shop Assistant. **RELATED KNOWLEDGE/ COURSES**—**Principles of Mechanical Devices:** Knowledge of machines and tools, including their designs, uses, repair, and maintenance. **Production and Processing:** Knowledge of raw materials, production processes, quality control, costs, and other techniques for maximizing the effective manufacture and distribution of goods. **Engineering and Technology:** Knowledge of the practical application of engineering science and technology. This includes applying principles, techniques, procedures, and equipment to the design and production of various goods and services. **Mathematics:** Knowledge of arithmetic, algebra, geometry, calculus, statistics, and their applications. **Computers and Electronics:** Knowledge of circuit boards, processors, chips, electronic equipment, and computer hardware and software, including applications and programming.

# Numerical Tool and Process Control Programmers

▲ Growth: 16.6%

▲ Annual Job Openings: 2,000

▲ Annual Earnings: $37,690

▲ Education/Training Required: Long-term on-the-job training

▲ Self-Employed: 0%

▲ Part-Time: 11.7%

**Develop programs to control machining or processing of parts by automatic machine tools, equipment, or systems.** Prepares geometric layout from graphic displays, using computer-assisted drafting software or drafting instruments and graph paper. Writes instruction sheets, cutter lists, and machine instructions programs to guide setup and encode numerical control tape. Analyzes drawings, specifications, printed circuit board pattern film, and design data to calculate dimensions, tool selection, machine speeds, and feed rates. Determines reference points, machine cutting paths, or hole locations and computes angular and linear dimensions, radii, and curvatures. Compares encoded tape or computer printout with original program sheet to verify accuracy of instructions. Draws machine tool paths on pattern film, using colored markers and following guidelines for tool speed and efficiency. Revises numerical control machine tape programs to eliminate instruction errors and omissions. Enters computer commands to store or retrieve parts patterns, graphic displays, or programs to transfer data to other media. Aligns and secures pattern film on reference table of optical programmer and observes enlarger scope view of printed circuit board. Moves reference table to align pattern film over circuit board holes with reference marks on enlarger scope. Depresses pedal or button of programmer to enter coordinates of each hole location into program memory. Loads and unloads disks or tapes and observes operation of machine on trial run to test taped or programmed instructions. Reviews shop orders to determine job specifications and requirements. Sorts shop orders into groups to maximize materials utilization and minimize machine setup. **SKILLS**—Mathematics. Programming. Reading Comprehension. Operations Analysis. Troubleshooting.

**GOE**—**Interest Area:** 02. Science, Math, and Engineering. **Work Group:** 02.08. Engineering Technology. **Other Job Titles in This Work Group:** Aerospace Engineering and Operations Technicians; Architectural and Civil Drafters; Architectural Drafters; Calibration and Instrumentation Technicians; Cartographers and Photogrammetrists; Civil Drafters; Civil Engineering Technicians; Construction and Building Inspectors; Drafters, All Other; Electrical and Electronic Engineering Technicians; Electrical and Electronics Drafters; Electrical Drafters; Electrical Engineering Technicians; Electro-Mechanical Technicians; Electronic Drafters; Electronics Engineering Technicians; Engineering Technicians, Except Drafters, All Other; Environmental Engineering Technicians; Industrial Engineering Technicians; Mapping Technicians; Mechanical Drafters; Mechanical Engineering Technicians; Pressure Vessel Inspectors; Surveying and Mapping Technicians; Surveying Technicians; Surveyors. **PERSONALITY TYPE**—Realistic. Realistic occupations frequently involve work activities that include practical, hands-on problems and solutions. They often deal with plants, animals, and real-world materials like wood, tools, and machinery. Many of the occupations require working outside and do not involve a lot of paperwork or working closely with others.

**EDUCATION/TRAINING PROGRAM(S)**—Business Machine Repairer; Communication Systems Installer and Repairer; Computer Programming; Data Processing Technologist/Technician; Industrial Electronics Installer and Repairer; Machine Shop Assistant. **RELATED KNOWLEDGE/COURSES**—**Computers and Electronics:** Knowledge of circuit boards, processors, chips, electronic equipment, and computer hardware and software, including applications and programming. **Mathematics:** Knowledge of arithmetic, algebra, geometry, calculus, statistics, and their applications. **Design:** Knowledge of design techniques, tools, and principles involved in production of precision technical plans, blueprints, drawings, and models. **Production and Processing:** Knowledge of raw materials, production processes, quality control, costs, and other techniques for maximizing the effective manufacture and distribution of goods. **Engineering and Technology:** Knowledge of the practical application of engineering science and technology. This includes applying principles, techniques, procedures, and equipment to the design and production of various goods and services.

# Nursing Aides, Orderlies, and Attendants

- ▲ Growth: 23.5%
- ▲ Annual Job Openings: 268,000
- ▲ Annual Earnings: $19,100
- ▲ Education/Training Required: Short-term on-the-job training
- ▲ Self-Employed: 3.6%
- ▲ Part-Time: 26.4%

**Provide basic patient care under direction of nursing staff. Perform duties, such as feed, bathe, dress, groom, or move patients or change linens.** Feeds patients unable to feed themselves. Sets up equipment, such as oxygen tents, portable X-ray machines, and overhead irrigation bottles. Prepares food trays. Bathes, grooms, and dresses patients. Measures and records food and liquid intake and output. Measures and records vital signs. Administers medication as directed by physician or nurse. Cleans room and changes linen. Stores, prepares, and issues dressing packs, treatment trays, and other supplies. Administers catheterizations, bladder irrigations, enemas, and douches. Sterilizes equipment and supplies. Administers massages and alcohol rubs. Transports patient to areas such as operating and X-ray rooms. Turns and re-positions bedfast patients, alone or with assistance, to prevent bedsores. Assists patient to walk. **SKILLS**—Social Perceptiveness. Active Listening. Reading Comprehension. Speaking. Service Orientation.

**GOE—Interest Area:** 14. Medical and Health Services. **Work Group:** 14.07. Patient Care and Assistance. **Other Job Titles in This Work Group:** Home Health Aides; Licensed Practical and Licensed Vocational Nurses; Psychiatric Aides; Psychiatric Technicians. **PERSONALITY TYPE**—Social. Social occupations frequently involve working with, communicating with, and teaching people. These occupations often involve helping or providing service to others.

**EDUCATION/TRAINING PROGRAM(S)**—Health Aide; Nurse Assistant/Aide. **RELATED KNOWLEDGE/COURSES**—**Customer and Personal Service:** Knowledge of principles and processes for providing customer and personal services. This includes customer needs assessment, meeting quality standards for services, and evaluation of customer satisfaction. **Medicine and Dentistry:** Knowledge of the information and techniques needed to diagnose and treat human injuries, diseases, and deformities. This includes symptoms, treatment alternatives, drug properties and interactions, and preventive health-care measures. **Chemistry:** Knowledge of the chemical composition, structure, and properties of substances and of the chemical processes and transformations that they undergo. This includes uses of chemicals and their interactions, danger signs, production techniques, and disposal methods. **Therapy and Counseling:** Knowledge of principles, methods, and procedures for diagnosis, treatment, and rehabilitation of physical and mental dysfunctions and for career counseling and guidance. **Public Safety and Security:** Knowledge of relevant equipment, policies, procedures, and strategies to promote effective local, state, or national security operations for the protection of people, data, property, and institutions.

# Occupational Therapist Assistants

▲ Growth: 39.7%
▲ Annual Job Openings: 3,000
▲ Annual Earnings: $34,860
▲ Education/Training Required: Associate's degree
▲ Self-Employed: 0%
▲ Part-Time: 24.9%

Assist occupational therapists in providing occupational therapy treatments and procedures. May, in accordance with state laws, assist in development of treatment plans, carry out routine functions, direct activity programs, and document the progress of treatments. Generally requires formal training. Assists occupational therapist to plan, implement, and administer educational, vocational, and recreational activities to restore, reinforce, and enhance task performances. Reports information and observations to supervisor verbally. Transports patient to and from occupational therapy work area. Maintains observed information in client records and prepares written reports. Prepares work material, assembles and maintains equipment, and orders supplies. Fabricates splints and other assistant devices. Assists educational specialist or clinical psychologist in administering situational or diagnostic tests to measure client's abilities or progress. Designs and adapts equipment and working-living environment. Helps professional staff demonstrate therapy techniques, such as manual and creative arts and games. Instructs or assists in instructing patient and family in home programs and basic living skills as well as care and use of adaptive equipment. Assists in evaluation of physically, developmentally, or mentally retarded or emotionally disabled client's daily living skills and capacities. **SKILLS**—Social Perceptiveness. Reading Comprehension. Active Listening. Speaking. Service Orientation.

**GOE**—**Interest Area:** 14. Medical and Health Services. **Work Group:** 14.06. Medical Therapy. **Other Job Titles in This Work Group:** Audiologists; Massage Therapists; Occupational Therapist Aides; Occupational Therapists; Physical Therapist Aides; Physical Therapist Assistants; Physical Therapists; Radiation Therapists; Recreational Therapists; Respiratory Therapists; Respiratory Therapy Technicians; Speech-Language Pathologists; Therapists, All Other. **PERSONALITY TYPE**—Social. Social occupations frequently involve working with, communicating with, and teaching people. These occupations often involve helping or providing service to others.

**EDUCATION/TRAINING PROGRAM(S)**—Occupational Therapy Assistant. **RELATED KNOWLEDGE/COURSES**—**Therapy and Counseling:** Knowledge of principles, methods, and procedures for diagnosis, treatment, and rehabilitation of physical and mental dysfunctions and for career counseling and guidance. **Education and Training:** Knowledge of principles and methods for curriculum and training design, teaching and instruction for individuals and groups, and the measurement of training effects. **Medicine and Dentistry:** Knowledge of the information and techniques needed to diagnose and treat human injuries, diseases, and deformities. This includes symptoms, treatment alternatives, drug properties and interactions, and preventive health-care measures. **Psychology:** Knowledge of human behavior and performance; individual differences in ability, personality, and interests; learning and motivation; psychological research methods; and the assessment and treatment of behavioral and affective disorders. **English Language:** Knowledge of the structure and content of the English language, including the meaning and spelling of words, rules of composition, and grammar. **Customer and Personal Service:** Knowledge of principles and processes for providing customer and personal services. This includes customer needs assessment, meeting quality standards for services, and evaluation of customer satisfaction.

# Office Clerks, General

> ▲ Growth: 15.9%
> ▲ Annual Job Openings: 676,000
> ▲ Annual Earnings: $22,290
> ▲ Education/Training Required: Short-term on-the-job training
> ▲ Self-Employed: 0.5%
> ▲ Part-Time: 30.7%

Perform duties too varied and diverse to be classified in any specific office clerical occupation that require limited knowledge of office management systems and procedures. Clerical duties may be assigned in accordance with the office procedures of individual establishments and may include a combination of answering telephones, bookkeeping, typing or word processing, stenography, office machine operation, and filing. Compiles, copies, sorts, and files records of office activities, business transactions, and other activities. Communicates with customers, employees, and other individuals to disseminate or explain information. Collects, counts, and disburses money, completes banking transactions, and processes payroll. Completes work schedules and arranges appointments for staff and students. Reviews files, records, and other documents to obtain information to respond to requests. Answers telephone, responds to requests, delivers messages, and runs errands. Orders materials, supplies, and services and completes records and reports. Transcribes dictation and composes and types letters and other correspondence, using typewriter or computer. Stuffs envelopes and addresses, stamps, sorts, and distributes mail, packages, and other materials. Completes and mails bills, contracts, policies, invoices, or checks. Operates office machines, such as photocopier, telecopier, and personal computer. Computes, records, and proofreads data and other information, such as records or reports. **SKILLS—** Reading Comprehension. Active Listening. Mathematics. Writing. Speaking.

**GOE—Interest Area:** 09. Business Detail. **Work Group:** 09.07. Records Processing. **Other Job Titles in This Work Group:** Correspondence Clerks; Court Reporters; Credit Authorizers; Credit Authorizers, Checkers, and Clerks; Credit Checkers; File Clerks; Human Resources Assistants, Except Payroll and Timekeeping; Information and Record Clerks, All Other; Insurance Claims and Policy Processing Clerks; Insurance Claims Clerks; Insurance Policy Processing Clerks; Medical Records and Health Information Technicians; Medical Transcriptionists; Procurement Clerks; Proofreaders and Copy Markers. **PERSONALITY TYPE—**Conventional. Conventional occupations frequently involve following set procedures and routines. These occupations can include working with data and details more than with ideas. Usually there is a clear line of authority to follow.

**EDUCATION/TRAINING PROGRAM(S)—**General Office/Clerical and Typing Services. **RELATED KNOWLEDGE/COURSES—Clerical Studies:** Knowledge of administrative and clerical procedures and systems such as word processing, managing files and records, stenography and transcription, designing forms, and other office procedures and terminology. **Customer and Personal Service:** Knowledge of principles and processes for providing customer and personal services. This includes customer needs assessment, meeting quality standards for services, and evaluation of customer satisfaction. **English Language:** Knowledge of the structure and content of the English language, including the meaning and spelling of words, rules of composition, and grammar. **Mathematics:** Knowledge of arithmetic, algebra, geometry, calculus, statistics, and their applications. **Computers and Electronics:** Knowledge of circuit boards, processors, chips, electronic equipment, and computer hardware and software, including applications and programming. **Economics and Accounting:** Knowledge of economic and accounting principles and practices, the financial markets, banking, and the analysis and reporting of financial data.

# Office Machine and Cash Register Servicers

- ▲ Growth: 14.2%
- ▲ Annual Job Openings: 24,000
- ▲ Annual Earnings: $32,860
- ▲ Education/Training Required: Post-secondary vocational training
- ▲ Self-Employed: 14.8%
- ▲ Part-Time: 1.8%

**Repair and service office machines, such as adding, accounting, calculating, duplicating, and typewriting machines. Includes the repair of manual, electrical, and electronic office machines.** Tests machine to locate cause of electrical problems, using testing devices, such as voltmeter, ohmmeter, and circuit test equipment. Disassembles machine and examines parts such as wires, gears, and bearings for wear and defects, using hand tools, power tools, and measuring devices. Operates machine, such as typewriter, cash register, or adding machine, to test functioning of parts and mechanisms. Assembles and installs machine according to specifications, using hand tools, power tools, and measuring devices. Cleans and oils mechanical parts to maintain machine. Reads specifications, such as blueprints, charts, and schematics, to determine machine settings and adjustments. Repairs, adjusts, or replaces electrical and mechanical components and parts, using hand tools, power tools, and soldering or welding equipment. Instructs operators and servicers in operation, maintenance, and repair of machine. **SKILLS**—Instructing. Reading Comprehension. Equipment Maintenance. Repairing. Installation. Troubleshooting. Learning Strategies.

**GOE—Interest Area:** 05. Mechanics, Installers, and Repairers. **Work Group:** 05.02. Electrical and Electronic Systems. **Other Job Titles in This Work Group:** Avionics Technicians; Battery Repairers; Central Office and PBX Installers and Repairers; Communication Equipment Mechanics, Installers, and Repairers; Computer, Automated Teller, and Office Machine Repairers; Data Processing Equipment Repairers; Electric Home Appliance and Power Tool Repairers; Electric Meter Installers and Repairers; Electric Motor and Switch Assemblers and Repairers; Electric Motor, Power Tool, and Related Repairers; Electrical and Electronics Installers and Repairers, Transportation Equipment; Electrical and Electronics Repairers, Commercial and Industrial Equipment; Electrical and Electronics Repairers, Powerhouse, Substation, and Relay; Electrical Parts Reconditioners; Electrical Power-Line Installers and Repairers; Electronic Equipment Installers and Repairers, Motor Vehicles; Electronic Home Entertainment Equipment Installers and Repairers; Elevator Installers and Repairers; Frame Wirers, Central Office; Home Appliance Installers; Home Appliance Repairers; Radio Mechanics; Signal and Track Switch Repairers; Station Installers and Repairers, Telephone; Telecommunications Equipment Installers and Repairers, Except Line Installers; Telecommunications Facility Examiners; Telecommunications Line Installers and Repairers; Transformer Repairers. **PERSONALITY TYPE**—Realistic. Realistic occupations frequently involve work activities that include practical, hands-on problems and solutions. They often deal with plants, animals, and real-world materials like wood, tools, and machinery. Many of the occupations require working outside and do not involve a lot of paperwork or working closely with others.

**EDUCATION/TRAINING PROGRAM(S)**—Building/Property Maintenance and Manager; Business Machine Repairer; Computer Installer and Repairer; Computer Maintenance Technologist/Technician. **RELATED KNOWLEDGE/COURSES—Principles of Mechanical Devices:** Knowledge of machines and tools, including their designs, uses, repair, and maintenance. **Computers and Electronics:** Knowledge of circuit boards, processors, chips, electronic equipment, and computer hardware and software, including applications and programming. **Engineering and Technology:** Knowledge of the practical application of engineering science and technology. This includes applying principles, techniques, procedures, and equipment to the design and production of various goods and services. **Education and Training:** Knowledge of principles and methods for curriculum

and training design, teaching and instruction for individuals and groups, and the measurement of training effects. **Design:** Knowledge of design techniques, tools, and principles involved in production of precision technical plans, blueprints, drawings, and models.

# Offset Lithographic Press Setters and Set-Up Operators

▲ Growth: 5.5%
▲ Annual Job Openings: 24,000
▲ Annual Earnings: $30,090
▲ Education/Training Required: Moderate-term on-the-job training
▲ Self-Employed: 2.6%
▲ Part-Time: 3.3%

**Set up or set up and operate offset printing press, either sheet or web fed, to print single and multicolor copy from lithographic plates. Examine job order to determine press operating time, quantity to be printed, and stock specifications.** Examines job order to determine quantity to be printed, stock specifications, colors, and special printing instructions. Installs and locks plate into position, using hand tools, to achieve pressure required for printing. Measures plate thickness and inserts packing sheets on plate cylinder to build up plate to printing height. Fills ink and dampening solution fountains and adjusts controls to regulate flow of ink and dampening solution to plate cylinder. Removes and cleans plate and cylinders. Loads paper into feeder or installs rolls of paper, adjusts feeder and delivery mechanisms, and unloads printed material from delivery mechanism. Applies packing sheets to blanket cylinder to build up blanket thickness to diameter of plate cylinder. Washes plate to remove protective gum coating. Measures paper thickness and adjusts space between blanket and impression cylinders according to thickness of paper stock. Makes adjustments to press throughout production run to maintain specific registration and color density. Starts press and examines printed copy for ink density, position on paper, and registration. **SKILLS**—Operation and Control. Operation Monitoring. Equipment Selection. Equipment Maintenance. Installation.

GOE—**Interest Area:** 08. Industrial Production. **Work Group:** 08.03. Production Work. **Other Job Titles in This Work Group:** Bakers, Manufacturing; Bindery Machine Operators and Tenders; Brazers; Cementing and Gluing Machine Operators and Tenders; Chemical Equipment Controllers and Operators; Chemical Equipment Operators and Tenders; Chemical Equipment Tenders; Cleaning, Washing, and Metal Pickling Equipment Operators and Tenders; Coating, Painting, and Spraying Machine Operators and Tenders; Coil Winders, Tapers, and Finishers; Combination Machine Tool Operators and Tenders, Metal and Plastic; Computer-Controlled Machine Tool Operators, Metal and Plastic; Cooling and Freezing Equipment Operators and Tenders; Crushing, Grinding, and Polishing Machine Setters, Operators, and Tenders; Cutters and Trimmers, Hand; Cutting and Slicing Machine Operators and Tenders; Cutting and Slicing Machine Setters, Operators, and Tenders; Design Printing Machine Setters and Set-Up Operators; Electrolytic Plating and Coating Machine Operators and Tenders, Metal and Plastic; Electrolytic Plating and Coating Machine Setters and Set-Up Operators, Metal and Plastic; Electrotypers and Stereotypers; Embossing Machine Set-Up Operators; Engraver Set-Up Operators; Extruding and Forming Machine Operators and Tenders, Synthetic or Glass Fibers; Extruding and Forming Machine Setters, Operators, and Tenders, Synthetic and Glass Fibers; Extruding, Forming, Pressing, and Compacting Machine

Operators and Tenders; Fabric and Apparel Patternmakers; Fiber Product Cutting Machine Setters and Set-Up Operators; Fiberglass Laminators and Fabricators; others. **PERSONALITY TYPE**—Realistic. Realistic occupations frequently involve work activities that include practical, hands-on problems and solutions. They often deal with plants, animals, and real-world materials like wood, tools, and machinery. Many of the occupations require working outside and do not involve a lot of paperwork or working closely with others.

**EDUCATION/TRAINING PROGRAM(S)**—Graphic and Printing Equipment Operator, General; Graphic and Printing Equipment Operators, Other; Printing Press Operator. **RELATED KNOWLEDGE/COURSES**— **Production and Processing:** Knowledge of raw materials, production processes, quality control, costs, and other techniques for maximizing the effective manufacture and distribution of goods. **Principles of Mechanical Devices:** Knowledge of machines and tools, including their designs, uses, repair, and maintenance. **Communications and Media:** Knowledge of media production, communication, and dissemination techniques and methods. This includes alternative ways to inform and entertain via written, oral, and visual media. **English Language:** Knowledge of the structure and content of the English language, including the meaning and spelling of words, rules of composition, and grammar. **Engineering and Technology:** Knowledge of the practical application of engineering science and technology. This includes applying principles, techniques, procedures, and equipment to the design and production of various goods and services. **Mathematics:** Knowledge of arithmetic, algebra, geometry, calculus, statistics, and their applications.

# Operating Engineers

- ▲ Growth: 6.9%
- ▲ Annual Job Openings: 25,000
- ▲ Annual Earnings: $36,170
- ▲ Education/Training Required: Moderate-term on-the-job training
- ▲ Self-Employed: 6.6%
- ▲ Part-Time: 2%

**Operate several types of power construction equipment, such as compressors, pumps, hoists, derricks, cranes, shovels, tractors, scrapers, or motor graders, to excavate, move and grade earth, erect structures, or pour concrete or other hard surface pavement. May repair and maintain equipment in addition to other duties.** Adjusts handwheels and depresses pedals to drive machines and control attachments, such as blades, buckets, scrapers, and swing booms. Turns valves to control air and water output of compressors and pumps. Repairs and maintains equipment. **SKILLS**—Operation and Control. Equipment Maintenance. Repairing. Troubleshooting. Operation Monitoring.

**GOE—Interest Area:** 06. Construction, Mining, and Drilling. **Work Group:** 06.02. Construction. **Other Job Titles in This Work Group:** Boat Builders and Shipwrights; Boilermakers; Brattice Builders; Brickmasons and Blockmasons; Carpenters; Carpet Installers; Ceiling Tile Installers; Cement Masons and Concrete Finishers; Commercial Divers; Construction Carpenters; Drywall and Ceiling Tile Installers; Drywall Installers; Electricians; Explosives Workers, Ordnance Handling Experts, and Blasters; Fence Erectors; Floor Layers, Except Carpet, Wood, and Hard Tiles; Floor Sanders and Finishers; Glaziers; Grader, Bulldozer, and Scraper Operators; Hazardous Materials Removal Workers; Insulation Workers, Floor, Ceiling, and Wall; Insulation Workers, Mechanical; Manufactured Building and Mobile Home Installers; Operating Engineers and Other Construction Equipment Operators; Painters, Construction and Maintenance; Paperhangers; Paving, Surfacing, and Tamping Equipment Operators; Pile-Driver Operators; Pipe Fitters; Pipelayers; Pipelaying Fitters; Plasterers and Stucco Masons; Plumbers; Plumbers, Pipefitters, and Steamfitters; Rail-Track Laying and Maintenance Equipment Operators; Refractory Materials Repairers, Except

Brickmasons; Reinforcing Iron and Rebar Workers; Riggers; Roofers; Rough Carpenters; Security and Fire Alarm Systems Installers; Segmental Pavers; Sheet Metal Workers; Ship Carpenters and Joiners; Stone Cutters and Carvers; Stonemasons; Structural Iron and Steel Workers; Tapers; Terrazzo Workers and Finishers; Tile and Marble Setters. **PERSONALITY TYPE**—Realistic. Realistic occupations frequently involve work activities that include practical, hands-on problems and solutions. They often deal with plants, animals, and real-world materials like wood, tools, and machinery. Many of the occupations require working outside and do not involve a lot of paperwork or working closely with others.

**EDUCATION/TRAINING PROGRAM(S)**—Construction Equipment Operator. **RELATED KNOWLEDGE/COURSES**—**Principles of Mechanical Devices:** Knowledge of machines and tools, including their de-

signs, uses, repair, and maintenance. **Building and Construction:** Knowledge of materials, methods, and tools involved in the construction or repair of houses, buildings, or other structures such as highways and roads. **Engineering and Technology:** Knowledge of the practical application of engineering science and technology. This includes applying principles, techniques, procedures, and equipment to the design and production of various goods and services. **Physics:** Knowledge and prediction of physical principles and laws and their interrelationships and applications to understanding fluid, material, and atmospheric dynamics and mechanical, electrical, atomic, and sub-atomic structures and processes. **Sales and Marketing:** Knowledge of principles and methods for showing, promoting, and selling products or services. This includes marketing strategy and tactics, product demonstration, sales techniques, and sales control systems.

# Order Fillers, Wholesale and Retail Sales

- ▲ Growth: 8.5%
- ▲ Annual Job Openings: 467,000
- ▲ Annual Earnings: $20,650
- ▲ Education/Training Required: Short-term on-the-job training
- ▲ Self-Employed: 0.2%
- ▲ Part-Time: 13.7%

**Fill customers' mail and telephone orders from stored merchandise in accordance with specifications on sales slips or order forms. Duties include computing prices of items, completing order receipts, keeping records of out-going orders, and requisitioning additional materials, supplies, and equipment.** Computes price of each group of items. Obtains merchandise from bins or shelves. Places merchandise on conveyor leading to wrapping area. Reads order to ascertain catalog number, size, color, and quantity of merchandise. **SKILLS**—Mathematics. Operation and Control. Coordination.

**GOE**—**Interest Area:** 09. Business Detail. **Work Group:** 09.08. Records and Materials Processing. **Other Job Titles in This Work Group:** Cargo and Freight Agents; Couriers and Messengers; Mail Clerks, Except Mail Machine Operators and Postal Service; Marking Clerks; Postal Service Mail Carriers; Postal Service Mail Sort-

ers, Processors, and Processing Machine Operators; Shipping, Receiving, and Traffic Clerks; Stock Clerks and Order Fillers; Stock Clerks—Stockroom, Warehouse, or Storage Yard; Weighers, Measurers, Checkers, and Samplers, Recordkeeping. **PERSONALITY TYPE**—Conventional. Conventional occupations frequently involve following set procedures and routines. These occupations can include working with data and details more than with ideas. Usually there is a clear line of authority to follow.

**EDUCATION/TRAINING PROGRAM(S)**—Food Products Retailing and Wholesaling Operations; General Retailing Operations; Home and Office Products Marketing Operations, Other. **RELATED KNOWLEDGE/COURSES**—**Clerical Studies:** Knowledge of administrative and clerical procedures and systems such as word processing, managing files and records, stenography and transcription, designing forms, and other office procedures and terminology. **English Language:** Knowledge of the structure and content of the English language, including the meaning and spelling of words, rules of composition, and grammar. **Mathematics:** Knowledge of arithmetic, algebra, geometry, calculus, statistics, and their applications. **Production and Processing:** Knowledge of raw materials, production processes, quality control, costs, and other techniques for maximizing the effective manufacture and distribution of goods.

# Packaging and Filling Machine Operators and Tenders

▲ Growth: 14.4%
▲ Annual Job Openings: 56,000
▲ Annual Earnings: $21,700
▲ Education/Training Required: Short-term on-the-job training
▲ Self-Employed: 0%
▲ Part-Time: 7.1%

**Operate or tend machines to prepare industrial or consumer products for storage or shipment. Includes cannery workers who pack food products.** Tends or operates machine that packages product. Starts machine by engaging controls. Adjusts machine tension and pressure and machine components according to size or processing angle of product. Removes finished packaged items from machine and separates rejected items. Stocks product for packaging or filling machine operation. Tests and evaluates product and verifies product weight or measurement to ensure quality standards. Attaches identification labels to finished packaged items. Stacks finished packaged items or packs items in cartons or containers. Counts and records finished and rejected packaged items. Cleans, oils, and makes minor repairs to machinery and equipment. Secures finished packaged items by hand tying, sewing, or attaching fastener. Stocks packaging material for machine processing. Inspects and removes defective product and packaging material. Observes machine operations to ensure quality and conformity of filled or packaged products to standards. Stops or resets machine when malfunction occurs and clears machine jams. Regulates machine flow, speed, or temperature. Operates mechanism to cut filler product or packaging material. **SKILLS**—Equipment Maintenance. Operation and Control. Operation Monitoring. Repairing. Quality Control Analysis.

**GOE—Interest Area:** 08. Industrial Production. **Work Group:** 08.03. Production Work. **Other Job Titles in This Work Group:** Bakers, Manufacturing; Bindery Machine Operators and Tenders; Brazers; Cementing and Gluing Machine Operators and Tenders; Chemical Equipment Controllers and Operators; Chemical Equipment Operators and Tenders; Chemical Equipment Tenders; Cleaning, Washing, and Metal Pickling Equipment Operators and Tenders; Coating, Painting, and Spraying Machine Operators and Tenders; Coil Winders, Tapers, and Finishers; Combination Machine Tool Operators and Tenders, Metal and Plastic; Computer-Controlled Machine Tool Operators, Metal and Plastic; Cooling and Freezing Equipment Operators and Tenders; Crushing, Grinding, and Polishing Machine Setters, Operators, and Tenders; Cutters and Trimmers, Hand; Cutting and Slicing Machine Operators and Tenders; Cutting and Slicing Machine Setters, Operators, and Tenders; Design Printing Machine Setters and Set-Up Operators; Electrolytic Plating and Coating Machine Operators and Tenders, Metal and Plastic; Electrolytic Plating and Coating Machine Setters and Set-Up Operators, Metal and Plastic; Electrotypers and Stereotypers; Embossing Machine Set-Up Operators; Engraver Set-Up Operators; Extruding and Forming Machine Operators and Tenders, Synthetic or Glass Fibers; Extruding and Forming Machine Setters, Operators, and Tenders, Synthetic and Glass Fibers; Extruding, Forming, Pressing, and Compacting Machine

Operators and Tenders; Fabric and Apparel Patternmakers; Fiber Product Cutting Machine Setters and Set-Up Operators; Fiberglass Laminators and Fabricators; others. **PERSONALITY TYPE**—Realistic. Realistic occupations frequently involve work activities that include practical, hands-on problems and solutions. They often deal with plants, animals, and real-world materials like wood, tools, and machinery. Many of the occupations require working outside and do not involve a lot of paperwork or working closely with others.

**EDUCATION/TRAINING PROGRAM(S)**—No data available. **RELATED KNOWLEDGE/ COURSES—Production and Processing:** Knowledge of raw materials, production processes, quality control, costs, and other techniques for maximizing the effective manufacture and distribution of goods. **Principles of Mechanical Devices:** Knowledge of machines and tools, including their designs, uses, repair, and maintenance. **Mathematics:** Knowledge of arithmetic, algebra, geometry, calculus, statistics, and their applications. **Physics:** Knowledge and prediction of physical principles and laws and their interrelationships and applications to understanding fluid, material, and atmospheric dynamics and mechanical, electrical, atomic, and sub-atomic structures and processes. **Public Safety and Security:** Knowledge of relevant equipment, policies, procedures, and strategies to promote effective local, state, or national security operations for the protection of people, data, property, and institutions. **Engineering and Technology:** Knowledge of the practical application of engineering science and technology. This includes applying principles, techniques, procedures, and equipment to the design and production of various goods and services.

# Packers and Packagers, Hand

- ▲ Growth: 19.3%
- ▲ Annual Job Openings: 242,000
- ▲ Annual Earnings: $17,030
- ▲ Education/Training Required: Short-term on-the-job training
- ▲ Self-Employed: 0.4%
- ▲ Part-Time: 16.1%

**Pack or package by hand a wide variety of products and materials.** Fastens and wraps products and materials, using hand tools. Seals containers or materials, using glues, fasteners, and hand tools. Assembles and lines cartons, crates, and containers, using hand tools. Places or pours products or materials into containers, using hand tools and equipment. Marks and labels containers or products, using marking instruments. Loads materials and products into package processing equipment. Cleans containers, materials, or work area, using cleaning solutions and hand tools. Tends packing machines and equipment that prepare and package materials and products. Removes and places completed or defective product or materials on moving equipment or specified area. Measures, weighs, and counts products and materials, using equipment. Records product and packaging information on specified forms and records. Examines and inspects containers, materials, and products to ensure packaging process meets specifications. Obtains and sorts products, materials, and orders, using hand tools. **SKILLS**—Operation and Control.

**GOE—Interest Area:** 08. Industrial Production. **Work Group:** 08.07. Hands-on Work: Loading, Moving, Hoisting, and Conveying. **Other Job Titles in This Work Group:** Conveyor Operators and Tenders; Crane and Tower Operators; Dragline Operators; Excavating and Loading Machine and Dragline Operators; Freight, Stock, and Material Movers, Hand; Hoist and Winch Operators; Industrial Truck and Tractor Operators; Irradiated-Fuel Handlers; Laborers and Freight, Stock, and Material Movers, Hand; Machine Feeders and Offbearers; Material Moving Workers, All Other; Pump Operators, Except Wellhead Pumpers; Refuse and Recyclable Material Collectors; Tank Car, Truck, and Ship

Loaders. **PERSONALITY TYPE**—Realistic. Realistic occupations frequently involve work activities that include practical, hands-on problems and solutions. They often deal with plants, animals, and real-world materials like wood, tools, and machinery. Many of the occupations require working outside and do not involve a lot of paperwork or working closely with others.

**EDUCATION/TRAINING PROGRAM(S)**—No data available. **RELATED KNOWLEDGE/COURSES**— **Production and Processing:** Knowledge of raw materials, production processes, quality control, costs, and other techniques for maximizing the effective manufacture and distribution of goods. **Clerical Studies:** Knowledge of administrative and clerical procedures and systems such as word processing, managing files and records, stenography and transcription, designing forms, and other office procedures and terminology. **Mathematics:** Knowledge of arithmetic, algebra, geometry, calculus, statistics, and their applications. **English Language:** Knowledge of the structure and content of the English language, including the meaning and spelling of words, rules of composition, and grammar.

# Painters and Illustrators

▲ Growth: 13.4%

▲ Annual Job Openings: 4,000

▲ Annual Earnings: $35,770

▲ Education/Training Required: Long-term on-the-job training

▲ Self-Employed: 56.7%

▲ Part-Time: 24%

**Paint or draw subject material to produce original artwork or illustrations, using watercolors, oils, acrylics, tempera, or other paint mediums.** Renders drawings, illustrations, and sketches of buildings, manufactured products, or models, working from sketches, blueprints, memory, or reference materials. Paints scenic backgrounds, murals, and portraiture for motion picture and television production sets, glass artworks, and exhibits. Etches, carves, paints, or draws artwork on material, such as stone, glass, canvas, wood, and linoleum. Develops drawings, paintings, diagrams, and models of medical or biological subjects for use in publications, exhibits, consultations, research, and teaching. Studies style, techniques, colors, textures, and materials used by artist to maintain consistency in reconstruction or retouching procedures. Removes painting from frame or paint layer from canvas to restore artwork, following specified technique and equipment. Examines surfaces of paintings and proofs of artwork, using magnifying device, to determine method of restoration or needed corrections. Installs finished stained glass in window or door frame. Assembles, leads, and solders finished glass to fabricate stained glass article. Applies select solvents and cleaning agents to clean surface of painting and remove accretions, discolorations, and deteriorated varnish. Performs tests to determine factors, such as age, structure, pigment stability, and probable reaction to various cleaning agents and solvents. Confers with professional personnel or client to discuss objectives of artwork and develop illustration ideas and theme to be portrayed. Brushes or sprays protective or decorative finish on completed background panels, informational legends, exhibit accessories, or finished painting. Integrates and develops visual elements, such as line, space, mass, color, and perspective, to produce desired effect. **SKILLS**—Active Listening. Operations Analysis. Speaking. Equipment Selection. Complex Problem Solving.

**GOE—Interest Area:** 01. Arts, Entertainment, and Media. **Work Group:** 01.04. Visual Arts. **Other Job Titles in This Work Group:** Cartoonists; Commercial and Industrial Designers; Designers, All Other; Exhibit Designers; Fashion Designers; Fine Artists, Including Painters, Sculptors, and Illustrators; Floral Designers; Graphic Designers; Interior Designers; Merchandise Displayers and Window Trimmers; Multi-Media Artists and Animators; Sculptors; Set and Exhibit Designers; Set Designers; Sketch Artists. **PERSONALITY TYPE**—Artistic. Artistic occupations frequently involve working with forms, designs, and patterns. They often require self-expression, and the work can be done without following a clear set of rules.

**EDUCATION/TRAINING PROGRAM(S)**—Art, General; Ceramics Arts and Ceramics; Drawing; Fine Arts and Art Studies, Other; Fine/Studio Arts; Intermedia; Medical Illustrating; Painting; Printmaking; Sculpture. **RELATED KNOWLEDGE/COURSES— Fine Arts:** Knowledge of the theory and techniques required to compose, produce, and perform works of music, dance, visual arts, drama, and sculpture. **Design:** Knowledge of design techniques, tools, and principles involved in production of precision technical plans, blueprints, drawings, and models. **Chemistry:**

Knowledge of the chemical composition, structure, and properties of substances and of the chemical processes and transformations that they undergo. This includes uses of chemicals and their interactions, danger signs, production techniques, and disposal methods. **Customer and Personal Service:** Knowledge of principles and processes for providing customer and personal services. This includes customer needs assessment, meeting quality standards for services, and evaluation of customer satisfaction. **Communications and Media:** Knowledge of media production, communication, and dissemination techniques and methods. This includes alternative ways to inform and entertain via written, oral, and visual media. **History and Archeology:** Knowledge of historical events and their causes, indicators, and effects on civilizations and cultures.

# Painters, Construction and Maintenance

- ▲ Growth: 19.1%
- ▲ Annual Job Openings: 67,000
- ▲ Annual Earnings: $29,610
- ▲ Education/Training Required: Moderate-term on-the-job training
- ▲ Self-Employed: 46.5%
- ▲ Part-Time: 9.2%

**Paint walls, equipment, buildings, bridges, and other structural surfaces, using brushes, rollers, and spray guns. May remove old paint to prepare surface prior to painting. May mix colors or oils to obtain desired color or consistency.** Paints surfaces, using brushes, spray gun, or rollers. Applies paint to simulate wood grain, marble, brick, or stonework. Cuts stencils and brushes and sprays lettering and decorations on surfaces. Sands surfaces between coats and polishes final coat to specified finish. Bakes finish on painted and enameled articles in baking oven. Washes and treats surfaces with oil, turpentine, mildew remover, or other preparations. Mixes and matches colors of paint, stain, or varnish. Fills cracks, holes, and joints with caulk putty, plaster, or other filler, using caulking gun or putty knife. Reads work order or receives instructions from supervisor or homeowner. Erects scaffolding or sets up ladders to work above ground level. Covers surfaces with dropcloths or

masking tape and paper to protect surface during painting. Burns off old paint, using blowtorch. Removes fixtures, such as pictures and electric switchcovers, from walls prior to painting. Sprays or brushes hot plastics or pitch onto surfaces. Smoothes surfaces, using sandpaper, scrapers, brushes, steel wool, or sanding machine. **SKILLS**—Mathematics. Reading Comprehension.

**GOE—Interest Area:** 06. Construction, Mining, and Drilling. **Work Group:** 06.02. Construction. **Other Job Titles in This Work Group:** Boat Builders and Shipwrights; Boilermakers; Brattice Builders; Brickmasons and Blockmasons; Carpenters; Carpet Installers; Ceiling Tile Installers; Cement Masons and Concrete Finishers; Commercial Divers; Construction Carpenters; Drywall and Ceiling Tile Installers; Drywall Installers; Electricians; Explosives Workers, Ordnance Handling Experts, and Blasters; Fence Erectors; Floor Layers, Except Carpet, Wood, and Hard Tiles; Floor Sanders and Finishers; Glaziers; Grader, Bulldozer, and Scraper Operators; Hazardous Materials Removal Workers; Insulation Workers, Floor, Ceiling, and Wall; Insulation Workers, Mechanical; Manufactured Building and Mobile Home Installers; Operating Engineers; Operating Engineers and Other Construction Equipment Operators; Paperhangers; Paving, Surfacing, and Tamping Equipment Operators; Pile-Driver Operators; Pipe Fitters; Pipelayers; Pipelaying Fitters; Plasterers and Stucco Masons; Plumbers; Plumbers, Pipefitters, and Steamfitters; Rail-Track Laying and Maintenance Equipment Operators; Refractory Materials Repairers, Except Brickmasons; Reinforcing Iron and Rebar Workers; Riggers; Roofers; Rough Carpenters; Security and Fire Alarm Systems Installers; Segmental Pavers; Sheet Metal Workers; Ship Carpenters and Joiners; Stone Cutters and Carvers; Stonemasons; Structural Iron and Steel Workers; Tapers; Terrazzo Workers and Finishers; Tile and Marble Setters. **PERSONALITY TYPE—** Realistic. Realistic occupations frequently involve work activities that include practical, hands-on problems and solutions. They often deal with plants, animals, and real-world materials like wood, tools, and machinery. Many of the occupations require working outside and do not involve a lot of paperwork or working closely with others.

**EDUCATION/TRAINING PROGRAM(S)—**Painter and Wall Coverer. **RELATED KNOWLEDGE/ COURSES—Building and Construction:** Knowledge of materials, methods, and tools involved in the construction or repair of houses, buildings, or other structures such as highways and roads. **Customer and Personal Service:** Knowledge of principles and processes for providing customer and personal services. This includes customer needs assessment, meeting quality standards for services, and evaluation of customer satisfaction. **Chemistry:** Knowledge of the chemical composition, structure, and properties of substances and of the chemical processes and transformations that they undergo. This includes uses of chemicals and their interactions, danger signs, production techniques, and disposal methods. **Principles of Mechanical Devices:** Knowledge of machines and tools, including their designs, uses, repair, and maintenance. **Fine Arts:** Knowledge of the theory and techniques required to compose, produce, and perform works of music, dance, visual arts, drama, and sculpture.

# Painters, Transportation Equipment

▲ Growth: 17.5%

▲ Annual Job Openings: 8,000

▲ Annual Earnings: $32,910

▲ Education/Training Required: Moderate-term on-the-job training

▲ Self-Employed: 7.4%

▲ Part-Time: 5.7%

**Operate or tend painting machines to paint surfaces of transportation equipment, such as automobiles, buses, trucks, trains, boats, and airplanes.** Pours paint into spray gun and sprays specified amount of primer, decorative, or finish coatings onto prepared surfaces. Paints designs, lettering, or other identifying information on vehicles, using paint brush or paint sprayer. Operates lifting and moving devices to move equipment or materials to access areas to be painted. Removes accessories from vehicles, such as chrome or mirrors, and masks other surfaces with tape or paper. Sets up portable ventilators, exhaust units, ladders, and scaffolding. Strips grease, dirt, paint, and rust from vehicle surface, using abrasives, solvents, brushes, blowtorch, or sandblaster. Lays out logos, symbols, or designs on painted surfaces according to blueprint specifications, using measuring instruments, stencils, and patterns. Regulates controls on portable ventilators and exhaust units to cure and dry paint or other coatings. Disassembles sprayer and power equipment, such as sandblaster, and cleans equipment and hand tools, using solvents, wire brushes, and cloths. Selects paint according to company requirements and matches colors of paint following specified color charts. Mixes, stirs, and thins paint or other coatings, using spatula or power mixing equipment. Paints areas inaccessible to spray gun or retouches painted surface, using brush. **SKILLS—** Operation and Control.

**GOE—Interest Area:** 05. Mechanics, Installers, and Repairers. **Work Group:** 05.03. Mechanical Work. **Other Job Titles in This Work Group:** Aircraft Body and Bonded Structure Repairers; Aircraft Engine Specialists; Aircraft Mechanics and Service Technicians; Airframe-and-Power-Plant Mechanics; Automotive Body and Related Repairers; Automotive Glass Installers and Repairers; Automotive Master Mechanics; Automotive Service Technicians and Mechanics; Automotive Specialty Technicians; Bicycle Repairers; Bridge and Lock Tenders; Bus and Truck Mechanics and Diesel Engine Specialists; Camera and Photographic Equipment Repairers; Coin, Vending, and Amusement Machine Servicers and Repairers; Control and Valve Installers and Repairers, Except Mechanical Door; Farm Equipment Mechanics; Gas Appliance Repairers; Hand and Portable Power Tool Repairers; Heating and Air Conditioning Mechanics; Heating, Air Conditioning, and Refrigeration Mechanics and Installers; Helpers—Electricians; Helpers—Installation, Maintenance, and Repair Workers; Industrial Machinery Mechanics; Keyboard Instrument Repairers and Tuners; Locksmiths and Safe Repairers; Maintenance and Repair Workers, General; Maintenance Workers, Machinery; Mechanical Door Repairers; Medical Appliance Technicians; Medical Equipment Repairers; Meter Mechanics; Millwrights; Mobile Heavy Equipment Mechanics, Except

Engines; Motorboat Mechanics; Motorcycle Mechanics; Musical Instrument Repairers and Tuners; Ophthalmic Laboratory Technicians; Optical Instrument Assemblers; Outdoor Power Equipment and Other Small Engine Mechanics; Percussion Instrument Repairers and Tuners; Precision Instrument and Equipment Repairers, All Other; others. **PERSONALITY TYPE—**Realistic. Realistic occupations frequently involve work activities that include practical, hands-on problems and solutions. They often deal with plants, animals, and real-world materials like wood, tools, and machinery. Many of the occupations require working outside and do not involve a lot of paperwork or working closely with others.

**EDUCATION/TRAINING PROGRAM(S)—**Auto/Automotive Body Repairer. **RELATED KNOWLEDGE/COURSES—Principles of Mechanical Devices:** Knowledge of machines and tools, including their designs, uses, repair, and maintenance. **Mathematics:** Knowledge of arithmetic, algebra, geometry, calculus, statistics, and their applications. **Design:** Knowledge of design techniques, tools, and principles involved in production of precision technical plans, blueprints, drawings, and models. **Fine Arts:** Knowledge of the theory and techniques required to compose, produce, and perform works of music, dance, visual arts, drama, and sculpture. **Chemistry:** Knowledge of the chemical composition, structure, and properties of substances and of the chemical processes and transformations that they undergo. This includes uses of chemicals and their interactions, danger signs, production techniques, and disposal methods.

# Paperhangers

- ▲ Growth: 20.2%
- ▲ Annual Job Openings: 3,000
- ▲ Annual Earnings: $32,490
- ▲ Education/Training Required: Moderate-term on-the-job training
- ▲ Self-Employed: 60.2%
- ▲ Part-Time: 9.2%

Cover interior walls and ceilings of rooms with decorative wallpaper or fabric or attach advertising posters on surfaces such as walls and billboards. Duties include removing old materials from surface to be pa-

**pered.** Applies thinned glue to waterproof porous surfaces, using brush, roller, or pasting machine. Measures and cuts strips from roll of wallpaper or fabric, using shears or razor. Trims rough edges from strips, using straightedge and trimming knife. Trims excess material at ceiling or baseboard, using knife. Smoothes strips or poster sections with brush or roller to remove wrinkles and bubbles and to smooth joints. Aligns and places strips or poster sections of billboard on surface to match adjacent edges. Mixes paste, using paste-powder and water, and brushes paste onto surface. Marks vertical guideline on wall to align first strip, using plumb bob and chalkline. Applies acetic acid to damp plaster to prevent lime from bleeding through paper. Staples or tacks advertising posters onto fences, walls, or poles. Measures walls and ceiling to compute number and length of strips required to cover surface. Fills holes and cracks with plaster, using trowel. Removes paint, varnish, and grease from surfaces, using paint remover and water soda solution. Erects and works from scaffold. Removes old paper, using water, steam machine, or chemical remover and scraper. Smoothes rough spots on walls and ceilings, using sandpaper. **SKILLS**—Mathematics. Reading Comprehension. Critical Thinking.

**GOE—Interest Area:** 06. Construction, Mining, and Drilling. **Work Group:** 06.02. Construction. **Other Job Titles in This Work Group:** Boat Builders and Shipwrights; Boilermakers; Brattice Builders; Brickmasons and Blockmasons; Carpenters; Carpet Installers; Ceiling Tile Installers; Cement Masons and Concrete Finishers; Commercial Divers; Construction Carpenters; Drywall and Ceiling Tile Installers; Drywall Installers; Electricians; Explosives Workers, Ordnance Handling Experts, and Blasters; Fence Erectors; Floor Layers, Except Carpet, Wood, and Hard Tiles; Floor Sanders and Finishers; Glaziers; Grader, Bulldozer, and Scraper Operators; Hazardous Materials Removal Workers; Insulation Workers, Floor, Ceiling, and Wall; Insulation Workers, Mechanical; Manufactured Building and Mobile Home Installers; Operating Engineers; Operating Engineers and Other Construction Equipment Operators; Painters, Construction and Maintenance; Paving, Surfacing, and Tamping Equipment Operators; Pile-Driver Operators; Pipe Fitters; Pipelayers; Pipelaying Fitters; Plasterers and Stucco Masons; Plumbers; Plumbers, Pipefitters, and Steamfitters; Rail-Track Laying and Maintenance Equipment Operators; Refractory Materials Repairers, Except Brickmasons; Reinforcing Iron and Rebar Workers; Riggers; Roofers; Rough Carpenters; Security and Fire Alarm Systems Installers; Segmental Pavers; Sheet Metal Workers; Ship Carpenters and Joiners; Stone Cutters and Carvers; Stonemasons; Structural Iron and Steel Workers; Tapers; Terrazzo Workers and Finishers; Tile and Marble Setters. **PERSONALITY TYPE**—Realistic. Realistic occupations frequently involve work activities that include practical, hands-on problems and solutions. They often deal with plants, animals, and real-world materials like wood, tools, and machinery. Many of the occupations require working outside and do not involve a lot of paperwork or working closely with others.

**EDUCATION/TRAINING PROGRAM(S)**—Painter and Wall Coverer. **RELATED KNOWLEDGE/COURSES**—**Building and Construction:** Knowledge of materials, methods, and tools involved in the construction or repair of houses, buildings, or other structures such as highways and roads. **Design:** Knowledge of design techniques, tools, and principles involved in production of precision technical plans, blueprints, drawings, and models. **Mathematics:** Knowledge of arithmetic, algebra, geometry, calculus, statistics, and their applications. **Chemistry:** Knowledge of the chemical composition, structure, and properties of substances and of the chemical processes and transformations that they undergo. This includes uses of chemicals and their interactions, danger signs, production techniques, and disposal methods. **Principles of Mechanical Devices:** Knowledge of machines and tools, including their designs, uses, repair, and maintenance.

# Paralegals and Legal Assistants

▲ Growth: 33.2%

▲ Annual Job Openings: 23,000

▲ Annual Earnings: $38,790

▲ Education/Training Required: Associate's degree

▲ Self-Employed: 3.5%

▲ Part-Time: 12.5%

**Assist lawyers by researching legal precedent, investigating facts, or preparing legal documents. Conduct research to support a legal proceeding, to formulate a defense, or to initiate legal action.** Gathers and analyzes research data, such as statutes, decisions, and legal articles, codes, and documents. Prepares legal documents, including briefs, pleadings, appeals, wills, contracts, and real estate closing statements. Prepares affidavits or other documents, maintains document file, and files pleadings with court clerk. Arbitrates disputes between parties and assists in real estate closing process. Answers questions regarding legal issues pertaining to civil service hearings. Presents arguments and evidence to support appeal at appeal hearing. Keeps and monitors legal volumes to ensure that law library is up to date. Directs and coordinates law office activity, including delivery of subpoenas. Calls upon witnesses to testify at hearing. Appraises and inventories real and personal property for estate planning. Investigates facts and law of cases to determine causes of action and to prepare cases. **SKILLS**—Reading Comprehension. Critical Thinking. Speaking. Writing. Negotiation. Persuasion. Active Listening.

**GOE**—**Interest Area:** 04. Law, Law Enforcement, and Public Safety. **Work Group:** 04.02. Law. **Other Job Titles in This Work Group:** Administrative Law Judges, Adjudicators, and Hearing Officers; Arbitrators, Mediators, and Conciliators; Judges, Magistrate Judges, and Magistrates; Law Clerks; Lawyers; Legal Support Workers, All Other; Title Examiners and Abstractors; Title Examiners, Abstractors, and Searchers; Title Searchers. **PERSONALITY TYPE**—Enterprising. Enterprising occupations frequently involve starting up and carrying out projects. These occupations can involve leading people and making many decisions. They sometimes require risk taking and often deal with business.

**EDUCATION/TRAINING PROGRAM(S)**—Paralegal/Legal Assistant. **RELATED KNOWLEDGE/COURSES**—**Law and Government:** Knowledge of laws, legal codes, court procedures, precedents, government regulations, executive orders, agency rules, and the democratic political process. **Clerical Studies:** Knowledge of administrative and clerical procedures and systems such as word processing, managing files and records, stenography and transcription, designing forms, and other office procedures and terminology. **English Language:** Knowledge of the structure and content of the English language, including the meaning and spelling of words, rules of composition, and grammar. **Computers and Electronics:** Knowledge of circuit boards, processors, chips, electronic equipment, and computer hardware and software, including applications and programming. **Administration and Management:** Knowledge of business and management principles involved in strategic planning, resource allocation, human resources modeling, leadership technique, production methods, and coordination of people and resources.

# Paving, Surfacing, and Tamping Equipment Operators

▲ Growth: 15.5%
▲ Annual Job Openings: 6,000
▲ Annual Earnings: $30,090
▲ Education/Training Required: Moderate-term on-the-job training
▲ Self-Employed: 0%
▲ Part-Time: 8.4%

Operate equipment used for applying concrete, asphalt, or other materials to road beds, parking lots, or airport runways and taxiways or equipment used for tamping gravel, dirt, or other materials. Includes concrete and asphalt paving machine operators, form tampers, tamping machine operators, and stone spreader operators. Operates machine or manually rolls surfaces to compact earth fills, foundation forms, and finished road materials according to grade specifications. Sets up forms and lays out guidelines for curbs according to written specifications, using string, spray paint, and concrete/water mix. Cleans, maintains, and repairs equipment according to specifications, using mechanics' hand tools, or reports malfunction to supervisor. Fills tank, hopper, or machine with paving materials. Installs dies, cutters, and extensions to screed onto machine, using hand tools. Drives machine onto truck trailer and drives truck to transport machine to and from job site. Lights burner or starts heating unit of machine and regulates temperature. Monitors machine operation and observes distribution of paving material to adjust machine settings or material flow. Starts machine, engages clutch, pushes and moves levers, and turns wheels to control and guide machine along forms or guidelines. Drives and operates curbing machine to extrude concrete or asphalt curbing. Operates machine to clean or cut expansion joints in concrete or asphalt and to rout out cracks in pavement. Operates machine to mix and spray binding, waterproofing, and curing compounds. Operates machine to spread, smooth, or steel-reinforce stone, concrete, or asphalt. SKILLS—Operation and Control. Equipment Selection. Equipment Maintenance. Operation Monitoring.

GOE—Interest Area: 06. Construction, Mining, and Drilling. Work Group: 06.02. Construction. Other Job

Titles in This Work Group: Boat Builders and Shipwrights; Boilermakers; Brattice Builders; Brickmasons and Blockmasons; Carpenters; Carpet Installers; Ceiling Tile Installers; Cement Masons and Concrete Finishers; Commercial Divers; Construction Carpenters; Drywall and Ceiling Tile Installers; Drywall Installers; Electricians; Explosives Workers, Ordnance Handling Experts, and Blasters; Fence Erectors; Floor Layers, Except Carpet, Wood, and Hard Tiles; Floor Sanders and Finishers; Glaziers; Grader, Bulldozer, and Scraper Operators; Hazardous Materials Removal Workers; Insulation Workers, Floor, Ceiling, and Wall; Insulation Workers, Mechanical; Manufactured Building and Mobile Home Installers; Operating Engineers; Operating Engineers and Other Construction Equipment Operators; Painters, Construction and Maintenance; Paperhangers; Pile-Driver Operators; Pipe Fitters; Pipelayers; Pipelaying Fitters; Plasterers and Stucco Masons; Plumbers; Plumbers, Pipefitters, and Steamfitters; Rail-Track Laying and Maintenance Equipment Operators; Refractory Materials Repairers, Except Brickmasons; Reinforcing Iron and Rebar Workers; Riggers; Roofers; Rough Carpenters; Security and Fire Alarm Systems Installers; Segmental Pavers; Sheet Metal Workers; Ship Carpenters and Joiners; Stone Cutters and Carvers; Stonemasons; Structural Iron and Steel Workers; Tapers; Terrazzo Workers and Finishers; Tile and Marble Setters. PERSONALITY TYPE—Realistic. Realistic occupations frequently involve work activities that include practical, hands-on problems and solutions. They often deal with plants, animals, and real-world materials like wood, tools, and machinery. Many of the occupations require working outside and do not involve a lot of paperwork or working closely with others.

EDUCATION/TRAINING PROGRAM(S)—Construction Equipment Operator. **RELATED KNOWLEDGE/COURSES—Principles of Mechanical Devices:** Knowledge of machines and tools, including their designs, uses, repair, and maintenance. **Transportation:** Knowledge of principles and methods for moving people or goods by air, rail, sea, or road, including the relative costs and benefits. **Building and Construction:** Knowledge of materials, methods, and tools involved in the construction or repair of houses, buildings, or other structures such as highways and roads. **Production and Processing:** Knowledge of raw materials, production processes, quality control, costs, and other techniques for maximizing the effective manufacture and distribution of goods. **Physics:** Knowledge and prediction of physical principles and laws and their interrelationships and applications to understanding fluid, material, and atmospheric dynamics and mechanical, electrical, atomic, and sub-atomic structures and processes.

# Personal and Home Care Aides

- ▲ Growth: 62.5%
- ▲ Annual Job Openings: 84,000
- ▲ Annual Earnings: $15,960
- ▲ Education/Training Required: Short-term on-the-job training
- ▲ Self-Employed: 1.5%
- ▲ Part-Time: 42.4%

Assist elderly or disabled adults with daily living activities at the person's home or in a daytime non-residential facility. Duties performed at a place of residence may include keeping house (making beds, doing laundry, washing dishes) and preparing meals. May provide meals and supervised activities at non-residential care facilities. May advise families, the elderly, and disabled on such things as nutrition, cleanliness, and household utilities. Advises and assists family members in planning nutritious meals, purchasing and preparing foods, and utilizing commodities from surplus food programs. Evaluates needs of individuals served and plans for continuing services. Prepares and maintains records of assistance rendered. Assists client with dressing, undressing, and toilet activities. Assists parents in establishing good study habits for children. Drives motor vehicle to transport client to specified locations. Types correspondence and reports. Obtains information for client for personal and business purposes. Assigns housekeeping duties according to children's capabilities. Gives bedside care to incapacitated individuals and trains family members to provide bedside care. Assists in training children. Explains fundamental hygiene principles. **SKILLS—**Service Orientation. Speaking. Social Perceptiveness. Learning Strategies. Active Listening.

**GOE—Interest Area:** 11. Recreation, Travel, and Other Personal Services. **Work Group:** 11.08. Other Personal Services. **Other Job Titles in This Work Group:** Cleaners of Vehicles and Equipment; Cooks, Private Household; Embalmers; Funeral Attendants; Personal Care and Service Workers, All Other. **PERSONALITY TYPE—**Social. Social occupations frequently involve working with, communicating with, and teaching people. These occupations often involve helping or providing service to others.

**EDUCATION/TRAINING PROGRAM(S)—**Elder Care Provider/Companion; Homemaker's Aide; Massage. **RELATED KNOWLEDGE/COURSES—Customer and Personal Service:** Knowledge of principles and processes for providing customer and personal services. This includes customer needs assessment, meeting quality standards for services, and evaluation of customer satisfaction. **Medicine and Dentistry:** Knowledge of the information and techniques needed to diagnose and treat human injuries, diseases, and deformities. This includes symptoms, treatment alternatives, drug properties and interactions, and preventive health-care measures. **Education and Training:** Knowledge of principles and methods for curriculum and training design, teaching and instruction for individuals and groups, and the measurement of training effects. **Clerical Studies:** Knowledge of administrative and clerical procedures and systems such as word processing, managing files and records, stenography and transcription, designing forms, and other office procedures and terminology. **Administration and Management:** Knowledge of business and management principles involved in strategic planning, resource allocation, human resources modeling, leadership technique, production methods, and coordination of people and resources.

# Pest Control Workers

- ▲ Growth: 22.1%
- ▲ Annual Job Openings: 7,000
- ▲ Annual Earnings: $24,020
- ▲ Education/Training Required: Moderate-term on-the-job training
- ▲ Self-Employed: 14%
- ▲ Part-Time: 30.4%

**Spray or release chemical solutions or toxic gases and set traps to kill pests and vermin, such as mice, termites, and roaches, that infest buildings and surrounding areas.** Sprays or dusts chemical solutions, powders, or gases into rooms, onto clothing, furnishings, or wood, and over marshlands, ditches, and catch-basins. Sets mechanical traps and places poisonous paste or bait in sewers, burrows, and ditches. Cuts or bores openings in building or surrounding concrete, accesses infested areas, inserts nozzle, and injects pesticide to impregnate ground. Directs and/or assists other workers in treatment and extermination processes to eliminate and control rodents, insects, and weeds. Cleans and removes blockages from infested areas to facilitate spraying procedure and provide drainage, using broom, mop, shovel, and rake. Digs up and burns or sprays weeds with herbicides. Cleans work site after completion of job. Records work activities performed. Drives truck equipped with power spraying equipment. Posts warning signs and locks building doors to secure area to be fumigated. Positions and fastens edges of tarpaulins over building and tapes vents to ensure air-tight environment and checks for leaks. Measures area dimensions requiring treatment, using rule, calculates fumigant requirements, and estimates cost for service. Studies preliminary reports and diagrams of infested area and determines treatment type required to eliminate and prevent recurrence of infestation. Inspects premises to identify infestation source, extent of damage to property, wall, and roof porosity, and access to infested locations. **SKILLS**—Mathematics. Reading Comprehension. Judgment and Decision Making. Operation and Control. Equipment Selection.

**GOE**—**Interest Area:** 03. Plants and Animals. **Work Group:** 03.03. Hands-on Work in Plants and Animals. **Other Job Titles in This Work Group:** Agricultural Equipment Operators; Fallers; Farmworkers and Laborers, Crop, Nursery, and Greenhouse; Farmworkers, Farm and Ranch Animals; Fishers and Related Fishing Workers; Forest and Conservation Technicians; Forest and Conservation Workers; General Farmworkers; Grounds Maintenance Workers, All Other; Hunters and Trappers; Landscaping and Groundskeeping Workers; Logging Equipment Operators; Logging Tractor Operators; Logging Workers, All Other; Nursery Workers; Pesticide Handlers, Sprayers, and Applicators, Vegetation; Tree Trimmers and Pruners. **PERSONALITY TYPE**—Realistic. Realistic occupations frequently involve work activities that include practical, hands-on problems and solutions. They often deal with plants, animals, and real-world materials like wood, tools, and machinery. Many of the occupations require working outside and do not involve a lot of paperwork or working closely with others.

**EDUCATION/TRAINING PROGRAM(S)**—Agricultural Supplies Retailing and Wholesaling. **RELATED**

KNOWLEDGE/COURSES—**Chemistry:** Knowledge of the chemical composition, structure, and properties of substances and of the chemical processes and transformations that they undergo. This includes uses of chemicals and their interactions, danger signs, production techniques, and disposal methods. **Principles of Mechanical Devices:** Knowledge of machines and tools, including their designs, uses, repair, and maintenance. **Mathematics:** Knowledge of arithmetic, algebra, geometry, calculus, statistics, and their applications. **Customer and Personal Service:** Knowledge of principles and processes for providing customer and personal services. This includes customer needs assessment, meeting quality standards for services, and evaluation of customer satisfaction. **Biology:** Knowledge of plant and animal organisms and their tissues, cells, functions, interdependencies, and interactions with each other and the environment.

# Pharmacy Technicians

- ▲ Growth: 36.4%
- ▲ Annual Job Openings: 22,000
- ▲ Annual Earnings: $21,600
- ▲ Education/Training Required: Moderate-term on-the-job training
- ▲ Self-Employed: 0%
- ▲ Part-Time: 22.9%

**Prepare medications under the direction of a pharmacist. May measure, mix, count out, label, and record amounts and dosages of medications.** Assists pharmacist to prepare and dispense medication. Receives and stores incoming supplies. Prepares intravenous (IV) packs, using sterile technique, under supervision of hospital pharmacist. Cleans equipment and sterilizes glassware according to prescribed methods. Counts stock and enters data in computer to maintain inventory records. Processes records of medication and equipment dispensed to hospital patient, computes charges, and enters data in computer. Mixes pharmaceutical preparations, fills bottles with prescribed tablets and capsules, and types labels for bottles. **SKILLS**—Reading Comprehension. Mathematics. Active Listening. Science. Writing.

**GOE—Interest Area:** 14. Medical and Health Services. **Work Group:** 14.02. Medicine and Surgery. **Other Job Titles in This Work Group:** Anesthesiologists; Family and General Practitioners; Internists, General; Medical Assistants; Obstetricians and Gynecologists; Pediatricians, General; Pharmacists; Pharmacy Aides; Physician Assistants; Physicians and Surgeons, All Other; Psychiatrists; Registered Nurses; Surgeons; Surgical Technologists. **PERSONALITY TYPE**—Conventional. Conventional occupations frequently involve following set procedures and routines. These occupations can include working with data and details more than with ideas. Usually there is a clear line of authority to follow.

EDUCATION/TRAINING PROGRAM(S)—Pharmacy Technician/Assistant. **RELATED KNOWLEDGE/COURSES—Clerical Studies:** Knowledge of administrative and clerical procedures and systems such as word processing, managing files and records, stenography and transcription, designing forms, and other office procedures and terminology. **Medicine and Dentistry:** Knowledge of the information and techniques needed to diagnose and treat human injuries, diseases, and deformities. This includes symptoms, treatment alternatives, drug properties and interactions, and preventive health-care measures. **Computers and Electronics:** Knowledge of circuit boards, processors, chips, electronic equipment, and computer hardware and software, including applications and programming. **Mathematics:** Knowledge of arithmetic, algebra, geometry, calculus, statistics, and their applications. **Chemistry:** Knowledge of the chemical composition, structure, and properties of substances and of the chemical processes and transformations that they undergo. This includes uses of chemicals and their interactions, danger signs, production techniques, and disposal methods.

# Photographers, Scientific

- ▲ Growth: 17%
- ▲ Annual Job Openings: 13,000
- ▲ Annual Earnings: $27,420
- ▲ Education/Training Required: Long-term on-the-job training
- ▲ Self-Employed: 51.9%
- ▲ Part-Time: 23.1%

**Photograph variety of subject material to illustrate or record scientific/medical data or phenomena, utilizing knowledge of scientific procedures and photographic technology and techniques.** Photographs variety of subject material to illustrate or record scientific or medical data or phenomena related to an area of interest. Sights and focuses camera to take picture of subject material to illustrate or record scientific or medical data or phenomena. Plans methods and procedures for photographing subject material and setup of required equipment. Observes and arranges subject material to desired position. Engages in research to develop new photographic procedure, materials, and scientific data. Sets up, mounts, or installs photographic equipment and cameras. Removes exposed film and develops film, using chemicals, touch-up tools, and equipment. **SKILLS**—Reading Comprehension. Equipment Selection. Active Learning. Science. Writing.

**GOE—Interest Area:** 02. Science, Math, and Engineering. **Work Group:** 02.05. Laboratory Technology. **Other Job Titles in This Work Group:** Biological Technicians; Chemical Technicians; Environmental Science and Protection Technicians, Including Health; Geological and Petroleum Technicians; Geological Data Technicians; Geological Sample Test Technicians; Nuclear Equipment Operation Technicians; Nuclear Technicians. **PERSONALITY TYPE**—Artistic. Artistic occupations frequently involve working with forms, designs, and patterns. They often require self-expression, and the work can be done without following a clear set of rules.

**EDUCATION/TRAINING PROGRAM(S)**—Commercial Photography; Film/Video and Photographic Arts, Other; Photography. **RELATED KNOWLEDGE/ COURSES—Fine Arts:** Knowledge of the theory and techniques required to compose, produce, and perform works of music, dance, visual arts, drama, and sculpture. **Chemistry:** Knowledge of the chemical composition, structure, and properties of substances and of the chemical processes and transformations that they undergo. This includes uses of chemicals and their interactions, danger signs, production techniques, and disposal methods. **Physics:** Knowledge and prediction of physical principles and laws and their interrelationships and applications to understanding fluid, material, and atmospheric dynamics and mechanical, electrical, atomic, and sub-atomic structures and processes. **Biology:** Knowledge of plant and animal organisms and their tissues, cells, functions, interdependencies, and interactions with each other and the environment. **Medicine and Dentistry:** Knowledge of the information and techniques needed to diagnose and treat human injuries, diseases, and deformities. This includes symptoms, treatment alternatives, drug properties and interactions, and preventive health-care measures. **Communications and Media:** Knowledge of media production, communication, and dissemination techniques and methods. This includes alternative ways to inform and entertain via written, oral, and visual media.

# Physical Therapist Aides

- ▲ Growth: 46.3%
- ▲ Annual Job Openings: 7,000
- ▲ Annual Earnings: $20,930
- ▲ Education/Training Required: Short-term on-the-job training
- ▲ Self-Employed: 0%
- ▲ Part-Time: 34.5%

**Under close supervision of a physical therapist or physical therapy assistant, perform only delegated, selected, or routine tasks in specific situations. These duties include preparing the patient and the treatment area.** Observes patients during treatment, compiles and evaluates data on patients' responses to treatments and progress, and reports to physical therapist. Administers active and passive manual therapeutic exercises, therapeutic massage, and heat, light, sound, water, and electrical modality treatments, such as ultrasound. Administers traction to relieve neck and back pain, using intermittent and static traction equipment. Provides routine treatments, such as hydrotherapy, hot and cold packs, and paraffin bath. Secures patients into or onto therapy equipment. Measures patient's range-of-joint motion, body parts, and vital signs to determine effects of treatments or for patient evaluations. Records treatment given and equipment used. Performs clerical duties, such as taking inventory, ordering supplies, answering telephone, taking messages, and filling out forms. Cleans work area and equipment after treatment. Transports patients to and from treatment area. Fits patients for orthopedic braces, prostheses, and supportive devices, such as crutches. Assists patients to dress, undress, and put on and remove supportive devices, such as braces, splints, and slings. Confers with physical therapy staff and others to discuss and evaluate patient information for planning, modifying, and coordinating treatment. Adjusts fit of supportive devices for patients as instructed. Trains patients in use and care of orthopedic braces, prostheses, and supportive devices, such as crutches. Safeguards, motivates, and assists patients practicing exercises and functional activities under direction of professional staff. Instructs, motivates, and assists patients to learn and improve functional activities, such as perambulation, transfer, ambulation, and daily-living activities. **SKILLS**—Reading Comprehension. Learning Strategies. Service Orientation. Active Listening. Instructing.

**GOE—Interest Area:** 14. Medical and Health Services. **Work Group:** 14.06. Medical Therapy. **Other Job Titles in This Work Group:** Audiologists; Massage Therapists; Occupational Therapist Aides; Occupational Therapist Assistants; Occupational Therapists; Physical Therapist Assistants; Physical Therapists; Radiation Therapists; Recreational Therapists; Respiratory Therapists; Respiratory Therapy Technicians; Speech-Language Pathologists; Therapists, All Other. **PERSONALITY TYPE**—Social. Social occupations frequently involve working with, communicating with, and teaching people. These occupations often involve helping or providing service to others.

**EDUCATION/TRAINING PROGRAM(S)**—Physical Therapy Assistant. **RELATED KNOWLEDGE/COURSES—Therapy and Counseling:** Knowledge of principles, methods, and procedures for diagnosis, treatment, and rehabilitation of physical and mental dysfunctions and for career counseling and guidance. **Customer and Personal Service:** Knowledge of principles and processes for providing customer and personal services. This includes customer needs assessment, meeting quality standards for services, and evaluation of customer satisfaction. **Education and Training:** Knowledge of principles and methods for curriculum and training design, teaching and instruction for individuals and groups, and the measurement of training effects. **Clerical Studies:** Knowledge of administrative and clerical procedures and systems such as word processing, managing files and records, stenography and transcription, designing forms, and other office procedures and terminology. **Psychology:** Knowledge of human behavior and performance; individual differences in ability, personality, and interests; learning and motivation; psychological research methods; and the assessment and treatment of behavioral and affective disorders. **Biology:** Knowledge of plant and animal organisms and their tissues, cells, functions, interdependencies, and interactions with each other and the environment.

# Physical Therapist Assistants

- ▲ Growth: 44.8%
- ▲ Annual Job Openings: 9,000
- ▲ Annual Earnings: $34,370
- ▲ Education/Training Required: Associate's degree
- ▲ Self-Employed: 0%
- ▲ Part-Time: 34.5%

**Assist physical therapists in providing physical therapy treatments and procedures. May, in accordance with state laws, assist in the development of treatment plans, carry out routine functions, document the progress of treatment, and modify specific treatments in accordance with patient status and within the scope of treatment plans established by a physical therapist. Generally requires formal training.** Records treatment given and equipment used. Fits patients for orthopedic braces, prostheses, and supportive devices, such as crutches. Transports patients to and from treatment area. Cleans work area and equipment after treatment. Performs clerical duties, such as taking inventory, ordering supplies, answering telephone, taking messages, and filling out forms. Administers active and passive manual therapeutic exercises, therapeutic massage, and heat, light, sound, water, and electrical modality treatments, such as ultrasound. Instructs, motivates, and assists patients to learn and improve functional activities, such as perambulation, transfer, ambulation, and daily-living activities. Safeguards, motivates, and assists patients practicing exercises and functional activities under direction of professional staff. Administers traction to relieve neck and back pain, using intermittent and static traction equipment. Secures patients into or onto therapy equipment. Measures patient's range-of-joint motion, body parts, and vital signs to determine effects of treatments or for patient evaluations. Assists patients to dress, undress, and put on and remove supportive devices, such as braces, splints, and slings. Confers with physical therapy staff and others to discuss and evaluate patient information for planning, modifying, and coordinating treatment. Adjusts fit of supportive devices for patients as instructed. Provides routine treatments, such as hydrotherapy, hot and cold packs, and paraffin bath. Trains patients in use and care of orthopedic braces, prostheses, and supportive devices, such as crutches. Observes patients during treatments, compiles and evaluates data on patients' responses to treatments and progress, and reports to physical therapist. **SKILLS**—Reading Comprehension. Learning Strategies. Service Orientation. Instructing. Active Listening.

**GOE—Interest Area:** 14. Medical and Health Services. **Work Group:** 14.06. Medical Therapy. **Other Job Titles in This Work Group:** Audiologists; Massage Therapists; Occupational Therapist Aides; Occupational Therapist Assistants; Occupational Therapists; Physical Therapist Aides; Physical Therapists; Radiation Therapists; Recreational Therapists; Respiratory Therapists; Respiratory Therapy Technicians; Speech-Language Pathologists; Therapists, All Other. **PERSONALITY TYPE**—Social. Social occupations frequently involve working with, communicating with, and teaching people. These occupations often involve helping or providing service to others.

**EDUCATION/TRAINING PROGRAM(S)**—Physical Therapy Assistant. **RELATED KNOWLEDGE/ COURSES—Therapy and Counseling:** Knowledge of principles, methods, and procedures for diagnosis, treatment, and rehabilitation of physical and mental dysfunctions and for career counseling and guidance. **Customer and Personal Service:** Knowledge of principles and processes for providing customer and personal services. This includes customer needs assessment, meeting quality standards for services, and evaluation of customer satisfaction. **Education and Training:** Knowledge of principles and methods for curriculum and training design, teaching and instruction for individuals and groups, and the measurement of training effects. **Clerical Studies:** Knowledge of administrative and clerical procedures and systems such as word processing, managing files and records, stenography and transcription, designing forms, and other office procedures and terminology. **Psychology:** Knowledge of human behavior and performance; individual differences in ability, personality, and interests; learning and motivation; psychological research methods; and the assessment and treatment of behavioral and affective disorders. **Biology:** Knowledge of plant and animal organisms and their tissues, cells, functions, interdependencies, and interactions with each other and the environment.

# Pile-Driver Operators

▲ Growth: 14%

▲ Annual Job Openings: 1,000

▲ Annual Earnings: $41,570

▲ Education/Training Required: Moderate-term on-the-job training

▲ Self-Employed: 0%

▲ Part-Time: 5.2%

**Operate pile drivers mounted on skids, barges, crawler treads, or locomotive cranes to drive pilings for retaining walls, bulkheads, and foundations of structures, such as buildings, bridges, and piers.** Moves hand and foot levers to control hoisting equipment to position piling leads, hoist piling into leads, and position hammer over piling. Moves levers and turns valves to activate power hammer or raise and lower drophammer which drives piles to required depth. **SKILLS**—Operation and Control. Operation Monitoring. Troubleshooting.

**GOE—Interest Area:** 06. Construction, Mining, and Drilling. **Work Group:** 06.02. Construction. **Other Job Titles in This Work Group:** Boat Builders and Shipwrights; Boilermakers; Brattice Builders; Brickmasons and Blockmasons; Carpenters; Carpet Installers; Ceiling Tile Installers; Cement Masons and Concrete Finishers; Commercial Divers; Construction Carpenters; Drywall and Ceiling Tile Installers; Drywall Installers; Electricians; Explosives Workers, Ordnance Handling Experts, and Blasters; Fence Erectors; Floor Layers, Except Carpet, Wood, and Hard Tiles; Floor Sanders and Finishers; Glaziers; Grader, Bulldozer, and Scraper Operators; Hazardous Materials Removal Workers; Insulation Workers, Floor, Ceiling, and Wall; Insulation Workers, Mechanical; Manufactured Building and Mobile Home Installers; Operating Engineers; Operating Engineers and Other Construction Equipment Operators; Painters, Construction and Maintenance; Paperhangers; Paving, Surfacing, and Tamping Equipment Operators; Pipe Fitters; Pipelayers; Pipelaying Fitters; Plasterers and Stucco Masons; Plumbers; Plumbers, Pipefitters, and Steamfitters; Rail-Track Laying and Maintenance Equipment Operators; Refractory Materials Repairers, Except Brickmasons; Reinforcing Iron and Rebar Workers; Riggers; Roofers; Rough Carpenters; Security and Fire Alarm Systems Installers; Segmental Pavers; Sheet Metal Workers; Ship Carpenters and Joiners; Stone Cutters and Carvers; Stonemasons; Structural Iron and Steel Workers; Tapers; Terrazzo Workers and Finishers; Tile and Marble Setters. **PERSONALITY TYPE**—Realistic. Realistic occupations frequently involve work activities that include practical, hands-on problems and solutions. They often deal with plants, animals, and real-world materials like wood, tools, and machinery. Many of the occupations require working outside and do not involve a lot of paperwork or working closely with others.

EDUCATION/TRAINING PROGRAM(S)—Construction Equipment Operator. **RELATED KNOWL-EDGE/COURSES—Building and Construction:** Knowledge of materials, methods, and tools involved in the construction or repair of houses, buildings, or other structures such as highways and roads. **Principles of Mechanical Devices:** Knowledge of machines and tools, including their designs, uses, repair, and maintenance. **Engineering and Technology:** Knowledge of the practical application of engineering science and technology. This includes applying principles, techniques,

procedures, and equipment to the design and production of various goods and services. **Physics:** Knowledge and prediction of physical principles and laws and their interrelationships and applications to understanding fluid, material, and atmospheric dynamics and mechanical, electrical, atomic, and sub-atomic structures and processes. **Public Safety and Security:** Knowledge of relevant equipment, policies, procedures, and strategies to promote effective local, state, or national security operations for the protection of people, data, property, and institutions.

# Pipe Fitters

- ▲ Growth: 10.2%
- ▲ Annual Job Openings: 49,000
- ▲ Annual Earnings: $40,170
- ▲ Education/Training Required: Long-term on-the-job training
- ▲ Self-Employed: 13.5%
- ▲ Part-Time: 5.5%

**Lay out, assemble, install, and maintain pipe systems, pipe supports, and related hydraulic and pneumatic equipment for steam, hot water, heating, cooling, lubricating, sprinkling, and industrial production and processing systems.** Plans pipe system layout, installation, or repair according to specifications. Operates motorized pump to remove water from flooded manholes, basements, or facility floors. Turns valve to shut off steam, water, or other gases or liquids from pipe section, using valve key or wrenches. Cuts and bores holes in structures such as bulkheads, decks, walls, and mains, using hand and power tools, prior to pipe installation. Coats nonferrous piping materials by dipping in mixture of molten tin and lead to prevent erosion or galvanic and electrolytic action. Inspects work site to determine presence of obstruction and ensure that holes will not cause structure weakness. Lays out full-scale drawings of pipe systems, supports, and related equipment, following blueprints. Inspects, examines, and tests installed systems and pipelines, using pressure gauge, hydrostatic testing, observation, or other methods. Attaches pipes to walls, structures, and fixtures such as radiators or tanks, using brackets, clamps, tools, or welding equipment. Modifies and maintains pipe systems

and related machines and equipment components following specifications, using hand tools and power tools. Selects pipe sizes and types and related materials, such as supports, hangers, and hydraulic cylinders, according to specifications. Assembles pipes, tubes, and fittings according to specifications. Measures and marks pipes for cutting and threading. Cuts, threads, and hammers pipe to specifications, using tools such as saws, cutting torches, and pipe threaders and benders. **SKILLS—Installation.** Quality Control Analysis. Equipment Selection. Operation and Control. Equipment Maintenance. Mathematics.

**GOE—Interest Area:** 06. Construction, Mining, and Drilling. **Work Group:** 06.02. Construction. **Other Job Titles in This Work Group:** Boat Builders and Shipwrights; Boilermakers; Brattice Builders; Brickmasons and Blockmasons; Carpenters; Carpet Installers; Ceiling Tile Installers; Cement Masons and Concrete Finishers; Commercial Divers; Construction Carpenters; Drywall and Ceiling Tile Installers; Drywall Installers; Electricians; Explosives Workers, Ordnance Handling Experts, and Blasters; Fence Erectors; Floor Layers, Except Carpet, Wood, and Hard Tiles; Floor Sanders and Finishers; Glaziers; Grader, Bulldozer, and Scraper Operators; Hazardous Materials Removal Workers; Insulation Workers, Floor, Ceiling, and Wall; Insulation Workers, Mechanical; Manufactured Building and Mobile Home Installers; Operating Engineers; Operating Engineers and Other Construction Equipment Operators; Painters, Construction and Maintenance; Paperhangers; Paving, Surfacing, and Tamping Equipment Operators; Pile-Driver Operators; Pipelayers; Pipelaying Fitters; Plasterers and Stucco Masons; Plumbers; Plumbers, Pipefitters, and Steamfitters; Rail-Track Laying and Maintenance Equipment Operators; Refractory Materials Repairers, Except Brickmasons; Reinforcing Iron and Rebar Workers; Riggers; Roofers; Rough Carpenters; Security and Fire Alarm Systems Installers; Segmental Pavers; Sheet Metal Workers; Ship Carpenters and Joiners; Stone Cutters and Carvers; Stonemasons; Structural Iron and Steel Workers; Tapers; Terrazzo Workers and Finishers; Tile and Marble Setters. **PERSONALITY TYPE**—Realistic. Realistic occupations frequently involve work activities that include practical, hands-on problems and solutions. They often deal with plants, animals, and real-world materials like wood, tools, and machinery. Many of the occupations require working outside and do not involve a lot of paperwork or working closely with others.

**EDUCATION/TRAINING PROGRAM(S)**—Plumber and Pipefitter. **RELATED KNOWLEDGE/COURSES—Building and Construction:** Knowledge of materials, methods, and tools involved in the construction or repair of houses, buildings, or other structures such as highways and roads. **Principles of Mechanical Devices:** Knowledge of machines and tools, including their designs, uses, repair, and maintenance. **Design:** Knowledge of design techniques, tools, and principles involved in production of precision technical plans, blueprints, drawings, and models. **Engineering and Technology:** Knowledge of the practical application of engineering science and technology. This includes applying principles, techniques, procedures, and equipment to the design and production of various goods and services. **Mathematics:** Knowledge of arithmetic, algebra, geometry, calculus, statistics, and their applications.

# Pipelayers

▲ Growth: 11.9%
▲ Annual Job Openings: 6,000
▲ Annual Earnings: $30,220
▲ Education/Training Required: Moderate-term on-the-job training
▲ Self-Employed: 13.4%
▲ Part-Time: 8.5%

Lay pipe for storm or sanitation sewers, drains, and water mains. Perform any combination of the following tasks: grade trenches or culverts, position pipe, or seal joints. Grades and levels base of trench, using tamping machine and hand tools. Lays out route of pipe, following written instructions or blueprints. Lays pipes in trenches and welds, cements, glues, or otherwise connects pieces together. Taps and drills holes into pipe to introduce auxiliary lines or devices. Covers pipe with earth or other materials. Digs trenches to desired or required depth by hand or using trenching tool. Checks slope, using carpenter's level or lasers. **SKILLS**—Equipment Selection. Operation and Control. Active Listening. Mathematics.

**GOE—Interest Area:** 06. Construction, Mining, and Drilling. **Work Group:** 06.02. Construction. **Other Job Titles in This Work Group:** Boat Builders and Shipwrights; Boilermakers; Brattice Builders; Brickmasons and Blockmasons; Carpenters; Carpet Installers; Ceiling Tile Installers; Cement Masons and Concrete Finishers; Commercial Divers; Construction Carpenters; Drywall and Ceiling Tile Installers; Drywall Installers; Electricians; Explosives Workers, Ordnance Handling Experts, and Blasters; Fence Erectors; Floor Layers,

Except Carpet, Wood, and Hard Tiles; Floor Sanders and Finishers; Glaziers; Grader, Bulldozer, and Scraper Operators; Hazardous Materials Removal Workers; Insulation Workers, Floor, Ceiling, and Wall; Insulation Workers, Mechanical; Manufactured Building and Mobile Home Installers; Operating Engineers; Operating Engineers and Other Construction Equipment Operators; Painters, Construction and Maintenance; Paperhangers; Paving, Surfacing, and Tamping Equipment Operators; Pile-Driver Operators; Pipe Fitters; Pipelaying Fitters; Plasterers and Stucco Masons; Plumbers; Plumbers, Pipefitters, and Steamfitters; Rail-Track Laying and Maintenance Equipment Operators; Refractory Materials Repairers, Except Brickmasons; Reinforcing Iron and Rebar Workers; Riggers; Roofers; Rough Carpenters; Security and Fire Alarm Systems Installers; Segmental Pavers; Sheet Metal Workers; Ship Carpenters and Joiners; Stone Cutters and Carvers; Stonemasons; Structural Iron and Steel Workers; Tapers; Terrazzo Workers and Finishers; Tile and Marble Setters. **PERSONALITY TYPE—Realistic.** Realistic occupations frequently involve work activities that include practical, hands-on problems and solutions. They often deal with plants, animals, and real-world materials like wood, tools, and machinery. Many of the occupations require working outside and do not involve a lot of paperwork or working closely with others.

**EDUCATION/TRAINING PROGRAM(S)—** Plumber and Pipefitter. **RELATED KNOWLEDGE/ COURSES—Principles of Mechanical Devices:** Knowledge of machines and tools, including their designs, uses, repair, and maintenance. **Building and Construction:** Knowledge of materials, methods, and tools involved in the construction or repair of houses, buildings, or other structures such as highways and roads. **Design:** Knowledge of design techniques, tools, and principles involved in production of precision technical plans, blueprints, drawings, and models. **Physics:** Knowledge and prediction of physical principles and laws and their interrelationships and applications to understanding fluid, material, and atmospheric dynamics and mechanical, electrical, atomic, and sub-atomic structures and processes. **Engineering and Technology:** Knowledge of the practical application of engineering science and technology. This includes applying principles, techniques, procedures, and equipment to the design and production of various goods and services.

# Pipelaying Fitters

▲ Growth: 10.2%
▲ Annual Job Openings: 49,000
▲ Annual Earnings: $40,170
▲ Education/Training Required: Long-term on-the-job training
▲ Self-Employed: 13.5%
▲ Part-Time: 8.5%

**Align pipeline section in preparation of welding. Signal tractor driver for placement of pipeline sections in proper alignment. Insert steel spacer.** Guides pipe into trench and signals hoist operator to move pipe until specified alignment with other pipes is achieved. Corrects misalignment of pipe using sledgehammer. Inserts spacers between pipe ends. Inspects joint to verify uniformity of spacing and alignment of pipe surfaces. **SKILLS—Equipment Selection.**

**GOE—Interest Area:** 06. Construction, Mining, and Drilling. **Work Group:** 06.02. Construction. **Other Job Titles in This Work Group:** Boat Builders and Shipwrights; Boilermakers; Brattice Builders; Brickmasons and Blockmasons; Carpenters; Carpet Installers; Ceiling Tile Installers; Cement Masons and Concrete Finishers; Commercial Divers; Construction Carpenters; Drywall and Ceiling Tile Installers; Drywall Installers; Electricians; Explosives Workers, Ordnance Handling Experts, and Blasters; Fence Erectors; Floor Layers,

Except Carpet, Wood, and Hard Tiles; Floor Sanders and Finishers; Glaziers; Grader, Bulldozer, and Scraper Operators; Hazardous Materials Removal Workers; Insulation Workers, Floor, Ceiling, and Wall; Insulation Workers, Mechanical; Manufactured Building and Mobile Home Installers; Operating Engineers; Operating Engineers and Other Construction Equipment Operators; Painters, Construction and Maintenance; Paperhangers; Paving, Surfacing, and Tamping Equipment Operators; Pile-Driver Operators; Pipe Fitters; Pipelayers; Plasterers and Stucco Masons; Plumbers; Plumbers, Pipefitters, and Steamfitters; Rail-Track Laying and Maintenance Equipment Operators; Refractory Materials Repairers, Except Brickmasons; Reinforcing Iron and Rebar Workers; Riggers; Roofers; Rough Carpenters; Security and Fire Alarm Systems Installers; Segmental Pavers; Sheet Metal Workers; Ship Carpenters and Joiners; Stone Cutters and Carvers; Stonemasons; Structural Iron and Steel Workers; Tapers; Terrazzo Workers and Finishers; Tile and Marble Setters. **PERSONALITY TYPE**—Realistic. Realistic occupations frequently involve work activities that include practical, hands-on problems and solutions. They often deal with plants, animals, and real-world materials like wood, tools, and machinery. Many of the occupations require working outside and do not involve a lot of paperwork or working closely with others.

**EDUCATION/TRAINING PROGRAM(S)**— Plumber and Pipefitter. **RELATED KNOWLEDGE/ COURSES**—**Principles of Mechanical Devices:** Knowledge of machines and tools, including their designs, uses, repair, and maintenance. **Building and Construction:** Knowledge of materials, methods, and tools involved in the construction or repair of houses, buildings, or other structures such as highways and roads. **Food Production:** Knowledge of techniques and equipment for planting, growing, and harvesting food products (both plant and animal) for consumption, including storage/handling techniques. **Production and Processing:** Knowledge of raw materials, production processes, quality control, costs, and other techniques for maximizing the effective manufacture and distribution of goods.

# Plasterers and Stucco Masons

- ▲ Growth: 11.9%
- ▲ Annual Job Openings: 7,000
- ▲ Annual Earnings: $35,170
- ▲ Education/Training Required: Long-term on-the-job training
- ▲ Self-Employed: 16.8%
- ▲ Part-Time: 8.4%

**Apply interior or exterior plaster, cement, stucco, or similar materials. May also set ornamental plaster.** Applies coats of plaster or stucco to walls, ceilings, or partitions of buildings, using trowel, brush, or spray gun. Mixes mortar to desired consistency and puts up scaffolds. Installs guidewires on exterior surface of buildings to indicate thickness of plaster or stucco. Molds and installs ornamental plaster pieces, panels, and trim. Directs workers to mix plaster to desired consistency and to erect scaffolds. Applies weatherproof, decorative covering to exterior surfaces of building. Creates decorative textures in finish coat, using sand, pebbles, or stones. **SKILLS**—Coordination. Monitoring. Time Management. Equipment Selection. Installation.

**GOE—Interest Area:** 06. Construction, Mining, and Drilling. **Work Group:** 06.02. Construction. **Other Job Titles in This Work Group:** Boat Builders and Shipwrights; Boilermakers; Brattice Builders; Brickmasons and Blockmasons; Carpenters; Carpet Installers; Ceiling Tile Installers; Cement Masons and Concrete Finishers; Commercial Divers; Construction Carpenters; Drywall and Ceiling Tile Installers; Drywall Installers; Electricians; Explosives Workers, Ordnance Handling Experts, and Blasters; Fence Erectors; Floor Layers,

Except Carpet, Wood, and Hard Tiles; Floor Sanders and Finishers; Glaziers; Grader, Bulldozer, and Scraper Operators; Hazardous Materials Removal Workers; Insulation Workers, Floor, Ceiling, and Wall; Insulation Workers, Mechanical; Manufactured Building and Mobile Home Installers; Operating Engineers; Operating Engineers and Other Construction Equipment Operators; Painters, Construction and Maintenance; Paperhangers; Paving, Surfacing, and Tamping Equipment Operators; Pile-Driver Operators; Pipe Fitters; Pipelayers; Pipelaying Fitters; Plumbers; Plumbers, Pipefitters, and Steamfitters; Rail-Track Laying and Maintenance Equipment Operators; Refractory Materials Repairers, Except Brickmasons; Reinforcing Iron and Rebar Workers; Riggers; Roofers; Rough Carpenters; Security and Fire Alarm Systems Installers; Segmental Pavers; Sheet Metal Workers; Ship Carpenters and Joiners; Stone Cutters and Carvers; Stonemasons; Structural Iron and Steel Workers; Tapers; Terrazzo Workers and Finishers; Tile and Marble Setters. **PERSONALITY TYPE**—Realistic. Realistic occupations frequently involve work activities that include practical, hands-on problems and solutions. They often deal with plants, animals, and real-world materials like wood, tools, and machinery. Many of the occupations require working outside and do not involve a lot of paperwork or working closely with others.

**EDUCATION/TRAINING PROGRAM(S)**—Construction Trades, Other. **RELATED KNOWLEDGE/ COURSES—Building and Construction:** Knowledge of materials, methods, and tools involved in the construction or repair of houses, buildings, or other structures such as highways and roads. **Mathematics:** Knowledge of arithmetic, algebra, geometry, calculus, statistics, and their applications. **Design:** Knowledge of design techniques, tools, and principles involved in production of precision technical plans, blueprints, drawings, and models. **English Language:** Knowledge of the structure and content of the English language, including the meaning and spelling of words, rules of composition, and grammar. **Principles of Mechanical Devices:** Knowledge of machines and tools, including their designs, uses, repair, and maintenance.

# Plastic Molding and Casting Machine Operators and Tenders

- ▲ Growth: 9.8%
- ▲ Annual Job Openings: 38,000
- ▲ Annual Earnings: $23,630
- ▲ Education/Training Required: Moderate-term on-the-job training
- ▲ Self-Employed: 0%
- ▲ Part-Time: 2.6%

**Operate or tend plastic molding machines, such as compression or injection molding machines, to mold, form, or cast thermoplastic materials to specified shape.** Starts machine that automatically liquefies plastic material in heating chamber, injects liquefied material into mold, and ejects molded product. Observes meters and gauges to verify specified temperatures, pressures, and press-cycle times. Turns valves and dials of machines to regulate pressure and temperature, to set press-cycle time, and to close press. Observes continuous operation of automatic machine and width and alignment of plastic sheeting to ensure side flanges.

Weighs prescribed amounts of material for molded part and finished product to ensure specifications are maintained. Removes product from mold or conveyor and cleans and reloads mold. Positions mold frame to correct alignment and tubs containing mixture on top of mold to facilitate loading of molds. Examines molded product for surface defects, such as dents, bubbles, thin areas, and cracks. Fills tubs, molds, or cavities of machine with plastic material in solid or liquid form prior to activating machine. Mixes and pours liquid plastic into rotating drum of machine that spreads, hardens, and shapes mixture. Pulls level and toggle latches to fill mold and regulate tension on sheeting and to release mold covers. Dumps plastic powder, preformed plastic pellets, or preformed rubber slugs into hopper of molding machine. Heats plastic material prior to forming product or cools product after processing to prevent distortion. Breaks seals that hold plastic product in molds, using hand tool, and removes product from mold. Feels stiffness and consistency of molded sheeting to detect machinery malfunction. Reports defect in molds to supervisor. Signals coworker to synchronize feed of materials into molding process. Trims flashing from product. Throws flash and rejected parts into grinder machine to be recycled. Stacks molded parts in boxes or on conveyor for subsequent processing or leaves parts in mold to cool. **SKILLS**—Operation and Control. Operation Monitoring. Quality Control Analysis. Mathematics. Equipment Selection.

**GOE**—**Interest Area:** 08. Industrial Production. **Work Group:** 08.02. Production Technology. **Other Job Titles in This Work Group:** Aircraft Rigging Assemblers; Aircraft Structure Assemblers, Precision; Aircraft Structure, Surfaces, Rigging, and Systems Assemblers; Aircraft Systems Assemblers, Precision; Bench Workers, Jewelry; Bindery Machine Setters and Set-Up Operators; Bindery Workers; Bookbinders; Buffing and Polishing Set-Up Operators; Casting Machine Set-Up Operators; Coating, Painting, and Spraying Machine Setters and Set-Up Operators; Coating, Painting, and Spraying Machine Setters, Operators, and Tenders; Combination Machine Tool Setters and Set-Up Operators, Metal and Plastic; Cutting, Punching, and Press Machine Setters, Operators, and Tenders, Metal and Plastic; Dental Laboratory Technicians; Drilling and Boring Machine Tool Setters, Operators, and Tenders, Metal and Plastic; Electrical and Electronic Equipment Assemblers; Electrical and Electronic Inspectors and Testers; Electromechanical Equipment Assemblers; Engine and Other Machine Assemblers; Extruding and Drawing Machine Setters, Operators, and Tenders, Metal and Plastic; Extruding, Forming, Pressing, and Compacting Machine Setters and Set-Up Operators; Extruding, Forming, Pressing,

and Compacting Machine Setters, Operators, and Tenders; Forging Machine Setters, Operators, and Tenders, Metal and Plastic; Foundry Mold and Coremakers; Gem and Diamond Workers; Grinding, Honing, Lapping, and Deburring Machine Set-Up Operators; Grinding, Lapping, Polishing, and Buffing Machine Tool Setters, Operators, and Tenders, Metal and Plastic; Heat Treating Equipment Setters, Operators, and Tenders, Metal and Plastic; others. **PERSONALITY TYPE**—Realistic. Realistic occupations frequently involve work activities that include practical, hands-on problems and solutions. They often deal with plants, animals, and real-world materials like wood, tools, and machinery. Many of the occupations require working outside and do not involve a lot of paperwork or working closely with others.

**EDUCATION/TRAINING PROGRAM(S)**—Aviation Systems and Avionics Maintenance Technologist/Technician; Dental Laboratory Technician; Machinist/Machine Technologist; Precision Metal Workers, Other. **RELATED KNOWLEDGE/COURSES**—**Production and Processing:** Knowledge of raw materials, production processes, quality control, costs, and other techniques for maximizing the effective manufacture and distribution of goods. **Principles of Mechanical Devices:** Knowledge of machines and tools, including their designs, uses, repair, and maintenance. **Mathematics:** Knowledge of arithmetic, algebra, geometry, calculus, statistics, and their applications. **Physics:** Knowledge and prediction of physical principles and laws and their interrelationships and applications to understanding fluid, material, and atmospheric dynamics and mechanical, electrical, atomic, and sub-atomic structures and processes. **English Language:** Knowledge of the structure and content of the English language, including the meaning and spelling of words, rules of composition, and grammar. **Engineering and Technology:** Knowledge of the practical application of engineering science and technology. This includes applying principles, techniques, procedures, and equipment to the design and production of various goods and services.

# Plastic Molding and Casting Machine Setters and Set-Up Operators

- ▲ Growth: 9.8%
- ▲ Annual Job Openings: 38,000
- ▲ Annual Earnings: $23,630
- ▲ Education/Training Required: Moderate-term on-the-job training
- ▲ Self-Employed: 0%
- ▲ Part-Time: 2.6%

**Set up or set up and operate plastic molding machines, such as compression or injection molding machines, to mold, form, or cast thermoplastic materials to specified shape.** Positions, aligns, and secures assembled mold, mold components, and machine accessories onto machine press bed and attaches connecting lines. Installs dies onto machine or press and coats dies with parting agent according to work order specifications. Presses button or pulls lever to activate machine to inject dies and compress compounds to form and cure specified products. Observes and adjusts machine setup and operation to eliminate production of defective parts and products. Weighs premixed compounds and dumps compound into die well or fills hoppers of machines that automatically supply compound to die. Reads specifications to determine setup and prescribed temperature and time settings to mold, form, or cast plastic materials. Sets machine controls to regulate molding temperature, volume, pressure, and time according to knowledge of plastics and molding procedures. Mixes catalysts, thermoplastic materials, and coloring pigments according to formula, using paddle and mixing machine. Repairs and maintains machines and auxiliary equipment, using hand tools and power tools. Trims excess material from part, using knife, and grinds scrap plastic into powder for reuse. Removes finished or cured product from dies or mold, using hand tools and airhose. Measures and visually inspects products for surface and dimension defects, using precision measuring instruments, to ensure conformance to specifications. **SKILLS**—Operation Monitoring. Operation and Control. Equipment Maintenance. Repairing. Troubleshooting. Reading Comprehension. Quality Control Analysis.

**GOE—Interest Area:** 08. Industrial Production. **Work Group:** 08.02. Production Technology. **Other Job Titles**

**in This Work Group:** Aircraft Rigging Assemblers; Aircraft Structure Assemblers, Precision; Aircraft Structure, Surfaces, Rigging, and Systems Assemblers; Aircraft Systems Assemblers, Precision; Bench Workers, Jewelry; Bindery Machine Setters and Set-Up Operators; Bindery Workers; Bookbinders; Buffing and Polishing Set-Up Operators; Casting Machine Set-Up Operators; Coating, Painting, and Spraying Machine Setters and Set-Up Operators; Coating, Painting, and Spraying Machine Setters, Operators, and Tenders; Combination Machine Tool Setters and Set-Up Operators, Metal and Plastic; Cutting, Punching, and Press Machine Setters, Operators, and Tenders, Metal and Plastic; Dental Laboratory Technicians; Drilling and Boring Machine Tool Setters, Operators, and Tenders, Metal and Plastic; Electrical and Electronic Equipment Assemblers; Electrical and Electronic Inspectors and Testers; Electromechanical Equipment Assemblers; Engine and Other Machine Assemblers; Extruding and Drawing Machine Setters, Operators, and Tenders, Metal and Plastic; Extruding, Forming, Pressing, and Compacting Machine Setters and Set-Up Operators; Extruding, Forming, Pressing, and Compacting Machine Setters, Operators, and Tenders; Forging Machine Setters, Operators, and Tenders, Metal and Plastic; Foundry Mold and Coremakers; Gem and Diamond Workers; Grinding, Honing, Lapping, and Deburring Machine Set-Up Operators; Grinding, Lapping, Polishing, and Buffing Machine Tool Setters, Operators, and Tenders, Metal and Plastic; Heat Treating Equipment Setters, Operators, and Tenders, Metal and Plastic; others. **PERSONALITY TYPE**—Realistic. Realistic occupations frequently involve work activities that include practical, hands-on problems and solutions. They often deal with plants, animals, and real-world materials like wood, tools, and machinery. Many of the occupations require working outside and do not involve a lot of paperwork or working closely with others.

EDUCATION/TRAINING PROGRAM(S)—Aviation Systems and Avionics Maintenance Technologist/Technician; Dental Laboratory Technician; Machinist/Machine Technologist; Precision Metal Workers, Other. **RELATED KNOWLEDGE/COURSES—Principles of Mechanical Devices:** Knowledge of machines and tools, including their designs, uses, repair, and maintenance. **Production and Processing:** Knowledge of raw materials, production processes, quality control, costs, and other techniques for maximizing the effective manufacture and distribution of goods. **Chemistry:** Knowledge of the chemical composition, structure, and properties of substances and of the chemical processes and transformations that they undergo. This includes uses of chemicals and their interactions, danger signs, production techniques, and disposal methods. **Mathematics:** Knowledge of arithmetic, algebra, geometry, calculus, statistics, and their applications. **Computers and Electronics:** Knowledge of circuit boards, processors, chips, electronic equipment, and computer hardware and software, including applications and programming.

# Plumbers

- ▲ Growth: 10.2%
- ▲ Annual Job Openings: 49,000
- ▲ Annual Earnings: $40,170
- ▲ Education/Training Required: Long-term on-the-job training
- ▲ Self-Employed: 13.5%
- ▲ Part-Time: 5.5%

**Assemble, install, and repair pipes, fittings, and fixtures of heating, water, and drainage systems according to specifications and plumbing codes.** Repairs and maintains plumbing by replacing defective washers, replacing or mending broken pipes, and opening clogged drains. Assembles pipe sections, tubing, and fittings, using screws, bolts, solder, plastic solvent, and caulking. Installs pipe assemblies, fittings, valves, and fixtures, such as sinks, toilets, and tubs, using hand and power tools. Cuts, threads, and bends pipe to required angle, using pipe cutters, pipe-threading machine, and pipe-bending machine. Directs workers engaged in pipe cutting and preassembly and installation of plumbing systems and components. Fills pipes or plumbing fixtures with water or air and observes pressure gauges to detect and locate leaks. Locates and marks position of pipe installations and passage holes in structures, using measuring instruments such as ruler and level. Cuts opening in structures to accommodate pipe and pipe fittings, using hand and power tools. Studies building plans and inspects structure to determine required materials and equipment and sequence of pipe installations. **SKILLS**—Installation. Coordination. Repairing. Equipment Selection. Operation and Control. Equipment Maintenance. Active Listening.

**GOE—Interest Area:** 06. Construction, Mining, and Drilling. **Work Group:** 06.02. Construction. **Other Job Titles in This Work Group:** Boat Builders and Shipwrights; Boilermakers; Brattice Builders; Brickmasons and Blockmasons; Carpenters; Carpet Installers; Ceiling Tile Installers; Cement Masons and Concrete Finishers; Commercial Divers; Construction Carpenters; Drywall and Ceiling Tile Installers; Drywall Installers; Electricians; Explosives Workers, Ordnance Handling Experts, and Blasters; Fence Erectors; Floor Layers, Except Carpet, Wood, and Hard Tiles; Floor Sanders and Finishers; Glaziers; Grader, Bulldozer, and Scraper Operators; Hazardous Materials Removal Workers; Insulation Workers, Floor, Ceiling, and Wall; Insulation Workers, Mechanical; Manufactured Building and Mobile Home Installers; Operating Engineers; Operating Engineers and Other Construction Equipment Operators; Painters, Construction and Maintenance; Paperhangers; Paving, Surfacing, and Tamping Equipment Operators; Pile-Driver Operators; Pipe Fitters; Pipelayers; Pipelaying Fitters; Plasterers and Stucco Masons; Plumbers, Pipefitters, and Steamfitters; Rail-Track Laying and Maintenance Equipment Operators; Refractory Materials Repairers, Except Brickmasons; Reinforcing Iron and Rebar Workers; Riggers; Roofers; Rough Carpenters; Security and Fire Alarm Systems Installers; Segmental Pavers; Sheet Metal Workers; Ship Carpenters and Joiners; Stone Cutters and Carvers; Stonemasons; Structural Iron and Steel Workers; Tapers; Terrazzo Workers and Finishers; Tile and Marble Setters. **PERSONALITY TYPE**—Realistic. Realistic occupations frequently involve work activities that include practical, hands-on problems and solutions. They often deal with plants, animals, and real-world materials like wood, tools, and machinery. Many of the occupations require working outside and do not involve a lot of paperwork or working closely with others.

**EDUCATION/TRAINING PROGRAM(S)**—Plumber and Pipefitter. **RELATED KNOWLEDGE/COURSES**—**Principles of Mechanical Devices:** Knowledge of machines and tools, including their designs, uses, repair, and maintenance. **Building and Construction:** Knowledge of materials, methods, and tools involved in the construction or repair of houses, buildings, or other structures such as highways and roads. **Engineering and Technology:** Knowledge of the practical application of engineering science and technology. This includes applying principles, techniques, procedures, and equipment to the design and production of various goods and services. **Mathematics:** Knowledge of arithmetic, algebra, geometry, calculus, statistics, and their applications. **Design:** Knowledge of design techniques, tools, and principles involved in production of precision technical plans, blueprints, drawings, and models.

# Police Detectives

- ▲ Growth: 16.4%
- ▲ Annual Job Openings: 4,000
- ▲ Annual Earnings: $49,830
- ▲ Education/Training Required: Work experience in a related occupation
- ▲ Self-Employed: 0%
- ▲ Part-Time: 1.5%

**Conduct investigations to prevent crimes or solve criminal cases.** Examines scene of crime to obtain clues and gather evidence. Records progress of investigation, maintains informational files on suspects, and submits reports to commanding officer or magistrate to authorize warrants. Reviews governmental agency files to obtain identifying data pertaining to suspects or establishments suspected of violating laws. Testifies before court and grand jury and appears in court as witness. Schedules polygraph test for consenting parties and records results of test interpretations for presentation with findings. Prepares assigned cases for court and charges or responses to charges according to formalized procedures. Observes and photographs narcotic purchase transaction to compile evidence and protect undercover investigators. Arrests or assists in arrest of criminals or suspects. Interviews complainant, witnesses,

and accused persons to obtain facts or statements; records interviews, using recording device. Investigates establishments or persons to establish facts supporting complainant or accused, using supportive information from witnesses or tangible evidence. Maintains surveillance of establishments to attain identifying information on suspects. **SKILLS**—Critical Thinking. Active Listening. Social Perceptiveness. Active Learning. Speaking.

**GOE**—**Interest Area:** 04. Law, Law Enforcement, and Public Safety. **Work Group:** 04.03. Law Enforcement. **Other Job Titles in This Work Group:** Animal Control Workers; Bailiffs; Child Support, Missing Persons, and Unemployment Insurance Fraud Investigators; Correctional Officers and Jailers; Criminal Investigators and Special Agents; Crossing Guards; Detectives and Criminal Investigators; Fire Investigators; Fish and Game Wardens; Forensic Science Technicians; Gaming Surveillance Officers and Gaming Investigators; Highway Patrol Pilots; Immigration and Customs Inspectors; Lifeguards, Ski Patrol, and Other Recreational Protective Service Workers; Parking Enforcement Workers; Police and Sheriff's Patrol Officers; Police Identification and Records Officers; Police Patrol Officers; Private Detectives and Investigators; Security Guards; Sheriffs and Deputy Sheriffs; Transit and Railroad Police. **PERSONALITY TYPE**—Enterprising. Enterprising occupations frequently involve starting up and carrying out projects. These occupations can involve leading people and making many decisions. They sometimes require risk taking and often deal with business.

**EDUCATION/TRAINING PROGRAM(S)**—Law Enforcement/Police Science. **RELATED KNOWLEDGE/COURSES**—**Public Safety and Security:**

Knowledge of relevant equipment, policies, procedures, and strategies to promote effective local, state, or national security operations for the protection of people, data, property, and institutions. **Law and Government:** Knowledge of laws, legal codes, court procedures, precedents, government regulations, executive orders, agency rules, and the democratic political process. **Psychology:** Knowledge of human behavior and performance; individual differences in ability, personality, and interests; learning and motivation; psychological research methods; and the assessment and treatment of behavioral and affective disorders. **English Language:** Knowledge of the structure and content of the English language, including the meaning and spelling of words, rules of composition, and grammar. **Clerical Studies:** Knowledge of administrative and clerical procedures and systems such as word processing, managing files and records, stenography and transcription, designing forms, and other office procedures and terminology.

# Police Identification and Records Officers

- ▲ Growth: 16.4%
- ▲ Annual Job Openings: 4,000
- ▲ Annual Earnings: $49,830
- ▲ Education/Training Required: Work experience in a related occupation
- ▲ Self-Employed: 0%
- ▲ Part-Time: 1.5%

**Collect evidence at crime scene, classify and identify fingerprints, and photograph evidence for use in criminal and civil cases.** Dusts selected areas of crime scene to locate and reveal latent fingerprints. Lifts prints from crime site, using special tape. Photographs, records physical description, and fingerprints homicide victims and suspects for identification. Submits evidence to supervisor. Develops film and prints, using photographic developing equipment. Classifies and files fingerprints. Photographs crime or accident scene to obtain record of evidence. **SKILLS**—Active Listening. Operation and Control. Equipment Selection. Science. Reading Comprehension. Writing.

**GOE—Interest Area:** 04. Law, Law Enforcement, and Public Safety. **Work Group:** 04.03. Law Enforcement.

**Other Job Titles in This Work Group:** Animal Control Workers; Bailiffs; Child Support, Missing Persons, and Unemployment Insurance Fraud Investigators; Correctional Officers and Jailers; Criminal Investigators and Special Agents; Crossing Guards; Detectives and Criminal Investigators; Fire Investigators; Fish and Game Wardens; Forensic Science Technicians; Gaming Surveillance Officers and Gaming Investigators; Highway Patrol Pilots; Immigration and Customs Inspectors; Lifeguards, Ski Patrol, and Other Recreational Protective Service Workers; Parking Enforcement Workers; Police and Sheriff's Patrol Officers; Police Detectives; Police Patrol Officers; Private Detectives and Investigators; Security Guards; Sheriffs and Deputy Sheriffs; Transit and Railroad Police. **PERSONALITY**

TYPE—Conventional. Conventional occupations frequently involve following set procedures and routines. These occupations can include working with data and details more than with ideas. Usually there is a clear line of authority to follow.

EDUCATION/TRAINING PROGRAM(S)—Law Enforcement/Police Science. RELATED KNOWLEDGE/COURSES—Public Safety and Security: Knowledge of relevant equipment, policies, procedures, and strategies to promote effective local, state, or national security operations for the protection of people, data, property, and institutions. Clerical Studies: Knowledge of administrative and clerical procedures and systems such as word processing, managing files and records, stenography and transcription, designing forms, and other office procedures and terminology. Law and Government: Knowledge of laws, legal codes, court procedures, precedents, government regulations, executive orders, agency rules, and the democratic political process. English Language: Knowledge of the structure and content of the English language, including the meaning and spelling of words, rules of composition, and grammar. Chemistry: Knowledge of the chemical composition, structure, and properties of substances and of the chemical processes and transformations that they undergo. This includes uses of chemicals and their interactions, danger signs, production techniques, and disposal methods.

# Police Patrol Officers

- ▲ Growth: 23.2%
- ▲ Annual Job Openings: 21,000
- ▲ Annual Earnings: $40,590
- ▲ Education/Training Required: Long-term on-the-job training
- ▲ Self-Employed: 0%
- ▲ Part-Time: 1.5%

**Patrol assigned area to enforce laws and ordinances, regulate traffic, control crowds, prevent crime, and arrest violators.** Patrols specific area on foot, horseback, or motorized conveyance. Draws diagram of crime or accident scene. Photographs crime or accident scene. Interviews principal witnesses and eyewitnesses. Renders aid to accident victims and other persons requiring first aid for physical injuries. Records facts and prepares reports to document activities. Testifies in court to present evidence or act as witness in traffic and criminal cases. Expedites processing of prisoners and prepares and maintains records of prisoner bookings and prisoner status during booking and pre-trial process. Relays complaint and emergency-request information to appropriate agency dispatcher. Provides road information to assist motorists. Investigates traffic accidents and other accidents to determine causes and to determine if crime has been committed. Evaluates complaint and emergency-request information to determine response requirements. Reviews facts to determine if criminal act or statute violation is involved. Directs traffic flow and reroutes traffic in case of emergencies. Monitors traffic to ensure motorists observe traffic regulations and exhibit safe driving procedures. Arrests perpetrator of criminal act or submits citation or warning to violator of motor vehicle ordinance. Maintains order, responds to emergencies, protects people and property, and enforces motor vehicle and criminal law. SKILLS—Active Listening. Critical Thinking. Service Orientation. Social Perceptiveness. Speaking. Judgment and Decision Making.

GOE—Interest Area: 04. Law, Law Enforcement, and Public Safety. Work Group: 04.03. Law Enforcement. Other Job Titles in This Work Group: Animal Control Workers; Bailiffs; Child Support, Missing Persons, and Unemployment Insurance Fraud Investigators; Correctional Officers and Jailers; Criminal Investigators and Special Agents; Crossing Guards; Detectives and Criminal Investigators; Fire Investigators; Fish and Game Wardens; Forensic Science Technicians; Gaming

Surveillance Officers and Gaming Investigators; Highway Patrol Pilots; Immigration and Customs Inspectors; Lifeguards, Ski Patrol, and Other Recreational Protective Service Workers; Parking Enforcement Workers; Police and Sheriff's Patrol Officers; Police Detectives; Police Identification and Records Officers; Private Detectives and Investigators; Security Guards; Sheriffs and Deputy Sheriffs; Transit and Railroad Police. **PERSONALITY TYPE**—Social. Social occupations frequently involve working with, communicating with, and teaching people. These occupations often involve helping or providing service to others.

**EDUCATION/TRAINING PROGRAM(S)**—Law Enforcement/Police Science. **RELATED KNOWLEDGE/COURSES**—**Public Safety and Security:** Knowledge of relevant equipment, policies, procedures, and strategies to promote effective local, state, or national security operations for the protection of people, data, property, and institutions. **Law and Government:** Knowledge of laws, legal codes, court procedures, precedents, government regulations, executive orders, agency rules, and the democratic political process. **English Language:** Knowledge of the structure and content of the English language, including the meaning and spelling of words, rules of composition, and grammar. **Medicine and Dentistry:** Knowledge of the information and techniques needed to diagnose and treat human injuries, diseases, and deformities. This includes symptoms, treatment alternatives, drug properties and interactions, and preventive health-care measures. **Psychology:** Knowledge of human behavior and performance; individual differences in ability, personality, and interests; learning and motivation; psychological research methods; and the assessment and treatment of behavioral and affective disorders.

# Postal Service Mail Carriers

- ▲ Growth: 2.4%
- ▲ Annual Job Openings: 13,000
- ▲ Annual Earnings: $36,830
- ▲ Education/Training Required: Short-term on-the-job training
- ▲ Self-Employed: 0%
- ▲ Part-Time: 8.6%

**Sort mail for delivery. Deliver mail on established route by vehicle or on foot.** Inserts mail into slots of mail rack to sort mail for delivery. Enters changes of address in route book and re-addresses mail to be forwarded. Sells stamps and issues money orders. Picks up outgoing mail. Completes delivery forms, collects charges, and obtains signature on receipts for delivery of specified types of mail. Delivers mail to residences and business establishments along route. Drives vehicle over established route. **SKILLS**—Reading Comprehension. Service Orientation.

**GOE**—**Interest Area:** 09. Business Detail. **Work Group:** 09.08. Records and Materials Processing. **Other Job Titles in This Work Group:** Cargo and Freight Agents; Couriers and Messengers; Mail Clerks, Except Mail Machine Operators and Postal Service; Marking Clerks; Order Fillers, Wholesale and Retail Sales; Postal Service Mail Sorters, Processors, and Processing Machine Operators; Shipping, Receiving, and Traffic Clerks; Stock Clerks and Order Fillers; Stock Clerks—Stockroom, Warehouse, or Storage Yard; Weighers, Measurers, Checkers, and Samplers, Recordkeeping. **PERSONALITY TYPE**—Conventional. Conventional occupations frequently involve following set procedures and routines. These occupations can include working with data and details more than with ideas. Usually there is a clear line of authority to follow.

**EDUCATION/TRAINING PROGRAM(S)**—No data available. **RELATED KNOWLEDGE/COURSES**—**Geography:** Knowledge of principles and methods for describing the features of land, sea, and air masses, including their physical characteristics, locations, interrelationships, and distribution of plant, animal, and human life. **Transportation:** Knowledge of principles and methods for moving people or goods by air, rail, sea, or road, including the relative costs and benefits. **Mathematics:** Knowledge of arithmetic, algebra, geometry, calculus, statistics, and their applications. **Clerical Studies:** Knowledge of administrative and clerical procedures and systems such as word processing, managing files and records, stenography and transcription, designing forms, and other office procedures and terminology. **English Language:** Knowledge of the structure and content of the English language, including the meaning and spelling of words, rules of composition, and grammar. **Customer and Personal Service:** Knowledge of principles and processes for providing customer and personal services. This includes customer needs assessment, meeting quality standards for services, and evaluation of customer satisfaction.

# Precision Printing Workers

▲ Growth: 5.5%
▲ Annual Job Openings: 24,000
▲ Annual Earnings: $30,090
▲ Education/Training Required: Moderate-term on-the-job training
▲ Self-Employed: 2.6%
▲ Part-Time: 6.3%

**Perform variety of precision printing activities, such as duplication of microfilm and reproduction of graphic arts materials.** Operates automatic processor to develop photographs, plates, or base material used in single or multicolor proofs. Sets up and operates bindery equipment to cut, assemble, staple, or bind materials. Maintains printing machinery and equipment. Examines and inspects printed material for clarity of print and specified color. Mixes powdered ink pigments, using matching book and measuring and mixing tools. Reviews layout and customer order to determine size and style of type. Measures density levels of colors or color guides on proofs, using densitometer, and compares readings to set standards. Prints paper or film copies of completed material from computer. Scans artwork, using optical scanner, which changes image into computer-readable form. Enters, positions, and alters size of text, using computer, to make up and arrange pages to produce printed materials. Hand rubs paper against printing plate to transfer specified design onto paper for use in etching glassware. Operates offset-duplicating machine or small printing press to reproduce single- or multicolor copies of line, drawings, graphs, or similar materials. Prepares microfiche duplicates of microfilm, using contact printer and developing machine. Positions and aligns negatives to assemble flats for re-production. Compares test exposures to quality control color guides or exposure guides to determine data for exposure settings. Puts flats into vacuum frame to produce aluminum plate, microfiche print, or single- or multicolor proof. Immerses exposed materials into chemical solutions to hand-develop single- or multicolor proofs or printing plates. Sets up and operates various types of cameras to produce negatives, photostats, or plastic or paper printing plates. **SKILLS**—Equipment Selection. Operation and Control. Quality Control Analysis. Reading Comprehension.

**GOE—Interest Area:** 08. Industrial Production. **Work Group:** 08.03. Production Work. **Other Job Titles in This Work Group:** Bakers, Manufacturing; Bindery Machine Operators and Tenders; Brazers; Cementing and Gluing Machine Operators and Tenders; Chemical Equipment Controllers and Operators; Chemical Equipment Operators and Tenders; Chemical Equipment Tenders; Cleaning, Washing, and Metal Pickling Equipment Operators and Tenders; Coating, Painting, and Spraying Machine Operators and Tenders; Coil Winders, Tapers, and Finishers; Combination Machine Tool Operators and Tenders, Metal and Plastic; Computer-Controlled Machine Tool Operators, Metal and Plastic; Cooling and Freezing Equipment Operators and

Tenders; Crushing, Grinding, and Polishing Machine Setters, Operators, and Tenders; Cutters and Trimmers, Hand; Cutting and Slicing Machine Operators and Tenders; Cutting and Slicing Machine Setters, Operators, and Tenders; Design Printing Machine Setters and Set-Up Operators; Electrolytic Plating and Coating Machine Operators and Tenders, Metal and Plastic; Electrolytic Plating and Coating Machine Setters and Set-Up Operators, Metal and Plastic; Electrotypers and Stereotypers; Embossing Machine Set-Up Operators; Engraver Set-Up Operators; Extruding and Forming Machine Operators and Tenders, Synthetic or Glass Fibers; Extruding and Forming Machine Setters, Operators, and Tenders, Synthetic and Glass Fibers; Extruding, Forming, Pressing, and Compacting Machine Operators and Tenders; Fabric and Apparel Patternmakers; Fiber Product Cutting Machine Setters and Set-Up Operators; Fiberglass Laminators and Fabricators; others. **PERSONALITY TYPE**—Realistic. Realistic occupations frequently involve work activities that include practical, hands-on problems and solutions. They often deal with plants, animals, and real-world materials like wood, tools, and machinery. Many of the occupations require working outside and do not involve a lot of paperwork or working closely with others.

**EDUCATION/TRAINING PROGRAM(S)**—Graphic and Printing Equipment Operator, General; Graphic and Printing Equipment Operators, Other; Printing Press Operator. **RELATED KNOWLEDGE/COURSES**—**English Language:** Knowledge of the structure and content of the English language, including the meaning and spelling of words, rules of composition, and grammar. **Computers and Electronics:** Knowledge of circuit boards, processors, chips, electronic equipment, and computer hardware and software, including applications and programming. **Production and Processing:** Knowledge of raw materials, production processes, quality control, costs, and other techniques for maximizing the effective manufacture and distribution of goods. **Chemistry:** Knowledge of the chemical composition, structure, and properties of substances and of the chemical processes and transformations that they undergo. This includes uses of chemicals and their interactions, danger signs, production techniques, and disposal methods. **Mathematics:** Knowledge of arithmetic, algebra, geometry, calculus, statistics, and their applications. **Communications and Media:** Knowledge of media production, communication, and dissemination techniques and methods. This includes alternative ways to inform and entertain via written, oral, and visual media.

# Pressure Vessel Inspectors

- ▲ Growth: 8.9%
- ▲ Annual Job Openings: 9,000
- ▲ Annual Earnings: $44,140
- ▲ Education/Training Required: Long-term on-the-job training
- ▲ Self-Employed: 0%
- ▲ Part-Time: 2.9%

**Inspect pressure vessel equipment for conformance with safety laws and standards regulating their design, fabrication, installation, repair, and operation.** Inspects drawings, designs, and specifications for piping, boilers, and other vessels. Performs standard tests to verify condition of equipment and calibration of meters and gauges, using test equipment and hand tools. Inspects gas mains to determine that rate of flow, pressure, location, construction, or installation conform to standards. Evaluates factors such as materials used, safety devices, regulators, construction quality, riveting, welding, pitting, corrosion, cracking, and safety valve operation. Calculates allowable limits of pressure, strength, and stresses. Examines permits and inspection records to determine that inspection schedule and remedial actions conform to procedures and regulations. Keeps records and prepares reports of inspections and investigations for administrative or legal authorities. Investigates accidents to determine causes and to develop methods of preventing recurrences. Confers with engineers, manufacturers, contractors, owners, and operators concerning problems in construction, operation, and repair. Witnesses acceptance and installation tests. Recommends or orders actions to correct violations of legal requirements or to eliminate unsafe conditions. **SKILLS**—Mathematics. Writing. Quality Control Analysis. Active Listening. Operations Analysis. Speaking. Operation Monitoring.

**GOE—Interest Area:** 02. Science, Math, and Engineering. **Work Group:** 02.08. Engineering Technology. **Other Job Titles in This Work Group:** Aerospace Engineering and Operations Technicians; Architectural and Civil Drafters; Architectural Drafters; Calibration and Instrumentation Technicians; Cartographers and Photogrammetrists; Civil Drafters; Civil Engineering Technicians; Construction and Building Inspectors; Drafters, All Other; Electrical and Electronic Engineering Technicians; Electrical and Electronics Drafters; Electrical Drafters; Electrical Engineering Technicians; Electro-Mechanical Technicians; Electronic Drafters; Electronics Engineering Technicians; Engineering Technicians, Except Drafters, All Other; Environmental Engineering Technicians; Industrial Engineering Technicians; Mapping Technicians; Mechanical Drafters; Mechanical Engineering Technicians; Numerical Tool and Process Control Programmers; Surveying and Mapping Technicians; Surveying Technicians; Surveyors. **PERSONALITY TYPE**—Realistic. Realistic occupations frequently involve work activities that include practical, hands-on problems and solutions. They often deal with plants, animals, and real-world materials like wood, tools, and machinery. Many of the occupations require working outside and do not involve a lot of paperwork or working closely with others.

**EDUCATION/TRAINING PROGRAM(S)**—Business Administration and Management, General; Construction/Building Technologist/Technician; Logistics and Materials Management; Material Engineering; Mechanical Engineering; Operations Management and Supervision; Purchasing, Procurement and Contracts Management; Systems Engineering. **RELATED KNOWLEDGE/COURSES**—**Public Safety and Security:** Knowledge of relevant equipment, policies, procedures, and strategies to promote effective local, state, or national security operations for the protection of people, data, property, and institutions. **Mathematics:** Knowledge of arithmetic, algebra, geometry, calculus, statistics, and their applications. **Physics:** Knowledge and prediction of physical principles and laws and their interrelationships and applications to understanding fluid, material, and atmospheric dynamics and mechanical, electrical, atomic, and sub-atomic structures and processes. **Principles of Mechanical Devices:** Knowledge of machines and tools, including their designs, uses, repair, and maintenance. **Engineering and Technology:** Knowledge of the practical application of engineering science and technology. This includes applying principles, techniques, procedures, and equipment to the design and production of various goods and services.

# Printing Press Machine Operators and Tenders

- ▲ Growth: 5.5%
- ▲ Annual Job Openings: 24,000
- ▲ Annual Earnings: $30,090
- ▲ Education/Training Required: Moderate-term on-the-job training
- ▲ Self-Employed: 2.6%
- ▲ Part-Time: 3.3%

Operate or tend various types of printing machines, such as offset lithographic presses, letter or letterset presses, or flexographic or gravure presses, to produce print on paper or other materials, such as plastic, cloth, or rubber. Pushes buttons, turns handles, or moves controls and levers to start printing machine or manually controls equipment operation. Turns, pushes, or moves controls to set and adjust speed, temperature, inkflow, and position and pressure tolerances of press. Selects and installs printing plates, rollers, screens, stencils, type, die, and cylinders in machine according to specifications, using hand tools. Loads, positions, and adjusts unprinted materials on holding fixture or in loading and feeding mechanisms of press. Reviews work order to determine ink, stock, and equipment needed for production. Accepts orders, calculates and quotes prices, and receives payments from customers. Discards or corrects misprinted materials, using ink eradicators or solvents. Dismantles and reassembles printing unit or parts, using hand and power tools, to repair, maintain, or adjust machine. Cleans and lubricates printing machine and components (e.g., rollers, screens, typesetting, reservoirs) using oil, solvents, brushes, rags, and hoses. Removes printed materials from press, using handtruck, electric lift, or hoist, and transports them to drying, storage, or finishing areas. Inspects and examines printed products for print clarity, color accuracy, conformance to specifications, and external defects. Pours or spreads paint, ink, color compounds, and other materials into reservoirs, troughs, hoppers, or color holders of printing unit. Blends and tests paint, inks, stains, and solvents according to type of material being printed and work order specifications. Monitors and controls operation of auxiliary equipment, such as cutters, folders, drying ovens, and sanders, to assemble and finish product. Directs and monitors activities of workers feeding, inspecting, and tending printing machines and materials. Keeps daily time and materials usage reports and records identifying information printed on manufactured products and parts. Packs and labels cartons, boxes, or bins of finished products. Monitors feeding, printing, and racking processes of press to maintain specified operating levels and detect malfunctions. **SKILLS**—Operation Monitoring. Operation and Control. Quality Control Analysis. Management of Personnel Resources. Equipment Maintenance.

**GOE**—**Interest Area:** 08. Industrial Production. **Work Group:** 08.03. Production Work. **Other Job Titles in This Work Group:** Bakers, Manufacturing; Bindery Machine Operators and Tenders; Brazers; Cementing and Gluing Machine Operators and Tenders; Chemical Equipment Controllers and Operators; Chemical Equipment Operators and Tenders; Chemical Equipment Tenders; Cleaning, Washing, and Metal Pickling Equipment Operators and Tenders; Coating, Painting, and Spraying Machine Operators and Tenders; Coil Winders, Tapers, and Finishers; Combination Machine Tool Operators and Tenders, Metal and Plastic; Computer-Controlled Machine Tool Operators, Metal and Plastic; Cooling and Freezing Equipment Operators and Tenders; Crushing, Grinding, and Polishing Machine Setters, Operators, and Tenders; Cutters and Trimmers, Hand; Cutting and Slicing Machine Operators and Tenders; Cutting and Slicing Machine Setters, Operators, and Tenders; Design Printing Machine Setters and Set-Up Operators; Electrolytic Plating and Coating Machine Operators and Tenders, Metal and Plastic; Electrolytic Plating and Coating Machine Setters and Set-Up Operators, Metal and Plastic; Electrotypers and Stereotypers; Embossing Machine Set-Up Operators; Engraver Set-Up Operators; Extruding and Forming Machine Operators and Tenders, Synthetic or Glass Fibers; Extruding and Forming Machine Setters, Operators, and Tenders, Synthetic and Glass Fibers; Extruding, Forming, Pressing, and Compacting Machine Operators and Tenders; Fabric and Apparel Patternmakers; Fiber Product Cutting Machine Setters and Set-Up Operators; Fiberglass Laminators and Fabricators; others. **PERSONALITY TYPE**—Realistic. Realistic occupations frequently involve work activities that include practical, hands-on problems and solutions. They often deal with plants, animals, and real-world materials like wood, tools, and machinery. Many of the occupations require working outside and do not involve a lot of paperwork or working closely with others.

**EDUCATION/TRAINING PROGRAM(S)**—Graphic and Printing Equipment Operator, General; Graphic and Printing Equipment Operators, Other; Printing Press Operator. **RELATED KNOWLEDGE/COURSES**—**Production and Processing:** Knowledge of raw materials, production processes, quality control, costs, and other techniques for maximizing the effective manufacture and distribution of goods. **Principles of Mechanical Devices:** Knowledge of machines and tools, including their designs, uses, repair, and maintenance. **English Language:** Knowledge of the structure and content of the English language, including the meaning and spelling of words, rules of composition, and grammar. **Mathematics:** Knowledge of arithmetic, algebra, geometry, calculus, statistics, and their applications. **Engineering and**

P

**Technology:** Knowledge of the practical application of engineering science and technology. This includes applying principles, techniques, procedures, and equipment to the design and production of various goods and services. **Chemistry:** Knowledge of the chemical composition, structure, and properties of substances and of the chemical processes and transformations that they undergo. This includes uses of chemicals and their interactions, danger signs, production techniques, and disposal methods.

# Private Detectives and Investigators

▲ Growth: 23.5%
▲ Annual Job Openings: 9,000
▲ Annual Earnings: $30,650
▲ Education/Training Required: Work experience in a related occupation
▲ Self-Employed: 39.3%
▲ Part-Time: 19.8%

**Detect occurrences of unlawful acts or infractions of rules in private establishment or seek, examine, and compile information for client.** Confers with establishment officials, security department, police, or postal officials to identify problems, provide information, and receive instructions. Alerts staff and superiors of presence of suspect in establishment. Writes reports and case summaries to document investigations or inform supervisors. Testifies at hearings and court trials to present evidence. Locates persons using phone or mail directories to collect money owed or to serve legal papers. Evaluates performance and honesty of employees by posing as customer or employee and comparing employee to standards. Assists victims, police, fire department, and others during emergencies. Enforces conformance to establishment rules and protects persons or property. Counts cash and reviews transactions, sales checks, and register tapes to verify amount of cash and shortages. Obtains and analyzes information on suspects, crimes, and disturbances to solve cases, identify criminal activity, and maintain public peace and order. Warns and ejects troublemakers from premises and apprehends and releases suspects to authorities or security personnel. Examines crime scene for clues or fingerprints and submits evidence to laboratory for analysis. Questions persons to obtain evidence for cases of divorce, child custody, or missing persons or individual's character or financial status. Observes employees or customers and patrols premises to detect violations and obtain evidence, using binoculars, cameras, and television. **SKILLS—** Active Listening. Critical Thinking. Speaking. Writing. Judgment and Decision Making.

**GOE—Interest Area:** 04. Law, Law Enforcement, and Public Safety. **Work Group:** 04.03. Law Enforcement. **Other Job Titles in This Work Group:** Animal Control Workers; Bailiffs; Child Support, Missing Persons, and Unemployment Insurance Fraud Investigators; Correctional Officers and Jailers; Criminal Investigators and Special Agents; Crossing Guards; Detectives and Criminal Investigators; Fire Investigators; Fish and Game Wardens; Forensic Science Technicians; Gaming Surveillance Officers and Gaming Investigators; Highway Patrol Pilots; Immigration and Customs Inspectors; Lifeguards, Ski Patrol, and Other Recreational Protective Service Workers; Parking Enforcement Workers; Police and Sheriff's Patrol Officers; Police Detectives; Police Identification and Records Officers; Police Patrol Officers; Security Guards; Sheriffs and Deputy Sheriffs; Transit and Railroad Police. **PERSONALITY TYPE—**Enterprising. Enterprising occupations frequently involve starting up and carrying out projects. These occupations can involve leading people and making many decisions. They sometimes require risk taking and often deal with business.

**EDUCATION/TRAINING PROGRAM(S)—**Law Enforcement/Police Science. **RELATED KNOWLEDGE/COURSES—Public Safety and Security:** Knowledge of relevant equipment, policies, procedures, and strategies to promote effective local, state, or national security operations for the protection of people, data, property, and institutions. **English Language:** Knowledge of the structure and content of the English language, including the meaning and spelling of words, rules of composition, and grammar. **Law and Government:** Knowledge of laws, legal codes, court procedures, precedents, government regulations, executive orders, agency rules, and the democratic political process. **Telecommunications:** Knowledge of transmission, broadcasting, switching, control, and operation of tele-

communications systems. **Customer and Personal Service:** Knowledge of principles and processes for providing customer and personal services. This includes customer needs assessment, meeting quality standards for services, and evaluation of customer satisfaction. **Communications and Media:** Knowledge of media production, communication, and dissemination techniques and methods. This includes alternative ways to inform and entertain via written, oral, and visual media.

# Production Helpers

- ▲ Growth: 11.9%
- ▲ Annual Job Openings: 143,000
- ▲ Annual Earnings: $19,350
- ▲ Education/Training Required: Short-term on-the-job training
- ▲ Self-Employed: 0%
- ▲ Part-Time: 16.2%

**Perform variety of tasks requiring limited knowledge of production processes in support of skilled production workers.** Cleans and lubricates equipment. Signals coworkers to facilitate moving product during processing. Measures amount of ingredients, length of extruded article, or work to ensure conformance to specifications. Replaces damaged or worm equipment parts. Tends equipment to facilitate process. Mixes ingredients according to procedure. Turns valves to regulate flow of liquids or air, to reverse machine, to start pump, and to regulate equipment. Starts machines or equipment to begin process. Marks or tags identification on parts. Observes operation and notifies equipment operator of malfunctions. Places or positions equipment or partially assembled product for further processing manually or using hoist. Removes product, machine attachments, and waste material from machine. Reads gauges and charts and records data. Loads and unloads processing equipment or conveyance used to receive raw materials or to ship finished products. Dumps materials into machine hopper prior to mixing. **SKILLS**—Equipment Maintenance. Operation and Control. Operation Monitoring. Repairing. Equipment Selection.

**GOE—Interest Area:** 08. Industrial Production. **Work Group:** 08.03. Production Work. **Other Job Titles in This Work Group:** Bakers, Manufacturing; Bindery Machine Operators and Tenders; Brazers; Cementing and Gluing Machine Operators and Tenders; Chemical Equipment Controllers and Operators; Chemical Equipment Operators and Tenders; Chemical Equipment Tenders; Cleaning, Washing, and Metal Pickling Equipment Operators and Tenders; Coating, Painting, and Spraying Machine Operators and Tenders; Coil Winders, Tapers, and Finishers; Combination Machine Tool Operators and Tenders, Metal and Plastic; Computer-Controlled Machine Tool Operators, Metal and Plastic; Cooling and Freezing Equipment Operators and Tenders; Crushing, Grinding, and Polishing Machine Setters, Operators, and Tenders; Cutters and Trimmers, Hand; Cutting and Slicing Machine Operators and Tenders; Cutting and Slicing Machine Setters, Operators, and Tenders; Design Printing Machine Setters and Set-Up Operators; Electrolytic Plating and Coating Machine Operators and Tenders, Metal and Plastic; Electrolytic Plating and Coating Machine Setters and Set-Up Operators, Metal and Plastic; Electrotypers and Stereotypers; Embossing Machine Set-Up Operators; Engraver Set-Up Operators; Extruding and Forming

Machine Operators and Tenders, Synthetic or Glass Fibers; Extruding and Forming Machine Setters, Operators, and Tenders, Synthetic and Glass Fibers; Extruding, Forming, Pressing, and Compacting Machine Operators and Tenders; Fabric and Apparel Patternmakers; Fiber Product Cutting Machine Setters and Set-Up Operators; Fiberglass Laminators and Fabricators; others. **PERSONALITY TYPE**—Realistic. Realistic occupations frequently involve work activities that include practical, hands-on problems and solutions. They often deal with plants, animals, and real-world materials like wood, tools, and machinery. Many of the occupations require working outside and do not involve a lot of paperwork or working closely with others.

**EDUCATION/TRAINING PROGRAM(S)**—Industrial Equipment Maintenance and Repairers, Other.

**RELATED KNOWLEDGE/COURSES—Production and Processing:** Knowledge of raw materials, production processes, quality control, costs, and other techniques for maximizing the effective manufacture and distribution of goods. **Principles of Mechanical Devices:** Knowledge of machines and tools, including their designs, uses, repair, and maintenance. **Engineering and Technology:** Knowledge of the practical application of engineering science and technology. This includes applying principles, techniques, procedures, and equipment to the design and production of various goods and services. **Mathematics:** Knowledge of arithmetic, algebra, geometry, calculus, statistics, and their applications. **English Language:** Knowledge of the structure and content of the English language, including the meaning and spelling of words, rules of composition, and grammar.

# Production Laborers

- ▲ Growth: 11.9%
- ▲ Annual Job Openings: 143,000
- ▲ Annual Earnings: $19,350
- ▲ Education/Training Required: Short-term on-job training
- ▲ Self-Employed: 0%
- ▲ Part-Time: 16.2%

**Perform variety of routine tasks to assist in production activities.** Carries or handtrucks supplies to work stations. Records information, such as number of product tested, meter readings, and date and time product placed in oven. Examines product to verify conformance to company standards. Mixes ingredients according to formula. Feeds item into processing machine. Inserts parts into partial assembly during various stages of assembly to complete product. Counts finished product to determine completion of production order. Washes machines, equipment, vehicles, and products, such as prints, rugs, and table linens. Folds parts of product and final product during processing. Separates product according to weight, grade, size, and composition of material used to produce product. Cuts or breaks flashing from materials or products. Places product in equipment or on work surface for further processing, inspecting, or wrapping. Positions spout or chute of storage bin to fill containers during processing. Breaks up defective products for reprocessing. Attaches slings, ropes, cables, or identification tags to objects such as pipes, hoses, and bundles. Weighs raw materials for distribution. Threads ends of items such as thread, cloth, and lace through needles and rollers and around takeup tube. Ties product in bundles for further processing or shipment, following prescribed procedure. Lifts raw materials, final products, and items packed for shipment manually or using hoist. Loads and unloads items from machines, conveyors, and conveyance. **SKILLS**—Equipment Selection.

**GOE—Interest Area:** 08. Industrial Production. **Work Group:** 08.03. Production Work. **Other Job Titles in This Work Group:** Bakers, Manufacturing; Bindery Machine Operators and Tenders; Brazers; Cementing and Gluing Machine Operators and Tenders; Chemical Equipment Controllers and Operators; Chemical Equipment Operators and Tenders; Chemical Equipment Tenders; Cleaning, Washing, and Metal Pickling Equipment Operators and Tenders; Coating, Painting, and Spraying Machine Operators and Tenders; Coil Winders, Tapers, and Finishers; Combination Machine Tool Operators and Tenders, Metal and Plastic; Computer-Controlled Machine Tool Operators, Metal and Plastic; Cooling and Freezing Equipment Operators and Tenders; Crushing, Grinding, and Polishing Machine Setters, Operators, and Tenders; Cutters and Trimmers, Hand; Cutting and Slicing Machine Operators and Tenders; Cutting and Slicing Machine Setters, Operators, and Tenders; Design Printing Machine Setters and Set-Up Operators; Electrolytic Plating and Coating Machine Operators and Tenders, Metal and Plastic; Electrolytic Plating and Coating Machine Setters and Set-Up Operators, Metal and Plastic; Electrotypers and Stereotypers; Embossing Machine Set-Up Operators; Engraver Set-Up Operators; Extruding and Forming Machine Operators and Tenders, Synthetic or Glass Fibers; Extruding and Forming Machine Setters, Operators, and Tenders, Synthetic and Glass Fibers; Extruding, Forming, Pressing, and Compacting Machine Operators and Tenders; Fabric and Apparel Patternmakers; Fiber Product Cutting Machine Setters and Set-Up Operators; Fiberglass Laminators and Fabricators; others. **PERSONALITY TYPE**—Realistic. Realistic occupations frequently involve work activities that include practical, hands-on problems and solutions. They often deal with plants, animals, and real-world materials like wood, tools, and machinery. Many of the occupations require working outside and do not involve a lot of paperwork or working closely with others.

**EDUCATION/TRAINING PROGRAM(S)**—Industrial Equipment Maintenance and Repairers, Other. **RELATED KNOWLEDGE/COURSES—Production and Processing:** Knowledge of raw materials, production processes, quality control, costs, and other techniques for maximizing the effective manufacture and distribution of goods. **Clerical Studies:** Knowledge of administrative and clerical procedures and systems such as word processing, managing files and records, stenography and transcription, designing forms, and other office procedures and terminology. **Mathematics:** Knowledge of arithmetic, algebra, geometry, calculus, statistics, and their applications.

# Production, Planning, and Expediting Clerks

- ▲ Growth: 17.9%
- ▲ Annual Job Openings: 36,000
- ▲ Annual Earnings: $32,520
- ▲ Education/Training Required: Short-term on-the-job training
- ▲ Self-Employed: 0.9%
- ▲ Part-Time: 18.8%

**Coordinate and expedite the flow of work and materials within or between departments of an establishment according to production schedule. Duties include reviewing and distributing production, work, and shipment schedules; conferring with department supervisors to determine progress of work and completion dates; and compiling reports on progress of work, inventory levels, costs, and production problems.** Reviews documents, such as production schedules, staffing tables, and specifications, to obtain information, such as materials, priorities, and personnel requirements. Compiles schedules and orders, such as personnel assignments, production, work flow, transportation, and maintenance and repair. Monitors work progress, provides services, such as furnishing permits, tickets, and union information, and directs workers to expedite work flow. Requisitions and maintains inventory of materials and supplies to meet production demands. Calculates figures, such as labor and materials amounts, manufacturing costs, and wages, using pricing schedules, adding machine, or calculator. Maintains files, such as maintenance records, bills of lading, and cost reports.

Arranges for delivery and distributes supplies and parts to expedite flow of materials to meet production schedules. Examines documents, materials, and products and monitors work processes for completeness, accuracy, and conformance to standards and specifications. Completes status reports, such as production progress, customer information, and materials inventory. Confers with establishment personnel, vendors, and customers to coordinate processing and shipping and to resolve complaints. **SKILLS**—Active Listening. Writing. Reading Comprehension. Monitoring. Time Management. Management of Material Resources.

**GOE—Interest Area:** 09. Business Detail. **Work Group:** 09.04. Material Control. **Other Job Titles in This Work Group:** Meter Readers, Utilities. **PERSONALITY TYPE**—Conventional. Conventional occupations frequently involve following set procedures and routines. These occupations can include working with data and details more than with ideas. Usually there is a clear line of authority to follow.

**EDUCATION/TRAINING PROGRAM(S)**—Accounting; Accounting Technician; Business Computer

Facilities Operator; Clothing, Apparel and Textile Workers and Managers, General; Commercial Garment and Apparel Worker; General Office/Clerical and Typing Services; Graphic and Printing Equipment Operator, General; Information Processing/Data Entry Technician; Mechanical Typesetter and Composer. **RELATED KNOWLEDGE/COURSES—Clerical Studies:** Knowledge of administrative and clerical procedures and systems such as word processing, managing files and records, stenography and transcription, designing forms, and other office procedures and terminology. **Production and Processing:** Knowledge of raw materials, production processes, quality control, costs, and other techniques for maximizing the effective manufacture and distribution of goods. **Mathematics:** Knowledge of arithmetic, algebra, geometry, calculus, statistics, and their applications. **Economics and Accounting:** Knowledge of economic and accounting principles and practices, the financial markets, banking, and the analysis and reporting of financial data. **Transportation:** Knowledge of principles and methods for moving people or goods by air, rail, sea, or road, including the relative costs and benefits.

# Professional Photographers

- ▲ Growth: 17%
- ▲ Annual Job Openings: 13,000
- ▲ Annual Earnings: $27,420
- ▲ Education/Training Required: Long-term on-the-job training
- ▲ Self-Employed: 51.9%
- ▲ Part-Time: 23.1%

**Photograph subjects or newsworthy events, using still cameras, color or black-and-white film, and variety of photographic accessories.** Frames subject matter and background in lens to capture desired image. Focuses camera and adjusts settings based on lighting, subject material, distance, and film speed. Selects and assembles equipment and required background properties according to subject, materials, and conditions. Directs activities of workers assisting in setting up photographic equipment. Arranges subject material in desired position. Estimates or measures light level, distance, and number of exposures needed, using measuring devices

and formulas. **SKILLS**—Equipment Selection. Monitoring. Coordination. Mathematics. Operation and Control.

**GOE—Interest Area:** 01. Arts, Entertainment, and Media. **Work Group:** 01.08. Media Technology. **Other Job Titles in This Work Group:** Audio and Video Equipment Technicians; Broadcast Technicians; Camera Operators, Television, Video, and Motion Picture; Film and Video Editors; Media and Communication Equipment Workers, All Other; Photographers; Radio Operators; Sound Engineering Technicians. **PERSON-**

ALITY TYPE—Artistic. Artistic occupations frequently involve working with forms, designs, and patterns. They often require self-expression, and the work can be done without following a clear set of rules.

EDUCATION/TRAINING PROGRAM(S)—Commercial Photography; Film/Video and Photographic Arts, Other; Photography. RELATED KNOWLEDGE/ COURSES—Fine Arts: Knowledge of the theory and techniques required to compose, produce, and perform works of music, dance, visual arts, drama, and sculpture. Chemistry: Knowledge of the chemical composition, structure, and properties of substances and of the chemical processes and transformations that they undergo. This includes uses of chemicals and their interactions, danger signs, production techniques, and disposal methods. Geography: Knowledge of principles and methods for describing the features of land, sea, and air masses, including their physical characteristics, locations, interrelationships, and distribution of plant, animal, and human life. Communications and Media: Knowledge of media production, communication, and dissemination techniques and methods. This includes alternative ways to inform and entertain via written, oral, and visual media. Mathematics: Knowledge of arithmetic, algebra, geometry, calculus, statistics, and their applications. English Language: Knowledge of the structure and content of the English language, including the meaning and spelling of words, rules of composition, and grammar.

# Public Transportation Inspectors

- ▲ Growth: 11.3%
- ▲ Annual Job Openings: 3,000
- ▲ Annual Earnings: $44,200
- ▲ Education/Training Required: Work experience in a related occupation
- ▲ Self-Employed: 9%
- ▲ Part-Time: 2.9%

Monitor operation of public transportation systems to ensure good service and compliance with regulations. Investigate accidents, equipment failures, and complaints. Observes employees performing assigned duties to note their deportment, treatment of passengers, and adherence to company regulations and schedules. Observes and records time required to load and unload passengers or freight volume of traffic on vehicle and at stops. Investigates schedule delays, accidents, and complaints. Inspects company vehicles and other property for evidence of abuse, damage, and mechanical malfunction and directs repair. Determines need for changes in service, such as additional vehicles, route changes, and revised schedules to improve service and efficiency. Drives automobile along route to detect conditions hazardous to equipment and passengers and negotiates with local governments to eliminate hazards. Submits written reports to management with recommendations for improving service. Reports disruptions to service. Assists in dispatching equipment when necessary. Recommends promotions and disciplinary actions involving transportation personnel. SKILLS— Writing. Monitoring. Reading Comprehension. Speaking. Operations Analysis.

GOE—Interest Area: 04. Law, Law Enforcement, and Public Safety. Work Group: 04.04. Public Safety. Other Job Titles in This Work Group: Agricultural Inspectors; Aviation Inspectors; Compliance Officers, Except Agriculture, Construction, Health and Safety, and Transportation; Emergency Medical Technicians and Paramedics; Environmental Compliance Inspectors; Equal Opportunity Representatives and Officers; Financial Examiners; Fire Fighters; Fire Inspectors; Fire Inspectors and Investigators; Forest Fire Fighters; Forest Fire Inspectors and Prevention Specialists; Government Property Inspectors and Investigators; Licensing Examiners and Inspectors; Marine Cargo Inspectors; Municipal Fire Fighters; Nuclear Monitoring Technicians; Occupational Health and Safety Specialists; Occupational Health and Safety Technicians. PERSONALITY

TYPE—Enterprising. Enterprising occupations frequently involve starting up and carrying out projects. These occupations can involve leading people and making many decisions. They sometimes require risk taking and often deal with business.

EDUCATION/TRAINING PROGRAM(S)—Operations Management and Supervision. RELATED KNOWLEDGE/COURSES—Transportation: Knowledge of principles and methods for moving people or goods by air, rail, sea, or road, including the relative costs and benefits. Public Safety and Security: Knowledge of relevant equipment, policies, procedures, and strategies to promote effective local, state, or national security operations for the protection of people, data, property, and institutions. Mathematics: Knowledge of arithmetic, algebra, geometry, calculus, statistics, and their applications. English Language: Knowledge of the structure and content of the English language, including the meaning and spelling of words, rules of composition, and grammar. Law and Government: Knowledge of laws, legal codes, court procedures, precedents, government regulations, executive orders, agency rules, and the democratic political process. Administration and Management: Knowledge of business and management principles involved in strategic planning, resource allocation, human resources modeling, leadership technique, production methods, and coordination of people and resources.

# Radiologic Technologists and Technicians

- ▲ Growth: 23.1%
- ▲ Annual Job Openings: 13,000
- ▲ Annual Earnings: $37,290
- ▲ Education/Training Required: Associate's degree
- ▲ Self-Employed: 0%
- ▲ Part-Time: 17.5%

Take X rays and CAT scans or administer nonradioactive materials into patient's bloodstream for diagnostic purposes. Includes technologists who specialize in other modalities, such as computed tomography and magnetic resonance. Includes workers whose primary duties are to demonstrate portions of the human body on X-ray film or fluoroscopic screen. SKILLS—No data available.

GOE—Interest Area: 14. Medical and Health Services. Work Group: 14.05. Medical Technology. Other Job Titles in This Work Group: Cardiovascular Technologists and Technicians; Diagnostic Medical Sonographers; Health Technologists and Technicians, All Other; Medical and Clinical Laboratory Technicians; Medical and Clinical Laboratory Technologists; Medical Equipment Preparers; Nuclear Medicine Technologists; Orthotists and Prosthetists; Radiologic Technicians; Radiologic Technologists. PERSONALITY TYPE—No data available.

EDUCATION/TRAINING PROGRAM(S)—Health and Medical Diagnostic and Treatment Services, Other; Medical Radiologic Technologist/Technician. RELATED KNOWLEDGE/COURSES—No data available.

# Railroad Inspectors

- ▲ Growth: 11.3%
- ▲ Annual Job Openings: 3,000
- ▲ Annual Earnings: $44,200
- ▲ Education/Training Required: Work experience in a related occupation
- ▲ Self-Employed: 9%
- ▲ Part-Time: 5.5%

**Inspect railroad equipment, roadbed, and track to ensure safe transport of people or cargo.** Inspects signals and track wiring to determine continuity of electrical connections. Examines roadbed, switches, fishplates, rails, and ties to detect damage or wear. Examines locomotives and cars to detect damage or structural defects. Inspects and tests completed work. Operates switches to determine working conditions. Tests and synchronizes rail-flaw-detection machine, using circuit tester and hand tools, and reloads machine with paper and ink. Starts machine and signals worker to operate rail-detector car. Prepares reports on repairs made and equipment, railcars, or roadbed needing repairs. Tags railcars needing immediate repair. Fills paint container on rail-detector car used to mark section of defective rail with paint. Directs crews to repair or replace defective equipment or to re-ballast roadbed. Places lanterns or flags in front and rear of train to signal that inspection is being performed. Seals leaks found during inspection that can be sealed with caulking compound. Replaces defective brake rod pins and tightens safety appliances. Notifies train dispatcher of railcar to be moved to shop for repair. Makes minor repairs. Packs brake bearings with grease. **SKILLS**—Troubleshooting. Quality Control Analysis. Repairing. Writing. Operation Monitoring.

**GOE—Interest Area:** 05. Mechanics, Installers, and Repairers. **Work Group:** 05.03. Mechanical Work. **Other Job Titles in This Work Group:** Aircraft Body and Bonded Structure Repairers; Aircraft Engine Specialists; Aircraft Mechanics and Service Technicians; Airframe-and-Power-Plant Mechanics; Automotive Body and Related Repairers; Automotive Glass Installers and Repairers; Automotive Master Mechanics; Automotive Service Technicians and Mechanics; Automotive Specialty Technicians; Bicycle Repairers; Bridge and Lock Tenders; Bus and Truck Mechanics and Diesel Engine Specialists; Camera and Photographic Equipment Repairers; Coin, Vending, and Amusement Machine Servicers and Repairers; Control and Valve Installers and Repairers, Except Mechanical Door; Farm Equipment Mechanics; Gas Appliance Repairers; Hand and Portable Power Tool Repairers; Heating and Air Conditioning Mechanics; Heating, Air Conditioning, and Refrigeration Mechanics and Installers; Helpers—Electricians; Helpers—Installation, Maintenance, and Repair Workers; Industrial Machinery Mechanics; Keyboard Instrument Repairers and Tuners; Locksmiths and Safe Repairers; Maintenance and Repair Workers, General; Maintenance Workers, Machinery; Mechanical Door Repairers; Medical Appliance Technicians; Medical Equipment Repairers; Meter Mechanics; Millwrights; Mobile Heavy Equipment Mechanics, Except Engines; Motorboat Mechanics; Motorcycle Mechanics; Musical Instrument Repairers and Tuners; Ophthalmic Laboratory Technicians; Optical Instrument Assemblers; Outdoor Power Equipment and Other Small Engine Mechanics; Painters, Transportation Equipment; Percussion Instrument Repairers and Tuners; others. **PERSONALITY TYPE**—Realistic. Realistic occupations frequently involve work activities that include practical, hands-on problems and solutions. They often deal with plants, animals, and real-world materials like wood, tools, and machinery. Many of the occupations require working outside and do not involve a lot of paperwork or working closely with others.

**EDUCATION/TRAINING PROGRAM(S)**—Operations Management and Supervision. **RELATED KNOWLEDGE/COURSES**—**Transportation:** Knowledge of principles and methods for moving people or goods by air, rail, sea, or road, including the relative costs and benefits. **Public Safety and Security:** Knowledge of relevant equipment, policies, procedures, and strategies to promote effective local, state, or national security operations for the protection of people, data, property, and institutions. **Principles of Mechanical Devices:** Knowledge of machines and tools, including their designs, uses, repair, and maintenance.

**Building and Construction:** Knowledge of materials, methods, and tools involved in the construction or repair of houses, buildings, or other structures such as highways and roads. **Engineering and Technology:** Knowledge of the practical application of engineering science and technology. This includes applying principles, techniques, procedures, and equipment to the design and production of various goods and services.

# Real Estate Brokers

- ▲ Growth: 9.6%
- ▲ Annual Job Openings: 8,000
- ▲ Annual Earnings: $60,080
- ▲ Education/Training Required: Work experience in a related occupation
- ▲ Self-Employed: 63.1%
- ▲ Part-Time: 16.6%

Operate real estate office or work for commercial real estate firm, overseeing real estate transactions. Other duties usually include selling real estate or renting properties and arranging loans. SKILLS—No data available.

GOE—**Interest Area:** 10. Sales and Marketing. **Work Group:** 10.03. General Sales. **Other Job Titles in This Work Group:** Parts Salespersons; Real Estate Sales Agents; Retail Salespersons; Sales Representatives, Wholesale and Manufacturing, Except Technical and Scientific Products; Service Station Attendants; Stock Clerks, Sales Floor; Travel Agents. **PERSONALITY TYPE**—No data available.

**EDUCATION/TRAINING PROGRAM(S)**—Real Estate. **RELATED KNOWLEDGE/COURSES**—No data available.

# Real Estate Sales Agents

- ▲ Growth: 9.5%
- ▲ Annual Job Openings: 28,000
- ▲ Annual Earnings: $37,950
- ▲ Education/Training Required: Post-secondary vocational training
- ▲ Self-Employed: 69.4%
- ▲ Part-Time: 16.6%

Rent, buy, or sell property for clients. Perform duties such as studying property listings, interviewing prospective clients, accompanying clients to property site, discussing conditions of sale, and drawing up real estate contracts. Includes agents who represent buyer. Displays and explains features of property to client and discusses conditions of sale or terms of lease. Prepares

real estate contracts, such as closing statements, deeds, leases, and mortgages, and negotiates loans on property. Oversees signing of real estate documents, disburses funds, and coordinates closing activities. Secures construction financing with own firm or mortgage company. Inspects condition of premises and arranges for or notifies owner of necessary maintenance. Reviews trade journals and relevant literature and attends staff and association meetings to remain knowledgeable about real estate market. Searches public records to ascertain that client has clear title to property. Investigates client's financial and credit status to determine eligibility for financing. Plans and organizes sales promotion programs and materials, including newspaper advertisements and real estate promotional booklets. Appraises client's unimproved property to determine loan value. Locates and appraises undeveloped areas for building sites based on evaluation of area market conditions. Collects rental deposit. Reviews plans, recommends to client construction features, and enumerates options on new home sales. Solicits and compiles listings of available rental property. Answers client's questions regarding work under construction, financing, maintenance, repairs, and appraisals. Interviews prospective tenants and records information to ascertain needs and qualifications. Contacts utility companies for service hookup to client's property. Conducts seminars and training sessions for sales agents to improve sales techniques. **SKILLS**—Active Listening. Persuasion. Speaking. Reading Comprehension. Mathematics. Judgment and Decision Making.

**GOE—Interest Area:** 10. Sales and Marketing. **Work Group:** 10.03. General Sales. **Other Job Titles in This Work Group:** Parts Salespersons; Real Estate Brokers; Retail Salespersons; Sales Representatives, Wholesale and Manufacturing, Except Technical and Scientific Products; Service Station Attendants; Stock Clerks, Sales Floor; Travel Agents. **PERSONALITY TYPE**—Enterprising. Enterprising occupations frequently involve starting up and carrying out projects. These occupations can involve leading people and making many decisions. They sometimes require risk taking and often deal with business.

**EDUCATION/TRAINING PROGRAM(S)**—Arts Management; Business Administration and Management, General; Business Administration and Management, Other; Business Management and Administrative Services, Other; Business, General; Community Organization, Resources and Services; Enterprise Management and Operation, General; Enterprise Management and Operation, Other; Entrepreneurship; Franchise Operation; Hospitality Services Management, Other; Non-Profit and Public Management; Public Administration; Real Estate; Travel-Tourism Management. **RELATED KNOWLEDGE/COURSES—Sales and Marketing:** Knowledge of principles and methods for showing, promoting, and selling products or services. This includes marketing strategy and tactics, product demonstration, sales techniques, and sales control systems. **Law and Government:** Knowledge of laws, legal codes, court procedures, precedents, government regulations, executive orders, agency rules, and the democratic political process. **Mathematics:** Knowledge of arithmetic, algebra, geometry, calculus, statistics, and their applications. **Economics and Accounting:** Knowledge of economic and accounting principles and practices, the financial markets, banking, and the analysis and reporting of financial data. **Administration and Management:** Knowledge of business and management principles involved in strategic planning, resource allocation, human resources modeling, leadership technique, production methods, and coordination of people and resources. **English Language:** Knowledge of the structure and content of the English language, including the meaning and spelling of words, rules of composition, and grammar.

# Receptionists and Information Clerks

▲ Growth: 23.7%

▲ Annual Job Openings: 269,000

▲ Annual Earnings: $20,780

▲ Education/Training Required: Short-term on-the-job training

▲ Self-Employed: 1.3%

▲ Part-Time: 35.1%

Answer inquiries and obtain information for general public, customers, visitors, and other interested parties. Provide information regarding activities conducted at establishment and location of departments, offices, and employees within organization. Greets persons entering establishment, determines nature and purpose of visit, and directs visitor to specific destination or answers questions and provides information. Provides information to public concerning available land leases, land classification, or mineral resources. Registers visitors of public facility, such as national park or military base, collects fees, explains regulations, and assigns sites. Answers telephone to schedule future appointments, provide information, or forward call. Provides information to public regarding tours, classes, workshops, and other programs. Transmits information or documents to customer, using computer, mail, or facsimile. Records, compiles, enters, and retrieves information by hand or using computer. Operates telephone switchboard to receive incoming calls. Performs duties such as taking care of plants and straightening magazines to maintain lobby or reception area. Monitors facility to ensure compliance with regulations. Receives payment and records receipts for services. Conducts tours or delivers talks describing features of public facility, such as historic site or national park. Hears and resolves complaints from customers and public. Files and maintains records. Enrolls individuals to participate in programs, prepares lists, notifies individuals of acceptance in programs, and arranges and schedules space and equipment for participants. Types memos, correspondence, travel vouchers, or other documents. Calculates and quotes rates for tours, stocks, insurance policies, and other products and services. Collects and distributes messages for employees of organization. Analyzes data to determine answer to customer or public inquiry. **SKILLS—** Reading Comprehension. Active Listening. Service Orientation. Speaking. Writing.

**GOE—Interest Area:** 09. Business Detail. **Work Group:** 09.05. Customer Service. **Other Job Titles in This Work Group:** Adjustment Clerks; Bill and Account Collectors; Cashiers; Counter and Rental Clerks; Customer Service Representatives; Customer Service Representatives, Utilities; Gaming Cage Workers; Gaming Change Persons and Booth Cashiers; New Accounts Clerks; Order Clerks; Tellers; Travel Clerks. **PERSONALITY TYPE—**Conventional. Conventional occupations frequently involve following set procedures and routines. These occupations can include working with data and details more than with ideas. Usually there is a clear line of authority to follow.

**EDUCATION/TRAINING PROGRAM(S)—**General Office/Clerical and Typing Services; Health Unit Coordinator/Ward Clerk; Receptionist. **RELATED KNOWLEDGE/COURSES—Clerical Studies:** Knowledge of administrative and clerical procedures and systems such as word processing, managing files and records, stenography and transcription, designing forms, and other office procedures and terminology. **Customer and Personal Service:** Knowledge of principles and processes for providing customer and personal services. This includes customer needs assessment, meeting quality standards for services, and evaluation of customer satisfaction. **English Language:** Knowledge of the structure and content of the English language, including the meaning and spelling of words, rules of composition, and grammar. **Telecommunications:** Knowledge of transmission, broadcasting, switching, control, and operation of telecommunications systems. **Mathematics:** Knowledge of arithmetic, algebra, geometry, calculus, statistics, and their applications.

# Refrigeration Mechanics

▲ Growth: 22.3%

▲ Annual Job Openings: 21,000

▲ Annual Earnings: $34,180

▲ Education/Training Required: Long-term on-the-job training

▲ Self-Employed: 20%

▲ Part-Time: 4.9%

**Install and repair industrial and commercial refrigerating systems.** Mounts compressor, condenser, and other components in specified location on frame, using hand tools and acetylene welding equipment. Assembles structural and functional components, such as controls, switches, gauges, wiring harnesses, valves, pumps, compressors, condensers, cores, and pipes. Replaces or adjusts defective or worn parts to repair system and reassembles system. Installs expansion and control valves, using acetylene torch and wrenches. Cuts, bends, threads, and connects pipe to functional components and water, power, or refrigeration system. Keeps records of repairs and replacements made and causes of malfunctions. Reads blueprints to determine location, size, capacity, and type of components needed to build refrigeration system. Tests lines, components, and connections for leaks. Lays out reference points for installation of structural and functional components, using measuring instruments. Dismantles malfunctioning systems and tests components, using electrical, mechanical, and pneumatic testing equipment. Observes system operation, using gauges and instruments, and adjusts or replaces mechanisms and parts according to specifications. Adjusts valves according to specifications and charges system with specified type of refrigerant. Lifts and aligns components into position, using hoist or block and tackle. Drills holes and installs mounting brackets and hangers into floor and walls of building. Fabricates and assembles components and structural portions of refrigeration system, using hand tools, powered tools, and welding equipment. Brazes or solders parts to repair defective joints and leaks. **SKILLS**—Installation. Repairing. Troubleshooting. Quality Control Analysis. Equipment Maintenance.

**GOE—Interest Area:** 05. Mechanics, Installers, and Repairers. **Work Group:** 05.03. Mechanical Work. **Other Job Titles in This Work Group:** Aircraft Body and Bonded Structure Repairers; Aircraft Engine Specialists; Aircraft Mechanics and Service Technicians; Airframe-and-Power-Plant Mechanics; Automotive Body and Related Repairers; Automotive Glass Installers and Repairers; Automotive Master Mechanics; Automotive Service Technicians and Mechanics; Automotive Specialty Technicians; Bicycle Repairers; Bridge and Lock Tenders; Bus and Truck Mechanics and Diesel Engine Specialists; Camera and Photographic Equipment Repairers; Coin, Vending, and Amusement Machine Servicers and Repairers; Control and Valve Installers and Repairers, Except Mechanical Door; Farm Equipment Mechanics; Gas Appliance Repairers; Hand and Portable Power Tool Repairers; Heating and Air Conditioning Mechanics; Heating, Air Conditioning, and Refrigeration Mechanics and Installers; Helpers—Electricians; Helpers—Installation, Maintenance, and Repair Workers; Industrial Machinery Mechanics; Keyboard Instrument Repairers and Tuners; Locksmiths and Safe Repairers; Maintenance and Repair Workers, General; Maintenance Workers, Machinery; Mechanical Door Repairers; Medical Appliance Technicians; Medical Equipment Repairers; Meter Mechanics; Millwrights; Mobile Heavy Equipment Mechanics, Except Engines; Motorboat Mechanics; Motorcycle Mechanics; Musical Instrument Repairers and Tuners; Ophthalmic Laboratory Technicians; Optical Instrument Assemblers; Outdoor Power Equipment and Other Small Engine Mechanics; Painters, Transportation Equipment; Percussion Instrument Repairers and Tuners; others. **PERSONALITY TYPE**—Realistic. Realistic occupations frequently involve work activities that include practical, hands-on problems and solutions. They often deal with plants, animals, and real-world materials like wood, tools, and machinery. Many of the occupations require working outside and do not involve a lot of paperwork or working closely with others.

**EDUCATION/TRAINING PROGRAM(S)**—Heating, Air Conditioning and Refrigeration Mechanic and Repair; Heating, Air Conditioning and Refrigeration Technologist/Technician. **RELATED KNOWLEDGE/ COURSES—Principles of Mechanical Devices:** Knowledge of machines and tools, including their designs, uses, repair, and maintenance. **Engineering and Technology:** Knowledge of the practical application of engineering science and technology. This includes applying principles, techniques, procedures, and equipment to the design and production of various goods and services. **Design:** Knowledge of design techniques, tools, and principles involved in production of precision technical plans, blueprints, drawings, and models. **Clerical Studies:** Knowledge of administrative and clerical procedures and systems such as word processing, managing files and records, stenography and transcription, designing forms, and other office procedures and terminology. **Building and Construction:** Knowledge of materials, methods, and tools involved in the con-

struction or repair of houses, buildings, or other structures such as highways and roads.

# Refuse and Recyclable Material Collectors

▲ Growth: 16.6%
▲ Annual Job Openings: 34,000
▲ Annual Earnings: $26,020
▲ Education/Training Required: Short-term on-the-job training
▲ Self-Employed: 1.7%
▲ Part-Time: 11%

**Collect and dump refuse or recyclable materials from containers into truck. May drive truck.** Drives truck. Starts hoisting device that raises refuse bin attached to rear of truck and dumps contents into opening in enclosed truck body. **SKILLS**—Operation and Control. Operation Monitoring. Troubleshooting.

**GOE—Interest Area:** 08. Industrial Production. **Work Group:** 08.07. Hands-on Work: Loading, Moving, Hoisting, and Conveying. **Other Job Titles in This Work Group:** Conveyor Operators and Tenders; Crane and Tower Operators; Dragline Operators; Excavating and Loading Machine and Dragline Operators; Freight, Stock, and Material Movers, Hand; Hoist and Winch Operators; Industrial Truck and Tractor Operators; Irradiated-Fuel Handlers; Laborers and Freight, Stock, and Material Movers, Hand; Machine Feeders and Offbearers; Material Moving Workers, All Other; Packers and Packagers, Hand; Pump Operators, Except Wellhead Pumpers; Tank Car, Truck, and Ship Load-

ers. **PERSONALITY TYPE**—Realistic. Realistic occupations frequently involve work activities that include practical, hands-on problems and solutions. They often deal with plants, animals, and real-world materials like wood, tools, and machinery. Many of the occupations require working outside and do not involve a lot of paperwork or working closely with others.

**EDUCATION/TRAINING PROGRAM(S)**—No data available. **RELATED KNOWLEDGE/COURSES—Transportation:** Knowledge of principles and methods for moving people or goods by air, rail, sea, or road, including the relative costs and benefits. **Principles of Mechanical Devices:** Knowledge of machines and tools, including their designs, uses, repair, and maintenance. **Geography:** Knowledge of principles and methods for describing the features of land, sea, and air masses, including their physical characteristics, locations, interrelationships, and distribution of plant, animal, and human life.

# Registered Nurses

▲ Growth: 25.6%
▲ Annual Job Openings: 140,000
▲ Annual Earnings: $46,410
▲ Education/Training Required: Associate's degree
▲ Self-Employed: 1.1%
▲ Part-Time: 26.3%

Assess patient health problems and needs, develop and implement nursing care plans, and maintain medical records. Administer nursing care to ill, injured, convalescent, or disabled patients. May advise patients on health maintenance and disease prevention or provide case management. Licensing or registration required. Includes advanced-practice nurses such as nurse practitioners, clinical nurse specialists, certified nurse midwives, and certified registered nurse anesthetists. Advanced-practice nursing is practiced by RNs who have specialized formal post-basic education and who function in highly autonomous and specialized roles. Provides health care, first aid, and immunization in facilities such as schools, hospitals, and industry. Observes patient's skin color, dilation of pupils, and computerized equipment to monitor vital signs. Administers local, inhalation, intravenous, and other anesthetics. Orders, interprets, and evaluates diagnostic tests to identify and assess patient's condition. Prescribes or recommends drugs or other forms of treatment, such as physical therapy, inhalation therapy, or related therapeutic procedures. Refers students or patients to community agencies furnishing assistance and cooperates with agencies. Delivers infants and performs postpartum examinations and treatment. Instructs on topics such as health education, disease prevention, childbirth, and home nursing and develops health improvement programs. Advises and consults with specified personnel concerning necessary precautions to be taken to prevent possible contamination or infection. Administers stipulated emergency measures and contacts obstetrician when deviations from standard are encountered during pregnancy or delivery. Informs physician of patient's condition during anesthesia. Discusses cases with physician or obstetrician. Provides prenatal and postnatal care to obstetrical patients under supervision of obstetrician. Contracts independently to render nursing care, usually to one patient, in hospital or private home. Directs and coordinates infection control program in hospital. Maintains stock of supplies. Conducts specified laboratory tests. Prepares rooms, sterile instruments, equipment, and supplies and hands items to surgeon. Prepares patients for and assists with examinations. Records patient's medical information and vital signs. **SKILLS**—Reading Comprehension. Active Listening. Speaking. Service Orientation. Instructing.

**GOE—Interest Area:** 14. Medical and Health Services. **Work Group:** 14.02. Medicine and Surgery. **Other Job Titles in This Work Group:** Anesthesiologists; Family and General Practitioners; Internists, General; Medical Assistants; Obstetricians and Gynecologists; Pediatricians, General; Pharmacists; Pharmacy Aides; Pharmacy Technicians; Physician Assistants; Physicians and Surgeons, All Other; Psychiatrists; Surgeons; Surgical Technologists. **PERSONALITY TYPE**—Social. Social occupations frequently involve working with, communicating with, and teaching people. These occupations often involve helping or providing service to others.

**EDUCATION/TRAINING PROGRAM(S)**—Nursing (R.N. Training); Nursing Anesthetist (Post-R.N.); Nursing Midwifery (Post-R.N.); Nursing Science (Post-R.N.); Nursing, Adult Health (Post-R.N.); Nursing, Family Practice (Post-R.N.); Nursing, Maternal/Child Health (Post-R.N.); Nursing, Other; Nursing, Pediatric (Post-R.N.); Nursing, Psychiatric/Mental Health (Post-R.N.); Nursing, Public Health (Post-R.N.); Nursing, Surgical (Post-R.N.). **RELATED KNOWLEDGE/ COURSES—Medicine and Dentistry:** Knowledge of the information and techniques needed to diagnose and treat human injuries, diseases, and deformities. This includes symptoms, treatment alternatives, drug properties and interactions, and preventive health-care measures. **Biology:** Knowledge of plant and animal organisms and their tissues, cells, functions, interdependencies, and interactions with each other and the environment. **Customer and Personal Service:** Knowledge of principles and processes for providing customer and personal services. This includes customer needs assessment, meeting quality standards for services, and evaluation of customer satisfaction. **Chemistry:** Knowledge of the chemical composition, structure, and properties of substances and of the chemical processes and transformations that they undergo. This includes uses of chemicals and their interactions, danger signs, production techniques, and disposal methods. **Therapy and Counseling:** Knowledge of principles, methods, and procedures for diagnosis, treatment, and rehabilitation of physical and mental dysfunctions and for career counseling and guidance.

# Reinforcing Iron and Rebar Workers

▲ Growth: 17.5%
▲ Annual Job Openings: 4,000
▲ Annual Earnings: $37,800
▲ Education/Training Required: Long-term on-the-job training
▲ Self-Employed: 0%
▲ Part-Time: 4.9%

Position and secure steel bars or mesh in concrete forms in order to reinforce concrete. Use a variety of fasteners, rod-bending machines, blowtorches, and hand tools. Determines number, sizes, shapes, and locations of reinforcing rods from blueprints, sketches, or oral instructions. Selects and places rods in forms, spacing and fastening them together, using wire and pliers. Bends steel rods with hand tools and rodbending machine. Cuts rods to required lengths, using hacksaw, bar cutters, or acetylene torch. Reinforces concrete with wire mesh. Welds reinforcing bars together, using arch-welding equipment. **SKILLS**—Active Listening.

**GOE—Interest Area:** 06. Construction, Mining, and Drilling. **Work Group:** 06.02. Construction. **Other Job Titles in This Work Group:** Boat Builders and Shipwrights; Boilermakers; Brattice Builders; Brickmasons and Blockmasons; Carpenters; Carpet Installers; Ceiling Tile Installers; Cement Masons and Concrete Finishers; Commercial Divers; Construction Carpenters; Drywall and Ceiling Tile Installers; Drywall Installers; Electricians; Explosives Workers, Ordnance Handling Experts, and Blasters; Fence Erectors; Floor Layers, Except Carpet, Wood, and Hard Tiles; Floor Sanders and Finishers; Glaziers; Grader, Bulldozer, and Scraper Operators; Hazardous Materials Removal Workers; Insulation Workers, Floor, Ceiling, and Wall; Insulation Workers, Mechanical; Manufactured Building and Mobile Home Installers; Operating Engineers; Operating Engineers and Other Construction Equipment Operators; Painters, Construction and Maintenance; Paperhangers; Paving, Surfacing, and Tamping Equipment Operators; Pile-Driver Operators; Pipe Fitters; Pipelayers; Pipelaying Fitters; Plasterers and Stucco Masons; Plumbers; Plumbers, Pipefitters, and Steamfitters; Rail-Track Laying and Maintenance Equipment Operators; Refractory Materials Repairers, Except Brickmasons; Riggers; Roofers; Rough Carpenters; Security and Fire Alarm Systems Installers; Segmental Pavers; Sheet Metal Workers; Ship Carpenters and Joiners; Stone Cutters and Carvers; Stonemasons; Structural Iron and Steel Workers; Tapers; Terrazzo Workers and Finishers; Tile and Marble Setters. **PERSONALITY TYPE**—Realistic. Realistic occupations frequently involve work activities that include practical, hands-on problems and solutions. They often deal with plants, animals, and real-world materials like wood, tools, and machinery. Many of the occupations require working outside and do not involve a lot of paperwork or working closely with others.

**EDUCATION/TRAINING PROGRAM(S)**—Construction and Building Finishers and Managers, Other. **RELATED KNOWLEDGE/COURSES—Building and Construction:** Knowledge of materials, methods, and tools involved in the construction or repair of houses, buildings, or other structures such as highways and roads. **Design:** Knowledge of design techniques, tools, and principles involved in production of precision technical plans, blueprints, drawings, and models. **Engineering and Technology:** Knowledge of the practical application of engineering science and technology. This includes applying principles, techniques, procedures, and equipment to the design and production of various goods and services. **Physics:** Knowledge and prediction of physical principles and laws and their interrelationships and applications to understanding fluid, material, and atmospheric dynamics and mechanical, electrical, atomic, and sub-atomic structures and processes. **Mathematics:** Knowledge of arithmetic, algebra, geometry, calculus, statistics, and their applications.

# Reservation and Transportation Ticket Agents

- ▲ Growth: 14.5%
- ▲ Annual Job Openings: 39,000
- ▲ Annual Earnings: $26,140
- ▲ Education/Training Required: Short-term on-the-job training
- ▲ Self-Employed: 5%
- ▲ Part-Time: 31.7%

**Make and confirm reservations for passengers and sell tickets for transportation agencies such as airlines, bus companies, railroads, and steamship lines. May check baggage and direct passengers to designated concourse, pier, or track.** Arranges reservations and routing for passengers at request of Ticket Agent. Examines passenger ticket or pass to direct passenger to specified area for loading. Plans route and computes ticket cost, using schedules, rate books, and computer. Reads coded data on tickets to ascertain destination, marks tickets, and assigns boarding pass. Assists passengers requiring special assistance to board or depart conveyance. Informs travel agents in other locations of space reserved or available. Sells travel insurance. Announces arrival and departure information, using public-address system. Telephones customer or Ticket Agent to advise of changes with travel conveyance or to confirm reservation. Sells and assembles tickets for transmittal or mailing to customers. Answers inquiries made to travel agencies or transportation firms, such as airlines, bus companies, railroad companies, and steamship lines. Checks baggage and directs passenger to designated location for loading. Assigns specified space to customers and maintains computerized inventory of passenger space available. Determines whether space is available on travel dates requested by customer. **SKILLS**—Service Orientation. Active Listening. Speaking. Reading Comprehension. Coordination.

**GOE—Interest Area:** 11. Recreation, Travel, and Other Personal Services. **Work Group:** 11.03. Transportation and Lodging Services. **Other Job Titles in This Work Group:** Baggage Porters and Bellhops; Concierges; Flight Attendants; Hotel, Motel, and Resort Desk Clerks; Reservation and Transportation Ticket Agents and Travel Clerks; Transportation Attendants, Except Flight Attendants and Baggage Porters. **PERSONALITY TYPE**—Conventional. Conventional occupations frequently involve following set procedures and routines. These occupations can include working with data and details more than with ideas. Usually there is a clear line of authority to follow.

**EDUCATION/TRAINING PROGRAM(S)**—Tourism and Travel Services Marketing Operations, Other; Tourism Promotion Operations; Travel Services Marketing Operations. **RELATED KNOWLEDGE/COURSES**—**Customer and Personal Service:** Knowledge of principles and processes for providing customer and personal services. This includes customer needs assessment, meeting quality standards for services, and evaluation of customer satisfaction. **Transportation:** Knowledge of principles and methods for moving people or goods by air, rail, sea, or road, including the relative costs and benefits. **Geography:** Knowledge of principles and methods for describing the features of land, sea, and air masses, including their physical characteristics, locations, interrelationships, and distribution of plant, animal, and human life. **Clerical Studies:** Knowledge of administrative and clerical procedures and systems such as word processing, managing files and records, stenography and transcription, designing forms, and other office procedures and terminology. **Computers and Electronics:** Knowledge of circuit boards, processors, chips, electronic equipment, and computer hardware and software, including applications and programming. **English Language:** Knowledge of the structure and content of the English language, including the meaning and spelling of words, rules of composition, and grammar. **Mathematics:** Knowledge of arithmetic, algebra, geometry, calculus, statistics, and their applications.

# Residential Advisors

▲ Growth: 24%

▲ Annual Job Openings: 9,000

▲ Annual Earnings: $21,600

▲ Education/Training Required: Moderate-term on-the-job training

▲ Self-Employed: 0%

▲ Part-Time: 18%

**Coordinate activities for residents of boarding schools, college fraternities or sororities, college dormitories, or similar establishments. Order supplies and determine need for maintenance, repairs, and furnishings. May maintain household records and assign rooms. May refer residents to counseling resources if needed.** Assigns room, assists in planning recreational activities, and supervises work and study programs. Orders supplies and determines need for maintenance, repairs, and furnishings. Ascertains need for and secures service of physician. Chaperons group-sponsored trips and social functions. Plans menus of meals for residents of establishment. Sorts and distributes mail. Answers telephone. Hires and supervises activities of housekeeping personnel. Escorts individuals on trips outside establishment for shopping or to obtain medical or dental services. Compiles records of daily activities of residents. Counsels residents in identifying and resolving social and other problems. **SKILLS**—Social Perceptiveness. Active Listening. Coordination. Speaking. Critical Thinking.

**GOE—Interest Area:** 12. Education and Social Service. **Work Group:** 12.02. Social Services. **Other Job Titles in This Work Group:** Child, Family, and School Social Workers; Clergy; Clinical Psychologists; Clinical, Counseling, and School Psychologists; Community and Social Service Specialists, All Other; Counseling Psychologists; Counselors, All Other; Directors, Religious Activities and Education; Marriage and Family Therapists; Medical and Public Health Social Workers; Mental Health and Substance Abuse Social Workers; Mental Health Counselors; Probation Officers and Correctional Treatment Specialists; Rehabilitation Counselors; Religious Workers, All Other; Social and Human Service Assistants; Social Workers, All Other; Substance Abuse and Behavioral Disorder Counselors. **PERSONALITY TYPE**—Social. Social occupations frequently involve working with, communicating with, and teaching people. These occupations often involve helping or providing service to others.

**EDUCATION/TRAINING PROGRAM(S)**—Child Care Provider/Assistant; Child Care Services Manager; Sport and Fitness Administration/Management. **RELATED KNOWLEDGE/COURSES—Customer and Personal Service:** Knowledge of principles and processes for providing customer and personal services. This includes customer needs assessment, meeting quality standards for services, and evaluation of customer satisfaction. **Psychology:** Knowledge of human behavior and performance; individual differences in ability, personality, and interests; learning and motivation; psychological research methods; and the assessment and treatment of behavioral and affective disorders. **Therapy and Counseling:** Knowledge of principles, methods, and procedures for diagnosis, treatment, and rehabilitation of physical and mental dysfunctions and for career counseling and guidance. **Administration and Management:** Knowledge of business and management principles involved in strategic planning, resource allocation, human resources modeling, leadership technique, production methods, and coordination of people and resources. **Personnel and Human Resources:** Knowledge of principles and procedures for personnel recruitment, selection, training, compensation and benefits, labor relations and negotiation, and personnel information systems.

# Respiratory Therapists

- ▲ Growth: 34.8%
- ▲ Annual Job Openings: 4,000
- ▲ Annual Earnings: $38,220
- ▲ Education/Training Required: Associate's degree
- ▲ Self-Employed: 0%
- ▲ Part-Time: 20.8%

**Assess, treat, and care for patients with breathing disorders. Assume primary responsibility for all respiratory care modalities, including the supervision of respiratory therapy technicians. Initiate and conduct therapeutic procedures; maintain patient records; and select, assemble, check, and operate equipment.** Sets up and operates devices such as mechanical ventilators, therapeutic gas administration apparatus, environmental control systems, and aerosol generators. Operates equipment to administer medicinal gases and aerosol drugs to patients following specified parameters of treatment. Reads prescription, measures arterial blood gases, and reviews patient information to assess patient condition. Monitors patient's physiological responses to therapy, such as vital signs, arterial blood gases, and blood chemistry changes. Performs pulmonary function and adjusts equipment to obtain optimum results to therapy. Inspects and tests respiratory therapy equipment to ensure equipment is functioning safely and efficiently. Determines requirements for treatment, such as type and duration of therapy and medication and dosages. Determines most suitable method of administering inhalants, precautions to be observed, and potential modifications needed, compatible with physician's orders. Performs bronchopulmonary drainage and assists patient in performing breathing exercises. Consults with physician in event of adverse reactions. Maintains patient's chart that contains pertinent identification and therapy information. Orders repairs when necessary. Demonstrates respiratory care procedures to trainees and other health care personnel. **SKILLS**—Reading Comprehension. Service Orientation. Active Listening. Monitoring. Critical Thinking. Active Learning.

**GOE—Interest Area:** 14. Medical and Health Services. **Work Group:** 14.06. Medical Therapy. **Other Job Titles in This Work Group:** Audiologists; Massage Therapists; Occupational Therapist Aides; Occupational Therapist Assistants; Occupational Therapists; Physical Therapist Aides; Physical Therapist Assistants; Physical Therapists; Radiation Therapists; Recreational Therapists; Respiratory Therapy Technicians; Speech-Language Pathologists; Therapists, All Other. **PERSONALITY TYPE**—Investigative. Investigative occupations frequently involve working with ideas and require an extensive amount of thinking. These occupations can involve searching for facts and figuring out problems mentally.

**EDUCATION/TRAINING PROGRAM(S)**—Respiratory Therapy Technician. **RELATED KNOWLEDGE/COURSES**—**Medicine and Dentistry:** Knowledge of the information and techniques needed to diagnose and treat human injuries, diseases, and deformities. This includes symptoms, treatment alternatives, drug properties and interactions, and preventive health-care measures. **Biology:** Knowledge of plant and animal organisms and their tissues, cells, functions, interdependencies, and interactions with each other and the environment. **Therapy and Counseling:** Knowledge of principles, methods, and procedures for diagnosis, treatment, and rehabilitation of physical and mental dysfunctions and for career counseling and guidance. **Chemistry:** Knowledge of the chemical composition, structure, and properties of substances and of the chemical processes and transformations that they undergo. This includes uses of chemicals and their interactions, danger signs, production techniques, and disposal methods. **Psychology:** Knowledge of human behavior and performance; individual differences in ability, personality, and interests; learning and motivation; psychological research methods; and the assessment and treatment of behavioral and affective disorders.

# Retail Salespersons

▲ Growth: 12.4%

▲ Annual Job Openings: 1,124,000

▲ Annual Earnings: $20,260

▲ Education/Training Required: Short-term on-the-job training

▲ Self-Employed: 4.1%

▲ Part-Time: 40.2%

**Sell merchandise, such as furniture, motor vehicles, appliances, or apparel, in a retail establishment.** Prepares sales slip or sales contract. Sells or arranges for delivery, insurance, financing, or service contracts for merchandise. Recommends, selects, and obtains merchandise based on customer needs and desires. Greets customer. Inventories stock. Rents merchandise to customers. Wraps merchandise. Estimates cost of repair or alteration of merchandise. Estimates and quotes trade-in allowances. Maintains records related to sales. Tickets, arranges, and displays merchandise to promote sales. Estimates quantity and cost of merchandise required, such as paint or floor covering. Fits or assists customers in trying on merchandise. Cleans shelves, counters, and tables. Requisitions new stock. Demonstrates use or operation of merchandise. Totals purchases, receives payment, makes change, or processes credit transaction. Describes merchandise and explains use, operation, and care of merchandise to customers. Computes sales price of merchandise. **SKILLS**—Active Listening. Service Orientation. Speaking. Mathematics. Writing.

**GOE—Interest Area:** 10. Sales and Marketing. **Work Group:** 10.03. General Sales. **Other Job Titles in This Work Group:** Parts Salespersons; Real Estate Brokers; Real Estate Sales Agents; Sales Representatives, Wholesale and Manufacturing, Except Technical and Scientific Products; Service Station Attendants; Stock Clerks, Sales Floor; Travel Agents. **PERSONALITY TYPE**—Enterprising. Enterprising occupations frequently involve starting up and carrying out projects. These occupations can involve leading people and making many decisions. They sometimes require risk taking and often deal with business.

**EDUCATION/TRAINING PROGRAM(S)**—Apparel and Accessories Marketing Operations, General; Apparel and Accessories Marketing Operations, Other; Fashion and Fabric Consultant; Food Products Retailing and Wholesaling Operations; General Retailing Operations; General Selling Skills and Sales Operations; Health Products and Services Marketing Operations; Home Products Marketing Operations. **RELATED KNOWLEDGE/COURSES—Sales and Marketing:** Knowledge of principles and methods for showing, promoting, and selling products or services. This includes marketing strategy and tactics, product demonstration, sales techniques, and sales control systems. **Customer and Personal Service:** Knowledge of principles and processes for providing customer and personal services. This includes customer needs assessment, meeting quality standards for services, and evaluation of customer satisfaction. **Mathematics:** Knowledge of arithmetic, algebra, geometry, calculus, statistics, and their applications. **English Language:** Knowledge of the structure and content of the English language, including the meaning and spelling of words, rules of composition, and grammar. **Clerical Studies:** Knowledge of administrative and clerical procedures and systems such as word processing, managing files and records, stenography and transcription, designing forms, and other office procedures and terminology.

# Roofers

▲ Growth: 19.4%
▲ Annual Job Openings: 38,000
▲ Annual Earnings: $31,670
▲ Education/Training Required: Moderate-term on-the-job training
▲ Self-Employed: 27.5%
▲ Part-Time: 13.8%

**Cover roofs of structures with shingles, slate, asphalt, aluminum, wood, and related materials. May spray roofs, sidings, and walls with material to bind, seal, insulate, or soundproof sections of structures.** Fastens composition shingles or sheets to roof with asphalt, cement, or nails. Cuts roofing paper to size and nails or staples paper to roof in overlapping strips to form base for roofing materials. Cleans and maintains equipment. Removes snow, water, or debris from roofs prior to applying roofing materials. Insulates, soundproofs, and seals buildings with foam, using spray gun, air compressor, and heater. Punches holes in slate, tile, terra cotta, or wooden shingles, using punch and hammer. Applies gravel or pebbles over top layer, using rake or stiff-bristled broom. Applies alternate layers of hot asphalt or tar and roofing paper until roof covering is completed as specified. Overlaps successive layers of roofing material, determining distance of overlap, using chalkline, gauge on shingling hatchet, or lines on shingles. Cuts strips of flashing and fits them into angles formed by walls, vents, and intersecting roof surfaces. Mops or pours hot asphalt or tar onto roof base when applying asphalt or tar and gravel to roof. Aligns roofing material with edge of roof. **SKILLS**—Coordination. Equipment Selection. Operation and Control. Repairing.

**GOE—Interest Area:** 06. Construction, Mining, and Drilling. **Work Group:** 06.02. Construction. **Other Job Titles in This Work Group:** Boat Builders and Shipwrights; Boilermakers; Brattice Builders; Brickmasons and Blockmasons; Carpenters; Carpet Installers; Ceiling Tile Installers; Cement Masons and Concrete Finishers; Commercial Divers; Construction Carpenters; Drywall and Ceiling Tile Installers; Drywall Installers; Electricians; Explosives Workers, Ordnance Handling Experts, and Blasters; Fence Erectors; Floor Layers, Except Carpet, Wood, and Hard Tiles; Floor Sanders and Finishers; Glaziers; Grader, Bulldozer, and Scraper Operators; Hazardous Materials Removal Workers; Insulation Workers, Floor, Ceiling, and Wall; Insulation Workers, Mechanical; Manufactured Building and Mobile Home Installers; Operating Engineers; Operating Engineers and Other Construction Equipment Operators; Painters, Construction and Maintenance; Paperhangers; Paving, Surfacing, and Tamping Equipment Operators; Pile-Driver Operators; Pipe Fitters; Pipelayers; Pipelaying Fitters; Plasterers and Stucco Masons; Plumbers; Plumbers, Pipefitters, and Steamfitters; Rail-Track Laying and Maintenance Equipment Operators; Refractory Materials Repairers, Except Brickmasons; Reinforcing Iron and Rebar Workers; Riggers; Rough Carpenters; Security and Fire Alarm Systems Installers; Segmental Pavers; Sheet Metal Workers; Ship Carpenters and Joiners; Stone Cutters and Carvers; Stonemasons; Structural Iron and Steel Workers; Tapers; Terrazzo Workers and Finishers; Tile and Marble Setters. **PERSONALITY TYPE**—Realistic. Realistic occupations frequently involve work activities that include practical, hands-on problems and solutions. They often deal with plants, animals, and real-world materials like wood, tools, and machinery. Many of the occupations require working outside and do not involve a lot of paperwork or working closely with others.

**EDUCATION/TRAINING PROGRAM(S)**—No data available. **RELATED KNOWLEDGE/COURSES—Building and Construction:** Knowledge of materials, methods, and tools involved in the construction or repair of houses, buildings, or other structures such as highways and roads. **Principles of Mechanical Devices:** Knowledge of machines and tools, including their designs, uses, repair, and maintenance. **Engineering and Technology:** Knowledge of the practical application of engineering science and technology. This includes applying principles, techniques, procedures, and equipment to the design and production of various goods and services.

# Rough Carpenters

- ▲ Growth: 8.2%
- ▲ Annual Job Openings: 161,000
- ▲ Annual Earnings: $35,100
- ▲ Education/Training Required: Long-term on-the-job training
- ▲ Self-Employed: 28.6%
- ▲ Part-Time: 8.1%

**Build rough wooden structures such as concrete forms, scaffolds, tunnel, bridge, or sewer supports, billboard signs, and temporary frame shelters according to sketches, blueprints, or oral instructions.** Assembles and fastens material together to construct wood or metal framework of structure, using bolts, nails, or screws. Erects forms of prefabricated forms, framework, scaffolds, hoists, roof supports, or chutes, using hand tools, plumb rule, and level. Anchors and braces forms and other structures in place, using nails, bolts, anchor rods, steel cables, planks, wedges, and timbers. Fabricates parts, using woodworking and metalworking machines. Digs or directs digging of post holes and sets pole to support structure. Examines structural timbers and supports to detect decay and replaces timber, using hand tools, nuts, and bolts. Installs rough door and window frames, subflooring, fixtures, or temporary supports in structures undergoing construction or repair. Bores boltholes in timber with masonry or concrete walls, using power drill. Studies blueprints and diagrams to determine dimensions of structure or form to be constructed or erected. Measures materials or distances, using square, measuring tape, or rule to lay out work. Cuts or saws boards, timbers, or plywood to required size, using handsaw, power saw, or woodworking machine. **SKILLS**—Installation. Operation and Control. Mathematics.

**GOE—Interest Area:** 06. Construction, Mining, and Drilling. **Work Group:** 06.02. Construction. **Other Job Titles in This Work Group:** Boat Builders and Shipwrights; Boilermakers; Brattice Builders; Brickmasons and Blockmasons; Carpenters; Carpet Installers; Ceiling Tile Installers; Cement Masons and Concrete Finishers; Commercial Divers; Construction Carpenters; Drywall and Ceiling Tile Installers; Drywall Installers; Electricians; Explosives Workers, Ordnance Handling Experts, and Blasters; Fence Erectors; Floor Layers, Except Carpet, Wood, and Hard Tiles; Floor Sanders and Finishers; Glaziers; Grader, Bulldozer, and Scraper Operators; Hazardous Materials Removal Workers; Insulation Workers, Floor, Ceiling, and Wall; Insulation Workers, Mechanical; Manufactured Building and Mobile Home Installers; Operating Engineers; Operating Engineers and Other Construction Equipment Operators; Painters, Construction and Maintenance; Paperhangers; Paving, Surfacing, and Tamping Equipment Operators; Pile-Driver Operators; Pipe Fitters; Pipelayers; Pipelaying Fitters; Plasterers and Stucco Masons; Plumbers; Plumbers, Pipefitters, and Steamfitters; Rail-Track Laying and Maintenance Equipment Operators; Refractory Materials Repairers, Except Brickmasons; Reinforcing Iron and Rebar Workers; Riggers; Roofers; Security and Fire Alarm Systems Installers; Segmental Pavers; Sheet Metal Workers; Ship Carpenters and Joiners; Stone Cutters and Carvers; Stonemasons; Structural Iron and Steel Workers; Tapers; Terrazzo Workers and Finishers; Tile and Marble Setters. **PERSONALITY TYPE**—Realistic. Realistic occupations frequently involve work activities that include practical, hands-on problems and solutions. They often deal with plants, animals, and real-world materials like wood, tools, and machinery. Many of the occupations require working outside and do not involve a lot of paperwork or working closely with others.

**EDUCATION/TRAINING PROGRAM(S)**—Carpenter; Marine Maintenance and Ship Repairer. **RELATED KNOWLEDGE/COURSES—Building and Construction:** Knowledge of materials, methods, and tools involved in the construction or repair of houses, buildings, or other structures such as highways and roads. **Engineering and Technology:** Knowledge of the practical application of engineering science and tech-

nology. This includes applying principles, techniques, procedures, and equipment to the design and production of various goods and services. **Design:** Knowledge of design techniques, tools, and principles involved in production of precision technical plans, blueprints, drawings, and models. **Principles of Mechanical Devices:** Knowledge of machines and tools, including their designs, uses, repair, and maintenance. **Mathematics:** Knowledge of arithmetic, algebra, geometry, calculus, statistics, and their applications.

# Sales Representatives, Agricultural

- ▲ Growth: 7.5%
- ▲ Annual Job Openings: 24,000
- ▲ Annual Earnings: $58,630
- ▲ Education/Training Required: Moderate-term on-the-job training
- ▲ Self-Employed: 5.2%
- ▲ Part-Time: 22.3%

**Sell agricultural products and services, such as animal feeds, farm and garden equipment, and dairy, poultry, and veterinarian supplies.** Solicits orders from customers in person or by phone. Demonstrates use of agricultural equipment or machines. Recommends changes in customer use of agricultural products to improve production. Prepares reports of business transactions. Informs customer of estimated delivery schedule, service contracts, warranty, or other information pertaining to purchased products. Displays or shows customer agricultural-related products. Compiles lists of prospective customers for use as sales leads. Prepares sales contracts for orders obtained. Consults with customer regarding installation, setup, or layout of agricultural equipment and machines. Quotes prices and credit terms. **SKILLS**—Speaking. Active Listening. Writing. Reading Comprehension. Mathematics. Persuasion.

**GOE—Interest Area:** 10. Sales and Marketing. **Work Group:** 10.02. Sales Technology. **Other Job Titles in This Work Group:** Advertising Sales Agents; Insurance Sales Agents; Sales Agents, Financial Services; Sales Agents, Securities and Commodities; Sales Representatives, Chemical and Pharmaceutical; Sales Representa-

tives, Electrical/Electronic; Sales Representatives, Instruments; Sales Representatives, Mechanical Equipment and Supplies; Sales Representatives, Medical; Sales Representatives, Services, All Other; Sales Representatives, Wholesale and Manufacturing, Technical and Scientific Products; Securities, Commodities, and Financial Services Sales Agents. **PERSONALITY TYPE**—Enterprising. Enterprising occupations frequently involve starting up and carrying out projects. These occupations can involve leading people and making many decisions. They sometimes require risk taking and often deal with business.

**EDUCATION/TRAINING PROGRAM(S)**—General Selling Skills and Sales Operations; Health Products and Services Marketing Operations; Office Products Marketing Operations. **RELATED KNOWLEDGE/ COURSES—Sales and Marketing:** Knowledge of principles and methods for showing, promoting, and selling products or services. This includes marketing strategy and tactics, product demonstration, sales techniques, and sales control systems. **Mathematics:** Knowledge of arithmetic, algebra, geometry, calculus, statistics, and their applications. **English Language:** Knowledge of the structure and content of the English language, including the meaning and spelling of words, rules of composition, and grammar. **Economics and Accounting:** Knowledge of economic and accounting principles and practices, the financial markets, banking, and the analysis and reporting of financial data. **Customer and**

**Personal Service:** Knowledge of principles and processes for providing customer and personal services. This includes customer needs assessment, meeting quality standards for services, and evaluation of customer satisfaction.

# Sales Representatives, Chemical and Pharmaceutical

- ▲ Growth: 7.5%
- ▲ Annual Job Openings: 24,000
- ▲ Annual Earnings: $58,630
- ▲ Education/Training Required: Moderate-term on-the-job training
- ▲ Self-Employed: 5.2%
- ▲ Part-Time: 22.3%

**Sell chemical or pharmaceutical products or services, such as acids, industrial chemicals, agricultural chemicals, medicines, drugs, and water treatment supplies.** Promotes and sells pharmaceutical and chemical products to potential customers. Explains water treatment package benefits to customer and sells chemicals to treat and resolve water process problems. Estimates and advises customer of service costs to correct water-treatment process problems. Discusses characteristics and clinical studies pertaining to pharmaceutical products with physicians, dentists, hospitals, and retail/wholesale establishments. Distributes drug samples to customer and takes orders for pharmaceutical supply items from customer. Inspects, tests, and observes chemical changes in water system equipment, utilizing test kit, reference manual, and knowledge of chemical treatment. **SKILLS**—Speaking. Active Listening. Reading Comprehension. Persuasion. Science. Critical Thinking. Social Perceptiveness.

**GOE—Interest Area:** 10. Sales and Marketing. **Work Group:** 10.02. Sales Technology. **Other Job Titles in This Work Group:** Advertising Sales Agents; Insurance Sales Agents; Sales Agents, Financial Services; Sales Agents, Securities and Commodities; Sales Representatives, Agricultural; Sales Representatives, Electrical/Electronic; Sales Representatives, Instruments; Sales Representatives, Mechanical Equipment and Supplies; Sales Representatives, Medical; Sales Representatives, Services, All Other; Sales Representatives, Wholesale

and Manufacturing, Technical and Scientific Products; Securities, Commodities, and Financial Services Sales Agents. **PERSONALITY TYPE**—Enterprising. Enterprising occupations frequently involve starting up and carrying out projects. These occupations can involve leading people and making many decisions. They sometimes require risk taking and often deal with business.

**EDUCATION/TRAINING PROGRAM(S)**—General Selling Skills and Sales Operations; Health Products and Services Marketing Operations; Office Products Marketing Operations. **RELATED KNOWLEDGE/ COURSES**—**Sales and Marketing:** Knowledge of principles and methods for showing, promoting, and selling products or services. This includes marketing strategy and tactics, product demonstration, sales techniques, and sales control systems. **Chemistry:** Knowledge of the chemical composition, structure, and properties of substances and of the chemical processes and transformations that they undergo. This includes uses of chemicals and their interactions, danger signs, production techniques, and disposal methods. **Mathematics:** Knowledge of arithmetic, algebra, geometry, calculus, statistics, and their applications. **English Language:** Knowledge of the structure and content of the English language, including the meaning and spelling of words, rules of composition, and grammar. **Economics and Accounting:** Knowledge of economic and accounting principles and practices, the financial markets, banking, and the analysis and reporting of financial data.

# Sales Representatives, Electrical/Electronic

▲ Growth: 7.5%
▲ Annual Job Openings: 24,000
▲ Annual Earnings: $58,630
▲ Education/Training Required: Moderate-term on-the-job training
▲ Self-Employed: 5.2%
▲ Part-Time: 22.3%

Sell electrical, electronic, or related products or services, such as communication equipment, radiographic-inspection equipment and services, ultrasonic equipment, electronics parts, computers, and EDP systems. Analyzes communication needs of customer and consults with staff engineers regarding technical problems. Trains establishment personnel in equipment use, utilizing knowledge of electronics and product sold. Recommends equipment to meet customer requirements, considering salable features such as flexibility, cost, capacity, and economy of operation. Negotiates terms of sale and services with customer. Sells electrical or electronic equipment, such as computers and data processing and radiographic equipment to businesses and industrial establishments. **SKILLS**—Persuasion. Active Listening. Instructing. Speaking. Operations Analysis. Negotiation. Equipment Selection.

**GOE—Interest Area:** 10. Sales and Marketing. **Work Group:** 10.02. Sales Technology. **Other Job Titles in This Work Group:** Advertising Sales Agents; Insurance Sales Agents; Sales Agents, Financial Services; Sales Agents, Securities and Commodities; Sales Representatives, Agricultural; Sales Representatives, Chemical and Pharmaceutical; Sales Representatives, Instruments; Sales Representatives, Mechanical Equipment and Supplies; Sales Representatives, Medical; Sales Representatives, Services, All Other; Sales Representatives, Wholesale and Manufacturing, Technical and Scientific

Products; Securities, Commodities, and Financial Services Sales Agents. **PERSONALITY TYPE**—Enterprising. Enterprising occupations frequently involve starting up and carrying out projects. These occupations can involve leading people and making many decisions. They sometimes require risk taking and often deal with business.

**EDUCATION/TRAINING PROGRAM(S)**—General Selling Skills and Sales Operations; Health Products and Services Marketing Operations; Office Products Marketing Operations. **RELATED KNOWLEDGE/ COURSES—Sales and Marketing:** Knowledge of principles and methods for showing, promoting, and selling products or services. This includes marketing strategy and tactics, product demonstration, sales techniques, and sales control systems. **Computers and Electronics:** Knowledge of circuit boards, processors, chips, electronic equipment, and computer hardware and software, including applications and programming. **Education and Training:** Knowledge of principles and methods for curriculum and training design, teaching and instruction for individuals and groups, and the measurement of training effects. **Economics and Accounting:** Knowledge of economic and accounting principles and practices, the financial markets, banking, and the analysis and reporting of financial data. **Mathematics:** Knowledge of arithmetic, algebra, geometry, calculus, statistics, and their applications.

# Sales Representatives, Instruments

- ▲ Growth: 7.5%
- ▲ Annual Job Openings: 24,000
- ▲ Annual Earnings: $58,630
- ▲ Education/Training Required: Moderate-term on-the-job training
- ▲ Self-Employed: 5.2%
- ▲ Part-Time: 22.3%

**Sell precision instruments, such as dynamometers and spring scales, and laboratory, navigation, and surveying instruments.** Assists customer with product selection, utilizing knowledge of engineering specifications and catalog resources. Evaluates customer needs and emphasizes product features based on technical knowledge of product capabilities and limitations. Sells weighing and other precision instruments, such as spring scales, dynamometers, and laboratory, navigational, and surveying instruments, to customer. **SKILLS**—Active Listening. Persuasion. Speaking. Reading Comprehension. Service Orientation. Instructing. Mathematics.

**GOE—Interest Area:** 10. Sales and Marketing. **Work Group:** 10.02. Sales Technology. **Other Job Titles in This Work Group:** Advertising Sales Agents; Insurance Sales Agents; Sales Agents, Financial Services; Sales Agents, Securities and Commodities; Sales Representatives, Agricultural; Sales Representatives, Chemical and Pharmaceutical; Sales Representatives, Electrical/Electronic; Sales Representatives, Mechanical Equipment and Supplies; Sales Representatives, Medical; Sales Representatives, Services, All Other; Sales Representatives, Wholesale and Manufacturing, Technical and Scientific Products; Securities, Commodities, and Financial Services Sales Agents. **PERSONALITY TYPE**—Enterprising. Enterprising occupations frequently involve starting up and carrying out projects. These occupations can involve leading people and making many decisions.

They sometimes require risk taking and often deal with business.

**EDUCATION/TRAINING PROGRAM(S)**—General Selling Skills and Sales Operations; Health Products and Services Marketing Operations; Office Products Marketing Operations. **RELATED KNOWLEDGE/COURSES—Sales and Marketing:** Knowledge of principles and methods for showing, promoting, and selling products or services. This includes marketing strategy and tactics, product demonstration, sales techniques, and sales control systems. **English Language:** Knowledge of the structure and content of the English language, including the meaning and spelling of words, rules of composition, and grammar. **Customer and Personal Service:** Knowledge of principles and processes for providing customer and personal services. This includes customer needs assessment, meeting quality standards for services, and evaluation of customer satisfaction. **Computers and Electronics:** Knowledge of circuit boards, processors, chips, electronic equipment, and computer hardware and software, including applications and programming. **Engineering and Technology:** Knowledge of the practical application of engineering science and technology. This includes applying principles, techniques, procedures, and equipment to the design and production of various goods and services. **Principles of Mechanical Devices:** Knowledge of machines and tools, including their designs, uses, repair, and maintenance.

# Sales Representatives, Mechanical Equipment and Supplies

- ▲ Growth: 7.5%
- ▲ Annual Job Openings: 24,000
- ▲ Annual Earnings: $58,630
- ▲ Education/Training Required: Moderate-term on-the-job training
- ▲ Self-Employed: 5.2%
- ▲ Part-Time: 22.3%

Sell mechanical equipment, machinery, materials, and supplies, such as aircraft and railroad equipment and parts, construction machinery, material-handling equipment, industrial machinery, and welding equipment. Recommends and sells textile, industrial, construction, railroad, and oil field machinery, equipment, materials, and supplies and services utilizing knowledge of machine operations. Computes installation or production costs, estimates savings, and prepares and submits bid specifications to customer for review and approval. Submits orders for product and follows up on order to verify material list accuracy and that delivery schedule meets project deadline. Appraises equipment and verifies customer credit rating to establish trade-in value and contract terms. Reviews existing machinery/equipment placement and diagrams proposal to illustrate efficient space utilization, using standard measuring devices and templates. Attends sales and trade meetings and reads related publications to obtain current market condition information, business trends, and industry developments. Inspects establishment premises to verify installation feasibility and obtains building blueprints and elevator specifications to submit to engineering department for bid. Demonstrates and explains use of installed equipment and production processes. Arranges for installation and test-operation of machinery and recommends solutions to product-related problems. Contacts current and potential customers, visits establishments to evaluate needs, and promotes sale of products and services. **SKILLS**—Active Listening. Reading Comprehension. Speaking. Equipment Selection. Operations Analysis.

**GOE—Interest Area:** 10. Sales and Marketing. **Work Group:** 10.02. Sales Technology. **Other Job Titles in This Work Group:** Advertising Sales Agents; Insurance Sales Agents; Sales Agents, Financial Services; Sales Agents, Securities and Commodities; Sales Representatives, Agricultural; Sales Representatives, Chemical and Pharmaceutical; Sales Representatives, Electrical/Electronic; Sales Representatives, Instruments; Sales Representatives, Medical; Sales Representatives, Services, All Other; Sales Representatives, Wholesale and Manufacturing, Technical and Scientific Products; Securities, Commodities, and Financial Services Sales Agents. **PERSONALITY TYPE**—Enterprising. Enterprising occupations frequently involve starting up and carrying out projects. These occupations can involve leading people and making many decisions. They sometimes require risk taking and often deal with business.

**EDUCATION/TRAINING PROGRAM(S)**—General Selling Skills and Sales Operations; Health Products and Services Marketing Operations; Office Products Marketing Operations. **RELATED KNOWLEDGE/COURSES**—**Sales and Marketing:** Knowledge of principles and methods for showing, promoting, and selling products or services. This includes marketing strategy and tactics, product demonstration, sales techniques, and sales control systems. **Mathematics:** Knowledge of arithmetic, algebra, geometry, calculus, statistics, and their applications. **Economics and Accounting:** Knowledge of economic and accounting principles and practices, the financial markets, banking, and the analysis and reporting of financial data. **Principles of Mechanical Devices:** Knowledge of machines and tools, including their designs, uses, repair, and maintenance. **Communications and Media:** Knowledge of media production, communication, and dissemination techniques and methods. This includes alternative ways to inform and entertain via written, oral, and visual media.

# Sales Representatives, Medical

- ▲ Growth: 7.5%
- ▲ Annual Job Openings: 24,000
- ▲ Annual Earnings: $58,630
- ▲ Education/Training Required: Moderate-term on-the-job training
- ▲ Self-Employed: 5.2%
- ▲ Part-Time: 22.3%

**Sell medical equipment, products, and services. Does not include pharmaceutical sales representatives.** Promotes sale of medical and dental equipment, supplies, and services to doctors, dentists, hospitals, medical schools, and retail establishments. Writes specifications to order custom-made surgical appliances, using customer measurements and physician prescriptions. Advises customer regarding office layout, legal and insurance regulations, cost analysis, and collection methods. Designs and fabricates custom-made medical appliances. Selects surgical appliances from stock and fits and sells appliance to customer. Studies data describing new products to accurately recommend purchase of equipment and supplies. **SKILLS**—Active Listening. Reading Comprehension. Writing. Speaking. Equipment Selection. Persuasion. Operations Analysis.

**GOE—Interest Area:** 10. Sales and Marketing. **Work Group:** 10.02. Sales Technology. **Other Job Titles in This Work Group:** Advertising Sales Agents; Insurance Sales Agents; Sales Agents, Financial Services; Sales Agents, Securities and Commodities; Sales Representatives, Agricultural; Sales Representatives, Chemical and Pharmaceutical; Sales Representatives, Electrical/Electronic; Sales Representatives, Instruments; Sales Representatives, Mechanical Equipment and Supplies; Sales Representatives, Services, All Other; Sales Representatives, Wholesale and Manufacturing, Technical and Scientific Products; Securities, Commodities, and Financial Services Sales Agents. **PERSONALITY TYPE**—Enterprising. Enterprising occupations frequently involve starting up and carrying out projects. These occupations can involve leading people and making many decisions. They sometimes require risk taking and often deal with business.

**EDUCATION/TRAINING PROGRAM(S)**—General Selling Skills and Sales Operations; Health Products and Services Marketing Operations; Office Products Marketing Operations. **RELATED KNOWLEDGE/COURSES**—**Sales and Marketing:** Knowledge of principles and methods for showing, promoting, and selling products or services. This includes marketing strategy and tactics, product demonstration, sales techniques, and sales control systems. **Mathematics:** Knowledge of arithmetic, algebra, geometry, calculus, statistics, and their applications. **Engineering and Technology:** Knowledge of the practical application of engineering science and technology. This includes applying principles, techniques, procedures, and equipment to the design and production of various goods and services. **Design:** Knowledge of design techniques, tools, and principles involved in production of precision technical plans, blueprints, drawings, and models. **Economics and Accounting:** Knowledge of economic and accounting principles and practices, the financial markets, banking, and the analysis and reporting of financial data.

# Sales Representatives, Wholesale and Manufacturing, Except Technical and Scientific Products

▲ Growth: 5.7%
▲ Annual Job Openings: 86,000
▲ Annual Earnings: $46,770
▲ Education/Training Required: Moderate-term on-the-job training
▲ Self-Employed: 5.5%
▲ Part-Time: 22.3%

**Sell goods for wholesalers or manufacturers to businesses or groups of individuals. Work requires substantial knowledge of items sold.** Contacts regular and prospective customers to solicit orders. Recommends products to customers, based on customer's specific needs and interests. Answers questions about products, prices, durability, and credit terms. Meets with customers to demonstrate and explain features of products. Prepares lists of prospective customers. Reviews sales records and current market information to determine value or sales potential of product. Estimates delivery dates and arranges delivery schedules. Completes sales contracts or forms to record sales information. Instructs customers in use of products. Assists and advises retail dealers in use of sales promotion techniques. Investigates and resolves customer complaints. Forwards orders to manufacturer. Assembles and stocks product displays in retail stores. Writes reports on sales and products. Prepares drawings, estimates, and bids to meet specific needs of customer. Obtains credit information on prospective customers. Oversees delivery or installation of products or equipment. **SKILLS**—Speaking. Active Listening. Writing. Persuasion. Service Orientation. Active Learning. Negotiation.

**GOE—Interest Area:** 10. Sales and Marketing. **Work Group:** 10.03. General Sales. **Other Job Titles in This Work Group:** Parts Salespersons; Real Estate Brokers; Real Estate Sales Agents; Retail Salespersons; Service Station Attendants; Stock Clerks, Sales Floor; Travel Agents. **PERSONALITY TYPE**—Enterprising. Enterprising occupations frequently involve starting up and carrying out projects. These occupations can involve leading people and making many decisions. They sometimes require risk taking and often deal with business.

**EDUCATION/TRAINING PROGRAM(S)**—Business and Personal Services Marketing Operations, Other; Fashion and Fabric Consultant; Fashion Merchandising; General Retailing and Wholesaling Operations and Skills, Other; Marketing Operations/Marketing and Distribution, Other; Office Products Marketing Operations. **RELATED KNOWLEDGE/COURSES—Sales and Marketing:** Knowledge of principles and methods for showing, promoting, and selling products or services. This includes marketing strategy and tactics, product demonstration, sales techniques, and sales control systems. **Customer and Personal Service:** Knowledge of principles and processes for providing customer and personal services. This includes customer needs assessment, meeting quality standards for services, and evaluation of customer satisfaction. **English Language:** Knowledge of the structure and content of the English language, including the meaning and spelling of words, rules of composition, and grammar. **Mathematics:** Knowledge of arithmetic, algebra, geometry, calculus, statistics, and their applications. **Communications and Media:** Knowledge of media production, communication, and dissemination techniques and methods. This includes alternative ways to inform and entertain via written, oral, and visual media.

# Screen Printing Machine Setters and Set-Up Operators

- ▲ Growth: 5.5%
- ▲ Annual Job Openings: 24,000
- ▲ Annual Earnings: $30,090
- ▲ Education/Training Required: Moderate-term on-the-job training
- ▲ Self-Employed: 2.6%
- ▲ Part-Time: 3.3%

**Set up or set up and operate screen printing machines to print designs onto articles and materials, such as glass or plasticware, cloth, and paper.** Sets and adjusts feed rollers, spindle reel, printing screens, and bolts to specifications. Starts dyeing oven and sets thermostat to temperature specified for printing run. Reviews print order to determine settings and adjustments required to set up manually controlled or automatic screen printing machine or decorating equipment. Determines from orders type and color of designs to print. Adjusts position of design or screen to ensure specified color print registration. Trains workers in use of printing equipment and in quality standards. Counts and records quantities printed in production log. Patrols printing area to monitor production activities and to detect problems, such as mechanical breakdowns or malfunctions. Inspects printing equipment and replaces damaged or defective parts, such as switches, pulleys, fixtures, screws, and bolts. Compares ink or paint prepared for printing run with master color swatch to confirm accuracy of match. Examines product for paint smears, position of design, or other defects and adjusts equipment. Mixes paints according to formula, using bench mixer. Measures, centers, and aligns and positions screen, using gauge and hand tools. **SKILLS**—Operation and Control. Equipment Maintenance. Instructing. Troubleshooting. Operation Monitoring. Repairing.

**GOE—Interest Area:** 08. Industrial Production. **Work Group:** 08.02. Production Technology. **Other Job Titles in This Work Group:** Aircraft Rigging Assemblers; Aircraft Structure Assemblers, Precision; Aircraft Structure, Surfaces, Rigging, and Systems Assemblers; Aircraft Systems Assemblers, Precision; Bench Workers, Jewelry; Bindery Machine Setters and Set-Up Operators; Bindery Workers; Bookbinders; Buffing and Polishing Set-Up Operators; Casting Machine Set-Up Operators; Coating, Painting, and Spraying Machine Setters and Set-Up Operators; Coating, Painting, and Spraying Machine Setters, Operators, and Tenders; Combination Machine Tool Setters and Set-Up Operators, Metal and Plastic; Cutting, Punching, and Press Machine Setters, Operators, and Tenders, Metal and Plastic; Dental Laboratory Technicians; Drilling and Boring Machine Tool Setters, Operators, and Tenders, Metal and Plastic; Electrical and Electronic Equipment Assemblers; Electrical and Electronic Inspectors and Testers; Electromechanical Equipment Assemblers; Engine and Other Machine Assemblers; Extruding and Drawing Machine Setters, Operators, and Tenders, Metal and Plastic; Extruding, Forming, Pressing, and Compacting Machine Setters and Set-Up Operators; Extruding, Forming, Pressing, and Compacting Machine Setters, Operators, and Tenders; Forging Machine Setters, Operators, and Tenders, Metal and Plastic; Foundry Mold and Coremakers; Gem and Diamond Workers; Grinding, Honing, Lapping, and Deburring Machine Set-Up Operators; Grinding, Lapping, Polishing, and Buffing Machine Tool Setters, Operators, and Tenders, Metal and Plastic; Heat Treating Equipment Setters, Operators, and Tenders, Metal and Plastic; others. **PERSONALITY TYPE**—Realistic. Realistic occupations frequently involve work activities that include practical, hands-on problems and solutions. They often deal with plants, animals, and real-world materials like wood, tools, and machinery. Many of the occupations require working outside and do not involve a lot of paperwork or working closely with others.

**EDUCATION/TRAINING PROGRAM(S)**—Graphic and Printing Equipment Operator, General; Graphic and Printing Equipment Operators, Other;

Printing Press Operator. **RELATED KNOWLEDGE/ COURSES—Production and Processing:** Knowledge of raw materials, production processes, quality control, costs, and other techniques for maximizing the effective manufacture and distribution of goods. **Principles of Mechanical Devices:** Knowledge of machines and tools, including their designs, uses, repair, and maintenance. **Mathematics:** Knowledge of arithmetic, alge-

bra, geometry, calculus, statistics, and their applications. **Education and Training:** Knowledge of principles and methods for curriculum and training design, teaching and instruction for individuals and groups, and the measurement of training effects. **Design:** Knowledge of design techniques, tools, and principles involved in production of precision technical plans, blueprints, drawings, and models.

# Sculptors

- ▲ Growth: 13.4%
- ▲ Annual Job Openings: 4,000
- ▲ Annual Earnings: $35,770
- ▲ Education/Training Required: Long-term on-the-job training
- ▲ Self-Employed: 56.7%
- ▲ Part-Time: 24%

**Design and construct three-dimensional art works, using materials such as stone, wood, plaster, and metal and employing various manual and tool techniques.** Carves objects from stone, concrete, plaster, wood, or other material, using abrasives and tools, such as chisels, gouges, and mall. Models substances, such as clay or wax, using fingers and small hand tools to form objects. Cuts, bends, laminates, arranges, and fastens individual or mixed raw and manufactured materials and products to form works of art. Constructs artistic forms from metal or stone, using metalworking, welding, or masonry tools and equipment. **SKILLS—**Monitoring. Equipment Selection.

**GOE—Interest Area:** 01. Arts, Entertainment, and Media. **Work Group:** 01.04. Visual Arts. **Other Job Titles in This Work Group:** Cartoonists; Commercial and Industrial Designers; Designers, All Other; Exhibit Designers; Fashion Designers; Fine Artists, Including Painters, Sculptors, and Illustrators; Floral Designers; Graphic Designers; Interior Designers; Merchandise Displayers and Window Trimmers; Multi-Media Artists and Animators; Painters and Illustrators; Set and Exhibit Designers; Set Designers; Sketch Artists. **PERSONALITY TYPE—**Artistic. Artistic occupations frequently involve working with forms, designs, and

patterns. They often require self-expression, and the work can be done without following a clear set of rules.

**EDUCATION/TRAINING PROGRAM(S)—**Art, General; Ceramics Arts and Ceramics; Drawing; Fine Arts and Art Studies, Other; Fine/Studio Arts; Intermedia; Medical Illustrating; Painting; Printmaking; Sculpture. **RELATED KNOWLEDGE/COURSES— Fine Arts:** Knowledge of the theory and techniques required to compose, produce, and perform works of music, dance, visual arts, drama, and sculpture. **Design:** Knowledge of design techniques, tools, and principles involved in production of precision technical plans, blueprints, drawings, and models. **Engineering and Technology:** Knowledge of the practical application of engineering science and technology. This includes applying principles, techniques, procedures, and equipment to the design and production of various goods and services. **Building and Construction:** Knowledge of materials, methods, and tools involved in the construction or repair of houses, buildings, or other structures such as highways and roads. **English Language:** Knowledge of the structure and content of the English language, including the meaning and spelling of words, rules of composition, and grammar.

# Security Guards

▲ Growth: 35.4%

▲ Annual Job Openings: 242,000

▲ Annual Earnings: $19,470

▲ Education/Training Required: Short-term on-the-job training

▲ Self-Employed: 1.4%

▲ Part-Time: 19.8%

**Guard, patrol, or monitor premises to prevent theft, violence, or infractions of rules.** Patrols industrial and commercial premises to prevent and detect signs of intrusion and ensure security of doors, windows, and gates. Operates detecting devices to screen individuals and prevent passage of prohibited articles into restricted areas. Monitors and adjusts controls that regulate building systems, such as air conditioning, furnace, or boiler. Escorts or drives motor vehicle to transport individuals to specified locations and to provide personal protection. Writes reports of daily activities and irregularities, such as equipment or property damage, theft, presence of unauthorized persons, or unusual occurrences. Answers telephone calls to take messages, answer questions, and provide information during non-business hours or when switchboard is closed. Drives and guards armored vehicle to transport money and valuables to prevent theft and ensure safe delivery. Inspects and adjusts security systems, equipment, and machinery to ensure operational use and to detect evidence of tampering. Monitors and authorizes entrance and departure of employees, visitors, and other persons to guard against theft and maintain security of premises. Answers alarms and investigates disturbances. Circulates among visitors, patrons, and employees to preserve order and protect property. Calls police or fire departments in cases of emergency, such as fire or presence of unauthorized persons. Warns persons of rule infractions or violations and apprehends or evicts violators from premises, using force when necessary. **SKILLS**—Active Listening. Critical Thinking. Writing. Speaking. Judgment and Decision Making. Monitoring. Social Perceptiveness.

**GOE—Interest Area:** 04. Law, Law Enforcement, and Public Safety. **Work Group:** 04.03. Law Enforcement.

**Other Job Titles in This Work Group:** Animal Control Workers; Bailiffs; Child Support, Missing Persons, and Unemployment Insurance Fraud Investigators; Correctional Officers and Jailers; Criminal Investigators and Special Agents; Crossing Guards; Detectives and Criminal Investigators; Fire Investigators; Fish and Game Wardens; Forensic Science Technicians; Gaming Surveillance Officers and Gaming Investigators; Highway Patrol Pilots; Immigration and Customs Inspectors; Lifeguards, Ski Patrol, and Other Recreational Protective Service Workers; Parking Enforcement Workers; Police and Sheriff's Patrol Officers; Police Detectives; Police Identification and Records Officers; Police Patrol Officers; Private Detectives and Investigators; Sheriffs and Deputy Sheriffs; Transit and Railroad Police. **PERSONALITY TYPE**—Social. Social occupations frequently involve working with, communicating with, and teaching people. These occupations often involve helping or providing service to others.

**EDUCATION/TRAINING PROGRAM(S)**—Security and Loss Prevention Services. **RELATED KNOWLEDGE/COURSES—Public Safety and Security:** Knowledge of relevant equipment, policies, procedures, and strategies to promote effective local, state, or national security operations for the protection of people, data, property, and institutions. **Law and Government:** Knowledge of laws, legal codes, court procedures, precedents, government regulations, executive orders, agency rules, and the democratic political process. **English Language:** Knowledge of the structure and content of the English language, including the meaning and spelling of words, rules of composition, and grammar. **Customer and Personal Service:** Knowledge of principles and processes for providing customer and personal services. This includes customer needs assessment, meeting quality standards for services, and evaluation of customer satisfaction. **Telecommunications:** Knowledge of transmission, broadcasting, switching, control, and operation of telecommunications systems.

# Self-Enrichment Education Teachers

- ▲ Growth: 18.5%
- ▲ Annual Job Openings: 34,000
- ▲ Annual Earnings: $31,070
- ▲ Education/Training Required: Work experience in a related occupation
- ▲ Self-Employed: 16.1%
- ▲ Part-Time: 42.5%

Teach or instruct courses other than those that normally lead to an occupational objective or degree. Courses may include self-improvement, nonvocational, and nonacademic subjects. Teaching may or may not take place in a traditional educational institution. Conducts classes, workshops, and demonstrations to teach principles, techniques, procedures, or methods of designated subject. Plans and conducts field trips to enrich instructional programs. Orders, stores, and inventories books, materials, and supplies. Writes instructional articles on designated subjects. Maintains records, such as student grades, attendance, and supply inventory. Confers with leaders of government and other groups to coordinate training or to assist students to fulfill required criteria. Evaluates success of instruction based on number and enthusiasm of participants and recommends retaining or eliminating course in future. Plans course content and method of instruction. Selects and assembles books, materials, and supplies for courses or projects. Observes students to determine and evaluate qualifications, limitations, abilities, interests, aptitudes, temperament, and individual characteristics. Directs and supervises student project activities, performances, tournaments, exhibits, contests, or plays. Prepares outline of instructional program and lesson plans and establishes course goals. Administers oral, written, and performance tests and issues grades in accordance with performance. Presents lectures and conducts discussions to increase students' knowledge and competence. **SKILLS**—Writing. Speaking. Reading Comprehension. Instructing. Active Listening.

**GOE—Interest Area:** 12. Education and Social Service. **Work Group:** 12.03. Educational Services. **Other Job Titles in This Work Group:** Adult Literacy, Remedial Education, and GED Teachers and Instructors; Agricultural Sciences Teachers, Postsecondary; Anthropology and Archeology Teachers, Postsecondary; Architecture Teachers, Postsecondary; Archivists; Area, Ethnic, and Cultural Studies Teachers, Postsecondary; Art, Drama, and Music Teachers, Postsecondary; Atmospheric, Earth, Marine, and Space Sciences Teachers, Postsecondary; Audio-Visual Collections Specialists; Biological Science Teachers, Postsecondary; Business Teachers, Postsecondary; Chemistry Teachers, Postsecondary; Child Care Workers; Communications Teachers, Postsecondary; Computer Science Teachers, Postsecondary; Criminal Justice and Law Enforcement Teachers, Postsecondary; Curators; Economics Teachers, Postsecondary; Education Teachers, Postsecondary; Educational Psychologists; Educational, Vocational, and School Counselors; Elementary School Teachers, Except Special Education; Engineering Teachers, Postsecondary; English Language and Literature Teachers, Postsecondary; Environmental Science Teachers, Postsecondary; Farm and Home Management Advisors; Foreign Language and Literature Teachers, Postsecondary; Forestry and Conservation Science Teachers, Postsecondary; Geography Teachers, Postsecondary; Graduate Teaching Assistants; Health Specialties Teachers, Postsecondary; History Teachers, Postsecondary; Home Economics Teachers, Postsecondary; Kindergarten Teachers, Except Special Education; Law Teachers, Postsecondary; Librarians;

Library Assistants, Clerical; others. **PERSONALITY TYPE**—Social. Social occupations frequently involve working with, communicating with, and teaching people. These occupations often involve helping or providing service to others.

**EDUCATION/TRAINING PROGRAM(S)**—Adult and Continuing Teacher Education. **RELATED KNOWLEDGE/COURSES**—**Education and Training:** Knowledge of principles and methods for curriculum and training design, teaching and instruction for individuals and groups, and the measurement of training effects. **English Language:** Knowledge of the structure and content of the English language, including the meaning and spelling of words, rules of composition, and grammar. **Administration and Management:** Knowledge of business and management principles involved in strategic planning, resource allocation, human resources modeling, leadership technique, production methods, and coordination of people and resources. **Mathematics:** Knowledge of arithmetic, algebra, geometry, calculus, statistics, and their applications. **Psychology:** Knowledge of human behavior and performance; individual differences in ability, personality, and interests; learning and motivation; psychological research methods; and the assessment and treatment of behavioral and affective disorders. **Sociology and Anthropology:** Knowledge of group behavior and dynamics, societal trends and influences, human migrations, ethnicity, cultures, and their history and origins. **Computers and Electronics:** Knowledge of circuit boards, processors, chips, electronic equipment, and computer hardware and software, including applications and programming.

# Semiconductor Processors

▲ Growth: 32.4%

▲ Annual Job Openings: 7,000

▲ Annual Earnings: $27,170

▲ Education/Training Required: Associate's degree

▲ Self-Employed: 0%

▲ Part-Time: 2.7%

**Perform any or all of the following functions in the manufacture of electronic semiconductors: load semiconductor material into furnace; saw formed ingots into segments; load individual segment into crystal growing chamber and monitor controls; locate crystal axis in ingot using X-ray equipment and saw ingots into wafers; clean, polish, and load wafers into series of special-purpose furnaces, chemical baths, and equipment used to form circuitry and change conductive properties.** Measures and weighs amounts of crystal-growing materials, mixes and grinds materials, and loads materials into container, following procedures. Forms seed crystal for crystal growing or locates crystal axis of ingot, using X-ray equipment, drill, and sanding machine. Aligns photo mask pattern on photoresist layer, exposes pattern to ultraviolet light, and develops pattern, using specialized equipment. Attaches ampoule to diffusion pump to remove air from ampoule and seals ampoule, using blowtorch. Places semiconductor wafers in processing containers or equipment holders, using vacuum wand or tweezers. Monitors operation and adjusts controls of processing machines and equipment to produce compositions with specific electronic properties. Manipulates valves, switches, and buttons or keys commands into control panels to start semiconductor processing cycles. Etches, laps, polishes, or grinds wafers or ingots, using etching, lapping, polishing, or grinding equipment. Operates saw to cut remelt into sections of specified size or to cut ingots into wafers. Cleans and dries materials and equipment, using solvent, etching or sandblasting equipment, and drying equipment to remove contaminants or photoresist. Studies work order, instructions, formulas, and processing charts to determine specifications and sequence of operations. Loads and unloads equipment chambers and transports finished product to storage or to area for further processing. Inspects materials, components, or products for surface defects and measures circuitry, using electronic test equipment, precision measuring instruments, and standard procedures. Counts, sorts, and weighs processed items. Stamps or etches identifying information on finished component. Maintains processing, production, and inspection information and reports. **SKILLS**—Operation Monitoring. Operation and Control. Science. Equipment Selection. Reading Comprehension. Mathematics. Writing.

**GOE—Interest Area:** 08. Industrial Production. **Work Group:** 08.03. Production Work. **Other Job Titles in This Work Group:** Bakers, Manufacturing; Bindery Machine Operators and Tenders; Brazers; Cementing and Gluing Machine Operators and Tenders; Chemical Equipment Controllers and Operators; Chemical Equipment Operators and Tenders; Chemical Equipment Tenders; Cleaning, Washing, and Metal Pickling Equipment Operators and Tenders; Coating, Painting, and Spraying Machine Operators and Tenders; Coil Winders, Tapers, and Finishers; Combination Machine Tool Operators and Tenders, Metal and Plastic; Computer-Controlled Machine Tool Operators, Metal and Plastic; Cooling and Freezing Equipment Operators and Tenders; Crushing, Grinding, and Polishing Machine Setters, Operators, and Tenders; Cutters and Trimmers, Hand; Cutting and Slicing Machine Operators and Tenders; Cutting and Slicing Machine Setters, Operators, and Tenders; Design Printing Machine Setters and Set-Up Operators; Electrolytic Plating and Coating Machine Operators and Tenders, Metal and Plastic; Electrolytic Plating and Coating Machine Setters and Set-Up Operators, Metal and Plastic; Electrotypers and Stereotypers; Embossing Machine Set-Up Operators;

Engraver Set-Up Operators; Extruding and Forming Machine Operators and Tenders, Synthetic or Glass Fibers; Extruding and Forming Machine Setters, Operators, and Tenders, Synthetic and Glass Fibers; Extruding, Forming, Pressing, and Compacting Machine Operators and Tenders; Fabric and Apparel Patternmakers; Fiber Product Cutting Machine Setters and Set-Up Operators; Fiberglass Laminators and Fabricators; others. **PERSONALITY TYPE**—Realistic. Realistic occupations frequently involve work activities that include practical, hands-on problems and solutions. They often deal with plants, animals, and real-world materials like wood, tools, and machinery. Many of the occupations require working outside and do not involve a lot of paperwork or working closely with others.

**EDUCATION/TRAINING PROGRAM(S)**—Industrial Electronics Installer and Repairer. **RELATED KNOWLEDGE/COURSES—Production and Processing:** Knowledge of raw materials, production processes, quality control, costs, and other techniques for maximizing the effective manufacture and distribution of goods. **Mathematics:** Knowledge of arithmetic, algebra, geometry, calculus, statistics, and their applications. **Principles of Mechanical Devices:** Knowledge of machines and tools, including their designs, uses, repair, and maintenance. **Engineering and Technology:** Knowledge of the practical application of engineering science and technology. This includes applying principles, techniques, procedures, and equipment to the design and production of various goods and services. **Computers and Electronics:** Knowledge of circuit boards, processors, chips, electronic equipment, and computer hardware and software, including applications and programming.

# Septic Tank Servicers and Sewer Pipe Cleaners

- ▲ Growth: 16.5%
- ▲ Annual Job Openings: 4,000
- ▲ Annual Earnings: $28,930
- ▲ Education/Training Required: Moderate-term on-the-job training
- ▲ Self-Employed: 0%
- ▲ Part-Time: 5.5%

**Clean and repair septic tanks, sewer lines, or drains. May patch walls and partitions of tank, replace damaged drain tile, or repair breaks in underground piping.** Rotates cleaning rods manually with turning pin. Installs rotary knives on flexible cable mounted on reel of machine according to diameter of pipe to be cleaned. Services, adjusts, and makes minor repairs to equipment, machines, and attachments. Drives pickup trucks to haul crew, materials, and equipment. Taps mainline sewers to install sewer saddles. Requisitions tools and equipment and prepares records showing actions taken. Notifies coworkers to dig out ruptured line or digs out shallow sewers, using shovel. Breaks asphalt and other pavement, using airhammer, pick, and shovel. Covers repaired pipe with dirt and packs backfilled excavation, using air and gasoline tamper. Inspects manholes to locate stoppage of sewer line and repaired sewer line joints to ensure tightness prior to backfilling. Measures distance of excavation site, using plumbers' snake, tapeline, or length of cutting head within sewer, and marks trenching area. Communicates with supervisor and other workers, using radio telephone. Updates sewer maps and manhole charting. Cleans and disinfects domestic basements and other areas flooded as result of sewer stoppages. Operates sewer cleaning equipment, including power rodder, high velocity water jet, sewer flusher, bucket machine, wayne ball, and vac-all. Cuts damaged section of pipe with cutters, removes broken section from ditch, and replaces pipe section, using pipe sleeve. Starts machine to feed revolving cable or rods into opening, stopping machine and changing knives to conform to pipe size. Withdraws cable and observes residue for evidence of mud, roots, grease, and other deposits indicating broken or clogged sewer line. Cleans sewage collection points and sanitary lines and repairs catch basins, manholes, culverts, and storm drains. **SKILLS**—Operation and Control. Installation. Mathematics. Repairing. Equipment Selection.

**GOE**—**Interest Area:** 06. Construction, Mining, and Drilling. **Work Group:** 06.04. Hands-on Work in Construction, Extraction, and Maintenance. **Other Job Titles in This Work Group:** Carpenter Assemblers and Repairers; Construction Laborers; Grips and Set-Up Workers, Motion Picture Sets, Studios, and Stages; Helpers, Construction Trades, All Other; Helpers—Brickmasons, Blockmasons, Stonemasons, and Tile and Marble Setters; Helpers—Carpenters; Helpers—Extraction Workers; Helpers—Painters, Paperhangers, Plasterers, and Stucco Masons; Helpers—Pipelayers, Plumbers, Pipefitters, and Steamfitters; Helpers—Roofers; Highway Maintenance Workers. **PERSONALITY TYPE**—Realistic. Realistic occupations frequently involve work activities that include practical, hands-on problems and solutions. They often deal with plants, animals, and real-world materials like wood, tools, and machinery. Many of the occupations require working outside and do not involve a lot of paperwork or working closely with others.

**EDUCATION/TRAINING PROGRAM(S)**—Plumber and Pipefitter. **RELATED KNOWLEDGE/COURSES**—**Principles of Mechanical Devices:** Knowledge of machines and tools, including their designs, uses, repair, and maintenance. **Building and Construction:** Knowledge of materials, methods, and tools involved in the construction or repair of houses, buildings, or other structures such as highways and roads. **Engineering and Technology:** Knowledge of the practical application of engineering science and technology. This includes applying principles, techniques, procedures, and equipment to the design and production of various goods and services. **Mathematics:** Knowledge of arithmetic, algebra, geometry, calculus, statistics, and their applications. **Physics:** Knowledge and prediction of physical principles and laws and their interrelationships and applications to understanding fluid, material, and atmospheric dynamics and mechanical, electrical, atomic, and sub-atomic structures and processes. **Economics and Accounting:** Knowledge of economic and accounting principles and practices, the financial markets, banking, and the analysis and reporting of financial data. **Clerical Studies:** Knowledge of administrative and clerical procedures and systems such as word processing, managing files and records, stenography and transcription, designing forms, and other office procedures and terminology.

# Sheet Metal Workers

▲ Growth: 23%
▲ Annual Job Openings: 13,000
▲ Annual Earnings: $35,050
▲ Education/Training Required: Moderate-term on-the-job training
▲ Self-Employed: 1%
▲ Part-Time: 4.4%

Fabricate, assemble, install, and repair sheet metal products and equipment, such as ducts, control boxes, drainpipes, and furnace casings. Work may involve any of the following: setting up and operating fabricating machines to cut, bend, and straighten sheet metal; shaping metal over anvils, blocks, or forms, using hammer; operating soldering and welding equipment to join sheet metal parts; inspecting, assembling, and smoothing seams and joints of burred surfaces. Sets up and operates fabricating machines, such as shears, brakes, presses, and routers, to cut, bend, block, and form materials. Selects gauge and type of sheet metal or nonmetallic material, according to product specifications. Inspects assemblies and installation for conformance to specifications, using measuring instruments such as calipers, scales, dial indicators, gauges, and micrometers. Determines sequence and methods of fabricating, assembling, and installing sheet metal products, using blueprints, sketches, or product specifications. Welds, solders, bolts, rivets, screws, clips, caulks, or bonds component parts to assemble products, using hand tools, power tools, and equipment. Trims, files, grinds, deburrs, buffs, and smoothes surfaces, using hand tools and portable power tools. Installs assemblies in supportive framework according to blueprints, using hand tools, power tools, and lifting and handling devices. Lays out and marks dimensions and reference lines on material, using scribes, dividers, squares, and rulers. Shapes metal material over anvil, block, or other form, using hand tools. **SKILLS**—Installation. Mathematics. Equipment Selection. Operation and Control. Coordination.

**GOE**—**Interest Area:** 06. Construction, Mining, and Drilling. **Work Group:** 06.02. Construction. **Other Job Titles in This Work Group:** Boat Builders and Shipwrights; Boilermakers; Brattice Builders; Brickmasons and Blockmasons; Carpenters; Carpet Installers; Ceiling Tile Installers; Cement Masons and Concrete Finishers; Commercial Divers; Construction Carpenters; Drywall and Ceiling Tile Installers; Drywall Installers; Electricians; Explosives Workers, Ordnance Handling Experts, and Blasters; Fence Erectors; Floor Layers, Except Carpet, Wood, and Hard Tiles; Floor Sanders and Finishers; Glaziers; Grader, Bulldozer, and Scraper Operators; Hazardous Materials Removal Workers; Insulation Workers, Floor, Ceiling, and Wall; Insulation Workers, Mechanical; Manufactured Building and Mobile Home Installers; Operating Engineers; Operating Engineers and Other Construction Equipment Operators; Painters, Construction and Maintenance; Paperhangers; Paving, Surfacing, and Tamping Equipment Operators; Pile-Driver Operators; Pipe Fitters; Pipelayers; Pipelaying Fitters; Plasterers and Stucco Masons; Plumbers; Plumbers, Pipefitters, and Steamfitters; Rail-Track Laying and Maintenance Equipment Operators; Refractory Materials Repairers, Except Brickmasons; Reinforcing Iron and Rebar Workers; Riggers; Roofers; Rough Carpenters; Security and Fire Alarm Systems Installers; Segmental Pavers; Ship Carpenters and Joiners; Stone Cutters and Carvers; Stonemasons; Structural Iron and Steel Workers; Tapers; Terrazzo Workers and Finishers; Tile and Marble Setters. **PERSONALITY TYPE**—Realistic. Realistic occupations frequently involve work activities that include practical, hands-on problems and solutions. They often deal with plants, animals, and real-world materials like wood, tools, and machinery. Many of the occupations require working outside and do not involve a lot of paperwork or working closely with others.

**EDUCATION/TRAINING PROGRAM(S)**—Sheet Metal Worker. **RELATED KNOWLEDGE/**

COURSES—**Production and Processing:** Knowledge of raw materials, production processes, quality control, costs, and other techniques for maximizing the effective manufacture and distribution of goods. **Principles of Mechanical Devices:** Knowledge of machines and tools, including their designs, uses, repair, and maintenance. **Design:** Knowledge of design techniques, tools, and principles involved in production of precision technical plans, blueprints, drawings, and models. **Computers and Electronics:** Knowledge of circuit boards, processors, chips, electronic equipment, and computer hardware and software, including applications and programming. **Building and Construction:** Knowledge of materials, methods, and tools involved in the construction or repair of houses, buildings, or other structures such as highways and roads.

# Sheriffs and Deputy Sheriffs

▲ Growth: 23.2%

▲ Annual Job Openings: 21,000

▲ Annual Earnings: $40,590

▲ Education/Training Required: Long-term on-the-job training

▲ Self-Employed: 0%

▲ Part-Time: 2.7%

**Enforce law and order in rural or unincorporated districts or serve legal processes of courts. May patrol courthouse, guard court or grand jury, or escort defendants.** Serves subpoenas and summonses. Executes arrest warrants, locating and taking persons into custody, and issues citations. Patrols and guards courthouse, grand jury room, or assigned areas to provide security, enforce laws, maintain order, and arrest violators. Confiscates real or personal property by court order and posts notices in public places. Takes control of accident scene to maintain traffic flow, assist accident victims, and investigate causes. Investigates illegal or suspicious activities of persons. Transports or escorts prisoners or defendants between courtroom, prison or jail, District Attorney's offices, and medical facilities. Questions individuals entering secured areas to determine purpose of business and directs or reroutes individuals to destinations. Maintains records and submits reports of dispositions and logs daily activities. Arranges delivery of prisoner's arrest records from criminal investigation unit at District Attorney's request. Notifies patrol units to take violators into custody or provide needed assistance or medical aid. **SKILLS**—Social Perceptiveness. Active Listening. Speaking. Judgment and Decision Making. Coordination. Reading Comprehension.

**GOE—Interest Area:** 04. Law, Law Enforcement, and Public Safety. **Work Group:** 04.03. Law Enforcement. **Other Job Titles in This Work Group:** Animal Control Workers; Bailiffs; Child Support, Missing Persons, and Unemployment Insurance Fraud Investigators; Correctional Officers and Jailers; Criminal Investigators and Special Agents; Crossing Guards; Detectives and Criminal Investigators; Fire Investigators; Fish and Game Wardens; Forensic Science Technicians; Gaming Surveillance Officers and Gaming Investigators; Highway Patrol Pilots; Immigration and Customs Inspectors; Lifeguards, Ski Patrol, and Other Recreational Protective Service Workers; Parking Enforcement Workers; Police and Sheriff's Patrol Officers; Police Detectives; Police Identification and Records Officers; Police Patrol Officers; Private Detectives and Investigators; Security Guards; Transit and Railroad Police. **PERSONALITY TYPE**—Social. Social occupations frequently involve working with, communicating with, and teaching people. These occupations often involve helping or providing service to others.

**EDUCATION/TRAINING PROGRAM(S)**—Law Enforcement/Police Science. **RELATED KNOWLEDGE/COURSES—Public Safety and Security:** Knowledge of relevant equipment, policies, procedures, and strategies to promote effective local, state, or national security operations for the protection of people, data, property, and institutions. **Law and Government:** Knowledge of laws, legal codes, court procedures, precedents, government regulations, executive orders, agency rules, and the democratic political process. **Psychology:** Knowledge of human behavior and performance; individual differences in ability, personality, and interests; learning and motivation; psychological research methods; and the assessment and treatment of behavioral and affective disorders. **Geography:** Knowledge of principles and methods for describing the features of land, sea, and air masses, including their physical characteristics, locations, interrelationships, and distribution of plant, animal, and human life. **Clerical Studies:** Knowledge of administrative and clerical procedures and systems such as word processing, managing files and records, stenography and transcription, designing forms, and other office procedures and terminology.

# Ship Carpenters and Joiners

- ▲ Growth: 8.2%
- ▲ Annual Job Openings: 161,000
- ▲ Annual Earnings: $35,100
- ▲ Education/Training Required: Long-term on-the-job training
- ▲ Self-Employed: 28.6%
- ▲ Part-Time: 8.1%

**Fabricate, assemble, install, or repair wooden furnishings in ships or boats.** Reads blueprints to determine dimensions of furnishings in ships or boats. Shapes and laminates wood to form parts of ship, using steam chambers, clamps, glue, and jigs. Repairs structural woodwork and replaces defective parts and equipment, using hand tools and power tools. Shapes irregular parts and trims excess material from bulkhead and furnishings to ensure fit meets specifications. Constructs floors, doors, and partitions, using woodworking machines, hand tools, and power tools. Cuts wood or glass to specified dimensions, using hand tools and power tools. Assembles and installs hardware, gaskets, floors, furnishings, or insulation, using adhesive, hand tools, and power tools. Transfers dimensions or measurements of wood parts or bulkhead on plywood, using measuring instruments and marking devices. Greases gears and other moving parts of machines on ship. **SKILLS—** Installation. Monitoring. Repairing. Mathematics. Equipment Selection.

**GOE—Interest Area:** 06. Construction, Mining, and Drilling. **Work Group:** 06.02. Construction. **Other Job Titles in This Work Group:** Boat Builders and Shipwrights; Boilermakers; Brattice Builders; Brickmasons and Blockmasons; Carpenters; Carpet Installers; Ceiling Tile Installers; Cement Masons and Concrete Finishers; Commercial Divers; Construction Carpenters; Drywall and Ceiling Tile Installers; Drywall Installers; Electricians; Explosives Workers, Ordnance Handling Experts, and Blasters; Fence Erectors; Floor Layers, Except Carpet, Wood, and Hard Tiles; Floor Sanders and Finishers; Glaziers; Grader, Bulldozer, and Scraper Operators; Hazardous Materials Removal Workers; Insulation Workers, Floor, Ceiling, and Wall; Insulation Workers, Mechanical; Manufactured Building and Mobile Home Installers; Operating Engineers; Operating Engineers and Other Construction Equipment Operators; Painters, Construction and Maintenance; Paperhangers; Paving, Surfacing, and Tamping Equipment Operators; Pile-Driver Operators; Pipe Fitters; Pipelayers; Pipelaying Fitters; Plasterers and Stucco Masons; Plumbers; Plumbers, Pipefitters, and Steamfitters; Rail-Track Laying and Maintenance Equipment Operators; Refractory Materials Repairers, Except Brickmasons; Reinforcing Iron and Rebar Workers; Riggers; Roofers; Rough Carpenters; Security and Fire Alarm Systems Installers; Segmental Pavers; Sheet Metal Workers; Stone Cutters and Carvers; Stonemasons; Structural Iron and Steel Workers; Tapers;

Terrazzo Workers and Finishers; Tile and Marble Setters. **PERSONALITY TYPE**—Realistic. Realistic occupations frequently involve work activities that include practical, hands-on problems and solutions. They often deal with plants, animals, and real-world materials like wood, tools, and machinery. Many of the occupations require working outside and do not involve a lot of paperwork or working closely with others.

EDUCATION/TRAINING PROGRAM(S)—Carpenter; Marine Maintenance and Ship Repairer. RELATED KNOWLEDGE/COURSES—**Building and Construction:** Knowledge of materials, methods, and tools involved in the construction or repair of houses, buildings, or other structures such as highways and roads. **Design:** Knowledge of design techniques, tools, and principles involved in production of precision technical plans, blueprints, drawings, and models. **Engineering and Technology:** Knowledge of the practical application of engineering science and technology. This includes applying principles, techniques, procedures, and equipment to the design and production of various goods and services. **Principles of Mechanical Devices:** Knowledge of machines and tools, including their designs, uses, repair, and maintenance. **Mathematics:** Knowledge of arithmetic, algebra, geometry, calculus, statistics, and their applications.

# Shipping, Receiving, and Traffic Clerks

- ▲ Growth: 9.3%
- ▲ Annual Job Openings: 133,000
- ▲ Annual Earnings: $23,340
- ▲ Education/Training Required: Short-term on-the-job training
- ▲ Self-Employed: 0.2%
- ▲ Part-Time: 9.6%

**Verify and keep records on incoming and outgoing shipments. Prepare items for shipment. Duties include assembling, addressing, stamping, and shipping merchandise or material; receiving, unpacking, verifying and recording incoming merchandise or material; and arranging for the transportation of products.** Examines contents and compares with records, such as manifests, invoices, or orders, to verify accuracy of incoming or outgoing shipment. Confers and corresponds with establishment representatives to rectify problems, such as damages, shortages, and nonconformance to specifications. Requisitions and stores shipping materials and supplies to maintain inventory of stock. Delivers or routes materials to departments, using work devices, such as handtruck, conveyor, or sorting bins. Computes amounts, such as space available and shipping, storage, and demurrage charges, using calculator or price list. Records shipment data, such as weight, charges, space availability, and damages and discrepancies, for reporting, accounting, and record-keeping purposes. Contacts carrier representative to make arrangements and to issue instructions for shipping and delivery of materials. Packs, seals, labels, and affixes postage to prepare materials for shipping, using work devices such as hand tools, power tools, and postage meter. Prepares documents such as work orders, bills of lading, and shipping orders to route materials. Determines shipping method for materials, using knowledge of shipping procedures, routes, and rates. **SKILLS**—Reading Comprehension. Critical Thinking. Mathematics. Service Orientation. Active Listening. Writing.

**GOE**—Interest Area: 09. Business Detail. **Work Group:** 09.08. Records and Materials Processing. **Other Job Titles in This Work Group:** Cargo and Freight Agents; Couriers and Messengers; Mail Clerks, Except Mail Machine Operators and Postal Service; Marking Clerks; Order Fillers, Wholesale and Retail Sales; Postal Service Mail Carriers; Postal Service Mail Sorters, Processors, and Processing Machine Operators; Stock Clerks and Order Fillers; Stock Clerks—Stockroom, Warehouse, or Storage Yard; Weighers, Measurers, Checkers, and Samplers, Recordkeeping. **PERSONALITY**

TYPE—Conventional. Conventional occupations frequently involve following set procedures and routines. These occupations can include working with data and details more than with ideas. Usually there is a clear line of authority to follow.

EDUCATION/TRAINING PROGRAM(S)—General Office/Clerical and Typing Services. RELATED KNOWLEDGE/COURSES—Transportation: Knowledge of principles and methods for moving people or goods by air, rail, sea, or road, including the relative costs and benefits. Clerical Studies: Knowledge of administrative and clerical procedures and systems such as word processing, managing files and records, stenography and transcription, designing forms, and other office procedures and terminology. Production and Processing: Knowledge of raw materials, production processes, quality control, costs, and other techniques for maximizing the effective manufacture and distribution of goods. Mathematics: Knowledge of arithmetic, algebra, geometry, calculus, statistics, and their applications. Computers and Electronics: Knowledge of circuit boards, processors, chips, electronic equipment, and computer hardware and software, including applications and programming. English Language: Knowledge of the structure and content of the English language, including the meaning and spelling of words, rules of composition, and grammar. Economics and Accounting: Knowledge of economic and accounting principles and practices, the financial markets, banking, and the analysis and reporting of financial data.

# Singers

▲ Growth: 20.1%

▲ Annual Job Openings: 33,000

▲ Annual Earnings: $44,520

▲ Education/Training Required: Long-term on-the-job training

▲ Self-Employed: 45.4%

▲ Part-Time: 53.5%

Sing songs on stage, radio, television, or motion pictures. Sings before audience or recipient of message as soloist or in group, as member of vocal ensemble. Memorizes musical selections and routines or sings following printed text, musical notation, or customer instructions. Observes choral leader or prompter for cues or directions in vocal presentation. Practices songs and routines to maintain and improve vocal skills. Interprets or modifies music, applying knowledge of harmony, melody, rhythm, and voice production, to individualize presentation and maintain audience interest. Sings a cappella or with musical accompaniment. SKILLS—Active Listening. Coordination. Speaking. Reading Comprehension. Active Learning.

GOE—Interest Area: 01. Arts, Entertainment, and Media. Work Group: 01.05. Performing Arts. Other Job Titles in This Work Group: Actors; Choreographers; Composers; Dancers; Directors—Stage, Motion Pictures, Television, and Radio; Music Arrangers and Orchestrators; Music Directors; Music Directors and Composers; Musicians and Singers; Musicians, Instrumental; Public Address System and Other Announcers; Radio and Television Announcers; Talent Directors. PERSONALITY TYPE—Artistic. Artistic occupations frequently involve working with forms, designs, and patterns. They often require self-expression, and the work can be done without following a clear set of rules.

EDUCATION/TRAINING PROGRAM(S)—Music - General Performance; Music - Piano and Organ Performance; Music - Voice and Choral/Opera Performance; Music, General; Music, Other. RELATED KNOWLEDGE/COURSES—Fine Arts: Knowledge of the theory and techniques required to compose, produce, and perform works of music, dance, visual arts, drama, and sculpture. English Language: Knowledge of the structure and content of the English language, including the meaning and spelling of words, rules of composition, and grammar. Communications and

**Media:** Knowledge of media production, communication, and dissemination techniques and methods. This includes alternative ways to inform and entertain via written, oral, and visual media. **Education and Training:** Knowledge of principles and methods for curriculum and training design, teaching and instruction for individuals and groups, and the measurement of training effects. **Mathematics:** Knowledge of arithmetic, algebra, geometry, calculus, statistics, and their applications.

# Sketch Artists

▲ Growth: 13.4%

▲ Annual Job Openings: 4,000

▲ Annual Earnings: $35,770

▲ Education/Training Required: Long-term on-the-job training

▲ Self-Employed: 56.7%

▲ Part-Time: 24%

**Sketch likenesses of subjects according to observation or descriptions either to assist law enforcement agencies in identifying suspects, to depict courtroom scenes, or for entertainment purposes of patrons, using mediums such as pencil, charcoal, and pastels.** Draws sketch, profile, or likeness of posed subject or photograph, using pencil, charcoal, pastels, or other medium. Assembles and arranges outlines of features to form composite image according to information provided by witness or victim. Alters copy of composite image until witness or victim is satisfied that composite is best possible representation of suspect. Poses subject to accentuate most pleasing features or profile. Classifies and codes components of image, using established system, to help identify suspect. Prepares series of simple line drawings conforming to description of suspect and presents drawings to informant for selection of sketch. Interviews crime victims and witnesses to obtain descriptive information concerning physical build, sex, nationality, and facial features of unidentified suspect. Measures distances and develops sketches of crime scene from photograph and measurements. Searches police photograph records, using classification and coding system, to determine if existing photograph of suspects is available. Operates photocopy or similar machine to reproduce composite image. **SKILLS**—Active Listening. Speaking. Social Perceptiveness. Monitoring. Complex Problem Solving.

**GOE—Interest Area:** 01. Arts, Entertainment, and Media. **Work Group:** 01.04. Visual Arts. **Other Job Titles in This Work Group:** Cartoonists; Commercial and Industrial Designers; Designers, All Other; Exhibit Designers; Fashion Designers; Fine Artists, Including Painters, Sculptors, and Illustrators; Floral Designers; Graphic Designers; Interior Designers; Merchandise Displayers and Window Trimmers; Multi-Media Artists and Animators; Painters and Illustrators; Sculptors; Set and Exhibit Designers; Set Designers. **PERSONALITY TYPE**—Artistic. Artistic occupations frequently involve working with forms, designs, and patterns. They often require self-expression, and the work can be done without following a clear set of rules.

**EDUCATION/TRAINING PROGRAM(S)**—Art, General; Ceramics Arts and Ceramics; Drawing; Fine Arts and Art Studies, Other; Fine/Studio Arts; Intermedia; Medical Illustrating; Painting; Printmaking; Sculpture. **RELATED KNOWLEDGE/COURSES**—**Fine Arts:** Knowledge of the theory and techniques required to compose, produce, and perform works of music, dance, visual arts, drama, and sculpture. **Design:** Knowledge of design techniques, tools, and principles involved in production of precision technical plans, blueprints, drawings, and models. **English Language:** Knowledge of the structure and content of the English language, including the meaning and spelling of words, rules of composition, and grammar. **Clerical Studies:** Knowledge of administrative and clerical procedures and systems such as word processing, managing files and records, stenography and transcription, designing forms, and other office procedures and terminology. **Public Safety and Security:** Knowledge of relevant equipment, policies, procedures, and strategies to promote effective local, state, or national security

operations for the protection of people, data, property, and institutions. **Communications and Media:** Knowledge of media production, communication, and dissemination techniques and methods. This includes alternative ways to inform and entertain via written, oral, and visual media.

# Social and Human Service Assistants

▲ Growth: 54.2%

▲ Annual Job Openings: 45,000

▲ Annual Earnings: $23,840

▲ Education/Training Required: Moderate-term on-the-job training

▲ Self-Employed: 1%

▲ Part-Time: 42.4%

**Assist professionals from a wide variety of fields, such as psychology, rehabilitation, or social work, to provide client services as well as support for families. May assist clients in identifying available benefits and social and community services and help clients obtain them. May assist social workers with developing, organizing, and conducting programs to prevent and resolve problems relevant to substance abuse, human relationships, rehabilitation, or adult daycare.** Visits individuals in homes or attends group meetings to provide information on agency services, requirements, and procedures. Interviews individuals and family members to compile information on social, educational, criminal, institutional, or drug history. Assists clients with preparation of forms, such as tax or rent forms. Assists in planning of food budget, utilizing charts and sample budgets. Meets with youth groups to acquaint them with consequences of delinquent acts. Observes and discusses meal preparation and suggests alternate methods of food preparation. Oversees day-to-day group activities of residents in institution. Cares for children in client's home during client's appointments. Keeps records and prepares reports for owner or management concerning visits with clients. Submits to and reviews reports and problems with superior. Informs tenants of facilities, such as laundries and playgrounds. Demonstrates use and care of equipment for tenant use. Explains rules established by owner or management, such as sanitation and maintenance requirements and park-

ing regulations. Transports and accompanies clients to shopping area and to appointments, using automobile. Consults with supervisor concerning programs for individual families. Observes clients' food selections and recommends alternate economical and nutritional food choices. Monitors free, supplementary meal program to ensure cleanliness of facility and that eligibility guidelines are met for persons receiving meals. Assists in locating housing for displaced individuals. Provides information on and refers individuals to public or private agencies and community services for assistance. Advises clients regarding food stamps, child care, food, money management, sanitation, and housekeeping. **SKILLS**—Social Perceptiveness. Service Orientation. Active Listening. Speaking. Reading Comprehension.

**GOE—Interest Area:** 12. Education and Social Service. **Work Group:** 12.02. Social Services. **Other Job Titles in This Work Group:** Child, Family, and School Social Workers; Clergy; Clinical Psychologists; Clinical, Counseling, and School Psychologists; Community and Social Service Specialists, All Other; Counseling Psychologists; Counselors, All Other; Directors, Religious Activities and Education; Marriage and Family Therapists; Medical and Public Health Social Workers; Mental Health and Substance Abuse Social Workers; Mental Health Counselors; Probation Officers and Correctional Treatment Specialists; Rehabilitation Counselors; Religious Workers, All Other; Residential

Advisors; Social Workers, All Other; Substance Abuse and Behavioral Disorder Counselors. **PERSONALITY TYPE**—Social. Social occupations frequently involve working with, communicating with, and teaching people. These occupations often involve helping or providing service to others.

**EDUCATION/TRAINING PROGRAM(S)**—Mental Health Services, Other. **RELATED KNOWLEDGE/COURSES**—**Customer and Personal Service:** Knowledge of principles and processes for providing customer and personal services. This includes customer needs assessment, meeting quality standards for services, and evaluation of customer satisfaction. **Therapy and Counseling:** Knowledge of principles, methods, and procedures for diagnosis, treatment, and rehabilitation of physical and mental dysfunctions and for career counseling and guidance. **Psychology:** Knowledge of human behavior and performance; individual differences in ability, personality, and interests; learning and motivation; psychological research methods; and the assessment and treatment of behavioral and affective disorders. **Education and Training:** Knowledge of principles and methods for curriculum and training design, teaching and instruction for individuals and groups, and the measurement of training effects. **Clerical Studies:** Knowledge of administrative and clerical procedures and systems such as word processing, managing files and records, stenography and transcription, designing forms, and other office procedures and terminology.

# Solderers

- ▲ Growth: 19.3%
- ▲ Annual Job Openings: 51,000
- ▲ Annual Earnings: $29,080
- ▲ Education/Training Required: Post-secondary vocational training
- ▲ Self-Employed: 5.8%
- ▲ Part-Time: 8.6%

**Solder together components to assemble fabricated metal products, using soldering iron.** Melts and applies solder along adjoining edges of workpieces to solder joints, using soldering iron, gas torch, or electric-ultrasonic equipment. Grinds, cuts, buffs, or bends edges of workpieces to be joined to ensure snug fit, using power grinder and hand tools. Removes workpieces from molten solder and holds parts together until color indicates that solder has set. Cleans workpieces, using chemical solution, file, wire brush, or grinder. Cleans tip of soldering iron, using chemical solution or cleaning compound. Melts and separates soldered joints to repair misaligned or damaged assemblies, using soldering equipment. Applies flux to workpiece surfaces in preparation for soldering. Heats soldering iron or workpiece to specified temperature for soldering, using gas flame or electric current. Dips workpieces into molten solder or places solder strip between seams and heats seam with iron to band items together. Aligns and clamps workpieces together, using rule, square, or hand tools, or positions items in fixtures, jigs, or vise. Melts and applies solder to fill holes, indentations, and seams of fabricated metal products, using soldering equipment. **SKILLS**—Operation and Control. Equipment Selection. Equipment Maintenance.

**GOE**—**Interest Area:** 08. Industrial Production. **Work Group:** 08.03. Production Work. **Other Job Titles in This Work Group:** Bakers, Manufacturing; Bindery Machine Operators and Tenders; Brazers; Cementing and Gluing Machine Operators and Tenders; Chemical Equipment Controllers and Operators; Chemical Equipment Operators and Tenders; Chemical Equipment Tenders; Cleaning, Washing, and Metal Pickling Equipment Operators and Tenders; Coating, Painting, and Spraying Machine Operators and Tenders; Coil Winders, Tapers, and Finishers; Combination Machine Tool Operators and Tenders, Metal and Plastic; Computer-Controlled Machine Tool Operators, Metal and Plastic; Cooling and Freezing Equipment Operators and

Tenders; Crushing, Grinding, and Polishing Machine Setters, Operators, and Tenders; Cutters and Trimmers, Hand; Cutting and Slicing Machine Operators and Tenders; Cutting and Slicing Machine Setters, Operators, and Tenders; Design Printing Machine Setters and Set-Up Operators; Electrolytic Plating and Coating Machine Operators and Tenders, Metal and Plastic; Electrolytic Plating and Coating Machine Setters and Set-Up Operators, Metal and Plastic; Electrotypers and Stereotypers; Embossing Machine Set-Up Operators; Engraver Set-Up Operators; Extruding and Forming Machine Operators and Tenders, Synthetic or Glass Fibers; Extruding and Forming Machine Setters, Operators, and Tenders, Synthetic and Glass Fibers; Extruding, Forming, Pressing, and Compacting Machine Operators and Tenders; Fabric and Apparel Patternmakers; Fiber Product Cutting Machine Setters and Set-Up Operators; Fiberglass Laminators and Fabricators; others. **PERSONALITY TYPE**—Realistic. Realistic occupations frequently involve work activities that include practical, hands-on problems and solutions. They often deal with plants, animals, and real-world materials like wood, tools, and machinery. Many of the occupations require working outside and do not involve a lot of paperwork or working closely with others.

**EDUCATION/TRAINING PROGRAM(S)**—Welder/ Welding Technologist. **RELATED KNOWLEDGE/ COURSES**—**Principles of Mechanical Devices:** Knowledge of machines and tools, including their designs, uses, repair, and maintenance. **Building and Construction:** Knowledge of materials, methods, and tools involved in the construction or repair of houses, buildings, or other structures such as highways and roads. **Production and Processing:** Knowledge of raw materials, production processes, quality control, costs, and other techniques for maximizing the effective manufacture and distribution of goods. **Engineering and Technology:** Knowledge of the practical application of engineering science and technology. This includes applying principles, techniques, procedures, and equipment to the design and production of various goods and services. **Chemistry:** Knowledge of the chemical composition, structure, and properties of substances and of the chemical processes and transformations that they undergo. This includes uses of chemicals and their interactions, danger signs, production techniques, and disposal methods.

# Soldering and Brazing Machine Operators and Tenders

- ▲ Growth: 15.1%
- ▲ Annual Job Openings: 9,000
- ▲ Annual Earnings: $29,730
- ▲ Education/Training Required: Moderate-term on-the-job training
- ▲ Self-Employed: 5.9%
- ▲ Part-Time: 8.6%

**Operate or tend soldering and brazing machines that braze, solder, or spot weld fabricated metal products or components as specified by work orders, blueprints, and layout specifications.** Operates or tends soldering and brazing machines that braze, solder, or spot weld fabricated products or components. Adds chemicals and materials to workpieces or machines, using hand tools. Cleans and maintains workpieces and machines, using equipment and hand tools. Reads and records operational information on specified production reports. Examines and tests soldered or brazed products or components, using testing devices. Removes workpieces and parts from machinery, using hand tools. Loads and adjusts workpieces, clamps, and parts onto machine, using hand tools. Moves controls to activate and adjust soldering and brazing machines. Observes meters, gauges, and machine to ensure solder or brazing process meets specifications. **SKILLS**—Operation Monitoring. Operation and Control. Equipment Maintenance. Equipment Selection. Quality Control Analysis.

**GOE**—**Interest Area:** 08. Industrial Production. **Work Group:** 08.03. Production Work. **Other Job Titles in This Work Group:** Bakers, Manufacturing; Bindery

Machine Operators and Tenders; Brazers; Cementing and Gluing Machine Operators and Tenders; Chemical Equipment Controllers and Operators; Chemical Equipment Operators and Tenders; Chemical Equipment Tenders; Cleaning, Washing, and Metal Pickling Equipment Operators and Tenders; Coating, Painting, and Spraying Machine Operators and Tenders; Coil Winders, Tapers, and Finishers; Combination Machine Tool Operators and Tenders, Metal and Plastic; Computer-Controlled Machine Tool Operators, Metal and Plastic; Cooling and Freezing Equipment Operators and Tenders; Crushing, Grinding, and Polishing Machine Setters, Operators, and Tenders; Cutters and Trimmers, Hand; Cutting and Slicing Machine Operators and Tenders; Cutting and Slicing Machine Setters, Operators, and Tenders; Design Printing Machine Setters and Set-Up Operators; Electrolytic Plating and Coating Machine Operators and Tenders, Metal and Plastic; Electrolytic Plating and Coating Machine Setters and Set-Up Operators, Metal and Plastic; Electrotypers and Stereotypers; Embossing Machine Set-Up Operators; Engraver Set-Up Operators; Extruding and Forming Machine Operators and Tenders, Synthetic or Glass Fibers; Extruding and Forming Machine Setters, Operators, and Tenders, Synthetic and Glass Fibers; Extruding, Forming, Pressing, and Compacting Machine Operators and Tenders; Fabric and Apparel Patternmakers; Fiber Product Cutting Machine Setters and Set-Up Operators; Fiberglass Laminators and

Fabricators; others. **PERSONALITY TYPE**—Realistic. Realistic occupations frequently involve work activities that include practical, hands-on problems and solutions. They often deal with plants, animals, and real-world materials like wood, tools, and machinery. Many of the occupations require working outside and do not involve a lot of paperwork or working closely with others.

**EDUCATION/TRAINING PROGRAM(S)**—Welder/ Welding Technologist. **RELATED KNOWLEDGE/ COURSES**—**Principles of Mechanical Devices:** Knowledge of machines and tools, including their designs, uses, repair, and maintenance. **Production and Processing:** Knowledge of raw materials, production processes, quality control, costs, and other techniques for maximizing the effective manufacture and distribution of goods. **Design:** Knowledge of design techniques, tools, and principles involved in production of precision technical plans, blueprints, drawings, and models. **Chemistry:** Knowledge of the chemical composition, structure, and properties of substances and of the chemical processes and transformations that they undergo. This includes uses of chemicals and their interactions, danger signs, production techniques, and disposal methods. **Clerical Studies:** Knowledge of administrative and clerical procedures and systems such as word processing, managing files and records, stenography and transcription, designing forms, and other office procedures and terminology.

# Soldering and Brazing Machine Setters and Set-Up Operators

▲ Growth: 15.1%

▲ Annual Job Openings: 9,000

▲ Annual Earnings: $29,730

▲ Education/Training Required: Moderate-term on-the-job training

▲ Self-Employed: 5.9%

▲ Part-Time: 8.6%

**Set up or set up and operate soldering or brazing machines to braze, solder, heat treat, or spot weld fabricated metal products or components as specified by work orders, blueprints, and layout specifications.** Selects torch tips, alloy, flux, coil, tubing, and wire, according to metal type and thickness, data charts, and records. Sets dials and timing controls to regulate elec-

trical current, gas flow pressure, heating/cooling cycles, and shut-off. Connects, forms, and installs parts to braze, heat-treat, and spot-weld workpiece, metal parts, and components. Positions, aligns, and bolts holding fixtures, guides, and stops onto or into brazing machine to position and hold workpieces. Cleans, lubricates, and adjusts equipment to maintain efficient operation, using airhose, cleaning fluid, and hand tools. Examines workpiece for defective seams, solidification, and adherence to specifications, and anneals finished workpiece to relieve internal stress. Disconnects electrical current and removes and immerses workpiece into water or acid bath to cool and clean component. Operates and trains workers to operate heat-treating equipment to bond fabricated metal components according to blueprints, work orders, or specifications. Manipulates levers to synchronize brazing action or to move workpiece through brazing process. Assembles, aligns, and clamps workpieces into holding fixture to bond, heat-treat, or solder fabricated metal components. Starts machine to complete trial run, readjusts machine, and records setup data. Fills hoppers and positions spout to direct flow of flux or manually brushes flux onto seams of workpieces. **SKILLS**—Operation and Control. Quality Control Analysis. Operation Monitoring. Instructing. Installation. Equipment Selection.

**GOE**—**Interest Area:** 08. Industrial Production. **Work Group:** 08.02. Production Technology. **Other Job Titles in This Work Group:** Aircraft Rigging Assemblers; Aircraft Structure Assemblers, Precision; Aircraft Structure, Surfaces, Rigging, and Systems Assemblers; Aircraft Systems Assemblers, Precision; Bench Workers, Jewelry; Bindery Machine Setters and Set-Up Operators; Bindery Workers; Bookbinders; Buffing and Polishing Set-Up Operators; Casting Machine Set-Up Operators; Coating, Painting, and Spraying Machine Setters and Set-Up Operators; Coating, Painting, and Spraying Machine Setters, Operators, and Tenders; Combination Machine Tool Setters and Set-Up Operators, Metal and Plastic; Cutting, Punching, and Press Machine Setters, Operators, and Tenders, Metal and Plastic; Dental Laboratory Technicians; Drilling and Boring Machine Tool Setters, Operators, and Tenders, Metal and Plastic; Electrical and Electronic Equipment Assemblers; Electrical and Electronic Inspectors and Testers; Electromechanical Equipment Assemblers; Engine and Other Machine Assemblers; Extruding and Drawing Machine Setters, Operators, and Tenders, Metal and Plastic; Extruding,

Forming, Pressing, and Compacting Machine Setters and Set-Up Operators; Extruding, Forming, Pressing, and Compacting Machine Setters, Operators, and Tenders; Forging Machine Setters, Operators, and Tenders, Metal and Plastic; Foundry Mold and Coremakers; Gem and Diamond Workers; Grinding, Honing, Lapping, and Deburring Machine Set-Up Operators; Grinding, Lapping, Polishing, and Buffing Machine Tool Setters, Operators, and Tenders, Metal and Plastic; Heat Treating Equipment Setters, Operators, and Tenders, Metal and Plastic; others. **PERSONALITY TYPE**—Realistic. Realistic occupations frequently involve work activities that include practical, hands-on problems and solutions. They often deal with plants, animals, and real-world materials like wood, tools, and machinery. Many of the occupations require working outside and do not involve a lot of paperwork or working closely with others.

**EDUCATION/TRAINING PROGRAM(S)**—Welder/Welding Technologist. **RELATED KNOWLEDGE/COURSES**—**Principles of Mechanical Devices:** Knowledge of machines and tools, including their designs, uses, repair, and maintenance. **Building and Construction:** Knowledge of materials, methods, and tools involved in the construction or repair of houses, buildings, or other structures such as highways and roads. **Engineering and Technology:** Knowledge of the practical application of engineering science and technology. This includes applying principles, techniques, procedures, and equipment to the design and production of various goods and services. **Design:** Knowledge of design techniques, tools, and principles involved in production of precision technical plans, blueprints, drawings, and models. **Physics:** Knowledge and prediction of physical principles and laws and their interrelationships and applications to understanding fluid, material, and atmospheric dynamics and mechanical, electrical, atomic, and sub-atomic structures and processes. **Education and Training:** Knowledge of principles and methods for curriculum and training design, teaching and instruction for individuals and groups, and the measurement of training effects.

# Statement Clerks

▲ Growth: 8.5%
▲ Annual Job Openings: 69,000
▲ Annual Earnings: $25,480
▲ Education/Training Required: Short-term on-the-job training
▲ Self-Employed: 0.3%
▲ Part-Time: 19.1%

**Prepare and distribute bank statements to customers, answer inquiries, and reconcile discrepancies in records and accounts.** Compares previously prepared bank statements with canceled checks, prepares statements for distribution to customers, and reconciles discrepancies in records and accounts. Keeps canceled checks and customer signature files. Encodes and cancels checks, using machine. Takes orders for imprinted checks. Posts stop-payment notices to prevent payment of protested checks. Routes statements for mailing or over-the-counter delivery to customers. Recovers checks returned to customer in error, adjusts customer account, and answers inquiries. Matches statement with batch of canceled checks by account number. Inserts statements and canceled checks in envelopes and affixes postage or stuffs envelopes and meters postage. **SKILLS**—Reading Comprehension. Active Listening. Mathematics. Speaking. Critical Thinking.

**GOE—Interest Area:** 09. Business Detail. **Work Group:** 09.03. Bookkeeping, Auditing, and Accounting. **Other Job Titles in This Work Group:** Billing and Posting Clerks and Machine Operators; Billing, Cost, and Rate Clerks; Bookkeeping, Accounting, and Auditing Clerks; Brokerage Clerks; Payroll and Timekeeping Clerks; Tax Preparers. **PERSONALITY TYPE**—Conventional.

Conventional occupations frequently involve following set procedures and routines. These occupations can include working with data and details more than with ideas. Usually there is a clear line of authority to follow.

**EDUCATION/TRAINING PROGRAM(S)**—Accounting Technician. **RELATED KNOWLEDGE/COURSES—Clerical Studies:** Knowledge of administrative and clerical procedures and systems such as word processing, managing files and records, stenography and transcription, designing forms, and other office procedures and terminology. **Mathematics:** Knowledge of arithmetic, algebra, geometry, calculus, statistics, and their applications. **Economics and Accounting:** Knowledge of economic and accounting principles and practices, the financial markets, banking, and the analysis and reporting of financial data. **Customer and Personal Service:** Knowledge of principles and processes for providing customer and personal services. This includes customer needs assessment, meeting quality standards for services, and evaluation of customer satisfaction. **Computers and Electronics:** Knowledge of circuit boards, processors, chips, electronic equipment, and computer hardware and software, including applications and programming.

# Station Installers and Repairers, Telephone

▲ Growth: -3.1%
▲ Annual Job Openings: 9,000
▲ Annual Earnings: $42,520
▲ Education/Training Required: Post-secondary vocational training
▲ Self-Employed: 6.2%
▲ Part-Time: 3.4%

**Install and repair telephone station equipment, such as telephones, coin collectors, telephone booths, and switching-key equipment.** Installs communication equipment, such as intercommunication systems and related apparatus, using schematic diagrams, testing devices, and hand tools. Assembles telephone equipment, mounts brackets, and connects wire leads, using hand tools and following installation diagrams or work order. Analyzes equipment operation, using testing devices to locate and diagnose nature of malfunction and ascertain needed repairs. Operates and tests equipment to ensure elimination of malfunction. Climbs poles to install or repair outside service lines. Disassembles components and replaces, cleans, adjusts, and repairs parts, wires, switches, relays, circuits, or signaling units, using hand tools. Repairs cables, lays out plans for new equipment, and estimates material required. **SKILLS**—Troubleshooting. Installation. Repairing. Quality Control Analysis. Mathematics. Equipment Maintenance.

**GOE—Interest Area:** 05. Mechanics, Installers, and Repairers. **Work Group:** 05.02. Electrical and Electronic Systems. **Other Job Titles in This Work Group:** Avionics Technicians; Battery Repairers; Central Office and PBX Installers and Repairers; Communication Equipment Mechanics, Installers, and Repairers; Computer, Automated Teller, and Office Machine Repairers; Data Processing Equipment Repairers; Electric Home Appliance and Power Tool Repairers; Electric Meter Installers and Repairers; Electric Motor and Switch Assemblers and Repairers; Electric Motor, Power Tool, and Related Repairers; Electrical and Electronics Installers and Repairers, Transportation Equipment; Electrical and Electronics Repairers, Commercial and Industrial Equipment; Electrical and Electronics Repairers, Powerhouse, Substation, and Relay; Electrical Parts Reconditioners; Electrical Power-Line Installers and Repairers; Electronic Equipment Installers and Repairers, Motor Vehicles; Electronic Home Entertainment Equipment Installers and Repairers; Elevator Installers and Repairers; Frame Wirers, Central Office; Home Appliance Installers; Home Appliance Repairers; Office Machine and Cash Register Servicers; Radio Mechanics; Signal and Track Switch Repairers; Telecommunications Equipment Installers and Repairers, Except Line Installers; Telecommunications Facility Examiners; Telecommunications Line Installers and Repairers; Transformer Repairers. **PERSONALITY TYPE**—Realistic. Realistic occupations frequently involve work activities that include practical, hands-on problems and solutions. They often deal with plants, animals, and real-world materials like wood, tools, and machinery. Many of the occupations require working outside and do not involve a lot of paperwork or working closely with others.

**EDUCATION/TRAINING PROGRAM(S)**—Communication Systems Installer and Repairer. **RELATED KNOWLEDGE/COURSES—Computers and Electronics:** Knowledge of circuit boards, processors, chips, electronic equipment, and computer hardware and software, including applications and programming. **Telecommunications:** Knowledge of transmission, broadcasting, switching, control, and operation of telecommunications systems. **Principles of Mechanical Devices:** Knowledge of machines and tools, including their designs, uses, repair, and maintenance. **Engineering and Technology:** Knowledge of the practical application of engineering science and technology. This includes applying principles, techniques, procedures, and equipment to the design and production of various goods and services. **Design:** Knowledge of design techniques, tools, and principles involved in production of precision technical plans, blueprints, drawings, and models.

# Stevedores, Except Equipment Operators

- ▲ Growth: 13.9%
- ▲ Annual Job Openings: 519,000
- ▲ Annual Earnings: $20,460
- ▲ Education/Training Required: Short-term on-the-job training
- ▲ Self-Employed: 1.1%
- ▲ Part-Time: 16.2%

Manually load and unload ship cargo. Stack cargo in transit shed or in hold of ship using pallet or cargo board. Attach and move slings to lift cargo. Guide load lift. Carries or moves cargo by handtruck to wharf and stacks cargo on pallets to facilitate transfer to and from ship. Stacks cargo in transit shed or in hold of ship as directed. Attaches and moves slings used to lift cargo. Guides load being lifted to prevent swinging. Shores cargo in ship's hold to prevent shifting during voyage. **SKILLS**—Active Listening. Reading Comprehension.

**GOE—Interest Area:** 07. Transportation. **Work Group:** 07.08. Support Work. **Other Job Titles in This Work Group:** Freight Inspectors; Railroad Yard Workers; Train Crew Members; Transportation Inspectors. **PERSONALITY TYPE**—Realistic. Realistic occupations frequently involve work activities that include practical, hands-on problems and solutions. They often deal with plants, animals, and real-world materials like wood, tools, and machinery. Many of the occupations require working outside and do not involve a lot of paperwork or working closely with others.

**EDUCATION/TRAINING PROGRAM(S)**—No data available. **RELATED KNOWLEDGE/ COURSES—Production and Processing:** Knowledge of raw materials, production processes, quality control, costs, and other techniques for maximizing the effective manufacture and distribution of goods. **Transportation:** Knowledge of principles and methods for moving people or goods by air, rail, sea, or road, including the relative costs and benefits. **Building and Construction:** Knowledge of materials, methods, and tools involved in the construction or repair of houses, buildings, or other structures such as highways and roads.

# Stock Clerks and Order Fillers

- ▲ Growth: 8.5%
- ▲ Annual Job Openings: 467,000
- ▲ Annual Earnings: $20,650
- ▲ Education/Training Required: Short-term on-the-job training
- ▲ Self-Employed: 0.2%
- ▲ Part-Time: 12.8%

Receive, store, and issue sales floor merchandise, materials, equipment, and other items from stockroom, warehouse, or storage yard to fill shelves, racks, tables, or customers' orders. May mark prices on merchandise and set up sales displays. **SKILLS**—No data available.

**GOE—Interest Area:** 09. Business Detail. **Work Group:** 09.08. Records and Materials Processing. **Other Job Titles in This Work Group:** Cargo and Freight Agents; Couriers and Messengers; Mail Clerks, Except Mail Machine Operators and Postal Service; Marking Clerks; Order Fillers, Wholesale and Retail Sales; Postal Service Mail Carriers; Postal Service Mail Sorters, Processors, and Processing Machine Operators; Shipping, Receiving, and Traffic Clerks; Stock Clerks—Stockroom, Warehouse, or Storage Yard; Weighers, Measurers, Checkers, and Samplers, Recordkeeping. **PERSONALITY TYPE**—No data available.

**EDUCATION/TRAINING PROGRAM(S)**—Food Products Retailing and Wholesaling Operations; General Retailing Operations; Home and Office Products Marketing Operations, Other. **RELATED KNOWLEDGE/COURSES**—No data available.

# Stock Clerks, Sales Floor

- ▲ Growth: 8.5%
- ▲ Annual Job Openings: 467,000
- ▲ Annual Earnings: $20,650
- ▲ Education/Training Required: Short-term on-the-job training
- ▲ Self-Employed: 0.2%
- ▲ Part-Time: 13.7%

Receive, store, and issue sales floor merchandise. Stock shelves, racks, cases, bins, and tables with merchandise and arrange merchandise displays to attract customers. May periodically take physical count of stock or check and mark merchandise. Receives, opens, and unpacks cartons or crates of merchandise and checks invoice against items received. Takes inventory or examines merchandise to identify items to be reordered or replenished. Requisitions merchandise from supplier based on available space, merchandise on hand, customer demand, or advertised specials. Stamps, attaches, or changes price tags on merchandise, referring to price list. Stocks storage areas and displays with new or transferred merchandise. Sets up advertising signs and displays merchandise on shelves, counters, or tables to attract customers and promote sales. Cleans display cases, shelves, and aisles. Itemizes and totals customer merchandise selection at checkout counter, using cash register, and accepts cash or charge card for purchases. Answers questions and advises customer in selection of merchandise. Cuts lumber, screening, glass, and related materials to size requested by customer. Packs customer purchases in bags or cartons. Transports packages to customer vehicle. **SKILLS**—Reading Comprehension. Active Listening. Service Orientation. Social Perceptiveness. Mathematics.

**GOE**—**Interest Area:** 10. Sales and Marketing. **Work Group:** 10.03. General Sales. **Other Job Titles in This Work Group:** Parts Salespersons; Real Estate Brokers; Real Estate Sales Agents; Retail Salespersons; Sales Representatives, Wholesale and Manufacturing, Except Technical and Scientific Products; Service Station Attendants; Travel Agents. **PERSONALITY TYPE**—Realistic. Realistic occupations frequently involve work activities that include practical, hands-on problems and solutions. They often deal with plants, animals, and real-world materials like wood, tools, and machinery. Many of the occupations require working outside and do not involve a lot of paperwork or working closely with others.

**EDUCATION/TRAINING PROGRAM(S)**—Food Products Retailing and Wholesaling Operations; General Retailing Operations; Home and Office Products Marketing Operations, Other. **RELATED KNOWLEDGE/COURSES**—**Clerical Studies:** Knowledge of administrative and clerical procedures and systems such as word processing, managing files and records, stenography and transcription, designing forms, and other office procedures and terminology. **Customer and Personal Service:** Knowledge of principles and processes for providing customer and personal services. This includes customer needs assessment, meeting quality standards for services, and evaluation of customer satisfaction. **Sales and Marketing:** Knowledge of principles and methods for showing, promoting, and selling products or services. This includes marketing strategy and tactics, product demonstration, sales techniques, and sales control systems. **Mathematics:** Knowledge of arithmetic, algebra, geometry, calculus, statistics, and their applications. **English Language:** Knowledge of the structure and content of the English language, including the meaning and spelling of words, rules of composition, and grammar.

# Stock Clerks— Stockroom, Warehouse, or Storage Yard

▲ Growth: 8.5%
▲ Annual Job Openings: 467,000
▲ Annual Earnings: $20,650
▲ Education/Training Required: Short-term on-the-job training
▲ Self-Employed: 0.2%
▲ Part-Time: 13.7%

**Receive, store, and issue materials, equipment, and other items from stockroom, warehouse, or storage yard. Keep records and compile stock reports.** Receives, counts, and stores stock items and records data manually or using computer. Assists or directs other stockroom, warehouse, or storage yard workers. Adjusts, repairs, assembles, or prepares products, supplies, equipment, or other items according to specifications or customer requirements. Examines and inspects stock items for wear or defects, reports damage to supervisor, and disposes of or returns items to vendor. Confers with engineering and purchasing personnel and vendors regarding procurement and stock availability. Purchases or prepares documents to purchase new or additional stock and recommends disposal of excess, defective, or obsolete stock. Receives and fills orders or sells supplies, materials, and products to customers. Prepares documents, such as inventory balance, price lists, shortages, expenditures, and periodic reports, using computer, typewriter, or calculator. Verifies computations against physical count of stock, adjusts for errors, or investigates discrepancies. Delivers products, supplies, and equipment to designated area and determines sequence and release of backorders according to stock availability. Drives truck to pick up incoming stock or deliver parts to designated locations. Cleans and maintains supplies, tools, equipment, instruments, and storage areas to ensure compliance to safety regulations. Compares office inventory records with sales orders, invoices, or requisitions to verify accuracy and receipt of items. Locates and selects material, supplies, tools, equipment, or other articles from stock or issues stock item to workers. Compiles, reviews, and maintains data from contracts, purchase orders, requisitions, and other documents to determine supply needs. Determines method of storage, identification, and stock location based on turnover, environmental factors, and physical capacity of facility. Packs, unpacks, and marks stock items using identification tag, stamp, electric marking tool, or other labeling equipment. Records nature, quantity, value, or location of material, supplies, or equipment received, shipped, used, or issued to workers. **SKILLS**—Mathematics. Reading Comprehension. Writing. Active Listening. Speaking.

**GOE—Interest Area:** 09. Business Detail. **Work Group:** 09.08. Records and Materials Processing. **Other Job Titles in This Work Group:** Cargo and Freight Agents; Couriers and Messengers; Mail Clerks, Except Mail Machine Operators and Postal Service; Marking Clerks; Order Fillers, Wholesale and Retail Sales; Postal Service Mail Carriers; Postal Service Mail Sorters, Processors, and Processing Machine Operators; Shipping, Receiving, and Traffic Clerks; Stock Clerks and Order Fillers; Weighers, Measurers, Checkers, and Samplers, Recordkeeping. **PERSONALITY TYPE**—Conventional. Conventional occupations frequently involve following set procedures and routines. These occupations can include working with data and details more than with ideas. Usually there is a clear line of authority to follow.

**EDUCATION/TRAINING PROGRAM(S)**—Food Products Retailing and Wholesaling Operations; General Retailing Operations; Home and Office Products Marketing Operations, Other. **RELATED KNOWLEDGE/COURSES—Clerical Studies:** Knowledge of administrative and clerical procedures and systems such as word processing, managing files and records, stenography and transcription, designing forms, and other office procedures and terminology. **Mathematics:** Knowledge of arithmetic, algebra, geometry, calculus, and content of the English language, including the meaning and spelling of words, rules of composition, and grammar. **Production and Processing:** Knowledge of raw materials, production processes, quality control, costs, and other techniques for maximizing the effective manufacture and distribution of goods.

# Stonemasons

- ▲ Growth: 20.8%
- ▲ Annual Job Openings: 2,000
- ▲ Annual Earnings: $32,380
- ▲ Education/Training Required: Long-term on-the-job training
- ▲ Self-Employed: 26.1%
- ▲ Part-Time: 8.7%

**Build stone structures, such as piers, walls, and abutments. Lay walks, curbstones, or special types of masonry for vats, tanks, and floors.** Shapes, trims, faces, and cuts marble or stone preparatory to setting, using power saws, cutting equipment, and hand tools. Mixes mortar or grout and pours or spreads mortar or grout on marble slabs, stone, or foundation. Cleans excess mortar or grout from surface of marble, stone, or monument, using sponge, brush, water, or acid. Lines interiors of molds with treated paper and fills molds with composition-stone mixture. Repairs cracked or chipped areas of ornamental stone or marble surface, using blowtorch and mastic. Drills holes in marble or ornamental stone and anchors bracket. Digs trench for foundation of monument, using pick and shovel. Removes sections of monument from truck bed and guides stone onto foundation, using skids, hoist, or truck crane. Positions mold along guidelines of wall, presses mold in place, and removes mold and paper from wall. Smoothes, polishes, and bevels surfaces, using hand tools and power tools. Finishes joints between stones, using trowel. Lays out wall pattern or foundation of monument, using straight edge, rule, or staked lines. Sets stone or marble in place according to layout or pattern. Aligns and levels stone or marble, using measuring devices such as rule, square, and plumbline. **SKILLS**—Equipment Selection. Operation and Control. Mathematics.

**GOE—Interest Area:** 06. Construction, Mining, and Drilling. **Work Group:** 06.02. Construction. **Other Job Titles in This Work Group:** Boat Builders and Shipwrights; Boilermakers; Brattice Builders; Brickmasons and Blockmasons; Carpenters; Carpet Installers; Ceiling Tile Installers; Cement Masons and Concrete Finishers; Commercial Divers; Construction Carpenters; Drywall and Ceiling Tile Installers; Drywall Installers; Electricians; Explosives Workers, Ordnance Handling Experts, and Blasters; Fence Erectors; Floor Layers, Except Carpet, Wood, and Hard Tiles; Floor Sanders and Finishers; Glaziers; Grader, Bulldozer, and Scraper Operators; Hazardous Materials Removal Workers; Insulation Workers, Floor, Ceiling, and Wall; Insulation Workers, Mechanical; Manufactured Building and Mobile Home Installers; Operating Engineers; Operating Engineers and Other Construction Equipment Operators; Painters, Construction and Maintenance; Paperhangers; Paving, Surfacing, and Tamping Equipment Operators; Pile-Driver Operators; Pipe Fitters; Pipelayers; Pipelaying Fitters; Plasterers and Stucco Masons; Plumbers; Plumbers, Pipefitters, and Steamfitters; Rail-Track Laying and Maintenance Equipment Operators; Refractory Materials Repairers, Except Brickmasons; Reinforcing Iron and Rebar Workers; Riggers; Roofers; Rough Carpenters; Security and Fire Alarm Systems Installers; Segmental Pavers; Sheet Metal Workers; Ship Carpenters and Joiners; Stone Cutters and Carvers; Structural Iron and Steel Workers; Tapers; Terrazzo Workers and Finishers; Tile and Marble Setters. **PERSONALITY TYPE**—Realistic. Realistic occupations frequently involve work activities that include practical, hands-on problems and solutions. They often deal with plants, animals, and real-world materials like wood, tools, and machinery. Many of the occupations require working outside and do not involve a lot of paperwork or working closely with others.

EDUCATION/TRAINING PROGRAM(S)—Mason and Tile Setter. **RELATED KNOWLEDGE/ COURSES—Building and Construction:** Knowledge of materials, methods, and tools involved in the construction or repair of houses, buildings, or other structures such as highways and roads. **Principles of Mechanical Devices:** Knowledge of machines and tools, including their designs, uses, repair, and maintenance. **Design:** Knowledge of design techniques, tools, and principles involved in production of precision technical plans, blueprints, drawings, and models. **Mathematics:** Knowledge of arithmetic, algebra, geometry, calculus, statistics, and their applications.

# Storage and Distribution Managers

- ▲ Growth: 20.2%
- ▲ Annual Job Openings: 13,000
- ▲ Annual Earnings: $58,200
- ▲ Education/Training Required: Work experience in a related occupation
- ▲ Self-Employed: 21.9%
- ▲ Part-Time: 6.1%

**Plan, direct, and coordinate the storage and distribution operations within an organization or the activities of organizations that are engaged in storing and distributing materials and products.** Establishes standard and emergency operating procedures for receiving, handling, storing, shipping, or salvaging products or materials. Examines products or materials to estimate quantities or weight and type of container required for storage or transport. Interacts with customers or shippers to solicit new business, answer questions about services offered or required, and investigate complaints. Prepares or directs preparation of correspondence, reports, and operations, maintenance, and safety manuals. Schedules air or surface pickup, delivery, or distribution of products or materials. Interviews, selects, and trains warehouse and supervisory personnel. Examines invoices and shipping manifests for conformity to tariff and customs regulations and contacts customs officials to effect release of shipments. Reviews invoices, work orders, consumption reports, and demand forecasts to estimate peak delivery periods and issue work assignments. Supervises the activities of worker engaged in receiving, storing, testing, and shipping products or materials. Inspects physical condition of warehouse and equipment and prepares work orders for testing, maintenance, or repair. Develops and implements plans for facility modification or expansion, such as equipment purchase or changes in space allocation or structural design. Negotiates contracts, settlements, and freight-handling agreements to resolve problems between foreign and domestic shippers. Plans, develops, and implements warehouse safety and security programs and activities. Confers with department heads to coordinate warehouse activities, such as production, sales, records control, and purchasing. **SKILLS—**Management of Personnel Resources. Negotiation. Writing. Coordination. Monitoring. Operations Analysis. Speaking.

**GOE—Interest Area:** 13. General Management and Support. **Work Group:** 13.01. General Management Work and Management of Support Functions. **Other Job Titles in This Work Group:** Chief Executives; Compensation and Benefits Managers; Farm, Ranch, and Other Agricultural Managers; Financial Managers; Financial Managers, Branch or Department; Funeral Directors; General and Operations Managers; Government Service Executives; Human Resources Managers; Human Resources Managers, All Other; Legislators; Managers, All Other; Postmasters and Mail Superintendents; Private Sector Executives; Property, Real Estate, and Community Association Managers; Public Relations Managers; Purchasing Managers; Training and Development Managers; Transportation, Storage, and Distribution Managers; Treasurers, Controllers, and Chief Financial Officers. **PERSONALITY TYPE—** Enterprising. Enterprising occupations frequently involve starting up and carrying out projects. These occupations can involve leading people and making many decisions. They sometimes require risk taking and often deal with business.

EDUCATION/TRAINING PROGRAM(S)—Aviation Management; Business Administration and Management, General; General Distribution Operations; Logistics and Materials Management; Public Administration. **RELATED KNOWLEDGE/COURSES—Administration and Management:** Knowledge of business and management principles involved in strategic planning, resource allocation, human resources modeling, leadership technique, production methods, and coordi-

nation of people and resources. **Personnel and Human Resources:** Knowledge of principles and procedures for personnel recruitment, selection, training, compensation and benefits, labor relations and negotiation, and personnel information systems. **Mathematics:** Knowledge of arithmetic, algebra, geometry, calculus, statistics, and their applications. **Transportation:** Knowledge of principles and methods for moving people or goods by air, rail, sea, or road, including the relative costs and benefits. **Production and Processing:** Knowledge of raw materials, production processes, quality control, costs, and other techniques for maximizing the effective manufacture and distribution of goods.

# Structural Iron and Steel Workers

- ▲ Growth: 18.4%
- ▲ Annual Job Openings: 12,000
- ▲ Annual Earnings: $39,140
- ▲ Education/Training Required: Long-term on-the-job training
- ▲ Self-Employed: 2.5%
- ▲ Part-Time: 4.9%

**Raise, place, and unite iron or steel girders, columns, and other structural members to form completed structures or structural frameworks. May erect metal storage tanks and assemble prefabricated metal buildings.** Guides structural-steel member, using tab line (rope), or rides on member in order to guide it into position. Fastens structural-steel members to cable of hoist, using chain, cable, or rope. Signals worker operating hoisting equipment to lift and place structural-steel member. Sets up hoisting equipment for raising and placing structural-steel members. Inserts sealing strips, wiring, insulating material, ladders, flanges, gauges, and valves, depending on type of structure being assembled. Cuts and welds steel members to make alterations, using oxyacetylene welding equipment. Bucks (holds) rivets while Riveter, Pneumatic uses air-hammer to form heads on rivets. Catches hot rivets tossed by Rivet Heater in bucket and inserts rivets in holes, using tongs. Verifies vertical and horizontal alignment of structural-steel members, using plumb bob and level. Bolts aligned structural-steel members in position until they can be permanently riveted, bolted, or welded in place. Pulls, pushes, or pries struc-

tural-steel member into approximate position while member is supported by hoisting device. Forces structural-steel members into final position, using turnbuckles, crowbars, jacks, and hand tools. Drives drift pins through rivet holes to align rivet holes in structural-steel member with corresponding holes in previously placed member. SKILLS—Coordination. Installation. Equipment Selection. Operation and Control.

GOE—Interest Area: 06. Construction, Mining, and Drilling. Work Group: 06.02. Construction. **Other Job Titles in This Work Group:** Boat Builders and Shipwrights; Boilermakers; Brattice Builders; Brickmasons and Blockmasons; Carpenters; Carpet Installers; Ceiling Tile Installers; Cement Masons and Concrete Finishers; Commercial Divers; Construction Carpenters; Drywall and Ceiling Tile Installers; Drywall Installers; Electricians; Explosives Workers, Ordnance Handling Experts, and Blasters; Fence Erectors; Floor Layers, Except Carpet, Wood, and Hard Tiles; Floor Sanders and Finishers; Glaziers; Grader, Bulldozer, and Scraper Operators; Hazardous Materials Removal Workers; Insulation Workers, Floor, Ceiling, and Wall; Insulation Workers, Mechanical; Manufactured Building and Mobile Home Installers; Operating Engineers; Operating Engineers and Other Construction Equipment Operators; Painters, Construction and Maintenance; Paperhangers; Paving, Surfacing, and Tamping Equipment Operators; Pile-Driver Operators; Pipe Fitters; Pipelayers; Pipelaying Fitters; Plasterers and Stucco Masons; Plumbers; Plumbers, Pipefitters, and Steamfitters; Rail-Track Laying and Maintenance Equipment Operators; Refractory Materials Repairers, Except Brickmasons; Reinforcing Iron and Rebar Workers; Riggers; Roofers; Rough Carpenters; Security and Fire Alarm Systems Installers; Segmental Pavers; Sheet Metal Workers; Ship Carpenters and Joiners; Stone Cutters and Carvers; Stonemasons; Tapers; Terrazzo Workers and Finishers; Tile and Marble Setters. **PERSONALITY TYPE**—Realistic. Realistic occupations frequently involve work activities that include practical, hands-on problems and solutions. They often deal with plants, animals, and real-world materials like wood, tools, and machinery. Many of the occupations require working outside and do not involve a lot of paperwork or working closely with others.

**EDUCATION/TRAINING PROGRAM(S)**—Construction Trades, Other. **RELATED KNOWLEDGE/ COURSES—Building and Construction:** Knowledge of materials, methods, and tools involved in the construction or repair of houses, buildings, or other structures such as highways and roads. **Principles of Mechanical Devices:** Knowledge of machines and tools, including their designs, uses, repair, and maintenance. **Public Safety and Security:** Knowledge of relevant equipment, policies, procedures, and strategies to promote effective local, state, or national security operations for the protection of people, data, property, and institutions. **Engineering and Technology:** Knowledge of the practical application of engineering science and technology. This includes applying principles, techniques, procedures, and equipment to the design and production of various goods and services. **Mathematics:** Knowledge of arithmetic, algebra, geometry, calculus, statistics, and their applications. **Physics:** Knowledge and prediction of physical principles and laws and their interrelationships and applications to understanding fluid, material, and atmospheric dynamics and mechanical, electrical, atomic, and sub-atomic structures and processes.

# Surgical Technologists

- ▲ Growth: 34.7%
- ▲ Annual Job Openings: 8,000
- ▲ Annual Earnings: $29,660
- ▲ Education/Training Required: Postsecondary vocational training
- ▲ Self-Employed: 0%
- ▲ Part-Time: 22.9%

**Assist in operations under the supervision of surgeons, registered nurses, or other surgical personnel. May help set up operating room, prepare and transport patients for surgery, adjust lights and equipment, pass instruments and other supplies to surgeons and surgeon's assistants, hold retractors, cut sutures, and help count sponges, needles, supplies, and instruments.** Places equipment and supplies in operating room and arranges instruments according to instruction. Maintains supply of fluids, such as plasma, saline, blood, and glucose, for use during operation. Cleans operating room.

Washes and sterilizes equipment, using germicides and sterilizers. Puts dressings on patient following surgery. Aids team to don gowns and gloves. Scrubs arms and hands and dons gown and gloves. Assists team members to place and position patient on table. Counts sponges, needles, and instruments before and after operation. Hands instruments and supplies to surgeon, holds retractors and cuts sutures, and performs other tasks as directed by surgeon during operation. **SKILLS**—Reading Comprehension. Active Listening. Coordination. Critical Thinking. Active Learning.

GOE—**Interest Area:** 14. Medical and Health Services. **Work Group:** 14.02. Medicine and Surgery. **Other Job Titles in This Work Group:** Anesthesiologists; Family and General Practitioners; Internists, General; Medical Assistants; Obstetricians and Gynecologists; Pediatricians, General; Pharmacists; Pharmacy Aides; Pharmacy Technicians; Physician Assistants; Physicians and Surgeons, All Other; Psychiatrists; Registered Nurses; Surgeons. **PERSONALITY TYPE**—Realistic. Realistic occupations frequently involve work activities that include practical, hands-on problems and solutions. They often deal with plants, animals, and real-world materials like wood, tools, and machinery. Many of the occupations require working outside and do not involve a lot of paperwork or working closely with others.

**EDUCATION/TRAINING PROGRAM(S)**—Surgical/Operating Room Technician. **RELATED KNOWLEDGE/COURSES**—**Medicine and Dentistry:**

Knowledge of the information and techniques needed to diagnose and treat human injuries, diseases, and deformities. This includes symptoms, treatment alternatives, drug properties and interactions, and preventive health-care measures. **Biology:** Knowledge of plant and animal organisms and their tissues, cells, functions, interdependencies, and interactions with each other and the environment. **Mathematics:** Knowledge of arithmetic, algebra, geometry, calculus, statistics, and their applications. **English Language:** Knowledge of the structure and content of the English language, including the meaning and spelling of words, rules of composition, and grammar. **Chemistry:** Knowledge of the chemical composition, structure, and properties of substances and of the chemical processes and transformations that they undergo. This includes uses of chemicals and their interactions, danger signs, production techniques, and disposal methods.

# Tapers

- ▲ Growth: 8.3%
- ▲ Annual Job Openings: 6,000
- ▲ Annual Earnings: $38,680
- ▲ Education/Training Required: Moderate-term on-the-job training
- ▲ Self-Employed: 20.7%
- ▲ Part-Time: 8.4%

**Seal joints between plasterboard or other wallboard to prepare wall surface for painting or papering.** Spreads sealing compound between boards, using trowel, broadknife, or spatula. Tapes joint, using mechanical applicator that spreads compound and embeds tape in one operation. Sands rough spots after cement has dried. Installs metal molding at corners in lieu of sealant and tape. Applies texturizing compound and primer to walls and ceiling preparatory to final finishing, using brushes, roller, or spray gun. Countersinks nails or screws below surface of wall prior to applying sealing compound, using hammer or screwdriver. Mixes sealing compound by hand or with portable electric mixer. Fills cracks and holes in walls and ceiling with sealing compound. Spreads and smoothes cementing material over tape, using trowel or floating machine to

blend joint with wall surface. Presses paper tape over joint to embed tape into sealing compound and seal joint. **SKILLS**—Coordination.

GOE—**Interest Area:** 06. Construction, Mining, and Drilling. **Work Group:** 06.02. Construction. **Other Job Titles in This Work Group:** Boat Builders and Shipwrights; Boilermakers; Brattice Builders; Brickmasons and Blockmasons; Carpenters; Carpet Installers; Ceiling Tile Installers; Cement Masons and Concrete Finishers; Commercial Divers; Construction Carpenters; Drywall and Ceiling Tile Installers; Drywall Installers; Electricians; Explosives Workers, Ordnance Handling Experts, and Blasters; Fence Erectors; Floor Layers, Except Carpet, Wood, and Hard Tiles; Floor Sanders and Finishers; Glaziers; Grader, Bulldozer, and Scraper Operators; Hazardous Materials Removal Workers;

Insulation Workers, Floor, Ceiling, and Wall; Insulation Workers, Mechanical; Manufactured Building and Mobile Home Installers; Operating Engineers; Operating Engineers and Other Construction Equipment Operators; Painters, Construction and Maintenance; Paperhangers; Paving, Surfacing, and Tamping Equipment Operators; Pile-Driver Operators; Pipe Fitters; Pipelayers; Pipelaying Fitters; Plasterers and Stucco Masons; Plumbers; Plumbers, Pipefitters, and Steamfitters; Rail-Track Laying and Maintenance Equipment Operators; Refractory Materials Repairers, Except Brickmasons; Reinforcing Iron and Rebar Workers; Riggers; Roofers; Rough Carpenters; Security and Fire Alarm Systems Installers; Segmental Pavers; Sheet Metal Workers; Ship Carpenters and Joiners; Stone Cutters and Carvers; Stonemasons; Structural Iron and Steel Workers; Terrazzo Workers and Finishers; Tile and Marble Setters. **PERSONALITY TYPE**—Realistic. Realistic occupations frequently involve work activities that include practical, hands-on problems and solutions. They often deal with plants, animals, and real-world materials like wood, tools, and machinery. Many of the occupations require working outside and do not involve a lot of paperwork or working closely with others.

**EDUCATION/TRAINING PROGRAM(S)**—Construction Trades, Other. **RELATED KNOWLEDGE/ COURSES**—**Building and Construction:** Knowledge of materials, methods, and tools involved in the construction or repair of houses, buildings, or other structures such as highways and roads. **Engineering and Technology:** Knowledge of the practical application of engineering science and technology. This includes applying principles, techniques, procedures, and equipment to the design and production of various goods and services. **Chemistry:** Knowledge of the chemical composition, structure, and properties of substances and of the chemical processes and transformations that they undergo. This includes uses of chemicals and their interactions, danger signs, production techniques, and disposal methods.

# Taxi Drivers and Chauffeurs

- ▲ Growth: 24.4%
- ▲ Annual Job Openings: 37,000
- ▲ Annual Earnings: $18,920
- ▲ Education/Training Required: Short-term on-the-job training
- ▲ Self-Employed: 27%
- ▲ Part-Time: 21.5%

**Drive automobiles, vans, or limousines to transport passengers. May occasionally carry cargo.** Drives taxicab, limousine, company car, hearse, or privately owned vehicle to transport passengers. Communicates with taxicab dispatcher by radio or telephone to receive requests for passenger service. Collects and documents fees, payments, and deposits determined by rental contracts or taximeter recordings. Assists passengers to enter and exit vehicle, assists with luggage, and holds umbrellas in wet weather. Maintains vehicle by performing such duties as regulating tire pressure and adding gasoline, oil, and water. Delivers automobiles to customers from rental agency, car dealership, or repair shop. Tests performance of vehicle accessories, such as lights, horn, and windshield wipers. Performs errands for customers, such as carrying mail to and from post office. Vacuums, sweeps, and cleans interior, and washes and polishes exterior of automobile. Makes minor repairs on vehicle, such as fixing punctures, cleaning spark plugs, or adjusting carburetor. **SKILLS**—Operation and Control. Service Orientation. Repairing. Operation Monitoring. Mathematics. Writing.

**GOE**—**Interest Area:** 07. Transportation. **Work Group:** 07.07. Other Services Requiring Driving. **Other Job Titles in This Work Group:** Ambulance Drivers and Attendants, Except Emergency Medical Technicians; Bus Drivers, School; Bus Drivers, Transit and Intercity;

Driver/Sales Workers; Parking Lot Attendants. **PERSONALITY TYPE**—Realistic. Realistic occupations frequently involve work activities that include practical, hands-on problems and solutions. They often deal with plants, animals, and real-world materials like wood, tools, and machinery. Many of the occupations require working outside and do not involve a lot of paperwork or working closely with others.

**EDUCATION/TRAINING PROGRAM(S)**—Truck, Bus and Other Commercial Vehicle Operator. **RELATED KNOWLEDGE/COURSES**—**Transportation:** Knowledge of principles and methods for moving people or goods by air, rail, sea, or road, including the relative costs and benefits. **Customer and Personal Service:** Knowledge of principles and processes for providing customer and personal services. This includes

customer needs assessment, meeting quality standards for services, and evaluation of customer satisfaction. **Geography:** Knowledge of principles and methods for describing the features of land, sea, and air masses, including their physical characteristics, locations, interrelationships, and distribution of plant, animal, and human life. **Principles of Mechanical Devices:** Knowledge of machines and tools, including their designs, uses, repair, and maintenance. **English Language:** Knowledge of the structure and content of the English language, including the meaning and spelling of words, rules of composition, and grammar. **Law and Government:** Knowledge of laws, legal codes, court procedures, precedents, government regulations, executive orders, agency rules, and the democratic political process.

# Teacher Assistants

- ▲ Growth: 23.9%
- ▲ Annual Job Openings: 256,000
- ▲ Annual Earnings: $18,770
- ▲ Education/Training Required: Short-term on-the-job training
- ▲ Self-Employed: 0%
- ▲ Part-Time: 46.8%

**Perform duties that are instructional in nature or deliver direct services to students or parents. Serve in a position for which a teacher or another professional has ultimate responsibility for the design and implementation of educational programs and services.** Presents subject matter to students, using lecture, discussion, or supervised role-playing methods. Helps students, individually or in groups, with lesson assignments to present or reinforce learning concepts. Prepares lesson outline and plan in assigned area and submits outline to teacher for review. Plans, prepares, and develops various teaching aids, such as bibliographies, charts, and graphs. Discusses assigned teaching area with classroom teacher to coordinate instructional efforts. Prepares, administers, and grades examinations. Confers with parents on progress of students. **SKILLS**— Active Listening. Learning Strategies. Speaking. Instructing. Reading Comprehension.

GOE—**Interest Area:** 12. Education and Social Service. **Work Group:** 12.03. Educational Services. **Other Job Titles in This Work Group:** Adult Literacy, Remedial Education, and GED Teachers and Instructors; Agricultural Sciences Teachers, Postsecondary; Anthropology and Archeology Teachers, Postsecondary; Architecture Teachers, Postsecondary; Archivists; Area, Ethnic, and Cultural Studies Teachers, Postsecondary; Art, Drama, and Music Teachers, Postsecondary; Atmospheric, Earth, Marine, and Space Sciences Teachers, Postsecondary; Audio-Visual Collections Specialists; Biological Science Teachers, Postsecondary; Business Teachers, Postsecondary; Chemistry Teachers, Postsecondary; Child Care Workers; Communications Teachers, Postsecondary; Computer Science Teachers, Postsecondary; Criminal Justice and Law Enforcement Teachers, Postsecondary; Curators; Economics Teachers, Postsecondary; Education Teachers, Postsecondary;

Educational Psychologists; Educational, Vocational, and School Counselors; Elementary School Teachers, Except Special Education; Engineering Teachers, Postsecondary; English Language and Literature Teachers, Postsecondary; Environmental Science Teachers, Postsecondary; Farm and Home Management Advisors; Foreign Language and Literature Teachers, Postsecondary; Forestry and Conservation Science Teachers, Postsecondary; Geography Teachers, Postsecondary; Graduate Teaching Assistants; Health Specialties Teachers, Postsecondary; History Teachers, Postsecondary; Home Economics Teachers, Postsecondary; Kindergarten Teachers, Except Special Education; Law Teachers, Postsecondary; Librarians; Library Assistants, Clerical; others. **PERSONALITY TYPE**—Social. Social occupations frequently involve working with, communicating with, and teaching people. These occupations often involve helping or providing service to others.

**EDUCATION/TRAINING PROGRAM(S)**— Teacher Assistant/Aide. **RELATED KNOWLEDGE/ COURSES**—**Education and Training:** Knowledge of principles and methods for curriculum and training design, teaching and instruction for individuals and groups, and the measurement of training effects. **English Language:** Knowledge of the structure and content of the English language, including the meaning and spelling of words, rules of composition, and grammar. **Mathematics:** Knowledge of arithmetic, algebra, geometry, calculus, statistics, and their applications. **Clerical Studies:** Knowledge of administrative and clerical procedures and systems such as word processing, managing files and records, stenography and transcription, designing forms, and other office procedures and terminology. **Customer and Personal Service:** Knowledge of principles and processes for providing customer and personal services. This includes customer needs assessment, meeting quality standards for services, and evaluation of customer satisfaction. **Psychology:** Knowledge of human behavior and performance; individual differences in ability, personality, and interests; learning and motivation; psychological research methods; and the assessment and treatment of behavioral and affective disorders.

# Telecommunications Facility Examiners

▲ Growth: -3.1%

▲ Annual Job Openings: 9,000

▲ Annual Earnings: $42,520

▲ Education/Training Required: Post-secondary vocational training

▲ Self-Employed: 6.2%

▲ Part-Time: 24.3%

**Examine telephone transmission facilities to determine equipment requirements for providing subscribers with new or additional telephone services.** Examines telephone transmission facilities to determine requirements for new or additional telephone services. Visits subscribers' premises to arrange for new installations, such as telephone booths and telephone poles. Designates cables available for use. Climbs telephone poles or stands on truck-mounted boom to examine terminal boxes for available connections. **SKILLS**—Equipment Selection. Operations Analysis. Quality Control Analysis.

**GOE**—**Interest Area:** 05. Mechanics, Installers, and Repairers. **Work Group:** 05.02. Electrical and Electronic Systems. **Other Job Titles in This Work Group:** Avionics Technicians; Battery Repairers; Central Office and PBX Installers and Repairers; Communication Equipment Mechanics, Installers, and Repairers; Computer, Automated Teller, and Office Machine Repairers; Data Processing Equipment Repairers; Electric Home Appliance and Power Tool Repairers; Electric Meter Installers and Repairers; Electric Motor and Switch Assemblers and Repairers; Electric Motor, Power Tool, and Related Repairers; Electrical and Electronics Installers and Repairers, Transportation Equipment; Electrical and Electronics Repairers, Commercial and Industrial Equipment; Electrical and Electronics Repairers, Powerhouse, Substation, and Relay; Electrical Parts Reconditioners; Electrical Power-Line Installers and Repairers; Electronic Equipment Installers and Repairers, Motor Vehicles; Electronic Home Entertainment Equipment Installers and Repairers; Elevator Installers and Repairers; Frame Wirers, Central Office; Home Appliance Installers; Home Appliance Repairers; Office Machine and Cash Register Servicers; Radio Mechanics; Signal and Track Switch Repairers; Station Installers and Repairers, Telephone; Telecommunications Equipment Installers and Repairers, Except Line Installers; Telecommunications Line Installers and Repairers; Transformer Repairers. **PERSONALITY TYPE**—Realistic. Realistic occupations frequently involve work activities that include practical, hands-on problems and solutions. They often deal with plants, animals, and real-world materials like wood, tools, and machinery. Many of the occupations require working outside and do not involve a lot of paperwork or working closely with others.

**EDUCATION/TRAINING PROGRAM(S)**—Communication Systems Installer and Repairer. **RELATED KNOWLEDGE/COURSES—Telecommunications:** Knowledge of transmission, broadcasting, switching, control, and operation of telecommunications systems. **Computers and Electronics:** Knowledge of circuit boards, processors, chips, electronic equipment, and computer hardware and software, including applications and programming. **English Language:** Knowledge of the structure and content of the English language, including the meaning and spelling of words, rules of composition, and grammar. **Engineering and Technology:** Knowledge of the practical application of engineering science and technology. This includes applying principles, techniques, procedures, and equipment to the design and production of various goods and services. **Customer and Personal Service:** Knowledge of principles and processes for providing customer and personal services. This includes customer needs assessment, meeting quality standards for services, and evaluation of customer satisfaction.

# Telecommunications Line Installers and Repairers

- ▲ Growth: 27.6%
- ▲ Annual Job Openings: 9,000
- ▲ Annual Earnings: $38,050
- ▲ Education/Training Required: Long-term on-the-job training
- ▲ Self-Employed: 1%
- ▲ Part-Time: 0.9%

**String and repair telephone and television cable, including fiber optics and other equipment for transmitting messages or television programming.** Installs terminal boxes and strings lead-in-wires, using electrician's tools. Ascends poles or enters tunnels and sewers to string lines and install terminal boxes, auxiliary equipment, and appliances, according to diagrams. Repairs cable system, defective lines, and auxiliary equipment. Pulls lines through ducts by hand or with use of winch. Collects installation fees. Explains cable service to subscriber. Cleans and maintains tools and test equipment. Fills and tamps holes, using cement, earth, and tamping device. Digs holes, using power auger or shovel, and hoists poles upright into holes, using truck-mounted winch. Installs and removes plant equipment, such as callboxes and clocks. Measures signal strength at utility pole, using electronic test equipment. Connects television set to cable system, evaluates incoming signal, and adjusts system to ensure optimum reception. Computes impedance of wire from pole to house to determine additional resistance needed for reducing signal to desired level. **SKILLS**—Installation. Repairing. Troubleshooting. Mathematics. Equipment Maintenance. Active Listening.

GOE—**Interest Area:** 05. Mechanics, Installers, and Repairers. **Work Group:** 05.02. Electrical and Electronic Systems. **Other Job Titles in This Work Group:** Avionics Technicians; Battery Repairers; Central Office and PBX Installers and Repairers; Communication Equipment Mechanics, Installers, and Repairers; Computer, Automated Teller, and Office Machine Repairers; Data Processing Equipment Repairers; Electric Home Appliance and Power Tool Repairers; Electric Meter Installers and Repairers; Electric Motor and Switch Assemblers and Repairers; Electric Motor, Power Tool, and Related Repairers; Electrical and Electronics Installers and Repairers, Transportation Equipment; Electrical and Electronics Repairers, Commercial and Industrial Equipment; Electrical and Electronics Repairers, Powerhouse, Substation, and Relay; Electrical Parts Reconditioners; Electrical Power-Line Installers and Repairers; Electronic Equipment Installers and Repairers, Motor Vehicles; Electronic Home Entertainment Equipment Installers and Repairers; Elevator Installers and Repairers; Frame Wirers, Central Office; Home Appliance Installers; Home Appliance Repairers; Office Machine and Cash Register Servicers; Radio Mechanics; Signal and Track Switch Repairers; Station Installers and Repairers, Telephone; Telecommunications Equipment Installers and Repairers, Except Line Installers; Telecommunications Facility Examiners; Trans-

former Repairers. **PERSONALITY TYPE**—Realistic. Realistic occupations frequently involve work activities that include practical, hands-on problems and solutions. They often deal with plants, animals, and real-world materials like wood, tools, and machinery. Many of the occupations require working outside and do not involve a lot of paperwork or working closely with others.

**EDUCATION/TRAINING PROGRAM(S)**—Communication Systems Installer and Repairer. **RELATED KNOWLEDGE/COURSES**—**Telecommunications:** Knowledge of transmission, broadcasting, switching, control, and operation of telecommunications systems. **Computers and Electronics:** Knowledge of circuit boards, processors, chips, electronic equipment, and computer hardware and software, including applications and programming. **Engineering and Technology:** Knowledge of the practical application of engineering science and technology. This includes applying principles, techniques, procedures, and equipment to the design and production of various goods and services. **Principles of Mechanical Devices:** Knowledge of machines and tools, including their designs, uses, repair, and maintenance. **Mathematics:** Knowledge of arithmetic, algebra, geometry, calculus, statistics, and their applications.

# Telemarketers

- ▲ Growth: 22.2%
- ▲ Annual Job Openings: 145,000
- ▲ Annual Earnings: $21,460
- ▲ Education/Training Required: Short-term on-the-job training
- ▲ Self-Employed: 17.3%
- ▲ Part-Time: 40.2%

**Solicit orders for goods or services over the telephone.** Contacts customers by phone, by mail, or in person to offer or persuade them to purchase merchandise or services. Delivers merchandise, serves customer, collects money, and makes change. Maintains records of accounts and orders and develops prospect lists. Sets up and displays sample merchandise at parties or stands. Orders or purchases supplies and stocks cart or stand. Distributes product samples or literature that details

products or services. Arranges buying party and solicits sponsorship of parties to sell merchandise. Explains products or services and prices and demonstrates use of products. Writes orders for merchandise or enters order into computer. Circulates among potential customers or travels by foot, truck, automobile, or bicycle to deliver or sell merchandise or services. **SKILLS**—Persuasion. Speaking. Social Perceptiveness. Service Orientation. Mathematics.

GOE—Interest Area: 10. Sales and Marketing. **Work Group:** 10.04. Personal Soliciting. **Other Job Titles in This Work Group:** Demonstrators and Product Promoters; Door-To-Door Sales Workers, News and Street Vendors, and Related Workers. **PERSONALITY TYPE**—Enterprising. Enterprising occupations frequently involve starting up and carrying out projects. These occupations can involve leading people and making many decisions. They sometimes require risk taking and often deal with business.

EDUCATION/TRAINING PROGRAM(S)—General Marketing Operations; General Selling Skills and Sales Operations; Home Products Marketing Operations. **RELATED KNOWLEDGE/COURSES—Sales and Marketing:** Knowledge of principles and methods for showing, promoting, and selling products or services. This includes marketing strategy and tactics, product demonstration, sales techniques, and sales control systems. **Customer and Personal Service:** Knowledge of principles and processes for providing customer and personal services. This includes customer needs assessment, meeting quality standards for services, and evaluation of customer satisfaction. **Economics and Accounting:** Knowledge of economic and accounting principles and practices, the financial markets, banking, and the analysis and reporting of financial data. **English Language:** Knowledge of the structure and content of the English language, including the meaning and spelling of words, rules of composition, and grammar. **Telecommunications:** Knowledge of transmission, broadcasting, switching, control, and operation of telecommunications systems. **Communications and Media:** Knowledge of media production, communication, and dissemination techniques and methods. This includes alternative ways to inform and entertain via written, oral, and visual media. **Mathematics:** Knowledge of arithmetic, algebra, geometry, calculus, statistics, and their applications.

# Tile and Marble Setters

- ▲ Growth: 15.6%
- ▲ Annual Job Openings: 5,000
- ▲ Annual Earnings: $36,580
- ▲ Education/Training Required: Long-term on-the-job training
- ▲ Self-Employed: 49.4%
- ▲ Part-Time: 8.4%

**Apply hard tile, marble, and wood tile to walls, floors, ceilings, and roof decks.** Positions and presses or taps tile with trowel handle to affix tile to plaster or adhesive base. Cuts and shapes tile, using tile cutters and biters. Measures and cuts metal lath to size for walls and ceilings, using tin snips. Installs and anchors fixtures in designated positions, using hand tools. Brushes glue onto manila paper on which design has been drawn and positions tile's finished side down onto paper. Mixes and applies mortar or cement to edges and ends of drain tiles to seal halves and joints. Wipes grout between tiles and removes excess, using wet sponge. Tacks lath to wall and ceiling surfaces, using staple gun or hammer. Selects tile and other items to be installed, such as bathroom accessories, walls, panels, and cabinets, according to specifications. Spreads mastic or other adhesive base on roof deck to form base for promenade tile, using serrated spreader. Measures and marks surfaces to be tiled and lays out work, following blueprints. Cuts tile backing to required size, using shears. Spreads plaster or concrete over surface to form tile base and levels to specified thickness, using brush, trowel and screed. **SKILLS**—Mathematics. Equipment Selection. Installation. Monitoring.

GOE—Interest Area: 06. Construction, Mining, and Drilling. **Work Group:** 06.02. Construction. **Other Job Titles in This Work Group:** Boat Builders and Shipwrights; Boilermakers; Brattice Builders; Brickmasons and Blockmasons; Carpenters; Carpet Installers; Ceiling Tile Installers; Cement Masons and Concrete Finishers;

Commercial Divers; Construction Carpenters; Drywall and Ceiling Tile Installers; Drywall Installers; Electricians; Explosives Workers, Ordnance Handling Experts, and Blasters; Fence Erectors; Floor Layers, Except Carpet, Wood, and Hard Tiles; Floor Sanders and Finishers; Glaziers; Grader, Bulldozer, and Scraper Operators; Hazardous Materials Removal Workers; Insulation Workers, Floor, Ceiling, and Wall; Insulation Workers, Mechanical; Manufactured Building and Mobile Home Installers; Operating Engineers; Operating Engineers and Other Construction Equipment Operators; Painters, Construction and Maintenance; Paperhangers; Paving, Surfacing, and Tamping Equipment Operators; Pile-Driver Operators; Pipe Fitters; Pipelayers; Pipelaying Fitters; Plasterers and Stucco Masons; Plumbers; Plumbers, Pipefitters, and Steamfitters; Rail-Track Laying and Maintenance Equipment Operators; Refractory Materials Repairers, Except Brickmasons; Reinforcing Iron and Rebar Workers; Riggers; Roofers; Rough Carpenters; Security and Fire Alarm Systems Installers; Segmental Pavers; Sheet Metal Workers; Ship Carpenters and Joiners; Stone Cutters and Carvers; Stonemasons; Structural Iron and Steel Workers; Tapers; Terrazzo Workers and Finishers. **PERSONALITY TYPE**—Realistic. Realistic occupations frequently involve work activities that include practical, hands-on problems and solutions. They often deal with plants, animals, and real-world materials like wood, tools, and machinery. Many of the occupations require working outside and do not involve a lot of paperwork or working closely with others.

**EDUCATION/TRAINING PROGRAM(S)**—Construction and Building Finishers and Managers, Other; Mason and Tile Setter. **RELATED KNOWLEDGE/COURSES—Building and Construction:** Knowledge of materials, methods, and tools involved in the construction or repair of houses, buildings, or other structures such as highways and roads. **Mathematics:** Knowledge of arithmetic, algebra, geometry, calculus, statistics, and their applications. **Design:** Knowledge of design techniques, tools, and principles involved in production of precision technical plans, blueprints, drawings, and models. **Principles of Mechanical Devices:** Knowledge of machines and tools, including their designs, uses, repair, and maintenance. **Physics:** Knowledge and prediction of physical principles, laws, and their interrelationships and applications to understanding fluid, material, and atmospheric dynamics and mechanical, electrical, atomic, and sub-atomic structures and processes.

# Tractor-Trailer Truck Drivers

▲ Growth: 19.8%

▲ Annual Job Openings: 240,000

▲ Annual Earnings: $32,810

▲ Education/Training Required: Moderate-term on-the-job training

▲ Self-Employed: 8.2%

▲ Part-Time: 9.9%

**Drive tractor-trailer truck to transport products, livestock, or materials to specified destinations.** Drives tractor-trailer combination, applying knowledge of commercial driving regulations, to transport and deliver products, livestock, or materials, usually over long distance. Maneuvers truck into loading or unloading position, following signals from loading crew as needed. Drives truck to weigh station before and after loading and along route to document weight and conform to state regulations. Maintains driver log according to I.C.C. regulations. Inspects truck before and after trips and submits report indicating truck condition. Reads bill of lading to determine assignment. Fastens chain or binders to secure load on trailer during transit. Loads or unloads or assists in loading and unloading truck. Works as member of two-person team driving tractor with sleeper bunk behind cab. Services truck with oil, fuel, and radiator fluid to maintain tractor-trailer. Obtains customer's signature or collects payment for services. Inventories and inspects goods to be moved.

Wraps goods, using pads, packing paper, and containers, and secures load to trailer wall, using straps. Gives directions to helper in packing and moving goods to trailer. **SKILLS**—Operation and Control. Reading Comprehension. Equipment Maintenance. Writing. Troubleshooting.

**GOE—Interest Area:** 07. Transportation. **Work Group:** 07.05. Truck Driving. **Other Job Titles in This Work Group:** Truck Drivers, Heavy; Truck Drivers, Heavy and Tractor-Trailer; Truck Drivers, Light or Delivery Services. **PERSONALITY TYPE**—Realistic. Realistic occupations frequently involve work activities that include practical, hands-on problems and solutions. They often deal with plants, animals, and real-world materials like wood, tools, and machinery. Many of the occupations require working outside and do not involve a lot of paperwork or working closely with others.

**EDUCATION/TRAINING PROGRAM(S)**—Truck, Bus and Other Commercial Vehicle Operator.

**RELATED KNOWLEDGE/COURSES—Transportation:** Knowledge of principles and methods for moving people or goods by air, rail, sea, or road, including the relative costs and benefits. **Geography:** Knowledge of principles and methods for describing the features of land, sea, and air masses, including their physical characteristics, locations, interrelationships, and distribution of plant, animal, and human life. **Principles of Mechanical Devices:** Knowledge of machines and tools, including their designs, uses, repair, and maintenance. **Law and Government:** Knowledge of laws, legal codes, court procedures, precedents, government regulations, executive orders, agency rules, and the democratic political process. **Public Safety and Security:** Knowledge of relevant equipment, policies, procedures, and strategies to promote effective local, state, or national security operations for the protection of people, data, property, and institutions.

# Transit and Railroad Police

- ▲ Growth: 16.5%
- ▲ Annual Job Openings: Fewer than 500
- ▲ Annual Earnings: $41,560
- ▲ Education/Training Required: Long-term on-the-job training
- ▲ Self-Employed: 0%
- ▲ Part-Time: 6.5%

**Protect and police railroad and transit property, employees, or passengers.** Directs security activities at derailments, fires, floods, and strikes involving railroad property. Examines credentials of unauthorized persons attempting to enter secured areas. Investigates or directs investigations of freight theft, suspicious damage to or loss of passenger's valuables, and other crimes on railroad property. Guards, patrols, and polices railroad yards, cars, stations, and other facilities to protect company property and shipments and to maintain order. Apprehends or coordinates with local enforcement personnel to apprehend or remove trespassers or thieves from rail property. Seals empty boxcars by twisting nails in door hasps, using nail twister. Directs and coordinates the daily activities and training of security staff.

Records and verifies seal numbers from boxcars containing high-pilferage items, such as cigarettes and liquor, to detect tampering. Interviews neighbors, associates, and former employers of job applicants to verify personal references and obtain work history data. Prepares reports documenting the results and activities concerned with investigations. Plans and implements special safety and preventive programs, such as fire and accident prevention. **SKILLS**—Active Listening. Speaking. Coordination. Writing. Critical Thinking.

**GOE—Interest Area:** 04. Law, Law Enforcement, and Public Safety. **Work Group:** 04.03. Law Enforcement. **Other Job Titles in This Work Group:** Animal Control Workers; Bailiffs; Child Support, Missing Persons, and Unemployment Insurance Fraud Investigators; Correctional Officers and Jailers; Criminal Investigators and Special Agents; Crossing Guards; Detectives and Criminal Investigators; Fire Investigators; Fish and Game Wardens; Forensic Science Technicians; Gaming Surveillance Officers and Gaming Investigators; Highway Patrol Pilots; Immigration and Customs Inspectors; Lifeguards, Ski Patrol, and Other Recreational Protective Service Workers; Parking Enforcement Workers; Police and Sheriff's Patrol Officers; Police Detectives; Police Identification and Records Officers; Police Patrol Officers; Private Detectives and Investigators; Security Guards; Sheriffs and Deputy Sheriffs. **PERSONALITY TYPE**—Enterprising. Enterprising occupations frequently involve starting up and carrying out projects. These occupations can involve leading people and making many decisions. They sometimes require risk taking and often deal with business.

**EDUCATION/TRAINING PROGRAM(S)**—Protective Services, Other; Security and Loss Prevention Services. **RELATED KNOWLEDGE/COURSES**— **Public Safety and Security:** Knowledge of relevant equipment, policies, procedures, and strategies to promote effective local, state, or national security operations for the protection of people, data, property, and institutions. **Law and Government:** Knowledge of laws, legal codes, court procedures, precedents, government regulations, executive orders, agency rules, and the democratic political process. **Administration and Management:** Knowledge of business and management principles involved in strategic planning, resource allocation, human resources modeling, leadership technique, production methods, and coordination of people and resources. **English Language:** Knowledge of the structure and content of the English language, including the meaning and spelling of words, rules of composition, and grammar. **Sociology and Anthropology:** Knowledge of group behavior and dynamics, societal trends and influences, human migrations, ethnicity, cultures, and their history and origins. **Clerical Studies:** Knowledge of administrative and clerical procedures and systems such as word processing, managing files and records, stenography and transcription, designing forms, and other office procedures and terminology. **Transportation:** Knowledge of principles and methods for moving people or goods by air, rail, sea, or road, including the relative costs and benefits.

# Transportation Managers

▲ Growth: 20.2%

▲ Annual Job Openings: 13,000

▲ Annual Earnings: $58,200

▲ Education/Training Required: Work experience in a related occupation

▲ Self-Employed: 21.9%

▲ Part-Time: 6.1%

**Plan, direct, and coordinate the transportation operations within an organization or the activities of organizations that provide transportation services.** Directs and coordinates, through subordinates, activities of operations department to obtain use of equipment, facilities, and human resources. Participates in union contract negotiations and settlement of grievances. Negotiates and authorizes contracts with equipment and materials suppliers. Oversees procurement process, including research and testing of equipment, vendor contacts, and approval of requisitions. Inspects or oversees repairs and maintenance to equipment, vehicles, and facilities to enforce standards for safety, efficiency, cleanliness, and appearance. Acts as organization representative before commissions or regulatory bodies during hearings, such as to increase rates and change routes and schedules. Oversees workers assigning tariff classifications and preparing billing according to mode of transportation and destination of shipment. Oversees process of investigation and response to customer or shipper complaints relating to operations department. Recommends or authorizes capital expenditures for acquisition of new equipment or property to increase efficiency and services of operations department. Enforces compliance of operations personnel with administrative policies, procedures, safety rules, and government regulations. Reviews transportation schedules, worker assignments, and routes to ensure compliance with standards for personnel selection, safety, and union contract terms. Conducts investigations in cooperation with government agencies to determine causes of transportation accidents and to improve safety procedures. Prepares management recommendations, such as need for increasing fares, tariffs, or expansion or changes to existing schedules. Oversees activities relating to dispatching, routing, and tracking transportation vehicles, such as aircraft and railroad cars. Analyzes expenditures and other financial reports to develop plans, policies, and budgets for increasing profits and improving services. Confers and cooperates with management and others in formulating and implementing administrative, operational and customer relations, policies and procedures. **SKILLS**—Coordination. Reading Comprehension. Management of Personnel Resources. Management of Material Resources. Judgment and Decision Making.

**GOE—Interest Area:** 07. Transportation. **Work Group:** 07.01. Managerial Work in Transportation. **Other Job Titles in This Work Group:** First-Line Supervisors/Managers of Transportation and Material-Moving Machine and Vehicle Operators; Railroad Conductors and Yardmasters. **PERSONALITY TYPE**—Enterprising. Enterprising occupations frequently involve starting up and carrying out projects. These occupations can involve leading people and making many decisions. They sometimes require risk taking and often deal with business.

**EDUCATION/TRAINING PROGRAM(S)**—Aviation Management; Business Administration and Management, General; General Distribution Operations; Logistics and Materials Management; Public Administration. **RELATED KNOWLEDGE/COURSES**—**Transportation:** Knowledge of principles and methods for moving people or goods by air, rail, sea, or road, including the relative costs and benefits. **Administration and Management:** Knowledge of business and management principles involved in strategic planning, resource allocation, human resources modeling, leadership technique, production methods, and coordination of people and resources. **Mathematics:** Knowledge of arithmetic, algebra, geometry, calculus, statistics, and their applications. **Economics and Accounting:** Knowledge of economic and accounting principles and practices, the financial markets, banking, and the analysis and reporting of financial data. **Personnel and Human Resources:** Knowledge of principles and procedures for personnel recruitment, selection, training, compensation and benefits, labor relations and negotiation, and personnel information systems.

# Travel Clerks

- ▲ Growth: 14.5%
- ▲ Annual Job Openings: 39,000
- ▲ Annual Earnings: $26,140
- ▲ Education/Training Required: Short-term on-the-job training
- ▲ Self-Employed: 5%
- ▲ Part-Time: 31.7%

Provide tourists with travel information, such as points of interest, restaurants, rates, and emergency service. Duties include answering inquiries, offering suggestions, and providing literature pertaining to trips, excursions, sporting events, concerts, and plays. May make reservations, deliver tickets, arrange for visas, or contact individuals and groups to inform them of package tours. Provides customers with travel suggestions and information such as guides, directories, brochures, and maps. Contacts motel, hotel, resort, and travel operators by mail or telephone to obtain advertising literature. Studies maps, directories, routes, and rate tables to determine travel route and cost and availability of accommodations. Calculates estimated travel rates and expenses, using items such as rate tables and calculators. Informs client of travel dates, times, connections, baggage limits, medical and visa requirements, and emergency information. Obtains reservations for air, train, or car travel and hotel or other housing accommodations. Confirms travel arrangements and reservations. Assists client in preparing required documents and forms for travel, such as visas. Plans itinerary for travel and accommodations, using knowledge of routes, types of carriers, and regulations. Provides information concerning fares, availability of travel, and accommodations, either orally or by using guides, brochures, and maps. Confers with customers by telephone, writing, or in person to answer questions regarding services and determine travel preferences. **SKILLS**—Service Orientation. Active Listening. Speaking. Reading Comprehension. Writing. Mathematics. Coordination.

**GOE**—**Interest Area:** 09. Business Detail. **Work Group:** 09.05. Customer Service. **Other Job Titles in This Work Group:** Adjustment Clerks; Bill and Account Collectors; Cashiers; Counter and Rental Clerks; Customer Service Representatives; Customer Service Representatives, Utilities; Gaming Cage Workers; Gaming Change Persons and Booth Cashiers; New Accounts Clerks; Order Clerks; Receptionists and Information Clerks; Tellers. **PERSONALITY TYPE**—Conventional. Conventional occupations frequently involve following set procedures and routines. These occupations can include working with data and details more than with ideas. Usually there is a clear line of authority to follow.

**EDUCATION/TRAINING PROGRAM(S)**—Tourism and Travel Services Marketing Operations, Other; Tourism Promotion Operations; Travel Services Marketing Operations. **RELATED KNOWLEDGE/ COURSES**—**Customer and Personal Service:** Knowledge of principles and processes for providing customer and personal services. This includes customer needs assessment, meeting quality standards for services, and evaluation of customer satisfaction. **Geography:** Knowledge of principles and methods for describing the features of land, sea, and air masses, including their physical characteristics, locations, interrelationships, and distribution of plant, animal, and human life. **Transportation:** Knowledge of principles and methods for moving people or goods by air, rail, sea, or road, including the relative costs and benefits. **Mathematics:** Knowledge of arithmetic, algebra, geometry, calculus, statistics, and their applications. **Telecommunications:** Knowledge of transmission, broadcasting, switching, control, and operation of telecommunications systems.

# Travel Guides

- ▲ Growth: 9.5%
- ▲ Annual Job Openings: 10,000
- ▲ Annual Earnings: $30,990
- ▲ Education/Training Required: Moderate-term on-the-job training
- ▲ Self-Employed: 13.9%
- ▲ Part-Time: 31.7%

**Plan, organize, and conduct long-distance cruises, tours, and expeditions for individuals and groups.** Plans tour itinerary, applying knowledge of travel routes and destination sites. Explains hunting and fishing laws to group to ensure compliance. Sells or rents equipment, clothing, and supplies. Administers first aid to injured group participants. Pilots airplane or drives land and water vehicles to transport tourists to activity/tour site. Pitches camp and prepares meals for tour group members. Arranges for transportation, accommodations, activity equipment, and services of medical personnel. Verifies quantity and quality of equipment to ensure prerequisite needs for expeditions and tours have been met. Instructs novices in climbing techniques, mountaineering, and wilderness survival and demonstrates use of hunting, fishing, and climbing equipment. Obtains or assists tourists to obtain permits and documents, such as visas, passports, and health certificates, and to convert currency. Selects activity tour sites and leads individuals or groups to location and describes points of interest. **SKILLS**—Service Orientation. Coordination. Active Listening. Management of Material Resources. Instructing. Time Management. Operation and Control.

**GOE—Interest Area:** 11. Recreation, Travel, and Other Personal Services. **Work Group:** 11.02. Recreational Services. **Other Job Titles in This Work Group:** Amusement and Recreation Attendants; Entertainment Attendants and Related Workers, All Other; Gaming and Sports Book Writers and Runners; Gaming Dealers; Gaming Service Workers, All Other; Motion Picture Projectionists; Recreation Workers; Slot Key Persons; Tour Guides and Escorts; Ushers, Lobby Attendants, and Ticket Takers. **PERSONALITY TYPE**—Enterprising. Enterprising occupations frequently involve starting up and carrying out projects. These occupations can involve leading people and making many decisions. They some-

times require risk taking and often deal with business.

**EDUCATION/TRAINING PROGRAM(S)**—Hospitality and Recreation Marketing Operations, General. **RELATED KNOWLEDGE/COURSES—Customer and Personal Service:** Knowledge of principles and processes for providing customer and personal services. This includes customer needs assessment, meeting quality standards for services, and evaluation of customer satisfaction. **Transportation:** Knowledge of principles and methods for moving people or goods by air, rail, sea, or road, including the relative costs and benefits. **Geography:** Knowledge of principles and methods for describing the features of land, sea, and air masses, including their physical characteristics, locations, interrelationships, and distribution of plant, animal, and human life. **English Language:** Knowledge of the structure and content of the English language, including the meaning and spelling of words, rules of composition, and grammar. **Communications and Media:** Knowledge of media production, communication, and dissemination techniques and methods. This includes alternative ways to inform and entertain via written, oral, and visual media.

# Tree Trimmers and Pruners

- ▲ Growth: 16.3%
- ▲ Annual Job Openings: 11,000
- ▲ Annual Earnings: $25,590
- ▲ Education/Training Required: Short-term on-the-job training
- ▲ Self-Employed: 14.2%
- ▲ Part-Time: 25.4%

**Cut away dead or excess branches from trees or shrubs to maintain right-of-way for roads, sidewalks, or utilities or to improve appearance, health, and value of tree. Prune or treat trees or shrubs using handsaws, pruning hooks, sheers, and clippers. May use truck-mounted lifts and power pruners. May fill cavities in trees to promote healing and prevent deterioration.** Cuts away dead and excess branches from trees, using handsaws, pruning hooks, sheers, and clippers. Climbs trees, using climbing hooks and belts, or climbs ladders to gain access to work area. Prunes, cuts down, fertil-

izes, and sprays trees as directed by tree surgeon. Uses truck-mounted hydraulic lifts and pruners and power pruners. Scrapes decayed matter from cavities in trees and fills holes with cement to promote healing and to prevent further deterioration. Applies tar or other protective substances to cut surfaces to seal surfaces against insects. **SKILLS**—Operation and Control.

**GOE—Interest Area:** 03. Plants and Animals. **Work Group:** 03.03. Hands-on Work in Plants and Animals. **Other Job Titles in This Work Group:** Agricultural

Equipment Operators; Fallers; Farmworkers and Laborers, Crop, Nursery, and Greenhouse; Farmworkers, Farm and Ranch Animals; Fishers and Related Fishing Workers; Forest and Conservation Technicians; Forest and Conservation Workers; General Farmworkers; Grounds Maintenance Workers, All Other; Hunters and Trappers; Landscaping and Groundskeeping Workers; Logging Equipment Operators; Logging Tractor Operators; Logging Workers, All Other; Nursery Workers; Pest Control Workers; Pesticide Handlers, Sprayers, and Applicators, Vegetation. **PERSONALITY TYPE—** Realistic. Realistic occupations frequently involve work activities that include practical, hands-on problems and solutions. They often deal with plants, animals, and real-world materials like wood, tools, and machinery. Many of the occupations require working outside and do not

involve a lot of paperwork or working closely with others.

**EDUCATION/TRAINING PROGRAM(S)—**Horticulture Services Operations and Management, Other. **RELATED KNOWLEDGE/COURSES—Principles of Mechanical Devices:** Knowledge of machines and tools, including their designs, uses, repair, and maintenance. **Biology:** Knowledge of plant and animal organisms and their tissues, cells, functions, interdependencies, and interactions with each other and the environment. **Chemistry:** Knowledge of the chemical composition, structure, and properties of substances and of the chemical processes and transformations that they undergo. This includes uses of chemicals and their interactions, danger signs, production techniques, and disposal methods.

# Truck Drivers, Heavy

- ▲ Growth: 19.8%
- ▲ Annual Job Openings: 240,000
- ▲ Annual Earnings: $32,810
- ▲ Education/Training Required: Moderate-term on-the-job training
- ▲ Self-Employed: 8.2%
- ▲ Part-Time: 9.9%

**Drive truck with capacity of more than three tons to transport materials to specified destinations.** Drives truck with capacity of more than three tons to transport and deliver cargo, materials, or damaged vehicle. Maintains radio or telephone contact with base or supervisor to receive instructions or be dispatched to new location. Maintains truck log according to state and federal regulations. Keeps record of materials and products transported. Position blocks and ties rope around items to secure cargo for transport. Cleans, inspects, and services vehicle. Operates equipment on vehicle to load, unload, or disperse cargo or materials. Obtains customer signature or collects payment for goods delivered and delivery charges. Assists in loading and unloading truck manually. **SKILLS—**Equipment Maintenance. Operation and Control. Operation Monitoring. Reading Comprehension. Writing.

**GOE—Interest Area:** 07. Transportation. **Work Group:** 07.05. Truck Driving. **Other Job Titles in This Work Group:** Tractor-Trailer Truck Drivers; Truck Drivers, Heavy and Tractor-Trailer; Truck Drivers, Light or Delivery Services. **PERSONALITY TYPE—**Realistic. Realistic occupations frequently involve work activities that include practical, hands-on problems and solutions. They often deal with plants, animals, and real-world materials like wood, tools, and machinery. Many of the occupations require working outside and do not involve a lot of paperwork or working closely with others.

**EDUCATION/TRAINING PROGRAM(S)—**Truck, Bus and Other Commercial Vehicle Operator. **RELATED KNOWLEDGE/COURSES—Transportation:** Knowledge of principles and methods for moving people or goods by air, rail, sea, or road, including the relative costs and benefits. **Geography:** Knowledge of principles and methods for describing the features of land, sea, and air masses, including their physical characteristics, locations, interrelationships, and distribution of plant, animal, and human life. **Principles of Mechanical Devices:** Knowledge of machines and tools, including their designs, uses, repair, and maintenance. **Clerical Studies:** Knowledge of administrative and clerical procedures and systems such as word processing, managing files and records, stenography and transcrip-

tion, designing forms, and other office procedures and terminology. **Public Safety and Security:** Knowledge of relevant equipment, policies, procedures, and strategies to promote effective local, state, or national security operations for the protection of people, data, property, and institutions. **Law and Government:** Knowledge of laws, legal codes, court procedures, precedents, government regulations, executive orders, agency rules, and the democratic political process.

# Truck Drivers, Light or Delivery Services

- ▲ Growth: 19.2%
- ▲ Annual Job Openings: 153,000
- ▲ Annual Earnings: $24,620
- ▲ Education/Training Required: Short-term on-the-job training
- ▲ Self-Employed: 8.9%
- ▲ Part-Time: 9.9%

**Drive a truck or van with a capacity of under 26,000 GVW, primarily to deliver or pick up merchandise or to deliver packages within a specified area. May require use of automatic routing or location software. May load and unload truck.** Drives truck, van, or automobile with capacity under three tons to transport materials, products, or people. Loads and unloads truck, van, or automobile. Communicates with base or other vehicles using telephone or radio. Maintains records such as vehicle log, record of cargo, or billing statements in accordance with regulations. Inspects and maintains vehicle equipment and supplies. Presents billing invoice and collects receipt or payment. Performs emergency roadside repairs. **SKILLS**—Equipment Maintenance. Operation and Control. Repairing. Operation Monitoring. Reading Comprehension. Writing.

**GOE**—**Interest Area:** 07. Transportation. **Work Group:** 07.05. Truck Driving. **Other Job Titles in This Work Group:** Tractor-Trailer Truck Drivers; Truck Drivers, Heavy; Truck Drivers, Heavy and Tractor-Trailer. **PERSONALITY TYPE**—Realistic. Realistic occupations frequently involve work activities that include practical, hands-on problems and solutions. They often deal with plants, animals, and real-world materials like wood,

tools, and machinery. Many of the occupations require working outside and do not involve a lot of paperwork or working closely with others.

**EDUCATION/TRAINING PROGRAM(S)**—Truck, Bus and Other Commercial Vehicle Operator. **RELATED KNOWLEDGE/COURSES**—**Transportation:** Knowledge of principles and methods for moving people or goods by air, rail, sea, or road, including the relative costs and benefits. **Principles of Mechanical Devices:** Knowledge of machines and tools, including their designs, uses, repair, and maintenance. **Geography:** Knowledge of principles and methods for describing the features of land, sea, and air masses, including their physical characteristics, locations, interrelationships, and distribution of plant, animal, and human life. **Public Safety and Security:** Knowledge of relevant equipment, policies, procedures, and strategies to promote effective local, state, or national security operations for the protection of people, data, property, and institutions. **Clerical Studies:** Knowledge of administrative and clerical procedures and systems such as word processing, managing files and records, stenography and transcription, designing forms, and other office procedures and terminology.

# Veterinary Technologists and Technicians

- ▲ Growth: 39.3%
- ▲ Annual Job Openings: 6,000
- ▲ Annual Earnings: $22,730
- ▲ Education/Training Required: Associate's degree
- ▲ Self-Employed: 0%
- ▲ Part-Time: 11.7%

Perform medical tests in a laboratory environment for use in the treatment and diagnosis of diseases in animals. Prepare vaccines and serums for prevention of diseases. Prepare tissue samples, take blood samples, and execute laboratory tests, such as urinalysis and blood counts. Clean and sterilize instruments and materials and maintain equipment and machines. **SKILLS**—No data available.

**GOE—Interest Area:** 03. Plants and Animals. **Work Group:** 03.02. Animal Care and Training. **Other Job**

**Titles in This Work Group:** Animal Breeders; Animal Trainers; Nonfarm Animal Caretakers; Veterinarians; Veterinary Assistants and Laboratory Animal Caretakers. **PERSONALITY TYPE**—No data available.

**EDUCATION/TRAINING PROGRAM(S)**—Veterinarian Assistant/Animal Health Technician. **RELATED KNOWLEDGE/COURSES**—No data available.

# Waiters and Waitresses

- ▲ Growth: 18.3%
- ▲ Annual Job Openings: 596,000
- ▲ Annual Earnings: $14,750
- ▲ Education/Training Required: Short-term on-the-job training
- ▲ Self-Employed: 0.2%
- ▲ Part-Time: 57%

**Take orders and serve food and beverages to patrons at tables in dining establishment.** Takes order from patron for food or beverage, writing order down or memorizing it. Observes patrons to respond to additional requests and to determine when meal has been completed or beverage consumed. Presents menu to patron, suggests food or beverage selections, and answers questions regarding preparation and service. Obtains and replenishes supplies of food, tableware, and linen. Computes cost of meal or beverage. Serves, or assists patrons to serve themselves, at buffet or smorgasbord table. Serves meals or beverages to patrons. Relays order to kitchen or enters order into computer.

Accepts payment and returns change or refers patron to Cashier. Removes dishes and glasses from table or counter and takes them to kitchen for cleaning. Prepares hot, cold, and mixed drinks for patrons and chills bottles of wine. Cleans and arranges assigned station, including side stands, chairs, and table pieces, such as linen, silverware, and glassware. Prepares salads, appetizers, and cold dishes, portions desserts, brews coffee, and performs other services as determined by establishment's size and practices. Fills salt, pepper, sugar, cream, condiment, and napkin containers. Carves meats, bones fish and fowl, and prepares special dishes and desserts at work station or patron's table. Garnishes and decorates dishes preparatory to serving. **SKILLS**—Active Listening. Service Orientation. Mathematics. Monitoring. Social Perceptiveness.

**GOE—Interest Area:** 11. Recreation, Travel, and Other Personal Services. **Work Group:** 11.05. Food and Beverage Services. **Other Job Titles in This Work Group:** Bakers; Bakers, Bread and Pastry; Bartenders; Butchers and Meat Cutters; Chefs and Head Cooks; Combined Food Preparation and Serving Workers, Including Fast Food; Cooks, All Other; Cooks, Fast Food; Cooks, Institution and Cafeteria; Cooks, Restaurant; Cooks, Short Order; Counter Attendants, Cafeteria, Food Concession, and Coffee Shop; Dining Room and Cafeteria Attendants and Bartender Helpers; Dishwashers; Food Preparation and Serving Related Workers, All Other; Food Preparation Workers; Food Servers, Nonrestaurant; Hosts and Hostesses, Restaurant, Lounge, and Coffee Shop. **PERSONALITY TYPE**—Social. Social occupations frequently involve working with, communicating with, and teaching people. These occupations often involve helping or providing service to others.

**EDUCATION/TRAINING PROGRAM(S)**—Waiter/Waitress and Dining Room Manager. **RELATED KNOWLEDGE/COURSES—Customer and Personal Service:** Knowledge of principles and processes for providing customer and personal services. This includes customer needs assessment, meeting quality standards for services, and evaluation of customer satisfaction. **Mathematics:** Knowledge of arithmetic, algebra, geometry, calculus, statistics, and their applications. **English Language:** Knowledge of the structure and content of the English language, including the meaning and spelling of words, rules of composition, and grammar. **Sales and Marketing:** Knowledge of principles and methods for showing, promoting, and selling products or services. This includes marketing strategy and tactics, product demonstration, sales techniques, and sales control systems. **Psychology:** Knowledge of human behavior and performance; individual differences in ability, personality, and interests; learning and motivation; psychological research methods; and the assessment and treatment of behavioral and affective disorders.

# Water and Liquid Waste Treatment Plant and System Operators

- ▲ Growth: 18.1%
- ▲ Annual Job Openings: 6,000
- ▲ Annual Earnings: $32,450
- ▲ Education/Training Required: Long-term on-the-job training
- ▲ Self-Employed: 0%
- ▲ Part-Time: 1.8%

**Operate or control an entire process or system of machines, often through the use of control boards, to transfer or treat water or liquid waste.** Operates and adjusts controls on equipment to purify and clarify water, process or dispose of sewage, and generate power. Collects and tests water and sewage samples, using test equipment and color analysis standards. Cleans and maintains tanks and filter beds, using hand tools and power tools. Directs and coordinates plant workers engaged in routine operations and maintenance activities. Maintains, repairs, and lubricates equipment, using hand tools and power tools. Records operational data, personnel attendance, and meter and gauge readings on specified forms. Inspects equipment and monitors operating conditions, meters, and gauges to determine load requirements and detect malfunctions. Adds chemicals, such as ammonia, chlorine, and lime, to disinfect and deodorize water and other liquids. **SKILLS**—Operation and Control. Operation Monitoring. Science. Reading Comprehension. Critical Thinking. Mathematics. Quality Control Analysis.

**GOE—Interest Area:** 08. Industrial Production. **Work Group:** 08.06. Systems Operation. **Other Job Titles in This Work Group:** Auxiliary Equipment Operators,

Power; Boiler Operators and Tenders, Low Pressure; Chemical Plant and System Operators; Gas Compressor and Gas Pumping Station Operators; Gas Compressor Operators; Gas Distribution Plant Operators; Gas Plant Operators; Gas Processing Plant Operators; Gas Pumping Station Operators; Gaugers; Nuclear Power Reactor Operators; Petroleum Pump System Operators; Petroleum Pump System Operators, Refinery Operators, and Gaugers; Petroleum Refinery and Control Panel Operators; Plant and System Operators, All Other; Power Distributors and Dispatchers; Power Generating Plant Operators, Except Auxiliary Equipment Operators; Power Plant Operators; Ship Engineers; Stationary Engineers; Stationary Engineers and Boiler Operators; Wellhead Pumpers. **PERSONALITY TYPE**—Realistic. Realistic occupations frequently involve work activities that include practical, hands-on problems and solutions. They often deal with plants, animals, and real-world materials like wood, tools, and machinery. Many of the occupations require working outside and do not involve a lot of paperwork or working closely with others.

**EDUCATION/TRAINING PROGRAM(S)**—Water Quality and Wastewater Treatment Technologist/Technician. **RELATED KNOWLEDGE/COURSES**— **Chemistry:** Knowledge of the chemical composition, structure, and properties of substances and of the chemical processes and transformations that they undergo. This includes uses of chemicals and their interactions, danger signs, production techniques, and disposal methods. **Principles of Mechanical Devices:** Knowledge of machines and tools, including their designs, uses, repair, and maintenance. **Production and Processing:** Knowledge of raw materials, production processes, quality control, costs, and other techniques for maximizing the effective manufacture and distribution of goods. **Mathematics:** Knowledge of arithmetic, algebra, geometry, calculus, statistics, and their applications. **Clerical Studies:** Knowledge of administrative and clerical procedures and systems such as word processing, managing files and records, stenography and transcription, designing forms, and other office procedures and terminology.

# Weighers, Measurers, Checkers, and Samplers, Recordkeeping

- ▲ Growth: 17.9%
- ▲ Annual Job Openings: 13,000
- ▲ Annual Earnings: $26,250
- ▲ Education/Training Required: Short-term on-the-job training
- ▲ Self-Employed: 0%
- ▲ Part-Time: 16.2%

**Weigh, measure, and check materials, supplies, and equipment for the purpose of keeping relevant records. Duties are primarily clerical by nature.** Weighs or measures materials or products, using volume meters, scales, rules, and calipers. Compares product labels, tags, or tickets; shipping manifests; purchase orders; and bills of lading to verify that the contents, quantity, or weight of shipments is accurate. Removes products or loads not meeting quality standards from stock and notifies supervisor or appropriate department of discrepancy or shortage. Transports materials, products, or samples to processing, shipping, or storage areas manually or by using conveyors, pumps, or handtrucks. Unloads or

unpacks incoming shipments or arranges, packs, or prepares materials and products for display, distribution, outgoing shipment, or storage. Fills orders for products and samples, following order tickets, and forwards or mails items. Collects and prepares product samples for laboratory analysis or testing. Maintains perpetual inventory of samples and replenishes stock to maintain required levels. Sorts products or materials into predetermined sequence or groupings for packing, shipping, or storage. Prepares measurement tables and conversion charts, using standard formulae. Computes product totals and charges for shipments, using calculator. Works with, signals, or instructs other workers to weigh, move, or check products. Communicates with customers and vendors to exchange information regarding products, materials, and services. Operates or tends machines to clean or sanitize equipment or manually washes equipment, using detergent, brushes, and hoses. Collects fees and issues receipts for payments. Examines blueprints and prepares plans, layouts, or drawings of facility or finished products to identify storage locations or verify parts assemblies. Collects, prepares, or attaches measurement, weight, or identification labels or tickets to products. Documents quantity, quality, type, weight, and value of materials or products to maintain shipping, receiving, and production records and files. Examines products or materials, parts, and subassemblies for damage, defects, or shortages, using specification sheets, gauges, and standards charts. Counts or estimates quantities of materials, parts, or products received or shipped. **SKILLS**—Operation and Control. Mathematics. Equipment Selection. Operation Monitoring. Coordination. Reading Comprehension.

**GOE—Interest Area:** 09. Business Detail. **Work Group:** 09.08. Records and Materials Processing. **Other Job Titles in This Work Group:** Cargo and Freight Agents; Couriers and Messengers; Mail Clerks, Except Mail Machine Operators and Postal Service; Marking Clerks; Order Fillers, Wholesale and Retail Sales; Postal Service Mail Carriers; Postal Service Mail Sorters, Proces-sors, and Processing Machine Operators; Shipping, Receiving, and Traffic Clerks; Stock Clerks and Order Fillers; Stock Clerks—Stockroom, Warehouse, or Storage Yard. **PERSONALITY TYPE**—Conventional. Conventional occupations frequently involve following set procedures and routines. These occupations can include working with data and details more than with ideas. Usually there is a clear line of authority to follow.

**EDUCATION/TRAINING PROGRAM(S)**—General Office/Clerical and Typing Services. **RELATED KNOWLEDGE/COURSES—Clerical Studies:** Knowledge of administrative and clerical procedures and systems such as word processing, managing files and records, stenography and transcription, designing forms, and other office procedures and terminology. **Mathematics:** Knowledge of arithmetic, algebra, geometry, calculus, statistics, and their applications. **Production and Processing:** Knowledge of raw materials, production processes, quality control, costs, and other techniques for maximizing the effective manufacture and distribution of goods. **Transportation:** Knowledge of principles and methods for moving people or goods by air, rail, sea, or road, including the relative costs and benefits. **Design:** Knowledge of design techniques, tools, and principles involved in production of precision technical plans, blueprints, drawings, and models.

# Welder-Fitters

- ▲ Growth: 19.3%
- ▲ Annual Job Openings: 51,000
- ▲ Annual Earnings: $29,080
- ▲ Education/Training Required: Post-secondary vocational training
- ▲ Self-Employed: 5.8%
- ▲ Part-Time: 2.6%

Lay out, fit, and fabricate metal components to assemble structural forms, such as machinery frames, bridge parts, and pressure vessels, using knowledge of welding techniques, metallurgy, and engineering requirements. Includes experimental welders who analyze engineering drawings and specifications to plan welding operations where procedural information is **unavailable.** Lays out, positions, and secures parts and assemblies according to specifications, using straightedge, combination square, calipers, and ruler. Tack-welds or welds components and assemblies, using electric, gas, arc, or other welding equipment. Cuts workpiece, using powered saws, hand shears, or chipping knife. Melts lead bar, wire, or scrap to add lead to joint or to extrude melted scrap into reusable form. Installs or repairs equipment, such as lead pipes, valves, floors, and tank linings. Observes tests on welded surfaces, such as hydrostatic, X-ray, and dimension tolerance, to evaluate weld quality and conformance to specifications. Inspects grooves, angles, or gap allowances, using micrometer, caliper, and precision measuring instruments. Removes rough spots from workpiece, using portable grinder, hand file, or scraper. Welds components in flat, vertical, or overhead positions. Heats, forms, and dresses metal parts, using hand tools, torch, or arc welding equipment. Ignites torch and adjusts valves, amperage, or voltage to obtain desired flame or arc. Analyzes engineering drawings and specifications to plan layout, assembly, and welding operations. Develops templates and other work aids to hold and align parts. Determines required equipment and welding method, applying knowledge of metallurgy, geometry, and welding techniques. **SKILLS**—Mathematics. Equipment Selection. Repairing. Equipment Maintenance. Quality Control Analysis.

**GOE—Interest Area:** 08. Industrial Production. **Work Group:** 08.03. Production Work. **Other Job Titles in This Work Group:** Bakers, Manufacturing; Bindery Machine Operators and Tenders; Brazers; Cementing and Gluing Machine Operators and Tenders; Chemical Equipment Controllers and Operators; Chemical Equipment Operators and Tenders; Chemical Equipment Tenders; Cleaning, Washing, and Metal Pickling Equipment Operators and Tenders; Coating, Painting, and Spraying Machine Operators and Tenders; Coil Winders, Tapers, and Finishers; Combination Machine Tool Operators and Tenders, Metal and Plastic; Computer-Controlled Machine Tool Operators, Metal and Plastic; Cooling and Freezing Equipment Operators and Tenders; Crushing, Grinding, and Polishing Machine Setters, Operators, and Tenders; Cutters and Trimmers, Hand; Cutting and Slicing Machine Operators and Tenders; Cutting and Slicing Machine Setters, Operators, and Tenders; Design Printing Machine Setters and Set-Up Operators; Electrolytic Plating and Coating Machine Operators and Tenders, Metal and Plastic; Electrolytic Plating and Coating Machine Setters and Set-Up Operators, Metal and Plastic; Electrotypers and Stereotypers; Embossing Machine Set-Up Operators; Engraver Set-Up Operators; Extruding and Forming Machine Operators and Tenders, Synthetic or Glass Fibers; Extruding and Forming Machine Setters, Operators, and Tenders, Synthetic and Glass Fibers; Extruding, Forming, Pressing, and Compacting Machine Operators and Tenders; Fabric and Apparel Patternmakers; Fiber Product Cutting Machine Setters and Set-Up Operators; Fiberglass Laminators and Fabricators; others. **PERSONALITY TYPE**—Realistic. Realistic occupations frequently involve work activities that include practical, hands-on problems and solutions. They often deal with plants, animals, and real-world materials like wood, tools, and machinery. Many of the occupations require working outside and do not involve a lot of paperwork or working closely with others.

**EDUCATION/TRAINING PROGRAM(S)—** Welder/Welding Technologist. **RELATED KNOWLEDGE/COURSES—Principles of Mechanical Devices:** Knowledge of machines and tools, including their designs, uses, repair, and maintenance. **Design:** Knowledge of design techniques, tools, and principles involved in production of precision technical plans, blueprints, drawings, and models. **Engineering and Technology:** Knowledge of the practical application of engineering science and technology. This includes applying principles, techniques, procedures, and equipment to the design and production of various goods and services. **Building and Construction:** Knowledge of materials, methods, and tools involved in the construction or repair of houses, buildings, or other structures such as highways and roads. **Production and Processing:** Knowledge of raw materials, production processes, quality control, costs, and other techniques for maximizing the effective manufacture and distribution of goods.

# Welders and Cutters

- ▲ Growth: 19.3%
- ▲ Annual Job Openings: 51,000
- ▲ Annual Earnings: $29,080
- ▲ Education/Training Required: Post-secondary vocational training
- ▲ Self-Employed: 5.8%
- ▲ Part-Time: 2.6%

**Use hand welding and flame-cutting equipment to weld together metal components and parts or to cut, trim, or scarf metal objects to dimensions as specified by layouts, work orders, or blueprints.** Welds metal parts or components together, using brazing, gas, or arc-welding equipment. Repairs broken or cracked parts, fills holes, and increases size of metal parts, using welding equipment. Welds in flat, horizontal, vertical, or overhead position. Cleans or degreases parts, using wire brush, portable grinder, or chemical bath. Inspects finished workpiece for conformance to specifications. Chips or grinds off excess weld, slag, or spatter, using hand scraper or power chipper, portable grinder, or arc-cutting equipment. Positions workpieces and clamps together or assembles in jigs or fixtures. Preheats workpiece, using hand torch or heating furnace. Ignites torch or starts power supply and strikes arc. Reviews layouts, blueprints, diagrams, or work orders in preparation for welding or cutting metal components. Selects and inserts electrode or gas nozzle into holder and connects hoses and cables to obtain gas or specified amperage, voltage, or polarity. Connects and turns regulator valves to activate and adjust gas flow and pressure to obtain desired flame. Selects and installs torch, torch tip, filler rod, and flux according to welding chart specifications or type and thickness of metal. Guides electrodes or torch along weld line at specified speed and angle to weld, melt, cut, or trim metal. **SKILLS—**Operation Monitoring. Operation and Control. Mathematics. Equipment Selection. Equipment Maintenance.

**GOE—Interest Area:** 08. Industrial Production. **Work Group:** 08.03. Production Work. **Other Job Titles in This Work Group:** Bakers, Manufacturing; Bindery Machine Operators and Tenders; Brazers; Cementing and Gluing Machine Operators and Tenders; Chemical Equipment Controllers and Operators; Chemical Equipment Operators and Tenders; Chemical Equipment Tenders; Cleaning, Washing, and Metal Pickling Equipment Operators and Tenders; Coating, Painting, and Spraying Machine Operators and Tenders; Coil Winders, Tapers, and Finishers; Combination Machine Tool Operators and Tenders, Metal and Plastic; Computer-Controlled Machine Tool Operators, Metal and Plastic; Cooling and Freezing Equipment Operators and Tenders; Crushing, Grinding, and Polishing Machine Setters, Operators, and Tenders; Cutters and Trimmers, Hand; Cutting and Slicing Machine Operators and Tenders; Cutting and Slicing Machine Setters, Operators, and Tenders; Design Printing Machine Setters and Set-Up Operators; Electrolytic Plating and Coating Machine Operators and Tenders, Metal and Plastic; Electrolytic Plating and Coating Machine Setters and Set-Up Operators, Metal and Plastic; Electrotypers and Stereotypers; Embossing Machine Set-Up Operators; Engraver Set-Up Operators; Extruding and Forming Machine Operators and Tenders, Synthetic or Glass Fibers; Extruding and Forming Machine Setters, Operators, and Tenders, Synthetic and Glass Fibers; Extruding, Forming, Pressing, and Compacting Machine Operators and Tenders; Fabric and Apparel Patternmakers; Fiber Product Cutting Machine Setters and Set-Up Operators; Fiberglass Laminators and Fabricators; others. **PERSONALITY TYPE—**Realistic. Realistic occupations frequently involve work activities that include practical, hands-on problems and solutions. They often deal with plants, animals, and real-world materials like wood, tools, and machinery. Many of the occupations require working outside and do not involve a lot of paperwork or working closely with others.

EDUCATION/TRAINING PROGRAM(S)—
Welder/Welding Technologist. **RELATED KNOWL-
EDGE/COURSES—Principles of Mechanical
Devices:** Knowledge of machines and tools, including
their designs, uses, repair, and maintenance. **Building
and Construction:** Knowledge of materials, methods,
and tools involved in the construction or repair of
houses, buildings, or other structures such as highways
and roads. **Production and Processing:** Knowledge of
raw materials, production processes, quality control,
costs, and other techniques for maximizing the effective manufacture and distribution of goods. **Design:**
Knowledge of design techniques, tools, and principles
involved in production of precision technical plans,
blueprints, drawings, and models. **Physics:** Knowledge
and prediction of physical principles and laws and their
interrelationships and applications to understanding
fluid, material, and atmospheric dynamics and mechanical, electrical, atomic, and sub-atomic structures and
processes. **Mathematics:** Knowledge of arithmetic, algebra, geometry, calculus, statistics, and their applications. **Engineering and Technology:** Knowledge of the
practical application of engineering science and technology. This includes applying principles, techniques,
procedures, and equipment to the design and production of various goods and services.

# Welders, Production

- ▲ Growth: 19.3%
- ▲ Annual Job Openings: 51,000
- ▲ Annual Earnings: $29,080
- ▲ Education/Training Required: Post-
  secondary vocational training
- ▲ Self-Employed: 5.8%
- ▲ Part-Time: 2.6%

**Assemble and weld metal parts on production line,
using welding equipment requiring only a limited
knowledge of welding techniques.** Welds or tack welds
metal parts together, using spot welding gun or hand,
electric, or gas welding equipment. Connects hoses from
torch to tanks of oxygen and fuel gas and turns valves
to release mixture. Ignites torch and regulates flow of
gas and air to obtain desired temperature, size, and color
of flame. Preheats workpieces preparatory to welding
or bending, using torch. Fills cavities or corrects mal-
formation in lead parts and hammers out bulges and
bends in metal workpieces. Examines workpiece for
defects and measures workpiece with straightedge or
template to ensure conformance with specifications.
Climbs ladders or works on scaffolds to disassemble
structures. Signals crane operator to move large
workpieces. Dismantles metal assemblies or cuts scrap
metal, using thermal-cutting equipment, such as flame-
cutting torch or plasma-arc equipment. Positions and
secures workpiece, using hoist, crane, wire and banding machine, or hand tools. Selects, positions, and secures torch, cutting tips, or welding rod, according to
type, thickness, area, and desired temperature of metal.
Guides and directs flame or electrodes on or across
workpiece to straighten, bend, melt, or build up metal.
Fuses parts together, seals tension points, and adds metal
to build up parts. **SKILLS—**Operation and Control.
Operation Monitoring. Equipment Selection. Equipment Maintenance. Mathematics.

**GOE—Interest Area:** 08. Industrial Production. **Work
Group:** 08.03. Production Work. **Other Job Titles in
This Work Group:** Bakers, Manufacturing; Bindery
Machine Operators and Tenders; Brazers; Cementing
and Gluing Machine Operators and Tenders; Chemi-
cal Equipment Controllers and Operators; Chemical
Equipment Operators and Tenders; Chemical Equip-
ment Tenders; Cleaning, Washing, and Metal Pickling
Equipment Operators and Tenders; Coating, Painting,
and Spraying Machine Operators and Tenders; Coil
Winders, Tapers, and Finishers; Combination Machine
Tool Operators and Tenders, Metal and Plastic; Com-

puter-Controlled Machine Tool Operators, Metal and Plastic; Cooling and Freezing Equipment Operators and Tenders; Crushing, Grinding, and Polishing Machine Setters, Operators, and Tenders; Cutters and Trimmers, Hand; Cutting and Slicing Machine Operators and Tenders; Cutting and Slicing Machine Setters, Operators, and Tenders; Design Printing Machine Setters and Set-Up Operators; Electrolytic Plating and Coating Machine Operators and Tenders, Metal and Plastic; Electrolytic Plating and Coating Machine Setters and Set-Up Operators, Metal and Plastic; Electrotypers and Stereotypers; Embossing Machine Set-Up Operators; Engraver Set-Up Operators; Extruding and Forming Machine Operators and Tenders, Synthetic or Glass Fibers; Extruding and Forming Machine Setters, Operators, and Tenders, Synthetic and Glass Fibers; Extruding, Forming, Pressing, and Compacting Machine Operators and Tenders; Fabric and Apparel Patternmakers; Fiber Product Cutting Machine Setters and Set-Up Operators; Fiberglass Laminators and Fabricators; others. **PERSONALITY TYPE**—Realistic. Realistic occupations frequently involve work activities that include practical, hands-on problems and solutions. They often deal with plants, animals, and real-world materials like wood, tools, and machinery. Many of the occupations require working outside and do not involve a lot of paperwork or working closely with others.

**EDUCATION/TRAINING PROGRAM(S)**— Welder/Welding Technologist. **RELATED KNOWLEDGE/COURSES**—**Principles of Mechanical Devices:** Knowledge of machines and tools, including their designs, uses, repair, and maintenance. **Production and Processing:** Knowledge of raw materials, production processes, quality control, costs, and other techniques for maximizing the effective manufacture and distribution of goods. **Building and Construction:** Knowledge of materials, methods, and tools involved in the construction or repair of houses, buildings, or other structures such as highways and roads. **Public Safety and Security:** Knowledge of relevant equipment, policies, procedures, and strategies to promote effective local, state, or national security operations for the protection of people, data, property, and institutions. **Physics:** Knowledge and prediction of physical principles and laws and their interrelationships and applications to understanding fluid, material, and atmospheric dynamics and mechanical, electrical, atomic, and subatomic structures and processes. **Mathematics:** Knowledge of arithmetic, algebra, geometry, calculus, statistics, and their applications.

# Welding Machine Operators and Tenders

▲ Growth: 15.1%
▲ Annual Job Openings: 9,000
▲ Annual Earnings: $29,730
▲ Education/Training Required: Moderate-term on-the-job training
▲ Self-Employed: 5.9%
▲ Part-Time: 2.6%

**Operate or tend welding machines that join or bond together components to fabricate metal products and assemblies according to specifications and blueprints.** Operates or tends welding machines that join or bond components to fabricate metal products and assemblies. Turns and presses knobs and buttons to adjust and start welding machine. Enters operating instructions into computer to adjust and start welding machine. Stops and opens holding device on welding machine, using hand tools. Reads production schedule and specifications to ascertain product to be fabricated. Positions and adjusts fixtures, attachments, or workpiece on machine, using hand tools and measuring devices. Observes and listens to welding machine and its controls to ensure welding process meets specifications. Inspects metal workpiece to ensure specifications are met, using measuring devices. Transfers components, metal products, and assemblies, using moving equipment. Cleans and maintains workpieces and welding machine parts, using hand tools and equipment. Adds chemicals or solutions to welding machine to join or bind components. Tends auxiliary equipment used in the welding process. **SKILLS**—Operation and Control. Operation Monitoring. Equipment Selection. Equipment Maintenance. Reading Comprehension. Mathematics. Quality Control Analysis.

**GOE—Interest Area:** 08. Industrial Production. **Work Group:** 08.03. Production Work. **Other Job Titles in This Work Group:** Bakers, Manufacturing; Bindery Machine Operators and Tenders; Brazers; Cementing and Gluing Machine Operators and Tenders; Chemical Equipment Controllers and Operators; Chemical Equipment Operators and Tenders; Chemical Equipment Tenders; Cleaning, Washing, and Metal Pickling Equipment Operators and Tenders; Coating, Painting, and Spraying Machine Operators and Tenders; Coil Winders, Tapers, and Finishers; Combination Machine Tool Operators and Tenders, Metal and Plastic; Computer-Controlled Machine Tool Operators, Metal and Plastic; Cooling and Freezing Equipment Operators and Tenders; Crushing, Grinding, and Polishing Machine Setters, Operators, and Tenders; Cutters and Trimmers, Hand; Cutting and Slicing Machine Operators and Tenders; Cutting and Slicing Machine Setters, Operators, and Tenders; Design Printing Machine Setters and Set-Up Operators; Electrolytic Plating and Coating Machine Operators and Tenders, Metal and Plastic; Electrolytic Plating and Coating Machine Setters and Set-Up Operators, Metal and Plastic; Electrotypers and Stereotypers; Embossing Machine Set-Up Operators; Engraver Set-Up Operators; Extruding and Forming Machine Operators and Tenders, Synthetic or Glass Fibers; Extruding and Forming Machine Setters, Operators, and Tenders, Synthetic and Glass Fibers; Extruding, Forming, Pressing, and Compacting Machine Operators and Tenders; Fabric and Apparel Patternmakers; Fiber Product Cutting Machine Setters and Set-Up Operators; Fiberglass Laminators and Fabricators; others. **PERSONALITY TYPE**—Realistic. Realistic occupations frequently involve work activities that include practical, hands-on problems and solutions. They often deal with plants, animals, and real-world materials like wood, tools, and machinery. Many of the occupations require working outside and do not involve a lot of paperwork or working closely with others.

**EDUCATION/TRAINING PROGRAM(S)**—Welder/Welding Technologist. **RELATED KNOWLEDGE/COURSES—Production and Processing:** Knowledge of raw materials, production processes, quality control, costs, and other techniques for maximizing the effective manufacture and distribution of goods. **Principles of Mechanical Devices:** Knowledge of machines and tools, including their designs, uses, repair, and maintenance. **Engineering and Technology:** Knowledge of the practical application of engineering science and technology. This includes applying principles, techniques, procedures, and equipment to the design and production of various goods and services. **English Language:** Knowledge of the structure and content of the English language, including the meaning and spelling of words, rules of composition, and grammar. **Chemistry:** Knowledge of the chemical composition, structure, and properties of substances and of the chemical processes and transformations that they undergo. This includes uses of chemicals and their interactions, danger signs, production techniques, and disposal methods. **Mathematics:** Knowledge of arithmetic, algebra, geometry, calculus, statistics, and their applications. **Computers and Electronics:** Knowledge of circuit boards, processors, chips, electronic equipment, and computer hardware and software, including applications and programming.

# Welding Machine Setters and Set-Up Operators

- ▲ Growth: 15.1%
- ▲ Annual Job Openings: 9,000
- ▲ Annual Earnings: $29,730
- ▲ Education/Training Required: Moderate-term on-the-job training
- ▲ Self-Employed: 5.9%
- ▲ Part-Time: 2.6%

**Set up or set up and operate welding machines that join or bond together components to fabricate metal products or assemblies according to specifications and blueprints.** Sets up and operates welding machines that join or bond components to fabricate metal products or assemblies. Feeds workpiece into welding machine to join or bond components. Observes and listens to welding machine and its gauges to ensure welding process meets specifications. Turns and presses controls, such as cranks, knobs, and buttons, to adjust and activate welding process. Operates welding machine to produce trial workpieces used to examine and test. Lays out, fits, or tacks workpieces together, using hand tools. Examines metal product or assemblies to ensure specifications are met. Tends auxiliary equipment used in welding process. Tests products and records test results and operational data on specified forms. Devises and builds fixtures used to bond components during the welding process. Cleans and maintains workpieces and welding machine parts, using hand tools and equipment. Adds components, chemicals, and solutions to welding machine, using hand tools. Stops and opens holding device on welding machine, using hand tools. Positions and adjusts fixtures, attachments, or workpieces on machine, using hand tools. **SKILLS**—Equipment Selection. Quality Control Analysis. Operation Monitoring. Operation and Control. Mathematics.

**GOE**—**Interest Area:** 08. Industrial Production. **Work Group:** 08.02. Production Technology. **Other Job Titles in This Work Group:** Aircraft Rigging Assemblers; Aircraft Structure Assemblers, Precision; Aircraft Structure, Surfaces, Rigging, and Systems Assemblers; Aircraft Systems Assemblers, Precision; Bench Workers, Jewelry; Bindery Machine Setters and Set-Up Operators; Bindery Workers; Bookbinders; Buffing and Polishing Set-Up Operators; Casting Machine Set-Up Operators; Coating, Painting, and Spraying Machine Setters and Set-Up Operators; Coating, Painting, and Spraying Machine Setters, Operators, and Tenders; Combination Machine Tool Setters and Set-Up Operators, Metal and Plastic; Cutting, Punching, and Press Machine Setters, Operators, and Tenders, Metal and Plastic; Dental Laboratory Technicians; Drilling and Boring Machine Tool Setters, Operators, and Tenders, Metal and Plastic; Electrical and Electronic Equipment Assemblers; Electrical and Electronic Inspectors and Testers; Electromechanical Equipment Assemblers; Engine and Other Machine Assemblers; Extruding and Drawing Machine Setters, Operators, and Tenders, Metal and Plastic; Extruding, Forming, Pressing, and Compacting Machine Setters and Set-Up Operators; Extruding, Forming, Pressing, and Compacting Machine Setters, Operators, and Tenders; Forging Machine Setters, Operators, and Tenders, Metal and Plastic; Foundry Mold and Coremakers; Gem and Diamond Workers; Grinding, Honing, Lapping, and Deburring Machine Set-Up Operators; Grinding, Lapping, Polishing, and Buffing Machine Tool Setters, Operators, and Tenders, Metal and Plastic; Heat Treating Equipment Setters, Operators, and Tenders, Metal and Plastic; others. **PERSONALITY TYPE**—Realistic. Realistic occupations frequently involve work activities that include practical, hands-on problems and solutions. They often deal with plants, animals, and real-world materials like wood, tools, and machinery. Many of the occupations require working outside and do not involve a lot of paperwork or working closely with others.

**EDUCATION/TRAINING PROGRAM(S)**—Welder/Welding Technologist. **RELATED KNOWLEDGE/COURSES**—**Principles of Mechanical Devices:** Knowledge of machines and tools, including their designs, uses, repair, and maintenance. **Production and Processing:** Knowledge of raw materials, production processes, quality control, costs, and other techniques for maximizing the effective manufacture and distribution of goods. **Chemistry:** Knowledge of the chemical composition, structure, and properties of substances and of the chemical processes and transformations that they undergo. This includes uses of chemicals and their interactions, danger signs, production techniques, and disposal methods. **Design:** Knowledge of design techniques, tools, and principles involved in production of precision technical plans, blueprints, drawings, and models. **Engineering and Technology:** Knowledge of the practical application of engineering science and technology. This includes applying principles, techniques, procedures, and equipment to the design and production of various goods and services.

# *Appendix*

# Explanation of Skills

In each of the descriptions for the best jobs found in Part II, we've included a listing of skills required for each job. This table contains specific definitions of each skill. Use it as a key to gathering more information about the jobs that interest you.

## Explanation of Skills

| Skill | Definition |
| --- | --- |
| **Basic Skills** | **Developed capacities that facilitate learning or the more rapid acquisition of knowledge** |
| Active Learning | Working with new material or information to grasp its implications |
| Active Listening | Listening to what other people are saying and asking questions as appropriate |
| Critical Thinking | Using logic and analysis to identify the strengths and weaknesses of different approaches |
| Learning Strategies | Using multiple approaches when learning or teaching new things |
| Mathematics | Using mathematics to solve problems |
| Monitoring | Assessing how well one is doing when learning or doing something |
| Reading Comprehension | Understanding written sentences and paragraphs in work related documents |
| Science | Using scientific methods to solve problems |
| Speaking | Talking to others to effectively convey information |
| Writing | Communicating effectively with others in writing as indicated by the needs of the audience |

*(continued)*

*(continued)*

| Skill | Definition |
|---|---|
| **Resource Management Skills** | **Developed capacities used to allocate resources efficiently** |
| Management of Financial Resources | Determining how money will be spent to get the work done, and accounting for these expenditures |
| Management of Material Resources | Obtaining and seeing to the appropriate use of equipment, facilities, and materials needed to do certain work |
| Management of Personnel Resources | Motivating, developing, and directing people as they work, identifying the best people for the job |
| Time Management | Managing one's own time and the time of others |
| **Social Skills** | **Developed capacities used to work with people to achieve goals** |
| Coordination | Adjusting actions in relation to others' actions |
| Instructing | Teaching others how to do something |
| Negotiation | Bringing others together and trying to reconcile differences |
| Persuasion | Persuading others to approach things differently |
| Service Orientation | Actively looking for ways to help people |
| Social Perceptiveness | Being aware of others' reactions and understanding why they react the way they do |
| **Systems Skills** | **Developed capacities used to understand, monitor, and improve socio-technical systems** |
| Judgment and Decision Making | Weighing the relative costs and benefits of a potential action |
| **Technical Skills** | **Developed capacities used to design, set up, operate, and correct malfunctions involving application of machines or technological systems** |
| Equipment Maintenance | Performing routine maintenance and determining when and what kind of maintenance is needed |
| Equipment Selection | Determining the kind of tools and equipment needed to do a job |

| Skill | Definition |
|---|---|
| Installation | Installing equipment, machines, wiring, or programs to meet specifications |
| Operation and Control | Controlling operations of equipment or systems |
| Operation Monitoring | Watching gauges, dials, or other indicators to make sure a machine is working properly |
| Operations Analysis | Analyzing needs and product requirements to create a design |
| Programming | Writing computer programs for various purposes |
| Repairing | Repairing machines or systems using the needed tools |
| Technology Design | Generating or adapting equipment and technology to serve user needs |
| Troubleshooting | Determining what is causing an operating error and deciding what to do about it |

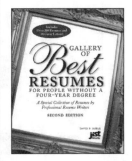
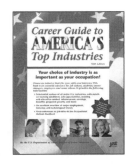